Rolf Rendtorff is Professor Emeritus,
University of Heidelberg. He has published extensively on the Pentateuch,
and particularly on Leviticus and topics
related to it.

Robert A. Kugler is the Paul S. Wright
Professor of Christian Studies at Lewis
& Clark College, Portland, Oregon. He
is the author of *Leviticus at Qumran* (Brill,
forthcoming).

THE BOOK OF LEVITICUS

SUPPLEMENTS

TO

VETUS TESTAMENTUM

EDITED BY
THE BOARD OF THE QUARTERLY

H.M. BARSTAD – PHYLLIS A. BIRD – R.P. GORDON
A. HURVITZ – A. ᴠᴀɴ ᴅᴇʀ KOOIJ – A. LEMAIRE
R. SMEND – J. TREBOLLE BARRERA
J.C. VANDERKAM – H.G.M. WILLIAMSON

VOLUME XCIII

FORMATION AND INTERPRETATION
OF OLD TESTAMENT LITERATURE

III

EDITED BY

CRAIG A. EVANS
ACADIA DIVINITY COLLEGE
Wolfville, Nova Scotia

PETER W. FLINT
TRINITY WESTERN UNIVERSITY
Langley, British Columbia

TUTA SUB AEGIDE PALLAS
· 1 6 8 3 ·

THE BOOK
OF LEVITICUS

COMPOSITION
AND RECEPTION

EDITED BY

ROLF RENDTORFF AND
ROBERT A. KUGLER

WITH THE ASSISTANCE OF

SARAH SMITH BARTEL

BRILL
LEIDEN · BOSTON
2003

This book is printed on acid-free paper.

Bibliographic information published by Die Deutsche Bibliothek

Die Deutsche Bibliothek lists this publication in the Deutsche
Nationalbibliographie; detailed bibliographic data are
available on the Internet at http://dnb.dde.de.

Library of Congress Cataloging-in-Publication Data

Library of Congress Cataloging-in-Publication Data is also available.

ISSN   0083-5889
ISBN   90 04 12634 1

PRINTED IN THE NETHERLANDS

CONTENTS

PART THREE

PRIESTHOOD IN LEVITICUS

PART FOUR

LEVITICUS IN TRANSLATION AND INTERPRETATION

INDICES

PREFACE

The Book of Leviticus: Composition and Reception contains, in addition to an Introduction, twenty-two essays on a range of topics in four sections: (a) Leviticus in its Literary Context; (b) Cult and Sacrifice; (c) Priesthood and Leviticus; and (d) Leviticus in Translation and Interpretation. The contributors were invited with a view to representing the spectrum of opinion on the current interpretation of the Book of Leviticus, over a range of subjects.

The Book of Leviticus: Composition and Reception is the third book in the series "The Formation and Interpretation of Old Testament Literature" (FIOTL), the purpose of which is to examine and explore the prehistory, contents, and themes of the books of the Old Testament, as well as their reception and interpretation in later Jewish and Christian literature. The first book to appear in the series was *Writing and Reading the Scroll of Isaiah: Studies in an Interpretive Tradition*, eds. Craig C. Broyles and Craig A. Evans (FIOTL 1.1–2 and VTSup 70.1–2, 1997).

It is appropriate to offer a brief note on the "*Index of Selected scriptural Citations and Ancient Sources.*" It intends in no way to be comprehensive; rather it lists only the chief passages from Leviticus discussed in the volume's essays, as well as the most important non-Leviticus texts associated by the authors with their discussion of Leviticus.

The editors extend thanks to four groups of people. First, to all the contributors for meeting various deadlines and working to render the editing process smooth and effective. Second, to Sarah Smith Bartel, a graduate assistant at Gonzaga University whose dedication and hard work proved indispensable to bringing the volume to completion. Thanks are also due to Professor André Lemaire and the VTSup Board for their support of the FIOTL volumes as part of the VTSup series. Finally, we are grateful to the team at Brill Academic Publishers, especially Desk Editor Mattie Kuiper for her guidance, encouragement, and patience in the production of this book.

12 June 2002

Rolf Rendtorff
University of Heidelberg (Emeritus)

Robert A. Kugler
Lewis & Clark College, Portland, OR

TERMS, SIGLA, AND ABBREVIATIONS

For most terms, sigla, and abbreviations of journals and other secondary sources, see P. H. Alexander et al. (eds.), *The SBL Handbook of Style for Ancient Near Eastern, Biblical, and Early Christian Studies* (Peabody, MA: Hendrickson, 1999). For Qumran sigla, see also J. A. Fitzmyer, *The Dead Sea Scrolls: Major Publications and Tools for Study* (rev. ed., SBLRBS 20; Atlanta: Scholars Press, 1990) 1–8.

Terms and Sigla

(?)	Some doubt exists as to the identification of a verse or reading.
[ ]	The bracketed portions are not extant, but were originally written.
[ ]	Space between fragments or where the leather surface is missing
[Baars W.]	In bibliographies, the square brackets denote that the name of the author or editor does not appear on the title page of the publication.
\	Division between lines in a manuscript
//	Two or more parallel texts (e.g. Ps 18//2 Sam 22)
°	Ink traces of an unidentified letter remain.
+	Word(s) or a verse have been added.
>	Word(s) or a verse have been omitted.
*	What the scribe originally wrote (e.g. 4QDan^{a}*)
*	The asterisk here indicates that not all of the verses are indicated (e.g. Dan 1:1–7:27*).
–	Denotes Hebrew pagination (e.g. "11QPsa^{a} המגילה," 123*–28*)
2:4–5	Dead Sea Scrolls: the second extant column of the manuscript, lines 4–5
2.5	Dead Sea Scrolls: fragment 2, line 5
10 ii.4–5	Dead Sea Scrolls: fragment 10, column 2, lines 4–5
2:23[24]	The number in square brackets is the Greek verse number.
§, §§	Section(s), especially in Josephus and Philo
א א א	A certain letter, a probable letter, a possible letter, respectively
AA	Animal Apocalypse
AB	Astronomical Book of Enoch
abbr.	Abbreviation
Adv. Haer.	*Adversus Haereses (Against Heresies)*
Ag. Ap.	Josephus, *Against Apion*
Ant.	Josephus, *Antiquities*
ar	Aramaic
AW	Apocalypse of Weeks
b.	The Babylonian Talmud (Bavli)
BG	Book of Giants
Beih.	Beihefte
BH	Biblical Hebrew
bis	Two times
BW	Book of Watchers
ca.	*circa*
cf.	*confer*, compare
Chr.	Chrysostom
col(s.)	Column(s)

Comm. in Dan.	*Commentary on Daniel*
Comm. in Matt.	*Commentary on Matthew*
corr.	*correctus, -a, um*, the corrected reading
Dem. Ev.	Eusebius, *Demonstratio evangelica* (*Demonstration of the Gospel*)
d.	died
ed(s).	Edition, editor(s), or edited
Ee	*Enuma Elish*
EE	Epistle of Enoch
e.g.	*exempli gratia*, for example
eras.	*erasum*, erased
esp.	especially
ET	English translation
et al.	*et alii*, and others
fin.	*finis*, end (e.g. 144:13^{fin})
frg(s).	Fragment(s)
𝔊 or LXX	The Old Greek (as in the Göttingen editions)
𝔊*	The (reconstructed) original reading of the Old Greek
θ′	Theodotion's version of the Septuagint
Heb.	Hebrew
HUBP	Hebrew University Bible Project
Hyp. Arch.	*Hypostasis of the Archons*
idem.	the same
i.e.	*id est*, that is
J. W.	Josephus, *The Jewish War*
L	Lucian Recension, *or* the Leningrad (St. Petersburg) Codex
La	The Vetus Latina or Old Latin translation of the LXX
Lev. Rab.	*Leviticus Rabbah*
LXX	The Septuagint
m.	Mishnah
𝔐 or MT	The Masoretic Text
𝔐^{ed}	An edition of the Masoretic Text (usually *BHS*)
𝔐^{L} or B$^{19\text{A}}$	The Leningrad (St. Petersburg) Codex
𝔐$^{\text{ms(s)}}$	Masoretic manuscript(s)
𝔐^{q}	*qere* for the Masoretic Text
m.	Mishnah
ms(s)	Individual manuscript(s)
MT	Masoretic Text
n.	*nota*, note
no.	Number
n.p.	No publisher (cited)
n.s.	New series
NT	New Testament
OG	The Old Greek (original Septuagint)
OG-Dan	Old Greek Daniel
orth.?	A form that may be only an orthographic variant
PAM	Dead Sea Scrolls: Palestine Archaeological Museum (photograph accession numbers)
par(s).	Parallel passage(s)
pl(s).	Plates(s)
Praep. Ev.	Eusebius, *Praeparatio Evangelica* (*Preparation for the Gospel*)
PRE	*Pirqe deRabbi Eliezer*
Ra	Rahlfs' edition of the Septuagint
recto	The front, inscribed side of a manuscript: the hair side of a leather scroll, or the side of a papyrus having horizontal ridges

repr.	Reprint(ed)
rev.	Revised
SP	Summary parenesis
s.v.	*sub verbo* ("under the word," dictonary entry)
Sanh.	*Sanhedrin*
SH	Syro-Hexapla
SP	Samaritan Pentateuch
Syh	Syrohexaplar
t.	Tosefta
T.	Testament, as in *T. Levi*, etc.
TE	Testament of Enoch
Tg.	Targum
Th. or Theod.	Theodotion
Th-Dan	Theodotion Daniel
Tht.	Theodoret
v(v).	Verse(s)
vacat	Indicates that the leather or papyrus was intentionally left blank
verso	The reverse side of a manuscript: the flesh side of a leather scroll, or the side of a papyrus having vertical ridges
Vg (Vlg)	Vulgate
vid.	*ut videtur, -entur*, as it seems, as they seem from the available evidence
Vorlage	Hebrew text used by the translator of the Greek or other Version
WE	*Words of Ezekiel*
y.	The Palestinian Talmud (Yerushalmi)

JOURNALS, BOOKS AND SERIES

AASOR	*Annual of the American Schools of Oriental Research*
AB	Anchor Bible
ABD	*The Anchor Bible Dictionary* (6 vols., New York: Doubleday, 1992), ed. D. N. Freedman
AfO	*Archiv für Orientforschung*
AfO Beih.	*Archiv für Orientforschung*, Beihefte
AGJU	Arbeiten zur Geschichte des antiken Judentums und des Urchristentums
AHw	*Akkadisches Handworterbuch* (3 vols., Wiesbaden, 1965–1981), by W. von Soden
AJP	*American Journal of Philology*
AnBib	Analecta biblica
ANEP	*The Ancient Near East in Pictures Relating to the OT* (Princeton: Princeton University Press, 1954), ed. J. B. Pritchard
ANET	*Ancient Near Eastern Texts Relating to the Old Testament* (3rd ed., Princeton: Princeton University Press, 1969), ed. J. B. Pritchard
ANRW	*Aufstieg und Niedergang der römischen Welt* (Berlin: de Gruyter, 1979–), ed. W. Haase and E. Temporini
ANTJ	Arbeiten zum Neuen Testament und Judentum
AOAT	Alter Orient und Altes Testament
ARM X	*Archives royales de Mari: La correspondance féminine*, ed. G. Dossin
ASNU	Acta seminarii neotestamentici upsaliensis
ASOR	American Schools of Oriental Research
AT	Altes Testament
ATAT	Arbeiten zu Text und Sprache im Alten Testament

ATANT	Abhandlungen zur Theologie des Alten und Neuen Testaments
ATD	Das Alte Testament Deutsch
BA	*Biblical Archaeologist*
BAR	*Biblical Archaeologist Reader*
BARev	*Biblical Archaeology Review*
BASOR	*Bulletin of the American Schools of Oriental Research*
BASORSup	*Bulletin of the American Schools of Oriental Research*, Supplements
BBR	*Bulletin for Biblical Research*
BETL	Bibliotheca ephemeridum theologicarum lovaniensium
BGBE	Beitrage zur Geschichte der biblischen Exegese
BHK	*Biblia Hebraica* (R. Kittel)
BHS	*Biblia Hebraica Stuttgartensia*
Bib	*Biblica*
BibOr	Biblica et orientalia
BIOSCS	*Bulletin of the International Organization for Septuagint and Cognate Studies*
BIS	Biblical Interpretation Series
BJS	Brown Judaic Studies
BK	Biblischer Kommentar
BKAT	Biblischer Kommentar: Altes Testament, eds. M. Noth and H. W. Wolff
BN	*Biblische Notizen*
BO	*Bibliotheca orientalis*
BZAW	Beihefte zur *ZAW*
BZNW	Beihefte zur *ZNW*
Cahiers RB	Cahiers de la *Revue Biblique*
CANE	*Civilizations of the Ancient Near East* (4 vols., New York: Charles Scribner's Sons, 1995), ed. J. Sasson
CAD	*The Assyrian Dictionary* of the Oriental Institute, University of Chicago
CAT	Commentaire de l'Ancien Testament
CBQ	*Catholic Biblical Quarterly*
CBQMS	Catholic Biblical Quarterly Monograph Series
CCSL	Corpus Christianorum: Series graeca
CCSL	Corpus Christianorum: Series latina
CCL	Classics of Christian Litererature
CJA	Christianity and Judaism in Antiquity
CNT	Commentaire du Nouveau Testament
ConB	Coniectanea biblica
ConBNT	Coniectanea biblica, New Testament
ConBOT	Coniectanea biblica, Old Testament
CRINT	Compendia rerum iudaicarum ad novum testamentum
CS	*The Context of Scripture*, eds. W. W. Hallo and K. Lawson Younger
CT	*Cuneiform Texts from Babylonian Tablets in the British Museum*
CT	*Christianity Today*
CTA	*Corpus des tablelettes en cunéiformes alphabétiques découvertes à Ras Shamra-Ugarit de 1929 à 1939* (Mission de Ras Shamra 10; Paris, 1963), ed. A. Herdner
DB	*Dictionnaire de la Bible* (5 vols., 1895–1912)
DBSup	*Dictionnaire de la Bible, Supplément*
DDD	*Dictionary of Deities and Demons in the Bible* (Leiden: Brill, 1995), ed. K. van der Toorn, B. Becking and P. W. van der Horst
DISO	*Dictionnaire des inscriptions semitiques de l'ouest* (Leiden: Brill, 1965), ed. Ch. F. Jean and J. Hoftijzer
DJD	Discoveries in the Judaean Desert
DJDJ	Discoveries in the Judaean Desert of Jordan

DSD	*Dead Sea Discoveries*
EB	Echter Bibel
Ebib	Études bibliques
EdF	Erträge der Forschung
ErIsr	*Eretz Israel*
ETL	*Ephemerides theologicae lovanienses*
EvT	*Evangelische Theologie*
FAT	Forschungen zum Alten Testament
FIOTL	The Formation and Interpretation of Old Testament Literature
FO	*Folia Orientalia*
FRLANT	Forschungen zur Religion und Literatur des Alten und Neuen Testaments
GCS	Griechischen christlichen Schriftsteller
GKC	*Gesenius' Hebrew Grammar* (ed. E. Kautzsch, tr. A. E. Cowley, 1910)
HAR	Hebrew Annual Review
HBC	*Harper's Bible Commentary*
HBD	*Harper's Bible Dictionary*
HDR	Harvard Dissertations in Religion
HKAT	Handkommentar zum Alten Testament
HNT	Handbuch zum Neuen Testament
HS	*Hebrew Studies*
HSM	Harvard Semitic Monographs
HSS	Harvard Semitic Studies
HTR	*Harvard Theological Review*
HTS	Harvard Theological Studies
HUCA	*Hebrew Union College Annual*
HUCMon	Hebrew Union College Monographs
ICC	International Critical Commentary
IDBSupp	*Interpreter's Dictionary of the Bible, Supplement*, ed. F. Crim et al.
IEJ	*Israel Exploration Journal*
IES	Israel Exploration Society
Int	*Interpretation*
IOS	Israel Oriental Society
Iraq	*Iraq*
JANESCU	*Journal of the Ancient Near Eastern Society of Columbia University*
JAOS	*Journal of the American Oriental Society*
JBL	*Journal of Biblical Literature*
JCS	*Journal of Cuneiform Studies*
JDS	Judaean Desert Studies
JECS	*Journal of Early Christian Studies*
JJS	*Journal of Jewish Studies*
JNES	*Journal of Near Eastern Studies*
JNSL	*Journal of Northwest Semitic Languages*
JNSLSup	*Journal of Northwest Semitic Languages*, Supplement Series
JQR	*Jewish Quarterly Review*
JQRMS	Jewish Quarterly Review Monograph Series
JSJ	*Journal for the Study of Judaism in the Persian, Hellenistic and Roman Period*
JSJSup	*Journal for the Study of Judaism in the Persian, Hellenistic and Roman Period, Supplement Series*
JSNT	*Journal for the Study of the New Testament*
JSNTSup	*Journal for the Study of the New Testament*, Supplement Series
JSOT	*Journal for the Study of the Old Testament*
JSOTSup	*Journal for the Study of the Old Testament*, Supplement Series
JSP	*Journal for the Study of the Pseudepigrapha*
JSPSup	*Journal for the Study of the Pseudepigrapha*, Supplement Series

JSS	*Journal of Semitic Studies*
JTS	*Journal of Theological Studies*
KAI	*Kanaanäische und Aramäische Inschriften*, eds. H. Donner and W. Röllig
KAT	Kommentaar zum Alten Testament
LCL	Loeb Classical Library
LDSS	Literature of the Dead Sea Scrolls
LEC	Library of Early Christianity
MDOG	Mitteilungen der Deutschen Orient-Gesellschaft
MSU	Mitteilungen des Septuaginta-Unternehmens
NCB	New Century Bible
NEA	*Near Eastern Archaeology*
NHS	Nag Hammadi Studies
NIB	New Interpreter's Bible
NJBC	*The New Jerome Biblical Commentary*, ed. R. E. Brown et al.
NovT	*Novum Testamentum*
NovTSup	*Novum Testamentum*, Supplements
NRSV	*The New Revised Standard Version*
ATD	Das Alte Testament Deutsch
NTOA	*Novum Testamentum et Orbis Antiquus*
NTS	*New Testament Studies*
OBO	Orbis biblicus et orientalis
Or	*Orientalia* (n.s.)
OTA	*Old Testament Abstracts*
OTL	Old Testament Library
OTP	*The Old Testament Pseudepigrapha*, ed. J. Charlesworth (2 vols., New York: Doubleday, 1983, 1985)
OTS	*Oudtestamentische Studiën*
PEQ	*Palestine Exploration Quarterly*
PL	*Patrologia latina*, ed. J. Migne
PTSDSS	The Princeton Theological Seminary Dead Sea Scrolls Project
QD	Quaestiones disputatae
RA	*Revue d'assyriologie et d'archeologie orientale*
RB	*Revue biblique*
RBib	Recherches Bibliques
REJ	*Revue des études juives*
RevQ	*Revue de Qumran*
RHR	*Revue de l'histoire des religions*
RivB	*Rivista biblica italiana*
RLA	*Reallexikon der Assyriologie*
RNT	Regensburger Neues Testament
SAA	State Archives of Assyria
SANT	Studien zum Alten und Neuen Testament
SB	Sources bibliques
SBLDS	Society of Biblical Literature Dissertation Series
SBLEJL	Society of Biblical Literature Early Judaism and Its Literature
SBLMasS	Society of Biblical Literature Masoretic Studies
SBLMS	Society of Biblical Literature Monograph Series
SBLSBS	Society of Biblical Literature Sources for Biblical Study
SBLSCS	Society of Biblical Literature Septuagint and Cognate Studies
SBLSP	*Society of Biblical Literature Seminar Papers*
SBLSS	Society of Biblical Literature Semeia Studies
SBLSym	Society of Biblical Literature Symposium Series
SBLTT	Society of Biblical Literature Texts and Translations
SBS	Stuttgarter Bibelstudien

SC	Sources chrétiennes
ScrHier	*Scripta hierosolymitana*
SDSRL	Studies in the Dead Sea Scrolls and Related Literature
Sem	*Semitica*
SFSHJ	South Florida Studies in the History of Judaism
SJLA	Studies in Judaism in Late Antiquity
SNTS	Society for New Testament Studies
SNTSMS	Society for New Testament Studies Monograph Series
ST	*Studia theologica*
STDJ	Studies on the Texts of the Desert of Judah
TSJTSA	Theological Studies of the Jewish Theological Seminary of America
TB	Theologische Bucherei: Neudrucke und Berichte aus dem 20. Jahrhundert
TCL	Textes cuneiformes, Musee de Louvre
TCL	Translations of Christian Literature
THKNT	Theologischer Handkommentar zum Neuen Testament
ThWAT	*Theologisches Wörterbuch zum Alten Testament* (Stuttgart, 1970–), ed. G. J. Botterweck and H. Ringgren
TLZ	*Theologische Literaturzeitung*
TRE	*Theologische Realenzyklopädie* (Berlin: de Gruyter, 1977–), ed. G. Krause and G. Müller
TSAJ	Texte und Studien zum antiken Judentum
TSK	*Theologische Studien und Kritiken*
TThZ	*Trierer theologische Zeitschrift*
TTZ	*Trierer theologische Zeitschrift*
TUAT	Texte aus der Umwelt des Alten Testaments
TWNT	*Theologisches Wörterbuch zum Neuen Testament*
TZ	*Theologische Zeitschrift*
UF	Ugarit-Forschungen
Ug	*Ugaritica*
VT	*Vetus Testamentum*
VTSup	*Vetus Testamentum*, Supplements
WBC	Word Biblical Commentary
WMANT	Wissenschaftliche Monographien zum Alten und Neuen Testament
WO	Die Welt des Orients
WUNT	Wissenschaftliche Untersuchungen zum Neuen Testament
ZA	*Zeitschrift für Assyriologie*
ZAW	*Zeitschrift für die alttestamentliche Wissenschaft*
ZBK	Zürcher Bibelkommentare
ZNW	*Zeitschrift für die neutestamentliche Wissenschaft*

LIST OF CONTRIBUTORS

A. Graeme Auld
Professor, University of Edinburgh

Gerhard Bodendorfer
Professor, Orientalisches Seminar/Judaistik, Freiburg

Calum Carmichael
Professor of Comparative Literature and Adjunct Professor of Law,
Cornell University

Bruce Chilton
Bernard Iddings Bell Professor of Religion, Bard College

Mary Douglas
Professor, University College London (Retired)

Peter Flint
Professor of Biblical Studies and Director of the Dead Sea Scrolls
Institute, Trinity Western University, Canada

Lester Grabbe
Professor of Hebrew Bible and Early Judaism, University of Hull,
England

Hannah K. Harrington
Professor of Old Testament, Patten College

The Rev. Dr. Walter J. Houston
Mansfield College, Oxford

Robert A. Kugler
Paul S. Wright Professor of Christian Studies, Lewis & Clark College

Rev. D. J. Lane
Overton Cottage, New Galloway, Castle Douglas, Great Britain

Baruch Levine
Skirball Professor Emeritus of Bible and Ancient Near Eastern Studies,
New York University

Alfred Marx
Professor, Faculty of Protestant Theology, University of Strasbourg

Martin McNamara, MSC
Professor Emeritus of Sacred Scripture, The Milltown Institute of
  Theology and Philosophy, Dublin, Ireland

Sarianna Metso
Assistant Professor of Religious Studies, Albion College

Jacob Milgrom
Professor Emeritus of Biblical Studies, University of California at
  Berkeley

René Péter-Contesse
Professor of Hebrew, Cantonal Gymnasium of Neuchâtel (Retired)

Rolf Rendtorff
Professor, University of Heidelberg (Emeritus)

Andreas Ruwe
Dr. theol., Wissenschaftlicher Assistent, Chair of Old Testament,
  Faculty of Theology at the Ernst-Moritz-Arndt University Greifswald

Linda Schearing
Associate Professor of Religious Studies, Gonzaga University

Adrian Schenker
Professor for Old Testament, Department of Biblical Studies, University
  of Fribourg, Switzerland

Eugene Ulrich
J. A. O'Brien Professor of Hebrew Scriptures, University of Notre
  Dame

James W. Watts
Associate Professor, Syracuse University

Judith Romney Wegner
Professor, Connecticut College (Retired)

INTRODUCTION

Rolf Rendtorff

In recent years a growing scholarly interest in the Book of Leviticus is to be observed. In particular, Leviticus as an individual book came in the view of scholars. In the last few years there appeared a number of books in which the "Book of Leviticus" figures in the title. In 1996 *Reading Leviticus*, subtitled *A Conversation with Mary Douglas*, appeared.[1] Mary Douglas herself published in 1999 *Leviticus as Literature*.[2] In the same year a number of German scholars brought out *Levitikus als Buch*.[3] The present volume—which appears in a series alongside other books on Genesis, Isaiah, Psalms, and Daniel—continues this specific interest in Leviticus as an individual book.

This is a very interesting development, because in the modern critical scholarship Leviticus is mainly taken as part of one of the "sources" of the Pentateuch, namely the "Priestly Code" (*Priesterschrift*). There were many discussions about the unity or disunity of the Priestly Code in which Leviticus was just one element among others. But when Leviticus was singled out as a specific part of the "Priestly" tradition or source there appeared a new problem with regard to its unity, because since the end of the eighteenth century Leviticus 17–26 was taken as a unit or even "source" of its own, the "Holiness Code" (*Heiligkeitsgesetz*). Thus Leviticus seemed to be composed from two originally independent "sources" or parts of them: the "Priestly Code" (P) and the "Holiness Code" (H). These theories, like any others in modern Pentateuchal research, have been developed by further division of the different sources, e.g. into P^G (*Grundschrift*), P^S (secondary additions), or P^1, P^2, etc. or even by a combination of P and H into P^H, etc.

---

[1] F. A. Sawyer (ed.), *Reading Leviticus. A Conversation with Mary Douglas* (JSOTSup 227; Sheffield: Sheffield Academic Press, 1996).

[2] M. Douglas, *Leviticus as Literature* (Oxford: University Press, 1999).

[3] H. J. Fabry and H. W. Jüngling (eds.), *Levitikus als Buch* (BBB 119; Berlin: Philo, 1999).

In the last two or three decades there began a new discussion on
the traditio-historical development of the Pentateuch.[4] One main
topic within this new trend is a new "canonical" interest in the given
structure of the Pentateuch which includes an interest in the character of the five individual "books" of the Pentateuch as they are
presented in the canonical Hebrew Scriptures.[5] Thus the new interest in the Book of Leviticus is part of a broader new development
in Pentateuchal studies. This discussion is still in its beginnings. In
addition scholars continue to work within different fields of the wide-
ranging area of Pentateuchal and priestly problems of which Leviticus
is an integral part.

This volume deals with certain relevant aspects of the present
scholarly discussions around the Book of Leviticus. We invited a
number of scholars who had published in this field or in parts of it
to contribute to this volume. Those who were able to accept our
invitation were more or less free to decide on the particular topic
of their contributions. Each of them approaches the problems from
his or her respective points of view, the result being a multivoiced
chorus of scholarly insights and positions in the field of Leviticus
studies. This demonstrates the ongoing vivid scholarly discussion in
this field, and at the same time the intensive endeavor to step forward
in illuminating the inner structure of the Book of Leviticus, its interrelations with the rest of biblical literature and traditions, its message,
and the wide range of interpretation to which it gave rise.

The essays are arranged in four sections. The first is *Leviticus in
its Literary Context*. This section deals with the literary formation of
the Book of Leviticus and with the question how it is related to the
rest of the books of the Pentateuch. There are, of course, different
possible approaches to this question. *Baruch Levine* chooses the question of the historical setting of the priestly literature of the Pentateuch,
using comparative material from the surrounding cultures. In doing
so, he necessarily touches one of the main aspects of the discussion
on the "priestly" traditions in Leviticus, namely the above mentioned
discrimination between the "Priestly Code" (P) as the main priestly
"source" and the "Holiness Code" (H, Leviticus 17–26), including

---

[4] See, e.g. R. Rendtorff, "Directions in Pentateuchal Studies" *Currents in Research:
Biblical Studies* 5 (1997) 43–65.

[5] I am using here the word "canonical" in a broader sense referring to the given
structure of the books, as distinct from source criticism or other attempts to reconstruct "earlier" and supposedly more "original" forms of the text.

the question of the interrelations between the two of them. In this respect there has been some discussion in recent years.[6] Hereby an additional aspect comes into play, namely the thesis, that there is not a "Holiness Code" as a clearly defined group of texts, but a "Holiness School" whose traces are discernible throughout the whole of the Pentateuch.[7] This thesis is vividly defended and expanded by *Jacob Milgrom* in his commentary on Leviticus,[8] and now also in his essay in this volume. It is closely connected with the question of the dating of the Priestly Code, which is controversial since the work of Yehezkel Kaufmann[9] who plead against Wellhausen[10] for a pre-exilic dating of P. Following Kaufmann, Milgrom takes the main corpus of the "Priestly Code" as being earlier than the "Holiness School," the latter being "the redactor of P." Levine, for his part, prefers the position "that H represents the primary stratum of the *Priesterschrift.*" It is obvious that in the question of dating the priestly traditions certain basic decisions about the development of the Israelite religion in pre- and postexilic times are involved, even if this is not always explicitly mentioned. Thus the different positions of Levine and Milgrom represent a controversy that is characteristic of at least one sector of present Old Testament scholarship.

Yet the question of dating Leviticus is not of central relevance for the majority of the essays in this volume. *Graeme Auld* continues to develop his view of the books of the Pentateuch which he first presented in his essay "Leviticus at the Heart of the Pentateuch?"[11] He shows the individual character of each "book," putting the whole question in a broader framework of Old Testament literature. *Andreas Ruwe*, who earlier published a book on *"Heiligkeitsgesetz" und "Priesterschrift,"*[12] offers a new proposal for understanding the Book of Leviticus

---

[6] For some scholars—myself included—it is no longer evident that Leviticus 17–26 has to be regarded as an independent collection; see R. Rendtorff, *The Old Testament. An Introduction* (Philadelphia: Fortress, 1986) 145; E. Gerstenberger, *Leviticus: A Commentary* (OTL; Louisville, Ky: Westminster John Knox, 1996) 17–19.

[7] I. Knohl, *The Sanctuary of Silence: The Priestly Torah and the Holiness Code* (Minneapolis: Fortress, 1995).

[8] J. Milgrom, *Leviticus 1–16* (AB 3; New York: Doubleday, 1991); idem, *Leviticus 17–22* (AB 3A; New York: Doubleday, 2000); idem, *Leviticus 23–27* (AB 3B; New York: Doubleday, 2001).

[9] Y. Kaufmann, *The Religion of Israel* (Hebrew, 8 vols. 1937–1956); abridged English translation: M. Greenberg, Chicago: The University of Chicago Press, 1960).

[10] J. Wellhausen, *Prolegomena zur Geschichte Israels* (Berlin: Reimer, 1883).

[11] In F. A. Sawyer (ed.), *Reading Leviticus*, 40–51.

[12] *"Heiligkeitsgesetz" und "Priesterschrift": literaturgeschichtliche und rechtssystematische*

as a "narrative text." He divides the book into two main parts: chapters 1–8 and 9–27, the latter one to be subdivided into four sections: 9:1–10:20; 11:1–15:31; 16:1–34 and 17:1–26:45. By this the
so-called "Holiness Code" (chapters 17–26) is kept as "a coherent,
fairly independent complex," now integrated into a broader narrative framework. Actually, this seems to be a negation of the existence of "H" as an independent source at all. *James Watts* investigates
the rhetorical character of the ritual instructions in Leviticus 1–7 by
comparing them with comparable texts from the ancient Near East.
He demonstrates the persuasive character of these texts which "intend
to persuade the people of Israel and their priests to perform their
religious offerings, and to do so correctly, as specified here."

   The second section contains essays on different aspects of *Cult and
Sacrifice* in Leviticus. The first essay by *Alfred Marx* deals again with
Leviticus 1–7, this time from the point of view of the theology of
sacrifice. In a detailed analysis of these chapters Marx explains the
central theological relevance of the sacrifices and the prominent position of these chapters which can be called "the pedestal on which
the remainder of the Book of Leviticus rests." *Mary Douglas* presents
a new interpretation of the "scapegoat." She shows that the current
understanding of the "scapegoat," as e.g. represented by René Girard,
is not based on the biblical text of Leviticus 16 but rather caused
by the Greek tradition. By stressing the fact that in the biblical tradition there are *two* goats, she compares it with the two birds in Lev
14:6–7, and, in particular, with the stories of the two brothers in
Genesis. By this comparison "nothing much is left of the idea of a
levitical scapegoat ceremony," which is mainly based on "random
misreading" of the biblical text.

   Walter Houston tries to find a new understanding of the "relationship between ritual laws and morality." He traces this question back
to Philo of Alexandria, and then to the contemporary authors Jacob
Milgrom and Mary Douglas; the positions of all three of them are
explained in detail. Finally the author presents "an attempt at integrated reading" which leads to the conclusion "that the dietary laws
are part of a much broader structure of moral and cosmological
thinking" and that "the distinction so characteristic of Christian inter-

---

Untersuchungen zu Leviticus 17,1–26,2 (FAT 26; Tübingen: J. C. B. Mohr [Paul Siebeck],
1999).

pretation, between ritual and moral, does not do justice" to the biblical material. *Adrian Schenker* presents a detailed exegetical study of Leviticus 18 und 20 as a collection as well as parts of the Pentateuch narrative. He sees a redactional process in several stages with a different linking of the texts with the respective concepts of the redactional layers of the Pentateuch with regard to certain stages of Israels early history.

In the third section one major topic of Leviticus is brought into focus: the *priesthood*. *René Péter-Contesse* unfolds the picture of the priests as presented in Leviticus, beginning with a terminological inventory, and then showing the different functions of the priests, which leads to the summarizing definition of the priest as a mediator and a representative between God and Israel. In an excursus the author takes up a detail which he had already dealt with in an earlier article: the laying on of the hands.[13] *Lester Grabbe* likewise approaches the topic of priesthood in the framework of the Book of Leviticus. He is mainly interested in the question to what purpose and for what audience Leviticus was written. This includes the question of when it was written and how the cultic details described in the book relate to cultic reality. He comes to the result that Leviticus was not written primarily for priests but contains also many details important for the laity. As a composition/compilation Leviticus belongs to the Persian period. With reference to Mary Douglas[14] (and Jacob Neusner) Grabbe claims that "the primary message of Leviticus seems to have been theological." Finally, *Calum Carmichael* deals with some particular aspects of priestly holiness and purity as treated in Leviticus 21. He discusses the exegetical and historical problems posed by the individual parts of this chapter, referring in detail to other texts, some of them outside the Book of Leviticus, such as Judges 19; 1 Samuel 2–4; Leviticus 10. In his Concluding Remarks he points to the "fiction that Moses delivers the laws during his lifetime," from that deducing the thesis of an "integral connection" between law and storytelling in the Hebrew Bible.

Almost half of the contributions are devoted to the section *Leviticus in Translation and Interpretation*. The first three essays deal with the

---

[13] R. Péter-Contesse, "L'imposition des mains dans l'Ancien Testament," *VT* 27 (1977) 48–55.

[14] *Leviticus as Literature* (see n. 2 above).

early translations of the Book of Leviticus: *Sarianna Metso* and *Eugene Ulrich* on the Old Greek Version, *Martin McNamara* on the Targums, and *D. J. Lane* on the Peshitta. It would go beyond the scope of this introductory essay to discuss details of these essays which are full of information. All three of them add a lot of information to the problem of the different stages of the formation of the Hebrew Text as seen from the side of the translations, and together with that they give some insights into the history of the respective community, Jewish and/or Christian, in which the individual translation originated and was used and transmitted through the generations. McNamara has also some pages on Halakah and Haggadic additions in the Targums.

The next two essays turn back to the Hebrew text, this time to the Dead Sea Scrolls. *Peter Flint* presents a detailed study of the seventeen Leviticus manuscripts from Qumran and other sites, their relations to the Masoretic text as well as to the Samaritan Pentateuch and the Septuagint and refers to some significant readings. He adds an extensive bibliography and three appendices including a complete list of all Leviticus texts preserved in the scrolls by chapter and verse. *Robert Kugler* goes a step further to the hermeneutical question in treating the notion of "scripture" in the Dead Sea Scrolls. He shows by a number of examples that for the Essenes there did not at all exist one uniform "biblical" text but rather several variant versions which they used with great freedom. For them "scripture" was a fluid concept, which they did not just interpret but developed further "in the effort to understand life in God's sight."

The following group of three essays examine certain aspects of the early interpretation of scripture, Christian and Jewish. *Bruce Chilton* challenges the common Christian, in particular liberal understanding of the New Testament's relation to purity. In a thorough exegetical study of the positions of Jesus, James, Peter and Paul he shows that while there is no completely unified position on questions of purity, impurity remains a fundamental category by the "equation of impurity and sin." *Hannah Harrington* examines the relation of Mishna, *Sifra* and *Leviticus Rabbah* to Scripture, in particular to Leviticus, extensively arguing with Jacob Neusner. She shows in detail the similarities and differences between these three texts or groups of texts in their respective use of Leviticus. The Rabbis "focused on settling ambiguity, not on restating the obvious message of the text." *Gerhard Bodendorfer* explains by a number of texts and from different views

the important hermeneutical function God's "self-introductory formula" אני יהוה serves in *Sifra*. Of particular relevance is the use of
the formula with regard to the Exodus from Egypt, which is closely
connected to the concept of holiness. "Exodus as sanctification means
separation and is connected to the radical acceptance of the commandments. . . . This is meant as warning and insistent exhortation;
at the same time however it contains an aspect of hope and consolation, especially in view of the apocalyptic redemption."

Finally, two essays are devoted to feminist interpretation, whose
importance had been more and more realized in recent years. *Linda
Schearing* explores the history of Leviticus 12's reception. From the
two millennia of interpretation she singles out: early and medieval
Judaism, patristic and medieval Christianity, and contemporary liturgical responses in Judaism and Christianity. She unfolds a broad
spectrum of traditions and opinions, sometimes rather controversial.
The contemporary discussion concentrates on the question whether
to "recover" 12:1–5 liturgically for contemporary women, or to invent
new rituals to replace it. The problems are far from being resolved.
Schearing quotes Rabbi Melissa Crespy: "perhaps these verses and
commentaries would not be so painful if the reality they reflect existed
only in the distant past. But this is not true." *Judith Wegner* examines the roots of the exclusion of women from the public domain of
the priestly cult. By scrutinizing several texts, in particular with regard
to the formula "before the Lord" (לפני יהוה), she demonstrates that
in the priestly texts women are totally excluded from any cultic activity that would bring them in the cultic presence of God. The far-
reaching impact of this approach to rabbinic and patristic rulings to
a large extent determines until today the behavior of Jewish and
Christian societies towards women.

This brief résumé of the essays collected in this volume shows a
multivoiced ensemble of approaches and opinions mirroring the present scholarly field with regard to Leviticus. Things are on the move,
and Leviticus is going to become a serious topic in the scholarly discussion on "The Formation and Interpretation of Old Testament
Literature."

PART ONE

LEVITICUS IN ITS LITERARY CONTEXT

LEVITICUS: ITS LITERARY HISTORY AND LOCATION IN BIBLICAL LITERATURE

Baruch A. Levine

The entire book of Leviticus is most probably composed of priestly literature. Attempts to find traces of the ubiquitous Deuteronomist in Leviticus have been less than convincing, and proceed from the questionable assumption that writers of the Deuteronomistic "school" were the final redactors of Torah literature. It is more likely that priestly writers were the last to contribute to the text of the Torah, and to edit it. We may gather as much from a series of priestly addenda appearing in the final chapters of Deuteronomy. We first encounter the priestly passage in Deut 31:23–30 that introduces Moses' poetic oration, הַאֲזִינוּ "Give ear!" (Deut 32:1–43) which, even if not fully priestly, was certainly edited by priests. Then comes a priestly postscript to that very poem, in Deut 32:48–52. Finally, there are the concluding verses of the entire book of Deuteronomy (34:6–12), which bear all the earmarks of priestly diction. This means, in effect, that the task of tracing the formation and redaction of Leviticus is part of the larger endeavor of reconstructing the transmission of priestly writings in the Torah, with a spin-off in the book of Joshua.

Since the beginnings of modern biblical research, the literary history of the Torah has been a subject of controversy between the traditionalists and the modernists within both Christian and Jewish scholarship, as well as among diverse modernists from both confessions, and critical scholars who would not regard themselves as religiously affiliated, at all. The discussion to follow is primarily intended to summarize my own views and methodology, within a publication where others are presenting diverse views. The basic positions taken here have been argued in detail in my publications, with progressive refinements and modifications, and the reader will be directed to the relevant literature in due course. These studies contain extensive bibliographies for reference. The challenge of preparing the present discussion has stimulated some new observations on my part.

The issues involved in tracing the formation of Torah literature ought to be engaged in two complementary ways: (1) Through inner-biblical investigation. This would include the identification of the

Pentateuchal "sources," and their alignment in chronological sequence, so as to approximate the dates, or periods of their compilation, and the *Sitz im Leben* of their respective authors. It would also involve tracing the development of biblical institutions and practices, in the case of priestly literature—the festivals, celebrations, and purifications characteristic of the cult; the roles of the clergy, the nature of sacred space, and much more. (2) Through comparative investigation. This would involve examining comparative evidence bearing on the language, structure, and substantive content of the Torah sources, all of which would help to fix their historical and cultural context. It would also include historical inquiry into the situation of the Israelite-Jewish people at various periods, into its socio-political status and cultural character.

In my view, it is unlikely that inner-biblical evidence alone, as enlightening as it may be, can enable us to reconstruct the formation of priestly literature, in particular. This is because Torah literature has been variously analyzed in terms of its distinctive language and themes, and the relationship of the *Priesterschrift* to the other sources, and there is no clear way to demonstrate the conclusiveness of any one reconstruction over the others. Biblical texts provide no colophons, and efforts to date them can only produce a relative chronology, at best. Ultimately, it is on the basis of comparative evidence that we may succeed in locating this textual material in a more or less definitive historical setting, because such external information, though limited, is available in its original form, and can often be dated, and its provenance identified quite precisely. The argument, based on inner-biblical considerations, as to whether the *Priesterschrift* is pre-exilic or post-exilic, has become stale, and it is time to look to comparative indications for resolution.

Inner-Biblical Considerations

At the present time, source criticism is hardly at the center of biblical research, with major attention being given rather to the study of the Hebrew Bible as literature. In recent years, historicism as a method of biblical study has come under attack by the so-called "minimalists," and the resulting ferment has inevitably affected efforts in the area of source criticism, which shares with historicism the objective of tracing the chronology of the biblical record. The emphasis

on literary approaches has also dampened interest in philology and
exegesis, directing scholarly focus to larger textual units in the quest
for structural insights. It should be conceded that source-criticism
had become progressively atomistic, breaking down discrete texts into
ever more minute units, and positing numerous sub-sections. At the
same time, the beginnings of a synthesis between archaeological discovery and textual interpretation are now clearly visible. This process
has a long way to go before producing coherent results, and what
is more, the dearth of written records among the archaeological finds
from Bible lands severely restricts our ability to relate material culture to texts.

And yet, we should not be too quick to dismiss the importance
of source criticism, if this method is pursued intelligently and applied
to the literary history of Leviticus, and of priestly literature, as a
whole. With penetrating insight, Julius Wellhausen effectively fixed
the order of the Torah sources as (1) J and E (= Jahwist and Elohist),
the oldest Torah sources, (2) D (= Deuteronomy), and P (= *Priesterschrift*).
He and other scholars of his time were very detailed in their analysis, but for the purposes of the present discussion, it will be sufficient
to limit ourselves to the relationship between D and P. Wellhausen
correctly understood that the requirements of Leviticus 17, the
Prologue to the Holiness Code (= H), were inevitably based on the
doctrine of cult centralization put forth in Deuteronomy, chapters
12 and 16. The rule that all sacrifices must be offered at the altar
standing at the opening of the Tent of Meeting makes sense only if
we assume that the authors of Leviticus 17 were endorsing, in a
retrojection of the wilderness period that portrays a tent-like, portable
Tabernacle, the Deuteronomic doctrine of cult centralization, in reality aimed at outlawing the many permanent cult installations of
ancient Israel.[1] A close reading of Leviticus 17, with its reference to
pouring out the blood of hunted animals, leads to the conclusion
that it is a veritable reflex of Deuteronomy 12. Wellhausen went
much further, however, in stressing that the entire regimen of worship and celebration as prescribed in P was based on the concept
of a unique altar and sanctuary. Focusing on the Tabernacle traditions
of Exodus 25–Leviticus 9, he notes: "The assumption that worship

---

[1] J. Wellhausen, *Prolegomena to the History of Ancient Israel* (1878; repr., Cleveland:
World Publishing, 1965) 34–38.

is restricted to one single centre runs everywhere throughout the entire document."[2]

The more recent studies by H. L. Ginsberg on the harvest festivals of biblical Israel, and on the early transmission of core-Deuteronomy to Judah from northern Israel, serve to corroborate Wellhausen's basic insight.[3] The deferral of the pilgrimage festival of First Fruits to a date seven weeks after the offering of the first sheaf during the Pesah-מצות festival, as ordained in Leviticus 23 (assigned to H, in its primary form), seems surely to be a response to the festival legislation of Deuteronomy 16. Once all sacrificial activity was restricted to a central temple, the long pilgrimage that was required of one if he were to be present at the sacrifice would be most inconvenient at the beginning of the spring, grain harvest. It is this new situation that explains the deferral legislated in Deuteronomy 16, and endorsed by priestly law in Leviticus 23. In Ginsberg's reconstruction, the Deuteronomic movement toward cult centralization, first proposed in northern Israel and encouraged by the prophecies of Hosea, was revived in Judah late in the reign of the heterodox king, Manasseh, and subsequently adopted by Josiah, king of Judah, as a practical program of cultic reform (2 Kings 22–23).

In contrast, the Herculean attempt of Yehezkel Kaufmann[4] to reverse the order of the two sources, dating P before D, runs into serious problems, especially if we accept the northern-Israelite hypothesis, according to Ginsberg. The first objection is raised by an analysis of language and diction. It is a curious fact that early attempts, by the likes of S. R. Driver,[5] for instance, to establish the textual limits of the *Priesterschrift* primarily on the basis of distinctive language, have held their ground, and are, with a few minor exceptions, acceptable even today. Notwithstanding all of the refinements in our knowledge of biblical Hebrew, it remains clear that priestly writings show evidence of lateness relative to the other sources. This can now be argued on a comparative basis, as will be clarified further on. How, then, are we to explain that texts which read so much

---

[2] Wellhausen, *Prolegomena*, 34.

[3] H. L. Ginsberg, *The Israelian Heritage of Judaism* (New York: Jewish Theological Seminary of America, 1982) 55–83.

[4] Y. Kaufmann, *The Religion of Israel from Its Beginnings to the Babylonian Exile* (trans. and ed. M. Greenberg; Chicago: University of Chicago Press, 1960).

[5] S. R. Driver, *Introduction to the Literature of the Old Testament* (Edinburgh: T&T Clark, 1894) 118–50.

like post-exilic biblical writings, like Ezra-Nehemiah and Chronicles, are allegedly to be assigned to a relatively early period? Specifically, some have pointed to the reign of Hezekiah, in the late eighth to early seventh centuries BCE, who is credited with having attempted to eliminate the local and regional high-places (במות, 2 Kgs 18:3–4, 22). However, the notion that early priestly texts were regarded as being so esoteric as not to be promulgated until a much later period, and then pervasively reformulated in the diction of later writings, is highly questionable.

If the precedence of D is accepted, and if the movement toward cult centralization it propounds was revived in Judah only in the mid-to-late seventh century BCE, then the earliest strata of the *Priesterschrift* would have been composed in the near-exilic period, or, as is more likely, subsequent to that time, during the exile or after the waves of return following 538 BCE, when the Cyrus edict was issued. When we examine the evidence of Ezekiel, especially of chapters 40–48, on the performance of the Jerusalem cult we are prompted to doubt that the author(s) of Ezekiel had very much of the *Priesterschrift* before them. This issue becomes more poignant when we apply source critical analysis to Ezekiel 40–48, in particular, and find that these chapters contain major interpolations, bringing us well into the exilic period, at the earliest. If we conclude, as we do, that Ezekiel 40–48 preceded the composition of at least most of the *Priesterschrift*, then we are well into the exile, more probably in post-exilic Jerusalem and Judea. Although it is possible that parts of the *Priesterschrift* were composed in Babylonia, it is more likely that such creativity occurred in the restored Jewish community, with the Temple of Jerusalem as its central institution. It has already been noted by many scholars that the daily burnt offering (עלת תמיד) of the evening, ordained in Exodus 29 and Numbers 28–29, is not mentioned in Ezekiel 40–48, or in Kings, for that matter, which knows only one daily burnt offering brought in the morning (2 Kgs 16:15). It is also suggestive that the notion of "release" (דרור), employed in Jeremiah 34 with reference to the manumission of slaves when the Chaldeans were at the gates of Jerusalem, becomes in Isa 61:1 a way of expressing the release of the Judeans after fifty years of exile. This could be what lies behind the theme of the Jubilee year so prominent in Leviticus 25 and 27. It is also worth noting that the verb גאל "to redeem, restore," so central to the exilic visions of national return to the homeland in Deutero- (and Trito-) Isaiah (Isa 41:14; 43:1; 14, 44:

22–24; 47:4; 48:17; 20; 49:7; 26; 51:10; 54:5; 8; 59:20; 60:16; 62:12;
63:4; 9) is prominent in Leviticus 25, where the subject at hand is
redemption of family land lost through default of debt. We must
concede, however, that the author of Ezek 46:17, part of a late interpolation in Ezekiel 40–48, who refers to "the year of release" (שנת
הדרור) as a known institution relevant to land tenure, may have had
Leviticus 25 and 27 before him.[6]

This last caveat leads us directly to a consideration of a rather
clear stratification within the *Priesterschrift,* itself, between what has
become known as the Holiness Code (= H), and the rest of this
source. Generally speaking, the Holiness Code is contained in Leviticus
17–27, minus its accretions, wherein the theme of קדוש "holy" is
prominent. Notwithstanding the recent attempts to argue that H is
largely redactional, and therefore subsequent to the core of the
Priesterschrift it is more likely that H represents the primary stratum
of the *Priesterschrift.* This can be shown by an analysis of a core section of H, the festival calendar of Leviticus 23. Within that chapter
we observe a series of interpolations which significantly alter the
character of the rites involved.

Representing H, Leviticus 23 had originally prescribed a sequence
of display offerings, beginning with the first sheaf (עמר) of new barley grain brought at some point during the Pesah festival (Lev 23:9–11,
14), and concluding with two further display offerings of new wheat
seven Sabbaths later (Lev 23:15–17, 20–22). The mode of display
offerings, or of presentation, expressed by the verb הניף "to raise,"
and the noun תנופה "raised offering," represents an early, typically
Near Eastern type of sacrifice. It is this mode which we observe in
the offering of first fruits as prescribed in Deuteronomy 26, for
instance, where the operative verb is הניח "to set down, present."
However, presentation as a mode of sacrifice lost ground in ancient
Israel to the burnt altar offering, and to similarly disposed rites, so
that even certain display offerings, themselves, were adapted to the
ascendant mode. In synch with this development in cultic practice,
Lev 23:12–13 and 18–20 were interpolated by a later priestly writer
so as to bring the festival rites of Leviticus 23 into conformity with

---

[6] B. A. Levine, "Late Language in the Priestly Source: Some Literary and Historical
Observations," in U. O. Schmelz, P. Glikson, and S. DellaPergola (eds.), *Proceedings
of the 8th World Congress of Jewish Studies (1981)* (Jerusalem: Hebrew University, 1983)
69–82.

what had become the prevailing pattern, a pattern evident, for example, in the sacrificial prescriptions of Leviticus 1–7. These verses add
the requirement of an עלה, and a burnt grain offering (מנחה) at the
beginning of the seven week period, and of an even more elaborate
combination of burnt altar sacrifices, including libations, at the end
of that period.[7]

This source-critical analysis argues for the primacy of H in the
Priesterschrift, showing that the rites as prescribed in H, representing
the earlier mode, were adapted to the later mode, which became
normal thereafter. When we encounter the קדוש theme in such redactional verses as Lev 11:44–45, at the end of the dietary code, it is
likely that we have the work of an even later priestly writer, expressing himself in the idiom of the Holiness Code. In late priestly writings, we note a widespread tendency toward anachronism, and the
blending of early and late traditions.

It is important to emphasize that the *Priesterschrift* contains both
ritual texts and legislation, on the one hand, and narratives, on the
other, and even preserves a poetic, or liturgical excerpt or two (Num
5:24–26, the priestly benediction; Num 10:35–36, the song of the
ark). Priestly law and ritual cannot be studied in detachment from
priestly narrative. True, the primary reality underlying the priestly
Torah texts was undoubtedly the cult, itself, with its sacred spaces,
edifices and appurtenances, and its sanctified clergy; its rites of
sacrifice, celebration, and purification, and its appointed times—
Sabbaths and festivals and other sacred occasions. More generally,
priestly law presents a coherent program for the constitution of
Israelite-Jewish society in which cult and celebration, and the personnel and institutions pertaining to them, were to play a central
role. In turn, this program was sanctioned by a recasting of Israelite
origins and early history in the priestly narratives of Genesis and
Exodus.

These narratives share the distinctive priestly vocabulary. Thus,
Leviticus 25 and 27, in discussing the legalities of land tenure, define
the status of land in Canaan as אחזה "acquired land," and the status of the Israelites who possess it as that of גרים ותושבים "resident
aliens, tenants." Compare these categories with the priestly narrative of Genesis 23, where we read that Abraham, self-defined as

---

[7] B. A. Levine, *Leviticus* (JPS Torah Commentary; Philadelphia: Jewish Publication
Society, 1989) 153–63.

גר ותושב, purchases a grave site as an אחזה. Or, with Genesis 34, an
account of negotiations on rights of residence with the Canaanites
of Shechem, where the denominative האחזו "to acquire the right of
אחזה" is used. In Genesis 47 we find similar terminology in recount-
ing Pharaoh's grant of land in Egypt to the clan of Jacob. As a further example, Lev 25:30 stipulates that urban real estate sold under
duress may be redeemed only up to a year after the sale, and if not
redeemed within that period of time becomes the permanent possession of the purchaser. This legal status is expressed by the verb
קום "to become legally valid," an Aramaistic connotation also present in Gen 23:17, where it conveys that Ephron's field and the cave
located within it have, indeed, become Abraham's property. Such
distinctive diction suggests a purposeful literary program intended to
offer an alternative version of Israelite origins in Canaan to that presented in JE and D.

More can be said about the place of Leviticus, and of the *Priesterschrift* within Torah literature, but the above discussion will suffice
to clarify the view that Leviticus is subsequent to core-Deuteronomy,
and even to the additions of the Deuteronomist. Within Leviticus,
itself, we can distinguish between the Holiness Code, and later priestly
ritual and law by tracing the adaptation of certain presentational
sacrifices to the ascendant mode of the burnt altar offering.

Comparative Considerations

We ought not to conclude from what has been said up to this point
that all of the priestly rites and laws of the Torah were introduced,
or originated in late biblical times. Even Wellhausen in his day realized that very ancient practices were preserved in the *Priesterschrift*,
itself a product of a later age. We now possess comparative evidence
indicating that burnt offerings like the עלה, and sacred meals like
the שלמים are known from Ugaritic rituals, dating from the Late
Bronze Age, where burnt offerings go by the name of *šrp* and sacred
meals by the same name as in the biblical cult, namely, *šlmm*. In
the Ebla texts of the late third millennium BCE there is mention of
burnt offerings known as *sarapati*.[8] Although such offerings are described
in earlier biblical texts, the elaborate ritual structure of Leviticus (and

---

[8] B. A. Levine and J.-M. de Tarragon "The King Proclaims the Day: Ugaritic
Rites for the Vintage (*KTU* 1.41//1.97)," *RB* 100 (1993) 76–115.

of Numbers), shows substantial development beyond what had been formerly introduced into practice. Whereas it is true that very ancient rites and legal practices often persisted over long periods of time (e.g. the law of release [דרור, Lev 25:10], and that which prohibits irretrievable sale [לצמתת, Lev 25:23]), it is from innovations, not from survivals, that we learn how relatively late certain patterns were.

In some respects, distinctive vocabulary and diction are inner-biblical features, as we have seen. And yet, they also provide comparative evidence on the dating and provenance of the *Priesterschrift*, and of Leviticus, in particular. This is because we now possess extra-biblical evidence on language that can be dated rather closely. Attention has already been called to the nuances of the verb קום "to arise, stand," which, in Aramaic legal parlance of the Persian period, means "to be legally valid, binding." These very nuances predominate in Numbers 30, the chapter on vows, where we also encounter the Aramaic term אסר "binding agreement," now attested in the Aramaic papyri from Wadi Daliyeh of the fourth century BCE.[9]

The *Priesterschrift's* distinctive term for the Israelite community, and for its representative assemblies, namely, עדה (Lev 4:15, 19:2, *et passim*), is attested in the Elephantine Aramaic papyri of the fifth century BCE.[10] The unit of three tribes called דגל in Numbers 2 and 10 is identical with Aramaic דגל, דגלא, used to designate the Persian military unit in the Elephantine papyri, a designation also attested at contemporary Saqqara, in Egypt. What is more, it has turned up at Arad, in Aramaic ostraca of the Persian period, which is closer to home.[11]

The significance of such terms as עדה and דגל is much more than linguistic, however. The case of דגל suggests that what is projected in Numbers as the Israelite encampment of the wilderness period is really a mirror-image of the Persian system of military colonies on the borders of the empire. The case of עדה is a bit more subtle. It directs our attention to Persian administration in the Babylonian cities, where the local assembly, called *puḫru*, in Akkadian, exercized considerable power. Now, Hebrew/Aramaic עדה is a semantic equivalent of Akkadian *puḫru*; it may even be a calque of it, for all we know.

[9] B. A. Levine, *Numbers 21–36* (AB 4A; New York: Doubleday, 2000) 425–41.
[10] B. A. Levine, *Leviticus*, 22; B. A. Levine, *Numbers 1–21* (AB 4; New York: Doubleday, 1993) 130–31, 411–13.
[11] B. A. Levine, *Numbers 1–21*, 142–50.

Another informative term is Hebrew נשיא, "chieftain," an early
tribal office (Exod 22:27), revived and modulated by the priestly writers, beginning with Ezekiel. It, too, leads us to comparative considerations. In Ezra 1:8, Sheshbazzar is called הנשיא ליהודה "the נשיא
for Judea." We read that he was given the temple vessels seized by
Nebuchadnezzar by the Persian authorities, and, indeed, in Ezra
5:14 we are told that the very same Sheshbazzar was appointed פחה
"governor." This equivalence suggests that the same official whom
the Persians called פחה, using an Aramaic form of the Akkadian
title, *bēl piḥati* "governor," was called פחה by the Judeans, and that
the priestly writers had, in fact, internalized a feature of Persian
administration. The title פחה appears frequently in the Aramaic
Elephantine papyri, and on Palestinian coins of the Persian period.
More recently, it has turned up in the Samaria papyri of the fourth
century BCE.[12]

This very equation: פחה = נשיא may lie behind the expanded role
of the נשיא envisioned in Ezekiel 40–48, and would explain why
David, whom God calls עבדי "my servant," is given the title נשיא in
Ezek 34:24, 37:25. The political organization of the Persian period
may also explain the fact that the Hivite ruler of Shechem is called
נשיא הארץ "the governor of the land" in Gen 34:2, within a priestly
text, and why the so-called Hittite ruler of Hebron calls Abraham
נשיא אלהים "a governor favored by God," in Genesis 23, another
priestly text.

Methodologically, it is research into the political, religious, and
institutional history of cities and provinces under Persian imperial
administration that may ultimately reveal the *Sitz im Leben* of priestly
literature. Information similar to what the Aramaic papyri from
Persian Egypt provide is to be found in Late-Babylonian sources,
and in records from other locations. The central role ascribed to the
priesthood and the functions of the Jerusalem temple projected in
Leviticus 25–27 accord well with what is known of Persian administration elsewhere. A give-away of post-exilic provenance is the exceptional provision of Lev 25:47 enjoining clan relatives to redeem land
lost through forfeiture to non-Israelites. This would be realistic in
the post-exilic period, as it reflects the problems of a mixed popu-

---

[12] J. Hoftijzer and K. Jongeling, *Dictionary of the Northwest-Semitic Inscriptions* (2 vols.;
Leiden: Brill, 1995) 904.

lation such as existed in Jerusalem and Judea, and the coastal areas during the Persian period. Generally, there is much in common between Leviticus 25 and 27 and Nehemiah 5, a chronicle of life under Persian administration. The comparative approach to the literary history of the *Priesterschrift* is only in its beginnings, and will undoubtedly benefit greatly from recent interest in the history of the Persian empire. In summary, comparative indications, when combined with inner-biblical considerations point to the Persian period as a time of priestly creativity in law, ritual and narrative.

The Composition of Leviticus and its Location

Once we acknowledge that the Holiness Code (H), contained within Leviticus 17–27, is the primary stratum of Leviticus we may proceed to an internal analysis of this major section of the book. Allowing for the usual prescriptive introductions and summary postscripts, we may identify the following as basic components of H: (1) Leviticus 17, the Prologue to the Holiness Code. Although there is evidence of internal redaction in Leviticus 17, as indicated by repetition and shifts in language, the principal thrusts of the chapter, namely, the idea of a single altar, and the emphatic statement of the blood *tabu* express the policy of H on proper sacrifice, a policy impacted by Deuteronomy. (2) Leviticus 18, the rules of incest, which define the limits of the nuclear family, and the prohibition of certain other sexual unions. The provisions of Lev 18:6–23 are undoubtedly primary vis-à-vis Leviticus 20, which restates the subject. (3) Leviticus 19, the basic teachings of the Holiness Code, commanding the Israelites to be קדושים "holy." (4) Leviticus 21, special rules governing the Israelite priesthood, including disqualifying blemishes. (5) Leviticus 22, a collection of regulations affecting the priesthood, including the priestly entitlements and the requirements of ritual purity. Also included are rules regarding sacrificial animals. It is unlikely, however, that all of this material belongs with the Holiness Code. (6) Leviticus 23, a calendar of annual festivals which shows considerable internal redaction. It has already been noted that some of the required sacrificial rites, originally presentational in their performance, have been accommodated to the ascendant mode of burnt altar offerings. We also note two versions of the rites celebrating the autumn harvest festival and the addition of a Sabbath law at the beginning of the chapter.

What is singular in Leviticus 23 is the emphasis on the Sabbath as
defining the week, a theme expanded in Leviticus 25 and 27, where
we read of periods of seven years' duration, even of seven-times-
seven. (7) Lev 24:15–23, an early collection of laws resembling the
Book of the Covenant of Exodus in its formulation. (8) Leviticus 25,
and its supplement, Leviticus 27, laws of land tenure, debt and inden-
ture, the Sabbatical year and the Jubilee, and the funding of the
sanctuary.

It would seem that (a) Leviticus 20, (b) unidentified parts of Leviticus
22, (c) certain insertions in Leviticus 23, (d) most of Leviticus 24,
and (e) Lev 26:3–46, the Epilogue to the Holiness Code, all represent later strata. What we have in Leviticus 17–27 is, therefore, a
blending of H and later strands of P, all expressive of priestly concerns, and addressed for the most part to the Israelite people. It is
worth mentioning that Leviticus 24:11–14 provide a narrative introduction to a previously unmentioned law governing blasphemy, as
if to say that the relevant law was occasioned by an actual incident.
We note the same literary device in Num 9:6–8, and 15:33–36. The
only truly prosaic contribution to Leviticus is to be found in the
Epilogue to the Holiness Code, Lev 26:3–26. This binary admonition
to the people of Israel resembles a blessing-curse section of a treaty,
and in some respects recalls the similar admonition of Deuteronomy
28. It reflects the progressive, ever deepening despair of the Judeans
in the Babylonian exile, but ends with the divine promise that the
God of Israel will remember his covenant with the Patriarchs, and
remember the desolate land, as well.[13]

The former part of Leviticus, chapters 1–16, pertains more specifically to the priesthood. An exception is Leviticus 11, the dietary
code, which expands on Deuteronomy 14. Although these dietary
regulations applied to all Israelites, the priests were the ones charged
with instructing the people in their proper observance. For the rest,
Leviticus 1–7 outline the various classes of sacrificial rites, whereas
Leviticus 8–10 record the installation of the Aaronide priesthood,
and the initiation of sacrificial worship in the Tabernacle. Leviticus
8–10 contain narrative elements, and this is particularly true of
Leviticus 10. There is an obvious logic to this sequence, whereby
the various types of sacrifices are first set forth, and then the initi-

---

[13] Levine, *Leviticus*, 275–81.

ation of the cult is recorded. Turning to purification, Leviticus 11–16 lay out the role of the priesthood in purifying afflicted Israelites. The priests are to instruct the Israelites in avoiding improper foods (Leviticus 11), and they undertake to maintain the purity of afflicted individual Israelites, and of the Sanctuary itself.

Although Leviticus is located between Exodus and Numbers, there are clear indications that most of the material included in the Tabernacle texts of Exodus 25–40 is subsequent to Leviticus, and that there is a clear link between Exodus 25–40 and the Tabernacle traditions of Numbers 1:1–10:28.

Most probably, it was a basic thrust of the priestly agenda to link the Tabernacle project to the Sinai theophany, and to embed Leviticus in the ongoing chronology of the wilderness period. In that traditional, priestly chronology, all that is recorded in the book of Leviticus took up one month's time. Thus, Exod 40:17 records that the Tabernacle was erected on the first day of the first month of the second year after the Exodus. Leviticus then sets forth the cultic regimen of the Tabernacle, most often called אהל מועד "the Tent of Meeting," and of its clergy. Numbers 1:1 is dated on the first day of the second month of the same year, when the ordering of the Israelite encampment around the Tabernacle commenced with a census. We may assume that the Leviticus material was encased in a subsequently composed rubric, which began in Exodus 25 and concluded in Num 10:28, when the encampment set forth on the march. In Leviticus there is no movement.

H_R IN LEVITICUS AND ELSEWHERE IN THE TORAH

Jacob Milgrom

The fundamental premise in unpacking Leviticus is that it comprises two priestly sources, P (chapters 1–16) and H (chapters 17–27) and that H is the redactor of P. In addition to the evidence cited by Knohl[1] I have found thirteen additional pieces of ammunition to add to his stockpile.[2] Among the most potent is H's festival calendar, Leviticus 23. The reference of the repeated formula והקרבתם אשה לה׳, "you shall offer food gifts to YHWH" (vv. 8, 23, 27, 36 [bis], 37) is Numbers 28–29 (P). When H agrees with Numbers 28–29 on sacrificial offerings it uses this formula. However, when H prescribes sacrifices for the grain festivals it enumerates all the requisite sacrifices (vv. 12–13, 18–19).

The reason is obvious. P's festival calendar (Numbers 28–29) has no firstfruits of barley offering; H (Lev 23:12–13) must therefore prescribe it. P does prescribe a firstfruits of wheat offering (Num 28:26–31). In this case H differs with P's sacrificial requirements. H must therefore prescribe its own version (Lev 23:18–19). Thus the logical (and chronological) relationship between Leviticus 23 (H) and Numbers 28–29 makes sense only if H is later than P. Indeed, if H were earlier than P why would two of its festivals list sacrifices and not the others? And what would be the referent of "you shall offer food gifts to YHWH"?

I cite, as an example of how the borrowing took place, the prescriptions for the festival of Alarm Blasts.[3]

---

[1] I. Knohl, *The Sanctuary of Silence* (Minneapolis: Fortress, 1995) 11–23.

[2] J. Milgrom, *Leviticus 17–22* (AB 3A; New York: Doubleday, 2000) 1349–51.

[3] For H's rewriting of P's texts on the Day of Purgation and the Festival of Booths, see J. Milgrom, *Leviticus 23–27* (AB 3B; New York: Doubleday, 2001) 2019–20, 2027.

Lev 23:23–25	Num 29:1–2a, 6b
<div dir="rtl">²³[וידבר ה' אל־משה לאמר ²⁴דבר אל בני ישראל לאמר] בחדש השביעי באחד לחדש יהיה לכם [שבתון זכרון] תרועה מקרא־קדש ²⁵כל־מלאכת עבדה לא תעשו [והקרבתם] אשה לה'</div>	<div dir="rtl">¹(ו)בחדש השביעי באחד לחדש מקרא קדש יהיה לכם כל־מלאכת עבדה לא תעשו יום תרועה (יהיה לכם ²ועשיתם עלה . . . ⁶ᵇלריח ניחח) אשה לה'</div>

Lev 23:23–25	Num 29:1–2a, 6b
²³[YHWH spoke to Moses saying, ²⁴"Speak to the Israelites thus:] 'In the seventh month, on the first day of the month, you shall observe a rest, [a sacred occasion, commemorated with] alarm blasts. ²⁵You shall do no laborious work, [and you shall present] a food-gift to YHWH'."	¹(And) in the seventh month, on the first day of the month, you shall observe a sacred occasion; you shall do no laborious work. (You shall observe a day of) alarm blasts. ²(You shall sacrifice a burnt offering . . . ⁶ᵇof pleasant aroma) a food gift to YHWH.

The parentheses in Numbers contain words deleted in Leviticus, while the brackets in Leviticus contain additions to Numbers. Leviticus 23 (H) takes for granted the sacrificial list detailed in Numbers 29, and it innovates two new terms, שבתון and זכרון. One must therefore conclude that the H legist had the actual text of P before him.

In my opinion, more than 95% of H's material is the product of the eighth century. It may be the work of a single generation of "young Turks," who radically changed priestly thought. Here I agree with Israel Knohl but I differ with him by rejecting his term "school" because I find no sign of continuous literary activity that would warrant it. There is only H and the remaining H_R (approximately 5%) composed in the Babylonian exile.

Leviticus 23 also testifies that H is not monolithic. It comprises four strata, two consisting of several (mainly partial) verses which were absorbed in H, labeled Pre-H₁ and Pre-H₂, and one exilic stratum H_R (vv. 1–3, 39–43) attached to the main text, the original calendar (H, vv. 4–38, 44).⁴ Thus, Leviticus 23 is totally the product of H. Against Haran and Knohl⁵ there is no original P in the entire

---

⁴ For details, see J. Milgrom, *Leviticus 23–27*, 1947–2053.
⁵ M. Haran, *Temples and Temple Service* (Oxford: Clarendon, 1978) 298, n. 27; Knohl, *The Sanctuary of Silence*, 8–52.

chapter. As indicated above, it only cites from P's cultic calendar
(Numbers 28–29) in order to compose its own.

The unifying theme of Leviticus 17–27 (H) is holiness. Its center
is chapter 19 which also provides its rationales. This chapter would
have introduced H, i.e. all the holiness materials, were it not for the
redactor H$_R$'s desire to make it the center of the entire book of
Leviticus by flanking it with two fairly similar collections of sexual
prohibitions (chapters 18–20) in chiastic order. These are followed
by holiness prohibitions for priests and laity (chapters 21–22), holiness of time (chapter 23), holy oil, holy bread and YHWH's name
(chapter 24), YHWH's land (chapter 25), YHWH's covenant (chapter 26) and consecrations (chapter 27).[6] The root קדש, "holy" appears
expressly or implicitly even in YHWH's name, land, and covenant.
Thus holiness appears throughout H except at H's beginning (chapters 17–18). Chapter 18, however, implies holiness by mentioning
the desecration (חלל) of YHWH's name, a common H motif (19:12,
20:6, 21:6, 22:2, 32). Anomalous chapter 17, containing no H motif,
even implicitly, was needed because its sacrificial laws befitted the
opening of a code (cf. Exod 20:22–26 [JE]; Deuteronomy 12 [D]),
because of its thematic and verbal associations with P's closing chapter 16, and because it served as a suitable bridge between P and H.
The theme of holiness thus accounts for the choice of these chapters
and justifies the use of the siglum H (holiness) to identify them.

Chapter 27 is an appendix. To be sure, it is linked to chapter 25
by the law of the jubilee (27:17–24; 25:10–54). However, it is likely
that it supplements and completes the laws of property desecration
(5:14–16). Both chapters 27 and 5:14–16 speak of a 20% fine; whereas
in chapter 27 it is a *charge* imposed for the *right* to convert the sacred
into the profane, in 5:14–16 it is a *penalty* for the *crime* of doing the
same. Thus all the cases of desanctification, legitimate and illegitimate, are covered. Nonetheless, chapter 27 remains an appendix. It
follows blessings and comminations (chapter 26) that normally ter-
minate a law corpus (e.g., Exod 23:20; Deuteronomy 28). Moreover,
both chapters 26 and 27 contain closing subscripts (26:46; 27:34).
Indeed, the subscript of chapter 26 contains the term תורה, found
only in P (6:2, 7, 18, 7:11; 13:58; 14:54–57; 15:32), indicating that
chapter 26, and not chapter 27, is H's closure to the book of Leviticus.

---

[6] The composition of H in Leviticus is spelled out in Milgrom, *Leviticus 17–22*,
1397–1400.

The appendix chapter 27 was probably chosen by H_R to close H's book of Leviticus because it deals with consecrations (and vows) to the sanctuary. It also complements sacrifices to the sanctuary, the content of the book's opening, chapters 1–7.[7] Thereby, chapter 27 provides a latch enclosing the book in a ring[8] as illustrated in Mary Douglas' diagram below, which I have slightly amended. I have also made provisions for its unnecessary tilt and bracketed the bulge formed by H_R's insertion of Leviticus 27 into Leviticus.

Leviticus in a Ring

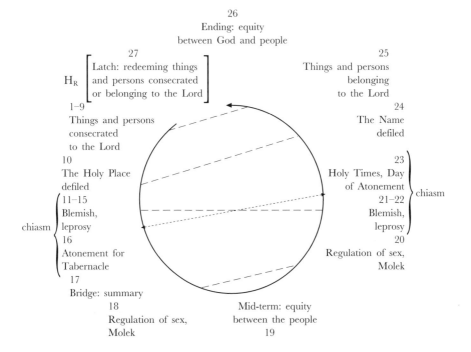

    ⁷ Cf. M. Douglas, "The Forbidden Animals in Leviticus," *JSOT* 59 (1993) 3–23; idem, "Poetic Structure in Leviticus," in D. P. Wright et al. (eds.), *Pomegranates and Golden Bells* (Winona Lake, IN: Eisenbrauns, 1995) 247–55.
    ⁸ Douglas' contribution is discussed in Milgrom, *Leviticus 17–22*, 1364–65 and *Leviticus 23–27*, 2407–9.

The virtues of Douglas' ring construction (overlooking its terminological imprecision) are, moving upward, as follows:

1. The central turning point (chapter 19) is flanked by two chapters of equivalent content (18 and 20) in chiastic relation.
2. The beginning of the central turning point (19:1–4) is matched
   in content (the Decalogue) by the beginning of the closing turning point (26:1–2) and offers a reason why the latter was inserted
   as a prefix to the chapter on blessings and curses (26:3–46). The
   two chapters are each enclosed by allusions to the Decalogue
   (19:30–32; 26:42–45).
3. Chapter 17 is not a summary, but a bridge between the two parts
   of Leviticus: chapters 1–16 and 18–27.
4. Chapters 11–16 and 21–23 form a giant introversion in the center of the ring (ABB'A'). Carcasses are innately "blemished" (chapter 11, שקץ or טמא)[9] as are certain sacrificial animals (22:22–25)
   and certain priests (21:16–23) (AA'). Carcasses of common animals also create "blemishes" (lit. טמאה, impurity) to persons
   (11:24–38), especially to priests (22:3a–9). Impure issues and scale
   diseases in laity (chapters 12–15) and priests (22:3–9) are identical
   in diagnosis and treatment; these form the center of the chiasm.
   The holiest day (chapter 16) corresponds with the holy (festival)
   days (chapter 23, BB').
5. The two narratives in Leviticus (10:1–4; 24:10–23) face each other
   in the ring; they also share a theme, defilement of the tabernac-
   cle (chapter 10) and God's name (chapter 24). Chapter 24 was
   placed in its present spot for the sake of this ring structure.[10]
6. Holy things, sacrifices (chapters 1–9) are complemented by holy
   land and its sabbatical and jubilee regulations (chapter 25).
7. The latch (chapter 27) was appended by H_R after the original
   ending (blessings and comminations, chapter 26) in order to lock
   with the opening topic (chapters 1–9). Both deal with sanctification: of sacrifices (chapters 1–7), persons, animals, houses, and
   lands (chapter 27).

H's distinctive style and terminology are clustered outside of Leviticus,
specially in its adjoining books Exodus and Numbers. They are
located exclusively in cultic and legal passages. To be sure, they can

---

[9] Milgrom, "Two Priestly Terms *šeqeṣ* and *ṭāmē*," *Maarav* 8/2 (1992) 107–16.
[10] For a detailed analysis, see Milgrom, *Leviticus 23–27*, 2105–6.

also be identified in priestly narratives but they lack terminological precision.[11] I therefore limit this study to priestly law and cult, in particular where they are inserts into P passages. These clearly are inserts because they interrupt the flow of the text and when removed the text runs smoothly. I shall focus on its occurrence in Leviticus and Numbers.[12] I shall cite four examples.

1. *Exodus 31:12–17; 35:1–3; Lev 23:2aβ-3; 26:1–2.* The first two sabbath injunctions lie between the prescriptions for the tabernacle construction and priestly consecration (Exod 25:1–31:11) and between the prescriptions for the manufacture of the Tabernacle furniture and priestly clothes (Exod 35:4–39:43). They contain H's quintes-sential idioms: אני ה' אלהיכם, "I YHWH your God"; אני ה' מקדשכם "I YHWH your sanctifier" (cf. Lev 20:8; 21:8, 15, 23, 22:6, 32) the plural construct שבתות (cf. Lev 16:31; 23:3, 32; 25:4, 5), and YHWH's direct address to Israel (Exod 31:13, 15; 35:2, 3 LXX).[13]

These two sabbath inserts share with a third sabbath insert at the head of H's festival calendar (Lev 23:1–3) the aim of highlighting the central importance of the sabbath. Since I hold that Lev 23:1–3 was composed and inserted by exilic H_R, the probability exists that the two sabbath insertions in Exodus also stem from the pen of H_R. The rabbis hold the latter's purpose is to warn Israel not to con-struct the tabernacle on the sabbath. A historical explanation is more likely. Deprived of its temple in the Babylonian exile, Israel is informed (by H_R) that the observance of the sabbath is just as acceptable to God as worship in the Temple.

The obvious editorial seams between Lev 23:1–3 and v. 4 leave no doubt that the former, more precisely vv. 2aβ-3, is an interpolation (cf. the mention of the sabbath in v. 28). That it was composed and inserted by exilic H_R is demonstrated by the following: 1. Nowhere else is the sabbath called a מועד, "festival." 2. Similarly, nowhere else is the sabbath "proclaimed" (תקראו) or called a מקרא קדש lit. "a holy proclamation." 3. It is the only festival in chapter 23 with-out a reference to sacrifices.

---

[11] Cf. Milgrom, *Leviticus 17–22*, 1334.
[12] Noted by A. Kuenen, *An Historical-Critical Inquiry into the Origin and Composition of the Hexateuch* (London: Macmillan, 1886); S. R. Driver, *Introduction to the Literature of the Old Testament* (New York: Charles Scribner's Sons, 1913) 48–51; M. Paran, *Forms of the Priestly Style in the Pentateuch* (Jerusalem: Magnes, 1989) 167; Knohl, *Sanctuary*, 16.
[13] Details in Milgrom, *Leviticus 17–22*, 1341–44.

The only *Sitz im Leben* that can explain all these factors is the Babylonian exile, when the lack of the Temple sacrifice suspended all the festivals with the exception of the sabbath (and a revised סכות, "Festival of Booths"). Thus the sabbath was put at the head of the cultic calendar of Leviticus 23, called exceptionally a מועד, proclaimed (קרא), and marked by no sacrifice ritual.

Leviticus 26:1–2 is clearly an insert. It intrudes between two major blocks, jubilee provisions (chapter 25) and covenant (chapter 26). Why was it inserted there? As explained in my commentary,[14] since it continues an applied summary of commandments 1, 2, and 5 of the Decalogue, it seems to be a proleptic allusion to chapter 26, thereby reinforcing the basic thrust of that chapter, namely that blessings or curses will accrue to Israel in the wake of its obedience or disobedience of the covenant. A strange motive for the insertion of these two verses is found in v. 2, "You shall keep my sabbaths and venerate my sanctuary." It is an exact quotation of Lev 19:30. It not only is an allusion to the fourth commandment, it also exposes the view of the legist that the exile is caused not only by the violation of the septennial sabbath (26:34–35), but also by the violation of the weekly sabbath.

2. *Numbers 3:11–13; 8:15b–19* are inserts; remove them and again the text reads smoothly. They bear the hallmark of H: YHWH's first person address with the subject אני (3:11, 13) and the object לי (3:12, 13; 8:16 [bis], 17 [bis]), the formal אני ה׳, כפר meaning ransom (8:19)[15] and the use of rationales (3:13; 8:16, 17). The latter verses state that the Levites were chosen to replace the firstborn, who had been consecrated by YHWH (הקדשתי 3:13; 18:17; cf. Exod 13:2) as his cultic servants. The reason is not stated, but it must be that the firstborn (i.e. priests) worshiped the golden calf in contrast to the loyalty of the Levites to YHWH (Exod 32:24–29)—one of several instances where H_R demonstrates familiarity with the JE corpus.[16]

3. *Exodus 29:38–46.* At the end of the passage on the seven-day purgation and consecration of the altar (Exod 29:36–37), H_R appends a prescription on the Tamid (vv. 38–42) and a rationale for the Tabernacle (vv. 43–46). The Tamid insert is copied and condensed mainly from Num 28:3–8 (P). A significant deletion in Exodus 29

---

[14] Milgrom, *Leviticus 23–27*, 2275–85.
[15] Cf. Milgrom, *Leviticus 1–16* (AB 3; New York: Doubleday, 1991) 369–71.
[16] Details in Milgrom, *Leviticus 17–22*, 1334, 1340–41.

is בקדש הסך נסך שכר לה', "To be poured as a libation of beer inside the sanctuary" (Num 28:7b), implying that beer[17] was poured on the incense altar, a cultic act which is emphatically forbidden by H (Exod 30:9 [H]). The golden libation vessels on the table of the bread of presence were intended for use אשר יסך בהן, "with which libations would be poured" (Exod 25:29; 37:16), and being of gold could be used only inside the Tent, that is, on the inside altar. H, however, eliminated the golden libation vessels from his recapitulation of the Tamid and expressly prohibited their use (Exod 30:9) because it would imply that YHWH imbibed drink in his chambers.[18] Since the passage on the Tamid (Exod 29:38–42) is borrowed from Num 28:3–8 (P), it contains no H expressions. The opposite holds for the remaining verses, 43–46. H's imprint is explicit throughout: YHWH speaks in first person and concludes with his formulaic signature אני ה' אלהיכם (bis).

4. *Numbers 15.* As demonstrated by Kuenen[19] all of chapter 15 is the product of H (if not H_R). This can be substantiated in each of its five pericopes, vv. 1–16, 17–21, 22–31, 32–36, 37–41.[20] But why did the redactor (H_R) place it here? Traditional commentaries[21] suggest that after the Exodus generation is sentenced to die in the wilderness (Num 14:32), they are given some laws that will take effect in the promised land. Thus they are comforted that their children will inherit the land (cf. 14:31). In my commentary on Numbers, I also noted a structural reason. The book of Numbers[22] consists of an alternation of law and narrative totaling twelve units: 1:1–10:10 (law); 10:11–14:43 (narrative); 15 (law); 16–17 (narrative); 18–19 (law); 20–25 (narrative); 26:1–27:11 (law); 27:12–23 (narrative); 28–30 (law); 31:1–33:49 (narrative); 33:50–36:13 (law).[23] Thus there can be no doubt that H_R is fully aware of the narrative blocs 10:11–14:43 and 16–17 that precede and follow chapter 15. That chapter 15 is an

---

[17] J. Milgrom, *The Book of Numbers* (Philadelphia: Jewish Publication Society, 1990) 240.

[18] Ibid.

[19] Cf. Kuenen, *An Historical-Critical Inquiry*, 96, n. 37.

[20] Details in Milgrom, *Leviticus 17–22*, 1341–44.

[21] Ibid., 1343.

[22] Milgrom, *The Book of Numbers*, XV–XVI.

[23] Douglas, "Forbidden Animals," 102–22 refines my observation in her extensive treatment, which demonstrates that twelve alternating units (differently divided) form a ring (cf. Milgrom, *Leviticus 17–22*, 1365) such that Numbers 15 matches chapters 18–19 in that both deal with cultic provisions and defilement.

insertion is also highlighted by its final pericope on tassels (vv. 37–41). This pericope ends not only chapter 15 but also the larger unit Numbers 13–14, the failure of YHWH's chosen scouts in their mission to Canaan. It forms an envelope with the unit's opening verse by the similar term תתרו, "scout" (13:2; 15:39; cf. v. 25; 14:34) and further on with זנה, "whore, lust" (14:33, 15:39). Also, "that you (Israel) should not lust (זנה) after what is scouted (תר) by your eyes" (עיניכם, v. 39) negates the report of the scouts ונהי בעינינו כחגבים "we became like grasshoppers in our own eyes" (Num 13:33). Thus keeping the blue-corded tassels in sight will prevent Israel from disobeying YHWH as did the scouts.[24]

The tassels pericope also points forward to the Korahite rebellions (chapter 16). Korah's argument against the Aaronides was his ostensibly irrefutable claim כל־העדה כלם קדשים literally "the entire congregation, all of them, are holy" (Num 16:3). Korah's theological challenge is not answered in what follows in chapter 16, but in what precedes—the tassels unit (15:37–41). The H redactor anticipates Korah's challenge by his quintessential kerygma: Israel can become holy only if it fulfills the divine commandments. Holiness is not hereditary; it is not genetically transmitted except in YHWH's chosen, the Aaronide priests.

The examples outside of Leviticus (Exod 29:38–46; 31:12–13; Num 3:11–13; 8:15b–19; 15) discussed above illustrate what I believe are certain H passages that were placed in their present position by H_R. Within the book of Leviticus, H_R chose P's laws on sacrifices (Leviticus 1–10) and impurities (chapters 11–16) out of a larger body of available P material[25] as the basis of its own (H) laws on sacrifices (e.g., 17; 19:5–8, 20–22) and impurities (e.g., 17:15–16; 18:19; 22:3–8). The body of P (1–16) was probably also annotated by H_R (3:16b–17; 6:12–18aα; 27:22–29a, 39b(?); 8:35;[26] 9:17b; 10:10–11; 11:43–45; 12:8; 14:34–53(?), 54–57(?); 15:31; 16:2bβ, 29, 34a).[27] However, some of these annotations may be the handiwork of P_2 who added them to the basic text P_1 (e.g., 11:24–38). Outside of Leviticus, other passages of H material may also have been placed in their present posi-

---

[24] Cf. Milgrom, *The Book of Numbers*, 127, 410–14; idem, "The Tassels Pericope, Num 15:37–41," *Beit Mikra* 92 (1983) 14–22 (Hebrew).

[25] Cf. Milgrom, *Leviticus 23–27*, 2440–42.

[26] Cf. Milgrom, *Leviticus 17–22*, 1326, n. 8.

[27] Cf. Milgrom, *Leviticus 1–16*, 61–63, though I am no longer sure of Lev 6:17–18ad; 7:28–29a; 9:17b and 12:8.

tion by H$_R$. These are: Exod 6:2–8; 12:7–20, 43–50; Num 3:40–51; 5:1–3; 9:9–14; 10:10; 19:10b–13; 28:2b; 29:39; 33:50–56: 35:1–36:13, though their attribution to H$_R$ has yet to be substantiated. The remaining passages in Knohl's list[28] are possibly H, but in my opinion the evidence is lacking.

The passages cited above are characterized by H formulas, vocabulary and ideology. Moreover, they do not disrupt P units or attempt to alter them but are attached to or inserted between P units. It should also be noted that P's narratives are at times integrated into JE passages. For example, Num 13:1–17a; 14:26–38[29] have been grafted onto JE (13:17b–14:25). Remove these P portions and JE forms a smoothly continuous story (13:17b–14:25, 39–45).[30]

Is H$_R$ also the redactor of Genesis and Deuteronomy? If H$_R$'s hand is detectable in Gen 17:7–8, 14(?); 23(?); 36(?)[31] and in Deut 32:48–52 and these are the final inserts in these two books, then possibly H$_R$ is the redactor of the entire Torah. Knohl thinks so.[32] But these verses are few and far between and they lack the strong evidential controls that cluster in the law codes.

In my recently published commentary,[33] I argued that Gen 2:2–3 must be attributed to H$_R$. I would like to strengthen this thesis by arguing that the entire priestly story of creation (Gen 1:1–2:4a) is the work of H$_R$ and then by demonstrating that one verse of the sabbath pericope (Gen 2:3) is the source for several passages in Exodus and Numbers which also bear the imprint of H$_R$.

Amit[34] has already observed that Gen 2:2–3 are marked by anthropomorphisms never found in P's descriptions of God, namely, עשה, קדש שבת, כלה, and ברך.[35] Moreover, these two verses contain multiple

---

[28] Knohl, *The Sanctuary of Silence*, 104–6.

[29] Which Knohl, *The Sanctuary of Silence*, 90–92 assigns to H.

[30] Details in Milgrom, *The Book of Numbers*, 113.

[31] As claimed by Knohl, *The Sanctuary of Silence*, 104.

[32] Ibid., 101–3.

[33] Milgrom, *Leviticus 17–22*, 1344.

[34] Y. Amit, "Creation and the Calendar of Holiness," in M. Cogan, B. L. Eichler, and J. H. Tigay (eds.), *Tehillah le-Moshe: Biblical and Judaic Studies in Honor of Moshe Greenberg* (Winona Lake, IN: Eisenbrauns, 1997) 13*–30* (Hebrew).

[35] One must be wary of using anthropomorphisms as an H criterion as do Amit, "Creation and the Calendar of Holiness," and E. Firmage, "Genesis 1 and the Priestly Agenda," *JSOT* 82 (1999) 97–115, in view of Knohl's demonstration (*Sanctuary of Silence*, 128–36) that P is thoroughly anthropomorphistic before the name YHWH is revealed (Exod 6:2). For example, that God has a form (Gen 1:26–27), allegedly an H (but not a P) characteristic, is repeated almost verbatim in Gen 9:6, a P passage!

occurrences of מלאכה... עשה[36] (three times) and ביום השביעי (twice).
To her lexical evidence I would like to add the rationale (v. 3b),
beginning with כי—a distinctive H_R characteristic.[37]

This sabbath pericope cannot be contrived as an isolated H_R composition. It is integrally bound to Genesis 1: it is essential to the latter as its seventh day, the number of perfection,[38] and its first week
of creation. Moreover, it is inseparable from Genesis 1 structurally.
Note that Gen 2:4a אלה תולדות השמים והארץ בהבראם is the inclusio
of Gen 1:1 בראשית ברא אלהים את השמים ואת הארץ in chiastic order,
thereby embracing and unifying Gen 1:1–2:4a.[39] Within this unit,
2:1 serves a dual function: it is a minor inclusio of the prior six
days,[40] and it is an introduction to the seventh day.

Thus, the structural evidence argues for the possibility that not
only Gen 2:1–4a is an H_R composition but also all of Gen 1. However,
what converts this possibility into probability is the unique agglomeration of polemics against the Babylonian creation epic within this
pericope. Such a list was first compiled by Cassuto[41] but it can be
expanded. I cite five examples.

1. תהום, "deep" (1:2), minus a definite article, an indication that it
   is a proper noun, namely, *tiāmat*, the Mesopotamian goddess of
   the deep, assisted by:
2. התנינם, "sea monsters" (1:21; cf. Isa 27:1; Ps 74:13), the only other
   named animals in the creation story and just as mythical; all the
   others are species.
3. The sun and moon are created on the fourth day. They constitute a polemic against two major Babylonian deities, *šamaš* and
   sîn, respectively. They dominate (משלים) the day and night (1:16),
   but they are not the sources of light, which was created on the
   first day. They are not even named but called the "great lights"
   (1:16). They are not independent powers. They are not in heaven
   but set in the firmament by their creator.

---

[36] The awkward לעשות at the end of Gen 2:3 is thereby explained structurally.
It was needed to link with the previous מאלכתו to make the third occurrence of
this idiom.

[37] Cf. Milgrom, *Leviticus 17–22*, 1371–75.

[38] Cf. U. Cassuto, *A Commentary on the Book of Genesis* (Jerusalem: Magnes, 1961)
12–13.

[39] For additional evidence that the seventh day is an integral part of the creation story, see Amit, "Creation," 14*–20*.

[40] See my diagram, *Leviticus 17–22*, 1344.

[41] Cassuto, *A Commentary on the Book of Genesis*.

4. For the creation of the human being, God counsels his divine
   assembly, "Let *us* make the human being in *our* image (בצלמנו)
   after *our* likeness (כדמותנו)" (1:26). This, I submit, is a polemic
   against the Babylonian creation epic, *Enuma Elish*. God does not
   create the first human being with the blood of an executed rebel
   god (*Enuma Elish* VI:5, 33). He seeks the counsel of angelic under-
   lings. He treats them, as it were, as partners. It is no accident
   that the two other references to God's consulting his divine assembly are in Genesis 1–11. The first is the story of the Babylonian
   Tower (Gen 11:7), a satire against Babylon's Tower-shrine as
   described in *Enuma Elish* VI:60–62.[42]

   The other reference is Gen 3:22, "And the God YHWH said:
   'Now that the man has become like one of us, knowing what is
   good and what is bad, what if he should stretch out his hand
   and take also from the Tree of Life and eat, and live forever.'"
   In my opinion, this verse is directed toward the millenial best
   seller of antiquity, Gilgamesh and his quest for immortality. After
   many heroic adventures Gilgamesh finds the immortality-yielding
   plant. The existence and location of this plant is revealed to him
   by Utnapishtim, "The Mesopotomian Noah." Through the intervention of one of the gods who defied the divine decree of a
   global flood, Utnapishtim survived and was granted divine immortality. However, unfortunately for Gilgamesh, a serpent steals the
   plant while he is asleep (*Enuma Elish* XI:1–310). In just one verse
   the Bible demolishes the theology of Gilgamesh. The fruit of the
   Tree of Life may be eaten only by those confined in the Garden
   of Eden who are simultaneously prohibited from eating from the
   Tree of Knowledge. However, the first human couple decides that
   the knowledge (i.e., creative powers) to determine one's own life
   despite its attendant risks is superior to a deathless but choiceless
   existence (Gen 2:4–3:24; *ANET* 93–97). The following contrasts
   are briefly noted;

   i. One God defying another in contrast to humans defying
      their God.
   ii. The heroic exploits of a superman in contrast to the moral
       choice of the first human beings.
   iii. The quest for life in contrast to the quest for knowledge
        (Gen 3:5a, 22).

---

[42] *ANET* 69; cf. E. A. Speiser, *Genesis* (AB 1; Garden City, N.Y.: Doubleday,
1964) 75–76, for the wordplay on their names.

iv. The serpent that steals the gift of immortality from the human being in contrast to the serpent that lies when it promises immortality to the human being (Gen 2:17; 3:4, 19). As can be shown the deeper message of the biblical story of the Garden is that the ultimate goal for humanity is not an endless, confined life but a creatively freer though shorter life.

5. God's creation of the sabbath on the seventh day (Gen 2:2–3) matches the Babylonian shrine Esagila atop the highest ziggurat of Babylon (above), built by the gods as a palace for victorious Marduk and as a place of rest (motel?) for the other gods (*Enuma Elish* VI:51–79). In contrast, Israel's God (not his assembly) also builds a palace, not in space but in time, called the sabbath. It is his day (שבת לה׳, Exod 16:25; 35:21; Lev 23:3) on which he rests (וישבת = וינח, "he rested," Exod 20:11).

What could be the *Sitz im Leben* for Genesis 1? Surely, it would have to be when Babylonian cosmology posed a powerful threat to Israel's belief system. Only the Babylonian exile, when a defeated, humiliated, and expatriated Israel was deluged by the theology of the victorious (gods of the) Babylonians, could have provided the incentive for a counter-deluge of polemics. It is hardly accidental that the only other agglomeration of anti-Babylonian polemics occurs in Second Isaiah, when Israel had been exiled to Babylonia. Thus structural and contextual deductions converge: The entire priestly story of creation, Gen 1:1–2:4a, must be assigned to the pen of the redactor, H$_R$.[43]

The first six days (Genesis 1) have not left many traces in the Bible (e.g., the forbidden animals, Leviticus 11,[44] Isa 45:18,[45] Jer 4:23–28).[46] The reverse is true for the sabbath of creation (Gen

---

[43] There is even lexical support in favor of H$_R$'s authorship of Genesis 1. I am reminded by my perceptive e-mail correspondent, Sol Tupper, that I have cited (*Leviticus 1–16*, 615) G. Hannemann's demonstration ("On the Preposition *bêt* in the Mishna and the Bible," *Leshonenu* 40 [1975–76] 33–53) that the idiom *bên . . . ûbên* changes in Late Biblical Hebrew to *bên . . . lĕ*, beginning with Ezekiel (cf. Ezek 22:26; 42:20; 44:23). Thus the occurrence of *bên . . . lĕ* in Genesis 1 points to an exilic (or postexilic) provenience for Genesis 1, which would accord with the time of H$_R$.

[44] Milgrom, "Two Priestly Terms."

[45] Cf. J. Ibn Kaspi (1279–1340), *Mikra'ot gedolot ha-Keter* (ed. M. Cohen; Ramat Gan: Bar-Ilan University Press, 1996) 229 (Hebrew).

[46] Cf. J. R. Lundbom, *Jeremiah 1–20* (AB 21A; New York: Doubleday, 1999) 356–63.

2:1–3). The reason is obvious: It has impacted sabbath law and observance. The sabbath passages Exod 31:12–17; 35:1–3; Lev 23:2aβ–3; 26:1–2 have already been discussed above, where it was shown that these passages are redactoral interpolations and, hence, attributable to H$_R$. Now that it has been shown that Gen 2:1–3 is also an H$_R$ composition, the deduction can be drawn that it was intended by H$_R$ to provide a precedent for additional H$_R$ interpolations in Scripture. As evidence I cite two major sabbath passages that can be ascribed to H$_R$.

Exod 16:23

Without siding with Dillmann[47] that Exod 16:4–5, 22–30 is P$_{2R}$ (= H$_R$), there is no doubt that v. 23, which contains the term שבתו and the phrase שבת קדש לה', is all or partially H$_R$. Though Frankel[48] has discerned an early P layer in chapter 16, it is noteworthy that his early P contains no mention of the sabbath, thereby leaving the remaining priestly text for H$_R$. To be sure, P acknowledges the sabbath as a cultic rite in the Tabernacle/Temple (Num 28:9–10), but it betrays no interest in its private observance. Of course, the sabbath passages (16:4–5, 22–30) could also be the work of H, and there are insufficient grammatical and lexical tools to distinguish between H and H$_R$. I therefore remain focused on v. 23, which, as just argued, is an H$_R$ composition. YHWH provided Israel with daily manna as soon as they entered the wilderness more than two months before reaching Mt. Sinai. Since YHWH was not going to work *on his day*, he provided a double portion on the sixth day. Israel too is bidden to rest on YHWH's rest day; the text states explicitly, ה' נתן לכם השבת, "YHWH has given you the sabbath" (v. 29). Thus, the manna episode provides the backdrop for the first occasion when Israel is commanded to observe the sabbath. The sabbath of creation (Gen 2:3), namely, the creation of the divine rest day, has led inexorably to Israel's rest day (Exod 16:29–30). Israel must rest on the day because it is now *its* sabbath.

---

[47] A. Dillmann and V. Ryssel, *Exodus and Leviticus* (Leipzig: S. Hirzel, 1897) 190.
[48] D. Frankel, "The Stories of Murmuring in the Desert in the Priestly School," Ph.D. dissertation, Hebrew University, 1994 (Hebrew).

Exod 20:11

כי ששת־ימים עשה ה׳ את־השמים
ואת־הארץ את־הים ואת־כל־אשר־בם *וינח* ביום השביעי
על־כן *ברך* ה׳ את־יום השבת *ויקדשהו*

> *For* in six days YHWH made heaven and earth, and sea, and all that
> is in them, and he *rested* on the seventh day; therefore YHWH *blessed*
> the sabbath day and *sanctified* it.

The four words (in italics) are found in one other verse, Gen 2:3,
an indication that it was the archetype for Exod 20:11. Then if, as
demonstrated, Gen 2:3 is an H_R composition, this must also be true
for Exod 20:11. Rashbam provides an incisive comment on the word
זכור "remember" (20:8) which deserves citation in full:

> Every "remember" responds to days that have passed: "Remember the
> days of old ... when the Most High appointed the nations" (Deut
> 32:7–8); "Remember this day" (Deut 13:3) forever, because in the past
> on this day you left Egypt; "Remember, do not forget that you angered
> YHWH your God ... and at Horeb you angered YHWH...." (Deut
> 9:7–8); "Remember your mercy and your faithfulness, O YHWH, for
> they are of old" (Ps 25:6). Here also "Remember the sabbath day"
> (Exod 20:8) of the six days of creation as the text states explicitly "for
> in six days YHWH made...." (20:10). Therefore it is written here
> "remember," in order to sanctify it (לקדשו) by ceasing from work.

Most commentators, both ancient[49] and modern,[50] claim that since
the object of זכור "remember" is לקדשו "to sanctify it" (v. 8), Israel
should remember to observe the sabbath in a sacred way, chiefly by
abstaining from labor. Rashbam was the first, to my knowledge, to
demonstrate that זכור always means to remember some event in the
past, and in this case, as the text specifically unfolds (vv. 9–11), the
sabbath of creation. From a critical stance, this means that H_R has
authored both the sabbath of creation and the entire sabbath commandment (Exod 20:8–11). One should note that the pericope of
the sabbath (the fourth) commandment is framed by the inclusio (in
italics): זכור *את יום השבת לקדשו* ... על־כן ברך ה׳ *את־יום השבת ויקדשהו*
"Remember *the sabbath day to sanctify it* (v. 8) ... Therefore, YHWH

---

[49] E. G. *Mekh. Baḥodeš*, par. 7; Rashi, Bekhor Shor, Sforno.
[50] E.g. S. R. Driver, *The Book of Exodus* (Cambridge: University of Cambridge,
1911) 196; J. I. Durham, *Exodus* (Waco, Tex.: World, 1987) 289; A. Cohen, *The
Book of Exodus* (2 vols.; Jerusalem: Mosad Harav Kook, 1991) 383 (Hebrew).

blessed *the sabbath day and sanctified it*" (v. 11b). Thus, there is no doubt that the sabbath commandment in its entirety (vv. 8–11, and not just v. 11) was modeled after the sabbath of creation (Gen 2:2–3).[51] Nevertheless, there is something lacking in this argument. All that can be derived from the ballooned exposition of the sabbath in the Decalogue is that God rested on the seventh day. But why should Israel do likewise? All of Rashbam's "remember" citations in Scripture refer to Israel's historic experience. But how should Israel "remember" creation?

I would suggest that זכור means that Israel should remember what it had experienced some three weeks earlier (Exod 16:1) during the manna episode (Exod 16:22–30)[52] when "YHWH gave (נתן) you the sabbath" (v. 29). Henceforth, the sabbath is not only YHWH's (v. 25) but also Israel's. Thereafter (על־כן), Israel has to rest on the sabbath (v. 30). Thus Israel was commanded to rest on the sabbath even before they received the Decalogue. At Sinai they were bidden to remember this manna-given commandment (Exod 20:8) and were provided with a divine etiology that the sabbath preexisted history, was embedded in cosmic time, and was sanctified by the Creator as his day of rest (Exod 20:9–11).

Thus, H_R divides the sabbath into three stages: YHWH's sabbath at creation (Gen 2:2–3), Israel's sabbath at the manna event (Exod 16:22–30)[53] and the fusion of both into a single commandment at Sinai (Exod 20:8–11). The latter constitutes an etiology of the sabbath of creation formulated for Israel in the Babylonian exile as one of the ten highest commandments.

To recapitulate: H_R inserted additions either in intercises (e.g., Num 3:11–13; 15) or termini (e.g., Gen 1:1–2:4a; Lev 2:1–3) of a received text. The text itself had congealed. Thus the redactoral process was one of arrangement and occasional insertion.[54] The proliferation of H_R in Exodus and Numbers provides sufficient evidence

---

[51] It is even possible that H_R altered Exod 20:8 by replacing שמור (cf. Deut 5:12) with זכור. That the deuteronomistic שמר may have been the original version; cf. Lev 19:3, 30 (H).

[52] First noted by Ḥazzequmi; cf. also Dillman *Exodus and Leviticus*, 235; U. Cassuto, *A Commentary on the Book of Exodus* (2 vols.; Jerusalem: Magnes, 1953) 1.169; B. S. Childs, *The Book of Exodus* (OTL; Philadelphia: Westminster, 1974) 416.

[53] The subdivisions of the priestly verses in Exodus 16 into P, H, and H_R are not clear.

[54] For a detailed description of the redactoral techniques in the Bible, cf. Y. Amit, *The Book of Judges: The Art of Editing* (Leiden: Brill, 1999) 1–24.

to conclude that these books were redacted by H_R. However, the absence of such hard evidence in Genesis (and Deuteronomy) calls for a negative conclusion. Even if the attribution of the priestly story (Gen 1:1–2:4a) to H_R proves correct, it does not mean that H_R's hand is visible in the rest of Genesis. It is even more probable that H_R attached his version of creation to the existing one (Gen 2:4b–25) at the beginning of the already completed book. Other scenarios are possible. Until the redactoral picture of Genesis is clarified, definitive conclusions are unwarranted.

LEVITICUS: AFTER EXODUS AND BEFORE NUMBERS

GRAEME AULD

In discussion of the five "books of Moses," it is often observed that the outer two are more different from the others than the inner three. Genesis is a very extended prologue relating to the time before Moses; and Deuteronomy is very much to itself. It is true that Deuteronomy, like the books of Exodus, Leviticus, and Numbers, is dominated by Moses. However, this fifth book is almost completely innocent of the priestly interests which are already manifest at the very beginning of Genesis and occasionally throughout that "book," and which are prevalent in Exodus-Numbers. The consensus of scholarship on the Pentateuch, or at least the books Genesis-Numbers, has attributed much of their material to a "Priestly School."

However complicated the drafting and supplementation of the contents of Exodus, Leviticus, and Numbers is supposed to be, it is held that it was accomplished by the same priestly authors and/or editors who had operated over the whole sweep of the material. And yet, at the end of a paper on "Leviticus at the Heart of the Pentateuch," I found myself sketching a proposal that these "books" had been conceived not together but serially, that each of Exodus, Leviticus, and Numbers might have been separately conceived, each starting afresh, not just in narrative location, but also in whole conception, from where the preceding one had left off.[1]

There is a good deal of scholarly interest in defining what ‏ספר‎ or "book" meant in the "biblical" world.[2] How much did that term imply of completeness and consistency? Did it merely describe what was written on a single manuscript or document? The successor traditions have sent out divergent signals. Calling the material "the five

---

[1] A. G. Auld, "Leviticus at the Heart of the Pentateuch?" in J. F. A. Sawyer (ed.), *Reading Leviticus. A Conversation with Mary Douglas* (JSOTSup 227; Sheffield: Sheffield Academic Press, 1996) 40–51 (esp. 49–51). I have not been able to consult, while preparing this contribution, H.-J. Fabry and H.-W. Jüngling (eds.), *Levitikus als Buch* (BBB 119; Berlin: Philo, 1999).

[2] See for example P. R. Davies, *Scribes and Schools. The Canonization of the Hebrew Scriptures* (Library of Ancient Israel; London: SPCK, 1998).

fifths of the Torah" focuses on the whole rather than the parts. Talking of "the five books of Moses" may suggest that each of the units has integrity in itself. It is clear that the names of the Pentateuchal books familiar in Christian tradition and derived from the Greek Bible are thematic: Exodus reports the departure from Egypt, Leviticus contains priestly or levitical teaching, and much of the content of Numbers is bracketed by two numberings of the people of Israel. It is often said by contrast that the Jewish names for these Torah "fifths" are simply their opening words (in four cases) or, in the case of "In the wilderness," a distinctive element from within the opening sentence of Num 1:1. And yet the manifest thematic appropriateness of "In the beginning" (Genesis), "In the wilderness" (Numbers), and "These are the words" (Deuteronomy), suggests we are dealing with more than happenstance and invites readers to inspect the thematic implications of "These are the names" (Exodus) and "And he called" (Leviticus).

The Torah or Pentateuch as a whole has often been described as a torso, a body lacking a head: Moses does not reach the land promised to Abraham; and settlement under his leadership is only tantalizingly embarked on, east of the Jordan.[3] Exodus reports Israel's paradigmatic deliverance, the key commands from the holy mountain, the discussion of the divine presence (to which Milgrom so rightly attaches prominence)[4] and the provision of an alternative, humanly constructed focus for the divine glory. Of course Exodus tells only a part of the whole story of deliverance and settlement with which we are now familiar. And yet, as understood above, Exodus is far less vulnerable than the Pentateuch itself to the charge that it is little more than a torso often directed at the Pentateuch "as a whole." Exodus can be plausibly claimed as more complete in itself than the whole Torah: it reports a people led from slavery in Egypt to free worship of their deity at a mountain of his choice, then through a first rebellion at the mountain to the fashioning there of a divinely appointed shrine. It may be sensible to consider it as complete in itself, and not another (smaller) torso without a head.

---

[3] D. J. A. Clines addresses this point directly with the proposal that the theme "is the partial fulfilment—which implies also the partial non-fulfilment—of the promise to or blessing of the patriarchs" (*The Theme of the Pentateuch* [JSOTSup 10; Sheffield: JSOT, 1978] 29).

[4] Even if his presentation of the whole "Hexateuch" as a vast palistrophe with Exodus 33 at its center is somewhat forced.

The opening of Leviticus, with its striking resumption (1:1) of the divine call (ויקרא) from the end of Exodus 24 (v. 16), makes plain that Yahweh's commanding and providing were not just mediated through Moses in forty days at the top of a holy mountain—God could and did continue to "convoke" and "proclaim" from within the new shrine. The divine provision for the (priestly mediated) cleanness and holiness of Israel before Yahweh, already instructed—and therefore implicitly realised—in Exodus, is reported in Leviticus. Accordingly Leviticus is the "book" which can properly and simply conclude with the words, "These are the commandments which the Lord commanded Moses for the people of Israel at Mt. Sinai." Conceived admittedly as a supplement to Exodus, it is still a supplement which is complete in itself.

And Numbers goes further. It also resumes its wilderness theme במדבר (x30)[5] from both Exodus (x12)[6] and Leviticus (x2)[7] and shows that God continued to teach his wandering people from the portable shrine even after it had left Mt. Sinai. In assessing Leviticus and Numbers, we might argue that categories important in Exodus remain normative, even when the original time and place are extended. As in Exodus, so in Leviticus and Numbers, Israel never reaches the promised land, though she continues to hear her God's call in the wilderness.

The interplay between the foundation traditions in Samuel/Kings and in the Pentateuch is obvious and has been explored from many angles. In each there is a mountain where Yahweh is to be encountered and from which his teaching goes forth: Zion and Sinai. In each there is a corresponding sanctuary, humanly constructed but under divine guidance: the divinely appointed temple in Jerusalem and the divinely appointed tent of meeting. Both Solomon and Moses have unmediated visionary access to their God, and speak to him for their people. There are twin foci of opposition: Jeroboam's golden calves and Aaron's golden calf, both humanly devised in opposition to the centerpiece of the divinely legitimated shrine. These several

---

[5] במדבר absolutely (x16) in Num 10:31; 14:2, 16, 29, 32, 33, 35; 15:32; 16:13; 21:5, 11, 13; 26:65; 27:3; 32:13, 15; and in construct (x14)—with סיני in Num 1:1, 19; 3:4, 14; 9:1, 5; 26:64; 33:15; with פארן in Num 10:12; 12:16; with צן in Num 27:14; 33:36; with אתם in Num 33:8; and with סין in Num 33:11.

[6] All (in the absolute) in Exod 3:18; 5:1, 3; 7:16; 8:23, 24; 14:11, 12; 15:22; 16:2, 32; 19:2.

[7] Absolutely in Lev 16:22, and as במדבר סיני in Lev 7:38.

points of comparison may add plausibility to an intertextual exploration of the larger narrative at the heart of the Pentateuch in the light of Solomon's prayer at the dedication of the temple.

Solomon envisages several situations in which people will want to seek the heavenly God via his earthly dwelling in Jerusalem. It is quite clear that these situations are in two sets. First of all 1 Kgs 8:31–40 offers examples of situations close to home which lead to prayer at the temple. Three are explored in a little detail in vv. 31–36: the judicial oath (vv. 31–32), supplication after defeat (vv. 33–34), and confession of sin (vv. 35–36). This first part of the text comes to a preliminary conclusion in (vv. 37–40) with an overview of several further typical situations, still plausibly within Solomon's time and place, where his people will be able to come to the shrine and pray there to Yahweh, and hope to be heard.

Then 1 Kgs 8:41–49 seeks to build on this assured foundation, and extend the significance of the Jerusalem sanctuary in different ways to three groups. In each case a negotiation seems to be implied between Solomon and Yahweh, not unlike the bargaining between Jeremiah and Yahweh in the case of Jerusalem (Jer 5:1) or Abraham and Yahweh over the fate of Sodom (Gen 18:23–33). If Israel may address Yahweh at his temple in Jerusalem (8:31–40), why not the foreigner as well (vv. 41–43)? After all, this will only add to Yahweh's international reputation. Then, if Israel when in distress at home, why not the army when temporarily abroad (vv. 44–45)? And finally, if Israel when suffering at home on account of their sins (vv. 33–36), then why not a future sinful Israel if sent into exile (vv. 46–49)? In all of these new cases too, Solomon suggests, people may direct their prayer to Yahweh towards his house in Jerusalem.

Yahweh may have chosen the mountain of Jerusalem to have a house built in which he may place his name; and Jerusalem may be part of the land granted to Israel—but the foreigner may still direct prayer there. And distance from Jerusalem of army or of exiles is in no way disruptive of access to Israel's god. We note that in each case the theological implications of, or extensions to an agreed position are being explored in direct address to the deity, whether by Solomon, Jeremiah, or Abraham.

Beyond the obvious synchronic comparisons between these texts as they stand, there are many legitimate diachronic questions. Does Jer 5:1 in all its brevity allude to and draw on a tradition of Abraham interceding for Sodom? Or was the more detailed story in Genesis of

Abraham's haggling developed from an idea suggested in Jeremiah?[8] Was Solomon's prayer spun as a piece of whole cloth, or stitched together from different pieces? Many scholars have held that 1 Kgs 8:40 marks the end of an earlier draft of this prayer. Solomon's argument certainly comes to at least an interim climax there. Whatever the date of its composition, this is the portion which can most easily be imagined as suitable to the period of the monarchy in Jerusalem. And yet, is the manifest shift in focus from home (vv. 31–40) to abroad (vv. 41–49) to be explained in terms of before and after, whether simply earlier and later or more precisely before and after the exile? Or is the shift not so much temporal as [theo]logical: from easier to more difficult, from agreed to more controversial? Or are both accounts true at the same time?

It is widely supposed that the foundation narrative of the monarchy in Jerusalem had been transposed and retrojected into the stories told in the Pentateuch of Moses and the earlier origins of the people of Israel. In addition to the points of comparison already noted, we might add the connection between David's fateful census in 2 Samuel 24 and the countings of Israel in Numbers 1 and 26.[9] All that said, the logic of the account across Exodus-Leviticus-Numbers of Moses' receipt of the priestly teaching can be presented as analogous, though in a somewhat upside-down way, to the logic of the structure and development of Solomon's prayer. Just as Yahweh could be addressed via the temple on Zion by whomever and from whatever distance, no less than once by Israel within the temple's very courts, so too Yahweh could continue to summon and command Moses from the tent, as he had once from the top of Mt. Sinai. And similarly, life in exile was no more cut off from Yahweh than had been life "in the desert" at an increasing remove from Sinai.

If the Hebrew names for Leviticus and Numbers are significant, and not merely accidental, then the reading which they signal of

---

[8] The fact that אולי יש חמשים צדיקם (Gen 18:24) and אם יש עשה משפט (Jer 5:1) share the distinctive יש strongly suggests that these questions to the deity are closely related.

[9] I become increasingly persuaded that the numbering of Israel urged by the deity on the founder of the Davidic line is a principal wellspring of the biblical story. For the relationship with Job, see some preliminary comments in A. G. Auld, "Prophets Shared—and Recycled" in T. Römer (ed.), *The Future of the Deuteronomistic History* (BETL 147; Leuven: Peeters, 2000) 21–22.

the larger plot which overarches these books may be illumined by
Solomon's pleadings. Yahweh is no less present in the shrine than
on the mountain of God; and there is no "too far" for Yahweh.
Indeed the logic of Exodus-Leviticus-Numbers, taken as a whole,
may bear the same relationship to the logic of Solomon's prayer, as
Abraham's bargaining to Jeremiah's. It is not unlikely that in each
pairing one text has influenced the other. However, we still have to
ask whether this holistic reading of the heart of the Pentateuch is
the only sensible one, or a better one than any rivals. The foundation stories of the monarchy may have exerted a controlling force
on the development of the Pentateuch. Yet need that imply unitary
composition of Exodus to Numbers? How does all this bear on the
notion that Exodus, or at least its core formulation, was conceived
in and for itself, with Leviticus and then Numbers added as supplements—rather than all drafted together, simply as three parts of
something bigger?

A second intertext—or should we call it an intratext?—is the "Song
of the Sea" in Exod 15:1–18. The larger part of this poem hymns
Yahweh as the deliverer of Israel from Egypt (vv. 1–12). The goal
of the deliverance is first adumbrated in v. 13: Yahweh leads the
people he has redeemed to his holy abode (אל נוה קדשך). Other peoples hear and fear, from the inhabitants of Philistia (v. 14) to those
of Canaan (v. 15). The dread of these others is emphasised (v. 16)
before the fuller statement in v. 17 of the climax already foreshad-
owed in v. 13:

you will bring them and plant them	תבאמו ותטעמו
on the mountain that is your inheritance	בהר נחלתך
the establishment for your habitation	מכון לשבתך
you, Yahweh, have made;	פעלת יהוה
the sanctuary, Lord,	מקדש אדני
your hands have established	כוננו ידיך

A brief doxology (v. 18) concludes the Song.

As goal of the deliverance by the sea Exod 15:13, 17 envisage
not a land of promise, but a holy mountain and a sanctuary which
Yahweh shall make. Songs and poems within biblical narrative regularly have summative or explanatory force. Like the Song of Hannah,
early in the books of Samuel, this poem looks forward in the narrative as well as backward—but how far forward? Read as a part
of, as a comment on the whole Mosaic corpus, it may remind the
reader how close to fulfilment in Jerusalem the Mosaic project reached.

Yet, if so, we have to recognise that the focus of the Song—on arrival at a holy place—is distinct from gaining a land and settling in it. However, it is worth pondering a rather different role for the song within Exodus alone, placed as it is immediately after the deliverance at the sea and immediately before Israel's arrival at the mountain of God. Part of the purpose of the "Song of the Sea" within Exodus may be to help the reader familiar with the Jerusalem sanctuary understand the "retrojection" of Mt. Zion into a holy mountain in the desert between Egypt and Jerusalem. The situation of Moses' Song precisely there in the Exodus narrative may be to help its readers understand that in coming to Sinai their ancestors had indeed arrived at their goal, and not just at a stage on the way. Put in other words, these readers should intuit that the promised mountain and sanctuary is neither Zion and its future temple nor Sinai and the tent shrine constructed there, but both at the same time. Solomon's prayer repeatedly insists on the close links between Jerusalem sanctuary and heaven as established "seat" or "dwelling" (שבת) of Yahweh (1 Kgs 8:27–30, and then within each separate petition). The correspondences between Zion and Sinai were no less real.

We may have assembled sufficient evidence for a *prima facie* case that the plot of Exodus was complete in itself. It was designed, at least in part, to comment on and correct some elements of the foundation story of Jerusalem sanctuary and Davidic line, as well as to provide a more ancient pedigree. It had been a Davidic initiative to build a house for Yahweh in Jerusalem (2 Sam 7:2), although the suggestion was immediately parried by his God (7:5–16). Then, although he was careful to repeat that heaven was Yahweh's established שבת (1 Kgs 8:39, 43, 49), Solomon still started his address with the claim that he had built an establishment for Yahweh's "seat" or "abode" (1 Kgs 8:13). By contrast, the initiative in Exodus came from Yahweh himself. What did result from divine initiative in the David/Solomon stories was David's fateful census of Israel (2 Samuel 24). This story is also taken up in Exodus, where making a count of Israel is again an explicit instruction from Yahweh (30:11–16), no less than in 2 Samuel 24, and the possibility of plague resulting from a census is mentioned at an early stage in the narrative (30:12). However, the provision of a poll-tax levied from every adult male counted should avert any anticipation of David's calamity.

Exodus does not lack closure; it does not require a sequel. It concludes with Yahweh's "glory" filling the new shrine (compare Exod

40:34 with 1 Kgs 8:11), just as earlier it had settled on the top of
the mountain (Exod 24:15–18). However, following the implicit claim
in Exodus of a divine origin for the Jerusalem sanctuary, Leviticus
opens with the concomitant assurance that "the tent of meeting"
(still then at Mt. Sinai, 7:38) was as suitable a locus for divine instruction of Moses as the shrouded peak of the mountain of God. After
Lev 1:1, there would be no further report of any divine "calling" to
Moses. That happened just once on the mountain and once at the
tent—sufficient to assert the equivalence of a humanly constructed
shrine and the very mountain of God itself.

We have already noted that the Hebrew name for Numbers is
not provided by the opening word(s) of that text. Two observations
may be made about its first sentence. The one is that it is remarkably rare for any further detail to be supplied to the very common
introductory formula, "And Yahweh spoke to Moses and/or Aaron."
The few instances are:

> Lev 1:1, "from the tent of meeting"
> Lev 16:1, "after the death of the two sons of Aaron"
> Num 1:1, "in the Sinai desert, in the tent of meeting, on the first day"
> Num 3:14, "in the Sinai desert"
> Num 9:1, "in the Sinai desert, in the first month"
> Num 33:50, "in the plains of Moab by the Jordan at Jericho"
> Num 35:1, "in the plains of Moab by the Jordan at Jericho"

The other was already noted: that the "desert," whether of Sinai or
Paran or Zin or whether unspecified, is a much bigger theme in
Numbers than in the rest of the Pentateuch. This remains so until
the anticipation towards the end of the book of the setting of
Deuteronomy "in the plains of Moab." The opening verse of Numbers
may not be quite as distinctive as the title verse of Leviticus; yet it
does combine two typical emphases of the book.

The introductions in Num 1:1 and 3:14 noted above both relate
to the countings which give the book its "Christian" name. The
beginning of Numbers returns in great detail to a theme we have
already seen handled in Exodus: the receipts from the poll-tax commanded in 30:11–16 have already been utilised in the construction
of the sanctuary (38:25–28). From that note we learn that the census had already been carried out. As an afterthought, Numbers now
reports on the count itself. We may remark that there is no immediate talk here in Numbers of the tax specified in Exodus for "cop-

ing with"[10] the perils inherent in such a tally. There is instead a special reckoning which involves the Levites. First of all, in Numbers 1
the Levites are not numbered among the rest of Israel but appointed
to special cultic duties (1:49–50): these include camping round the
tabernacle to prevent "wrath" (קֶצֶף) on the wider congregation (v.
53). Double word-play draws attention to the continuity alongside
the discontinuity: Moses is not to "lift" the Levites' heads (an idiom
for taking a census) like all the rest of Israel; they rather will "lift"
the divine tabernacle. Moses is not to "muster" them (פָּקַד [qal]), but
is rather to "appoint" them (פָּקַד [hip'il]) to their duties.[11] But then
in Numbers 3–4 the Levites are first taken by Yahweh in place of
all the first-born of Israel (3:11–13), and then numbered in very precise detail (3:14–4:49). Only as part of this calculation does a version of the census poll-tax in Exodus 30 reappear: because there
were more first-born males in Israel than the total of male Levites,
the surplus Israelites would be redeemed (פָּדָה) at the rate specified
in Exodus 30. All of this suggests not so much the development in
a later section of a theme already introduced in an earlier section
of one and the same work—but rather a new work in a new situation re-presenting or re-developing or re-appropriating an element
from a previous work.

From this perspective, it is very curious that it is to the third
"book" of Moses that the name "Leviticus" has become attached;
for Leviticus would be even more appropriate as the name for the
fourth than Numbers. Moving from Moses' second and third "books"
to this fourth is like moving into a new world—like moving from
Samuel and Kings to Chronicles. In that novel milieu, tales which
had been told quite successfully in Samuel or Kings without mention of the Levites are now thoroughly retold, like the wholesale
recasting in 1 Chronicles 13–16 of David's bringing of the ark into
Jerusalem as reported in 2 Samuel 6.[12] Here, after only scarce mention

---

[10] I choose a deliberately non-specific expression for the much discussed כֶּפֶר.

[11] B. A. Levine draws attention to the second but not the first, in *Numbers 1–20*
(AB 4; New York: Doubleday, 1993) 140.

[12] Strictly it was not from 2 Samuel 6 as we know it that the Chronicler worked
(A. G. Auld, "What if the Chronicler did use the Deuteronomistic History?" *BibInt*
8 [2000] 137–50); however, like 2 Samuel 6 his source knew nothing of any role
for the Levites.

in the previous books of Moses,[13] the Levites are specifically, and
often repeatedly mentioned in each of chapters 1, 2, 3, 4, 7, 8, 16,
17, 18, 26, 31, 35 of the book of Numbers. (Note well their appearance at the beginning, in the middle, and at the end.)

Much of the detailed evidence for the novelty of Numbers has
already been presented and argued by Knohl—but differently
assessed—within his argument that a "Holiness School" was responsible for substantial reworking of the earlier "Priestly Torah."[14] Knohl
claims that earlier scholarship had doubly misunderstood the relationship between P and H: H was not a source available to P, but
in fact a development from P; and H was not restricted to the
"Holiness Code" identified by earlier scholarship (Leviticus 17–26)—
rather the Holiness School had contributed material throughout the
P-corpus, and especially in Numbers.[15] He has ascribed mostly to
later strata of material from his Holiness School the material on the
prominence of the Levites. Exodus 38:21, for example, is distinctive
within "P," not just in its unique mention of Levites in the account
of the tabernacle-making, but also in its naming the tabernacle by
the rare and late expression משכן העדת. However, the key question
to be put to Knohl must be whether such Levitical texts do not represent a more radical development than he allows of the "Holiness"
material as most cohesively presented in Leviticus.

It may depend on one's point of view whether "radical" is the
right word to use for the shift I am trying to describe. Development
in the usage of קדש ("holy"), as Knohl and Milgrom describe it,
from being restricted in "priestly torah" to the divine and the realm
of the priests to application within the "holiness school" to Israel
generally, is certainly a radical move. It is a move reflected in
Deuteronomy, where Israel is עם קדוש ליהוה (7:6), and in Exodus,
where much the same is said (גוי קדוש) and is then reinforced by
ממלכת כהנים (19:6). However, Numbers is innocent of such bold usage
of priestly language for the whole people: establishing the Levites as

---

[13] Gen 29:34; 34:25, 30; 35:23; 49:5; Exod 1:2; 2:1; 4:14; 6:16, 19, 25; 32:26,
28; 38:21; Lev 25:32, 33.
[14] I. Knohl, *The Sanctuary of Silence. The Priestly Torah and the Holiness School* (Minneapolis: Fortress, 1995).
[15] This argument, first defended in Knohl's Hebrew University dissertation (1988),
was adopted with small modifications and given wider currency by Jacob Milgrom,
Leviticus 1–16 (AB 3; New York: Doubleday, 1991); see now also his *Leviticus 17–22*
(AB 3A; New York: Doubleday, 2000) 1319–67.

"adjunct clergy," while "radical" in terms of novelty, appears rather to resile from the boldness of the metaphor applied elsewhere in the Pentateuch to Israel as a whole. The alternative metaphor of the fourth fifth of the Torah is offered by Moses in the story of Eldad and Medad: "Would that all Yahweh's people were prophets" (Num 11:30).

The references to Levi and Levites in the first three books of the Bible[16] are of two sorts. Levi in Genesis and in Exod 1:2 is a member of Jacob's family like the others. Most if not all of the other mentions of Levi in Exodus and Leviticus are secondary additions, and reflect the new view presented in Numbers. Three examples may suffice: 1. The sole mention of Levites in all of the book that now bears their name (Lev 25:32–33) is an exception to the rules about redemption of property, and will constitute a footnote to the extended rules in Leviticus 25 about redemption, added in the light of Numbers 35 and the related material in 1 Chronicles 6 and Joshua 21. 2. The Levites have been added in Exod 38:21 to the instructions Moses gave in 31:1–11 concerning Bezalel and Oholiab.[17] 3. The assistance provided by Levites to Moses in the aftermath of the making of the golden calf (Exod 32:25–29) is unknown to the version presented by Deuteronomy 9, is described as ("priestly") ordination,[18] and will hardly belong to a pre-"Priestly" stratum of the Pentateuch. Indeed the boldness of comparing the bloody purge by Levites to priestly ordination by blood may go beyond and so be subsequent to what Numbers reports about a separation of the Levites to a service that is carefully distinguished from the priestly.

---

[16] See n. 13 above.

[17] It has of course long been argued that the report of the making of the tabernacle as a whole (Exodus 35–40) was drafted (much) later than the report of the instructions in Exodus 25–31. R. Nurmela (*The Levites. Their Emergence as a Second-Class Priesthood* [SFSHJ 193; Atlanta: Scholars, 1998] 114) observes that "[t]he notion of the Levites as a *clerus minor* belongs ... apparently to a later level of P than that of the Aaronic priesthood and the tabernacle. Above all, it is an indisputable fact that the second-class priesthood is overlooked in the passages where priesthood and worship are introduced in P. Neither has a later redaction made any attempts to add this notion into the context of priesthood and worship, except the mention of the Levites in Exodus 38:21."

[18] Although מלאו here is pointed *qal*, but *pi'el* elsewhere of priestly ordination, יד is nowhere else the object of מלא (*qal*). At the very least, it is sensible to see a comparison being offered here to the ordination of priests; but it is more than likely that a stronger claim was intended, but toned down in the tradition by alternative pointing.

This changing portrayal of Levites is found also in the development of the narratives about the monarchy; and hence these can
function together as a third "comparator," since not strictly a single
"intertext." At one end of the process, Levites are absent from the
oldest forms of the ark traditions still witnessed in 2 Samuel 6 and
1 Kgs 8:1–5 (LXX), and in fact from the entirety of the "Book of
Two Houses."[19] At the other, Levites are very heavily represented
in the books of Chronicles, as also in Ezra-Nehemiah. In between,
the beginning of 1 Kings 8 has been adjusted so that the first five
verses in MT now agree with the fuller "Levite-friendly" Chronicler's
text in 2 Chron 5:2–6; and increasing interest in the Levites has led
to unobtrusive but telling mentions of their responsibility for moving the ark in 1 Sam 6:15 and 2 Sam 15:24. Whether these three
texts in Samuel-Kings anticipate the situation in Chronicles, or are
influenced by it, or simply stem from the same "late biblical" world,
need not concern us here.

Elsewhere in the Former Prophets, we should recall that the exceptional role accorded the Levites in Joshua 13–21 is regularly attributed to later phases in the development of that book. Similarly, in
Josh 3:3, "the Levites" will be a supplement to an existing text. This
addition is mostly understood as a clarification that the "priests" who
feature prominently in carrying the ark (3:6, 8, 13, 14, 15, 17; 4:3,
9, 10, 11, 16, 17, 18) were in fact "levitical" priests. The phrase
הכהנים הלוים is repeated in Josh 8:33. Indeed it is far from impossible that the addition of הלוים to Josh 3:3[20] was intended not so much
as a "clarification" but rather as a correction of the earlier text. If
so, הכהנים הלוים might be better rendered "the priests (read 'the
levites')." Only in the later portions of Judges (17–20), itself possibly
the latest "book" in the Former Prophets,[21] do we arrive at a situation in which there are stories about individual Levites.

"In the wilderness" (Num 1:1) does not have the same rarity value
as the title "And he called" (Lev 1:1). It is the sudden arrival in
Numbers, as in Chronicles and Ezra-Nehemiah, of the Levites in

---

[19] The "synoptic" material shared by Samuel-Kings and Chronicles.

[20] The same may be true of Josh 8:33; however, since 8:30–35 as a whole is
widely recognised as one of the latest passages in Joshua, the composite הכהנים הלוים
may be part of the original draft there.

[21] A. G. Auld, "The Deuteronomists between History and Theology," in A. Lemaire
and M. Saebø (eds.), *Congress Volume. Oslo 1998* (VTSup 66; Leiden: Brill, 2000)
353–67.

force that demonstrates that we have moved on from Leviticus to a
new "book" from a new period, that we are now in a new world.
Of course matters are less tidy than this sketch of the origins of the
middle books of the Pentateuch might appear to suggest. The proposal is simply that *in conception* the books of Exodus, Leviticus, and
Numbers are more different from each other than would be expected
of three parts of a larger whole; and that they were conceived one
after the other and not together. They do represent stages in the
same broad tradition; and ripples from the later did roll over the
earlier: it was not only the Levites that washed back from Numbers
into Exodus and Leviticus.

The relative priority of Exodus 29 and Leviticus 8 on the ordination of Aaron and his sons, and of Leviticus 23 and Numbers
28–29 on the festival calendar, may continue to be debated backwards and forwards. And in each of these cases it may be better to
think of separate development from a common original than dependence of one present form of the text on the other. Several other
instances of material inconsistency—or at least updating rules to correspond to later cultic practice—have long been discussed, such as
the development of Leviticus 4 in Numbers 15.[22] Similarly, it is natural to portray the four separate תורות in Numbers[23] as loosely dependent on the two sets of five תורות each in Leviticus 6–7 and 11–15.
The scholarly consensus in most such cases is that the more recent
practice is attested in a subsequent "fifth" of the Torah: in Leviticus
rather than Exodus, or in Numbers rather than Leviticus. A serial
approach to the actual conception of these books offers a fresh context for discussion of such developments.

The proposal that we should read Numbers in and for itself, as
an entity separate from Leviticus, is far from new. It has been discussed on other grounds by Wenham and others.[24] What I have
missed in such discussion has been attention to the novelty within
the broad "Priestly" tradition of the concentration on the Levites we
find in Numbers, and of the intimate connection between this new
role of the Levites and the very business of "numbering." To decouple

---

[22] M. Fishbane, *The Garments of Torah. Essays in Biblical Hermeneutics* (Bloomington,
Ind.: Indiana University Press, 1989) 9; Knohl, *Sanctuary of Silence*, 53.

[23] Num 5:29; 6:13, 21; 19:14.

[24] For a convenient recent orientation, see G. J. Wenham, *Numbers* (OTG; Sheffield:
Sheffield Academic Press, 1997) 14–15, 75–79.

Numbers from Exodus and Leviticus and to note how much the
new Levitical interests of Numbers are shared with Chronicles-Ezra-
Nehemiah is to point to a later date for the book than either
Wenham[25] or Knohl and Milgrom will find congenial.

One of the most pleasant results of working on this paper has
been to discover that Mary Douglas was there already. Of course
and in one sense I was not unaware of that, because I had enjoyed
her *In the Wilderness*[26] and discussed it with her. However, much as
I admired her account of Numbers as a unified priestly essay critical
of Nehemiah's government policies, I could not accept it: I remained
and remain persuaded[27] of my own earlier argument that much of
the final quarter of Numbers depended on later elements in Joshua
depicting tribal relationships which in turn had drawn on materials
in Chronicles.[28] A measure of stylistic distinctiveness cannot be ignored
within the closing chapters of Numbers. However, to decouple
Numbers from Exodus and Leviticus permits the broad unity of
Numbers to be more readily glimpsed. It is a book which develops
themes found in Exodus and Leviticus within a world also shared
with Chronicles-Ezra-Nehemiah and later strands in Joshua.

What these prolegomena imply for the reading of ויקרא/Λευιτικον
as a "book" must await a further study.

---

[25] *Numbers*, 84.

[26] M. Douglas, *In the Wilderness. The Doctrine of Defilement in the Book of Numbers*
(JSOTSup 158; Sheffield: Sheffield Academic Press) 1993.

[27] As I admitted in "Leviticus at the Heart of the Pentateuch?" (see above, n. 1),
47.

[28] A. G. Auld, *Joshua, Moses and the Land* (Edinburgh: T&T Clark, 1980), especially pp. 72–87. That earlier work is summarized, and much of its argument
extended in *Joshua Retold. Synoptic Perspectives* (Edinburgh: T&T Clark, 1998).

THE STRUCTURE OF THE BOOK OF LEVITICUS IN THE NARRATIVE OUTLINE OF THE PRIESTLY SINAI STORY (EXOD 19:1–NUM 10:10*)

Andreas Ruwe

I. *Methodological Preconditions and Topic Definition*

Clarifying the literary history of the book of Leviticus is closely connected with clarifying the literary history of the formation of the
priestly material in the Pentateuch. Because in Leviticus there are
no passages to be found that belong to the nonpriestly sources of
the books of Genesis to Deuteronomy, there results—in the face of
the obvious closeness of the texts of Leviticus to the formation of the
priestly material—already the problem in what manner the texts are
to be related to the so-called "Priestly Code": Do they belong to
the heart of this literary source in the Pentateuch or to its pre- or
posthistory? Research agrees that its relation to the "Priestly Code"
is the central, literary historical problem of Leviticus. However, there
are major differences when it comes to solving this problem. Many
authors take for granted the *Grundschrift-Ergänzung-Hypothese* that has
dominated the scientific discussion on the priestly material at least
since J. Wellhausen; they ask which texts of Leviticus are part of the
Priestergrundschrift ("P^g," etc.) and which texts belong to the "supplementary layer" or "supplementary layers" ("P^s," "P^{ss}," etc.).[1] In his
still decisive commentary, K. Elliger maintains that only "a little bit
of chapters 8–10" belongs to the *Priestergrundschrift*[2] while the other
parts "have their own history which usually starts before its integration into the P-composition and is not at all finished with this
act."[3] Other authors, like T. Pola, E. Otto and C. Frevel, also starting

---

[1] Cf. J. Wellhausen, *Composition des Hexateuch* (3rd ed.; Berlin: G. Reimer, 1899) 81.
[2] K. Elliger, *Leviticus* (HAT I/4; Tübingen: J. C. B. Mohr [Siebeck], 1966) 10;
quotation transl. by A. Ruwe. In contrast to his earlier essay, "Sinn und Ursprung
der priesterlichen Geschichtserzählung," *ZThK* 49 (1952) 121–43, Elliger considers
Lev 8:1, 2a, 3, 4–8, 9*, 10aα, 12*, 13–14, 15*, 16–23, 24b*, 25a, 26a, 27*, 28,
31a, 32, 36*; 9:3*, 4–5 (6), 7a, 8a, 15b, 16, 17a, 18, 19, 20b, 21b, 22, 23b, 24b;
10:1–7 (8–9) as belonging to the *Priestergrundschrift*.
[3] Ibid., 9.

from the *Grundschrifthypothese*, have denied recently that there are any texts from "Pᵍ" within Leviticus at all; they regard Leviticus as late- or post-priestly.[4] Others—I. Knohl and J. Milgrom—substitute the traditional literary critical differentiation between "Pᵍ" and "Pˢ" by the assumption that the shape of the text at issue originates in two priestly schools ("Priestly Torah" and "Holiness School") that are supposed to have followed different concepts of cult and ethics.[5] Yet others—e.g. R. Rendtorff, E. Blum, F. Crüsemann and E. Gersten- berger—consider the differentiation between different priestly layers or schools as questionable because of the lack of sufficient factual and linguistic criteria; they explain the lack of text unity in Leviticus as the result of flowing tradition processes.[6] Finally there are authors who try to make the text order of Leviticus comprehensible as a meaningful composition; they try to avoid diachronic differentiations at all.[7]

Thus an agreement on the genesis of Leviticus still seems to be a long time off. In the face of this situation it is in my opinion nec- essary to name the methodological and hermeneutic aspects of the analysis of these texts before analyzing them. Clarifying the method- ological preconditions of the analysis might contribute to improving the possibility of a consensus. In analyzing Leviticus, I start from the following assumptions:

---

[4] T. Pola, *Die ursprüngliche Priesterschrift. Beobachtungen zur Literarkritik und Traditionsgeschichte von Pᵍ* (WMANT 70; Neukirchen-Vluyn: Neukirchener Verlag, 1995), esp. pp. 351–54; E. Otto, "Forschungen zur Priesterschrift," *TRu* 62 (1997) 1–50, esp. pp. 27, 36; C. Frevel, "Kein Ende in Sicht? Zur Priestergrundschrift im Buch Leviticus," in H.-J. Fabry and H.-W. Jüngling (eds.), *Levitikus als Buch* (BBB 119; Berlin: Philo, 1999) 85–123, esp. 117–20; idem, *Mit Blick auf das Land die Schöpfung erinnern. Zum Ende der Priestergrundschrift* (Herders biblische Studien 23; Freiburg: Herder, 2000).

[5] Cf. I. Knohl, *The Sanctuary of Silence. The Priestly Torah and the Holiness School* (Minneapolis: Fortress, 1995) passim; J. Milgrom, *Leviticus 1–16. A New Translation with Introduction and Commentary* (AB 3; New York: Doubleday, 1991) 13–35.

[6] R. Rendtorff, "Is it Possible to Read Leviticus as a Separate Book?," in J. F. A. Sawyer (ed.), *Reading Leviticus. A Conversation with Mary Douglas* (JSOTSup 227; Sheffield: Sheffield Academic Press, 1996) 22–35, esp. p. 34; E. Blum, *Studien zur Komposition des Pentateuch* (BZAW 189; Berlin: de Gruyter, 1990) 219ff.; F. Crüsemann, *Die Tora. Theologie und Sozialgeschichte des alttestamentlichen Gesetzes* (München: Kaiser, 1992) 328–29; E. Gerstenberger, *Das dritte Buch Mose. Leviticus* (ATD 6; Göttingen: Vandenhoeck & Ruprecht, 1993) 5.

[7] E.g. M. Douglas, "Poetic Structure in Leviticus," in D. P. Wright, D. N. Freedman and A. Hurvitz (eds.), *Pomegranates and Golden Bells. Studies in Biblical, Jewish, and Near Eastern Ritual, Law and Literature in Honor of Jacob Milgrom* (Winona Lake, Ind.: Eisenbrauns, 1995) 239–56; idem, "The Forbidden Animals in Leviticus," *JSOT* 59 (1993) 2–23, and C. R. Smith, "The Literary Structure in Leviticus," *JSOT* 70 (1996) 17–32.

1. The twenty seven chapters of Leviticus form a narrative context. It is true that the narrative level of the text in Leviticus stays
in the background compared to the level of direct speech, and is
limited to Lev 8:1–10:20; 21:24; 23:44; 24:10–23, the summaries in
Lev 7:37–38; 26:46 and 27:34 and to the thirty seven so-called divine
speech formulae.[8] However, it cannot be denied that Leviticus is a
narrative text. One generally has to consider that the many commands and instructions in Leviticus are phrased in the form of divine
speeches. The direct speech, however, as "mimetic" form" of the
presentation of speeches, is a constitutive element of narration.[9]
Therefore the tendency in research, prevailing since J. Wellhausen,
to identify the priestly narrative mainly with the narrative level of
the text, cannot be taken as a starting point for the analysis of these
texts.[10] The differentiation between "narrative" and "law"—and thus
the differentiation between "P^g" and "P^s"—as a basic model of literary history has to be questioned.

2. It follows from the thoroughly narrative character of Leviticus
that the interpretation of these texts has to start consistently from
those factors that structure the "narrated world" of this text. First
of all, however, "narrated worlds" are organized by details about
time and place as well as about the characters.[11] An adequate analysis

---

[8] Lev 1:1; 4:1; 5:14, 20; 6:1, 12, 17; 7:22, 28; 8:1; 10:8; 11:1; 12:1; 13:1; 14:1,
33; 15:1; 16:1–2; 17:1; 18:1; 19:1; 20:1; 21:1, 16; 22:1, 17, 26; 23:1, 9, 23, 26, 33;
24:1, 13; 25:1; 27:1.

[9] Cf. G. Genette, *Figures III* (Paris: Editions du Seuil, 1972).

[10] There exists a widespread habit to differentiate between "priestly narrative"
and the "legislative material" presented in the divine speeches. This trend, however, is problematic insofar as it fails to consider that the so-called "legislative material" itself is substantially determined by the fictional elements of the frame of the
surrounding story. (1) For many commandments in Leviticus, the topography of the
מחנה is constitutive, which characterizes the Priestly passages of the exodus-, desert-
and Sinai-narrative as a whole (cf. Lev 4:12, 21; 6:4; 13:46; 14:3, 8; 16:26, 27, 28;
17:3). (2) Many regulations in Leviticus that refer to the cult offer—in accordance
with the desert setting of the surrounding Priestly narrative sequences—the term
אהל מועד (Lev 1:3, 5; 3:2, 8, 13; 4:4, 5, 7 (twice), 14, 16, 18 (twice); 6:9, 19, 23;
8:31, 33, 35; 10:7, 9; 12:6; 14:11, 23; 15:14, 29; 16:7, 16, 17, 20, 23, 33; 17:4, 5,
6, 9; 19:21; 24:3). Vice versa there are no directions in Leviticus that mention a
temple (בית or comparable). (3) In many commands and instructions of Leviticus
the priests are called, by analogy with Aaron's particular position within the priestly
narrative context of Sinai, בני אהרון (Lev 1:5, 7, 8, 11; 2:2; 3:2, 5, 8, 13; 6:7, 11;
7:10, 33). (4) Some directions in Leviticus refer directly to Moses. (5) Four collections of laws in Leviticus open with so-called *historisierende Gebotseinleitungen* (Lev 14:33;
19:23; 23:10; 25:2) and are thus determined by the fiction of the frame narrative.

[11] Cf. C. Hardmeier, *Prophetie im Streit vor dem Untergang Judas. Erzählkommunikative
Studien zur Entstehungssituation der Jesaja- und Jeremiaerzählungen II Reg 18–20 und Jer
37–40* (BZAW 187; Berlin: de Gruyter, 1989) 23–86.

of Leviticus therefore should not superficially concentrate on the contents of the divine speeches. Moreover the analysis of these texts has to start from a consistent recording of those structural elements that constitute the "narrated world" in Leviticus. Especially the stereotypical divine speech formulae in Leviticus are to be considered. Once the outline of the *general shape* of the narrative at issue has been established on the basis of the analysis of these narrative elements—only then is there a methodological reason for beginning with the literary-historical or content-related analysis.

3. Leviticus obviously is not an independent narrative, but is part of the priestly narrative context of the Sinai pericope, Exod 19:1–Num 10:10, which is itself part of the Tetra- or Pentateuch. The priestly narrative context of Exod 19:1–Num 10:10 is the primary literary context of Leviticus. Independently of the disputed question whether the priestly formation of the Pentateuch is an independent narrative work[12] or serves as a supplement to the nonpriestly formation of the Pentateuch,[13] it is necessary in any case to examine the inner coherence, the narrative structure and the thematic profile of this formation. Many elements of Leviticus become comprehensible only by contextualizing them with the other priestly texts of the Sinai narrative or with the priestly texts as such. An analysis of Leviticus that is satisfying with regard to the narrative respect, should therefore in any case start from the consideration of the immediate narrative context of Exod 19:1–Num 10:10.

This essay is an attempt to develop—in keeping with the text—the structure of the book of Leviticus on the basis of the methodological principles mentioned above. Since, as is well known, details of time are very relevant for the priestly texts, the chronological system of the priestly Sinai story shall be dealt with first and the chronologisms in the book of Leviticus examined (II). As a second step, the structure developing from this examination shall be consulted regarding contents and intentions (III).

---

[12] Cf. e.g. the recent work of E. Otto, "Forschungen zur Priesterschrift," 1–50; and A. de Pury, "Der priesterliche Umgang mit der Jakobsgeschichte," in R. G. Kratz, T. Krüger, and K. Schmidt (eds.), *Schriftauslegung in der Schrift. Festschrift für Odil Hannes Steck zu seinem 65. Geburtstag* (BZAW 300; Berlin: de Gruyter, 2000) 33–60, esp. pp. 34–40.

[13] Cf. e.g. E. Blum, *Studien zur Komposition des Pentateuch*; and R. Rendtorff, *Kanonische Grundlegung* (vol. 1 of *Theologie des Alten Testaments. Ein kanonischer Entwurf*; Neukirchen-Vluyn: Neukirchener Verlag, 1999) 10–11.

II. *The Details of Time in the Priestly Sinai Narrative and the Basic Structure of Leviticus*

Through the two related travel notices in Exod 19:1–2 and Num 10:11–12, the priestly Sinai story in Exod 19:1–Num 10:10 is revealed as a coherent narrative context containing shape-giving initial and final marks. According to Exod 19:1–2; Num 10:10–12 the Israelites came ממצרים ארץ in the third month (Exod 19:1). They settled במדבר (Exod 19:2a) and continued בשנה השנית בחדש השני בעשרים from there (ממדבר) again (Num 10:11–12). With these details Exod 19:1–2 and Num 10:11–12 take up the chronological structure of the priestly formation in the Tetrateuch.[14] Exodus 19:1–2 and Num 10:11–12 contain the decisive pieces of information for the temporal classification of the events belonging to the priestly Sinai story. All events that are being narrated in the texts between Exod 19:1–2 and Num 10:11–12 are, in accordance with these two notices, situated between the third month (of the first year) and the twentieth day of the second month of the second year after the exodus from Egypt. But the details in Exod 19:1–2 and Num 10:11–12 also provide a temporal orientation for the events narrated in Leviticus. This follows from the fact that the narrative context, begun in Exodus 19, continues in Leviticus without interruption and that there are no details in Leviticus which have a comparable function of providing orientation like Exod 19:1–2 and Num 10:11–12. Without these details Leviticus lacks necessary narrative information. Already for this reason alone, Leviticus can only be regarded as part of the priestly Sinai story.

Through the further chronological details in Exod 40:17; Lev 7:35–38; 8:32–36; 9:1, 4; 10:19; 16:1 and Num 1:1, the events narrated in the book of Leviticus are classified in even more detail. In Exod 40:17 the setting up of the sanctuary is dated on the first day of the first month of the second year (בחדש הראשון השנה השנית בחדש). Because in Leviticus in many instances it is required that the Tent of Meeting (אהל מועד) be available for use, it follows that the events narrated in Leviticus are situated *after* this date (the first day of the first month of the second year).[15] On the other hand, the events

---

[14] Cf. T. Pola, *Die ursprüngliche Priesterschrift*, 108–16 and the literature quoted there.

[15] The אהל מועד is mentioned as existing and usable in the book of Leviticus in

narrated in Numbers 1–10 (the revelation of the ordering of the camp, etc.) are connected with the first day of the second month of the second year (Num 1:1). Through the chronological notices in Exod 19:1–2; 40:17; Num 1:1; 10:11–12, consisting of details of months and sometimes days and years, the whole priestly narrative context of Sinai is structured conclusively. First of all, the building and setting up of the sanctuary is set; these events are located between the third month (of the first year) (Exod 19:1–2) and the first day of the first month of the second year (Exod 40:17). On the other hand the chain of events that concludes the Sinai context, the revelation and setting up of the order of the camp (Numbers 1–10*) is placed between the first day of the second month of the second year (Num 10:1) and the twentieth day of the second month of the second year (Num 10:11). The events narrated in Leviticus, finally, are situated between the day of the setting up of the sanctuary (the first day of the first month of the second year; Exod 40:17) and the day when the command is given to take a census of the people (the first day of the second month of the second year; Num 1:1). All events of Leviticus therefore are assigned to the first month of the second year; the book of Leviticus all in all "takes place" in this month. Distinguishing Leviticus as a book exactly corresponds with the temporal structuring of the priestly Sinai narrative which is externally limited through the details in Exod 19:1–2 and Num 10:10ff. and internally structured through the details in Exod 40:17 and Num 1:1.

Besides these "external" chronologisms there are narrative details of time within Leviticus only in Lev 7:35–38;[16] 9:1; and 16:1. Apart from that, for the temporal organization one has to consider the detail היום that marks the "Origo"[17] in the direct speeches in Lev

---

general in Lev 1:1, 3, 5; 3:2, 8, 13; 4:4, 5, 7 (twice), 14, 16, 18 (twice); 6:9, 19, 23; 8:3, 4, 31, 33, 35; 9:5, 23; 10:7, 9; 12:6; 14:8, 11, 23; 15:14, 29; 16:7, 16, 17, 20, 23, 33; 17:4, 5, 6, 9; 19:21; 24:3.

[16] Assigning Lev 7:35–38 to the narrative level of the text, however, is not completely without doubt. It arises from the following observations. The instructions concerning the priestly portions relative to the זבח שלמים certainly reach as far as 7:34, because v. 34 is clearly part of the divine speech in 7:29bff. because of the first person singular. On the other hand, vv. 37–38 certainly belong to the narrative level, because they do not contain a first person narrative but deal with יהוה and Moses in the third person (v. 38). Since in vv. 35–36—as opposed to v. 34—יהוה is represented in the third person as well, v. 35 presumably belongs to the narrative level of the text.

[17] The term "Origo" that serves to indicate the different ways of marking the speaker's position in a text was first used by K. Bühler, *Sprachtheorie. Die Darstellungsfunktion der Sprache* (3rd ed.; Stuttgart: Lucius & Lucius, 1999) 102–20.

9:4 and 10:19. Among these chronologisms within Leviticus, the detail of date in 9:1, ביום השמיני, is particularly to be taken into account, which however raises questions as to its context. Many authors assume that it refers back to the end of the consecration of the sanctuary and the Aaronites, narrated in Lev 8:1–36.[18] Towards the end of the consecration, Moses instructs Aaron that he and his sons shall stay at the entrance of the אהל מועד for seven days for the purpose of ordination (8:33–35). When 8:36 summarily states that Aaron and his sons do everything which they were instructed by Moses to do, the observance of this waiting period of seven days by the Aaronites is expressed (implicitly). The detail of time ביום השמיני thus can very well be identified with the first day after the end of the seven-day consecration. However, one has to take into account that an eighth day is not considered at all in the speech of Moses in 8:31–35. Thus ביום השמיני is not an immediate continuation of the time horizon opened up in 8:33–36. Systematically, this detail moreover takes up Exod 40:17 and is therefore immediately connected with the larger chronological system of the priestly Sinai narrative (Exod 19:1–2; 40:17, etc.). Concretely meant is the eighth day of the first month of the second year, which is at the same time the first day after completing the consecration.[19]

It is important to realize that the chronological notice in Lev 9:1 is the only one within Leviticus that refers back to the larger date structure of the priestly narrative consisting of Exod 19:1–2; 40:17; Num 1:1; 10:11–12. This circumstance is of highest importance for structuring Leviticus: because the chronological notices in Exod 19:1–2; 40:17; Num 1:1; 10:11–12 are of basic relevance for structuring the priestly Sinai story in marking the main sections of the narrative, one can assume that Lev 9:1 has got an analogous function for structuring Leviticus. The structure usually imposed on the book of Leviticus—chapters 1–7 being the first major part and chapters 8–10 the second etc.[20]—ignores this temporal caesura. This structure, oriented towards the differentiation between "law" and "narrative," does

---

[18] Cf. the early publication of D. Hoffmann, *Das Buch Leviticus übersetzt und erklärt. Erster Halbband Lev 1–17* (Berlin: Poppelauer, 1905) 284; further J. Milgrom, *Leviticus 1–16*, 571, and many others.

[19] That Lev 9:1 depends on Exod 40:17 is already noticed by M. Noth, *Das dritte Buch Mose. Leviticus* (2nd ed.; ATD 6; Göttingen: Vandenhoeck & Ruprecht, 1966) 62.

[20] Cf. E. Zenger, "Das Buch Leviticus als Teiltext der Tora/des Pentateuch," in H.-J. Fabry and H.-W. Jüngling (eds.), *Levitikus als Buch*, 62–64; also J. Milgrom, *Leviticus 1–16*, v–x.

not consider the narrative structure of the text; moreover, it does
not recognize that the divine speech formula in 8:1 continues without interruption the divine speech formulae in 1:1–2; 4:1–2; 5:20;
6:1–2, 12, 17–18; 7:22–23, 28–29 which mark the sections in Leviticus
1–7. Leviticus 9:1 does, however, mark a temporal caesura and is
therefore crucial to structuring Leviticus as such. The fact that the
chronologism in 9:1 refers back to the date structure of the priestly
Sinai narrative results—in view of the structural analysis of Leviticus—
in the following thesis: *Leviticus consists of two main parts, of Leviticus
1–8 on the one hand and of Leviticus 9–27 on the other*. This thesis has
to be verified through further observations below. First of all, though,
the other chronological notices in Leviticus shall be considered: Lev
7:35–38; 9:4; 10:19 and 16:1.

1. The details in Lev 7:35 (ביום הקריב אתם לכהן); Lev 7:36 (אתם
ביום צותו את בני ישראל להקריב את קרבניהם) und Lev 7:38 (ביום משחו
are not quite clear in their composition.[21] First of all it is only certain that the phrase ביום משחו אתם in v. 36 refers to the day of the
consecration of the sanctuary (Leviticus 8). At the end of the regulations for sacrifice in Leviticus 1–7, sights are thus set on the consecration in 8:1–36 (as already in 6:13). The collection of sacrificial
regulations is related to the consecration in 8:1–36. The second summary in 7:37–38 is completely unclear. About these sentences it is
so far only possible to say that—because of the order of the kinds
of offerings in 7:37—they function as a summary of the partial synopsis of offering prescriptions in 6:1–7:35 and that they do not possess a resuming function for Leviticus 1–7 as a whole.[22] The major
problem with this second summary concerns the question: with which
command of God in the preceding narrative context of Sinai should
we identify the instruction to the Israelites, mentioned in v. 38b, to
offer their קרבניהם ליהוה? This instruction serves in v. 38b as a time
reference point for the תורת העלה that is being announced in Leviticus
6–7. In my opinion, this can only be the collection of sacrificial regulations in Lev 1:1–5:26*, directed towards all Israelites. The fol-

---

[21] It is unclear in particular what the subject of the verb is that has to be supplemented and what the pronoun is related to. Cf. M. Noth, *Das dritte Buch Mose*,
41, 53.
[22] This is how J. Milgrom, *Leviticus 1–16*, 436, and R. Rendtorff, *Leviticus* (BK
III; Neukirchen-Vluyn: Neukirchener Verlag, 1985–) 231, correctly judge. However,
difficulties are provided by the מלואים in 7:37; cf. the different solutions in J. Milgrom,
Leviticus 1–16, 436–37.

lowing observations give reason for this claim. On the one hand, addressing the aforementioned instructions to the בני ישראל (7:38b) corresponds with the general addressing of the sacrificial rules in 1:1–5:26. On the other hand the sacrifice terminology in v. 38b corresponds with the corresponding terminology in 1:2–3; 2:1 and 3:1.[23]

But if it is clear that the phrasing in Lev 7:37 decidedly refers to Leviticus 6–7 and that the instruction, mentioned in 7:38b, has to be identified with 1:1–5:26, then the detail of time in 7:38b is a notice of synchronity, emphasizing that the sacrificial regulations for the priests (Leviticus 6–7) were issued at the same time as the instructions for all Israelites (1:1–5:26).[24] But why was it important to emphasize the synchronity of the announcement of instructions for sacrifice for all Israelites on the one hand and for the priests on the other? In my opinion, through this emphasis of synchronity the following complex that is central for the general composition of the priestly Sinai narrative is stressed: the sacrificial instructions, issued in 1:1–5:26, are according to 1:1 qualified by that fact that the Lord called them *"from the Tent of Meeting"* (מאהל מועד) out to Moses. Immediately after setting up the sanctuary it was not possible for Moses to go into the Tent of Meeting because the cloud (הענן) covered it and the כבוד filled the tabernacle (Exod 40:34–35). This inaccessibility of the אהל מועד for Moses, conditioned by the indwelling of the כבוד, is being evoked anew through the conspicuous phrasing in 1:1.[25] Following the first communal offering (9:22–24), the possibilities of entering the אהל מועד for Moses and Aaron are later shown to have fundamentally changed nevertheless. Moses and Aaron are indeed allowed to enter the אהל מועד after the celebration of the offerings and after Aaron has blessed the people (9:22–23). Also the further announcement of laws to Moses in the following passage takes place באהל מועד (*"in the Tent of Meeting"*) (though this is mentioned explicitly no earlier than in Num 1:1). Thus it becomes clear that the events narrated in 9:1–24 function to initiate a new phase of the priestly Sinai narrative with regard to a theology of encounter. When setting up the Tent of Meeting, the כבוד יהוה did fill the tabernacle. But he

---

[23] The phrase הקריב קרבן appears in the torah in Lev 1:2 (twice); 2:1, 4; 3:6, 7, 14; 7:13, 14, 38; 9:15; 17:4; 22:18; 27:9, 11; Num 6:14; 7:10, 11, 19; 9:7; 15:4 (twice); 31:50.
[24] A comparable result is achieved by J. Milgrom, *Leviticus 1–16*, 438.
[25] Cf. in this context and for Lev 1:1 in general J. Milgrom, *Leviticus 1–16*, 134–37.

was shielded by a cloud; a direct encounter with יהוה is thus impossible. As soon as the first communal offering is celebrated, the encounter between the Lord and Moses, Aaron and the people (העם) really takes place. Through the composition of the narrative, developing from Exod 40:34–35 to Lev 9:22–24, it is made clear: not through the mere existence and setting up of the sanctuary, but only through the complete establishment of the sacrificial cult does the promised presence of God in Israel become reality. The theology of encounter in the priestly texts thus receives the accentuation of a theology of sacrifice.[26]

Now the chronological notice in Lev 7:37–38, in my opinion, emphasizes this overall concept of God's closeness to Israel. The sacrificial regulations announced to the priests (Leviticus 6–7) are synchronized in 7:38b with the regulations for the Israelites in 1:1–5:26 for the following reason: the announcement of all regulations is explicitly located within the time of the Tent of Meeting's inaccessibility, described in Exod 40:34–35.[27] The details of time in Lev 7:35–38 bring the announcement of the sacrificial regulations in Leviticus 1–7 and the celebration of the consecration (8:1–36) into *one* period of time that is characterized by the "not yet" of the immediate presence of God before the Israelites. Thus in view of 7:35–38 the above formulated thesis that the chronological notice in 9:1 creates a far-reaching caesura within Leviticus is confirmed. The announcement of the sacrificial regulations and the consecration belong to the *preparation* for the immediate encounter of God with the Israelites, but not to the encounter itself that takes place separately on the "eighth

---

[26] This already follows from the central text of the priestly texts in Exod 29:42–46, where it is emphasized that the Lord will reveal himself to the Israelites particularly at the "entrance of the Tent of Meeting," i.e. in the area of the sacrificial cult. The "entrance of the Tent of Meeting" is nearly identical with the place of the Altar of Burnt Offering.

[27] Following D. Hoffmann, *Das Buch Leviticus*, 19–28 J. Milgrom, *Leviticus 1–16*, 438, has attempted a different interpretation of Lev 7:37–38. Both authors take for granted that the detail of place בהר סיני is to be interpreted in the sense of "upon Mount Sinai" and thus they differentiate between the announcement of laws in the priestly texts that were issued on Mont Sinai and those that were issued in the Tent (cf. J. Milgrom, *Leviticus 1–16*, 436ff.). In my opinion, however, the detail of place בהר סיני in the priestly texts can—for reasons from within the texts—mean "at Mount Sinai" only. (1) There is no sound differentiation between "Sinai laws" and "Tent laws" visible in the texts. (2) In Lev 26:46 the detail of place בהר סיני can mean "at Mount Sinai" only since the text deals with the issuing of the laws towards the Israelites, which is to be situated at the foot of Mount Sinai only. Accordingly, all other records of בהר סיני in the priestly texts are to be translated as "at Mount Sinai."

day" after the absolute completion of the consecration of sanctuary and priests.

2. Now we will deal with the next set of chronologisms in Leviticus, the marking of the "Origo" in the direct speeches in Lev 9:4 and 10:19. The presentation of the reason כי היום יהוה נראה עליכם following Lev 9:2–4a in 9:4b connects the revelation of the Lord before the people of Israel explicitly with Moses' order, issued to Aaron on the eighth day, to offer a series of sacrifices (9:1–2). Because in the context there are no further temporal caesuras noted, it follows that besides the Mosaic command to sacrifice also the celebration of the sacrifices and the revelation of the כבוד יהוה, connected with it, are assigned to the "eighth day." All the events narrated in 9:1–24 therefore take place on the "eighth day."

Against the background of this temporal assignment of the events narrated in Lev 9:1–24 is the marking of the "Origo" in 10:19 to be considered. This marking is located at the end of a discussion between Moses and Aaron about the consumption of the priestly portions of the חטאת. In this discussion Aaron justifies himself for having refrained from consuming the priestly portions—a failure criticized by Moses—with reference to his bitter fate (i.e. the death of his sons Nadab and Abihu). Although his sons have offered their offerings (את חטאתם ואת עלתם) היום ("today"), these things have happened to him. For this reason he has "today" refrained from consuming the portions of the חטאת due him. The sacrifice of sin-offering and the whole burnt offering through the Aaronites, indicated in this justification, can hardly be identified with anything other than the first part of the sequence of offerings mentioned in Lev 9:1–24. For the offering dealt with in Lev 9:1–24 consists of two parts: first Aaron, assisted by his sons, offers for himself (Lev 9:2, 8b–14); then he offers for the people (Lev 9:3b–4a, 15–21). The offerings for the people consist of עלה, חטאת, זבה השלמים, and מנחה, while the ones for Aaron or the Aaronites, however, are only חטאת and עלה. The correspondence between the termini named in Lev 10:19 and in Lev 9:2, 8b–14 indicates very clearly that Aaron's argument against Moses (הן היום הקריבו את חטאתם ואת עלתם לפני יהוה ותקראנה אתי כאלה, Lev 10:19a) refers to the first part of the sequence of offerings, described in 9:2, 8b–14, the one for the Aaronites.[28] If this is true, the marking

---

[28] This is what D. Hoffmann, *Das Buch Leviticus*, 299, and J. Milgrom, *Leviticus 1–16*, 626, think as well.

of the "Origo" (היום) in 10:19, however, indicates that the events depicted in 10:1–20 also belong to the "eighth day" and that 9:1–24 and 10:1–20 thus create a connected complex in temporal, and therefore also in compositional respect.

The assumption that Lev 9:1–24 and 10:1–20 create a compositional unity can be supported by further observations. On the one hand there are no details within 10:1–20 that mark a temporal caesura between the events narrated in 9:1–24 and the ones in 10:1–20. Especially the opening sentence in 10:1 continues the narrative sequence of 9:1–24 without interruption. On the other hand in his speech to Moses (10:19), Aaron looks back upon the priestly offering of the beginning (9:8b–14) as well as upon the death of Nadab and Abihu (ותקראנה אתי כאלה) and locates both events היום.

All of the events narrated in Lev 9:1–10:20—including the above mentioned discussion between Moses and Aaron—belong to the "eighth day."[29] Leviticus 9:1–10:20 is to be considered as a narrative unity that is clearly distinguished from 1:1–8:36.

3. Against this background finally the last detail of time in the book of Leviticus has to be considered, the narrative detail in Lev 16:1. Other than the "eighth day" in 9:1, this chronological notice is not part of the date structure that covers the priestly Sinai story (Exod 19:1; 40:17; Num 1:1; Num 10:11–12). It is a subordinate mark that is *related to a particular event*. The divine speech concerning the יום הכפורים (announced in 16:2–34a) is through this detail closely connected with the death of Nadab and Abihu (narrated in 10:1–20), since it is classified as having been issued after this event. It is not possible to decide whether the detail of time, אחרי מות שני בני אהרן,

---

[29] If Lev 9:1–24 and 10:1–20 are considered as a narrative unity, many problems concerning the interpretation of 10:1–20 are resolved. The whole passage about dealing with the priestly portions in 10:12–20, that is hardly comprehensible in this place if 10:1–20 were isolated from 9:1–24, becomes clear when connecting 9:1–24 and 10:1–20: the presentation of these priestly portions in 10:12–20 refers back to the offering of sacrifices for the people, narrated in 9:3–4a, 15–21. In particular, the Mosaic orders concerning the מנחה (10:12–13) refer back to the burning of the cereal offering, narrated in 9:17. Otherwise the specifying term המנחה הנותרת in 10:12 would hardly be comprehensible. The orders concerning the consumption of the חזה התנופה and the שוק התרומה (10:13–15) refer to the offering of the זבח שלמים (cf. 7:32–34), narrated in 9:18–21. Finally the sequence of the consumption of the שעיר החטאת (10:16–20) refers to 9:15. Apart from the עלה, where due to the system there are no consumable portions for the priests, 10:12–20 conclusively deals with the complete series of offerings for the people, described in 9:3–4a, 15–21, under the aspect of the priestly consumption.

has to be considered within the horizon of the "eighth day" or whether a distance of a day or a week has to be thought of. Independently of this question, however, it is obvious in any case that the events narrated in 16:1–34 are connected to the events of 9:1–10:20 or to the "eighth day" through this detail of time. Because there are, apart from the analyzed pieces of evidence (9:1, 4; 10:19 and 16:1), no further chronological details in 9:1–27:34, it follows that all chronologisms in 9:1–27:34 refer to the "eighth day" or to events related to it and thus constitute a fairly closed period of time. All in all the thesis raised above is thus confirmed: Leviticus 9:1 creates the decisive caesura for the structuring of Leviticus. Leviticus therefore is structured into two main parts, Leviticus 1–8 on the one hand and Leviticus 9–27 on the other.

III. *The Aspects of Content of Lev 1:1–8:36 and Lev 9:1–27:34**

The consecration narrated in Lev 8:1–36 is already reflected in Exod 29:1–37 and Exod 40:9–15, in fact in the shape of divine instructions. Leviticus 8:1–36 is related to these instructions as an "executing sequence."[30] The priestly texts concerning the sanctuary (Exodus 25–40) thus finally come to an end in Lev 8:1–36. The celebration of the first communal sacrifices, narrated in Lev 9:1–24, however, has no corresponding material in the divine instructions (Exodus 25–40). This observation also confirms that with 9:1–24 a new thematic context begins within the outline of the priestly Sinai texts. Leviticus 1:1–8:36 and 9:1–27:34 are also for this reason to be considered as the two main parts of Leviticus. If the necessity of this structure is thus evident for various compositional reasons, then the question arises which intentions are being expressed with this structure of Leviticus. This crucial question shall now be dealt with in several steps.

1. The intention that lies behind connecting the sacrificial instructions (Leviticus 1–7) and the consecration (Leviticus 8:1–36) to one narrative section, is still fairly obvious. Both contexts deal with the *preparation* of the offering, crucial to the presence of God in Israel,

---

[30] Concerning the general relationship between the section of orders (Exodus 25–31) and the section of execution (Exodus 35–40), compare the important considerations of B. Jacob, *Das Buch Exodus* (Stuttgart: Calwer, 1997) 992–96, who formulates arguments, worth considering, for the originally literary connection between the two sections.

before the entire people. On the one hand the celebration of the offering for the whole of Israel presupposes the consecration of the Aaronites and the sanctuary as well as its accoutrements, especially the altar for the burnt offering. That is what 8:1–36 is about. On the other hand it presupposes the knowledge of the various sacrificial rituals. That is what 1:1–7:37 is about. The sacrifice regulations in 1:1–7:37, however, have not got anything to do with the series of offerings celebrated by Moses in the context of the consecration (8:14–29), since this sequence of offerings has already been ordered in the instructional portion of the priestly texts concerning the sanctuary in detail (cf. Exod 29:10–28 in connection with Exod 40:9–15).[31] The sacrificial regulations in 1:1–7:37, however, refer only to the first offering of Israel through Aaron and the Aaronites, celebrated *following the consecration,* and all further offerings of the people. For these reasons the narrative sequence about the consecration as well as the one about the announcement of the offering regulations clearly reflect events that prepare for the first communal offering of the Israelites. But because both of these subsections, 1:1–7:37 and 8:1–36, deal with this preparation, they have been connected to one narrative unit.

2. The intentions that lie behind connecting Lev 9:1–27:34 to one narrative unit are, however, less obvious, since 9:1–27:34 is thematically much more complex than 1:1–8:36. Thus first of all the basic structure of 9:1–27:34 is to be described, as it follows from the above mentioned structural features.

Leviticus 9:1–10:20 shows a concluding element through the final conversation between Moses and Aaron about the use of the portions (10:12–20) of the offerings described in 9:15–24, and thus forms a fairly independent narrative section.

Apart from this, it is obvious that the divine speech concerning the יום הכפורים (Lev 16:1–34) constitutes a section of its own due to the chronological notice in 16:1 and due to the exclusive address of the instructions to Aaron (cf. 16:2) that deviates from the context

---

[31] Concerning the relation between Exodus 29 and Leviticus 8, see J. Milgrom, "The Consecration of the Priests: A Literary Comparison of Leviticus 8 and Exodus 29," in D. R. Daniels, U. Glessmer and M. Rösel (eds.), *Ernten, was man sät* (Neukirchen-Vluyn: Neukirchener Verlag, 1991) 273–86; K. Elliger, *Leviticus,* 106–15; C. Frevel, "Kein Ende in Sicht?" 96–97.

(Leviticus 11–26).[32] This address refers back to 9:1–10:20 in particular and continues this narrative unit in a particular way.[33]

Thirdly, it is clear that Lev 11:1–15:33 also forms a fairly self-
contained unit, dealing with the topic of purity. In its center there
are instructions for the diagnosis and ritual remediation of צרעת of
humans and of houses (13:1–14:56). These speeches are framed by
two sections on forms of impurity that are related to sexuality: 12:1–8
and 15:1–33. The extensive section 11:1–46, containing instructions
on how to deal with pure and impure animals, the particular emphasis of which is marked by the only parenetical passage within the
whole section on impurities (11:45–46), is set apart and opens the
whole complex. Apart from the introductory section, Lev 11:1–46,
Lev 11:1–15:33 shows a concentric structure and is thus also recognizable as a fairly independent complex within 9:1–27:34.

Finally, there is the thematically complex end of the book of
Leviticus, Lev 17:1–27:34. Of this section, 24:10–24 and 27:1–34
can be set aside as these sections are presumably later supplements.[34]
Against recent denials, one can, however, assume that the sequence
of chapters Leviticus 17–26 is a coherent, fairly independent complex.[35] The following formal observations alone are in favor of this

---

[32] The decrees in Leviticus 11–15 are announced to Moses or to Moses and
Aaron and are directed towards the Israelites (cf. Lev 12:2; 15:2). The decrees in
Leviticus 17–27 are directed to various addressees (the Israelites, Aaron and his
sons, the Israelites only, the priests only or Aaron only etc.).

[33] The references of Lev 16:1–34 to Lev 9:1–10:20 are mentioned by C. Frevel,
"Kein Ende in Sicht?" 92, in particular. Frevel, however, starts from Lev 10:1ff.
as a reference text for Lev 16:1–34 only, leaving the aspect of the presence of God
(cf. Lev 16:2b), already mentioned in Lev 9:4, unconsidered.

[34] Concerning Lev 24:10–24, cf. F. Crüsemann, *Die Tora*, 121–26, and A. Ruwe,
*"Heiligkeitsgesetz" und "Priesterschrift". Literaturgeschichtliche und rechtssystematische Untersuchungen
zu Lev 17,1–26,2* (FAT 26; Tübingen: J. C. B. Mohr [Siebeck], 1999) 56–57; Lev
27:1–34 certainly is a text of transition that thematically already belongs to Numbers
1–10; cf. A. Ruwe, *"Heiligkeitsgesetz"*, 44, n. 21. It is also questionable if the summary in Lev 26:46 belongs to the original composition or if it was added secondarily in connection with Lev 27:34 and Num 36:13.

[35] The new proposal regarding structure by E. Zenger, "Das Buch Levitikus als
Teiltext der Tora/des Pentateuch," in H.-J. Fabry and H. W. Jüngling (eds.), *Levitikus
als Buch*, 47–83. esp. pp. 64–76, proposes a division of the book of Leviticus into
seven sections with Leviticus 16–17 as the center and Leviticus 1–7; 8–10; 11–15;
16–17; 18–20; 21–23; 23–26 (27) as constitutive subunits (see p. 65). One has to
object, however, that in Zenger, the numerous internal references of Leviticus 17–26
as well as the conspicuous changes of addressees between Leviticus 16 and Leviticus
17 are left unconsidered.

structure:[36] (1) The parenetic passages in Lev 18:2b–5, 24–30; 19:1aβb, 19α?, 37; 20:7–8, 22–27; 21:6, 12, 23b; 22:2, 9, 15–16, 31–33; 25:18–22, 23b, 38, 42a, 55 constitute an argumentative context that covers all of Leviticus 17–26 apart from its introductory paragraph that deals with cultic problems (17:1–16).[37] (2) Seemingly scattered, but thematically connected decrees in 17:1–26:2 shape it into a fairly dense texture: the decrees of 19:5–8 are coupled with the regulation of 22:29–30;[38] 19:3, 30 is repeated in 23:22 with small deviations; 19:3, 30 is reformulated in 26:2. (3) The divine speech formulae in Lev 17:1; 22:18–19 show that the sections 17:1–16 and 22:18–31 belong together. Thus it becomes obvious that Lev 17:1–26:2 has got a clearly outlined general structure with 17:1–22:31 as its first and 23:1–25:55 as its second part, 26:1–2 being the summary and 26:3–45 being the concluding parenesis of the complex.[39] The order of the different divine speech formulae in Leviticus 17–26 actually makes clear that 17:1–26:45 is a fairly independent complex within 9:1–27:34.[40] (4) The extensive text containing blessings and curses in Leviticus 26, decidedly thematizing the keeping and following of the חקות, מצות and משפטים of the Lord (cf. 26:3, 14–15), marks the end of a larger complex which also extends at least until 18:1–30.[41]

---

[36] Concerning Lev 17:1–26:2 and its structure, cf. A. Ruwe, "*Heiligkeitsgesetz*", passim. With many authors, I assume that Lev 17:1–26:45 is a thematically independent complex within the priestly texts (analogous to the Torah on purity in Leviticus 11–15). Against many authors, however, it is my opinion that this complex is genuinely priestly and that it belongs neither to the prehistory of the priestly literature nor to late redactional levels of the Pentateuch.

[37] Although Lev 17:1–16 does not contain any parenesis and אני יהוה formulae, typical of the other sections of Leviticus 18–25, it is in my opinion without doubt that the Holiness-Torah starts with Lev 17:1–16, because the divine speech formula in 17:1–2 is exclusively identical with the one in 22:17–18, and the content dealing with permitted animals is close to 22:18–33.

[38] In their connection both texts refer back to Lev 7:15–18. I. Knohl, *Sanctuary of Silence*, 116, 118, and J. Milgrom, *Leviticus 1–16*, 14–15, think that Lev 7:15–18 and 19:5–8 and 22:29–30 belong to different literary formations. In my opinion, however, there are no differences of *content* between 7:12–18 and 19:5–8; 22:29–30. The terminological differences between both texts are possibly due to the places of composition (especially the evaluation as קדש in the so-called "Holiness Code," 19:8). They are not necessarily signs of different literary levels.

[39] Cf. A. Ruwe, "*Heiligkeitsgesetz*," 79–120.

[40] The divine speech formula in Lev 17:1–2 shows with v. 2 a special introductory formula (cf. Exod 16:16, 32; 35:1, 4; Lev 8:5; 9:6; Num 30:2, 17; 36:6). With the conspicuous detail of place, בהר סיני, Lev 25:1 marks the end of the complex.

[41] Lev 26:14 refers with its deictic phrase כל המצות האלה back to a sum of מצות. The term מצוה, however, within the priestly Sinai texts before (apart from 4:2, 13,

This short overview intends to have shown that the second main part of Leviticus, Lev 9:1–26:45, consists of four sections all in all: 9:1–10:20; 11:1–15:31; 16:1–34 and 17:1–26:45. But what is the general topic of this major narrative section?

In my opinion, the first unit of this major narrative section, Lev 9:1–10:20, is of central importance for determining the question of the general topic of 9:1–26:45. Therefore this part of the text shall be dealt with in detail in the following. Independently of the literary critical analysis of it, it is conspicuous that through this text some special notes are struck within the book of Leviticus. First of all, Lev 9:1–10:20 is a decisive text because it widely develops the topic of the closeness and presence of the כבוד יהוה in Israel.[42] Apart from Lev 9:1–10:20, this topic that is crucial for the whole priestly formation of the Pentateuch is nowhere dealt with in the book of Leviticus.[43] In 9:4 the appearance of the Lord before Israel is announced through Moses. In accordance with this announcement, 9:22–24 narrates that—after the celebration of the offerings as well as the blessing of the Israelites through Aaron and Moses—the appearance of the כבוד יהוה before the whole people takes place.[44] Concretely,

---

22, 27; 5:17), can only be found in the parenetic sequence in Lev 22:31 which is at the end of the first main part of the so-called "Holiness Code" and which thus has a central compository position. Also the terms חקה und משפט can only be found in Leviticus 18–26. On the other hand, the term תורה is (apart from the secondary summary, 26:46) only used in 6:2, 7, 18; 7:1, 7, 11, 37; 11:46; 12:7; 13:59; 14:2, 36, 54, 57; 15:32, but not in Leviticus 17–26. This fact indicates that the parenesis of 26:3–45, unaffected by major compositional relations, is indeed related back to the complex Leviticus 17–26. Cf. H.-U. Steymans, "Verheißung und Drohung: Lev 26," in H.-J. Fabry and H.-W. Jüngling (eds.), *Levitikus als Buch*, 263–301, esp. pp. 267–70.

[42] Cf. only B. Janowski, "Tempel und Schöpfung. Schöpfungstheologische Aspekte der priesterlichen Heiligtumskonzeption," in *Gottes Gegenwart in Israel. Beiträge zur Theologie des Alten Testaments* (Neukirchen-Vluyn: Neukirchener, 1993) 214–46; E. Blum, *Studien zur Komposition des Pentateuch*, 294–300; and R. Rendtorff, *Theologie des Alten Testaments*, 60ff.

[43] There is also Lev 16:2 to consider, but that verse is about the revelation and presence of the Lord in the tabernacle, disguised by the cloud (cf. Exod 40:34–35) and not about his revealed presence in Israel.

[44] The section Lev 9:22–24 is arranged very concisely. Particularly the motive of the double blessing attracts attention. On the one hand Aaron blesses the people at the end of the communal offering, doing so from the altar (9:22a). Then Aaron and Moses together bless the people after they have left the אהל מועד again (9:23a). The duplication of the blessing is no reason for the assumption that this text has been secondarily revised. This special form of the double blessing has obviously got to be seen in connection with the priestly concept of the presence of God, according to which the Lord reveals himself particularly at the two exposed places of the

the manifestation of the כבוד יהוה is expressed as an event of fire. In the place that describes the theophany, it is concretely expressed that a fire starts from the presence of the Lord which consumes the offering pieces that have been offered at the altar (Lev 9:24a).[45] Here it is important to realize that the consumption of the offering pieces in this narrative context is not the only action of the fire that embodies the כבוד יהוה. Immediately following the manifestation narrated in 9:22–24, there is set a second one in 10:1. In 10:1–2 it is said that after the incense offering of Aaron's sons Nadab and Abihu, another fire comes from the Lord now intended to consume Nadab and Abihu who offered a "foreign" (זרה), "unauthorized" (לא צוה) fire before יהוה (10:1b). Both appearances of the godly fire parallel each other since both cases are phrased identically (ותצא אש מלפני יהוה ותאכל; Lev 9:24a//Lev 10:2). Leviticus 9:1–10:20 thus describes a decidedly twofold or two-phase manifestation of the כבוד יהוה.

What is the intention behind this structure of the text? Apparently, Lev 9:22–23 marks the climax of the priestly Sinai story. Here for the first time within the Sinai story it is recounted that the כבוד יהוה appears before the whole people. The meeting between the Lord and Israel as a people, which is intended as early as in the first mentioning of the Tent of Meeting (אהל מועד) in Exod 27:21, is being realized in this place. The Lord's promises, related to the people and formulated in Exod 29:45–46, to live amongst the Israelites and to be their God, are fulfilled here. In Lev 10:1–2 next to the first healing manifestation of the כבוד יהוה, a second one is set which, however, proves deadly for Aaron's sons Nadab and Abihu because they approach the Lord with an "unauthorized" (לא צוה) incense offering (10:1b). Thus it is underscored that the healing appearance

---

sanctuary, the altar and inner of the Tent. Through this blessing the expiating and atoning impact of offering and Tent spread over the whole people. Israel is thus being prepared for the immediately forthcoming meeting with God. The people are—as it were—sanctified through the double blessing, which is hardly surprising since the blessing has generally got a sanctifying impact in the priestly theology (cf. Gen 2:3a).

[45] The revelation of the כבוד יהוה before the Israelites is concretely reported in Lev 9:23b–24. Verse 23b serves here as a summarizing headline in between, and v. 24 offers the actual report about the revelation. Verse 24a specifically deals with the theophany itself, whereas v. 24b describes the impact of the presence of God on the Israelites. But if it is true that v. 24a is a concrete rendering of the event of the theophany, then it is obvious that the revelation of the glory of the Lord in this text is concretely described as a phenomenon of fire.

of the כבוד יהוה in Israel is ethically conditioned. The healing presence of the כבוד יהוה is thus clearly connected with the obligation to the Lord and his laws imparted through Moses. Through offering an "unauthorized" incense offering, however, Nadab and Abihu do not comply with God and his laws. Correspondingly, the dangerous aspect of the godly כבוד is demonstrated with them. Leviticus 9:1–10:20 is the decisive text concerning the appearance of the כבוד יהוה before the people of Israel. At the same time this text insists that the healing presence of the glory of God is an event conditioned *by obedience toward the laws*, particularly by the obedience of the Aaronites towards the Mosaic legal tradition.

Leviticus 9:1–10:20 is principally a treatise on the topic of the Aaronites "obedience" toward the Mosaic legal tradition in view of the presence of the כבוד יהוה.[46] This "obedience" is formally and materially defined in 9:1–10:20 through the constitution of narrative models. That the "obedience" of the Aaronites toward the laws issued through Moses is the central topic of 9:1–10:20 becomes obvious when interpreting it against the background of the general composition of Exod 25:1–40:34a; Lev 8:1–36. In Exod 25:1–40:34; Lev 8:1–36, the plot is always the same. God issues instructions to Moses which he is to announce to the Israelites, so that they live accordingly; or God provides Moses with orders which he is to carry out. Thus each of Moses' actions represented in these texts—either verbal or nonverbal—relates back to a word of God, *presented in direct speech*. The passages referring to the Tent of Meeting in Exod 25:1–40:34a; Lev 8:1–36 therefore consist of two parts, a "section of orders" presenting the godly laws and orders in direct speech (Exod 25:1–31:17, 40:1–15), and a "section of execution" dealing with the fulfilling of the corresponding godly orders through Moses (Ex 35:1–39:43; 40:16–34a; Lev 8:1–36). The very redundancy of this arrangement of the text obviously serves the pragmatic aim to make clear in detail the correspondence between God's orders and Moses' execution of them. In the days of the primary addressees of the priestly texts, presumably belonging to the Babylonian or early Persian epoch, the material in Exod 25:1–40:34a; Lev 8:1–36 with its obvious double

---

[46] This aspect is, in my opinion, too little regarded by W. Houston in his essay, "Tragedy in the Courts of the Lord: A Socio-Literary Reading of the Death of Nadab and Abihu," *JSOT* 90 (2000) 31–39.

structure presumably functioned as a plea for the conformity of revelation and thus the authority of the Mosaic legal tradition. As B. Jacob has rightly made clear, the aim was not to propagate the "literal conformity and identity" between godly order and its Mosaic execution. Moreover, "comparison and analogy" are stressed as decisive features of the fulfilling of the godly orders through Moses.[47] Thus in Exod 25:1–40:34a; Lev 8:1–36 creativity and freedom are emphasized as central moments of the Mosaic "obedience."

The narrative unit Lev 9:1–10:20 continues this topic of obedience, but now in the sense that, in supplement and continuation of Exod 25:1–40:34a; Lev 8:1–36, the "obedience" of the Aaronites is defined in a narrative model towards the law-issuing Moses. In exilic and post-exilic times, the question if and to what extent the decisive clan of priests is bound to the Mosaic legal tradition—if only Moses holds the right of receiving revelation or if the leading priests themselves hold the status of immediacy concerning the godly issuing of laws—presumably was at least as significant as the question of the conformity of the Mosaic torah tradition to revelation.[48] To clarify this second aspect of the problem of obedience is the specific function of Lev 9:1–10:20 subsequent to Exod 25:1–40:34a; Lev 8:1–36.

Leviticus 9:1–10:20 only presents Moses' orders. These do relate to godly orders, but only in a general way (cf. 9:7, 10, 16). Words of God, presented in direct speech and prefiguring Moses' orders in detail, are not to be found in Lev 9:1–10:20, as opposed to Exod 25:1–40:34a; Lev 8:1–36. But how is the "obedience" of the Aaronites toward Moses exactly defined? The death of Nadab and Abihu makes clear that the Mosaic cultic and legal tradition is supposed to be of a generally normative meaning for the Aaronites. For Nadab and Abihu's high-handedness, having offered an "unauthorized fire" before the Lord, had caused their destruction through the כבוד יהוה. Also in the passages that report the removal of Nadab's and Abihu's corpses of this incident (Lev 10:4–7) it is emphasized that the other

---

[47] B. Jacob, *Das Buch Exodus*, 995. Quotations transl. by A. Ruwe.
[48] This assumption is supported by the deuteronomic concept of the supreme court that implies a far-reaching torah competence of the priests (cf. Deut 17:8–13, 18). One possibly has to consider in this context also Ezekiel's so-called outline constitution in Ezekiel 40–48 as an example of the vigor of non-Mosaic torah revelation in exilic or post-exilic times (cf. especially Ezek 40:4; 44:5).

Aaronites do exactly as Moses has said (v. 5b, 7b). Thus the compliance of the Aaronites to Mosaic orders is underlined. The discussion between Aaron and Moses concerning the consumption of the portions of the חטאה concluding the section Lev 10:1–20, and Moses' tacit agreement to Aaron's decision not to consume the חטאה portions (which itself is conditioned by the whole situation) (10:16–20), however, show that regardless of their obedience to Moses, there does exist a certain independence in competence on the part of the Aaronites toward the Mosaic orders at the same time.[49] It is possible to assume that in 9:1–10:20, "obedience" of the Aaronites toward Moses is in the same way defined by the moments of freedom and creativity as Exod 25:1–40:34a; Lev 8:1–36 defines Moses' "obedience" towards the Lord and his issuing of orders.

Against this background it is now possible to make clear how far the narrative section Lev 9:1–10:20 prefigures the general outline of the second main part of the book of Leviticus, 9:1–26:45. In the centre of 9:1–10:20 there is the word of God in 10:8–11.[50] This word is already crucial because it is the only word of God in the whole context and the only one directly and exclusively directed toward Aaron in the book of Leviticus.[51] The importance of this word lies in the fact that thereby the teaching competences of the Aaronites are recorded through the authoritative shape of the word of God. Concretely the Aaronites are ordered not to consume any

---

[49] The speech of Moses in Lev 10:12–15 has the function of underlining in this context again that Moses' decrees relate to corresponding decrees of the Lord (cf. vv. 13b, 15b).

[50] When I. Knohl thinks that Lev 10:8–11 interrupts the story about the death of the two sons of Aaron and is therefore secondary (cf. I. Knohl, *The Sanctuary of Silence*, 51–52, 105), he ignores the thoroughly concentric structure of Lev 10:1–20. The speech of God in Lev 10:8–11 is exactly at the center of the whole structure, thus it is simply consequent that it should interrupt the speech of Moses in Lev 10:6–7, 12ff.; this observation is no literary critical argument. On the structure of Lev 10:1–20 cf. T. Staubli, *Die Bücher Levitikus, Numeri* (NSKAT 3; Stuttgart: Verlag Katholisches Bibelwerk, 1996) 85–87; and C. Frevel, "Kein Ende in Sicht?" 93. Thus it follows that two concise narrative passages—Lev 10:1–5 (A) on the one hand and Lev 10:16–20 (A') on the other—open and finish the context of Lev 10:1–20. Two speeches of Moses that are parallel because they are directed toward the same addressees (namely Aaron and his other two sons Eleazar and Itamar) form parallel units in Lev 10:6–7 (B) and Lev 10:12–15 (B'). The word of God in Lev 10:8–11 (C) thus forms exactly the center of Lev 10:1–20.

[51] Speeches of God that are exclusively directed towards Aaron are mentioned only in Exod 4:27 and Num 18:1, 8, 20. However, the statement that the Lord speaks to Moses and Aaron appears quite often (cf. Exod 6:13; 7:8; 9:8; 12:1; Lev 11:1; 13:1; 14:33; 15:1; Num 2:1; 4:1, 17; 12:4, 14:26; 16:20; 19:1; 20:12, 23; 26:1).

wine or fermented drink before entering the Tent of Meeting (v. 9). Thus special personal conditions are imposed on them when administering in the area of the holy. More general than the prohibition of alcohol are the prescriptions following in vv. 10–11 which, however, because of their conspicuous infinitives seem to depend on the alcohol taboo.[52] These prescriptions assign two important tasks to the Aaronites: on the one hand they shall distinguish "between the holy and the common" (בין הקדש ובין החל) and "between the clean and the unclean" (בין הטהור ובין הטמא) (v. 10). On the other hand they shall teach the Israelites "all laws" (כל החקים) that God has given them through Moses (v. 11). According to the general flow of 9:1–10:20 shown above, the Aaronites are bound to the Mosaic laws particularly through v. 11, since they shall teach the Israelites exactly what the Lord said through Moses. On the other hand they are provided with a certain independence of competence at the same time which lies in distinguishing between "holy/common" and "clean/unclean" (v. 10).

How central the obligation of the Aaronites to observe the Mosaic tradition really is in Lev 10:10–11 becomes visible when comparing this text with its immediate parallel, Ezek 44:23–24. Between these two words of God that concern the priestly office there certainly exists a relation of reception; in my opinion Lev 10:10–11 has been formulated on the basis of Ezek 44:23–24.[53] In Ezek 44:24 the priests are given tasks of jurisdiction (v. 24a).[54] Also they are requested to keep the godly תורות and חקות of all feasts (v. 24b). In Lev 10:11 this decree is rephrased in favor of an obligation to teach *all* of the חקים imparted through Moses. Thus the singular contents of the Aaronite תורה are supposed to be the חקים imparted through Moses. This bond with Moses cannot be found in Ezek 44:23. As regards the second decree dealing with the priests distinguishing between

---

[52] The syntactic problem of Lev 10:9–11 can be left aside: cf. the various solutions in J. Milgrom, *Leviticus 1–16*, 615; M. Noth, *Das dritte Buch Mose*, 72, and K. Elliger, *Leviticus*, 134.

[53] J. Wellhausen, *Prolegomena zur Geschichte Israels* (5th ed.; Berlin: G. Reimer, 1899) 199–224, has said basic things on the relation between the priestly prescriptions of the priestly texts and of the Book of Ezekiel. Cf. also M. Noth, *Leviticus*, passim; or, differently, J. Milgrom, *Leviticus 1–16*, passim. On the priority of Ezek 44:20, 22, 25–27 over Lev 21:1–3, 5, 7, 10, 11, 13ff., cf. A. Ruwe, *"Heiligkeitsgesetz"*, 255–64.

[54] This corresponds with the tasks that the priests are to perform in Deuteronomy (cf. Deut 17:8–13; 21:5).

"holy/common" and "clean/unclean" (Lev 10:10//Ezek 44:23), the emphasis is rather the other way around: in Ezek 44:23 this is made the topic of the priestly teaching of the people (which also corresponds with traditional ideas),[55] whereas in Lev 10:10 the Aaronites are only requested to *distinguish* between those bipolarities but not to *teach* them. To put it simply: Lev 10:10–11 modifies Ezek 44:23–24 in the way that the usual priestly competence of teaching concerning "holy/common" and "clean/unclean" is turned into a tradition-bound teaching of the Mosaic "laws." Only the actual differentiation between "holy/common" and "clean/unclean" is the task of the Aaronites according to Lev 10:10–11. The theme of the teaching of the people shall only be the Mosaic "laws," and this is presumably the case because the Mosaic tradition, as it is rendered in the priestly texts, contains itself a teaching on the differentiation between "holy/common" and "clean/unclean."

Against the background of the word of God in Lev 10:9–11 it is certainly no coincidence that the two major parts following 9:1–10:20 in the book of Leviticus, the Torah on purity in Leviticus 11–15 and the so-called "Holiness Code" in Leviticus 17–26, are exactly a teaching, imparted through Moses, on the differentiation between "holy/common" and "clean/unclean." Leviticus 11:1–15:33 contains decrees on the topic of "uncleanness and cleanness" only, which already becomes clear through the fact that the section is dominated by the expressions טהור and טמא. And Lev 17:1–26:45, being thematically more complex than 11:1–15:33, is clearly dominated by the expressions קדש and חלל and is to be understood as a Mosaic teaching on "holy/common" concerning Israel.[56] The emphasized divine decrees in 10:11–12 are thus a summary of the topic of the following major sections in 11:1–26:45.[57] The decrees on the יום הכפ ורים in 16:1–34, which are decidedly to be imparted to Aaron, are connected to 9:1–10:20 directly: on the one hand, after the deadly meeting of Nadab and Abihu with the כבוד יהוה, Aaron is prescribed to enter the inner part of the sanctuary only once a year because God appears above the כפרת, and on the other hand regulations

---

[55] Cf. Deut 24:8.

[56] The expressions "holy/common" dominate this text, even if they do not appear in all the subordinate passages.

[57] This connection is already assumed by K. Elliger, *Leviticus*, 134. On the whole context cf. also A. Ruwe, "*Heiligkeitsgesetz*", 45–52.

are offered on how the sanctuary and the priests can regularly be cleaned from the transgressions (פשעיהם and הטאתם) and impurities (טמאתם) of the Israelites (16:16, 19). If one takes this into account, it becomes clear that 11:1–26:45 serves to formulate conditions under which the healing presence of the כבוד יהוה in Israel is possible. The thesis mentioned above, according to which the book of Leviticus is structured into two major sections, 1:1–8:36 and 9:1–26:45 is thus confirmed. Leviticus 1:1–8:36 presents the preparatory measures that have to be taken in view of the forthcoming revelation of the כבוד יהוה in Israel. Leviticus 9:1–26:45 on the other hand reports on the event of this realization and offers the Mosaic teaching on the conditions under which the presence of the כבוד יהוה in Israel is a healing one.

THE RHETORIC OF RITUAL INSTRUCTION
IN LEVITICUS 1–7

James W. Watts

Formal and structural features of Leviticus 1–7 distinguish these chapters as some of the most systematic texts in the Hebrew Bible. In a collection of literature otherwise noted for its sweeping narratives and urgent sermons, these methodical instructions for the performance of five kinds of offerings, presented twice in different arrangements, have suggested to many interpreters that they preserve examples of an ancient genre of ritual instruction. However, the identification of a ritual genre in these chapters (and elsewhere in the Pentateuch) has failed to account for all the features of this material. The present form of Leviticus 1–7 can be better understood as a product of the same process of generic mixture and allusion apparent in many other biblical texts.

I have argued elsewhere that the large-scale structure of the Pentateuch and several of its constituent parts has been shaped by a rhetorical strategy that combines diverse materials for persuasive effect. Thus the narratives of Genesis and Exodus ground the authority of the divine law-giver on the basis of past acts of creation, blessing and salvation, the laws and instructions of Exodus, Leviticus, and Numbers stipulate behavior in the present, while the blessings and curses that conclude Leviticus and Deuteronomy, and which in the larger context characterize Deuteronomy as a whole, depict the possible futures determined by Israel's response to the laws. This story-list-sanction pattern can be recognized in some other ancient Near Eastern texts of various types, and reflects a strategy employed in various literary genres to increase their persuasive impact. Thus the macro-structure of the Pentateuch seems designed to maximize its persuasive impact on ancient Jews who read it or, more likely, heard it read.[1]

---

[1] J. W. Watts, *Reading Law: The Rhetorical Shaping of the Pentateuch* (Biblical Seminar 59; Sheffield: Sheffield Academic Press, 1999).

Persuasion has been a traditional subject of rhetoric, its theories and its modes of analysis.[2] Though rhetoric has come to be associated in biblical studies with purely literary analysis of structure and style, ancient and modern rhetoric has usually addressed such issues from the larger perspective of argumentation, asking how speakers and writers influence their listeners and readers. Literary study then becomes more than an analysis of the text itself; it aims to understand texts as transactions between authors and audiences.[3] Rhetoric therefore calls attention to both the literary features of a text and the real writers and readers whose ideas motivated its formation. When biblical texts give overt indications of being formulated for persuasive purposes, and most do, rhetorical analysis provides the means for bringing together critical observations from both historical and literary studies to explain their form and function.

Leviticus 1–7 furthers the Pentateuch's persuasive agenda and was designed for that purpose. Of course, these chapters also instruct, but instruction frequently involves persuasion as well. Leviticus 1–7 has been shaped not only to instruct worshipers and priests how to perform various offerings, but also to persuade them to do exactly as these texts stipulate and to accept these texts as the ultimate authority for such ritual performances.[4] To demonstrate these claims regarding the form and function of Leviticus 1–7, I will first argue that previous efforts to describe their form and function on the basis of genre have not accounted for the text as it appears in the Hebrew Bible. I will then compare the rhetorical features of these chapters

---

[2] For a survey and discussion of the history of rhetoric in terms of persuasion, see K. Burke, *A Rhetoric of Motives* (Berkeley: University of California, 1950) 49–55, 61–62.

[3] See D. Patrick and A. Scult, *Rhetoric and Biblical Interpretation* (JSOTSup 82; Sheffield: Almond, 1990), esp. p. 12.

[4] More than a decade ago, Baruch J. Schwartz argued similarly for the persuasive formulation of biblical law: "The 'laws' in the Torah form part of a story, according to which they were spoken in order to be proclaimed, they were to be proclaimed in order to convince, they were to convince in order to be observed, and they were to be observed in fulfillment of the Sinai covenant . . . the laws, as well as the story in which they are contained, were composed in order to be read publicly and understood, to have a lasting, pedagogical, persuasive influence on later generations of listeners" ("The Prohibitions Concerning the 'Eating' of Blood in Leviticus 17," in G. A. Anderson and S. M. Olyan [eds.], *Priesthood and Cult in Ancient Israel* [JSOTSup 125; Sheffield: JSOT, 1991] 35 [34–66]; idem, *Selected Chapters of the Holiness Code—A Literary Study of Leviticus 17–19* [Hebrew] [Ph.D. Dissertation, Hebrew University of Jerusalem, 1987], 1–24).

with other ancient Near Eastern texts dealing with rituals, to lay the basis for describing their rhetorical function in the context of Leviticus and the Pentateuch as a whole.

The Search for Ritual Genres

In twentieth-century criticism, the genre of ritual instructions has been analyzed from two different directions: form-critical reconstruction of its oral form and comparative analysis of its ancient parallels. Each approach, however, produced a reconstructed genre quite different from the texts of Leviticus 1–7. The latter was then presumed to have been modified in distinctive ways to fit new social or literary contexts. Reviewing these theories will illustrate the difficulties that genre analysis encounters in Leviticus 1–7.

Interpreters in the mid-twentieth century mounted a major effort to isolate and analyze the forms of oral priestly teaching and categorize them by genre.[5] This movement found its fullest and most direct application to Leviticus 1–7 in Rolf Rendtorff's monograph, *Die Gesetze in der Priesterschrift* (1954).[6] Rendtorff isolated in chapters 1 and 3 a genre of short instructions for the performance of offerings that he labeled "ritual." It is characterized by stereotypical short verbal sentences formulated in impersonal perfect verbs except for an introductory imperfect, and by concluding formulas.[7] Chapters 2, 4 and 5 reflect this form to a lesser extent, so Rendtorff concluded that this material originally took other forms that were secondarily adapted to the "ritual" pattern. Chapters 6–7 do not reflect this form or any other, and probably had a scribal origin.[8] Klaus Koch built on Rendtorff's analysis, but defined the ritual genre on the basis of sequences of converted perfect verbs alone, which allowed him to find it in more texts in Leviticus 1–7 and in Exodus 25–40.[9] Rendtorff

---

[5] E.g. J. Begriff, *Die priesterliche Tora* (BZAW 66; Berlin: De Gruyter, 1936); G. von Rad, *Deuteronomium-Studien* (rev. ed.; Göttingen: Vandenhoeck & Ruprecht, 1948), translated by D. Stalker as *Studies in Deuteronomy* (SBT 9; London: SCM, 1953).

[6] R. Rendtorff, *Die Gesetze in der Priesterschrift: eine gattungsgeschichtliche Untersuchung* (FRLANT 44; Göttingen: Vandenhoeck & Ruprecht, 1954).

[7] Ibid., 12.

[8] Ibid., 14, 19, 20, 33–34.

[9] K. Koch, *Die Priesterschrift von Exodus 25 bis Leviticus 16: eine überlieferungsgeschichtliche und literarkritische Untersuchung* (FRLANT 53; Göttingen: Vandenhoeck & Ruprecht, 1959) 46–76.

admitted that it is difficult to reconstruct the original setting of the
"ritual" genre, because its social context is not reflected in Leviticus
1–7 or almost anywhere else in the Hebrew Bible. He suggested, however, that the strict stylization and stereotypical repetition notable in
chapters 1 and 3 suggest that they were intended for oral recitation,
perhaps as sentences spoken to accompany offerings.[10]

Two difficulties hindered this form-critical attempt to establish the
genre of these ritual texts. First, it was not able to establish convincing evidence for the original settings in which ritual genres of
instruction developed.[11] Rendtorff himself has since backed away from
any attempt to identify these original settings, preferring to speak of
a "ritual style" rather than an oral genre.[12] Second, the observation
that much of this material stemmed from editorial modifications of
the hypothetical original genres raised the question of whether there
ever was an oral tradition behind these edited texts. Rolf Knierim
dismissed the case for a ritual genre because it did not account for
the form of the present text. He argued that the casuistic ("if . . .
then . . .") formulation of Lev 1:2b–9 must be taken seriously for
genre analysis, in which case the material can only be classified as
case law.[13] Casuistic law is a scribal genre, so there was never an
oral form of this material.[14] Yet Knierim, like Rendtorff and Koch,
abstracted the material's genre out of the context in God's instructions through Moses (vv. 1–2a). He justified doing so by arguing
that, though case-law can be used for didactic purposes, that use
does not explain why the material was formulated this way.[15] However,
his grounds for this conclusion, that the material's impersonal style
does not fit instruction, remained purely impressionistic. Thus Knierim's
modification of the form-critical project by focusing on the extant
text and on scribal genres still abstracted the text's genre from its
role in its literary context. As such, it did not contribute much
towards explaining why the text was chosen or written to function
within the book of Leviticus as it stands.

---

[10] Rendtorff, *Gesetze*, 22–23.

[11] See the critique of K. Elliger, *Leviticus* (HAT 4; Tübingen: J. C. B. Mohr [Paul Siebeck], 1966) 30–31.

[12] See his *Leviticus* (BKAT 3/1; Neukirchen-Vluyn: Neukirchener Verlag, 1985) 18–19.

[13] R. P. Knierim, *Text and Concept in Leviticus 1:1–9: A Case in Exegetical Method* (FAT 2; Tübingen: J. C. B. Mohr [Paul Siebeck], 1992) 10, 65, 95.

[14] Ibid., 103.

[15] Ibid., 7, 98–100, 106.

The second approach to ritual genre has emphasized scribal practices from the start. Comparative studies of ancient ritual texts have
sought to explain the material's form and arrangement through a
scenario of textual development. In a series of articles, Baruch Levine
has argued that ancient ritual texts began as archival records of
offerings. Out of these records the genre of "descriptive ritual" developed, composed of texts that record in indicative verbs the performance of liturgies and rites. Such descriptive rituals appear in
Akkadian, Hittite and Ugaritic sources, and probably served as instructions for priests and other liturgical actors. Only much later, however, did such texts get recast in a more hortatory form as prescriptive
rituals to reflect their didactic role.[16] In the Hebrew Bible, Levine
focused his attention on texts such as Exodus 35–39, Leviticus 8–9,
and Num 7:10–88, that describe past ritual events rather than pre-
scribing future ritual actions. His analysis suggested that passages
such as Leviticus 1–7 stand at the end of a long process of textual
development from temple archive through descriptive rituals to prescriptive rituals.

Levine's isolation of the descriptive ritual genre depended on a
survey of texts from a wide variety of cultures, which is both his
theory's strength and its weakness. The number of texts strengthens
the argument that this form reflects a genre, that is, a recognizable
group of literary conventions governing the text's form and contents.
The label "descriptive," however, depends on interpreting verbal
forms as indicatives that can and have been read otherwise. Some
of Levine's Ugaritic examples in particular have been interpreted as
prescriptive rituals, despite his arguments to the contrary.[17] The comparative evidence allowed Levine to point to specific examples of
each stage of development, which otherwise would be lacking in the

---

[16] B. A. Levine, "Ugaritic Descriptive Rituals," *JCS* 17 (1963) 105–11; idem,
"The Descriptive Tabernacle Texts of the Pentateuch," *JAOS* 85 (1965) 307–318;
idem, "The Descriptive Ritual Texts from Ugarit: Some Formal and Functional
Features of the *Genre*," in C. L. Meyers and M. O'Conner (eds.), *The Word of the
Lord Shall Go Forth: Essay in Honor of David Noel Freedman* (Winona Lake: Eisenbrauns,
1983) 467–75; idem, *Numbers 1–20* (AB 4; Garden City: Doubleday, 1993) 81–82;
idem, with W. W. Hallo, "Offerings to the Temple Gates at Ur," *HUCA* 38 (1967)
17–58; idem, with J.-M. de Tarragon, "The King Proclaims the Day: Ugaritic Rites
for the Vintage (*KTU* 1.41//1.87)," *RB* 100 (1993) 76–115.

[17] J. C. de Moor argued that "The ritual texts of Ugarit are usually of the prescriptive type, listing in a very terse style instructions for knowledgeable people,
apparently priests" and translated them accordingly (*An Anthology of Religious Texts
from Ugarit* [Nisaba 16; Leiden: Brill, 1987] 157).

biblical material. The Bible does not preserve any examples of the original archival form, which must be hypothesized on the basis of texts from other ancient cultures.[18] Comparative analysis of ritual texts, however, has been able to find parallels for only some of the features of biblical prescriptive texts. It has so far been unable to present good parallels to the divine voicing and hortatory address of these ritual instructions, and has been forced to depend on hypothetical developments in the genre to account for them.[19]

Rendtorff, Koch, Knierim and Levine worked by identifying a genre that then became the basis for analyzing the text. Whether using inductive form-critical analysis or comparisons of ancient ritual texts, they attempted to explain the present text as derived from hypothetical oral or written antecedents described on the basis of genre. However, both the form-critical and comparative methods end up as analyses of ideal types rather than of actual biblical texts, because some features of the extant text do not conform to the proposed genres. Invariably they describe the present form of the biblical text as having undergone further textual development that differentiates it from the ritual genres they have described.

These approaches to biblical ritual texts use an overly strict understanding of genre. Even Knierim, who aimed to analyze genre within the present text rather than applying an *a priori* genre to the text, ended up doing so anyway because his conception of the case-law genre was too inflexible.[20] The Hebrew Bible demonstrates a flair for juxtaposing and mixing various genres (narrative, law, instruction, oracle, etc.) and modes (prose, poetry) of expression in the same compositions. Psalms and other poems appear in contexts of narra-

---

[18] "Except for brief descriptions of ritual acts in poetic passages ritual content in the Bible is always treated either as a divine command presented prescriptively, or as an event presented in narrative form" (Levine, "Descriptive Tabernacle Texts," 314).

[19] I must note that Levine's goal in describing "descriptive rituals" was to establish a better basis for describing ancient cult practices; he argued that descriptive rituals are more reliable depictions of actual performances than are prescriptive texts that are frequently idealistic (Levine and Hallo, "Offerings to the Temple Gates," 17–18). Thus he isolated the genre for purposes of reconstructing the history of religion, not originally to explain the present form of biblical texts.

[20] Similarly E. Gerstenberger, who despite emphasizing the hortatory features of Leviticus, nevertheless regarded them as secondary, because "where in the world are legal books composed in direct, admonitory address?" (*Leviticus: A Commentary* [trans. D. W. Stott; OTL; Louisville: Westminster, 1996] 25). See, however, the examples of second person address cited below.

tive prose (Genesis 49, Exodus 15, 1 Samuel 2, etc.) and prophetic poetry (Habakkuk 3).[21] Narrative always surrounds collections of laws in the Pentateuch. These are only some of the most obvious examples of juxtaposed genres in the Hebrew Bible, and they reflect practices also attested in other ancient Near Eastern literatures. Though some inset genres, such as psalmody, are well attested in independent compositions, others seem to conventionally appear as insets in other frameworks, ancient law collections being a notable example. Therefore the large-scale features of Hebrew and other ancient literatures should warn interpreters to expect the juxtaposition of genres and their literary conventions in many texts.

Genres are not immutable forms, but rather repertoires of literary conventions available to speakers and writers that allow them to play on the expectations of their audiences.[22] Descriptions of genres are useful for describing the cultural expectations that readers and hearers have of texts. Such expectations come into play in the reading of any text and the hearing of any speech, regardless of how far that text or speech may deviate from conventional forms. Deviations from genre use these conventions no less than do rigid reproductions of a traditional form; they just aim for a different effect on their audience, as David Damrosch noted:

> Genre is the narrative covenant between author and reader, the framework of norms and expectations shaping both the composition and the reception of the text. Genre is always a shaping force, though never a determining one in the case of truly creative work, and it can be studied in its uses, its adaptations, its transformations, and even its repressions, over the history of the composition and rewriting of biblical narrative.[23]

---

[21] For analysis of these combinations, see J. W. Watts, *Psalm and Story: Inset Hymns in Hebrew Narrative* (JSOTSup 139; Sheffield: JSOT Press, 1992); idem, "Psalmody in Prophecy: Habakkuk 3 in Context," in J. W. Watts and P. R. House (eds.), *Forming Prophetic Literature: Essays on Isaiah and the Twelve in Honor of John D. W. Watts* (JSOTSup 235, Sheffield: Sheffield Academic Press, 1996) 209–23.

[22] For a convenient survey of genre theory and its application to ancient texts, see T. Longman III, *Fictional Akkadian Autobiography: A Generic and Comparative Study* (Winona Lake, IN: Eisenbrauns, 1991) 3–21. An ambitious attempt to write a genre history linking Mesopotamian and Hebrew literatures can be found in D. Damrosch, *The Narrative Covenant: Transformations of Genre in the Growth of Biblical Literature* (San Francisco: Harper & Row, 1987). I find Damrosch's understanding of genre and his comparative method very congenial, but am not convinced that Hebrew narrative developed out of epic (see my *Psalm and Story*, 194–96).

[23] Damrosch, *Narrative Covenant*, 2.

Genre identification depends on the comparison of large numbers of texts from the same literary culture. The lack of extant extra-biblical Hebrew literature from the centuries in which the biblical texts were composed greatly hampers the identification of genres, because of the small number of examples available. It is no accident, then, that the description of psalm genres rests on much firmer grounds, because of the larger number of examples, than does genre analysis of almost any other kind of Hebrew literature, and it is relatively easy to isolate a psalm within a larger work.[24] Detailed descriptions of rituals do not appear nearly as frequently in biblical literature, so describing their various genres and distinguishing them from their frameworks cannot proceed with the same confidence. However, even without knowing which forms were recognized as genres by ancient audiences and which represent creative modifications and amalgamations of diverse genre elements, one can still describe some of the effects that certain literary conventions were intended to have on their audiences by observing their use in other literatures. Such texts often state overtly some of the motives for their composition. Comparisons with other ancient literatures can therefore show how particular devices tended to be used, even if we cannot be sure whether they conventionally appeared together as part of a recognizable genre or not.[25] Description of the rhetorical effects produced by conventional features of the text will produce a better understanding of the extant text than will reconstructing some original genre within it.

Rhetorical Features of Leviticus 1–7

Both form-critical and comparative methods have found support from features of Leviticus 1–7 (and other collections of ritual instructions

---

[24] For the latter, see J. W. Watts, "'This Song': Conspicuous Poetry in Hebrew Prose," in J. C. de Moor and W. G. E. Watson (eds.), *Verse in Ancient Near Eastern Prose* (AOAT 42; Neukirchen-Vluyn: Neukirchener Verlag, 1993) 345–58; idem, "Psalmody in Prophecy," 209–23.

[25] Koch reevaluated his earlier form-critical efforts on the basis of such comparisons ("Alttestamentliche und altorientalische Rituale," in E. Blum et al. [eds.], *Die Hebräische Bibel und ihre zweifache Nachgeschichte: Festschrift für Rolf Rendtorff* [Neukirchen-Vluyn: Neukirchener Verlag, 1990] 75–85). On the basis of Akkadian parallels, he produced a much more flexible definition of ritual genre to include casuistic structures and second person address, rather than just a sequence of perfect verbs. He considered these parallels to be confirmation of the existence of such an originally oral ritual genre. However, on the basis this handful of texts, one cannot tell whether the ancients would have recognized this as a distinct genre or simply as a combination of conventions used to describe rituals in various genres.

in the Pentateuch): while various of its formal features suggest oral composition and delivery, its structure and contents remind one of ritual texts from ancient Near Eastern archives. However, the narrative framework that casts Leviticus 1–7 as divine prescriptions delivered through Israel's paradigmatic law-giver, Moses, highlights the persuasive intent behind this text's formulation as it stands.

The narrative frame depicts this material as oral instruction. Like all the other instructions and laws in the Pentateuch, these chapters portray themselves as speeches. God is the speaker, as in most of Exodus 20 through Numbers. The immediate audience is Moses, but he is told to repeat these instructions to the people of Israel (1:1; 4:2; 7:23, 29) or to the priests, Aaron and his sons (6:2, 18 [LXX vv. 9, 25]), who are all then the intended recipients within the story. Interpreters are no doubt correct in finding behind the rhetoric of this story the historical conditions and political hierarchies of early Second Temple Judaism, or late monarchic Judea at the earliest: God's voice delivers the prescriptions of priestly and provincial (or royal) powers to Jews whom the Pentateuch repeatedly urges to identify themselves with Israel of the exodus and wilderness period (e.g. Exod 12:14–27; 13:3–16; 23:9; Lev 19:34; Deut 5:15; 29:14–16; etc.). Casting this material as oral instruction fits such later historical contexts just as well as the period of wilderness wandering depicted in the story, for the Hebrew Bible depicts *torah* even in these later periods being read aloud from written texts to large assemblies of people (2 Kgs 22–23; Nehemiah 8).[26] Thus the frequent mention of "you/your" in these chapters seems intended to reinforce in the intended audience the sense of authoritative instructions directed at them.[27]

That does not mean they originated as oral compositions. Biblical narratives describe law *readings*, that is, secondary orality based on written texts (Exod 24:3–7; Deut 31:9–11; Josh 8:30–35; 2 Kgs 22–23//2 Chr 34; Nehemiah 8). The Sinai traditions themselves vacillate between depicting the original revelation of divine law as written on tablets (Exod 20:12; 31:18; 32:16; 34:1; Deut 5:22; 9:10) or as delivered orally to Moses who then wrote it down (Exod 20:4; Deut 31:9; 34:27–28). This reminder that the interaction between

---

[26] On public readings of law and their rhetorical significance, see Watts, *Reading Law*, 15–60.

[27] So rightly Gerstenberger (*Leviticus*, 26), though his arguments for placing this audience exclusively in the Persian-period diaspora are not convincing.

oral and written compositions ran in both directions should warn interpreters against too sharp a distinction between the modes of presentation. And of course, despite the formal features and explicit evocation of oral rhetoric, comparative analysis of oral origins is ultimately forced to depend on written texts, since that is all that survives, and is therefore limited to whatever oral forms the texts happen to preserve.

Increasing numbers of Ugaritic, Hittite, and Akkadian ritual texts (most recently, those from Emar) have been published and anthologized, providing an opportunity to place Leviticus' ritual instructions within a wider cultural context. Yet the prescriptive and hortatory cast of Leviticus 1–7, as well as most other biblical texts containing ritual instructions, does not allow one to simply include them within the same textual genre. Rather than limiting the comparison to texts of a predetermined genre, a comparison of Leviticus 1–7 with *any* ancient texts exhibiting similar features and contents will be more helpful for assessing its rhetorical effect. By not restricting comparisons in advance on the basis of genre, the whole range of literary conventions at work in these chapters can be assessed and their effects analyzed. I will discuss the major literary features of Leviticus 1–7, focusing first on the narrative framework (God tells Moses to tell Israel or the priests), and then turning to the form and style of the contents.

Framework

Leviticus 1:1–2 depicts the material that follows as quoted direct speech by God through Moses to people and priests, and similar introductions that appear with increasing frequency in these chapters (4:1; 5:14, 20; 6:1, 12, 17 [LXX vv. 8, 19, 24], 7:22, 28) keep drawing this scenario to readers' and hearers' attention. Comparative analysis suggests that they do so to increase the text's persuasiveness.

Divine voicing of laws and instructions is the norm in the Hebrew Bible, but rare in other ancient Near Eastern texts. There divine prescriptions appear most often in narratives, where deities are likely to issue orders to each other and humans. As one would expect, such commands tend to be occasional, limited to the situation depicted in the story, such as when Ea or YHWH orders Utnapishtim or Noah to build a boat (Gilgamesh xi; Gen 6:11–9:17). Sometimes deities prescribe cultic acts in such stories, such as when El commands offerings to start a military campaign in the Ugaritic legend of Keret. More commonly humans present offerings and prayers on their own initiative, such as Utnapishtim/Noah do at the end of the flood stories. The deities' role is to respond appropriately. This pattern of human initiative and divine response appears in many other stories involving cultic worship. Even in Keret where a deity commands offerings, the plot turns not on El's command of offerings but on Keret's initiative in vowing gifts to the goddess Athirat that he later forgets to provide, and so suffers that deity's anger as a consequence.[28]

Instructional, legal, and didactic literatures are more likely to be presented in human, rather than divine, voices. Kings such as Hammurabi voice the Mesopotamian law codes, though they claim divine support for doing so. Some Hittite ritual texts begin, "Thus says X: if/when ... then I do as follows ...,"[29] and the Punic tariffs begin by citing a committee of prominent citizens that established them: "Tariff of priestly revenues set up by the thirty men who are in charge of the revenues, in the time when Hillesba'l the mayor, was head."[30] More often, the authorities behind ritual instructions remain anonymous.

However, ritual instructions also appear within royal dedicatory inscriptions from various ancient Near Eastern cultures. Here kings regularly claim credit for instituting one or more cults and sometimes for ordaining the rites to be performed there, especially the kinds and amounts of offerings. Thus in a second millennium Akkadian inscription, the Kassite king Kurigalzu reported that, to accompany his land grant to an Ishtar temple, "3 kor of bread, 3 kor of fine wine, 2 (large measures) of date cakes, 30 quarts of imported dates, 30 quarts of fine(?) oil, 3 sheep per day did I establish as the regular offering for all time."[31] Similar cultic mandates are found in New Kingdom Egyptian inscriptions, e.g. "I assigned to [Amun] thousands of oxen, so as to present their choice cuts,"[32] and in the 8th

---

[28] *KTU* 1.14–1.16; translated by N. Wyatt, *Religious Texts from Ugarit: The Words of Ilimilku and his Colleagues* (Biblical Seminar 53; Sheffield: Sheffield Academic Press, 1998) 176–243; and by D. Pardee in *COS* 1.102.

[29] *CTH* 407, 410, 757; translation by B. J. Collins in *COS* 1.62, 1.63, 1.64.

[30] *KAI* 69; translation by D. Pardee in *COS* 1.98.

[31] *HKL* 1.136; translation in B. Foster, *Before the Muses: An Anthology of Akkadian Literature* (2 vols.; Bethesda, MD: CDL, 1993) 1:278–79.

[32] A stela of Amenhotep III from his mortuary temple in Thebes; translation by

century Luwian/Phoenician bilingual inscription of Azatiwada: "a yearly sacrifice: an ox; and at the time (season) of plowing: a sheep; and at the time (season) of reaping/harvesting: a sheep."[33] The fourth century Naucratis stela depicts Pharaoh Nectanebo I ordering on behalf of the temple of Neith that "one shall make one portion of an ox, one fat goose, and five measures of wine . . . as a perpetual daily offering . . . My majesty has commanded to preserve and protect the divine offering of my mother Neith."[34] These texts testify to royal interests in cultic matters, especially the quantities of offerings to various temples. Priests, on the other hand, rarely claim to be the authorities behind cultic teachings, though the Hittite texts mentioned above are a notable exception.[35]

Oracular texts are the most likely ancient genre to portray a deity mandating offerings and other rites, as YHWH does in the Pentateuch. Thus an occasional ritual command appears among the oral oracles reported to the king in the eighteenth century Mari letters: ". . . The god sent me. Hurry, write to the king that they are to offer the mortuary-sacrifices for the sha[de] of Yahdun-Li[m]" and "Write to your lord that in the coming month, on the fourteenth day, the sacrifice for the dead is to be performed. Under no circumstances are they to omit this sacrifice."[36] The goddess Ishtar addresses the Assyrian king Esarhaddon in a similar fashion in one of the seventh century oracles of her priestesses: "Why did you not act on the earlier oracle which I gave you? Now you shall act on this one. Praise me! When the day declines, let them hold torches facing (me). Praise me!"[37]

It must be noted, however, that oracles more often portray deities ordering military and building campaigns than issuing cultic instructions, an observation that applies to the narrative and prophetic texts of the Hebrew Bible as well. In this respect, oracular texts mirror the concerns of royal inscriptions, which probably reflect the inter-

---

M. Lichtheim, *Ancient Egyptian Literature* (3 vols.; Berkeley: University of California, 1973–80) 2:46.

[33] H. Çambel, *Corpus of Hieroglyphic Luwian Inscriptions* (Berlin: de Gruyter, 1999) vol. 2; translations by J. D. Hawkins and K. Lawson Younger, Jr., in *COS* 2.21, 2.31.

[34] Translation by Lichtheim, *Ancient Egyptian Literature*, 3:88–89.

[35] At Ugarit, while colophons to the major epics credit priests—Ilimilku "the sacrificer" wrote or copied both the Baal cycle (*KTU* 1.6 vi) and Keret (*KTU* 1.16 vi)—no such colophons appear on the ritual texts.

[36] ARM 3.40, 2.90; translations by W. B. Moran in *ANET*, 624.

[37] H. C. Rawlinson, *The Cuneiform Inscriptions of Western Asia* (London: Harrison, 1861–1864), vol. 4 plate 68; translation by R. D. Biggs in *ANET*, 605.

ests at work in the preservation of these texts more than the inherent tendencies of oracles. The oracles were recorded in the Mari letters and were preserved in Esarhaddon's archive because they dealt with royal concerns. Private oracular pronouncements, which were no doubt very common, were less likely to be written down and preserved. The degree to which they may have dealt with ritual matters can therefore not be ascertained. There is one text, however, that suggests that the royal and oracular genres may have influenced each other and that the speeches of kings and of gods could be interchangeable. The ambiguous "Marduk Prophecy," probably from the twelfth century, ends with the god Marduk mandating a schedule of offerings, apparently for King Nebuchadnezzar (!), that reads:

> 40 quarts [ ], of 40 quarts [ ], of 10 quarts of flour, 1 quart of [ ], 1 quart of honey, 1 quart of butterfat, 1 quart of figs(?), 1 quart of raisins, 1 quart of alabstron [oil], 1 quart of finest [ ] without alkali(?), 1 regular sheep, a fatted calf will be burned for this spirit. Month, day, and year I will bless him![38]

If this interpretation of the last column is correct, then king and deity here reverse places, with the deity mandating (funerary) offerings on behalf of the king in exactly the same manner that kings mandate divine offerings in royal commemorative inscriptions. Since gods were traditionally thought of as royalty, and some kings were portrayed as gods, the merging of divine and royal voices should come as no surprise.[39]

The framework of Leviticus 1–7, which periodically introduces God issuing instructions through Moses, resembles not so much the form of ancient ritual texts narrowly defined as it does the forms of expression used in royal and oracular texts dealing with cultic matters among other things. Therefore considerations of the chapters' literary genre need to include this wider range of texts. Furthermore, the royal and oracular genres make explicit rhetorical claims that ritual texts, especially Levine's "descriptive" rituals, may not: they clearly aim to *persuade* their audience to undertake a particular course

---

[38] R. Borger, "Gott Marduk und Gott-König Šulgi als Propheten," *BO* 28 (1971) 3–24; translation by Foster, *Before the Muses*, 1:307; cf. Longman, *Fictional Akkadian Autohiography*, 132–42.

[39] Borger compared the Marduk Prophecy with the Prophecy of Shulgi as similar texts: the first has a royal deity speak and the second a deified king ("Gott Marduk," 3–24).

of action, usually to preserve the temple or the king's other accomplishments, particularly the inscription itself. The framework's evocation of royal and oracular genres should not be viewed as applying the conventions of some other genre to a basically "ritual" text, for ritual prescriptions are at home in these genres as well. Rather, the writers of Leviticus 1–7 used various literary conventions traditionally associated with ritual concerns to shape a text to serve their purposes. Their use of royal and oracular rhetoric in the framework emphasizes by literary convention the royal authority of the divine speaker and demonstrates the persuasive intent behind their work.

Contents and Style

Royal and oracular texts, however, contain nothing to compare with Leviticus 1–7's detailed stipulation of ritual performance. For such descriptions, we must turn to those texts usually classified by the term "ritual." Yet even among ritual texts from other ancient cultures, nothing has so far been found that matches the form and content of these chapters. That is less surprising when one notes the diversity of form and content among ancient ritual texts. There is no single ritual genre into which all these texts fit. They share only an emphasis on the details of cultic ritual, and it is therefore for reasons of contents rather than form that they tend to be classified together.

The prescriptive formulation of most rituals in the Bible contrasts with the predominance of descriptive rituals in other ancient cultures, as Levine has demonstrated. Nevertheless, prescriptive rituals are not unknown in Ugaritic, Akkadian and Punic sources. These sources also parallel specific features of Leviticus 1–7. The systematic repetition that characterizes especially Leviticus 1–3 can also be found in Punic tariffs that consist principally of repeated introductory phrases: "In (the case of) a X, (whether it be) a whole offering, or a presentation offering, or a whole wellbeing offering, the priests receive Y. . . ."[40] An atonement ritual from Ugarit repeats six times an almost identical liturgy applied to three types of offerings (ox?, sheep, donkey) and two kinds of worshipers (men, women).[41]

---

[40] *KAI* 69; translation by Pardee in *COS* 1.98.
[41] *KTU* 1.40; translation by Wyatt, *Religious Texts*, 342–47.

The casuistic ("if/when . . ., then . . .") formulation that is character-istic of priestly style throughout P's legal and instructional corpus also appears as a prominent structural feature of some Hittite and Ugaritic descriptive rituals. Several Hittite texts begin: "If the troops are defeated by the enemy, then they prepare the 'behind the river' ritual as follows" or "When [they] cleanse a house . . ., its treatment is as follows. . . ."[42] Among the Ugaritic corpus, a prescriptive list of required offerings and actions begins, "When Athtart-of-the-Window enters the pit in the royal palace, pour a libation . . .," and another list of offerings ends with a liturgy introduced casuistically: "Here begins (the liturgy): If a strong one attacks your gates, a warrior your walls, raise your eyes to Baal (saying)."[43]

Even the second person address, "you shall . . .," that appears fre-quently in Leviticus 1–7 as well as other ritual instructions in the Hebrew Bible, appears also in ritual materials from other ancient cultures, such as the Ugaritic list of offerings (*KTU* 1.119), otherwise in third person, that ends with the second person liturgy quoted above. The Ugaritic atonement rite (*KTU* 1.40) mixes first and sec-ond person exhortations in its casuistic introductions ("whenever you sin . . . this is the sacrifice we make . . .") and continues to alternate between them throughout. Several Akkadian texts from the Seleucid era describing rituals for repairing temples are consistently structured in second person casuistic form.[44]

Though many ancient ritual texts focus on just one aspect of a ritual, others reflect the same range of interests as Leviticus 1–7: types of offering, nature of the animals, worshiper's duties, priestly duties, priestly prebends, etc. Thus some of the rituals from Emar list the types and amounts of offerings due every deity on particu-lar days, but also describe the course and timing of processions, var-ious ritual actions, and the distribution of offered meats and other commodities, including priestly prebends.[45]

These comparisons illustrate that the literary features of Leviticus 1–7 also appear in ancient texts dealing with rituals in other Near

---

[42] *CTH* 426, 446; translation by Collins in *COS* 1.61, 1.68.

[43] *KTU* 1.43, 1.119; translations by Wyatt, *Religious Texts*, 357–59, 416–22.

[44] F. Thureau-Dangin, *Rituels accadiens* (Paris: E. Leroux, 1921) 34ff., translated by A. Sachs, *ANET* 339–42. For other Akkadian rituals in the second person, see ibid., 334–38, 343–45.

[45] *Emar* 3 73, 3 85, 3 87, 446; translated by D. Fleming, *COS* 1.123, 1.124, 1.126.

Eastern cultures, but dispersed throughout various texts in such a way as to undermine efforts to identify specific genres by constellations of features. There is no evidence, therefore, that the priestly writers started with some pure genre, whether oral or written, and then modified it through successive scribal additions taken from other literary contexts. That does not mean that no genre conventions influenced the writing of these chapters, but simply that every writer and editor who left a mark on these chapters worked, as we should expect, with various literary conventions traditionally used to portray rituals. Every stage of the text's development was influenced by such genre conventions. Though this conclusion might seem like an obvious observation about the constraints on virtually any writer or editor of any culture, it has a negative consequence for critical study of biblical texts: genre distinctions cannot be used as evidence for editorial modifications of texts. If writers and editors could use and mix genre conventions at will, and evidence from many parts of the Hebrew Bible suggest that they could and did, then hypothetical reconstructions of the original text or tradition that exemplified the "pure" genre are creative fantasies. I do not mean by this to deny that editorial modifications of biblical texts occurred. Other evidence suggests that they are pervasive throughout the biblical books, but genre analysis provides no basis for recognizing them.[46] Comparative analysis of literary conventions does, however, provide a powerful tool for exposing the intentions that shaped the extant text.

The Rhetorical Purpose of Leviticus 1–7

Interpreters have offered many suggestions for what purpose the instructions in Leviticus 1–7 may have originally served. Some of the more recent comments show the range and nature of the opinions. For example, Anson F. Rainey described chapters 1–5 as a "Handbook for Priests."[47] Similarly, Meir Paran suggested that this material was designed to facilitate rote memorization by priests.[48] Martin Noth ventured the opinion that the original audience for

---

[46] Contra Koch, "Alttestamentliche und altorientalische Rituale," 78.
[47] "The Order of Sacrifices in Old Testament Ritual Texts," *Bib* 51 (1970) 487.
[48] *Forms of the Priestly Style in the Pentateuch: Patterns, Linguistic Usages, Syntactic Structures* (Jerusalem: Magnes, 1989) xiii (Hebrew).

these instructions in oral or written form were lay people needing instruction on how to make their offerings.[49] David W. Baker concluded that, like the Punic tariffs, this material was inscribed on a monument at the sanctuary to inform both laity (chapters 1–5) and priests (chapters 6–7).[50] Rendtorff suggested tentatively that the material's strict stylization and stereotypical repetition suggest that it was intended for liturgical recitation, perhaps as sentences to accompany the offerings.[51] Knierim argued that ritual case-law was written to systematize ritual performance.[52]

What these suggestions all share in common is an attempt to find the *original* purpose for this material, that is, before it was excerpted into Leviticus and the Pentateuch and therefore before it was refashioned to fit this context. Evaluations of its purpose in its present context tend to be mechanical and topical, noting that the instructions for offerings must logically precede the stories about those offerings in Leviticus 8–10. Though this explanation for the position of these chapters is no doubt correct, it offers no insight into how their present shape and contents were intended to affect their audiences. All the efforts to imagine the purpose served by these texts have focused on their presumed original rather than their actual shape, under the influence of the idea that only from the pure genre can the text's setting and purpose be discerned. However, if all features of the present text were written under the influence of genre conventions, as I have argued above, then the shape of the present text should also be intended to evoke certain kinds of responses, and should theoretically offer clues as to what motivated its construction in this form. Furthermore, reconstruction of the form and function of earlier strata in the text can only proceed confidently if the form and function of the extant text has been fully analyzed first, for only then (if at all) can editorial seams be distinguished from intentional literary features.

Because of their focus on hypothetical original genres, the suggestions listed above miss the persuasive orientation of Leviticus 1–7.

---

[49] *Leviticus: A Commentary* (OTL; Philadelphia: Westminster, 1965) 20.

[50] "Leviticus 1–7 and the Punic Tariffs: A Form Critical Comparison," *ZAW* 99 (1987) 193–94; see also "Division Markers and the Structure of Leviticus 1–7," in E. A. Livingstone (ed.), *Studia Biblica* 1978 (JSOTSup 11; Sheffield: JSOT, 1979) 193–94.

[51] *Gesetze*, 22–23.

[52] *Text and Concept*, 103–6.

Comparisons with other biblical texts also obscures this persuasive element, because within the Hebrew Bible, Leviticus 1–7 looks less hortatory than, e.g. Deuteronomy, the Wisdom literature, the prophets, or the priestly Holiness Code (Leviticus 17–27). As a result, readers of the Bible are struck by these chapters' systematic, impersonal, and repetitive style. Knierim, for example, argued that "Deuteronomy's appeals to joy are based on the parenetic and therefore inevitably psychological language and intentionality of Deuteronomy. The priestly legal corpus is composed in 'legislative' language. It is not parenetic."[53] Mary Douglas took this distinction further, arguing that Leviticus contains only analogic reasoning of a mytho-poetic form, in contrast to Deuteronomy's discursive and abstract logic. Only in the latter is speech "used for persuasion, challenge, and argument."[54] If, however, one shifts the basis of comparison to other ancient Near Eastern ritual texts, the picture changes. Many ancient descriptive rituals and temple records outdo Leviticus 1–7 for mechanical repetition of detail and the absence of all hortatory devices.[55] On the other hand, those texts that parallel these chapters' use of an authoritative royal/divine speaker also make explicit their persuasive agenda: royal and oracular texts clearly express their goal of persuading readers and hearers to engage in certain behaviors and not others.

Once we have noted the persuasive shaping of Leviticus 1–7, the systematic and repetitive style appears in a different light. Repetition that may well seem redundant to a silent reader can sound very motivating to a skilled speaker's audience. The repetition of structural elements and of refrains have a long history in oral rhetoric because they help an audience anticipate a speaker's direction and respond appropriately to the speaker's cues. Within such repetition, slight variation can convey considerable emphasis.[56] Therefore the systematic and repetitive character of these chapters can be under-

---

[53] *Text and Concept*, 81.

[54] M. Douglas, *Leviticus as Literature* (Oxford: Oxford University, 1999) 40; see also 20, 29, 36–38, 41–65.

[55] See Levine's discussion of Ugaritic administrative records of rituals, such as *KTU* 1.91 and 1.104 ("Ugaritic Ritual Texts," 468), and of descriptive rituals in all his publications listed in n. 16 above.

[56] The Roman theorist, Quintilian, emphasized the need for repetition in legal argumentation: "We shall frequently repeat anything which we think the judge has failed to take in as he should" (*Inst. Orat.* 8.2.22–24). For a discussion of the rhetorical function of repetition and variation throughout the Pentateuch, see Watts, *Reading Law*, 68–74.

stood as bearing out, rather than conflicting with, the framework's presentation of them as oral speeches.[57] God is represented as a speaker who, through Moses, urges people and priests to engage in specific behaviors. If these speeches seem much less vivid than other biblical texts, that is only because the hortatory emphasis is even more pronounced elsewhere.

Leviticus 1–7 has been composed of repetitive structures bounded by refrains (e.g. אשה ריח ניחוח ליהוה "a fire-offering of soothing scent for YHWH" 1:9, 13, 17; 2:2, 9, 11, 16; 3:5, 16; כפר עלהם הכהן ונסלח להם "the priest will make atonement for them and they will be forgiven" 4:20, 26, 31, 35; 5:6, 10, 13, 16, 18, 26 [LXX 6:7]), with minor variations in the structure and refrains marking changing emphases and subjects (e.g. the pronouns in the refrain of forgiveness punctuating chapters 4–5). Major shifts in structure draw special attention and mark climaxes, such as the prohibition on consuming fat and blood (3:16b–17) that breaks out of and concludes the description of routine offerings in chapters 1–3. Damrosch rightly noted that the three-fold structure of Leviticus 1–3 "gives these chapters a certain lyrical aspect" and that the presentation of the offerings is staged dramatically.[58] Despite the longstanding tradition of reading such repetitive structures as dull and uninspiring, their effect in oral readings would instead be exciting and motivating. Indeed, since repetition and refrains often mark the climax of speeches, their appearance here provides further evidence that the Pentateuch reaches its climax in Leviticus.[59]

To whom was Leviticus 1–7's persuasive rhetoric addressed, and to what end? Is the intended audience composed of religious professionals like the priests, diviners, and exorcists for whom many of the Ugaritic, Hittite, and Emar ritual texts seem to be intended? Or are they lay people, such as those to whom the Punic tariffs, most royal inscriptions,[60] and perhaps even a few of the Ugaritic rituals

---

[57] Contra Knierim, *Text and Concept*, 7, 99–100.

[58] D. Damrosch, "Leviticus," in R. Alter and F. Kermode (eds.), *The Literary Guide to the Bible* (Cambridge, Mass.: Belknap/Harvard, 1987) 67–68.

[59] For other arguments for this conclusion, see J. Blenkinsopp, *The Pentateuch: An Introduction to the First Five Books of the Bible* (New York: Doubleday, 1992) 47; R. P. Knierim, *The Task of Old Testament Theology: Method and Cases* (Grand Rapids: Eerdmans, 1995) 367; Watts, *Reading Law*, 59.

[60] Royal inscriptions that employ the story-list-sanction strategy usually address other kings and royal officials, and a less defined lay audience beyond them; see J. W. Watts, "Story-List-Sanction: A Cross-Cultural Strategy of Ancient Persuasion"

were aimed? Clearly, ancient texts with ritual contents could address either group or both, so neither of the audiences mentioned in Leviticus is inherently improbable. In fact, if it were not for the fact that Leviticus explicitly distinguishes between these two audiences (Moses is directed to the people in 1:2; 4:1; 7:22, 28; to the priests in 6:2, 18 [LXX 6:9, 25]), one might think the sharp distinction between them to be anachronistic.

One effect of presenting the major sacrifices twice, once explicitly addressed to the people of Israel as a whole (chapters 1–5) and once explicitly addressed to the priests (6:1–7:21), is to subject both groups to the words that God spoke to Moses, that is, to *this* law. That may explain why the phrase זאת תורת "this is the law for . . ." appears exclusively in the materials directed at priests (6:2, 7, 18 [LXX vv. 9, 14, 25]; 7:1, 11).[61] Perhaps תורה here does not name a genre, as many interpreters have thought, but rather serves to emphasize the authority of these instructions over the priests, precisely those who are mandated to teach divine law (Lev 10:10–11). The point then would be to insist that *this*, and not anything else, is the authoritative regulation governing each particular offering. The prominence of negative stipulations—what should *not* be done (6:5, 6, 10, 16, 23 [LXX 6:12, 13, 17, 23, 30]; 7:15, 18, 19, 23, 24, 26)—in these latter chapters and their rarity in chapters 1–5 (only 3:17) confirms that these rules were written to supplant competing practices: "this is torah (not that)."

The text asserts its authority over those who teach it. No one in Israel can claim to be exempt from its provisions or to have other instructions that supersede it. That is not to say that these instructions cannot be supplemented; their incomplete character in fact requires supplementation in many ways. Among other things, nowhere in these chapters or elsewhere in the Bible is it specified exactly how the animals are to be killed, what prayers or liturgies (if any) are to be spoken or sung to accompany the offerings, etc. But by addressing explicitly both religious professionals and laity, Leviticus 1–7 enhances its own authority over all who participate in the cult and

---

in R. Binkley and C. Lipson (eds.), *Rhetoric Before/Beyond the Greeks* (Albany: SUNY Press, forthcoming).

[61] Though 7:11–21 seem to be aimed at the worshiper despite the superscription in 6:18.

so reinforces its status as authoritative cultic legislation. Despite the technical nature of many of these instructions, they address all Israel to persuade the people not only to perform the offerings as instructed, but even more to recognize and accept this text's authority to dictate religious obligations. The address to the priests, framed as it is within the divine speeches directed to the people, simply reinforces this claim by making clear that even the cultic professionals in the performance of their office are not exempt from this text's authority. For example, by saying זאת תורת העלה "this is the law of the ʿolā-offering," Lev 6:2 [LXX v. 9] requires what 1 Chr 16:40 reports, that the priests להעלות עלות . . . לכל הכתוב בתורת יהוה אשר צוה על ישראל "offer the ʿolā-offering . . . in accordance with everything written in the law of YHWH which he commanded Israel."

No doubt these chapters, like the royal and oracular texts that their framework evokes, intend to persuade the people of Israel and their priests to perform their religious offerings, and to do so correctly, as specified here. However, within the wider context of the priestly writings and the Pentateuch as a whole, these chapters aim also to reinforce the authority of Torah, specifically its authority over religious performance in the Jerusalem Temple. By publicly stipulating the forms of Israel's offerings, they position priests and laity to monitor each other's performance with the text as arbiter of correct practice. Thus an ironic consequence of Leviticus 1–7's role in the Pentateuch was to shift cultic authority from the priesthood to the book. Of course, the priests continued to wield enormous influence, because they not only controlled the Temple rites but also were authoritative interpreters of the book. But the presence of ritual legislation in the Pentateuch made the basis for their performances available to the public and therefore open to public scrutiny. The record of fierce debates over cultic practice between temple priests, Pharisees and Qumran covenanters in later Second Temple times shows that this rhetorical potential in the Pentateuch's ritual texts did not go unrecognized.[62]

---

[62] See e.g. the halakhic letter from Qumran, 4QMMT (E. Qimron and J. Strugnell, *Qumran Cave 4. V. Miqṣat Maʿase ha-Torah* [DJD 10; Oxford: Clarendon, 1994]), and Josephus, *Ant.* 12§297; 18§15.

Conclusion

Like any other composition, Leviticus 1–7 weaves together various literary conventions to affect its audience. The framework that repeatedly and with increasing frequency designates the speaker as YHWH claims not only divine but also royal authority for these instructions. Its designation of the intended audience as all Israel, with the priests explicitly included, specifies these laws' jurisdiction over all proper cultic performance. The contents' repetitive formulation in prescriptive casuistic style lends a heightened intensity to its provisions that is reminiscent of oral rhetoric. The frequent second person forms of address make clear the direct application to its intended audience.

All of these features of Leviticus 1–7 fit comfortably in the range of literary conventions typical of ancient ritual texts. None are likely to have been considered unusual or exceptional by Leviticus' intended audience. Though there is insufficient comparative evidence to determine if their combination produced a recognizable genre in Hebrew literature, neither is there any evidence that they were written through some dramatic modification of prevailing genres, whether oral or written.

These chapters were shaped to be read aloud to Jews as part of the larger Pentateuch. They contribute to the Pentateuch's rhetoric by emphasizing the supreme authority and jurisdiction of this Torah in Israel, especially over Israel's worship in the Temple. They therefore do more than instruct readers and hearers in proper religious performance. They aim to persuade them that these instructions must be normative, along with the rest of Pentateuchal law.[63]

---

[63] This article has benefited from the comments and suggestions of Carol Babiracki, Gay Washburn, Tazim Kassam, and Dixie Evatt, for which I am most grateful.

PART TWO

CULT AND SACRIFICE

THE THEOLOGY OF THE SACRIFICE ACCORDING TO LEVITICUS 1–7*

Alfred Marx

Leviticus 1–7 is assuredly the primary source for a study of P's sacrificial system. It is nonetheless a very deceptive source. Contrary to what might be expected, this text offers no full treatment of the sacrificial system. It does not review the entire set of sacrifices known by P. For instance, the incense offering, קְטֹרֶת, which the high priest is required to offer daily on the golden altar in the inner part of the sanctuary (Exod 30:7–8), is never referred to, nor is the drink offering, נֶסֶךְ, even though it is to be offered twice a day to YHWH, in addition to the whole offering and the cereal offering (Exod 29:38–42a). The ordination offering, מִלֻּאִים, which is of major importance for the priestly ordinations, is mentioned only once, in Lev 7:37. Moreover the circumstances in which the various sacrifices are to be offered are only indicated for some of them, and even then only partially. In fact, except for two instances (Lev 4:13–21; 6:12–16), only the private sacrifices are considered. As for the sacrifices listed, Leviticus 1–7 does not even give a full description of the ritual to be performed.[1] For, as has been demonstrated by R. Knierim, the literary genre of Leviticus 1–7 is not ritual, but "case law,"[2] so that it would be quite impossible to perform sacrifices using its guidance alone. It is especially frustrating that none of the various rites are explained. Neither does P develop a general theory of sacrifice. The only scraps of theology are given by two recurrent stereotyped formulas: the sacrifice may be a pleasant fragrance, רֵיחַ נִיחֹחַ, for YHWH, or it may serve to atone, כִּפֶּר *pi'el.*

---

* I would like to thank Mrs. Cheryl Cloyd for her assistance in translation of the text.

[1] R. P. Knierim, *Text and Concept in Leviticus 1:1–9. A Case in Exegetical Method* (FAT 2; Tübingen: J. C. B. Mohr [Paul Siebeck], 1992) 17–18, 23–28.

[2] Knierim, *Text*, 91–97. But cf. K. Koch, "Alttestamentliche und altorientalische Rituale," in E. Blum, C. Macholz, E. W. Stegemann (eds.), *Die Hebräische Bibel und ihre zweifache Nachgeschichte* (Neukirchen-Vluyn: Neukirchener Verlag, 1990) 75–85. Reply by Knierim, *Text*, 106–11.

However, what might be considered at first glance to be a serious handicap, proves in fact to be advantageous. The kinds of sacrifices reviewed are those which the common Israelite would offer most habitually. The rites mentioned are those which are the most significant, indicative of the distinctive feature of each kind of sacrifice, and which thus give a clue as to their respective function. Even the literary genre of Leviticus 1–7 may be considered positively. Law texts are especially characterized by their utmost precision, their accurate terminology, their eagerness to classify. So that special attention to the literary devices used by P in order to delineate, the distinctions he establishes, and the variation of vocabulary, may at least allow the proposal of a precise description of the essentials of the private sacrificial system, and of its function.

On the other hand, the place of Leviticus 1–7 in its larger context, the type of material offered to YHWH, the verbs used to express the act of sacrificing, added to the stereotyped formulas expressing the expected result of sacrifice, may more especially help to discover the underlying theology of sacrifice.

As is commonly considered, the book of Leviticus can be schematically divided into two main parts, Leviticus 1–16, on the one hand, and, on the other, Leviticus 17–26, the so-called Holiness Code, to which Leviticus 27 is appended.[3] A clue as to this division is given by the concluding formula in Lev 26:46, החקים והמשפטים (words which, except for Lev 10:11, are never used in the plural in Leviticus 1–16) referring more precisely to Leviticus 17–26, התורה (which is never used in Leviticus 17–26) referring to Leviticus 1–16.[4]

Leviticus 1–16 can itself be subdivided into two main sections, first the section on sacrifice, chapters 1–7, second, chapters 11–15 which review various agents of uncleanness and the corresponding rites of reinstatement of those who had become unclean. These two sections are separated by two narratives, the first, chapters 8–9, on

[3] On the structure of Leviticus see recently C. R. Smith, "The Literary Structure of Leviticus," *JSOT* 70 (1996) 17–32; M. Douglas, *Leviticus as Literature* (Oxford: Oxford University, 1999); W. Warning, *Literary Artistry in Leviticus* (BIS 35; Leiden: Brill, 1999); E. Zenger, "Das Buch Levitikus als Teiltext der Tora/des Pentateuch. Eine synchrone Lektüre mit kanonischer Perspektive," in H.-J. Fabry and H.-W. Jüngling (eds.), *Levitikus als Buch* (BBB 119; Berlin: Philo, 1999) 47–83 (esp. 62–76).

[4] Cf. J. E. Hartley, *Leviticus* (WBC 4; Dallas: Word, 1992) 471; and for an altogether other interpretation, G. Auld, "Leviticus at the Heart of the Pentateuch?" in J. F. A. Sawyer (ed.), *Reading Leviticus. A Conversation with Mary Douglas* (JSOTSup 227; Sheffield: JSOT Press, 1996) 40–51 (esp. 43–46).

the ordination of the high priest and the priests (in fulfilment of the instructions given by YHWH to Moses, Exod 29:1–37), to which is connected the story immediately following of YHWH's entrance into the Tent of Meeting (an expansion of Exod 40:34–38); the second, chapter 10, the episode of the sin of Nadab and Abihu, to which are appended, in a narrative context, various instructions to the priests. Leviticus 1–16 culminates in chapter 16 with the description of the ritual of the Day of Atonement. This ritual is of special importance, as it gives Israel, at the turning point of every year, the possibility of removing all the sins and impurities which had polluted Israel in the past year, so that YHWH can again be fully present among his people.

The book of Leviticus thus has a structure which is roughly parallel to that of Exodus 19–24 : a theophany, Exodus 19//the coming of YHWH, Exod 40:34–38, followed by a divine discourse on sacrifice, Exod 20:22–26//Leviticus 1–16 (Leviticus laying special stress on the ritual terms of YHWH's presence), concluded by the instructions, המשפטים, respectively החקים והמשפטים, of YHWH to his people, Exodus 21–23//Leviticus 17–25, on the basis of which a covenant is concluded, Exodus 24//blessings and "curses,"[5] Leviticus 26.

The section on sacrifice, Leviticus 1–7, is clearly set apart.

Leviticus 1:1 opens with the unique reference to the summons of Moses by YHWH, ויקרא אל משה, never mentioned again in Leviticus, and with the additional information that YHWH called Moses מאהל מועד, thus linking this section with the story of YHWH's entrance into the Tent of Meeting, Exod 40:34–38, which immediately precedes it. These two pieces of information frame the classical introductory formula in Leviticus וידבר יהוה אל.[6] Evidently, there is more here than just a mere chronological sequence. This sequence suggests, as a matter of fact, a correlation between YHWH's presence and the sacrificial cult. Such a correlation is clearly demonstrated in Exod 29:38–46, where the daily sacrifices, vv. 38–42a, are at the same time Israel's answer to, and the condition for the presence of YHWH, vv. 42b–46.

---

[5] The quotation marks draw attention to the mostly overlooked fact that, contrarily to Deuteronomy, Leviticus 26 does not use the verb "curse" or its derivatives.

[6] For a review of all the introductory formulas in Exod 25:1 to Num 10:10, see A. Ruwe, *"Heiligkeitsgesetz" und "Priesterschrift". Literaturgeschichtliche und rechtssystematische Untersuchungen zu Leviticus 17,1–26,2* (FAT 26; Tübingen: J. C. B. Mohr [Paul Siebeck], 1999) 369–72.

The section on sacrifice concludes with a twofold formula, 7:37–38. As in Lev 14:54 (see also זאת תורת, Lev 11:46; 12:7; 13:59; 14:32, 57; 15:32), it begins with the summarizing phrase זאת התורה ל, followed by a reference to the content of the section, here the list of the various types of sacrifice reviewed, Lev 7:37. But unlike the other texts, this is the only instance where the summarizing phrase concludes a whole section, and not just the data concerning one particular case. The second part of the formula is unique. It repeats the information given in the introductory formula in 1:1, and expands upon it in three ways. First, whereas 1:1 uses the verb דבר, Lev 7:38 insists that these discourses are a commandment, using the verb צוה in place of the verb דבר, 7:38aβα. Secondly, we are told that these instructions were given to Moses בהר סני, 7:38aβ, במדבר סני, 7:38bβ, an indication found elsewhere in Leviticus only in 25:1, and in the concluding formulas of the book of Leviticus, 26:46—the החקים והמשפטים והתורת are given, נתן, by YHWH, literally "between him and between the sons of Israel" on Mount Sinai—and 27:34—the מצות had been commanded, צוה, there to them by YHWH. It is hard to imagine that this detail is given simply to tell the reader that the Tent of Meeting is located on Mount Sinai. On the contrary, it clearly sets apart the instructions about sacrifices, and underlines their special authority. Thirdly, expanding on Lev 1:2a, this concluding formula summarizes the content of the instructions with the phrase הקריב קרבן ליהוה, Lev 7:38bβ. We shall return to this later on. Notice that the characteristic terms צוה, סני and קרבן are each repeated twice.

Leviticus 1–7 is thus given a prominent position. Its unique features underline its great importance. To borrow the temple metaphor used—but there in a different sense—by Mary Douglas in her recent book *Leviticus as Literature*, the section on sacrifice might be called the Holy of Holies in the book of Leviticus. The instructions on the sacrifices are not simply a set of divine instructions among others. The requirement to bring these sacrifices to YHWH is of fundamental importance, as it is directly related to the fact that YHWH resides in the midst of Israel. Only if sacrifices are brought to him will YHWH remain among his people and bless them (cf. on the contrary 2 Chr 29:6–9). All of the other requirements stated in Leviticus flow from this divine presence: they are merely a consequence of it.

A close view of the introductory formulas in Leviticus 1–7 will enable us to better understand the way P considers the sacrifice. These formulas do not only introduce the content. Their primary purpose is, in fact, to distinguish the various kinds of sacrifices. The variations in their formulations are thus highly significant.[7]

First, P subdivides Leviticus 1–7 into two large sections, Leviticus 1–5 and Leviticus 6–7.

The first section is introduced as a discourse which Moses is commanded by YHWH to address to the sons of Israel, דבר אל בני ישראל ואמרת אלהם, Lev 1:2aα. It reviews all the kinds of sacrifices which the common Israelites may offer to YHWH, focusing on YHWH's share of each one.

The second section, on the other hand, is introduced as a commandment which Moses must relay to the priests, צו את אהרן ואת בניו, Lev 6:2aα, no provision being made for its content to be relayed to the common Israelites. Only the last part of this section is introduced similarly to Lev 1:1b2aα, וידבר יהוה אל משה...דבר אל בני ישראל, Lev 7:22, 28. Unlike the first, this section is concerned mainly with what may be called the "residual substance," that is, what is left after YHWH has received his part of the sacrifice. In his examination of the various kinds of sacrifices, P follows here a different order from Leviticus 1–5, proceeding from the lesser to the greater: first the whole offering, which is entirely devoted to YHWH, and of which the only remains are the ashes, Lev 6:1–6; then those sacrifices which are shared out among YHWH and the priests—the cereal offering and the sacrifices for atonement—Lev 6:7–7:7; and finally, that sacrifice which is divided among YHWH, the priests and the offerer, Lev 7:11–36, the respective share of each being distinctly set apart by the use of specific introductory formulas (vv. 22–23a, 28–29a). P, however, makes clear the separation between the latter sacrifice and the former by supplementing, in 7:8–10, information about the "residual substance" of the first two kinds of sacrifice listed, respectively the hide of the whole offering, 7:8, and the apportionment of

---

[7] On the various division markers in Leviticus 1–7 see D. W. Baker, "Division Markers and The Structure of Leviticus 1–7," in E. A. Livingstone (ed.), *Studia Biblica 1978. I: Papers on Old Testament and Related Themes. Sixth International Congress on Biblical Studies: Oxford 3–7 April 1978* (JSOTSup 11; Sheffield: JSOT Press, 1979) 9–15 (esp. 14–15).

the two main types of cereal offering between the officiating priest
and the other priests, 7:9–10. Through this concentric device, he
thus sets clearly apart those sacrifices which are shared only by
YHWH and the priests. Moreover, at the very center of this section, he mentions the cereal offering which the high priest must bring
daily[8] to YHWH on behalf of all the priests, Lev 6:12–15. That special kind of sacrifice, wholly dedicated to YHWH as is the whole
offering, is thus given an especially prominent position.

Only two kinds of sacrifice do not fit into this general structure:
the cereal offering, of which it is expressly stated already in Leviticus
2 that the remainder, after YHWH has received his share, belongs to
the priests, vv. 3, 10; and the reparation offering, for which YHWH's
precise share is merely specified in Leviticus 7, and not, as expected,
in Leviticus 1–5.

It follows that P, on the one hand, establishes a clear hierarchy
distinctly separating both YHWH from humanity, and the priests
from the common Israelites. But on the other hand, P unites YHWH
and the priests, and YHWH, the priests and the common Israelites,
underlining in that way the mediation role of the priests. P thus con-
ceives of the sacrifices as a three-tiered pyramidal system, of which
the top level is exclusively reserved for YHWH, the middle level for
the priests, and the bottom level for the common Israelites. These
different levels communicate only from top to bottom, never the
other way. It is not without interest to notice that this three-tiered
system parallels the floor plan of the Tent of Meeting, with its Holy
of Holies reserved for YHWH alone (accessible to the high priest,
but only once a year), its Holy accessible to the priests, but never
to the common Israelites, and its outer court open to the common
Israelites. As with the sacrifices, YHWH has access to all three areas,
whereas the priests have access only to the second and the third,
and the common Israelites only to the third. This parallel reinforces
the close relationship established between the presence of YHWH
in the Tent of Meeting, and the sacrificial ritual.

P then subdivides again, this time in the first section, in order to
divide into two sets the various kinds of sacrifices listed in Leviticus
1–5.

---

[8] Note that this offering is called מנחה תמיד, a perpetual offering, Lev 6:13. As
for instance in Lev 7:35, 36, ב has here the meaning of מן.

The first set of sacrifices, Leviticus 1–3, is introduced as follows: אדם כי יקריב מכם קרבן ליהוה, Lev 1:2aβ. The sacrifices reviewed here are those which the common Israelite may freely offer to YHWH. These are, ostensibly listed in decreasing order, the whole-offering, עלה, Leviticus 1, devolved in its entirety (except for the hide) on YHWH, the cereal offering, מנחה, Leviticus 2, divided between YHWH and the priests, and the well-being offering, זבח שלמים, Leviticus 3, which is divided into three shares. Each kind of offering is described according to the decreasing order of its material: cattle, flocks (distinguishing, in the case of the well-being offering, between sheep and goat) and, for the whole offering, doves, either turtledoves or pigeons; and, in the case of the cereal offering, the various modes of its preparation: raw, cooked, or roasted. Except for the doves, and the variety of the modes of preparation of the cereal offering, this list is traditional. All three kinds of offerings are termed אשה, fire (offering), Lev 1:9, 13, 17; 2: 2, 3, 9, 10, 16; 3:3, 5, 9, 11, 14, 16. They are all considered as an offering of pleasing aroma to YHWH, ריח ניחוח ליהוה, Lev 1:9, 13, 17; 2:2, 9; 3:5, 16.

In contrast to these offerings, the second set of sacrifices, Leviticus 4–5, are each introduced with נפש כי, followed by a reference to the sin which has been committed, Lev 4:2aβ. P distinguishes between two kinds of sins. First the חטאת, that is the transgression of a prohibitive commandment, מצות יהוה אשר לא תעשינה, Lev 4:2, 13, 22, 27, to which are appended, likewise introduced by נפש כי, three specific transgressions, Lev 5:1–4. Second the מעל, the trespass against property, Lev 5:15, 21, to which must be added the special case of Lev 5:17–19.

To these two kinds of sins correspond two kinds of sacrifices, respectively the חטאת, the sin offering, and the אשם, the reparation offering. This latter is clearly distinguished from the former by its introductory formula וידבר יהוה אל, Lev 5:14—which P has already used to introduce, first Leviticus 1–7, then Leviticus 4–5—followed, as in Lev 4:2, by the characteristic formula נפש כי, Lev 5:15.

Unlike the first set of offerings, these sacrifices are compulsory. They are required by YHWH, and that, in a very precisely determined case, and their material is clearly defined. The various types of חטאת are reviewed in descending order according to the status of the offender: the high priest, Lev 4:3–12, the congregation, 4:13–21, the leader, 4:22–26, and the common Israelite, 4:27–35. Special provisions are made for the specific transgressions listed in Lev 5:1–4,

5:5–13. In the case of a אשם, P follows the descending order of the trespass, trespass against YHWH's own property (first material, Lev 5:14–16, second, in a figurative sense, Lev 5:17–19), then trespass against the property of a fellow Israelite, Lev 5:20–26. The function of both of these kinds of sacrifices is to atone, כפר על *pi'el*, in order that the offender may be forgiven, (חטאת) על/מן . . . ל סלח *niphal*, Lev 4:20, 26, 31, 35; 5:10, 13, 16, 18, 26 (cf. 5:6). It must be emphasized that, unlike the first set of offerings, these sacrifices are never explicitly said to have any influence on YHWH, the object of כפר being always, either the offender or the transgression, but never YHWH.

P thus draws a clear distinction between these two sets of sacrifices. This conclusion is reinforced by another observation. With the exception only of Lev 7:5, the sacrifices for atonement are never termed אשה, although both sets of sacrifices are burnt; and Lev 4:31 is the only case where a sacrifice for atonement is said to be a pleasing aroma to YHWH. Whereas conversely, except for Lev 1:4, the first set of sacrifices is never said to have as its purpose to atone, כפר על *piel*.[9]

Interestingly, the cereal offering is clearly set apart from all the others. Framed by the whole offering, on the one hand, and the well-being offering, on the other, it is located at the very center of Leviticus 1–3. And, unlike the whole offering and the well-being offering, it is specifically introduced, Lev 2:1aα, so as to attract special attention. Moreover, the introductory formula itself underlines its particularity by drawing both on the introductory formula of the offerings of pleasing aroma to YHWH, and on that of the sacrifices for atonement. From the former, it borrows the second part of the introduction, קרב *hip'il* ליהוה . . . קרבן. From the latter, it borrows the first part, ונפש כי.[10] We may add that the priestly share of the cereal offering is termed קדש קדשים, Lev 2:3, 10; 6:10, like their share of the sacrifices for atonement, Lev 6:18, 22; 7:1, 6.

---

[9] Similarly, in Leviticus 6–7, אשה and ריח ניחוח always refer to the first set of sacrifices (respect. Lev 6:10, 11; 7:25, 30, 35 and Lev 6:8, 14), whereas, conversely, כפר על always pertains to the sacrifices for atonement (Lev 6:23; 7:7). For an exhaustive study of כפר see B. Janowski, *Sühne als Heilsgeschehen. Studien zur Sühnetheologie der Priesterschrift und zur Wurzel KPR im Alten Orient und im Alten Testament* (WMANT 55; Neukirchen-Vluyn: Neukirchener Verlag, 1982).

[10] On the respective characteristics of נפש כי and אדם כי, see R. Rendtorff, *Leviticus* (BKAT 3; Neukirchen-Vluyn: Neukirchener Verlag, 1990) 85–86. The latter is also commented on in Knierim, *Text*, 14–16.

At this point, two conclusions may be drawn.

The first is that a distinct line must be drawn between the offerings of pleasant aroma and the sacrifices for atonement. Only the first establish communication with YHWH: as the specific introductory formula emphasizes, they are offered to YHWH, קרב . . . ליהוה‎ hip̄ʿil, and as a result (pointed out by the concluding formula) they become his "fire," אשי יהוה‎, Lev 2:3, 10; 6:11; 7:30, 35, אשה ליהוה‎, Lev 2:11, 16; 3:3, 9, 11, 14; 7:25 (cf. Lev 6:10), and are a pleasing aroma for YHWH. Conversely, there seems to be a reluctance to say that the sacrifices for atonement are brought to YHWH: with YHWH as the addressee, קרב ל‎ hip̄ʿil is used only once, in Lev 4:3;[11] and with בוא‎ hip̄ʿil, only in Lev 5:6, 7, 15, 25, but here with אשם‎ as its object. Moreover, YHWH is never the subject, neither of כפר על‎ piʿel (whose subject, as is systematically stated, is always the officiating priest), nor of the verb סלה‎. Only the first set of sacrifices can thus be considered as an offering *stricto sensu*.

The second conclusion is that atonement is not the primary purpose of the sacrificial cult. Its major purpose, reported at the outset and indicated by the verb קרב‎ hip̄ʿil, is to establish a relationship with YHWH by means of an offering. Conversely, the scope of the sacrifices for atonement is restricted to only a few definite occasions. Their function is only a negative one. They have as their object to obtain pardon for an offense against YHWH's prohibitions or property, to break thus with a faulty past, and restore the possibility for an untroubled relationship with YHWH. Their function is thus a subsidiary one, which does not mean that they are only of minor importance. In fact, most of the first part of the book of Leviticus, Leviticus 1–16, addresses those who have sinned under special conditions, Leviticus 4–5, or have become impure, Leviticus 11–15, listing the rites by which the offender can be restored to their full membership in the community. The sacrifices for atonement are the necessary prerequisite for the offerings. They are not an end in themselves.

The distinctive feature of the whole-offering, the cereal offering and the well-being offering is pointed out by the verb קרב‎ hip̄ʿil with YHWH as its explicit object. Although this verb is used inclusively in Lev 7:38 (as is also its derivate קרבן‎), it specifically introduces Leviticus 1–3, as we have already noted. Moreover, Leviticus 1–3

---

[11] In the only other cases where the verb קרב‎ hip̄ʿil is used in this sense, it has as its object the priest, Lev 5:18, or the Tent of Meeting, Lev 4:14.

repeatedly makes use of it to describe the action of bringing an offering to YHWH, Lev 1:3, 10, 14; 2:1, 4, 11, 14; 3:1, 6, 7; see also 6:13; 7:8b, 11, 12, 13, 14, 16, 18, 25, 29, while it is mentioned only three times in relation to a sacrifice for atonement, Lev 4:3, 14; 5:8. And whereas these offerings are designated about two dozen times by its derivate קָרְבָּן, Lev 1:3, 10, 14; 2:1, 4, 5, 7, 13; 3:1, 2, 6, 7, 8, 12, 14; 6:13; 7:13, 14, 15, 16, 29, Leviticus 1–7 uses it only four times in relation to a sacrifice for atonement, and only with the חטּאת, Lev 4:23, 28, 32; 5:11.

This use of קרב *hipᶜil* supersedes the older terminology where עלה *hipᶜil* is used with predilection in relation to the עֹלָה, and זבח with the זֶבַח. P thus downplays the specificity of each of these offerings and stresses their common denominator: they are brought to YHWH, or, more precisely, they are made to draw near to YHWH. This is not haphazard. Indeed, the implication of this choice of a new terminology is twofold. Although קרב *hipᶜil* may be used especially in relation to the bringing of a tribute (Judg 3:17, 18; Ps 72:10; Mal 1:8; cf. Judg 5:25), קרב *hipᶜil* must here be taken literally. It underlines YHWH's proximity: YHWH is no longer the God who comes from heaven in order to receive the offering: he is present in the Tent of Meeting. Significantly, in Lev 9:24 the fire which eats the offerings does not fall from heaven as in 1 Kgs 18:38 (see also 1 Chr 21:26; 2 Chr 7:1): it comes for from, יצא מלפני, YHWH. But, on the other hand, the use of the *hipᶜil* also underlines the distance between the offerer and YHWH. It signifies that the offerer only brings near his offering, which the priest, in his turn, brings near to YHWH/his altar (Lev 1:5, 13, 15; 3:3, 9, 14; 6:7, 14; 7:8a, 9,33). YHWH's presence does not preclude his transcendence.

What the Israelites offer to YHWH are animals and plants, but among them, only those which form part of their usual (cereal, olive oil) or exceptional (animals) diet, and, more precisely, which are the main product of their agriculture or their livestock. These are brought to him not as raw materials, but ready to be prepared for a meal: the animals are skinned and carved up, the intestines and legs are washed; cereals are ground into flour and mixed with olive oil, or even baked into bread, or roasted. This points to the fact that the offerings are considered meals which are either presented solely to YHWH (whole offering) or shared among YHWH, the priests, and the offerer (well-being offering). As is expressly stated in connection with the latter offering, the part burnt on the altar is YHWH's food, לחם, Lev 3:11, 16.

But P, here again, insists on the distance which separates YHWH from the Israelites. As we have already noted, he makes a clear distinction among YHWH's share, Leviticus 1–3, the priest's share, Lev 6:7–7:10; Lev 7:28–34, and the share of the offerer, Lev 7:11–21. But that is not all. He also defines exactly the proper share of each of the guests. He strictly sets apart YHWH's share: to YHWH exclusively belong the blood and the fat—and what is considered fat is tediously listed, Lev 3:3–4, 9–10, 14–15—which are strictly forbidden to the Israelites, Lev 3:17, on pain of exclusion, Lev 7:23–27; and in the case of a whole offering, no part of the meat is eaten by either the priests or the offerer, the meat being, on the other hand, burned, and not boiled in water as when it is prepared for the Israelites. Concerning the latter, P strictly distinguishes, in the case of a well-being offering, what is specifically assigned to the priests— the right leg and the breast, Lev 7:30–34—and what to the offerer— the remainder of the animal—both parties preparing and eating their meal separately. YHWH and the human guests thus never partake of the same kind of animal food. Although the regulation imposed on the priests and the offerer clearly point to the holiness of the sacrificial meal (see respectively Lev 6:19–22; 7:6, and Lev 7:15–21), P tends to play down this traditional aspect of a communal meal which unites YHWH and his faithful, insisting more on YHWH's otherness.

Likewise, P stresses the fact that the offering is a gift to YHWH. The ritual procedure itemizes the successive stages of the gift. The offerer brings, קרב *hipʿil*, his gift to the entrance of the Tent of Meeting, before YHWH (Lev 1:3; 3:1, 7, 12), to the priest (Lev 2:8); in the case of an animal, he then lays his hand upon its head, סמך; and then kills it, שחט. These successive rites express the negative aspect of gift, the giving up by the offerer of what had belonged to him,[12] which is made definitive through the killing of the animal. Significantly, the positive aspect of gift, its handing over to YHWH, is the exclusive responsibility of the priest. This is accomplished in the burning, קטר *hipʿil*, upon the altar, hence, the designation אשה.[13] It is this precise portion which is called קרב, Lev 3:14. Although all offerings and sacrifices are burnt on the altar, the fact that the result

---

[12] On the laying on of hands see, similarly, Rendtorff, *Leviticus*, 32–48; Knierim, *Text*, 34–40, but cf. Hartley, *Leviticus*, 19–21.

[13] Concerning אשה, see J. Hoftijzer, "Das sogenannte Feueropfer," in B. Hartmann et al. (eds.), *Hebräische Wortforschung* (VTSup 16; Leiden: Brill, 1967) 114–34; Rendtorff, *Leviticus*, 63–69; Knierim, *Text*, 67–77.

of the offerings is directly related to the burning—אשה is almost always linked to ריח ניחוח ליהוה—may account for the fact that only the offerings are called אשה.

In the cereal offering these two aspects of gift and communion are given their utmost importance.[14] As indicated by its very name מנחה, the cereal offering, especially in its raw state (which is considered as the מנחה par excellence), is a gift, a tribute of homage offered to YHWH in order to express surrender. Whereas the bread offering, in which YHWH and the human guests partake of strictly the same food, prepared in the same manner, at the same place, realizes the most intimate communion which unites men to YHWH. This kind of communion, however, is the exclusive privilege of the priests. Interestingly, it is the cheapest form of offering that develops these aspects, and the one in which YHWH's share—a handful of flour, a piece of bread—is the smallest, both in nature and quantity.

It thus seems difficult to reduce the cereal offering to a mere surrogate of, or an appendix to, the animal offerings: when the cereal offering functions as a surrogate, its composition is a different one (Lev 5:11); and when it is appended to a whole or a well-being offering, its mode of preparation differs (Num 15:1–16). The importance of the cereal offering is also demonstrated by the fact that, whereas the private whole offerings and well-being offerings must always be offered with a cereal offering, Num 15:1–16, the cereal offering is the only kind of offering which can be offered to YHWH in its own rite. And whereas the daily offering brought by the priests on behalf of Israel consists in a whole, a cereal, and a drink offering, Exod 29:38–42a//Num 28:3–8, the daily offering of the priest, brought by the high priest himself, is a bread offering, Lev 6:12–16.

Whatever the reason for bringing an offering to YHWH—and Leviticus 1–7 does not give any information at all on that point (except for the vague statement על תודה, for thanksgiving, Lev 7:12)—what is important is the assumption that any Israelite might wish, whatever the circumstance, to offer something to YHWH and experience his nearness.

The whole, cereal, and well-being offerings are freely brought to YHWH by the offerer, who also decides the kind of offering he

---

[14] On the cereal offering, see A. Marx, *Les offrandes végétales dans l'Ancien Testament. Du tribut d'hommage au repas eschatologique* (VTSup 57; Leiden: Brill, 1994).

would like to offer as well as its material. The sacrifices for atone-ment, however, are a sort of penalty imposed as a result of a trans-gression, and the kind of sacrifice and the material required for it, are prescribed according to the nature of the transgression. Although the purpose of both the חטאת and the אשם is to atone, כפר על *pi'el*, their respective scope is clearly defined.

A חטאת is required in the case of a transgression of a divine prohibition, מצות יהוה אשר לא תעשינה, provided that the transgres-sion had been committed inadvertently, בשגגה, or unconsciously, נעלם דבר, Lev 4:2, 13–14, 22–23, 27–28. If the transgression were on purpose, ביד רמה, no atonement would be possible, and the offender would have to be cut off from his people, Num 15:30–31. This pro-vision plainly shows that P cannot be accused of ritualism: only in the case of a transgression of a divine prohibition, and not in the case of a transgression of a divine commandment, and only in very restrictive instances, can a transgression be atoned for by a sacrifice. The older translation "sin offering" is thus misleading, and should be discarded altogether. The kind of animal required for the חטאת varies in accordance with the importance of the offender: a bull, if the offender is the high priest, Lev 4:3, or the congregation, Lev 4:14; a male goat, if he is a leader, Lev 4:23; a female goat or lamb, if he is an ordinary Israelite, Lev 4:28, 32.

To the transgressions listed in chapter 4, Lev 5:1–4 adds three particular instances: the failure to give evidence in court; an uncon-scious contact with impurity, so that the required purification rites are omitted; a rash, self-imposed oath which unconsciously is not fulfilled. When the offender becomes conscious of his failure, he must first confess his failure, Lev 5:5, then bring a female sheep or goat, Lev 5:6, or, if he cannot afford these, two doves, one for the חטאת, and the other for a whole offering, Lev 5:7. If he is even too poor to afford these, he may bring an ephah of flour, Lev 5:11. This lat-ter is clearly distinguished from the cereal offering: it is not termed מנחה, and no oil is mixed with the flour.

As with the offerings, the offender brings the required animal to the priest—an action designated by the verb בוא *hip'il* (Lev 4:4, 14; cf. 4:23, 28, 32; 5:6, 7, 11) and not, as for an offering, by קרב *hip'il*[15]—lays his hand on its head, and then kills it. Likewise, as in

---

[15] בוא *hip'il* is only used in Lev 2:2; 7:29–30.

the case of a well-being offering, its fat is burned on the altar, Lev 4:8–10, 19–20, 26, 31, 35. Its flesh, however, is either burned with the hide and the intestines outside the camp, in a pure place, or it must be eaten in the court of the Tent of Meeting by the officiating priest and his sons, depending on whether the חטאת is intended to atone for the high priest or the congregation, Lev 4:11–12, 21; 6:23, or whether it serves to atone for an individual Israelite, Lev 6:19–22. The eating of the flesh, which is most holy, קדש קדשים, is not just a priestly prerogative, as in the case of a well-being offering. It is a holy obligation (see also Lev 10:16–18), in order to remove something which is holy.

Yet, what characterizes the חטאת is the peculiar use which is made of the blood. Whereas in a whole offering or a well-being offering the blood is splashed, זרק . . . סביב, all around the altar, Lev 1:5, 11; 3:2, 8, 13, in the case of a חטאת, the procedure is quite different, and it varies according to the nature of the offender. If the offender is the high priest or the congregation, the high priest first sprinkles, נזה hipʿil, some of the blood seven times on the curtain which separates the Holy Place from the Holy of Holies, then puts, נתן על, some of it on the horns of the incense altar, and finally pours out, שפך אל, the remainder at the foot of the altar in the Outer court, where the regular offerings are performed, Lev 4:5–7, 16–18. However, if the offender is a leader or an ordinary Israelite, the rite is performed by an ordinary priest in the outer court, with blood applied to, נתן על, the horns of the altar, and the remainder poured out, שפך אל, at its foot, Lev 4:25, 30, 34. The blood rite thus follows a movement which goes from the most holy to the less holy, and from top to bottom. These differences in the form of the rite indicate that it has a different function from the one it has in case of a whole or a well-being offering.

The importance of that blood rite is already underlined by its complexity. It is also demonstrated by the fact that this is the only instance where a part of an offering is brought into the sanctuary. When the ritual of the Day of Atonement is performed, the high priest even brings the blood into the Holy of Holies, Lev 16:14. But, most importantly, as is explicitly stated in Lev 6:23, it is through the blood that the distinctive function of the חטאת is achieved: it is precisely the blood which carries out the כפר על piʿel (see also Exod 30:10; Lev 16:15–18, 27), the means by which the offender is forgiven. This is only true in the case of a חטאת.

Leviticus 1–7 does not elaborate, beyond the stereotyped formula כפר על *pi'el*, on the exact function of the blood rite. The following point, however, should be emphasized. Even though the כפר על *pi'el* is precisely related to the blood rite, it results as a matter of fact both from the blood rite and the burning of the fat, and is thus always mentioned at the end of the whole sacrificial procedure, Lev 4:20, 26, 31, 35; 5:6, 10, 13. The distinctive function of the burning of the fat is pointed out in Lev 4:31: as in the case of the offerings, it is ריח ניחוח ליהוה, a pleasing aroma to YHWH. Thus each חטאת revolves around two poles. The first is negative: The actual כפר על *pi'el* removes, through the blood rite, what hinders the relationship with YHWH; as with the blood put on the doorposts and the lintel, Exod 12:7, 22, it has a repellant function. The second is positive: the restoration, through the fat offering, of the relationship with YHWH which had been broken by the offender. This may account for the designation קרבן in Lev 4:23, 28, 32. Although the atonement through the blood is its distinctive feature, the חטאת thus surpasses mere atonement.

These two poles can be addressed, as in the case of the dove חטאת, by two kinds of sacrifices: on the one hand the חטאת, and on the other, the whole offering, Lev 5:8–10. In fact, with the single exception of those instances mentioned in Lev 4:1–5:4, P always relates the חטאת to a whole offering. This is consistent with the characteristics of the *rite de passage*, which centers around the two poles of separation and integration. Thus my former proposal to interpret the חטאת as the first, the negative stage of a *rite de passage*.[16]

Most importantly, this demonstrates again that atonement is not the principal aim of the sacrificial cult. Atonement is only a prerequisite, although a necessary one. The chief aim is actually achieved through the offerings which are intended to establish a relationship with YHWH.

---

[16] For details see A. Marx, "Sacrifice pour les péchés ou rite de passage? Quelques réflexions sur la fonction du *hatta't*," *RB* 96 (1989) 27–48. For a different interprétation, see J. Milgrom, "Sin-Offering or Purification-Offering?" *VT* 21 (1971) 237–39; idem, "Israel's Sanctuary: The Priestly 'Picture of Dorian Gray,'" *RB* 83 (1976) 390–99; idem, "The *hatta't* A Rite of Passage?" *RB* 98 (1991) 120–24; idem, *Leviticus 1–16* (AB 3; New York: Doubleday; 1991) 226–318; idem, "Further on the Expiatory Sacrifices," *JBL* 115 (1996) 511–514; and A. Schenker, "Interprétations récentes et dimensions spécifiques du sacrifice *hattat*," *Bib* 75 (1994) 59–70; idem, "Welche Verfehlungen und welche Opfer in Lev 5:1–6?" in H.-J. Fabry and H.-W. Jüngling (eds.), *Levitikus als Buch* (BBB 119; Berlin: Philo, 1999) 249–61.

The second sacrifice for atonement is the אשם, the reparation offering. Whereas the חטאת is required in the case of a transgression,
חטאת, of a divine prohibition, the reparation offering is a penalty
exacted from the one who has trespassed, מָעַל מַעַל, Lev 5:15, 21
against someone's property, which is considered one kind of חטאת.
The injured property may belong to YHWH, and may consist in
"holy things," קדשי יהוה, Lev 5:15, such as temple furniture or, more
likely, precious metal or artifacts which should be given to the temple treasury (see Num 7:84–86; 31:50–54) or, probably more often,
first-born animals, firstfruits, the tithe, the priests' share, and all goods
previously dedicated to YHWH. Surprisingly, the owner may also
be a fellow Israelite, who has been lied to, either about a deposit
or a lost property, or whose property has been robbed or extorted
from him, Lev 5:21–22. In Lev 5:17–19, the Israelite who has transgressed a divine prohibition is also required to make a reparation
offering.

In order to obtain forgiveness, סלח, Lev 5:16, 18, 26—in the first
instance, provided the trespass has been committed inadvertently—
the offender must restore to its owner what he has stolen, with a
compensation equivalent to one fifth of its value. He thus fictitiously
redeems what he has stolen (see Lev 27:13, 15, 19, 27, 31). But
then, he gives it back to its owner, so that the theft is symbolically
cancelled and changed into a gift. Additionally, the offender must
bring to the priest a ram, the symbolic equivalent of the value of
the stolen property, Lev 5:16, 24–25. This ram—which is also required
in addition to the חטאת, Lev 5:18—is specifically a reparation, אשם,
due to YHWH, who is considered the ultimate owner of everything.
It is the act of the giving of the ram to the priest which obtains the
כפר על *pi'el* (see especially Lev 5:16b).

The reparation offering is thus clearly different from all the others. It is basically a reparation. It is significant that there is no reference in Leviticus 5 to any blood rite or burning.[17] The reparation
offering is primarily part of a legal procedure involving the offender,
the owner, and the priest, who represents YHWH. Contrary to the
other sacrifices, its ritual is not described in Leviticus 1–5, but only
in Lev 7:1–7. The sacrificial procedure is confined to the bare min-

---

[17] See G. J. Wenham, *The Book of Leviticus* (NICOT 3; Grand Rapids: Eerdmans,
1981) 105: "The value of the animal presented was more important than the procedure at the altar."

imum. Only the blood and the fat, which in any case belong solely to YHWH, Lev 7:23–27, are offered to him. As in the case of a well-being offering, the blood is splashed, ‏זרק ... סביב‎, all around the altar, Lev 7:2, whereas the fat is burned on the altar, Lev 7:3–5. But here all of the flesh is allotted to the officiating priest, as in the case of a first-born offering (Num 18:15–18). The involvement of YHWH as one of the injured parties to whom reparation is due may explain the use of ‏אשה‎ in Lev 7:5.[18]

These instructions on the offerings and sacrifices are not only intended to be a reference book for the priests. They are for the common Israelites as well, and are passed on orally, so that all have access to them. They concern every Israelite. Sacrifice is not only a public affair under the responsibility of the priests. It is surely not haphazard that almost no reference is made in Leviticus 1–7 to the public sacrifices. Each Israelite is called to draw near to YHWH with his offerings, and to enjoy YHWH's presence. And YHWH's presence has repercussions for each Israelite who must behave in perfect accordance with YHWH's commandments, and is in this way ultimately responsible for YHWH's presence or absence among His people.

The scope of this paper has been deliberately limited to the data given in Leviticus 1–7. It is obvious that P's theology of sacrifice cannot be reconstituted from that information alone. The shortcomings of this data as source material have already been noted in the introduction above. Obviously, all of the P texts on sacrifice should be considered together, with appropriate attention given to the various occasions where sacrifices are required, especially the public sacrifices. The reader must also guard against allowing the biased point of view in Leviticus 1–7 to lead to a picture of the sacrifice only as a demonstration of personal piety.

But even though our approach may be termed an artificial one, it is not entirely illegitimate. As has been emphasized, Leviticus 1–7

---

[18] For details, see A. Marx, "Sacrifice de réparation et rites de levée de sanction," *ZAW* 100 (1988) 183–98. But see J. Milgrom, *Cult and Conscience. The ASHAM and the Priestly Doctrine of Repentance* (SJLA 18; Leiden: Brill, 1976); A. Schenker, "Der Unterschied zwischen Sündopfer *Chattat* und Schuldopfer *Ascham* im Licht von Lv 5,17–19 und 5,1–6", in C. Brekelmans and J. Lust (eds.), *Pentateuchal and Deuteronomistic Studies* (BETL 94; Leuven: Peeters, 1989) 115–23; idem, "Die Anlässe zum Schuldopfer Ascham" in A. Schenker (ed.), *Studien zu Opfer und Kult im Alten Testament* (FAT 3; Tübingen: J. C. B. Mohr [Paul Siebeck], 1992) 45–66.

is not just one part of Leviticus among others; rather it has a prominent position in the book. In close correlation with Exod 40:34–38,
it constitutes the pedestal on which the remainder of the book of
Leviticus rests. What these chapter say about offerings and sacrifices
is thus of primary importance, at least in the eyes of P.[19]

---

[19] An exhaustive bibliography can be found in S. Lyonnet and L. Sabourin, *Sin, Redemption, and Sacrifice. A Biblical and Patristic Study* (AnBib 48; Rome: Biblical Institute, 1970) 299–332, and in V. Rosset, "Bibliographie 1969–91 zum Opfer in der Bibel," in A. Schenker (ed.), *Studien zu Opfer und Kult im Alten Testament* (FAT 3; Tübingen: J. C. B. Mohr [Paul Siebeck], 1992) 107–51. In addition, see especially I. Willi-Plein, *Opfer und Kult im alttestamentlichen Israel. Textbefragungen und Zwischenergebnisse* (SBS 153; Stuttgart: Katholisches Bibelwerk, 1993); V. Fritz, "Bis an die Hörner des Altars. Erwägungen zur Praxis des Brandopfers in Israel," in P. Mommer (ed.), *Gottesrecht als Lebensraum* (Neukirchen-Vluyn: Neukirchener Verlag, 1993) 61–70; W. Zwickel, "Zur Frühgeschichte des Brandopfers in Israel," in W. Zwickel (ed.), *Biblische Welten* (OBO 123; Freiburg, Göttingen; Universitätsverlag, 1993) 231–48; Marx, *Les offrandes végétales*; Schenker, "Interprétations récentes," 59–70; W. Zwickel, *Der Tempelkult in Kanaan und Israel. Studien zur Kultgeschichte Palästinas von der Mittelbronzezeit bis zum Untergang Judas* (FAT 10; Tübingen: J. C. B. Mohr [Paul Siebeck], 1994); H. Utzschneider, "Vergebung im Ritual. Zur Deutung des *hatta't*-Rituals im Sündopfer" in R. Riess (ed.), *Abschied von der Schuld? Zur Anthropologie und Theologie von Schuldbewusstsein, Opfer und Versöhnung* (Stuttgart-Berlin-Köln: Kohlhammer, 1995) 96–119; A. I. Baumgarten, "*Hatta't* Sacrifices," *RB* 103 (1996) 337–42; J. Milgrom, "Further on the Expiatory Sacrifices," 511–14; A. Marx, "La place du sacrifice dans l'ancien Israël," in J. A. Emerton (ed.), *Congress Volume. Cambridge 1995* (VTSup 56; Leiden: Brill, 1997) 203–17; A. Schenker, "Once Again, the Expiatory Sacrifices," *JBL* 116 (1997) 697–99; idem "Keine Versöhnung ohne Anerkennung der Haftung für verursachten Schaden. Die Rolle von Haftung und Intentionalität in den Opfern *hattât* und *'asam* (Lev 4–5)," *ZABR* 3 (1997) 164–73; idem "Welche Verfehlungen," 249–61; P. Heger, *The Three Biblical Altar Laws: Developments in the Sacrificial Cult in Practice and Theology; Political and Economic Background* (BZAW 279; Berlin, New York: De Gruyter, 1999); A. Marx, "Opferlogik im alten Israel," in B. Janowski and M. Welker (eds.), *Opfer. Theologische und kulturelle Kontexte* (Suhrkamp Taschenbuch Wissenschaft 1454; Frankfurt a.M.: Suhrkamp, 2000) 129–49; R. Rendtorff, "Priesterliche Opfertora in jüdi-scher Auslegung," in Janowski and Welker (eds.), *Opfer*, 178–90; I. Willi-Plein, "Opfer und Ritus im kultischen Lebenszusammenhang," in Janowski and Welker (eds.), *Opfer*, 150–77.

THE GO-AWAY GOAT

Mary Douglas[1]

Bible scholars are divided on the meaning of the scapegoat, which should not be a surprise to the anthropologist. More surprising, the accepted meanings of "scapegoat" are at variance with the original biblical piece in which the scapegoat figures. In common usage "to scapegoat" has become a verb meaning to persecute or to blame. Réné Girard uses it in this sense when he develops the idea that slaughter, blood and killing have always been the central element of religion, the main form of communication with the gods.[2] He uses "scapegoat" to refer to a variety of persecutory behaviours, whose unity he says we grasp intuitively. However, he cannot possibly get this meaning from the biblical rite where the scapegoat is not attacked, shamed nor harmed. The English word comes from Tyndale's 1530 translation of the Bible, meaning the goat that is *not* sacrificed, or the goat that *escapes* from being killed as a sacrificial victim. It follows a Hebrew interpretation of "Azazel," taken to mean the "go-away goat"—in secular terms you might say, "the lucky goat" compared with his fellow who stays and is killed for a sacrifice.

Where does Girard get the scapegoat as an image of persecution? Apparently from a Greek rite, *pharmakos*, which has nothing to do with goats though in English it is called the "scapegoat" rite. Robert Parker's *Miasma, Pollution and Purification in Early Greek Religion*,[3] gives an account of Greek "scapegoat rituals," but these rites, though they correspond well to Girard's idea, do not look remotely like the Bible instance except they both seem to have a common object, to rid a

[1] I warmly thank Simon Hornblower, Horst Seebass, Shmuel Trigano, K. Jenner, J. G. Oosten, Hyam Maccoby, John Sawyer and John North for much help and advice on early versions of this text, and I am also grateful to Joseph Blenkinsopp for the invitation to present it to the meeting of the SOTS in Oxford on 24 July 2000. I have tried to incorporate the many suggestions in the present version.

[2] R. Girard and J. Smith, *Violent Origins* (Stanford: Stanford University Press, 1987) 73–148.

[3] R. Parker, *Miasma: Pollution and Purification in Early Greek Religion* (Oxford: Clarendon, 1983) 257–70.

city of impurity.[4] So it turns out that when talking about scapegoats in everyday parlance we are drawing upon Greek rituals to rid the city of scum, discarded elements, useless and dirty people. For the Bible there is only this one text, which richly prescribes the rites of the Day of Atonement; the Greek sources have no prescriptive text, they are rich in brief descriptions of a customary rite being performed, in different places, at different times, with varying details, sometimes historical and mostly legendary.

Greek and Hebrew Compared

In Leviticus 16 the Yom-Kippur ceremony requires two goats, one to be sacrificed and one released. Both are real *goats*, the escapee is a goat, not a person, whereas the Greek riddance ceremonies focus on a *human* (not a goat), who may probably not escape. The Greek rituals humiliate the scape-person, often cruelly; in mythical versions he is even killed. However, no violence whatever is committed against the Leviticus scapegoat. The latter is one of a pair, the Greek "scape-person" is usually one individual. In the biblical ceremony both goats are involved in an elaborate and important sacrificial rite, but not the Greek "scape-person." He tends to be a subversive or marginal person picked from among miserable wretches, the very poor and ugly, marginal categories, or non-Greeks.[5] He is sent out of the city with a procession, discordant music is played, he may be whipped with wild plants, a humiliating rite at the very least. In the Greek case the rite has a punitive aspect, the "scape-person" is a representative of the evil that is being expelled, he carries the blame and guilt with him. But in fact no stigma is attached to the Bible scapegoat, he is chosen randomly by lot from a pair of goats, both can be assumed to be unblemished when they are chosen since it is not known which will be sacrificed and which will escape, and each is to be presented to the Lord. It is true that the sins of the people of Israel are formally laid on the scapegoat, which is then led away to a distant place, but there is nothing obviously punitive about the levitical rite. Seeking for similarities between the Greek and the Bible

---

[4] R. Girard, *The Scapegoat* (London: Athlone, 1986); the original French is *Le Bouc Emissaire* (Paris: Bernard Grasset, 1982).
[5] R. Parker, *Miasma*, 257–70.

instances, Jan Bremmer picks out the fact that in some (but not all) Greek versions the selected scape-person is decorated, which he sees as parallel to a biblical rule that the goat's horns shall be bound with scarlet thread.[6] However, this rule is post-biblical, a rabbinical touch. It does not appear anywhere in the text of chapter 16, but even if it did, the comparison would be misplaced. Scarlet thread figures without a decorative function in other rituals, as in the purification rites for cleansing from leprosy, or in the preparation of ashes from a red cow where it is produced to be burnt (Num 19:6). In effect, there are fewer similarities between the two so-called scapegoat rites than differences. Between Jerusalem and Athens the concept has moved from a might-have-been animal victim who has definitely escaped death, to a real human victim who will surely be hurt and may be killed. Part of my argument is going to be that the punitive elements not found in the biblical description have been imported, perhaps from Greece or Mesopotamia, by late interpreters. The more important question is whether a single category of scapegoat rites can be justified at all.

Category Problems in Studying Religion

Frazer's *Golden Bough,* after comparing scapegoat rituals round the world, concludes that the rite was originally a fertility cult.[7] Perhaps he was right and the biblical ceremony should not be classed with riddance ceremonies at all. The solution will lie within Leviticus itself and not in indiscriminate comparisons. Imagine a research assistant of James Frazer in modern times. He is trained to pick out similarities. When he has attended a number of weddings he will notice the focus on a big white cake. He recalls a white cake at Christmas, and more white cakes for birthdays and christenings. Soon a category of "white cake ceremonies" emerges in his mind, like the Kava drinking ceremonies of Melanesia, or the Peace-pipe smoking of the American Indians, he may even be tempted to class Cake-Communion with the Eucharist. In this spirit Jan Bremmer recently announced

---

[6] *"pharmakos"* in S. Hornblower and A. Spawforth (eds.), *The Oxford Classical Dictionary* (Oxford: Oxford University Press, 1996).

[7] J. Frazer, *The Golden Bough: A Study in Magic and Religion* (3rd ed.; London: Macmillan and Co., 1913), vol. 9, Part VI.

in the Harvard Studies in Classical Philology note on the scapegoat, "a hitherto neglected parallel from Tibet, which shows a striking resemblance with the Greek ritual."[8] The search for parallels allows the Greek idea of riddance or elimination of evil to dominate the discussion, and dubious solutions lend support to each other. S. Talmon's old essay on "The 'Comparative Method' in Biblical Interpretation—Principles and Problems" gives a thorough-going trouncing of what he calls "comparatist approaches" on the grand scale.[9]

Walter Burkert said, "blood and violence lurk fascinatingly at the very heart of religion," and claimed that sacrificial killing underlies the experience of the sacred.[10] About the same time Réné Girard placed the same emphasis on human cruelty in *Violence and the Sacred*.[11] Their writings, which in our time have colored so heavily the interpretation of ancient religion, are themselves colored by their own period. First the guilt of the Holocaust, and then revulsion against violence and cruelty during the Vietnam War and after. Yes, we must agree that humans tend to be violent and persecutory, and also that religion tends to be pervasive. We can agree that violence and religion will be likely to coincide in human history. But does that account for the basic experience of the sacred? With as much right others would offer different candidates for a basic religious experience: search for truth, longing for ecstatic union, the idea of an external moral imperative, the desire to make sense of existence, to experience a transcendent reality.

In Oxford in the 1950s anthropologists used to deride the "If-I-were-a-horse" principle of interpretation.[12] "If I were a horse, I would regard my rider as a divinity, I would irrationally believe in the value of rituals such as horse races, I would do my best to win, supposing my salvation depended on it." Arguing on these lines Burkert and Girard can believe that if I were an ancient Hebrew I would superstitiously perform sacrifice, though feeling horror and guilt at the bloodshed. Burkert exemplifies "If-I-were a horse" thinking with

---

[8] J. Bremmer, "Scapegoat Rituals in Ancient Greece," *HSCP* 87 (1983) 299–320, esp. 306.

[9] S. Talmon, "The Comparative Method in Biblical Interpretation: Principles and Problems," in W. Zimmerli (ed.), *Congress Volume: Göttingen, 1977* (VTSup 29; Leiden: Brill, 1978) 320–356.

[10] W. Burkert, *Homo necans; Interpretationen altgriechischen Opferriten und Mythen* (Berlin: de Gruyter, 1972) 5.

[11] R. Girard, *Violence and the Sacred* (Baltimore: Johns Hopkins, 1977).

[12] F. Steiner, *Taboo* (New York: Philosophical Library, 1956).

his idea that the inventors of the biblical scapegoat rite intended to express rejection or at least reserve about the violence of blood sacrifice, and by adding a goat that purifies without dying they intended to release the congregation from feelings of anxiety and guilt.[13] He himself is the one who is feeling horror and guilt. Furthermore, not all the religions of the world require blood sacrifices. As for the smell of roasting meat, it usually suggests the pleasing prospect of a convivial meal. Saying grace consecrates a meal: if Girard and Burkert were to count all types of consecrated meat-eating as sacrificial violence they would certainly stretch the idea of sacrifice. (It would make sense if they are vegetarians).

Azazel

What follows is an attempt to honor the levitical purification ceremony in its full integrity without importing assumptions from other similar-seeming purification rites. But first observe that purifications rites are poly-semic, they have many meanings: purification is a prerequisite for coronations, marriages, initiations, reconciliations and many other situations. The rite confers status, it affirms identity, sometimes for a group, sometimes for a single person, and in a major rite opportunity is generally taken to re-enact the historic identity of the group. To focus simply on the preparatory riddance of evil impoverishes the interpretation. A recent survey[14] which challenges current interpretations of the biblical scapegoat rite finds it incongruous that a creature treated as "scum" should be able to remove our sins. In such a muddied field, this seems to be a sensible starting point.

In the text used as basis for the annual atonement ceremony, Aaron is instructed to wash himself and put on the holy garments (Lev 16:4). He must offer a bull as a sin offering for himself and for his house (16:6, 11), a ram for a burnt offering and two male goats, one of which will be sacrificed for the sin-offering for the people of Israel and one which will go free:

---

[13] W. Burkert, *Structure and History in Greek Mythology and Ritual* (Berkeley: University of California Press, 1979).

[14] B. Janowski and G. Wilhelm, "Der Bock, der die Sünden hinausträgt. Zur Religionsgeschichte des Azazel-Ritus Lev 16, 10,21ff.," in B. Janowski, K. Koch and G. Wilhelm (eds.), *Religionsgeschichtliche Beziehungen zwischen Kleinasien, Nordsyrien und dem Alten Testament* (Göttingen: Vandenhoeck & Ruprecht, 1993) 106–69.

He shall take the two goats and set them before the Lord at the door
of the tent of meeting; and Aaron shall cast lots upon the two goats,
one lot for the Lord and the other lot for Azazel (16:6–8). And Aaron
shall present the goat on whom the lot fell for the Lord, and offer it
as a sin offering; but the goat on which the lot fell for Azazel shall
be presented alive before the Lord, to make atonement over it, that
it may be sent away into the wilderness to Azazel. (Lev 16:9–10)

Who or what is Azazel? The word has been disputed since antiquity. In Hebrew there are no compounds that are not proper names.
In recognition of this philological fact it is spelt in English as a name,
with a capital initial, Azazel, and so for that reason only it has been
assumed that it is the name for either a person or a place. Levine
gives three possible interpretations.[15]

The simplest interpretation (which is followed here) is that Azazel
is the name which designates the goat that is chosen to go away,
the go-away goat. According to Levine[16] this is an old interpretation
followed in both the Septuagint and the Vulgate and underlies the
rabbinic characterization of "the goat that is dispatched"[17] so well
rendered in the French, *le bouc emissaire*. The second is that Azazel
is an unexplained place in the wilderness, expected to be the habitation of demons (e.g., Isa 13:21; 34:14). The third is that Azazel is
the name of the demon ruler of the wilderness.[18] The differences
rest on very slight shifts among the prepositions "for" and "to" in
16:8, 10, 22 and 26, mostly depending on whether the word Azazel
or the phrase "goat for the scapegoat" is used. These are the only
places in the Pentateuch where the word Azazel is mentioned. It
has to be said that the claims for Azazel as demon in the wilderness rest on shaky grounds. There are no other biblical contexts
which can explain a gift or the payment of tribute to a demon ruler
out there. But this, the third view, is currently the most accepted.
In its support *1 Enoch* 1:5–7 is cited because it names Azazel among
the rebellious angels, but *1 Enoch* itself may been written under Greek
influence or the writer may have got the word from Leviticus 16.

---

[15] B. Levine, *Leviticus* (Philadelphia: Jewish Publication Society, 1989) 102–257.
[16] Levine, *Leviticus*, 102.
[17] Ibid., 102.
[18] J. Milgrom, *Leviticus 1–16* (AB 3; New York: Doubleday, 1991) 1020, notes
that this reading is dominant in the Midrashic literature dating back to the early
post-biblical period; but see also Levine, *Leviticus*, 102, 257.

Levine finds the word meaning the name of the goat or the name of a place "over-contrived."[19] If his own preference rests mainly on pre-biblical angelology, it is weak. Moreover, his description of the system of casting lots suggests support for the Septuagint and Tyndale's solution that Azazel is the name given to the goat. He explains that for the casting of lots in v. 8 two stones would have been prepared as lots, one with an inscription "For the Lord," or "Belonging to the Lord," and the other, "For Azazel," or "Belonging to Azazel."[20] This would correspond to the practice of assigning an animal to be sacrificed with a formal declaration and a name. The *Sifra* cited by Rashi explains the procedure as follows: "When he [the High priest] places the lot upon it [the goat] he gives it a name and states, 'To the Lord as a sin offering'."[21] So after all the goat has a name! This suggests that "the goat as Azazel" could be inscribed on the lot as a compound word to designate the goat that the lot will choose to be the "go-away goat," or "the scape-goat." Consequently there is no need to invent a gift for a Goat-Lord of the wilderness, which would anyway be completely out of character for the book of Leviticus. For in the very next chapter, Lev 17:7 gives a strong injunction against what is assumed to be a popular custom of sacrificing to demons, satyrs, spirits, in the fields. That Aaron be told in the middle of this very important rite for the consecration of the tabernacle to send a messenger or a gift to the demon Azazel is a very implausible translation.

The etymologies of the word do little to favor one interpretation over another, and the decision rests mainly on willingness to dabble in conjectural pre-biblical cosmology. Most of the arguments in favour of the demon solution depend on late sources, *1 Enoch* and certain Qumran documents which mention a fallen angel with a satanic role.[22] To depend on these later sources is awkward; it either implies that there has been unbroken continuity of the tradition of reading from the date of the redaction, which should be seriously

---

[19] Levine, *Leviticus*, 102.

[20] Ibid., 251, says that it had currency in late antiquity, referring to *1 Enoch* (6–13) where Azazel was considered to be one of the fallen angels.

[21] Ibid., 50–51, 103.

[22] G. W. E. Nickelsburg "The Bible Rewritten and Expanded," in M. E. Stone (ed.), *Jewish Writings of the Second Temple Period* (CRINT 2; Philadelphia: Fortress, 1984) 89–156.

disputed, or it involves establishing a much later date of redaction than is commonly accepted. With so much against the demon in the desert, even after two thousand years of argument, the anthropological preference for over-all coherence would support the view that Azazel is quite simply the name for the goat chosen by lot: "This is the goat that will be chosen to be the 'Go-Away Goat'."

Atonement

After the mention of Azazel follows the account of the sacrifices which Aaron makes for atonement. Aaron has contributed a bull which he sacrifices to make atonement for himself and his house, the people of Israel have contributed two male goats for a sin-offering and one ram[23] for a burnt offering (16:3–5). He sacrifices one of the goats for the people (16:9, 15). He sprinkles the blood of these two sacrifices on the holy of holies to "make atonement for the holy place because of the uncleannesses of the people of Israel, because of their transgressions, all their sins, and he shall do so for the tent of meeting which abides with them in the midst of their uncleannesses," and the same for the altar (16:15–20). By this time he has made atonement for himself, for his house, that is for his fellow priests, for all the assembly of Israel (16:17), and also for three places, the tabernacle, the altar and the holy of holies. The ceremony has come to a pause, it says he has "made an end of atoning" or finished atoning (16:20). Now he turns to the live goat that has been waiting. Since the atonement seems to have been completed, we can expect to have reached the central element in the ritual sequence.

> And when he has made an end of atoning for the holy place and the tent of meeting and the altar, he shall present the live goat; and Aaron shall lay both his hands upon the head of the live goat, and confess over him all the iniquities of the people of Israel, and all their transgressions, all their sins; and he shall put them upon the head of the goat, and send him away into the wilderness by the hand of a man who is in readiness. The goat shall bear all their iniquities upon him to a solitary land; and he shall let the goat go in the wilderness. (Lev 16:20–22)

---

[23] Nothing more is said about the ram.

Note that the scapegoat ceremony is set within a complex series of sacrifices: the goat has been moved forward and back, now with his brother goat and now without, and presented to the Lord for atonement for the holy place, etc. Now Aaron lays both hands on the goat and confesses the sins of Israel over its head. (We do not know which sins he confesses; it could be sins not included in the earlier atonement rites.) After this Aaron has no further contact with the goat. He takes off the ritual garments and washes (v. 24), and apparently supervises the disposal of the carcasses of the burnt offerings, the bull and the other goat.

The man who led away the goat and the man who has carried out the burning of the skin and flesh of the sin offerings both have likewise to wash before returning to the camp (vv. 26–29). To make too much of the act of washing has the unwarranted implication that it has a magical effect. Like assuming that the desert is a punitive exile for the goat, it suggests more Hellenic influence. The idea that Aaron has to wash because he has had contact with something very foul completely contradicts the solemn act of presentation to God. It is probably enough to interpret the washings as marking a clean break in the ceremonial sequence. The washings would be like punctuation marks; they show that the ceremony has been concluded, they wrap it up. The strong focus of the rite was the transfer of sins on to an animal, which has not yet been done. But what sins? Atonement for places has been done on a comprehensive scale. Whose sins? Atonement for living persons has been done comprehensively.

The Transfer of Sins

Why do the iniquities of Israel need to be transferred at all? Are they different from the iniquities that have already been atoned? We keep it in mind as a question: Whose sins are laid on the goat? What is involved in "bearing sin"? Is it possible that the simple transfer of sins is not the main motive of the scapegoat rite? It could be that the significant element is neither the sacrifice of the one goat, nor the sending away of the other, but something about the two goats initially seen as a pair and then separated. We first must examine closely what the bearing of sins means.

Biblical theology makes a strong distinction between sin and guilt, requiring different animals for a sin offering and a guilt offering, and

different actions to be done for them. The word for bearing sin is
נשׂא. When someone incurs guilt, he, the sinner, bears it; the metaphor
suggests a burden for him to carry around. But this is perhaps a
too material interpretation of guilt, for when guilt is transferred to
another it is not like the shifting of a heavy weight from one person to another. Baruch Schwartz explains it as a change of character: what was a weight, once transferred, has stopped being a weight.
It is not to be carried on the shoulders of the second person. It is
just blotted out, cancelled. He says, the terms for bearing sin,

> [A]lways mean precisely what they say: "to bear," that is, to hold up,
> haul about, carry sin. . . . . In this particular idiom, sin is a burden, a
> load that must be borne. When the sinner himself "bears" his sin, he
> *may* suffer its consequences if such there be. . . . . However, when and
> if another party—most often, but not necessarily, God, "bears"—the
> sinner's burden, it no longer rests on the shoulders of the wrongdoer;
> the latter is relieved of his load and of its consequences once again if
> such there be. . . . In this . . . usage the "bearing" of the sin by another
> is a metaphor for the guilty party's release from guilt. . . . [T]he sin
> ner whose burden someone else bears has not transferred its weight
> to another; the bearer is not weighted down by the weight of the sin
> as the sinner formerly was.[24]

On this interpretation the word "to bear" has two senses; one means
"to carry about," "to be laden with," which applies to the sinner
before purification, and the other, used for relieving the sinner of
his burden, means "to carry off, take away, to remove,"[25] or cancel. If through both stages we stay with the meaning of the word
"to bear," to "lift" the burden of sin, "to remove" sin, "to blot it
out," "to cancel it," there is not need for a sequence in which it is
transformed from a material to a spiritual meaning. The goat which
bears the sins of the congregation would, by having them transferred
to itself, simply lift off the sins, blot them out, remove or eliminate
them, etc.[26] There would not be any necessity for interpreting the

---

[24] B. Schwartz, "The Bearing of Sin in the Priestly Literature," in D. Wright,
D. Freedman, and A. Hurvitz (eds.), *Pomegranates and Golden Bells: Studies in Biblical,
Jewish, and Near Eastern Ritual, Law, and Literature in Honor of Jacob Milgrom* (Winona
Lake, Ind.: Eisenbrauns, 1995) 9–10.

[25] Ibid., 10.

[26] "More significantly, the most prominent epithet of God in His role of forgiver
is *nose' 'avon/het/pesha'*, lit. he who 'lifts off sin'; Exod 34:7, Num 14:18"; see "Forgiveness," in C. Roth (ed.), *Encyclopedia Judaica* (16 vols.; Philadelphia, Coronet Books,
1971) 6.1434.

rite as making the scapegoat materially carry them on its shoulders to the desert.

Aaron has to bear transgressions against the holy things of God (Exod 28:38), but in doing so he does not take on the liability or punishment for the sins of the community. It is enough that he is charged with their removal, elimination.[27] This teaching corrects a very material idea of sin and an unduly magical concept of transferring sins. Both are changed to a teaching more in keeping with the austerely spiritual religion of Leviticus. For someone else to bear his guilt is equivalent to the sinner being forgiven. The guilt is no more, the guilt is cancelled, blotted out, obliterated, forgotten. According to the anthropological reading of this book[28] God is not punitive, he is not obsessed with sin but expects to make a lasting covenant with his people. If a ritual transfer eliminates the sin, it means that when the sins of Israel are transferred to the scapegoat, that is an end of them, so that he is not being made to carry the sins of others away with him into the desert. The sins are no more—a great contrast with the Greek *pharmakos*. By being received on the shoulders of the scapegoat the sins (which have already been atoned) are now cancelled. The goat is the medium of atonement (16:16) and forgiveness. His role would therefore be honourable, to say the least.

While the comparison with the despised Greek scape-person begins to look very wild, other elements of the ritual gain in sense. For example, Aaron is told to lay his hands on the head of the goat (16:20). The verb means to lean on, or to press it down strongly. It is a ritual gesture known as שמיכה, the laying on of hands. For a sacrifice the person making the offering has to press one hand down on the head of the animal being offered (Lev 1:4, 4:4); the gesture assigns a sacrificial victim. Once assigned in this way, the offering is sacred and belongs to God.[29]

Evidently the scapegoat is assigned to God, since the same words are used for bringing him forward, near to the altar, making him stand before the Lord,[30] and having the priest's hands laid on his

---

[27] Milgrom, *Leviticus 1–16*, 54–55, 512, 623, 1045 (quoted in Schwartz, "The Bearing of Sin," 16).

[28] Douglas, *Leviticus as Literature* (Oxford: Oxford University, 1999).

[29] Levine, *Leviticus*, 6.

[30] The JPS translation offers instead of "shall be presented alive before the Lord," "shall be left standing before the Lord" (16:9).

head.[31] D. P. Wright says succinctly, the rite of laying on hands is
"the means of designating the focus of the ritual action ... in the
case of the scapegoat it signifies: 'This goat is the recipient of the
sins of the people.'"[32] The scapegoat has been consecrated to God
after its brother has been sacrificed, and its role must have something to do with receiving the sins of Israel. It would have made
sense for the goat to be sent away punitively to an inhospitable
region (though the text does not justify that translation) if by receiving the sins it has now become a guilty creature (an example of the
meaning pre-empted by prior assumptions). But if it is not guilty,
and not shameful, and is not going to be carrying a burden of sins
around with it, why should it be sent away to a fiercely hostile environment? The question can be resolved by starting with the parallel rite of two birds, one sacrificed, one freed, and noting that the
one that is not sacrificed goes free, not to a desert.

We do not know how far back goes the idea that the exile in the
desert is a punishment for the sin-bearing animal. It may go back
to the Hellenic period or further back still. The text itself goes back
long before the sages returned to Judah after the second destruction
of the temple by the Romans. The original editors would have been
deceased some four or five hundred years earlier. The sages could
have made use of unwritten traditions based on ancient local memories of the Hittite civilization whose ruins are still evident in Palestine
and Syria. In the Hittite rite the priest's hand was laid upon the
scape-goat, it was sent out to the plains, as an offering to the god
out there. Moshe Weinfeld[33] also mentions that the Hittite rite for
the scape-goat purification closely paralleled the biblical rite with two
birds. Similar purification rites are reported from contemporary
Babylon.[34] However, the interpretative style that picks parallels from
the region has to be supplemented with close examination of the
text itself. These other ceremonies may have been more condem-
natory and punitive,[35] more like the Greek *pharmakos*. But there is

---

[31] This passage has drawn a rather confused response from the commentators;
see Milgrom, *Leviticus 1–16*, 1043.

[32] D. Wright, "The Gesture of Hand-Placement in the Hebrew Bible and in
Hittite Literature," *JAOS* 106 (1986) 436.

[33] M. Weinfeld, "Traces of Hittite Cult in Shiloh, Bethel and in Jerusalem," in
in Janowski, Koch, and Wilhelm (eds.), *Religionsgeschichtliche Beziehungen*, 455–72.

[34] H. Krümmel, "Ersatzkönig und Sündenbock," *ZAW* 80 (1968) 289–318.

[35] Janowski and Wilhelm, "Der Bock, der die Sünden hinausträgt," in Janowski,
Koch and Wilhelm (eds.), *Religionsgeschichtliche Beziehungen*, passim.

nothing to guarantee that the editors of the Hebrew Bible did not adapt the antique rite to their own purposes.

Parallels within Leviticus: Two Birds

It is time to pay attention to the clues within Leviticus itself, starting with the parallel rites, the two goats and the two birds. When a leper has been cured, the rite of cleansing which prepares him to re-enter the community requires the priest to take two birds, and to sacrifice one of them:

> He shall take the living bird with the cedarwood and the scarlet stuff and the hyssop, and dip them and the living bird in the blood of the bird that was killed over the running water; and he shall sprinkle it seven times over him who is to be cleansed of leprosy, *and shall let the living bird go into the open field.* (Lev 14:6–7)

Then the same for the cleansing of a house, the lesson is repeated: two birds again, one of them killed, the other dipped in its blood and set free:

> And he shall let the living bird go out of the city into the open field. (Lev 14:53)

Notice that the same language is used for the freeing of the scapegoat: "*he shall let the living bird go,*" and he "*shall let the goat go.*" The same form and word, שלח, are used in Exodus for a strong imperative when Moses was told to say to Pharaoh, "*Let my people go!*" (Exod 10:3). Neither bird that is released is being sent to its death, or even condemned to a hard life; going out of the city even suggests going to a better situation. If the bird is set free to fly into the open fields we can revise the interpretation of the place in which the scapegoat is released. Is it the inhospitable desert, or just somewhere remote from human habitation?

There is a choice among the meanings of wilderness, but the treatment accorded to the Greek-style scapegoat preempts other interpretations, so that it is generally assumed nowadays to refer to the true desert. Talmon[36] distinguishes three sub-groups in the geo-physical

---

[36] S. Talmon, "The Desert Motif in the Bible and in the Qumran Literature," in *Literary Studies in the Hebrew Bible: Form and Content: Collected Studies* (Jerusalem: Magnes, 1993) 216–54.

reference to מדבר. One, it designates agriculturally un-exploited areas, mainly in the foothills of South Palestine, which serve as grazing land for the flocks and cattle for the agrarian population; this would be delightful for a goat set free. Two, it is the borderland between cultivated land and desert, thinly inhabited spaces on the outskirts of a permanent settlement; this also would suit a goat well. Three, it is true desert, arid zones beyond the edge of the cultivated land, a place of utter desolation unfit for human habitation (Lam 5:9). Those who espouse the persecutory meaning of scapegoat have adopted unquestioningly the last, the arid zone of parched earth. This is one of the biased choices which supports the desert-demon interpretation and supports the other wobbly assumptions. The teacher responds to questioning by saying: "It makes sense that they should send it into the desert or kill it out there, since they are repudiat-ing the iniquities with which it is laden. If I were a horse, or an ancient Israelite, I would send it to a nasty place." But since we have rejected the desert demon Azazel and raised doubts about the transfer of sins, we can also hesitate before reading מדבר as a des-olate arid zone. The first meaning, the wilderness as simply the pas-ture which lies outside the camp, has sometimes been adopted along with the idea that the scapegoat rite originates with the nomadic period of Israel's early history. Problems about nomadism and about early Israel have caused it to be discredited.[37] But the goat set free, either in outlying pastures or in the outskirts of settlements, can still figure in an interpretation shorn of conjectural history. Goats are hardier than sheep. It could live well in outlying pastures, and since this reading of מדבר keeps the goat rite in line with the bird rite it is the most compatible with an argument based primarily on the Leviticus text.

Parallels in Genesis: Two Brothers

Having dispensed with the demon god, and also with the arid desert in which he reigns, we are in danger of making nonsense of the whole rite, since we have apparently removed the motive for sending

---

[37] Janowski and Wilhelm, "Der Bock, der die Sünden hinausträgt," in Janowski, Koch and Wilhelm (eds.), *Religionsgeschichtliche Beziehungen*, passim.

the goat away. If the goat is not carrying the sins of the people of Israel, why should it be driven out at all? We have paid some attention to how the book sets certain rites in parallel to each other. Until we have checked parallel themes of the Pentateuch it is premature to look for explanations in *1 Enoch*, or in Hittite, Greek, Babylonian, or Tibetan rites.

As ever, the right place to start is Genesis, where the theme of conspicuously uneven destinies occurs prominently. Isaac and Ishmael, Jacob and Esau, of two brothers one is chosen and the other is not. On this showing the Leviticus rite of atonement points to the central theological theme of the Pentateuch, a chosen people and the contrast with the people who have not been chosen. The Genesis stories are about the eldest sons, Ishmael and Esau, being superseded. Their respective younger brothers, Isaac and Jacob, destined before birth to the disciplines of the covenant, would parallel the goat or the bird on which the lot of the Lord fell. Ishmael and Esau would parallel the bird and the goat not chosen, set free in a remote uncultivated land. The analogy between these stories and the two goats on the Day of Atonement is obscured by the Hellenist focus on guilt carried by the scape-goat. But if we accept the teaching that guilt transferred is guilt expunged, the scape-goat is as guiltless as Ishmael or Esau. It is important to know that in Genesis each of the escaped persons goes free and receives honor.

Ishmael's mother has run away from her harsh mistress but is sent back. The angel of the Lord prophesies that her unborn son will have innumerable progeny, he will grow up to be a "wild ass of a man, his hand against every man and every man's hand against him" (Gen 17:20). "Wild ass" is not an insult in a warrior culture, nor a pejorative term. Here it is an animal which cannot be domesticated, like a lion "born free." The narrative makes a big point that Ishmael grew up beloved of both Abraham and God, for when Abraham prays for a favor on his behalf God replies:

> As for Ishmael, I have heard you; behold I will bless him and make him fruitful and multiply him exceedingly; and he shall be the father of twelve princes and I will make of him a great nation. But I will establish my covenant with Isaac, whom Sarah will bear to you at this season next year.... (Gen 17:20)

After Isaac was born, Sarah wants to get rid of Ishmael lest he prejudice the rights of her son. Abraham does not want to cast him out, but the Lord promises to look after the mother and child. Accordingly Abraham "sent her away" to the wilderness, the same word as that in Leviticus for "sending away" (שׁלח) and the same place as the scapegoat went to. Against the dichotomy of wilderness as place of demons and tabernacle as place of God, notice that "God was with the boy, and he grew up; he dwelt in the wilderness, became a bowman" (Gen 21:20). The Bible thus recognizes him as son of Abraham; he was circumcised by his father, his descendants were not idolaters. The implication is that God is with them, even though he has not given them a covenant.

The text contrasts freedom with the covenant. As between the goat that is for the Lord and the goat that gets away, in a religious context the higher destiny is obviously being consecrated. Normally only unfit animals are not sacrificed. The ancestor who fails to become a patriarch does quite well in his life. Ishmael and Esau do become great rulers. Ishmael died as a patriarch of the Arab peoples, Esau became the mighty ruler of Edom.

So it is suggested here that the two goats on the Day of Atonement stand for the two pairs of brothers, in each pair only one becomes a patriarch of Israel. Isaac was chosen before he was born, it was no merit on his part that earned him God's choice, and no lack of merit caused the unborn Ishmael to be sent away. It was also foretold of Esau or Jacob, before either was born, that the older would serve the younger (Gen 25:23). The strong parallel confirms that the idea of the wilderness in the scapegoat rite of the day of Atonement means precisely what is said, a place outside the habitations of Israel. Among the people who live in that wilderness some are descendants of Abraham and Isaac, but not of Jacob. They do not come under the covenant, but they are not for that reason unblessed.

It has been objected that the anthropologist herself has fallen face-first into the "white-cake fallacy" in taking the pair of goats for figures of pairs of patriarchs: "Pairs of brothers abound in Genesis. What about Cain and Abel, one of them was killed and the other favoured? The vaunted anthropological method seems to give free rein to the imagination!" In practice this is not so. The rule is to stick closely to the text, and to find the interpretation that fits most closely the editor's usage. There is nothing sacrificial, expiatory or covenantal about the killing of Abel and the exile of Cain. By the time Isaac and Jacob come into the Genesis story the covenant has been established. The scapegoat rite takes place in the precincts of the tabernacle, the contrast between sacrificed and not-sacrificed refers essentially to the formally instituted cult. Leviticus is strongly grounded in covenantal thinking. In the pairs indicated by this rule, the one who has been chosen and the one who gets away are distinguished by the fact that to one the hard rules of the covenant will apply, and not to the other. Cain and Abel are right outside this comparison because they lived before the covenant. And it should be noticed that this interpretation is compatible with an early one that has been displaced by the desert-demon thesis, the version of the goat that is to be dispatched, as accepted in the Septuagint and early rabbinic reading, giving rise to Tyndale's translation of "the scapegoat."

In some ways Joseph is a better parallel to the go-away-goat. When the first three sons of Leah had been passed over in the succession to Jacob, the eldest son of Rachel might well have been chosen as heir to Jacob instead of Judah. But the brothers got rid of him to Egypt, a land which was certainly very remote, though not inhospitable to him, and where he eventually succored his father, Jacob, and his brothers. Calum Carmichael's vivid analysis of the story of Joseph makes the patriarchs' sin of dispatching their brother the origin of the scape-goat rituals.

> The drama of the brothers' actions becomes a ritualized annual confession of the historic sin. The performance telescopes all the individual transgressions of all the Israelites living at any one time into the manageable form of their ancestor's offence.[38]

His emphasis is on the performance aspect of the rite, and on the confession bringing forgiveness, and on teaching the lessons of history on the Day of Atonement. This is the point at which the purification rite is transformed into a rite of affirming identity and dramatizing Israel's history. The scapegoat rite can recall other historic splittings and divisions among the patriarchs, and also perennial family quarrels about succession.

In the fifth century BCE the people of Judah were overwhelmed with political problems from neighbors who either had no common origins or others of the tribes of Israel who were descended from Joseph or other sons of Jacob. The Book of Numbers insisted that the sons of Joseph were co-heirs of the covenant. In that period it

---

[38] C. Carmichael, "The Origin of the Scapegoat Ritual," *VT* 50 (2000) 167–182.

could have been seen as a subversive teaching, because of hostility
to Samaria, where the Josephites had been established before the
Assyrian invasion, deportation and re-population of the province.
Among some of the many communities and sects of Judah in the
post-exilic period there was a tradition that associated the Day of
Atonement with Joseph. We find it in the second century BCE *Book
of Jubilees*. Its author believed that the sons of Jacob had the strong
duty to be at peace with one another, but absolutely forbade inter-
marriage or even contact with other peoples. He rewrote the Genesis
story of Dinah seduced by prince Hamor of Sechem (*Jubilees* 30),
saying nothing about Levi and Simeon perfidiously breaking Jacob's
promise of peace (Gen 49:5–7), and he evidently approved of their
destroying the foreign city. He changed the Genesis story of Esau
to justify enmity with Idumaea (35:1–27). Surprisingly, he was fair
to Ishmael (*Jub* 20:12–13), but left out his splendid funeral though
Genesis' full description shows how effectively God had been with
him in his life.

When it comes to Joseph, the author of *Jubilees* approved of a
Day of Atonement set aside every year to do penance for the sinfulness of the brothers who sold him into Egypt:

> For this reason it is ordained for the children of Israel that they should
> afflict themselves on the tenth of the seventh month—on the day that
> the news which made him weep for Joseph came to Jacob his father—
> that they should make atonement for themselves thereon with a young
> goat on the tenth of the seventh month, once a year, for their sins;
> for they had grieved the affection of their father regarding Joseph his
> son. And this day hath been ordained that they should grieve thereon
> for their sins, and for all their transgressions, and for all their errors,
> so that they might cleanse themselves on that day once a year. (*Jub.*
> 34:18–9)

The ceremony described in *Jubilees* is a straightforward sin-offering
with one goat, so either it comes from a very old source, before the
more elaborate rite of Leviticus 16, or later, the author having
dropped the scapegoat ceremony with the two goats and the casting of lots upon them. What is striking for the argument here advanced
is this connection between atonement and the tears of Jacob. The
sin which made Jacob weep was not covered by the atonements
done by Aaron for all the living members of the assembly of Israel.
There was something left over, the sins of the forefathers and the
tensions on the question of the children being punished for them.

The redactors' views of political obligations between the sons of Jacob were very sensitive. Numbers, Leviticus and Deuteronomy insist that the "sojourner" residing in the land has the right to join in the major rituals; none of these books forbids marriage with outsiders.[39] Their views would have been contested by certain contemporary groups, in circumstances described in the books of Ezra and Nehemiah. It would have been in keeping for the priestly editors to have set up the ritual of the second goat to salute the tribes who were not chosen. Speculatively, one of the meanings of the scapegoat rite could be to recall that Judah should be at peace with the descendants of the other sons of Jacob now living in the region. A mission of peace to separated brethren would be a worthy assignation. To perform it, the goat would have to be sent away, not to a shameful death, but an envoy formally dispatched to the outlying borders of Israel. This line of interpretation is strongly against the derogatory versions of the scapegoat's role widely accepted by scholars and sages. It certainly needs further justification.

The Commission

The laying of hands on the goat assigned it to a function. When an animal is offered for sacrifice, the giver must put one hand on its head; this is the rite of assigning it to God. But the scapegoat is not offered for sacrifice. Moreover, Aaron is told to perform the rite with both hands. This difference is not for nothing. It makes the assigning of the scapegoat more like the commissioning of the Levites. In the Book of Numbers the Israelites are told to bring the Levites forward to the Lord, and to lay hands[40] on the Levites, for their consecration to God's service (Num 8:9–10). Then the Levites, thus solemnly dedicated to their task, must similarly assign the bulls to be sacrificed by laying hands on the animals' heads (Num 8:12). The parallel between Levites and the sacrificial offerings is explicit. As the Levites were commissioned, so was the animal assigned to be

---

[39] I developed this view in my book on Numbers, *In the Wilderness*, (JSOTSup 158; Sheffield: JSOT, 1993); and in *Leviticus as Literature*, passim.

[40] The text is ambiguous, it allows of this action being in the plural either because many people are laying one hand on the Levites or because many people are doing it with both hands.

sacrificed, but the Levites were not going to be sacrificed, any more than the scapegoat. The two-handed laying on of hands commissioned the Levites for a role. The other parallel is the two-handed commissioning of Joshua. When Moses commissioned Joshua to succeed himself, God told him to:

> ... single out Joshua, son of Nun, an inspired man, and lay your hand upon him. *Have him stand* before Eleazar, the priest and before the whole community, and commission him in their sight. (Num 27:18–19)

> And Moses did as the Lord commanded him: he took Joshua and *caused him to stand* before Eleazar the priest and the whole congregation, and he laid his hands on him, and commissioned him as the Lord directed. (Num 27:22–28)

We conclude that by the same gesture the live goat was formally assigned to a commission before the Lord. But what was the commission? On the reading constructed above, its role was to represent the former kinsmen of Judah an envoy of peace to the surrounding peoples. To enact this role it had to go to live outside the habitations of Israel. Also, as a figure of Esau who (in Genesis 33) forgave Jacob, and of Joseph who forgave his brothers, the scapegoat who has lifted the past sins of Israel is charged to pardon Israel for driving it out, and charged to stay at peace in their border marches. Remember Jacob's bitter reproaches to Simeon and Levi who had made him odious to his neighbors: "My numbers are few and if they attack me I shall be destroyed, I and my household" (Gen 34:30). These are grave enough matters for a Day of Atonement.

Conclusion

To return to the original question, nothing much is left of the idea of a levitical scapegoating ceremony. One could suppose that random misreading is the natural course of interpretation. But the transformation of a consecrated animal into the persecutory meanings of scapegoat is more interesting. If the text of Leviticus suggests a rite of reconciliation on the Day of Atonement, that would explain why it came to be misread so drastically by people who did not believe in the possibility of reconciliation and were therefore ready to accept the Hellenized distortion. In the period of redaction, which here is taken to be the sixth and fifth centuries, the rite would have had international political implications. Repatriates from Babylon, who sympathized with the exclusionary religious policy of governors such as Ezra/Nehemiah and those priests who were on their side, would have been very hostile to the open liberal political stance of the priestly editors. In those circumstances a banal, foreign-inspired interpretation, even though full of contradictions, would have had the advantage of papering over the cracks between the political parties.

Wellhausen's perception of the priests as remote from the concerns of their congregation survives in a Protestant prejudice against the cult.[41] The argument outlined above rests on another version of the priestly editors' concerns: they were deeply interested in politics and morals,[42] but discreet, perhaps to a fault. Not wishing to cause trouble for their flock, they wrote deviously in parables, but dramatized their teaching in vivid rituals.

---

[41] S. Geller, *Sacred Enigmas: Literary Religion in the Hebrew Bible* (New York: Routledge, 1996).

[42] Douglas, *In the Wilderness*, passim.

TOWARDS AN INTEGRATED READING OF
THE DIETARY LAWS OF LEVITICUS

WALTER J. HOUSTON

Can Leviticus be read as a book? To do that we would have to establish some connection between the "ritual" laws which dominate most of it and the moral teaching which emerges towards the end. But to attempt this goes against the main current of both traditional Christian and scholarly interpretation, which tend to draw a precise distinction between bodies of ritual and moral teaching, and in various ways seek to downgrade the importance of the ritual. Wellhausen's idea of the priestly cult as a "pedagogic instrument of discipline . . . estranged from the heart"[1] could be said to have dominated twentieth-century interpretation, with incalculable effects on Jewish-Christian relationships.

Precisely to make such a connection is the object of Mary Douglas's most recent and most extensive venture into the study of the Hebrew Bible.[2] The goal of her argument, as stated at the outset, is to show that "the religion of Leviticus" is "not very different from that of the prophets which demanded humble and contrite hearts."[3]

Douglas, however, is not a lone pioneer. Various, predominantly Jewish, interpreters have argued for a relationship between ritual laws and morality. In ways varying according to the school of interpretation the laws symbolize, represent or enforce rules or ideals of morality and religion. Philo of Alexandria's was perhaps the first systematic attempt to interpret all the laws of the Pentateuch as parts of a single system, derived in his case from Platonic idealism; he was indeed anticipated by Pseudo-Aristeas in certain respects, but not in the systematic character of his work.[4] Recently, Jacob Milgrom has argued that the dietary rules—for most a particularly hard case—

---

[1] J. Wellhausen, *Prolegomena to the History of Ancient Israel* (Gloucester, MA: Peter Smith, 1973) 425.
[2] M. Douglas, *Leviticus as Literature* (Oxford: Oxford University Press, 1999).
[3] Ibid., 1.
[4] *Philo* (ed. and trans. F. H. Colson and G. H. Whitaker; LCL; 10 vols., with 2 supp. vols.; London: Heinemann, 1929–53).

should be interpreted as symbolizing, or even literally enforcing, ideals of compassion and justice.[5]

That is not to say that Jewish interpreters in general take this line. The recent important work of Jonathan Klawans[6] argues for a sharp separation in the Pentateuch between ritual impurity, as exemplified in Leviticus 12–15, and moral impurity, as in Leviticus 18 and 20, and denies that one can be read as metaphorical or symbolic of the other. Yet Klawans is forced to acknowledge that in the dietary laws the two systems appear to overlap.[7] In 11:43–5 and 20:24–6 the eating of unclean animals is seen as a threat to the holiness of Israel in the same way as the sexual sins prohibited in chapters 18 and 20.

My object in this article is to examine the interpretations of Philo, Milgrom and Douglas and evaluate their persuasiveness as attempts to view the ritual and morality of Leviticus as parts of a unified whole rather than as unrelated systems; and then to offer my own reflections on the issue. The dietary laws are the most obvious point of entry to the question, as is evident from the above summaries. In an earlier work, I considered what I called the "moral-symbolic" interpretation of the law of Leviticus 11 (and Deut 14:3–20),[8] and offered my own understanding of the context in which this might be understood as having ethical significance.[9] However, the publication of Douglas's work creates the need, and this article gives me the opportunity, to tackle this aspect of their interpretation at greater length, to bring in other laws in Leviticus, and to revise my own views.[10]

The writers whom I study here all present their interpretations as expressing the authorial intention discoverable in the laws. Philo speaks of Moses, Milgrom of P or H and Douglas of the Priestly Writer or Writers. Their ideas of the authorial intention of these laws may not be correct in all cases; but this does not necessarily mean that their proposals for interpretation are unpersuasive. Whether with

---

[5] See especially J. Milgrom, *Leviticus 1–16: A New Translation with Introduction and Commentary* (AB 3; New York: Doubleday, 1991) 704–42.

[6] J. Klawans, *Impurity and Sin in Ancient Judaism* (New York: Oxford University Press, 2000).

[7] Ibid., 31–32.

[8] W. Houston, *Purity and Monotheism* (Sheffield: JSOT, 1993) 74–78.

[9] Ibid., 253–58.

[10] See also W. J. Houston, "Food Laws," in *Dictionary of the Old Testament: Pentateuch* (Downers Grove, Il. IVP, forthcoming); W. J. Houston, review of M. Douglas, *Leviticus as Literature*, *JJS* 51 (2000) 323–6.

postmodern interpreters in general one denies that authorial intention is the sole locus of meaning, or with E. D. Hirsch[11] distinguishes
meaning, intended by the author, from significance, discovered by
the reader, the task is to find interpretation that is coherent, persuasive and illuminating.

Philo of Alexandria

It is a mistake to categorize Philo as a mere allegorist. He uses allegory, but it is only one of a battery of interpretative methods which
he deploys in order to demonstrate the rationality of Moses' law and
its moral and spiritual superiority to the laws of other nations. In
the treatise known generally by its Latin title *De Specialibus Legibus*[12]
Philo groups a great many of the particular laws of the Pentateuch
under the heading of one or other of the Ten Commandments as
detailed applications of it. Here most of the dietary laws fall under
the tenth commandment οὐκ ἐπιθυμήσεις (Exod 20:17 LXX). Philo's
omission of the object with its specification of "your neighbor's" wife
and property enables him to broaden the moral application. Desire
is a danger to the health and peace of the soul, an offence against
temperance rather than justice. He holds that Moses ordained the
dietary laws to restrain gluttony as the leading example of desire,[13]
encouraging frugality and taking a middle path between the auster-
ity of the Spartans and the luxury of the Sybarites.[14]

More specifically he believes that it is those animals with the rich-
est and most appetizing flesh, those therefore that are the most dangerous in encouraging over-indulgence, that are forbidden, and asserts
that this is true of the pig and of water creatures without scales (here
he must be thinking mainly of such delicacies as oysters and crayfish).[15]
Needless to say he does not stay to examine the deliciousness of
hyrax, hoopoe or hydra, since he has several other cards up his
sleeve. In truth this consideration seems to apply only to those forbidden foods that are actually eaten by other nations. One may well

---

[11] E. D. Hirsch, *Validity in Interpretation* (New Haven: Yale University Press, 1967).
[12] *Philo*, 8.6ff.
[13] Philo, *Spec. Leg.* 4.96
[14] Ibid., 4.102.
[15] Ibid., 4.100.

imagine Philo's Gentile friends teasing him with how much he is missing in not eating pork or oysters!

The flesh of carnivorous beasts is forbidden on the to us surprising grounds that to eat animals guilty of devouring human flesh might encourage the sense of vengeance and the passion of anger; and this excludes all carnivores by association.[16]

Although this naturally leads to asserting the inoffensiveness of herbivores, Philo does not leave it at that, but goes on to find meaning in the criteria set out in the law (Lev 11:3) for identifying permitted beasts.[17] He recognizes two such despite the three participles in the biblical Greek text. Both of them symbolize good educational method: chewing the cud is a symbol of memorizing, reflection and exercise, the cloven hoof of clear discrimination between vice and virtue. In a similar way he finds meaning successively in all the criteria found in Leviticus 11 and Deuteronomy 14.[18]

Obviously, the hermeneutic he uses here is allegory. Allegory is a means of interpreting texts, and it is Leviticus 11 and Deuteronomy 14 as texts that he is interpreting in this way rather than the commandment as commandment. The allegories are various and ad hoc, and like the one just quoted they do not all appear to have a direct relevance to the issue of desire and indulgence. But they are clearly subordinate within his discourse to the general point, to which he returns at the end of his discussion of the distinctions of animal kinds, that by withdrawing various species from use "like fuel from a fire," Moses σβέσιν τῆς ἐπιθυμίας ἀπεργάζεται.[19]

He proceeds to consider the prohibition of eating carrion (cf. Lev 17:15; 22:8).[20] The reasons he finds for this are in fact not directly related to the issue of desire. It is not fitting to eat flesh torn by wild beasts, because "a human being ought not to share a table with savage beasts"; while as for animals which have died of themselves, it is fitting (ἁρμόττον) that one should "respect the natural fate which has overtaken them" (αἰδουμένους τὰς φύσεως ἀνάγκας αἷς προκατελήφθη).[21]

---

[16] Ibid., 4.103–4.
[17] Ibid., 4.106–9.
[18] Ibid., 4.110–15.
[19] Ibid., 4.118.
[20] Ibid., 4.119–121.
[21] Ibid. The criticism of hunters which Philo adds here seems irrelevant at first, but the link with the law discussed appears to be the sharing of the flesh between the hounds and the hunters.

Philo goes on to deal with the blood prohibition (Lev 17:10–12).[22]
In keeping with his theme, he introduces this by noting that "certain Sardanapaluses," in the search for novel ways of self-indulgence,
have chosen to feed on strangled beasts.[23] Philo's explanation is based
on the biblical identification of the blood with the ψυχή, and this
on the basis of Gen 2:7 he sees as "divine spirit" (πνεῦμα θεῖον).
The fat prohibition, on the other hand, he traces back once again
to Moses' desire to teach self-control.

This brief survey of Philo's comments on the dietary laws[24] shows
very clearly that he understands them as teaching and enforcing the
central virtues of temperance, self-control and humanity. That they
embody these values he considers relatively self-evident: they do not
require allegorization. Allegory is rather a subordinate mode of interpretation which finds meaning in the details of the text. Its use is in
effect an admission that the moral sense of the laws is not evident
in the *details* of the law of Leviticus 11, and the fragmentation of the
interpretation thus imposed on it seriously detracts from what is otherwise a quite persuasive case.

Philo argues, of course, from the point of view of an affluent urban
intellectual, whose food comes from the market in ample sufficiency,
and whose temptation is the search for titillation by continual novelty of sensation. His is not a morality adapted to the half-starved
peasant who would be glad of any addition to his meager daily dish.
But it is evident that in this respect he stood much closer to the
authors of the biblical text, and certainly also to most of the readers of this essay. Obviously, the biblical writers did not have the
Hellenistic virtues as such in mind in compiling the laws. But it is
equally obvious that the disciplined appetite, which Philo takes the
laws to be teaching, is essential for their observance, even if not their
original purpose. Therefore the lesson he draws from them is a not
inappropriate application of the text to the lives of his contempo-
raries, and indeed ours also. However, as is underlined by his use of

---

[22] Ibid., 4.122–3.

[23] This shows, incidentally, that the Jewish and biblical conviction of the universal validity of this prohibition (cf. Gen 9:4) is well founded on general ancient
custom: it was normal among Greeks as among Jews to slaughter by slitting the
throat; see E. P. Sanders, *Judaism: Practice and Belief 63 BCE–66 CE* (London: SCM;
Philadelphia: Trinity, 1992) 216.

[24] Omitting his treatment of the non-Levitical kid law (Exod 23:19b; 34:26b;
Deut 14:21b) in *de Virtutibus* 142–4.

allegory, this moral purpose cannot be observed in the detailed categorization of animals as clean and unclean, abhorrent and permitted.

Philo is compelled to interpret the laws in this way because he is
an observant Jew, in whose life the dietary laws loom large, but also
a Hellenistic intellectual with a strongly moralistic sense of the way
in which the universe works and of the human place in it. It should
be no surprise that it is above all Jewish interpreters who have taken
a similar path: for instance Maimonides and S. R. Hirsch, as well
as Jacob Milgrom.[25] As it is Milgrom who has worked this out in
our day with the most thorough consistency, his approach will form
the next part of this study.

Jacob Milgrom

Jacob Milgrom has argued for the ethical significance of the dietary
laws since his article of 1963, "The Biblical Diet Laws as an Ethical
System"[26]—note the "system"!—and it is a line that he has developed
considerably in more recent work. His most substantial statement is
his "Comment" on Leviticus 11 in his commentary on Leviticus.[27]
Throughout this, Milgrom seeks to show that the biblical dietary
laws are a consistent whole, teaching the ethical value of respect for
life. It is divided into four sections, dealing respectively with the
blood prohibition, "ritual slaughter" in the Jewish sense, the forbidden
animals, and the kid prohibition. Only the first and third deal directly
with laws in Leviticus and will be treated here.

It is easy to see why Milgrom places the blood prohibition first.
Not only is it the most important of the dietary laws in the Bible,
seen as binding on all humanity, but it offers the clearest example
of what he wishes to prove, for its rationale is stated in the biblical
text several times over (Gen 9:4; Lev 17:11, 14; Deut 12:23): "the
blood is the life" of the animal. The implicit message is "Mankind

---

[25] Cf. Houston, *Purity and Monotheism*, 74–8.

[26] J. Milgrom, *Int* 17 (1963) 288–301; reprinted in J. Milgrom, *Studies in Cultic Theology and Terminology* (SJLA 36; Leiden: Brill, 1983) 104–18.

[27] Milgrom, *Leviticus 1–16*, 704–42. Large parts of this appear also in J. Milgrom, "Ethics and Ritual: The Foundations of the Biblical Dietary Laws," in E. B. Firmage, B. G. Weiss, and J. W. Welch (eds.), *Religion and Law: Biblical-Judaic and Islamic Perspectives* (Winona Lake, IN: Eisenbrauns, 1990) 159–91; parts of earlier works are also drawn on.

has a right to nourishment, not to life."[28] Milgrom interprets the prohibition in the context of the priestly narrative of creation and flood, in which human beings are intended at the start to be vegetarian (Gen 1:29), but after the flood are given the concession of animal food, but only on condition that they do not eat the blood (Gen 9:3–4); and he notes that in Israel's case, according to H (Lev 17:3–4), there is the further condition that a domestic animal must be brought to the sanctuary for sacrifice. If this is not done, the act is equivalent to murder, as Lev 17:4b distinctly states. Milgrom includes a detailed argument,[29] which need not detain us, that the atonement stated in v. 11 to be worked by the blood is for the crime of killing the animal itself.

But whereas Philo could assume that the ψυχή was a quasi-material substance conferred on the animal by God, withdrawn from human use and returned to God, Milgrom must assign the blood a purely symbolic significance as representing life, the gift of God which must be returned to God. "The human being must never lose sight of the fundamental tenet for a viable human society. Life is inviolable; it may not be treated lightly. Mankind has a right to nourishment, not to life. Hence the blood, the symbol of life, must be drained, returned to the universe, to God."[30] And there is a logical problem here in that in point of fact life has been taken when the animal is slain; it is only a symbol that is returned. However, the connection made both in Gen 9:3–4 and in Lev 17:4 between the prohibition of murder and the prohibition of eating blood makes it highly likely that the latter is, in priestly thought, symbolic of the value placed on the life of all living creatures. Plants are not seen as living in Hebrew; there is however an anomaly in the fact that the blood prohibition is not applied to fish or to locusts, which are not slaughtered in such a way as to expel the blood. This is in harmony with the likely origins of the prohibition in the sacrificial ritual,[31] in which these creatures never figured, but not with the ethical-theological grounding that it is given in these two passages. But broadly speaking, Milgrom can be seen to have a strong case on this issue.

---

[28] Milgrom, *Leviticus 1–16*, 713.
[29] Previously stated in J. Milgrom, "A Prolegomenon to Lev 17:11," *JBL* 90 (1971) 149–156; reprinted in Milgrom, *Studies in Cultic Theology*, 96–103.
[30] Milgrom, *Leviticus 1–16*, 713.
[31] Houston, "Food Laws."

I have briefly dealt with Milgrom's argument about Leviticus 11 before.[32] But it is worth setting out at slightly greater length. He notes that in all the places where forbidden foods are mentioned holiness is part of the interpretative framework: Exod 22:30; Lev 11:44–5; Lev 20:26; Deut 14:2, 21. And in the Bible holiness implies *imitatio Dei*, as in Lev 19:2 and 20:26 just cited: and it is clear from Leviticus 19 and other places that this implies an ethical ideal. But what ideal is implied here? As impurity (so he argues) stems from things which "symbolize the forces of death," so holiness "stands for the forces of life"[33]; "therefore, there can be no doubt that the list of prohibited animals must be part of the same unified and coherent dietary system whose undergirding rationale is reverence for life."[34] Hence the purpose of the limitation of permitted species is to limit Israelites' access to the animal kingdom.

There seems to be a failure of logic here. The unclean animals symbolize *the forces of death*, yet the purpose of forbidding access to them is to maintain reverence for life *by limiting the exploitation of life*. Either of the two italicized phrases may be capable of making sense of the law as a consistent principle, though, as I have shown, neither accounts for its details; but taken together they are hopelessly contradictory. And the contradiction remains even if one does not accept Milgrom's understanding of the unclean as symbolizing the forces of death. As his student David Wright[35] points out, "The laws talk about inedible animals (in particular, their carcasses) in very negative terms"; he mentions the use of the terms טמא, שקץ and תועבה. Israelites are exhorted not to "make themselves abominable" (אל־תשקצו את־נפשתיכם) with teeming things or make themselves unclean with them (Lev 11:43). "This negative characterization of nonpermitted animals seems to me not to support a desire to inculcate a reverence for animal life." Israel is to maintain holiness by avoiding creatures as unclean or abominable, not by reverencing them as holy. The idea that animals could be understood as holy is well known in Israel's environment.[36] There are obvious reasons why this

---

[32] Houston, *Purity and Monotheism*, 76–78.
[33] Milgrom, *Leviticus 1–16*, 733.
[34] Ibid.
[35] D. P. Wright, "Observations on the Ethical Foundations of the Biblical Dietary Laws: A Response to Jacob Milgrom," in *Religion and Law: Biblical-Judaic and Islamic Perspectives* (Winona Lake, IN: Eisenbrauns, 1990) 197.
[36] Houston, *Purity and Monotheism*, 212–14.

idea should be unacceptable to the writers of the Hebrew Bible: but without such an idea it is difficult to see how a law mandating the avoidance of particular animals could inculcate reverence for life.

Further, as Wright also points out, no restrictions on permitted species can be said to encourage reverence for life if there is no restriction on the number of permitted animals one is allowed to kill. Milgrom's reply[37] is that the average Israelite could not afford to eat meat often. My response to this was: "In that case the *average* Israelite did not need the lesson taught by the law, but the rich did!"[38]—and of course they would not learn it from this law.

If the attainment of holiness which is the goal of the law in Leviticus 11 is held to involve *imitatio Dei*, it would seem to make more sense to argue that Israel is commanded to avoid what is unworthy of the presence of God. It is notable that the Holiness text which provides the parenetic conclusion to Leviticus 11, vv. 43–45 (also Lev 20:25), intermingles the terms שׁקץ and טמא which the main body of the text uses in discrete pericopes. It may be argued that for this editor there is no distinction between them:[39] all flesh to be avoided is unclean, and makes the eater unclean, and therefore unfit for the presence of God in the sanctuary. At least it is clear that this is a very natural way to read the passage and consequently the chapter as a whole. *Why* the animals to be avoided are seen in this way is another question, and I can only refer the reader to my earlier work for an attempt at an answer.[40]

Milgrom can hardly be said to have proved his case that the biblical dietary laws form an ethical *system*. It is not demonstrable that all the laws teach reverence for life. But that that lesson may be drawn from some of them is an entirely reasonable way to read them.

Mary Douglas

Over many years and through repeated and varying attempts at interpretation, it has been Mary Douglas's concern to place "the abominations of Leviticus," to quote the title of her first essay on

---

[37] Milgrom, *Leviticus 1–16*, 735.
[38] Houston, *Purity and Monotheism*, 77, n. 1.
[39] For the distinction in the body of the text, see Milgrom, *Leviticus 1–16*, 656–59.
[40] Houston, *Purity and Monotheism*, esp. 181–200.

the subject,[41] in a broader framework of interpretation. Her latest work takes up the entire book of Leviticus, and in it "the main new feature of this interpretation is the attitude to animal life. In this new perspective, Leviticus has to be read in line with Ps 145:8–9: the God of Israel has compassion for all he has made."[42]

This is a very firm statement of moral significance. In fact, as we shall see, her interpretation of Leviticus 11 in this book is a little more complicated than that. But it certainly contrasts with her earlier attempts, which could not generally be said to argue for moral significance in the rules.[43] It is the more striking that, when after a number of years she returned to the question in the early 90s, this was the main burden of her work. In the meantime she had become convinced that ethnographic parallels were of no use in interpreting the purity rules of Leviticus. Whereas in societies studied by anthropologists purity rules serve to discriminate between people and to ground accusations through which feuds can be carried on and groups excluded, in the Bible nothing of this appears: impurity is a fate that happens to all, and it can be purified by simple measures.[44] The rules in Leviticus have no social function, and have to be treated from a literary point of view (hence the title of her latest work) as analogical anticipations of the moral teaching which is developed in the latter part of the book.

The negative aspect of this assessment is dubious. Douglas is not comparing like with like. On the one hand we have a systematic presentation of the purity rules of a society; on the other anthropological investigation of the practical working of purity rules in daily life.

However, it is the positive assertion that concerns us here. In her 1993 essay,[45] the key to the entire scheme is the problem of predation, the existence of violence and bloodshed and injustice in God's creation. Like Milgrom and me[46] she takes note of the vegetarian

---

[41] In M. Douglas, *Purity and Danger: An Analysis of the Concepts of Pollution and Taboo* (London: Routledge, 1966) 41–57.

[42] M. Douglas, *Leviticus as Literature*, 1.

[43] Douglas, *Purity and Danger*, 41–57; M. Douglas, *Natural Symbols: Explorations in Cosmology* (2nd ed.; London: Barrie and Jenkins, 1973) 60–63; idem, "Deciphering a Meal" in M. Douglas, *Implicit Meanings* (London: Routledge, 1975) 249–75; idem, "Self-evidence," in ibid., 276–318.

[44] M. Douglas, "The Forbidden Animals in Leviticus," *JSOT* 59 (1993) 3–23, especially 7–8; cf. *Leviticus as Literature*, vii–viii.

[45] Douglas, "The Forbidden Animals in Leviticus."

[46] Houston, *Purity and Monotheism*, 253–58.

utopia in Gen 1:29–30, and relates to this the blood prohibition and
the exclusion of predators, as in "Deciphering a Meal." However,
she notes that this does not cover all the forbidden animals: the
water creatures, the swarming creatures of the air and the creeping
things of the ground remain to be explained. In a bold move, she
makes these "stand for the victims of predation."[47] Harking back to
her 1966 analysis that saw something deficient in the animals that
failed to meet the criteria, she argues that these creatures should be
seen as damaged or blemished; and Lev 24:19 provides the proof
that blemish can be understood as the result of assault. These are
creatures that labor under unfair burdens, "the chameleon with its
lumpy face, the high humped tortoise and beetle, and the ants labor-
ing under their huge loads. Think of the blindness of worms, and
bats, the vulnerability of fish without scales. Think of their human
parallels, the labourers, the beggars, the orphans and the defence-
less widows."[48] These animals, then, represent the poor and the vulnerable, and it is a matter of compassion to spare them.

Douglas attempts to avoid the charge of Philonic allegorizing by
pointing out that "the permitted animals do not stand for any
virtues . . . and the forbidden animals do not represent vices in their
own bodies, but the effects of vicious actions on the part of others."[49] However, in a characteristic phrase, she says that the purity
code "multiplies allegories of justice for all."[50] Philonic it may not
be, but allegorical the proposed interpretation clearly is. Readings
of this kind cannot be proved or disproved, only felt as convincing
or unconvincing. But it is difficult to fit the uncleanness of eight
creeping things (Lev 11:29–30) into this scheme, or the polluting
effect of them all implied in 11:43–44. I know of no one whom this
interpretation has convinced, and Douglas herself seems to be no
exception, for it is barely nodded to in *Leviticus as Literature*, her work
of 1999, to which we now turn.

Douglas deals with the rules of Leviticus 11 in two successive chapters in this book, occupying over 40 pages.[51] The two chapters deal
with different parts of Leviticus 11 and suggest that entirely different

---

[47] Douglas, "The Forbidden Animals in Leviticus," 18.
[48] Ibid., 22.
[49] Ibid., 23.
[50] Ibid.
[51] Douglas, *Leviticus as Literature*, 134–75.

principles underlie them. The first[52] deals with land animals (Lev 11:2b–8, 24–45). Douglas's treatment of the rules concerning these is dominated by two concepts: the analogy of body, table and altar, an idea which has often appeared in her works;[53] and the covenant. The covenant is interpreted as a feudal relationship. The people of Israel and their herds and flocks are within the covenant (Exod 20:8; 13:2ff.), protected by God on condition of their loyalty. "No one is allowed to harm God's people or use God's things, nor must his followers harm each other, or harm the other living beings on his territory without his express permission. This he gives [only, it is implied] for the killing of herd animals in sacrifice, and use of their carcasses."[54] No meat is eaten ("theoretically") except at God's table,[55] hence the act of eating is an act through which loyalty may be shown. "The table, and all who eat at it, and everything that has been cooked for them to eat, are under the same law of holiness,"[56] so that "the rules which protect the purity of the tabernacle are paralleled by rules which protect the worshipper,"[57] and what defiles the one defiles the other also. The full meaning of the rules, Douglas argues,[58] does not emerge until later in the book: in Leviticus 17 we learn that the dietary laws "support the law against unconsecrated killing," and the animal corpse pollution rules emerge as an example of the reverence for life also expressed on a human level in Lev 19:16: "Thou shalt not stand upon [profit from] another's blood."[59]

From the two basic principles Douglas derives both the blood prohibition and the rules of cleanness and uncleanness in animals. According to Lev 17:11, the blood of sacrificial animals is provided for the protection of the worshippers by atonement, as the condition for their use of the blood-drained flesh. And this teaches the sanctity of life (compare Milgrom), since the life is in the blood.[60]

On the other hand, the eating or touching of the carcasses of animals outside the covenant is a challenge to the honour of God. The

---

[52] Ibid., 134–51.
[53] E.g., in Douglas, *Implicit Meanings*, 263ff.
[54] Douglas, *Leviticus as Literature*, 136.
[55] Ibid., 149. The reference to Lev 17:3–4 is not explicit, but necessary.
[56] Ibid., 138.
[57] Ibid., 139.
[58] Ibid., 151.
[59] As quoted by Douglas, ibid.
[60] Ibid., 137.

flesh of such animals would defile the altar, and hence it defiles the
body of the worshipper. Douglas develops her feudal analogy by
comparing the language of contagious impurity with the discourse
of honour.[61] Any insult to the honour of God's people or things is
also an insult to him, and impurity such as is implied in the eating
or touching of unclean things is such an insult.

Thus so far as the rules about land animals are concerned, Douglas's
interpretation makes them bearers of the moral values of loyalty and
honour. There are significant insights here, but there are also problems. There are undoubtedly analogies between the discourses of
purity and honour, but the latter is also found in the Hebrew Bible,[62]
in religious contexts as well as secular, for example in Exod 20:7,
and the entirely different vocabulary of purity damages the analogy.
Impurity in P has a material character which is difficult to ignore
or dismiss, as Douglas attempts to do,[63] when the non-material language of honour is known to have been available.

Again, that the clean beasts in Leviticus 11 are based on the analogy of the sacrificial animals is an important principle which was
proposed by Firmage[64] and developed by me.[65] But Douglas applies
the principle in a crude and demonstrably inaccurate manner. In
more than one place she appears to say that Leviticus permits only
sacrificial animals, or only domestic animals, to be eaten, despite
referring to Lev 17:13 almost in the same breath. She makes a point
of contrasting Deuteronomy's list of permissible game animals (Deut
14:5) with the lack of any mention of them in Leviticus, and adds,
"Were Leviticus explicitly to permit secular slaughter, it would undermine the covenant basis of the Levitical rules constraining humans
from eating animals that they have not reared."[66] This is muddled:
the prohibition of slaughter away from the altar in Lev 17:3–4 does
not exclude the slaughter of game animals in the field, as v. 13
shows. That Lev 11:2–3 gives no list of permissible animals, but only
a set of criteria, inescapably implies that *all* animals that meet the

---

[61] Ibid., 146–49.

[62] See a number of the essays in *Semeia* 68: *Honor and Shame in the World of the Bible* (1996).

[63] Douglas, *Leviticus as Literature*, 148.

[64] E. B. Firmage, "The Biblical Dietary Laws and the Concept of Holiness," in J. A. Emerton (ed.), *Studies in the Pentateuch* (VTSup 41; Leiden: Brill, 1990) 177–208.

[65] Houston, *Purity and Monotheism*, 114–20, 230–34. Neither of us receives an acknowledgement from Douglas.

[66] Douglas, *Leviticus as Literature*, 140; cf. also 139.

criteria, domestic or wild, are permissible. Douglas's idea of the covenantal restriction of the table therefore needs to be reformulated to allow for this.

Despite such reservations, Douglas's general understanding of the rules as intended to ensure that the Israelite at table honours covenant loyalty to God is surely perfectly sound. What seems strange is that Douglas does not extend this understanding to the whole chapter, but explains the rules about water and air creatures (Lev 11:9–23) in a different and less satisfactory way.[67] They are certainly distinguished by their use of שקץ rather than טמא, as she emphasizes, following Milgrom,[68] but both terms are used in the rhetorical conclusion to the chapter (vv. 43–45) which makes the rules expressions of holiness. Douglas is in fact embarrassed by this passage, and inclined to call in aid source criticism, which she generally rejects, to dismiss it.[69] However, her eventual solution is to suggest that "It is fully in accord with Leviticus' literary style to weave together two strands, one about the cult, one about life, and to bring them together at the end. It consistently teaches that both cult and life come under the rubric of holiness."[70] This is hard to apply to Leviticus 11. טמא is a cultic term, but all sections of the chapter are "about life," and they are closely similar in structure.

One of the difficulties in the interpretation of Leviticus 11 is that it appears to condemn as "abominable" or "unclean" creatures which are all pronounced "good" in Genesis 1. We saw above that David Wright uses this fact as an argument against Milgrom's view of the law as teaching reverence for life. It is hard to evade the pejorative force of טמא, but Douglas argues for translating שקץ in a non-pejorative way.[71] The designation does not point to any inherent character of the creatures in themselves, but simply marks them out to be strictly avoided by Israelites. However, unless vv. 43–45 are excluded from the interpretation of the chapter, it must be taken into account that the root is used in a clearly pejorative way there. According to Douglas, they are to be avoided not because they are bad, but primarily because of a good quality: their teeming fertility.

---

[67] Ibid., 152–75.
[68] Milgrom, *Leviticus 1–16*, 656–59.
[69] Douglas, *Leviticus as Literature*, 156.
[70] Ibid.
[71] Ibid., 166–69.

She concentrates in her treatment of Lev 11:9–23 almost exclusively on the references to swarming things. She contemptuously dismisses the usual explanations of the unclean birds as moralistic (this would have to apply to her own explanations right down to 1993!), yet offers nothing to put in their place. As far as birds are concerned, her only contribution in this book is an attempt to show that the anger of the Lord in Numbers 11 is accounted for by quails counting as "swarming things."[72] It is generally agreed that the phrase שרץ העוף in Lev 11:20–23 refers to flying insects, and Douglas offers no adequate justification for including quails, whose resemblance to other commonly eaten birds such as partridges is obvious.

She does deal briefly[73] with water creatures without fins and scales, essentially in the same way as in her 1993 essay:[74] their lack of natural protection and easy locomotion makes them vulnerable, so that their prohibition is a measure of divine protection. She then goes on to point out that "they are all swarmers." So it would seem (Lev 11:10); but unfortunately for Douglas's argument, so are those with fins and scales: as I have shown,[75] in that verse "all the swarming things of the water and all the living creatures in water" is a hendiadys, simply describing all water creatures. All water creatures are swarmers, but only some are without fins and scales and therefore to be avoided.

This is fatal to Douglas's attempt to deal with all swarming things as a single category, which I have criticized before.[76] In her new book, the argument is that their teeming is a sign of fertility and thereby "antithetical to consecrated things."[77] On this ground she also explains the fact that leaven and honey are not acceptable as altar offerings.[78] Why is fertility thus the antithesis of consecration? Douglas's argument is here very obscure, and all I can do is to present it in her own words: "Remember that the holy of holies is traditionally a place of fertility. There can be protection for, but no covenant with, teeming things. If they cannot be offered to God, it

---

[72] Ibid., 169–71.
[73] Ibid., 168–69.
[74] See above.
[75] Houston, *Purity and Monotheism*, 104–5. On p. 105, lines 4 and 8, for נפש read שרץ.
[76] Houston, *Purity and Monotheism*, 104–6.
[77] Douglas, *Leviticus as Literature*, 163.
[78] Ibid., 163–66.

is that they are his already: 'All that moves is mine' (Ps 50:11), which is: 'All that has life in it is mine.'"[79] The reference to Psalm 50 is particularly odd, since the grounds quoted are part of an argument against the sacrifice of the normal sacrificial animals. If "*all* that has life in it is mine," how are שרץ specifically referred to? A rather more comprehensible version of the same argument (if it is the same) appears a few pages later.[80] "Eating the teeming creatures offends God's avowed concern for fertility. The ancient association of the temple with fertility supports the idea that harming the teeming creatures is wrong." This comes close to her earlier argument that the avoidance of these creatures should be seen as an expression of compassion, and before the end of the chapter she appears to have reverted to this, though without resurrecting the idea that the animals to be avoided are symbols of victimhood. "Covenant and fertility are two contrasted principles" whose rules express God's justice and his compassion respectively.[81] The main problem with this, apart from the difficulty of applying it to *all* that is שרץ, is that the more fertile a species is, the less it would appear to need protection.

As I have suggested, it would seem better in view of the chapter's peroration (Lev 11:43–45) to bring all the creatures with which it deals (that is, all creatures, as Douglas often stresses)[82] under her first principle, which is there explicitly stated. It is closely paralleled by my own formulation[83] that the function of the law in Leviticus is to preserve the people's holiness in the sense of their dedication to their one God, Yahweh. It is important for our present purpose to understand that this *religious* idea, as we would understand it, is also an *ethical* idea. Loyalty to one's superior is a key moral duty in most ancient societies. That it may not be such for many modern people will certainly make it difficult for them to read Leviticus as a work with an ethical message, since it is in fact the book's dominant demand. But those who do not wish to have their understanding of morality challenged will not read ancient literature, or only "against the grain."

---

[79] Ibid., 163.
[80] Ibid., 168.
[81] Ibid., 174.
[82] E.g. ibid., 139–40.
[83] Houston, *Purity and Monotheism*, 248–53.

An Attempt at an Integrated Reading

How could this ethical understanding of the dietary laws be more broadly supported? It is apparent that the interpretations of the dietary laws found in Lev 11:43–45; 17:11, 14; 20:24b–6 belong to the Holiness stratum.[84] And it is clear that this body of practical theology (despite Klawans)[85] draws no distinction such as we are used to between "ritual" and "moral" commands. All it recognizes are expressions of holiness. It is particularly notable that the parenetic conclusion of Leviticus 20 (vv. 22–26), which lists penalties for mainly sexual crimes, employs the symbol of the distinction between clean and unclean flesh to underline the distance to be kept from the immoral practices of the ejected nations. The condemnations of sexual offences in Leviticus 18 and 20 have themselves been understood by modern interpreters as ritual in character, or belonging to the purity code,[86] in that they are not supported by considerations of the harm the offences might cause, but by expressions indicating the ways in which they symbolically threaten the fundamental structure of society. Purity language is used extensively in the peroration in 18:24–30 as well as in 20:22–26: Israel is defiled by consuming unclean flesh as by violating the sexual code. But the latter passage uses the positive encouragement to holiness as well as the negative warning against impurity. And this language of holiness, as well as echoing 11:43–45, has in the meanwhile been introduced in 19:1ff., where it supports a series of commands normally seen by modern interpreters as "moral" or concerned with justice and righteousness.

We cannot simply say that the dietary commands are "symbolic" of the call to holiness more literally fulfilled by moral commands. Where would we place the sexual codes in such a categorization, foreign as it is to the material? All the commands warn against literal defilement,[87] admittedly understood in a broader way than in Leviticus 12–15, and exhort to holiness. All of them, I would argue,

---

[84] Cf. Milgrom, *Leviticus 1–16*, 13–14, 696; Houston, *Purity and Monotheism*, 248; I. Knohl, *The Sanctuary of Silence: The Priestly Torah and the Holiness School* (Minneapolis: Fortress Press, 1995) 69. With Knohl, I take this as a redactional layer in P rather than a pre-existing "code."

[85] Klawans, *Impurity and Sin.*

[86] Cf. L. W. Countryman, *Dirt, Greed and Sex: sexual ethics in the New Testament and their implications for today* (London: SCM, 1989) 28–39.

[87] Here I am in complete agreement with Klawans (*Impurity and Sin,* esp. 32–36).

inform Israel how they may live in such a way as to be in conformity with Yahweh's ordering of the cosmos.

Thus, we have already noted that obedience to the dietary code
by avoidance of the unclean may be understood, following Lev
11:43–45, as an expression of loyalty to the covenant Lord, loyalty
which is particularly demanded of Israel to Yahweh, but which is
of the same character as is recognized as a universal duty by all.
Lev 18:24–25 and 20:23 imply that the sexual code is not special
to Israel, but should have been followed by the nations who preceded them in the land. The motivations in Leviticus 18 mark out
each offence as contrary to natural order in its own way: incest
transgresses the boundaries of family structure marked by the designa-
tions of the male family member to whom the "nakedness" of each
of the female members belongs; the other offences are תועבה, תבל
and so on.

Now though the dietary code, except for the blood prohibition,
is presented as a peculiar ordinance for Israel, there is evidence that
the editors may have understood it as deriving from universal categories in the same way. The writer (usually referred to as J) in Gen
7:2 assumes that the distinctions of clean and unclean beasts with
which he was familiar were known in the primeval period (and for
birds cf. Gen 8:20). At least one ancient Hebrew writer, then, regarded
them as universal.[88] Again, in Deuteronomy this code is brought
under the rubric of eating תועבה (Deut 14:3), which I have interpreted, following Weinfeld,[89] as anything which would offend the
sensibility of the well brought up person.[90] This is likely to refer to
people of all nations, since, as I have shown,[91] the distinction of
acceptable and forbidden meats closely follows custom, especially
sacrificial custom, well established in the surrounding region by the
Iron Age. Thus, although it cannot be established with assurance, it
seems very likely that when the Holiness writers use expressions like
אל־תשקצו את־נפשתיכם (Lev 11:43, cf. 20:25) or לא תטמאו את־נפשתיכם
(11:44), they imply the existence of some objective (not necessarily
material) character of שקץ or of טמאה in the creature by which the

---

[88] Cf. Houston, *Purity and Monotheism*, 145–48.
[89] M. Weinfeld, *Deuteronomy and the Deuteronomic School* (Oxford: Oxford University
Press, 1972) 226.
[90] Houston, *Purity and Monotheism*, 59–60.
[91] Ibid., 124–80.

eater may be affected. These properties take their places in a cosmological pattern and not merely a legal one.

Moving now into a broader context, how would this square with the fact, emphasized by Douglas,[92] that all creatures are declared good by God himself in Genesis 1? Yes, all are good, but *each for its own purpose*. Some are fit for human food, following the concession made by God in Gen 9:3; others are not, though they have their own functions in the divine economy. It is only when each creature observes its place in the cosmic order, and humanity, in dominion over them all, preserves the place of each, that justice and harmony can be maintained in the world. This is clearly not the full harmony, free of violence or predation, envisaged primevally in Gen 1:26–30 or eschatologically in Isa 11:6–9, but it is an acceptable substitute. It is also in accordance with this that human beings are forbidden to taste blood: for the life of each creature, which resides in the blood, is reserved to God its maker alone. In the Holiness system this is recognized every time an animal is slaughtered for food: cattle, sheep and goats are taken to the door of the tent of meeting (Lev 17:3–4) as an offering to Yahweh and their blood placed on the altar; the blood of game animals is deliberately covered (Lev 17:13–14).

The priestly historian's projection of a primitive vegetarianism as God's intention in creation (Gen 1:29),[93] and his school's emphasis on the gift of life, embodied in the blood, as a divine prerogative, show that they did understand that eating cannot be separated from morality, that human appetites need to be restrained, and that God's creatures must be treated with respect. At least the final intention of the text is to place the dietary rules in a moral framework.

We thus arrive at the conclusion that the dietary laws are part of a much broader structure of moral and cosmological thinking, and serve to maintain not only the specific holiness of Israel in relation to Yahweh, but cosmic righteousness or right order in general, in the sense developed by H. H. Schmid.[94] In this they take their place

---

[92] Douglas, *Leviticus as Literature*, 166.

[93] See Houston, *Purity and Monotheism*, 253–58. Cf. also A. Marx, *Les offrandes végétales dans l'ancien Testament* (VTSup 57; Leiden: Brill, 1994) 139–49.

[94] Cf. H. H. Schmid, *Gerechtigkeit als Weltordnung: Hintergrund und Geschichte der alttestamentlichen Gerechtigkeitsbegriffes* (BHT 40; Tübingen: J. C. B. Mohr [Paul Siebeck], 1968).

alongside the social injunctions of Leviticus 19, the sexual ones of 18 and 20, and the ritual ones of 17 and 21–23. The distinction so characteristic of Christian interpretation, between ritual and moral, does not do justice to the character of this material. The dietary laws do not symbolize, but exemplify, justice and righteousness. In their broad contentions, Philo, Milgrom and Douglas may be accounted correct.

We have not had the space in this essay to extend the investigation to the purity laws of Leviticus 12–15, the primary context of the ritual impurity which Klawans declares quite unconnected with the moral impurity of the Holiness Code. It would, however, be possible to develop an argument along the above lines, that there is a connection at the deep level of cosmic structure.

This conclusion does not, admittedly, enable us to read Leviticus easily as moral guidance for the present age. We have been taught to separate "facts" (cosmology) from "values" (ethics) and to understand morality as a human creation relative to particular societies. But maybe that is not the point. Precisely because the "values" of Leviticus are relative to ancient Judaism, in reading it we enter a moral world quite strange to us, but not so strange as not to be able to challenge our own unexamined assumptions. This may be an exercise necessary even for the very survival of the world of creatures and of the human race among them, which does require a moral (and not merely "factual") understanding of the coherence and interdependence of the world and all its creatures—what the World Council of Churches has called "the integrity of creation." Perhaps the most important moral lesson we need to learn is that to preserve the "integrity of creation" we must discipline our appetites, place limits upon our desires, even more now that there appears to be no limit to our power to satisfy them. And that is the lesson of the dietary laws of Leviticus as interpreted by Philo of Alexandria!

WHAT CONNECTS THE INCEST PROHIBITIONS WITH THE OTHER PROHIBITIONS LISTED IN LEVITICUS 18 AND 20?

Adrian Schenker

Question and Method

In Leviticus 18 and 20 incest prohibitions stand together with other prohibitions, mainly of a sexual nature, but not exclusively so. What led the author or redactors to put together precisely these prohibitions?

We can think of two answers. Either they were put together under a common point of view concerning the contents—to be discovered— or with an arbitrary or associative compilation without any common criterion as far as the contents are concerned. Both opinions are found in research.[1]

The guiding hypothesis of the present examination is the supposition that the single precepts and their systematic order in Leviticus 18 and 20 are rationally transparent, because ancient oriental law in general and biblical law in particular follow rational principles,[2] which means that they are logical and can be understood. Hence it

---

[1] The literary unity of both lists, however, is rarely defended; we find it in C. F. Keil and F. Delitzsch, "Leviticus," in *Biblical Commentary on the Old Testament* (Clark's Foreign Theological Library; Edinburgh: T&T Clark, 1885) 123, 126; J. P. Lange, *Leviticus oder das dritte Buch Mosis* (Theologisch-homiletisches Bibelwerk; Leipzig: Velhagen u. Klasing, 1877) 194; D. Hoffmann, *Das Buch Leviticus* (vol. 2; Berlin: Poppelauer, 1906), and, recently, A. Ruwe, *"Heiligkeitsgesetz", und "Priesterschrift": literaturgeschichtliche und rechtssystematische Untersuchungen zu Leviticus* (FAT 26; Tübingen: J. C. B. Mohr [Paul Siebeck], 1999): "In der vorliegenden Untersuchung soll ... durch konsequent strukturbezogene Analyse gezeigt werden, dass auch das Heiligkeitsgesetz eine hohe systematische Kohärenz aufweist," 162ff., 224–29: this is valid also for Lev 18 and 20; J. Milgrom, *Leviticus 17–22* (AB 3A; New York: Doubleday, 2000) 1516–17. Most of the commentators reckon with successive additions to and redactions of both lists; e.g. among the most recent commentators, J. P. Budd, *Leviticus* (NCB; Grand Rapids: Eerdmans, 1996) 252; K. Grünwaldt, *Das Heiligkeitsgesetz Levitikus 17–26* (BZAW 271; Berlin: de Gruyter, 1999) 34–39.

[2] A. Schenker, *Versöhnung und Widerstand. Bibeltheologische Untersuchung zum Strafen Gottes und der Menschen, besonders im Lichte von Exodus 21–22* (SBS 139; Stuttgart: Verl. Kath. Bibelwerk, 1990) 15–23, 66–73; E. Otto, *Wandel der Rechtsbegründungen in der Gesellschaftsgeschichte des antiken Israel. Eine Rechtsgeschichte des "Bundesbuches" Ex XX 22–XXIII 13* (StudBib 3; Leiden: Brill, 1988) 66–68.

is methodologically necessary for the interpretation to look in every case for an intelligible principle, although such seems at first sight to be lacking, and also for methodological reasons, to avoid such terms as "archaic," "magic" and similar expressions in order to explain biblical commandments.

With this method the question that will be resolved here is what the literary unity of the lists of prohibitions of Leviticus 18 and 20 consists of. I do not exclude but include redactional changes and developments in these chapters, for this methodological principle is valid for the first authors as well as for redactors, since both stand in a process of tradition, which in both its starting point and in its course is indebted to rationality.[3]

Two Groups of Forbidden Sexual Relations in Leviticus 18:6–18

Leviticus 18 consists of a series of fourteen prohibitions of sexual intercourse, which are usually called incest prohibitions, and which are placed under a heading that is the only general prohibition, v. 6, and which comprehends all subsequent single prohibitions (vv. 6–18). This series is followed by five further mixed prohibitions (vv. 19–23). The whole lot is surrounded by a redactional frame (vv. 1–5, 24–30) embedding the chapter in the overall narrative of the Pentateuch. The series of fifteen prohibitions (vv. 6–18) is clearly structured: the general principle or heading in v. 6 is followed by two sequences of ten and four prohibitions of sexual intercourse (vv. 7–16, 17–18). The speech is directed to the Israelite *paterfamilias* as a man who may still have his mother or stepmothers, that is wives of his polygamous father (vv. 7–8), sisters (v. 9), granddaughters (v. 10), half-sisters (v. 11), aunts by the father's or mother's side (vv. 12–14), daughters-in-law (v. 15) and sisters-in-law (v. 16). With those women he is not allowed to have sexual intercourse ("to uncover their nakedness").

The forbidden relations split into the two groups of vv. 7–16 and 17–18.[4] The first one mentions ten women the *paterfamilias* is not allowed to marry, neither in monogamous nor in polygamous marriage, because they are related by blood (as mother, v. 7, sister, v. 9,[5]

---

[3] Cf. n. 1 about the commentators who suppose redactions.
[4] Different classifications are arrived at by Milgrom, *Leviticus 17–22*, 1523–27.
[5] Milgrom, *Leviticus 17–22*, 1527–28, seems to exclude the sister, because in v. 9

granddaughter, v. 10, half-sister, v. 11, aunt by the father's or mother's side, vv. 12–13) or by marriage (as stepmother, v. 8, married aunt, v. 14, daughter-in-law, v. 15 or sister-in-law, v. 16). Consanguinity and relationship by marriage are obstacles, when they are of first or second degree (second degree as granddaughter in v. 10 and as aunts in vv. 12–14, first degree everywhere else). The definition of the natural relationship and of the relationship by marriage includes the direct line (as mother, v. 7, as stepmother, v. 8, as granddaughter, v. 10, as daughter-in-law, v. 15) as well as the collateral line (as sister, v. 9, half-sister, v. 11, aunts, vv. 12–14 and sister-in-law, v. 16). Natural relationship and relationship by marriage in the direct line can be ascendant (as mother in v. 7, step-mother in v. 8) or descendent (as granddaughter in v. 10, as daughter-in-law in v. 15).

Why is the Daughter Missing?

Here the question arises as to why precisely the daughter is missing (natural relationship in direct line of first degree in descent) while the granddaughters in v. 10 (natural relationship of the second degree in descent) and the daughter-in-law in v. 15 are mentioned *expressis verbis* (relationship by marriage of the first degree in descent).[6] In reality the daughter is only apparently missing! For she turns up in

---

only the half-sisters are mentioned; but in his comment on v. 9 he reckons with the possibility that v. 9 includes the full sister (Milgrom, *Leviticus 17–22*, 1539). In my opinion this is the only possible interpretation of v. 9, because a prohibition of sexual contact with half-sisters and the permission of such contacts with full sisters at the same time would be absurd.

[6] The missing daughter is explained in different ways. Recently J. Joosten, "La non-mention de la fille en Lévitique 18. Essai sur la rhétorique du Code de Sainteté," *ETR* 75 (2000) 419–20, interpreted the non-mention of the daughter with rhetorical reasons. Ruwe, "*Heiligkeitsgesetz*", 168–72, on the contrary states that in incest *prescriptions* (in contrast to current incest *taboos*) in Deut 23:1; 27:20, 22–23 as well as in Lev 18:6–18 only more distant degrees of relationship are enumerated. That is why the full sister and the daughter can be omitted. F. Fechter, *Die Familie in der Nachexilszeit: Untersuchung zur Bedeutung der Verwandtschaft in ausgewählten Texten des Alten Testaments* (BZAW 264; Berlin and New York: de Gruyter, 1998) 177–88; E. Estévez, "Sexualidad, familia y pureza. El incesto en la legislación levítica," *Miscelanea Comillas* 57 (1999) 368–69; Milgrom, *Leviticus 17–22*, 1527–30, put the different models of explanation together. Seifert's explanation, *Tochter und Vater im Alten Testament. Eine ideologiekritische Untersuchung zur Verfügungsgewalt von Vätern über ihre Töchter* (Neukirchener theologische Dissertationen und Habilitationen 9; Neukirchen-Vluyn: Neukirchener Verlag, 1997) 222–23, seems extremely unlikely; cf. Ruwe's counter-arguments, "*Heiligkeitsgesetz*", 172–73.

the first prohibition of the second group (v. 17) where for a polygamous household the *paterfamilias* is forbidden to marry the mother
and daughter simultaneously. This implies as a consequence the prohibition to take the daughter as spouse![7]

The second group indeed designates four women that the *paterfamilias* must not marry in polygamous marriage because they are
related with another wife of the husband by blood (as mother and
daughter or grandmother and granddaughter, v. 17, or as sisters,
v. 18) or by marriage (as mother and daughter-in-law, v. 17). Here too,
the first and second degree are taken into account (grandmother and
granddaughter in the second, in the three other cases in the first
degree), also the direct (v. 17) and the collateral line (sisters, v. 18).

What is Prohibited: Sexual Intercourse or Matrimonial Relationship?

In the preceding paragraph the prohibitions in Lev 18:7–18 have
been explained as the interdiction of certain matrimonial relations
of the *paterfamilias* with related or allied women. Is this what the biblical text means? Does the expression "to uncover the nakedness of
a woman" not rather mean sexual intercourse as such, detached
from the matrimonial relationship? Verse 18 however has marriage
in view, as we can see from the context. The distinction between
sexual intercourse in general and sexual intercourse in marriage is
apparently not a concern of the text! Both are meant.[8]

Summarizing we can say that the double series of the fourteen
prohibitions in vv. 6–18 restricts the possibilities of marriage because
of certain types of relationship and alliance between the women and
the *paterfamilias* and between the women themselves.

---

[7] Cf. Estévez, "Sexualidad," 368 n. 90. For the possible objection that not only
a *simultaneous* (polygamous) marriage, but also *successive* (monogamous) marriages of
sisters are prohibited, see n. 9.

[8] So Milgrom, *Leviticus 17–22*, 1532. Differently A. Tosato, "The Law of Leviticus
18:18: A Reexamination," *CBQ* 46 (1984) 206: "Lev 18:18 is the only verse of the
chapter—together with the extension of v. 17b—to state an expressedly matrimonial prohibition...." For Tosato, "Law," 203–8, v. 18 as far as the form and the
contents are concerned does not belong to the series of the incest prohibitions in
vv. 7–17 any more, but already to the series in vv. 18–23. About Tosato's interpretation of v. 18 see n. 9 below.

The Meaning of the Fourteen Prohibitions of Sexual Relations

Relationship and alliance affect related and allied persons in a deep, definite and specific way. That is why they are incompatible with matrimonial relationship, which would add, with its sexually and affectively determined nature a totally different kind of relationship. The imposition of the specifically affective-erotic matrimonial relationship on a kindred relationship and alliance would make it impossible for the individuals and for the family group as a whole to play their own social part relative to one another. Am I a sister or a wife? Am I the son or the husband of my mother? Such conflicts concerning the parts to play would profoundly disturb family life in whose own interest it is to have clear relations.

It would be degrading and cruel to make out of a mother and her daughter or out of two sisters a couple of spouses of the same man, because they would inevitably be driven into a rivalry in relation to their common husband which would be in contradiction to their birth given natural relationships (cf. Prov 17:17).[9]

In view of all this, the purpose of such prohibitions is the peace of the whole family group which is based on clear, unmixed relationships among its members.[10] The sexual potential which in virtue

---

[9] Tosato, "Law," 206–7, interprets v. 18 as a polygamy prohibition: "This motivation shows that the act legislated against is deemed criminal, not in itself (and thus it is not a case of an incestuous union; nor more generally of a sexual union retained intrinsically perverse), but is deemed criminal in relation to the man's first wife who would be damaged. In addition, the harm which the law wants avoided is such (rivalry, enmity) that any woman (and not necessarily a sister of the first wife) is capable of causing it, once taken as a second wife, whether in bigamous marriage or in monogamous marriage after the dissolution of the previous marriage through divorce." Cf. A. Tosato, *Il Matrimonio Israelitico* (AnBib 100; Rome: Biblical Institute, 1982) 209–10. In the first clause quoted, Tosato eloquently points out the very reason of the interpretation of Lev 18:18 propounded here too. His second statement, however, may well be true in itself, but it goes beyond the text. What v. 18 explicitly aims at is the exclusion of rivalry, *within the same family group*, of sisters who were simultaneously spouses of one and the same husband. For two sisters could not be considered as rivals if one of them were the divorced wife of the husband and the other his second wife, married after the divorce of the first one, because they would not live in the same family. The bitter feelings of the divorced first wife against the second, her sister, are no rivalry in the full sense of the term since the two sisters do not live together under the roof of one husband like, e.g. Hannah and Peninna in 1 Samuel 1. And why would two non-related women married with one husband, either simultaneously, or successively after the divorce from the first one, be called sisters? Nowhere in the Old Testament is such a meaning for "sister" attested; Gen 20:12 is a totally different case.

[10] K. Elliger, "Das Gesetz in Levitikus 18," *ZAW* 67 (1955) 8: ". . . das Zusammen-

of erotic attraction is capable of creating new promising relations for the future is consciously and intentionally kept away from existing family relations in order to preserve from confusion the clear social order, which is an absolute necessity for the family.

This implies that sexual-affective tendencies are not always allowed to follow their own dynamics, but in the interest of the larger group and the security of all members of a family they have to give way to definite, preexisting and long-practiced relationships unless one wants to open the door to social and psychological chaos.[11]

The Five Additional Prohibitions in Lev 18:19–23

The following five prohibitions go beyond the exclusive sphere of inner family relationships. They are of a mixed nature. Verse 19 prohibits sexual intercourse with a menstruating woman, v. 20 adultery, v. 22 male homosexual intercourse and v. 23 male and female sexual intercourse with an animal (sodomy or bestiality). In the middle of these four prohibitions is inserted the prohibition against giving a child to Molech for burning (v. 21).

Is there a common characteristic between these five prohibitions?[12] Their first common trait is obviously the limitation of sexual activity

---

leben der Grossfamilie: es soll nicht in ein Durcheinander der Geschlechtsgemeinschaft ausarten, und der Friede innerhalb der Wohn- und Wirtschaftsgemeinschaft soll an einem empfindlichen Punkte gesichert werden" (idem, *Leviticus*, 239); Milgrom, *Leviticus 17–22*, 1530, mentions those who support this explanation (Ibn Kaspi, Abravanel and others), but rejects it. For him as for Ramban the intention of Leviticus 18; 20 is the protection of procreation.

[11] M. Douglas, "Justice as the Cornerstone. An Interpretation of Leviticus 18–20," *Int* 53 (1999) 345–47, explains all prohibitions of Leviticus 18 and 20 as interdictions of foreign cults with incestuous, sodomite and homosexual practices. Thus the prohibitions are denied a proper inherent meaning, and consequently the prohibitions are only interpreted in light of their literary frame in Leviticus 18 and 20, not in themselves. This explanation is not sufficient since there is a rationality in the prohibitions themselves. The same objection may be raised against the explanation of C. M. Carmichael, *Law, Legend, and Incest in the Bible: Leviticus 18–20* (Ithaca, NY: Cornell University Press, 1997), who derives the precepts of Leviticus 18 and 20 from the patriarchal stories of Genesis.

[12] The relation of the sexual prohibitions with the prohibition of v. 21, i.e. the prohibition to kill children for Molech, is especially difficult to interpret. Despite the tendency of the commentators to consider the verse as a later insertion just motivated by the connection of catchwords נתן and זרע, according to Grünwaldt, *Heiligkeitsgesetz*, 34–35, v. 21 is original and constitutes the consciously constructed middle of the paragraph; Ruwe, *"Heiligkeitsgesetz"*, 176–78, points out the careful, consistent structure of vv. 19–23 on the literary level and their syntactical connection with vv. 6–18; Milgrom, *Leviticus 17–22*, 1558–89, sees the reason for the combination

within the monogamous and polygamous marriage and at its borders.[13] Inside, menstruation creates a zone of sexual continence,[14] outside, the prohibitions of adultery, both inside and outside, homosexual intercourse of men and sodomy or bestiality of men and women do so.

In these four forms of sexual intercourse the man's procreative capacity gets lost. With respect to female sodomy or bestiality, the woman remains sterile. Fecundity is a wonderful capacity given to man by God (Gen 1:28; 9:1). This may moreover explain why the prohibition to kill a child for Molech, v. 21, is inserted into this context. For this would be a misuse of the fruit of procreation and the birth of the child, which belongs just as much or even more to God, YHWH, than to the parents. That is why they are not allowed to kill it, since it is not YHWH who requires such a thing, but the idol Molech. Common to these five prohibitions is, accordingly, the attempt to preserve the human capacity of procreation and giving birth in

---

of the prohibited sacrifice of children to Molech with sexual prohibitions in the fact that the Canaanites practiced both.

[13] Thus Ruwe, *"Heiligkeitsgesetz"*, 17; Milgrom, *Leviticus 17–22*, 1549, thinks that v. 19 together with v. 20 (adultery), v. 22 (homosexuality), and v. 23 (sodomy) designate sexual intercourse with *non-relatives*. This is too narrow. Adultery may occur among relatives by alliance, that is in the large family, and homosexuality within the family. These kinds of sexual intercourse are prohibited in general, both inside and outside the family.

[14] The prohibition of sexual contact with a menstruating woman is sometimes interpreted in the light of Lev 20:18. According to E. S. Gerstenberger, *Das 3. Buch Mose: Leviticus* (ATD 6; Göttingen: Vandenhoeck & Ruprecht, 1993) 231, the laying bare of *her flow of blood*, or respectively of *her flow* mentioned there, is the reason for the man's impurity. For Ruwe, *"Heiligkeitsgesetz"*, 180, "wäre das Aufdecken des Blutes im Sexualverkehr während der Periode ... ein Öffentlich-Machen des Lebens der Frau selbst. Dies soll vermieden werden." In my opinion, this identification of the *flow of blood* with the life or the personal existence of *the woman* (in the light of Leviticus 17) is not substantiated by the text. On the contrary, Grünwaldt, *Heiligkeitsgesetz*, 185, correctly interprets that the "Monatsblut die Möglichkeit der Fruchtbarkeit dokumentiert und dem Ursprung des Lebens entspringt." This explains the prohibition of coitus during the time when the "possibility of fecundity" flows away and procreation is not possible. Milgrom, *Leviticus 17–22*, 1550, takes the defilement by the menstrual blood according to Lev 15:24 as the explanation of the prohibition. In this view, however, the prohibition would lose its common characteristic with all other prohibitions in Leviticus 20, because they are all dealing with something else than mere ritual impurity. The tension between Lev 15:24 on the one hand and Lev 18:19; 20:18 on the other is to be explained differently, namely, either Leviticus 15 belongs to P, another source than H, or it has to do with a menstruation surprisingly occurring (Leviticus 15) which would defile, and a regular menstruation that can be foreseen (Leviticus 20) and may therefore be declared an obstacle for sexual intercourse.

its original purpose and to keep it away from what is certainly a barren use.[15] But there is still another common characteristic of all the prohibitions of Leviticus 18.

Connection between Lev 18:6–18 and 19–23

If we go from Lev 18:6–18 further to the five following prohibitions in vv. 19–23, they appear in a new light. In the same way as the relationships in the larger family have to be clear, there is also a need for clarity between husband and wife (sexually she is not absolutely and always at his disposal, v. 19!) as well as between internal and external relationships. The external relationships are articulated into four parts: other married women, Molech, men, and animals. Married women are forbidden because peace between families requires protection in the interest of the larger society (Exod 20:14; Deut 5:28). The power of the religious cult of Molech to decimate families is absolutely forbidden.[16] Sexual intercourse between man and man, between man and animal as well as between woman and animal is not only barren, but it also troubles the relationships in the house of the extended family where men and animals live closely together almost as brothers and sisters,[17] and where the seeds of conflicts among many brothers and male relatives are already numerous, e.g. in the families of Isaac, Jacob, Esau, Laban and his sons, of Jacob's sons or David's family. Sexual relations between men with all of its confusion, would lead to further complications of relationship and heavily endanger the unity of the family because of their passionate character. Moreover, the family hardly has means at its disposal to discipline its unruly members as can be seen from Jacob's inevitable flight (Genesis 28) or from the crimes within Jacob's (Genesis 37) and David's families, which give eloquent testimony to the family's weakness when it comes to restaining violence that breaks out in its midst (cf. Deut 21:18–21). From this perspective the prohibition against surrendering a child to Molech provides children

---

[15] Ruwe, *"Heiligkeitsgesetz"*, 178 shows that "fast alle Sexualbestimmungen in 18,19–23 . . . die Zuspitzung auf Koitus und Begattung gemeinsam [haben]."

[16] Grünwaldt, *Heiligkeitsgesetz*, 189, sees in the prohibition of the sacrifice to Molech a "Schutzgebot für Familie."

[17] Cf. 2 Sam 12:3 as an example for the living together of man and animal.

with safety from danger on the part of their parents. The prohibition of adultery warrants peace for the spouse.[18]

Thus, the negative commandments in Lev 18:6–23 taken together form a series of taboos and firm rules that aim at safeguarding the unity, peace and clarity of the parts played by each member of the family. They try to avoid from the outset a whole series of conflicts and rivalries. They consist of four parts: a principle, v. 6, governing the list of vv. 7–16, which is a topography of the relations of kinship and alliance between man and wife, outlining a space in which sexual relations are forbidden; then follows in vv. 17–18 a list of certain relations of kinship and alliance which must not occur between spouses of a polygamous marriage because these would be degrading and cruel relationships; and finally in vv. 19–23 there are five cases of incorrect use of the capacity of procreation and birth-giving which at the same time would heavily damage the peace and unity of the family and of the larger social community.

Leviticus 20: Complicity in Transgressions against the Family and the Larger Community, Sanctioned by the Death Penalty

Two common characteristics in Leviticus 20 connect the specific incest prohibitions with the other prohibitions of the same chapter. On the one hand it is the Israelite family,[19] in which there must exist relationships that are untouched by specific sexual relations. On the other hand it is capital punishment which has to be applied to all persons who are actively involved in the transgression of these prohibitions. (Only v. 21, prohibited marriage with one's brother's wife, is an exception.) All transgressions, indeed, are acts that can never be committed by one person alone, but naturally involve an *accomplice*.[20] In vv. 2–5 a father delivers up a child to Molech. The

---

[18] Ruwe's interpretation goes in a similar direction, *"Heiligkeitsgesetz"*, 181–82. According to him in vv. 19–23 the "kulturell bedeutsame(n) Basisunterscheidungen" (man and woman, human and animal etc.) have to be protected: "Das zentrale Rechtssatzkorpus 18,5–23 besteht damit nach seinen beiden Teilen (18,6–18 und 18,19–23) aus Bestimmungen, die das priesterliche Anliegen der Scheidung und Ordnungsstiftung verfolgen." It ought to be stressed, however, that the need for clear relationships in human groups corresponds not only to special priestly conceptions. It is generally a vital necessity for harmony within such groups and a condition of their happy social life.

[19] Cf. Grünwaldt, *Heiligkeitsgesetz*, 49–50.

[20] Ruwe, *"Heiligkeitsgesetz"*, 228: "Die Sonderstellung dieser Bestimmungen hängt

family and the whole society would become accomplices of the deed by tacitly tolerating the crime. Therefore they are to accuse and judge it. By their personal participation in stoning the guilty father, they assume the double liability for the punishment of transgressions in Israel and for the lawfulness of their condemnation of the culprit. Wherever forbidden mantic activity is practiced (vv. 6 and 27), complicities between those who practice manticism and the society which tolerates (and uses) it in its fold, are certain (cf. 1 Sam 28:9–10). Here again, those responsible in the community are called upon to intervene, just as Saul had done, and to stone the culprits in order not to become guilty of the illicit manticism themselves. If children, according to v. 9, curse their parents they must be put to death. This can only be realized if the witnesses of the cursing—and that could also be the parents themselves to whom the curse was addressed—do not cover the offense with silence which would make them guilty of the curse as well (cf. Lev 5:1).

In vv. 10–21, then, the matter is deliberate sexual intercourse between two persons or between a person and an animal (vv. 15–16). Hence both participants are guilty and both are punished with death, including even the animals (vv. 15–16).

Now, what is the common characteristic of the incest prohibitions and the other prohibitions in vv. 10–21? Again, it is certain sexual relations that create social unrest and conflicts inside a family and inside a village and thus threaten their survival. According to vv. 11–12 a *paterfamilias* as a lover would enter into competition with his own father (cf. Gen 35:22; 49:4; 2 Sam 16:21–22), or with his own son, and this in the same family, where everybody is seeing it and suffering from it. In vv. 17, 19–20 the head of the family would intrude into the marriage of his brother-in-law, his related or allied uncle and brother. An adultery must lead to bitter hatred between the families of the same village (v. 10). Sexual relations between men (v. 13) would hopelessly confuse the existing family relations, since an adult man is usually married and already has a wife, and, above all, because it would needlessly increase jealousy and conflicts between brothers and relatives or between villagers. The redactor of Leviticus

---

offenkundig damit zusammen, dass es sich durchweg um solche Sätze handelt, die die *Familiensolidarität* und die *Loyalität zu JHWH* in massiver Weise unterlaufenden Delikte betreffen . . .”; Milgrom, *Leviticus 17–22*, 1755 (especially in the case of a menstruating woman).

20 seems to understand the immolation of a child for Molech at the initiative of its own parents, illicit manticism, and the cursing of the parents, as analogous confusions of the social relationships in Israel. There would be something perverse in such deeds.

In any case the list of the twelve prohibitions with its sanction for each one in vv. 10–21 is in itself a unity, to which the three other prohibitions in vv. 2–5 (Molech), vv. 6 and 27 (manticism), and v. 9 (cursing of the parents) were added.[21] They differ in their formulation from vv. 10–21.

In vv. 10–21 we can recognize a systematic structure. Its content concerns inadmissible sexual intercourse for a man. In the first mentioned cases he hurts other marriages, first of all outside the family (adultery, v. 10), then inside in direct line of alliance of the first degree ascendant (father's wife, v. 11) and descendant (son's wife, v. 12). Then the passage addresses illicit sexual intercourse that does not hurt other marriages, in four forms: with a man (v. 13), with mother and daughter as simultaneous spouses of a polygamous man (v. 14), and male and—as supplement—also female bestiality (vv. 15–16). Finally five illicit relations with women related or allied in the collateral line, first with relatives of the first degree (half-sister, v. 17) and of the second degree (aunts in the blood line, v. 19), then with relatives by marriage of the second degree (uncle's wife on the father's side, v. 20) and of the first degree (with the sister-in-law, v. 21),[22] but also with a menstruating woman in marriage (v. 18; see below!).[23]

Verse 21 is the only one in the series of vv. 10–21 to contain no human punishment; the transgression is punished by YHWH alone through barrenness of the marriage. The reason for this exception might be the levirate law which under certain circumstances (after

---

[21] Regardless of its different formulation v. 9 is sometimes taken together with vv. 10–21. Thus Ruwe, *"Heiligkeitsgesetz"*, 228–9; Grünwaldt, *Heiligkeitsgesetz*, 47–50.

[22] For Grünwaldt, *Heiligkeitsgesetz*, 47, no "erkennbare Gliederung" can be seen in vv. 9–21; Ruwe, *"Heiligkeitsgesetz"*, 229–31, on the contrary, sees a structure in the different forms of punishment, 231: "Das Korpus teilt sich insofern in zwei Unterteile, in 20,9–16 einerseits und 20,17–21 andererseits." Milgrom, *Leviticus 17–22*, 1743–44 offers possible systematizations of the list.

[23] Milgrom, *Leviticus 17–22*, 1744, seems to imply that every menstruating woman except the menstruating wife is concerned (because of Lev 15:24; see n. 14 above). The formulation of the text, however, is general: every woman, spouse and non-spouse.

the brother's death) can be required (Deut 25:5–6). Thus, such a marriage is not completely forbidden.[24]

Two concluding observations concerning the sequence of vv. 17–21. With regard to the degrees of kinship and alliance the disposition is chiastic: half-sister—aunt//aunt—sister-in-law. Furthermore between the two prohibitions of marriage with relatives (vv. 17 and 19) the forbidden intercourse with the menstruating woman has been inserted: half-sister, menstruating woman (v. 18), aunt in the blood line. The reason for this is probably that the commandment to consider one's own wife as unapproachable during her period of menstrual blood creates a kind of temporarily limited "matrimonial fallowness" during which the wife is like a prohibited relative.

Recapitulating we may say that Leviticus 20, beside the redactional supplements (vv. 7–8, 24a as well as 24b–27) and the three mixed prohibitions of vv. 2–6, 9, 27, consists of a list of twelve prohibited sexual relationships. It differs from the list in Leviticus 18 in the regularly pronounced death penalty that concerns both persons involved in the transgression (exception v. 21). The twelve prohibitions occur all in the list of Lev 18:6–23 as well.[25] Leviticus 20 adds the sanction for all persons involved in the transgression, even for animals in the case of sodomy (Leviticus 18 does not speak of penalties). The interest of this list can be seen in the light of Lev 18:29: through the punishment Israel clearly rejects the transgressions and the liability for them. If there was no punishment Israel would thereby agree upon the crimes and would have to bear the responsibility for them.[26] Leviticus 20 on the other hand does not add any new reason for the prohibitions as such.

---

[24] Similarly Ruwe, *"Heiligkeitsgesetz"*, 240.

[25] Cf. the careful (and tabular) comparisons in Grünwaldt, *Heiligkeitsgesetz*, 172–208 and Fechter, *Familie*, 222.

[26] Ruwe, *"Heiligkeitsgesetz"*, 245–46, interprets the meaning of these sanctions in a slightly different way: "Lev 20,1–27 bildet den Abschluss der *allgemeinen Heiligkeitsbestimmungen*. Dass dieser Sanktionsteil ausnahmslos auf die in Lev 18 verbotenen Sexualdelikte sowie auf wenige Delikte gegen die Familiensolidarität (v. 2–5.9.6.27) konzentriert ist, zeigt nochmals deutlich, wie zentral die Fragen der Begründung von Familien- und Nächstenliebe für den gesamten Komplex der allgemeinen Heiligkeitsbestimmungen (Lev 18,1–20,27) sind ... Dass gerade die Inzest- und Sexualvergehen den Sanktionsteil derartig dominieren, hängt offenbar damit zusammen, dass gerade diese Delikte den Zusammenhalt der Gesellschaft und damit die Voraussetzungen für das Entstehen jener Solidaritätskreise empfindlich treffen."

The Redactional Parts of Leviticus 18 and 20

Leviticus 18 is anchored in the Pentateuchal narrative through vv. 2–5 and 24–30. These two sections are related together. Verses 2 and 30 contain first of all the authority formula "I am YHWH your God,"[27] which occurs again in v. 4 (and in its abbreviated form in vv. 5, 21). It states the authority of YHWH to claim obedience for his commandments on the part of Israel (cf. Gen 41:44). YHWH's authority formula frames Leviticus 18. It shows the divine origin of these claims on Israel.

Leviticus 18:2–5, the opening section of the narrative frame, is built upon the opposition between YHWH's ordinances and the norms and customs of Egypt which Israel is leaving and of Canaan to which it is going (v. 3). Four times YHWH calls on Israel to follow his law and three times to leave those of Egypt and Canaan. These seven calls or claims of YHWH flow, as it were, into the promise of reward that by satisfying YHWH's claims one shall live (v. 5).

The final section of the narrative frame, Lev 18:24–30, is characterized by a double *inclusion*. The first one concerns *personal defilement* from which the Israelites may be preserved (v. 24, purity as a commandment; v. 30, the consequence and reward of keeping the commandment). The condition is thereby to observe the twenty prohibitions of Leviticus 18 (respectively twenty-one if we take v. 6 as a separate prohibition and not as the heading of the whole series).

The second inclusion consists on the one hand of the *prohibition* against defiling oneself by violating the ordinances of Leviticus 18, and on the other hand, of its negative explanation: YHWH is presently casting out the defiled inhabitants before the Israelites precisely because they transgressed these very commandments (v. 24). Thus the *prohibition* with its *negative* explanation concerning the history of the nations in relation to Israel has its symmetrical correspondence at the end in the twofold obligation to keep positively YHWH's ordinances and not to commit the prohibited acts in order that the Israelites remain pure (v. 30).[28]

---

[27] On this "Authority formula" (*Vollmachtsformel*), see A. Schenker, "Der Monotheismus im ersten Gebot, die Stellung der Frau im Sabbatgebot und zwei andere Sachfragen zum Dekalog," in *Text und Sinn im Alten Testament. Textgeschichtliche und bibeltheologische Studien* (OBO 103, Göttingen: Vandenhoeck & Ruprecht, 1991) 188–92.

[28] Cf. Ruwe, *"Heiligkeitsgesetz"*, 184; Milgrom, *Leviticus 17–22*, 1576–77, discusses

In the middle of this double inclusion there is the central section concerning the *defiled* land, consistent in itself and divided in four sections. In v. 25 YHWH first of all announces the defilement of the *land*; thus YHWH had to punish the land and the land already has vomited out its inhabitants. This example of punishment in the past motivates YHWH's claim on Israel in v. 26 to keep his commandments and not to transgress the prohibitions of Leviticus 18. This claim concerns the Israelites as well as the aliens who reside among them. Verses 27–28 further reinforce this commandment and prohibition of v. 26 with the threat that the land will vomit out its inhabitants anew in the future if they were to defile it again. Verse 29 eventually explains how the land can be kept pure from defilement in case some of its inhabitants were to defile it by individual transgression of the prohibition; this would happen by cutting off the individual culprits.

The redactional frame of Lev 20:22–24 takes up, with some variation,[29] the motive of the vomiting land, embedding Leviticus 20 into the whole Pentateuchal narrative, as the framing paragraphs of vv. 3–4 and 24–30 did for Leviticus 18. In Lev 20:22 YHWH recalls that he is bringing at present Israel to the land which would, however, vomit Israel out if they were to transgress YHWH's commandments. In v. 23 he accordingly adds that he is driving out the nations before Israel precisely because they have transgressed these prohibitions, while in v. 24 he gives the reason for his promise of the land to Israel: the bad customs of the previous inhabitants of the land. Because they did such things YHWH could dispose of the land—a land flowing with milk and honey—for the benefit of Israel. However it should be noted that there is no question here of *defilement of the land*, not even of the personal defilement of its inhabitants.

The course of the argument in this section is as follows: since the nations which inhabited Israel's land practiced reprehensible things YHWH takes their land away and therefore has a land at his free disposal. Consequently he promises it to the people of Israel that he is just bringing to this newly allotted land and thus he is driving out the previous inhabitants before Israel. The argument pursues two purposes: it interweaves Leviticus 20 with the whole Pentateuchal

---

the structure of 18:24–30 and the relation of this section with the Holiness Code in its entirety.

[29] Cf. Grünwaldt, *Heiligkeitsgesetz*, 208–22, who carefully analyses the narrative frame of Leviticus 18 and 20 and assigns them their place in the *Redaktionsgeschichte*.

narration and motivates the acceptance of the commandments of Leviticus 20 as necessary conditions for inheriting the land.

Leviticus 20:24b–26 and v. 27 add two further commandments: Israel is to make a distinction between clean and unclean food and to abstain from illicit mantic activity. They have to be considered as equally important as the preceding ordinances of vv. 9–21, and consequently they too represent necessary conditions for Israel's remaining in the land.

Leviticus 20:6 and v. 27 moreover form an inclusion (the same prohibition of mantic practices which bypass the legitimate priestly means for knowing the future) to this prohibition.

Leviticus 20:7–8 furthermore marks a text division with one of the concentric formulas A-B-A' that are characteristic for the Holiness Code (cf. Lev 17:10–12; 17:11; 20:24b–26; 24:17–21 etc.). This subdividing formula of vv. 7–8 is redactional too.[30]

The Latest Redaction of Leviticus 18 and 20:
The Land Vomiting Out Its Inhabitants

Both Lev 18:24–30 and 20:22–24 present the common motive of the land vomiting out its inhabitants. This motive occurs only in these two places in the whole Bible. It embraces the whole of Israelite history from the promise of the land till the conquest by driving out its previous population which, by the way, is not specified by proper names (20:22–24). Thus it presupposes the whole Pentateuchal narrative. Furthermore, Lev 18:25, 27–28 already looks back at the expulsion of the population living there as if at the point in time when the narrator speaks in Leviticus 18 it were already realized. Remarkable too is the presentation of the land as an acting person: it vomits out its inhabitants (18:25, 28; 20:22), a notion somewhat similar to 26:34–35 where the land celebrates the sabbath as if it were a person.

The theme of the land vomiting out its population accomplishes three functions in Leviticus 18 and 20. The *first one* is literary-redactional. It makes out of Leviticus 18–20 a unit, giving all the commandments of these three chapters the weight of conditions necessary

---

[30] Grünwaldt, *Heiligkeitsgesetz*, 47, together with others, argues on the grounds of v. 6 and v. 27 for a concentric structure of Lev 20:6–27.

for the possession of the land. Leviticus 18 is already tied to Leviticus 19 by the use of the authority formula (18:2, 4, 30; 19:3, 4, 10, 25, 31, 34, 36; in its abbreviated form, 18:5, 21; 19:12, 14, 18, 28, 30, 32, 37), while Leviticus 19 on the other hand is closely attached to Leviticus 20 by the common theme of YHWH's and Israel's holiness (19:2; 20:7–8,26).[31] The theme of the personified land vomiting out its inhabitants embraces the two double sections Leviticus 18–19 and Leviticus 19–20 and makes an overall unit out of them. A second theme holds Leviticus 18–20 together like a hoop, namely the purity and impurity of the inhabitants and the land (18:24–30 and 20:24–26).

The *second* function of the land vomiting out its inhabitants is narrative and theological. It roots the commandments of Leviticus 18–20 into the Pentateuchal narrative. At the same time it explains why the promise and gift of the land to Israel at the expense of the resident population is not unjust. This population has lost its claim to dwell there by its contempt of the correct family relationships. It lived in contradiction to Leviticus 18–20. All this reflects the same conception as that of Gen 15:16.[32]

The interpretation of the loss of a land because its population despises the true rules of social life of Leviticus 18–20 within and outside the family implies that these rules are known to all peoples. How should we understand this implication? The most simple explanation seems to be that the authors of Lev 18:24–30; 20:22–24 held these rules to be common sense. They were regarded as obvious. According to the authors, these were rules for social life that YHWH recalled here, but which were, or could have been, accessible for everybody. They were convinced that the divine commandments concerning family relations were rational rules and therefore were generally accessible and, accordingly, compulsory for all men.

The *third* function of the redactor's idea of the land vomiting out its population is parenetical and ethical. If the precepts of Leviticus

---

[31] Cf. Ruwe, *"Heiligkeitsgesetz"*, 242–3 and esp. 242 n. 49.

[32] Ruwe interprets, however, the peoples mentioned in the narrative frame of Leviticus 18 and 20 as Israel itself, because, in the priestly interpretation, these sections explain the catastrophe of the exile; he writes in *"Heiligkeitsgesetz"*, 245, "Anders als die Autoren des DtrG führen diese Autoren den Verlust des Landes nicht auf den Götzendienst Israels zurück (vgl. Deut 12,29–31). Sie halten vielmehr die Unterlassung der eigenen Vorfahren, die Einheit der Gesellschaft durch die Prinzipien der Trennung und Scheidung und Zuordnung zu organisieren, für die eigentliche Ursache der Katastrophe."

18–20 are understood as necessary conditions for land possession they become of decisive importance, even though they are not part of the Decalogue and other commandments revealed on Mount Sinai. The redaction speaking in Lev 18:24–30; 20:22–24 revalorizes the rules of Leviticus 18–20 by connecting them with the land. The observance of the rules of Leviticus 18–20 entitles Israel to possess the land, their disregard leads to its loss. The inspiration for combining commandments concerning family relationships with the possession or the loss of the land may have originated from the commandment to honor the parents in the Decalogue (Exod 20:12; Deut 5:16).

According to Lev 18:24–30 the observance of the rules of Lev 18:6–23 creates *purity* for the inhabitants (vv. 24, 30) and for the land (vv. 25, 28), while their transgression defiles both, the transgression of the prohibitions in Lev 18:20–23 being qualified as defilement. The only other place in the Bible that presents the promised land the Israelites are to enter as completely *defiled* by the hitherto resident population is Ezra 9:11–12![33] There too, the strict consequence is that Israel must absolutely not enter into any *family relations* with this population (a prohibition which the Israelites did not observe at all). Ezra is apparently frightened about the mixed marriages precisely because they submit Israelite men and women to other rules of family life (i.e., to other incest and sexual rules) than those given in Leviticus 18 and 20 which, according to Lev 18:24–30, are decisive for the possession of the land. Neither Lev 18:24–30 nor Ezra 9:1–2, 11–12 warn against mixed marriages to avoid idolatry (but cf. Exod 23:24, 32–33; 34:11–16). In Ezra's eyes, it is the defilement of the land as a result of incorrect family relationships in contradiction with Leviticus 18 and 20 that is the danger.[34]

---

[33] It is interesting to note in this regard that Fechter, *Familie*, 203, supposes the series Lev 18:7–16 "sei erst nach 538 v.Chr. in den Zusammenhang der mosaischen Autorität gestellt worden. . . . In nachexilischer Zeit erst gewann jene Reihe ihr Gewicht. Und dies kann nur daran liegen, dass in dieser Situation der zugrundeliegenden Sozialform besondere Aufmerksamkeit zuteil wurde. Sie wurde in den Rang eines gesellschaftlichen Wertes erhoben, den es unter allen Umständen zu schützen galt."

[34] Milgrom, *Leviticus 17–22*, 1584–86, considers Ezra 9 as a halakhic midrash created in order to prohibit mixed marriages between Israelites and non-Israelites. In my opinion the prohibition of mixed marriages is already implied in the incest prohibitions of Leviticus 18 and 20, since other nations may observe other incest rules, and thus bring sexual relationships into the Israelite families that do not cor-

Thus, Ezra 9 corresponds to the redaction of Leviticus 18 and 20 which develops the idea of the defiled land vomiting out its defiled inhabitants because of incorrect relationships within the family and the larger society. This concept is only to be found at these two places in the Bible. Idolatry is implied only marginally with Molech (Lev 18:21; 20:2–5) and with manticism (Lev 20:6, 27). The principal source of defilement is the confusion of the right sexual order in family and society.

The Earlier Redaction in Leviticus 18:2–5: The Reward of Life

Leviticus 18:3–4 is in a subtly camouflaged way inconsistent with 18:24–30. In vv. 3–4 YHWH looks back at the land of Egypt in the past (Israel just left it) and forward at the land of Canaan in the future (YHWH will bring Israel there). Here the two geographical names are mentioned in contrast to vv. 24–30 which is a paragraph without proper names. Both countries behave according to principles which contradict those of YHWH. But YHWH does not punish either of the two countries. It could not be the thought of casting out the population as a punishment for their abominable customs since this would not fit Egypt whose inhabitants YHWH never drove away from their soil in favor of Israel. Nor is it mentioned in the case of the inhabitants of Canaan. The question of the guilt of these countries is not raised here.

The interest of this redactor points much more towards the distinction of Israel from these peoples. According to him, Israel has now to choose between their customs and YHWH's "customs" (laws). The choice in favor of YHWH's principles, accordingly, is the confession of YHWH on the practical level of the right order in family and society. The stimulus for this choice in the positive way is the benefit and the advantage it brings: life (v. 5). There is no threat in case of future disobedience (loss of the land).

Confessional contexts in which Israel must choose YHWH as an alternative to the gods and the advantages of the other nations

---

respond to the Israelite laws; see, e.g. the prohibition of sexual contact with a menstruating woman. Ezra did not have to invent any new prohibition by way of midrash since the prohibition of mixed marriages is already implied in Leviticus 18 and 20.

because with YHWH there is life are typical for the deuteronomic-deuteronomistic writers (see e.g., Deut 30:15–20; Joshua 24 etc.).

The time span of this redactional embedding of the command-ments of Leviticus 18 reaches from Egypt to Canaan. The promise of the land to the fathers lies beyond its horizon. The narrative moment—lying in the middle of the timeline, between the depar-ture from Egypt and the entrance into Canaan—coincides exactly with the moment of confession: Israel is not in Egypt any more, nor in Canaan yet. Here Israel is to make her choice because she is standing in the neutral space between both lands as well as in the presence of YHWH who is proposing a third possibility to Israel beside the Egyptian and Canaanite way of life: a divine one. This concept of choosing YHWH after Egypt and at the gates of the promised land, in the form of the promise to obey his Torah, cor-responds to deuteronomic-deuteronomistic theology.[35]

Results

The main results of the preceding study may be summarized as follows.

First: Leviticus 18 forbids the *paterfamilias* of a large family fourteen sexual unions with women who either belong to his family or are related or allied to one another. They would be incestuous unions, as is stated in the general heading, v. 6, in the opening of the list. Five subsequent prohibitions are attached to them, four of which prohibit certain forms of sexual intercourse too, which are not, how-ever, of an incestuous kind. The fifth one prohibits the *paterfamilias* from killing his own child for Molech. This second series of five pro-hibitions differs from the first one in content and form. The two lists clearly differ with regard to their history of tradition and redaction.

Second: In an analogous way Lev 20:10–21 offers a series of twelve prohibitions of illicit sexual intercourse. In this list incestuous and other illegitimate unions occur side by side without distinction between them. Moreover three (or four) further prohibitions were added to the basic list of twelve through tradition and redaction history: the prohibition of killing a child for Molech (vv. 2–5), of illicit mantic

---

[35] Thus also Grünwaldt, *Heiligkeitsgesetz*, 213–14.

practices (vv. 6 and 27), and of cursing the parents (v. 9) (and of unclean food [vv. 25–26]).

Third: The two basic series, Lev 18:6–18 and 20:10–21, differ in form. Leviticus 18 directly addresses the *paterfamilias* in the second person, in a formulaic language (except for the general principle in the title, v. 6), prohibits the forbidden sexual union in the protasis and motivates the prohibition in the apodosis. The regularity of the formulas, however, is not absolute. Leviticus 20:10–21 defines in casuistic formulation in the third person (always with "man" as subject, except in v. 16 where the woman is subject) the transgression in the protasis and the punishment (legal consequence) in the apodosis. But here too, the regularity suffers from exceptions (second person singular in v. 19).

The additional prohibitions in Lev 18:19–23 and Lev 20:2–6, 9, 25–27 vary from case to case without pattern. The regularity is most prominent in Lev 18:19–23 (direct speech in the second person, except for v. 23b).

Fourth: The specific focus of the basic series of Lev 18:6–18 is the prohibition of sexual unions that would confuse the social roles within the family so that it would become impossible for its members to clearly situate themselves in the community. The violation of existing and long-practiced, well-known kinship relations and alliances by new sexual and matrimonial relationships would lead to social and individual psychological chaos.

Fifth: The specific focus of the basic series of Lev 20:10–21, on the other hand, is the punishment that will fall on both persons involved in forbidden sexual intercourse, even animals in the case of bestiality (vv. 15–16). The penalty means that the whole community disproves of the transgressions, but will not be held guilty for those faults or crimes.

Sixth: The focus of the five additional prohibitions, which in Lev 18:19–23 are added to the basic series of vv. 6–18, seems to be first of all on the stolen capacity of procreation and birth-giving (which God bestows on men in a special authorization, Gen 1:28; 9:1). But since these five additional prohibitions follow without transition those of the basic series, vv. 6–18, they extend the number of human relationships in which sexual relations should be prohibited in the interest of the family and its larger social environment, in order to preserve them from chaos, cruelty and additional conflicts.

Seventh: The relation between the five additional prohibitions, vv. 19–23, and those of the basic series, vv. 6–21, with regard to their function, can be shown also in the interpretation of the five pre-scriptions as such: *adultery*, v. 20, tears to pieces the social net between the families; killing one's own *child*, v. 21 deeply hurts the security children are to experience in their home, a security all members of the family require; *sodomy* or *bestiality*, v. 23, destroys the human dig-nity of sexuality, a dignity which must characterize all other sexual and non-sexual relations of the family; *menstruating women*, v. 19, requires a man's continence during his wife's menstruation and lim-its his absolute right to dispose of his wife. This in turn becomes a sign that sexual needs lose their claim to satisfaction under any cir-cumstance. Hence male *homosexual* intercourse is to be interpreted in an analogous way (v. 22): special relationships of pairs of loving men would run against the matrimonial and family relationships in which such adult men stand, and would introduce additional seeds of conflict into the extended family where all kinds of tensions already exist. Taking into account the passionate quality of loving relationships it is easy to perceive the complexity and explosive power of such rela-tions between wives, husbands and their male lovers. The social hori-zon of the prohibition of homosexuality here refers to a limited group of persons, i.e. the extended family group and the totality of extended families in the village and in the region. All five prohibitions of vv. 19–23 have the same purpose as the incest prohibitions: they pre-serve clear social relationships and safeguard the people against chaos.

Eighth: Leviticus 20 confirms the interpretation proposed in con-clusion seven; there the incest prohibitions from Lev 18:6–18 as well as the five additional prohibitions in vv. 19–23 appear as one basic series without internal distinction (vv. 10–21). Thus the authors—or perhaps the redactors—of the series in Lev 20:10–21 did not make a distinction in the prohibitions between incest and other prohibi-tions and subjected both to the same penalty of death. They seem to imply one common characteristic in all these prohibitions.

Ninth: The additional prohibitions of Lev 20:1–5, 6, 9, 17, and perhaps also vv. 25–26, are different by nature. What seems to be common to them is the fact that they apparently require, like the prohibitions of the basic series, accomplices in order to be carried out and that they must be punished by order of the whole com-munity which would become guilty if it tolerated them silently.

Tenth: Sexual intercourse in Leviticus 18 and 20 seems to mean in each case the act itself as well as the corresponding matrimonial union. This is shown by the comparison of Lev 18:17–18; 20:14 (matrimonial union) and Lev 18:19; 20:18 etc. (sexual act). Where sexual intercourse is legitimate in principle, there the corresponding marriage *can* be legitimate and vice-versa; i.e. where the sexual act is illicit, e.g. with an already married woman, no legitimate marriage is conceivable. To the prohibition of sexual intercourse with X corresponds the prohibition of any marriage with X.

Eleventh: Leviticus 18 does not forbid explicitly sexual intercourse and marriage with a personal daughter of the husband, but this is implied in the first of the four prohibitions of vv. 17–18, which prohibit certain types of kinship relations between the spouses of a husband in a polygamous marriage. In the first prohibition of v. 17 the mother and daughter pair is excluded from the several wives of the husband and, accordingly, there must be no sexual intercourse between the husband and the two women. Therefore the husband's daughters and step-daughters are *ipso facto* illicit wives for him.

Twelfth: Two clearly recognizable distinct redactions anchor the basic lists and additional prohibitions of Leviticus 18 and 20 in the narrative context. The more recent one comprises Lev 18:24–30; 20:22–24a. It is characterized by the metaphor of the land vomiting out its inhabitants which appears only in these two places in the Old Testament. For this redaction the whole narrative context implied begins with the promise of the land and ends with the land which has vomited out its autochthonous populations and to which YHWH is now bringing Israel. The horizon of the future which corresponds to the past narrated in the Pentateuch is the possibility for the land to vomit out its Israelite inhabitants if they were to defile it by transgressing the prohibitions of Leviticus 18 and 20.

Thirteenth: This theme gives us two hints concerning the absolute chronology of this redaction. First of all it presupposes the Pentateuch in its actual shape, reaching from the promise of the land until the expulsion out of the indigenous peoples before the coming Israelites; secondly the conviction that disregarding the prohibitions of Leviticus 18 and 20 defiles the land and its inhabitants and therefore seriously endangers Israel's possession of the land can only be found at two places in the whole Bible, namely in Lev 18:24–30 and Ezra 9. This points to Ezra's time.

Fourteenth: This redaction achieves three goals: it makes of Leviticus 18, 19 and 20 a literary and redactional unit; it gives the laws of these three chapters, although they didn't come from Mount Sinai, the heavy weight of a *conditio sine qua non* for Israel's remaining in the land; it motivates the observance of these commandments with the threat that Israel will lose the land if the Israelites do not observe precisely these laws.

Fifteenth: The early redaction, Lev 18:2–5, on the contrary, implies a more narrow Pentateuchal narrative: it reaches from the exodus from Egypt, viewed in Leviticus 18 as a past event, until the entrance of Israel to Canaan, which is still lying ahead. There is no mention of casting out the indigenous peoples. YHWH rather places Israel before the choice either to follow YHWH's laws or those of Egypt and Canaan. By choosing YHWH's ordinances the reward is life (Lev 18:5). The motivation is positive, the promise of life, not negative, the threat of loosing the land. Such a perspective is very close to deuteronomic-deuteronomistic texts.

Sixteenth and last: The present examination leaves open some particular questions, which would have to be discussed in a complete commentary. Here the question to be answered was the meaning of the prohibitions compiled in Leviticus 18 and 20 as a collection, and also as parts of the Pentateuchal narrative in which they are located. It is hoped that this inquiry into an exegetical problem, the interpretation of the coherence of the prohibitions of Leviticus 18 and 20, will shed light on the important and much debated theological questions concerning family, sexuality, homosexuality, etc.

Select Bibliography of Works not Cited

Bigger, S. F. "The Family Laws of Leviticus 18 in their setting," *JBL* 98 (1979) 187–203.

Daube, D. *Studies in Biblical Law* (Cambridge: University Press, 1947).

———. *Leviticus* (HAT 4; Tübingen: J. C. B. Mohr [Paul Siebeck], 1966).

Epstein, L. M. *Marriage Laws in the Bible and in the Talmud* (Cambridge Ma.: Harvard University Press, 1942).

Joosten, J. *People and Land in the Holiness Code. An Exegetical Study on the Ideational Framework of the Law in Leviticus 17–26* (VTSup 67; Leiden: Brill, 1996).

Kugler, R. A. "Holiness, Purity, the Body and Society: the Evidence for Theological Conflict in Leviticus," *JSOT* 76 (1997) 3–27.

Lafont, S. *Femmes, Droit et Justice dans l'Antiquité orientale. Contribution à l'étude du droit pénal au Proche-Orient ancien* (OBO 165; Göttingen: Vandenhoeck & Ruprecht, 1999).

Levine, B. *Leviticus* (The JPS Torah Commentary; Philadelphia: The Jewish Publication Society, 1991).

Neufeld, E. *Ancient Hebrew Marriage Laws with Special References to General Semitic Laws and Customs* (London: Longmans, Green & Co., 1944).

Noth, M. *Das Dritte Buch Mose. Leviticus* (ATD 6; Göttingen: Vandenhoeck & Ruprecht, 1966).

Otto, E. "Homosexualität im Alten Orient und im Alten Testament," in *Kontinuum und Proprium: Studien zur Sozial- und Rechtsgeschichte des Alten Orients und des Alten Testaments* (Orientalia Biblica et Christiana 8; Wiesbaden: Harrassowitz, 1996) 322–30.

Péter-Contesse, R. *Lévitique 1–16* (CAT IIIa; Genève: Labor et Fides, 1993).

Richter, H.-F. *Geschlechtlichkeit, Ehe und Familie im Alten Testament und seiner Umwelt* (Frankfurt a.M.: Lang, 1978).

PART THREE

PRIESTHOOD IN LEVITICUS

LE SACERDOCE

René Péter-Contesse

Une lecture, même superficielle, du livre du Lévitique laisse appa-
raître le rôle fondamentalement médiateur du prêtre israélite. Les
prêtres forment une classe particulière au sein de la communauté,
servant d'intermédiaires obligés entre Dieu et son peuple. Cette classe
sacerdotale comprendra aussi, à d'autres époques, les lévites, lesquels
cependant ne sont mentionnés qu'une seule fois dans le Lévitique,
de manière quasi fortuite, dans la Loi de sainteté (25:32–33).[1]

Le vocabulaire

Le mot כֹּהֵן = "prêtre" apparaît 194 fois dans le livre du Lévitique,[2]
mais jamais, de manière à première vue surprenante, dans les chapitres 8–10 qui parlent pourtant de la consécration des prêtres, de
leur entrée en fonction et de certaines particularités de leurs tâches.
En fait, si le titre en question ne figure pas dans cette section, c'est
que les prêtres concernés y sont désignés à trente-trois reprises par
leur nom (Aaron) ou par leur filiation (les fils d'Aaron/ses fils). Dans
quarante-sept autres passages du livre, Aaron et/ou ses fils sont mentionnés, dont onze fois conjointement avec le titre de כֹּהֵן. Si l'on
compte encore deux emplois du verbe כָּהַן = "exercer le sacerdoce",
on trouve donc plus de 260 mentions du sacerdoce dans le livre du
Lévitique. C'est dire le rôle prépondérant qu'il y joue.

La conception moderne du sacerdoce (catholique) ou du ministère
(réformé) est basée sur une notion de vocation individuelle, acceptée
par une personne et reconnue par la communauté. Le prêtre juif au
contraire n'est pas l'objet de la part de Dieu d'un appel particulier.
Comme le montre ce qui vient d'être dit à propos du vocabulaire

---

[1] Le nom *Lévitique*, dérivé, par l'intermédiaire de la Vg (*liber*) *leviticus*, du titre
donné au livre dans la LXX (λευ[ε]ιτικον), pourrait laisser croire à certains que ce
livre va parler des *lévites*. Or en fait il parle surtout des prêtres, descendants d'Aaron,
lui-même issu de la tribu de *Lévi* (Ex 6:16–25), d'où le nom de *Lévitique*.

[2] Soit plus du quart des 750 occurrences du mot dans l'Ancien Testament.

("le prêtre Aaron et ses fils", "les prêtres, fils d'Aaron"), le prêtre juif est l'objet d'une vocation collective, qui remonte à l'ancêtre de la lignée; c'est en tant que membre d'une branche particulière de la tribu de Lévi qu'il est investi d'une charge et de privilèges sacerdotaux.[3]

La hiérarchie sacerdotale

Celui qui deviendra ultérieurement le "grand-prêtre" de la communauté juive commence à être distingué des simples prêtres dans le Lévitique. Il occupe une fonction de chef, de responsable à l'égard de ses collègues et de l'ensemble de la communauté, bien qu'il ne porte pas encore un titre précis. Il est mentionné en 4:3, 5, 16 comme משיח הכהן = "le prêtre consacré par l'onction" (sur l'onction des prêtres, voir le paragraphe suivant), et en 21:10 comme הכהן הגדול מאחיו = "le prêtre plus grand que ses frères"; ces deux appellations sont de type descriptif,[4] et non pas des titres officiels comme le deviendra הכהן הגדול en Agg 1:1; Zach 3:8; Néh 3:1 et 2 Chr 34:9. Dans la fiction littéraire du Lévitique, c'est Aaron, frère de Moïse, qui est le "grand-prêtre", bien que ce titre ne lui soit jamais appliqué explicitement; les autres prêtres, subalternes, sont souvent appelés "fils d'Aaron".

L'onction sacerdotale

Comme cela vient d'être signalé, l'expression descriptive הכהן המשיח (4:3, 5, 16) désigne le "grand-prêtre" ou le chef des prêtres. Cette formulation implique que lui seul recevait l'onction, à l'exclusion des simples prêtres. On retrouve cette perspective en 8:12; 16:32 et 21:12; voir également Ex 29:7, 29. Mais une autre tradition, attestée en Lév 8:30 et 10:7 (de même qu'en Ex 28:41; 29:21; 30:30; 40:15; Nomb 3:3) étend l'onction à tous les prêtres.

---

[3] D'autres traditions vétérotestamentaires parlent du prêtre Sadoq (sous la règne de David et de Salomon) et de sa descendance, constituant une famille sacerdotale. C'est tardivement que cette lignée, d'origine inconnue, fut rattachée généalogiquement à la famille d'Aaron (1 Chr 5:27–41; 6:35–38; 24:1–3).

[4] Comme le sera encore (ה)כהן (ה)ראש = "le prêtre en chef" en 2 Rois 25:18; Esd 7:5; 1 Chr 27:5–41 et 2 Chr 19:11).

Il est probable que l'onction généralisée des prêtres (si elle a jamais été pratiquée?) a succédé à celle du seul grand-prêtre; l'onction de ce dernier n'est intervenue elle-même qu'après l'exil, à l'époque où il n'y avait plus de roi en Israël. Le grand-prêtre apparaît alors comme le véritable chef de la nation, réunissant sur ses épaules l'autorité religieuse et l'autorité politique. Il semble donc que l'onction du grand-prêtre soit intervenue à cette époque comme un transfert sur lui de l'onction royale, clairement attestée pour l'époque pré-exilique (1 Sam 16:13; 2 Sam 19:11; 1 Rois 1:39; 19:16; etc.). Cette onction du grand-prêtre est d'ailleurs accompagnée de la remise d'un turban et d'un insigne (Lév 8:9), qui faisaient antérieurement partie des attributs royaux (מצנפת = "turban", voir Éz 21:31; נזר = "insigne"/"diadème", voir 2 Sam 1:10; 2 Rois 11:12; Ps 89:40; 132:18).

Les tâches sacerdotales

Tâches du grand-prêtre

Le Lévitique n'attribue explicitement au grand-prêtre que deux tâches particulières.

A) Il est chargé d'offrir le sacrifice pour le péché lorsque l'ensemble du peuple est concerné (4:13–21).[5]

B) Il accomplit le rituel annuel du Jour du Grand Pardon. Le 10e jour du 7e mois (de l'année commençant au printemps,[6] donc vers fin septembre ou début octobre; voir 16:29; 23:27, 32; 25:9), le grand-prêtre accomplit une double cérémonie, en vue de purifier le sanctuaire et d'obtenir pour le peuple le pardon des péchés qui n'auraient pas été effacés par les rites ordinaires. Tout d'abord il accomplit certains rites sacrificiels (holocaustes, sacrifices pour le péché) et apporte du sang et une cassolette de parfum jusque dans le lieu très saint. Ensuite il procède à un rituel tout à fait particulier: il place ses deux

---

[5] En 4:3–12, le grand-prêtre n'agit pas en tant que grand-prêtre, mais en tant qu'individu qui a péché, même si, comme le dit le v. 3, sa faute entraîne le peuple dans la culpabilité.

[6] Dans le calendrier antérieur, où l'année commençait en automne, ce rituel prenait donc place au début de la nouvelle année. Lors du changement de calendrier, l'insertion automnale de la cérémonie aura prévalu sur le lien avec le début de l'année.

mains sur la tête d'un bouc et confesse sur lui tous les péchés du peuple, afin que ce bouc les emporte au loin dans le désert et en débarrasse ainsi l'ensemble de la communauté.[7] Contrairement à l'opinion défendue par certains, il ne s'agit pas là d'un sacrifice, mais d'un rituel tout à fait différent. De deux boucs, acceptables pour un sacrifice pour le péché, l'un a été désigné par le sort "pour Yahvé" (et il sera effectivement offert en sacrifice), et l'autre "pour Azazel", probablement un démon hantant les lieux désertiques. Mais il est impensable que les Israélites offrent un sacrifice à un démon: au contraire le grand-prêtre le charge, indirectement, des péchés commis par la nation, en lui envoyant le bouc "vivant" (16:20–22) porteur des péchés.[8]

Excursus 1: Moïse était-il prêtre?

On s'est parfois posé la question de savoir si Moïse était lui-même prêtre pour pouvoir présenter légitimement des sacrifices à l'autel et surtout procéder à la consécration sacerdotale d'Aaron et de ses fils (Lév 8).[9] Il semble que l'on puisse répondre clairement non à cette question. Même si la tradition sacerdotale a eu tendance, dans le domaine sacrificiel, à restreindre progressivement le rôle des laïcs au profit de celui des prêtres, en réservant exclusivement à ces derniers certaines tâches spécifiques, l'auteur sacerdotal ne pouvait pas ignorer l'antique prérogative des laïcs habilités autrefois à officier dans le rituel sacrificiel; il n'avait donc pas absolument besoin de faire de Moïse un prêtre au sens strict pour lui attribuer le rôle qui est le sien dans Lév 8. La situation est encore plus claire en ce qui concerne

---

[7] Sur le rite d'"imposition des mains", voir plus bas, p. 201–8.

[8] En Lév 9:22–23, à la fin de la cérémonie solennelle d'entrée en fonction des prêtres, Aaron prononce la bénédiction en élevant les mains en direction du peuple; il pénètre ensuite en compagnie de Moïse dans la Tente de la rencontre, et enfin, à leur sortie, ils bénissent conjointement le peuple. Il ne faudrait pas tirer de ce récit la conclusion que la *bénédiction* serait une des tâches du grand-prêtre en tant que tel; il s'agit d'une tâche sacerdotale, qui n'est pas mentionnée ailleurs dans le Lévitique, mais que l'on trouve en Nomb 6:22–27; Deut 21:5 et 1 Chr 23:13. Si en Lév 9, Aaron seul bénit le peuple, sans participation explicite de ses fils, cela est conforme à la ligne de l'ensemble du chapitre, où c'est Aaron qui préside personnellement tout le rituel sacrificiel, ses fils n'apparaissant que comme des acolytes à son service. Pourtant, au travers d'Aaron, c'est bien toute la classe sacerdotale qui entre en fonction et qui s'initie au rôle sacrificiel avec lui. Il en va certainement de même en ce qui concerne la bénédiction, tâche (et privilège) de la classe sacerdotale dans son ensemble.

[9] Voir A. Cody, *A History of Old Testament Priesthood* (AnBib 35; Rome: Pontifical Biblical Institute, 1969) 41–50.

la consécration proprement dite. À la base, le récit de Lév 8 traite manifestement de "l'institution du sacerdoce", et non de la simple consécration d'un grand-prêtre parmi d'autres; nous sommes, dans l'optique de P, à l'origine de la fonction sacerdotale en Israël. Si donc Aaron est le *premier* grand-prêtre et ses fils les *premiers* prêtres, il est évident que Moïse ne pouvait être ni l'un ni l'autre.

En fait, pour P, Moïse transcende la figure du prêtre israélite; il agit spécifiquement comme prêtre lors de cette cérémonie, sans l'être institutionnellement. Mais cela fait partie de la dimension particulière que les traditions vétérotestamentaires attribuent à cet homme: il est parfois appelé "prophète" (Deut 18:15, 18; 34:10), alors même qu'il transcende la figure traditionnelle du prophète hébreu; enfin l'on peut rappeler encore son rôle "judiciaire" (Ex 18:13–26) et son rôle politique à la tête d'Israël, même s'il n'est jamais appelé ni "juge" ni "roi". Moïse est tout cela à la fois, sans l'être vraiment, et surtout sans que l'on puisse l'enfermer dans une catégorie ou une autre. Il est ainsi, à sa manière, préfiguration du Christ, lui aussi grand-prêtre (même sans être prêtre, voir Hébr 8:1–4), prophète (Matt 21:11; Luc 7:16), législateur (Jean 13:34) et chef du peuple nouveau qu'est l'Église (Éph 1:21–22).

Tâches des prêtres

Le Lévitique mentionne trois rôles du prêtre, en tant qu'intermédiaire entre Dieu et son peuple: un rôle cultuel, un rôle de discernement et d'enseignement, et un rôle oraculaire. Ces trois rôles sont énumérés dans l'ordre décroissant de leur importance dans le Lévitique, mais nous allons les examiner dans l'ordre inverse.

Rôle oraculaire

Le fonction oraculaire de prêtre, qui semble avoir eu une certaine importance avant l'exil (voir 1 Sam 14:36–37, 41–42; 22:10; 23:9–12; 28:6) n'apparaît plus que sous une forme atrophiée et symbolique dans le Lévitique. Lév 8:8 est le seul verset du livre à y faire allusion en signalant la présence de l'"Ourim" et du "Toummim" dans le "pectoral", pièce d'habillement qui fait partie de l'équipement vestimentaire d'apparat du grand-prêtre. Ces deux objets, Ourim et Toummim, dont on ignore la forme précise et le mode d'utilisation, étaient des instruments divinatoires au moyen desquels on pouvait interroger Dieu; on obtenait ainsi des informations sur les événements à venir et des directives sur la conduite à adopter. Ils sont mentionnés, outre 1 Sam 14:41 (LXX) et 28:6 déjà cités ci-dessus, en Ex 28:30; Nomb 27:21; Deut 33:8; Esd 2:63 et Néh 7:65; ils semblent avoir été utilisés de manière analogue aux "flèches" au moyen desquelles le roi de Babylone cherche des présages en Éz 21:26.

Si ce rôle particulier des prêtres s'est amenuisé avec le temps, pour ne plus être dans le Lévitique qu'une sorte de vestige archéologique subsistant dans un ornement vestimentaire, c'est que peu à peu les "voyants", précurseurs des "prophètes" (voir 1 Sam 9:6–11, 18–19) ont assumé cet aspect de la médiation entre Dieu et Israël.

Rôle de discernement et d'enseignement

Lév 10:8–9 interdit à Aaron, en tant que grand-prêtre, et à ses fils, en tant que prêtres, de consommer des boissons alcooliques au moment d'entrer dans la Tente de la rencontre (c'est-à-dire dans le sanctuaire). Les v. 10–11 justifient cette prescription en disant: "C'est pour être à même de distinguer le sacré du profane, ce qui est impur de ce qui est pur, et d'enseigner aux fils d'Israël tous les décrets que le Seigneur a édictés pour eux par l'intermédiaire de Moïse".

Le discernement. L'articulation entre "sacré/profane" d'une part, et "pur/impur" d'autre part, n'est pas facile à saisir. Dans notre commentaire de Lévitique 1–16,[10] nous avons présenté un diagramme, qui n'est peut-être pas le dernier mot sur la question, mais qui nous semble pouvoir aider au moins à clarifier quelques aspects de cette relation et à éviter certaines fausses interprétations. L'essentiel en tout cas, c'est de ne pas identifier "sacré" (ou sainteté) et "pureté" d'un côté et "profane" (ou non-sainteté = péché) et "impureté" de l'autre. Il s'agit dans les deux cas ("sacré/profane" et "pur/impur") de deux approches globales du réel, de deux conceptions du monde, qui ne coïncident pas dans leur découpage de la réalité. Mais ce n'est pas ici le lieu d'examiner plus en détail cette question.[11] Ce qui nous intéresse, c'est le rôle du prêtre, chargé de prononcer une décision en cas de situation litigieuse; il doit permettre aux membres du peuple de Dieu d'éviter, autant que faire se peut, un état d'impureté (qui les exclurait de la communauté et donc de la communion avec Dieu) ou une intrusion dans la sphère de la sainteté divine (qui les disqualifierait tout aussi certainement). Si dans la plupart des événements de la vie des Israélites, il était facile pour tout

---

[10] R. Péter-Contesse, *Lévitique 1–16* (Genève: Labor et Fides, 1993) 240–44.
[11] [Text]

un chacun de savoir s'il était en état d'impureté ou s'il pénétrait indûment dans la sphère de la sainteté, il y avait aussi des cas limites où le prêtre était appelé à user de son discernement pour trancher dans un sens ou un autre (voir l'exemple concret dont parle le prophète en Agg 2:11–13). Lév 11–15, et tout particulièrement les chapitres 13–14, constituent un aide-mémoire des prêtres, qui doit leur permettre de prendre des décisions correctes et bénéfiques pour la communauté.

L'enseignement. La tâche d'enseignement des prêtres recouvre partiellement leur tâche de discernement; ils doivent en effet communiquer aux Israélites le résultat de leur examen des cas particuliers qui leur ont été soumis. Mais ils doivent en plus enseigner aux laïcs les prescriptions divines, les חקים, transmises par Dieu à Israël, généralement par l'intermédiaire de Moïse (10:11). Le prêtre Esdras (voir Esd 7:10) est un bon témoin de cette tâche sacerdotale, dans la période post-exilique.

Dans le Lévitique, les chapitres 1–7 et 11–15, ainsi que l'essentiel de la Loi de sainteté (chapitres 16–26) et le chapitre 27 (annexe), constituent un ensemble bien structuré de ces prescriptions divines que les prêtres doivent enseigner aux fidèles tout en veillant à ce qu'ils les appliquent. On y trouve aussi bien des aspects liturgiques ou cultuels que moraux et sociaux. Dans toutes ces dimensions, le but final de l'activité sacerdotale est de favoriser la cohésion, par exemple la cohésion du couple par le rejet des unions illégitimes (chapitres 18 et 20), la cohésion de la famille, par le respect à l'égard des parents (19:3) et des enfants (19:29), la cohésion sociale, par l'attitude à l'égard des éléments les plus faibles de la communauté (19:13–16, 32–36; 25:35–54), et enfin la cohésion dans l'alliance entre Dieu et son peuple (tout particulièrement le chapitre 26).

La tâche d'enseignement dévolue aux prêtres sera dans la suite progressivement assumée par les lévites (voir Néh 8:7–9; 2 Chr 17:7–9; 35:3).

Rôle cultuel

Alors qu'avant l'exil, il n'était pas rare que des non-prêtres exercent certaines fonctions cultuelles,[12] après l'exil, les prêtres se réservèrent

---

[12] Noé offre des sacrifices à la fin du Déluge (Gen 8:20); de même Abraham (Gen 22:13), Gédéon (Jug 6:26) et Achaz (2 Rois 16:12–13); Salomon préside toute une cérémonie de consécration du Temple (1 Rois 8), qu'il termine en prononçant une bénédiction solennelle sur le peuple (v. 55–61).

peu à peu ces tâches. Ils concentrèrent leur intérêt sur cette dimension du ministère de médiation, abandonnant parallèlement et progressivement leur rôle oraculaire aux prophètes et leur rôle d'enseignement
aux lévites.

Il est possible de distinguer trois aspects dans le rôle cultuel du
sacerdoce:

La bénédiction. De la part de Dieu, le prêtre prononce une parole
agissante, une parole porteuse de sens, de force et de vie. Elle rappelle le lien qui unit Dieu au peuple qu'il s'est choisi, et Israël à
son Dieu. Le Lévitique ne rapporte pas de formule proprement dite
de bénédiction, mais mentionne qu'Aaron et Moïse ont béni le peuple au terme de la cérémonie d'entrée en fonction des prêtres
(9:22–23).[13]

La formule de bénédiction sacerdotale bien connue de Nomb
6:24–26 est intéressante, en ce qu'elle est introduite par le v. 23,
adressé "à Aaron et à ses fils", donc spécifiquement à la classe sacerdotale, et en ce qu'elle est suivie du v. 27 "Ils apposeront ainsi mon
nom sur les fils d'Israël, et moi, je les bénirai". Le "nom" est ici un
signe de propriété pour Dieu, et d'appartenance pour le peuple, donc
le signe d'un lien très fort; de plus, dans la même ligne, Dieu s'engage
personnellement ("et moi, je les bénirai") dans la parole prononcée
par les prêtres.

L'offrande de parfum. Il va de soi qu'il s'agit là d'une prérogative des
prêtres, puisque l'autel du parfum[14] est situé à l'intérieur de la Tente
de la rencontre (ou du Temple), dans la première partie du sanctuaire, devant le rideau de séparation intérieur (voir Ex 30:1–6; 1
Rois 6:22), et que seuls les prêtres ont le droit de pénétrer dans le
sanctuaire.[15]

L'offrande des sacrifices. C'est ce domaine-là que les prêtres juifs ont
petit à petit monopolisé. Bien que le vocabulaire hébreu ne soit pas

---

[13] En 26:3–13, Moïse énumère les bienfaits que Dieu accordera à son peuple,
"si vous suivez mes lois, si vous gardez mes commandements et les mettez en pratique". Il s'agit là d'une liste de "bénédictions" promises (suivie d'une liste parallèle de malédictions, v. 14–39; voir le texte formellement semblable de Deut 28:1–14,
15–68), mais pas d'une formule liturgique de bénédiction.

[14] De nombreuses versions françaises de la Bible et de dictionnaires bibliques parlent traditionnellement de l'autel "des parfums" (probablement à cause du pluriel
הסמים); en réalité, il s'agit "du parfum", קטרת, "des aromates", הסמים (voir Ex
30:34–35); ce parfum, unique, était obtenu par un mélange de plusieurs aromates.

[15] Ainsi s'explique l'épisode relatif au roi Ozias (2 Chr 26:16–20), frappé de lèpre
pour avoir osé pénétrer dans le Temple afin d'y offrir de l'encens.

encore unifié, l'idée de "s'approcher" (קרב, נגש) de l'autel (אל המזבח), ou du sanctuaire, ou du Seigneur, est une caractéristique du statut sacerdotal (voir Ex 28:43; 30:20; Lév 9:7–8; 10:3; Éz 40:46; 44:15–16). Les prêtres, qui ont été consacrés tout comme l'autel et la Tente de la rencontre, ont partie liée avec ces deux édifices et sont seuls admis à y accéder, car il faut être "saint" pour accéder à un endroit "saint".

Au prêtre sont donc réservés un certain nombre d'actes sacrificiels bien précis: apporter le sang de la victime pour en asperger le pourtour de l'autel, allumer (ou maintenir allumé) le feu sur l'autel, disposer les morceaux de la victime sur les bûches enflammées de l'autel (Lév 1:5, 7, 8, 9; de même Lév 3 et Lév 4).[16] Dans le cas de l'offrande végétale (Lév 2), le prêtre intervient également lorsqu'il s'agit d'apporter à l'autel la partie de l'offrande qui doit y être brûlée (v. 2–3, 8–9).

Dans le cadre du rituel relatif au "sacrifice pour le péché" (חטאת), le prêtre (ou le prend-prêtre suivant les cas) assume un rôle particulier. Il s'agit du rite de כפר. À la fin de quatre des cinq rituels énumérés en Lév 4, il est dit que וכפר עלהם/עליו הכהן, généralement rendu par "le prêtre fait le rite d'absolution sur eux/lui" (4:20, 26, 31, 35). Le verbe כפר apparaît quarante-neuf fois en tout dans le Lévitique, en particulier dans les chapitres 4, 5, 14 et 16. La racine en question a été étudiée et analysée de manière approfondie par B. Janowski.[17] Comme nous l'avons souligné dans notre commentaire du Lévitique[18] et comme Janowski l'avait montré également, plusieurs problèmes se posent à propos de ce verbe (par exemple l'étymologie, et la construction du verbe avec son complément [on trouve six prépositions différentes!]). À notre avis cependant, le problème principal est de savoir si כפר résume en un mot le rituel précédent ou s'il désigne un rite particulier accompli par le prêtre, à la suite de la mise à mort de la victime et de l'offrande de la chair sur l'autel. La plupart des commentateurs ne se posent pas cette question et par conséquent n'y apportent pas de réponse. Plusieurs,

---

[16] Selon le texte hébreu de Lév 1:5, c'est l'offrant qui égorge la victime; selon la LXX (verbe au pluriel), ce sont les prêtres qui accomplissent ce geste (de même que dans le texte hébreu de 2 Chr 29:22–24). En Éz 44:11 et 2 Chr 35:6, ce sont les lévites que en sont chargés. C'est l'indice d'une pratique fluctuante, qui va certainement dans le sens d'une augmentation des prérogatives sacerdotales.

[17] B. Janowski, *Sühne als Heilsgeschehen* (WMANT 55; Neukirchen-Vluyn: Neukirchener Verlag, 1982).

[18] R. Péter-Contesse, *Lévitique 1–16*, 81–83.

dont Janowski, considèrent que כפר résume le rituel précédent. Pour notre part, d'accord en cela avec G. Gerleman,[19] nous préférons y voir un rite spécifique, pour les deux raisons suivantes: 1. l'emploi de la préposition על, la plus fréquente après le verbe כפר, et qui a plusieurs fois une valeur clairement locale, nous semble aller dans ce sens-là; 2. l'absence de la formule וכפר עליו הכהן à la fin du premier rituel du chapitre 4 (v. 3–12) se justifie dans le sens où il n'est guère vraisemblable que le grand-prêtre accomplisse le rite en question sur lui-même. Si כפר ne faisait que résumer le rituel précédent, il n'y aurait pas de raison pour qu'il ne figure pas au v. 12. Il faudrait dans ce cas donner une explication valable de cette absence.[20]

Si l'auteur ne décrit pas spécifiquement le rite de כפר, c'est que pour ses contemporains et coreligionnaires, le déroulement en était suffisamment connu et n'avait pas besoin d'être décrit. Nous ne pouvons plus aujourd'hui que l'imaginer. Nous ne serions probablement pas loin de la réalité en supposant qu'un geste particulier, peut-être une aspersion d'eau lustrale au moyen d'une branche d'hysope (voir Ps 51:9) accompagnait une formule déclarative dans le genre de נסלח לך = "il t'est pardonné" = "Dieu te pardonne".[21]

Conclusion: Le prêtre, médiateur et représentant

Parler du sacerdoce dans le Lévitique, c'est parler d'une fonction tout à la fois de médiation et de représentation.[22]

La médiation est le fait d'une personne neutre, que s'entremet entre deux interlocuteurs pour établir un contact. Lorsque le dialogue a été instauré, le médiateur devient parfois superflu: le courant peut passer directement entre les interlocuteurs.

---

[19] G. Gerleman, "Die Wurzel *kpr* im Hebräischen" in *Studien zur alttestamentlichen Theologie* (Franz Delitzsch Vorlesungen; Heidelberg: Schneider, 1980).

[20] K. Elliger (*Leviticus* [HAT; Tübingen: J. C. B. Mohr {Paul Siebeck}, 1966] 70) se borne à constater que cette absence est bizarre; M. Noth (*Das dritte Buch Mose: Leviticus* [ATD; Göttingen: Vandenhoeck & Ruprecht, 1966] 31) pense que la formule de conclusion a dû figurer primitivement à la fin des v. 3–12, mais a disparu par suite d'une inadvertance. De telles explications, superficielles, ne sont guère convaincantes.

[21] En Matt 9:2, 5 (et les parallèles), Jésus déclare au paralytique αφιενται σου αι αμαρτιαι; il est possible qu'il ait repris la formule déclarative du rituel (voir la rétroversion hébraïque de F. Delitzsch נסלחו לך הטאתיך), sur quoi ses adversaires lui auraient reproché d'usurper une fonction exclusive du prêtre.

[22] Voir G. Auzou, "Connaissance du Lévitique", *Cahiers sioniens* 7 (1953) 291–319, en particulier p. 301.

La représentation n'est pas identique; le représentant peut remplacer un des interlocuteurs empêché d'être présent. Il peut même arriver que les deux parties se fassent représenter pour un dialogue par personnes interposées.

Le prêtre du Lévitique est à la fois un médiateur et un représentant.[23] Comme médiateur, il établit le contact entre Dieu et Israël, sans toutefois jamais devenir un élément superflu du dialogue; il reste un passage obligé de la relation. C'est ce qu'exprime la dimension de représentation qu'il assume conjointement. La particularité de sa position de représentant est qu'il est "double face", chargé aussi bien de représenter Dieu face au peuple, que le peuple face à Dieu.

C'est dans son rôle de "discernement" que le prêtre est le plus clairement le médiateur entre Dieu et son peuple. Dans son rôle oraculaire primitif (8:8), dans son rôle d'enseignement (le Lévitique en général) et dans son rôle de porte-parole de la bénédiction divine (9:22–23), le prêtre est le représentant de Dieu devant Israël; à l'inverse, dans ses tâches sacrificielles (particulièrement chapitre 9), purificatrices (14:3–20 par exemple) et expiatoires (chapitre 16 essentiellement), il fonctionne comme représentant d'Israël devant Dieu.

Excursus 2: L'imposition des mains[24]

Dans plusieurs passages du Lévitique, Aaron et ses fils, ou Aaron seul (grand-prêtre), pratiquent un geste rituel particulier consistant à placer une main ou les mains sur la tête d'un animal. Quelle est la signification de ce geste?

On parle généralement du rite d'"imposition des mains"; mais comme le montrera l'analyse qui suit, il faut en fait distinguer deux rites distincts, l'un d'"imposition des (deux) mains", l'autre d'"imposition de la main".

La plupart des auteurs qui ont étudié ce problème ont noté que les textes de l'Ancien Testament ne donnaient pas une image claire et précise de ce rite. Le verbe le plus souvent employé est סמך, mais on rencontre aussi occasionnellement deux autres verbes; le sujet est tantôt un individu, tantôt une collectivité; tantôt un prêtre, tantôt un laïc; tantôt un chef; tantôt un simple citoyen; l'objet est tantôt

---

[23] C'est le grand-prêtre que résume en lui-même cette double fonction; les prêtres ordinaires "participent" collectivement à son ministère.

[24] La section qui suit est la reprise, quelque peu remaniée, de R. Péter-Contesse, "L'imposition des mains dans l'Ancien Testament," *VT* 27 (1977) 48–55.

une main, tantôt les deux mains; enfin le destinataire est tantôt un animal, tantôt un être humain; tantôt un homme que l'on "consacre", tantôt un coupable que l'on voue à la mort.

La très grande variété de ces éléments ne facilitait pas l'étude de la question. Il en résultait que l'on trouvait chez certains auteurs qui l'avaient abordée, soit des affirmations très générales, qui ne rendaient pas compte des différences essentielles,[25] soit une présentation analytique qui ne faisait pas suffisamment ressortir les relations fondamentales existant entre ces éléments divers.[26] Les auteurs plus récents ont généralement tenu compte, dans une mesure plus ou moins grande, des résultats auxquels arrivait notre article de *Vetus Testamentum*.[27]

A) La combinaison du verbe סמך et du substantif יד (comme complément d'objet direct) se rencontre vingt-cinq fois dans l'Ancien Testament. Mais d'emblée nous pouvons laisser de côté deux cas qui ne concernent pas notre recherche: Ps 37:24, où la main n'est pas celle du sujet (le Seigneur soutient la main de celui qui est tombé) et Amos 5:19, où le texte décrit un simple geste physique, sans valeur rituelle (un homme appuie sa main contre le mur, et un serpent le mord).

Par contre l'examen de la LXX nous permet de relever quelques autres cas intéressants,[28] dont deux sont spécifiquement dans la ligne

---

[25] M. Bernoulli, "Imposition des mains", dans J.-J. von Allmen (éd.), *Vocabulaire biblique* (Neuchâtel: Delachaux & Niestlé, 1954) 130–31; "Imposition des mains," *Encyclopédie de la Bible* (Bruxelles, 1961) 121.

[26] J. Coppens, "Handauflegung", dans B. Reike et L. Rost, *Biblisch-historisches Handwörterbuch: Landeskunde, Geschichte, Religion, Kultur* (Göttingen: Vandenhoeck & Ruprecht, 1962–1965) col. 632–36. E. Ferguson, "Selection and Installation to Office in Roman, Greek, Jewish and Christian Antiquity", *TZ* 30 (1974) 273–84 (surtout p. 283–84). H. Lesêtre, "Imposition des mains", dans F. Vigouroux (éd.), *Dictionnaire de la Bible* (Paris: Letouzey, 1912) col. 847–50. E. Lohse, *Die Ordination im Spätjudentum und im Neuen Testament* (Göttingen: Vandenhoeck & Ruprecht, 1951) 19–27. C. Maurer, "*tithemi*, etc.", *ThWNT* 8, 152–70 (surtout p. 160–61). M. H. Shepherd, "Hands, Laying on of", *IDB* 521–22. H. D. Wendland, "Handauflegung II. Biblisch", *RGG*[3], col. 53–54. Elliger (*Leviticus*) était à l'époque l'auteur qui s'exprimait de la manière la plus nuancée sur le sujet (voir p. 34, 215–16, 334), bien qu'il cherchât finalement à faire entrer tous les textes dans un schéma unique d'imposition de la main.

[27] Voir tout particulièrement Janowski, *Sühne*, R. Rendtorff, *Leviticus* (vol. 3.1; Neukirchen-Vluyn: Neukirchener Verlag, 1985) 32–35. D. P. Wright, J. Milgrom & H. J. Fabry, "סמך", *ThWAT* 5, col. 880–89.

[28] La LXX traduit régulièrement סמך יד/ידים par επιτιθεναι την/ται χειρα/χειρας, sauf dans les deux cas laissés de côté, où elle a bien senti qu'il s'agissait d'autre chose: αντιστηριζει en Ps 37(36):24, et απερεισηται en Amos 5:19. Par contre

de cette étude; ceci ramène donc la liste à 25 occurrences de l'expression: Ex 29:10, 15, 19; Lév 1:4, 10 (LXX); 3:2, 8, 13; 4:4, 15, 24, 29, 33; 8:14, 18, 22; 16:21; 24:14; Nomb 8:10, 12; 27:18, 23; Deut 34:9; 2 Chr 29:23; *Susanne* (= *Daniel grec* 13) 34 (LXX).

Une chose frappe dans cette liste: tous les textes sauf deux appartiennent à la source P;[29] mais si 2 Chr 29:23 n'en fait pas partie, on connaît néanmoins les affinités de P et du Chroniqueur. Et, quant à *Susanne* 34 (LXX), nous constatons que ce geste est manifestement inspiré du récit de Lév 24:14. L'unité d'origine de ce geste n'a d'ailleurs rien d'étonnant: il est normal que ce soit dans le milieu sacerdotal qu'on parle d'un rite aussi caractéristique.

Comme il ne se pose de problème de classification littéraire des textes, nous pouvons immédiatement établir le tableau synoptique de la page suivante, donnant, sur trois colonnes, a) l'identité du sujet de סמך, b) le nombre grammatical de l'objet direct (יד) de סמך, et c) l'identité du destinataire de ce geste. De l'examen de ce tableau, nous pouvons retirer de nombreuses constatations intéressantes.

	a) sujet	b) objet	c) destinataire
Ex 29:10	Aaron et ses fils	duel	taureau (sacr. péché)
15	Aaron et ses fils	duel	bélier (holocauste)
19	Aaron et ses fils	duel	bélier (sacr. investiture)
Lév 1:4	un offrant	singulier	gros bétail (holocauste)
10 (LXX)	un offrant	singulier	petit bétail (holocauste)
3:2	un offrant	singulier	gros bétail (sacr. comm.)
8	un offrant	singulier	mouton (sacr. comm.)
13	un offrant	singulier	chèvre (sacr. comm.)
4:4	le grand-prêtre	singulier	taureau (sacr. péché)
15	les anciens du peuple	duel	taureau (sacr. péché)
24	un chef	singulier	bouc (sacr. péché)
29	un simple citoyen	singulier	chèvre (sacr. péché)
33	un simple citoyen	singulier	brebis (sacr. péché)
8:14	Aaron et ses fils	duel	taureau (sacr. péché)
18	Aaron et ses fils	duel	bélier (holocauste)
22	Aaron et ses fils	duel	bélier (sacr. investiture)
16:21	Aaron	duel	bouc ("pour Azazel")
24:14	tous ceux qui ont entendu	duel	blasphémateur

l'emploi de ἐπιτιθέναι nous permet d'ajouter deux autres cas à la liste des emplois de סמך יד en hébreu. (Sur d'autres emplois de ἐπιτιθέναι dans la LXX, voir le paragraphe B ci-après).

[29] L'attribution de Deut 34:9 à P n'est pratiquement pas contestée.

Table (*cont.*)

	a) sujet	b) objet	c) destinataire
Nomb 8:10	les fils d'Israël	duel	lévites
12	les lévites	duel	taureaux (sacr. péché et holoc.)
27:18	tu (Moïse)	singulier	Josué
23	Moïse	duel	Josué
Deut 34:9	Moïse	duel	Josué
2 Chr 29:23	le roi et l'assemblée	duel	boucs (sacr. péché)
Susanne 34 (LXX)	les anciens et juges	pluriel	Susanne

La première sur laquelle nous nous arrêtons concerne les trois textes relatifs à Josué, entre lesquels il y a un désaccord: alors qu'en Nomb 27:18, Moïse reçoit l'ordre d'imposer *sa main* à Josué, au v. 23 il nous est dit qu'il lui impose *ses mains*, et c'est également ainsi que Deut 34:9 se réfère à l'événement. Les versions anciennes ne présentent pas toutes cette même difficulté: la LXX dit trois fois τας χειρας; le texte samaritain, au contraire, a les trois fois le singulier; le Targum et la Vulgate représentent fidèlement l'état actuel du texte massorétique; enfin la version syriaque (édition de Mossoul) a deux fois le singulier en Nomb 27, mais maintient le duel en Deut 34. On pourrait soupçonner, dans les traditions samaritaine, grecque et syriaque, des tentatives d'harmonisation, poussées plus ou moins loin, à partir d'un texte hébreu présentant au départ un désaccord.[30] Il nous semble plus vraisemblable de supposer qu'au départ il n'y avait pas désaccord en hébreu, mais simplement un emploi ambigu de la *scriptio defectiva* ידך en Nomb 27:18;[31] la LXX l'aura reconnu comme une forme défective du duel avec suffixe, et traduit en conséquence par un pluriel. Par contre une harmonisation en sens inverse aura été faite, partiellement par le traducteur syriaque (au v. 23, mais pas dans le Deutéronome), et totalement par le copiste samaritain, sur la base du ידך de Nomb 27:18, lu comme un singulier avec suffixe.

Si l'on admet l'hypothèse ci-dessus, à savoir que dans le cas de Josué, il est question d'une imposition *des (deux) mains* par Moïse, on découvre que les vingt-cinq textes du tableau précédent s'ordonnent

---

[30] Rachi *Les Nombres* (vol. 4 dans *Le Pentateuque avec commentaires de Rachi* [Paris: la Fondation O. & S. Levy, 1968]) commente Nomb 27:23 comme suit: "*Il posa ses mains sur lui.* Avec grande générosité; il a fait beaucoup plus que ce qui lui avait été ordonné, car Dieu lui avait dit: 'tu lui imposeras ta main', et, lui, il l'a fait de ses deux mains. Il l'a rempli de sa sagesse, généreusement, comme on remplit un récipient jusqu'au bord".

[31] Comparer les cas analogues de *scriptio defectiva* de 2 Sam 3:34; Jér 40:4 (ידך) et de Lév 16:21 (שתי ידו).

sans trop de difficultés en deux catégories clairement distinctes, se rapportant à deux rites différents: "imposition de la main" (ou "d'une main") et "imposition des mains" (ou "des deux mains.") Les cas déterminants sont ceux où le sujet est singulier: en Lév 1:4, 10 (LXX); 3:2, 8, 13; 4:4, 24, 29, 33, il est question de l'imposition *d'une main*; en Lév 16:21; Nomb 27:18 (corrigé d'après la LXX), 23; Deut 34:9, il est question de l'imposition *des deux mains*.

Dans la première série de textes, le geste est un élément constitutif du rituel sacrificiel (holocauste, sacrifice de communion, sacrifice pour le péché). Dans la seconde série, le geste est indépendant du rituel sacrificiel; il implique le transfert de quelque chose d'un être sur un autre: transfert du péché de la communauté sur le bouc "pour Azazel" (Lév 16:21–22), ou transfert de pouvoir et d'autorité de Moïse sur Josué (Nomb 27; Deut 34). Ce transfert, lorsqu'il concerne le péché et s'effectue sur un animal, exclut même toute utilisation sacrificielle de l'animal; le bouc "pour Azazel" n'est pas sacrifié, mais est conduit vivant dans le désert.[32]

Par opposition à cette valeur symbolique de l'imposition des deux mains, l'imposition d'une main n'exprime pas une idée de transfert,[33] mais une idée d'identification entre l'offrant et l'animal offert: l'offrant affirme par ce geste que c'est bien lui qui offre l'animal, et, en quelque sorte, qu'il s'offre lui-même au travers de la victime.[34]

---

[32] Comparer Deut 21:1–9, où les anciens se lavent les mains (manifestement *les deux mains*) עַל הָעֶגְלָה "au-dessus de la génisse" dont ils ont brisé la nuque. Briser la nuque est une méthode d'abattage qui se différencie expressément du rite sacrificiel.

[33] Nous refusons l'idée exprimée par certains exégètes, par exemple W. Rudolph, *Chronikbücher* (HAT; Tübingen: J. C. B. Mohr [Paul Siebeck], 1955) 297 (commentaire sur 2 Chr 29:23); E. Dhorme, *La Bible* I. *L'Ancien Testament* (Paris: La Pléiade, 1956) 295 (note sur Lév 1:4); Noth, *Das dritte Buch Mose*, 13, 28 (commentaires sur 1:4 et 4:4); G. von Rad, *Theologie des Alten Testaments* 1 (dritte Auflage Einführung in die evangelische Theologie 1; München: Kaiser Verlag, 1961) 247 = *Théologie de l'Ancien Testament* 1 (Nouvelle série théologique 12; Genève: Labor et Fides, 1963) 218. Ces théologiens interprètent, avec ou sans nuances, l'imposition de la main dans le rituel sacrificiel comme impliquant un transfert du péché de l'offrant sur la victime animale. Comme à R. de Vaux, *Les institutions de l'Ancien Testament* 2 (Paris: Cerf, 1960) 292, cette interprétation nous paraît absolument invraisemblable; il est impensable que l'on puisse offrir à Dieu en sacrifice un animal *porteur de péché*, et que les prêtres puissent en manger la chair (comparer précisément la manière dont est traité le bouc "pour Azazel", Lév 16:21). Voir aussi, dans le même sens, W. Kornfeld, *Das Buch Leviticus* (Die Welt der Bibel; Kleinkommentare zur Heiligen Schrift KK 15; Düsseldorf: Patmos Verlag, 1972) 20; H. Ringgren, *Israelitische Religion* (Die Religionen der Menschheit; Stuttgart: W. Kohlhammer, 1963) 153–54 = *La Religion d'Israël* (Paris: Payot, 1966) 181–82; Rendtorff, *Leviticus*, 34–35.

[34] Le rituel de l'holocauste d'oiseau (Lév 1:14–17) ne prescrit pas d'imposition

Dans les textes où le sujet est pluriel, il subsiste en principe un ambiguïté, car l'objet direct est évidemment à une forme grammaticale de pluriel/duel; en effet le nombre de mains en action est de toute manière supérieur à un. Un cas pourtant est d'emblée non ambigu; en Lév 4:15, il est évident par le contexte (même rite qu'en 4:4, 24, 29, 33) que les anciens n'imposent chacun qu'une seule main sur la tête du taureau.[35] Il est donc vraisemblable que dans les autres textes où le sujet est pluriel et où le contexte est sacrificiel, le mot ידהם doive être compris comme impliquant que les participants imposent chacun une seule main sur la victime: Ex 29:10, 15, 19; Lév 8:14, 18, 22; Nomb 8:12; 2 Chr 29:23. En Lév 24:14 par contre, ידיהם (de même que τὰς χεῖρας αὐτῶν de *Susanne* 34) doit être compris comme indiquant que chaque participant impose les deux mains au coupable, car il y a transfert de quelque chose: en entendant le blasphème proféré par le fils de Shelomit (ou en voyant la [prétendue] inconduite de Susanne), les témoins ont été en quelque sorte "souillés" par la faute commise; ils se déchargent donc de cette responsabilité sur le coupable "de base" en lui imposant les deux mains, ensuite de quoi la communauté le lapide (Lév 24:16, 23), pour éviter tout contact avec lui, même dans le rite d'exécution. (On peut supposer que la même forme de châtiment était réservée à Susanne, et qu'elle fut administrée aux faux témoins).

Seul le texte de Nomb 8:10 nous paraît vraiment ambigu; on peut le comprendre aussi bien comme une imposition *des mains* (consécration, par transfert de la "fonction" ou de la "position" de premier-né sur les lévites) ou comme une imposition *de la main* (identification, les Israélites s'offrant eux-mêmes à Dieu au travers des lévites). Avec la majorité des commentateurs, nous pensons qu'il faudrait y voir plutôt une idée de substitution ou d'identification que de consécra-

---

de la main. La raison en est probablement que l'offrant tenait déjà la tourterelle ou le pigeon dans sa main pour l'apporter au prêtre, ce qui soulignait suffisamment qu'il s'agissait bien de son offrande. C'est sans doute pour une raison semblable que, dans le rituel de purification de Lév 14, il n'y a pas non plus d'imposition des mains sur l'oiseau qui sera lâché dans la campagne, bien que le rituel en question rappelle sur bien des points celui du bouc "pour Azazel" de Lév 16.

[35] En hébreu biblique, on ne trouve aucun exemple du pluriel de יד (si ce n'est ידות, dans un sens dérivé). La seule forme attestée est celle du duel ידים (à l'état construit et dans les formes avec suffixe, le duel et le pluriel étant identiques, il n'est pas possible de savoir si l'hébreu classique connaissait une forme de pluriel de יד [par exemple *ידים]; il est plus probable que le duel était utilisé dès qu'il y avait multiplicité de mains; voir les exemples cités dans Joüon §91e et GKC §88f.).

tion: tout le vocabulaire sacrificiel du contexte (surtout le v. 11) semblerait l'indiquer, de même que le fait que ceux qui imposent les mains sont les fils d'Israël en général, et pas spécifiquement les premiers-nés auxquels les lévites sont substitués (v. 16). Toutefois il ne nous semble pas que l'on puisse trancher de manière absolument nette, et il n'est pas exclu que le rédacteur ait laissé ici, consciemment ou inconsciemment, subsister l'ambiguïté.

B) La LXX emploie l'expression ἐπιτίθεναι τὴν/τὰς χεῖρα/χεῖρας pour traduire d'autres formules hébraïques que סמך יד/ידים. Dans la plupart des cas, il s'agit d'un rite ou d'un geste autre que l'imposition de la main ou des mains: "mettre la main sur sa bouche", geste exprimant l'idée de se taire (Jug 18:19; Mich 7:16; verbe שׂים) ou geste d'adoration (Job 31:27; verbe נשׁק); "mettre la main sur sa (propre) tête", geste de désespoir (2 Sam 13:19; verbe שׂים), etc. Trois textes seulement de la tradition grecque nous intéressent dans le cadre de cette analyse:

a) En 2 Rois 13:16, Élisée, mourant, place (וישׂם) ses mains sur celles du roi qui se prépare à tirer de l'arc: manifestement, il veut par ce geste (des deux mains) communiquer au roi une part de la puissance divine qui est en lui. (Comparer également, en 2 Rois 4:34, le geste d'Élisée lors de la résurrection du fils de la Sunamite: וישׂם...וכפיו—ἔθηκεν ... τὰς χεῖρας; transfert de la puissance de vie.)

b) En Gen 48:18, ἐπίθες τὴν δεξιάν σου traduit שׂים ימינך; c'est le geste rituel de la bénédiction, qu'on retrouve en Lév 9:22 sous la forme וישׂא אהרן את ידו (K ידו = singulier ?)—καὶ ἐξάρας Ααρων τὰς χεῖρας. Il semble donc bien que le geste rituel de la bénédiction doive être distingué à la base d'autres gestes d'imposition des mains: le contact de la main (ou des mains) avec le destinataire est possible (Gen 48), mais pas indispensable (Lév 9), contrairement aux cas où est employé le verbe סמך, lequel implique un contact physique.

c) En 2 Rois 5:11, καὶ ἐπιθήσει τὴν χεῖρα αὐτοῦ traduit (de façon approximative) והניף ידו; ce qui est devenu par la suite le geste rituel de la guérison (attesté ainsi dans la LXX) n'était probablement à l'origine qu'un geste magique (הניף = agiter), n'impliquant même pas forcément un contact physique.[36]

---

[36] Il est probable que, dans la mesure où le geste de guérison a été compris comme une *imposition de la main* (ce que laissait supposer la traduction grecque de 2 Rois 5:11), il a été ensuite ressenti comme impliquant un transfert (de vitalité, de

C) En conclusion, le rite d'imposition des mains, tel qu'il est attesté dans le Nouveau Testament par exemple, avec ses significations diverses, a ses racines dans l'Ancien Testament.

Les gestes de bénédiction et de guérison y sont rarement attestés, et le vocabulaire utilisé dans ces cas ne semble pas avoir une valeur technique spécifique.

Par contre, en ce qui concerne le rite d'imposition proprement dit, le verbe y est pris dans un sens technique, largement attesté dans la couche sacerdotale. Dans ces cas-là, il faut distinguer deux rites différents dans leur forme et leur signification:

    a) celui de *l'imposition d'une main*, exprimant l'identification de l'offrant à la victime, dans le rituel sacrificiel (Ex 29:10, 15, 19: Lév 1:4, 10 [LXX]; 3:2, 8, 13; 4:4, 15, 24, 29, 33; 8:14, 18, 22; Nomb 8:10 [?], 12; 2 Chr 29:23);

    b) celui de *l'imposition des (deux) mains*, exprimant le transfert de quelque chose du sujet sur le destinataire, en dehors du rituel sacrificiel (Lév 16:21; 24:14; Nomb [8:10??]; 27:18 [corrigé avec la LXX], 23; Deut 34:9; *Susanne* 34 [LXX]; comparer 2 Rois 4:34; 13:16).

---

santé), d'où l'emploi le plus fréquent dans le Nouveau Testament de l'expression ἐπιτίθεναι τὰς χεῖρας (Marc 5:23; 6:5; 8:23, 25; 16:18; Luc 4:40 13:13; Act 28:8), alors que ἐπιτίθεναι τὴν χεῖρα ne se trouve que deux fois (Matt 9:18; Marc 7:32).

THE PRIESTS IN LEVITICUS—IS THE MEDIUM
THE MESSAGE?

Lester L. Grabbe

When we ask about the priests in Leviticus, the question immediately arises as to what is meant by "Leviticus." Leviticus is traditionally considered a part of the Priestly Document (P) which would also include portions of Exodus and Numbers. Would it be more appropriate to speak of the priesthood in P? However, Leviticus is also traditionally divided into P (Leviticus 1–16) and the Holiness Code (H: Leviticus 17–26), though the relationship of H and P is still discussed. These days, however, there is less of a consensus about many of these points than there once was. Apart from the dating of P—very much in discussion in some recent studies—there are questions of whether P postdates H[1] or H depends on P[2] or even whether H exists at all.[3] Although a study of the priesthood in P would be perfectly legitimate, it is also just as warranted to investigate the subject in the book of Leviticus alone.[4] The Pentateuch is not just a continuous text but has been divided up into several different "books" as far back as one can go. If this division into books is secondary, we have no direct evidence of it. To investigate Leviticus alone therefore seems justified, though this study will not stop there. I propose to address several related issues: (1) what the text of Leviticus says about priests; (2) a comparison of the views of Leviticus with those about priests in other texts; (3) the text's

---

[1] The standard view; e.g., S. R. Driver, *An Introduction to the Literature of the Old Testament* (ITL; Edinburgh: T&T Clark, 1913) 47–59.

[2] I. Knohl, "The Priestly Torah Versus the Holiness School: Sabbath and the Festivals," *HUCA* 58 (1987) 65–117; *The Sanctuary of Silence: The Priestly Torah and the Holiness School* (Minneapolis: Fortress, 1995).

[3] E.g., E. S. Gerstenberger, *Leviticus: A Commentary* (OTL; Louisville, KY: Westminister John Knox, 1996) 17–19.

[4] Cf. R. Rendtorff, "Is It Possible to Read Leviticus as a Separate Book?" in John F. A. Sawyer (ed.), *Reading Leviticus: A Conversation with Mary Douglas* (JSOTSup 227; Sheffield: Sheffield Academic Press, 1996) 22–35, and the response by Kathryn Gutzwiller (pp. 36–39); Gerstenberger, *Leviticus*, 2–6.

208

relation to the actual practice of the priesthood; and (4) the purpose of the book.[5]

Survey of Leviticus's Perspective on Priests

The traditional Greek title for the book is *Leuitikon* "the Levitical book," but in fact the Levites as such are referred to only once (Lev 25:32–34). A cursory look at Leviticus shows that much of it seems to talk about some aspect of the priesthood. The book begins with a description of the sacrificial system. A glaring omission is immediately obvious: a priest cannot function without a temple, and no temple or altar is described—they are simply presupposed. This fits with the present place of Leviticus in the biblical text, immediately following Exodus 35–40 which describes the building of a cult shrine and the place of sacrifices in great detail.

Leviticus 1–5 lists the main sorts of sacrifices and tells how to carry them out. The description given is from the sacrificer's point of view, though the priest is essential for handling the blood of the sacrifice. In Leviticus 6–7 some of the same ground seems to be covered; however, in these the portions of the sacrifice are described: those that are burned on the altar and those that go to the priests. Although the focus is on the different types of sacrifice, the priests would be intimately concerned with the details of how these were to be carried out, especially with regard to their own role in the process. Thus, much of these two chapters seems to be from a priestly standpoint.

These are followed by Leviticus 7–8 which tell of how Aaron and his sons were consecrated as priests. Surely, this should have come first in the book, shouldn't it? From a modern point of view, it would make sense to begin with Aaron and his sons' anointing to become

---

[5] Inevitably, some of these topics have already been covered in some of my writings on Leviticus; see L. Grabbe, *Leviticus* (OTG; Sheffield: Sheffield Academic Press, 1993); idem, "The Book of Leviticus," *Currents in Research: Biblical Studies* 5 (1997) 91–110; idem, "Leviticus," in J. Barton and J. Muddiman (eds.), *Oxford Bible Commentary* (Oxford: Oxford Universty Press, 2001). In some cases, this allows me to summarize without repeating in detail what I have already said elsewhere. I shall not debate the question of authorial intent except to say that when postmodernists dispute authorial intent, they seem themselves to have an authorial intent and expect readers to heed it.

priests, but evidently this was not the ancient writer's logic. He is likely to have thought, how can Aaron offer sacrifices as a part of his consecration ceremony if the sacrificial system has not already been initiated?[6] Part of what is described is one of the ceremonies to be enacted by Aaron and sons at their consecration (Lev 6:13 [ET 6:20]).

One of the most curious passages immediately follows the consecration of Aaron and his sons; this is the episode of the "strange fire" and the deaths of two of Aaron's sons Nadab and Abihu (ch. 10). The problem is that no one knows what "strange fire" (אש זרה) is. A number of explanations have been offered, some of them quite plausible, but none has been widely accepted in scholarship.[7] The sin seemed to be some sort of cultic breach. Whatever it was, the point of the story in the context is the sacredness of the priestly office. The conventions and needs of ordinary life are superseded by the demands of the priesthood: there is to be no normal mourning during bereavement (10:6–7, 12–20), no wine is to be drunk while on duty (10:8–11), and even the eating of the sacrificial portions has a sacral function (10:12–20).

Chapter 11 on the creatures fit for food was an important section for cultic purity, but the priest is not mentioned in it. On the other hand, the whole people are analogous to priests and must observe the laws because of their holiness (11:44–45). Chapter 12 focuses on forms of impurity, and in chapters 12–14 the concentration is on

---

[6] M. Douglas (*Leviticus as Literature* [Oxford: Oxford University Press, 1999] 195–217) argues that this section, along with the other narrative section in 24:10–23, serves to mark off the text in the way that the screens mark the tabernacle into sections.

[7] The episode is very puzzling since the "sin" of the two sons is never clearly indicated, with the result that the passage generated many explanations in later Judaism; see R. Hecht, "Patterns of Exegesis in Philo's Interpretation of Leviticus," *SPhilo* 6 (1979–80) 77–155; R. Kirschner, "Rabbinic and Philonic Exegesis of the Nadab and Abihu Incident (Lev 10:1–6)," *JQR* 73 (1982–83) 375–93. Thus, as with the Golden Calf episode, one must ask what lies behind the story. Those who date this part of Leviticus late usually look for some event in the exilic or post-exilic period; for example, Noth (*Leviticus: A Commentary* [OTL; London: SCM, 1977] 84) thought he saw internal disputes between different priestly groups. However, others are willing to ascribe the background to one or other event during the time of the monarchy. Milgrom (*Leviticus 1–16* [AB 3, Garden City, NY: Doubleday, 1991] 628–33) suggests that it is a polemic against private offerings of incense. W. Houston ("Tragedy in the Courts of the Lord: A Socio-Literary Reading of the Death of Nadab and Abihu," *JSOT* 90 [2000] 31–39) points out that the example of a father's being shamed by his sons is a widespread folklore motif.

various diseases and their relationship to the cultic purity system. Once again the priest is central, because the declaration of a priest can cut someone off from the community, and it requires a priest to pronounce the person (or house, object, etc.) pure or clear of the disease. The priest is not a primitive medic as is sometimes assumed, since his role is to declare ritually clean or unclean, not effect a cure. As with the sacrifices, his function is cultic. Similarly, chapter 15 discusses various bodily discharges and whether they make the person clean or unclean; here the priest's duty is to offer the appropriate sacrifices in the purification process. The ceremonies to take place on the Day of Atonement, as described in chapter 16, are unique in giving central place to the high priest. The high priest is recognized in Leviticus and elsewhere, but few special functions are ascribed to him by the legal parts of the Bible.[8] One of the few is his central role on the Day of Atonement (יום הכפורים).

The last part of Leviticus (17–26, often ascribed to a separate source called H or the Holiness Code; chapter 27 is often seen as an appendix) has the appearance of treating a variety of different topics without any clear sequence or organization.[9] Priests appear episodically in this section.

Chapter 17 is mainly about the slaughter of animals, and the priests figure only in that any animal killed for food is to be brought to the Tent of Meeting to be sacrificed before it can be eaten. In the laws about sexual relations in chapter 18, the priests are not mentioned. The next two chapters (19–20) cover a number of different commandments, being in part parallel to the Ten Commandments and with some repetitions. The only reference to the priests is with regard to bringing a guilt offering for a particular infraction (19:20–22).

Chapters 21–22 are specifically addressed to "the priests, the sons of Aaron." All relate to the conduct of the priests, with regard to mourning, sex and marriage, bodily defects, and the eating of the holy things (at 22:17, the subject shifts to general instructions about offerings that apply to all Israelites). Of particular interest is a pas-

---

[8] On the high priest during the period of the monarchy, see L. Grabbe, *Priests, Prophets, Diviners, Sages: A Socio-historical Study of Religious Specialists in Ancient Israel* (Valley Forge, PA: Trinity Press International, 2000) 60–62.

[9] This statement represents a modern viewpoint, of course, since the original compiler may have had a very specific structure in mind. Cf. Douglas, *Leviticus as Literature* (especially 218–51) who argues for an intricate structure to the entire book.

sage on the high priest who is not allowed to mourn even for close relatives and who is to marry only a virgin (21:10–15). The chapter on the holy days (Leviticus 23) seems to be given from the lay Israelite point of view, the priests occurring only incidentally with regard to ceremonies to be observed; nevertheless, a couple of priestly activities are mentioned: the priest is to wave the first sheaf of harvest (23:10–11) and to elevate (הניף) the offerings designated for the Festival of Weeks (23:20). Priestly activity is also implied by the various sacrifices, but the actions of the priests are not specifically mentioned.

Leviticus 24:1–9 describes the lamps and oil to burn continously in the tabernacle, for which Aaron is responsible, and the show bread, which goes to the priests when it is replaced with fresh bread. The rest of the chapter (24:10–23) is about a blasphemer, with no reference to the priests. The next chapter (25) describes the sabbatical and jubilee years. These mainly concern ordinary Israelites, but the one reference in the book to Levites is found here (25:32–34): the Levites have the right of redemption of the houses in their cities, regardless of the jubilee. In the chapter on blessings for obedience and curses for disobedience (26), the priests are not specifically mentioned. The last chapter (27) talks mainly about redeeming vows, with the priest having a central job to assess the value and the payment (27:8, 12, 14, 18, 21, 23). Non-redeemable land is said to go to the priest at the jubilee (27:21).

Analysis and Comparison

As described in the preceding section, priests are referred to in Leviticus in a variety of passages. A large portion of these can be subsumed under the four themes which are discussed in this section. Relevant biblical passages outside Leviticus will also be considered here.

Priestly Duties

The main function of the priests according to Leviticus is service at the altar. Priests must logically have had other functions, though, as even Leviticus itself indicates. For example, the priest had to pronounce on whether a person or object infected with "leprosy" was clean or not (Leviticus 13–14). One might extrapolate from this that

one of their responsibilities was to rule on cultic and purity matters
(cf. Hag 2:11–13). Other parts of the Old Testament suggest that
there were also other responsibilities: they were responsible for religious law, and even a lot which we would characterize as civil law.
According to Deuteronomy they (here called the "Levitical priests")
were also to act as judges (Deut 17:8–12; 19:17; 21:5). They were
responsible for promulgating the law of Moses (Deut 31:9–13) and
in general to be teachers (Deut 24:8; 27:9–10). Leviticus is silent on
much of this. It may very well presuppose such activity, but we cannot be certain. It is plausible that the priests were supposed to do
much more than just serve at the altar, and the analogies of other
religious systems and priests supports this, but Leviticus—for whatever reason—saw no need to expound on this question explicitly.

Levites

Leviticus mentions the Levites only once (25:32–34), but their existence is taken for granted. Scholars have generally assumed that
Leviticus's concept of the priesthood is that of the P document.[10] If
so, this passage would be explained by and in harmony with such
passages as Num 8:5–26 and 18:6–7: only the sons of Aaron were
to preside at the altar; only they were priests properly speaking.[11]

---

[10] In Deuteronomy we find the common phrase "levitical priests" (17:9: הכהנים
הלוים) or "priests, sons of Levi" (21:5; 31:9: הכהנים בני לוי). This indicates to many
scholars that Deuteronomy considers all Levites to be priests. This view is not uni-
versally held, however; see R. Abba ("Priests and Levites in Deuteronomy," *VT* 27
[1977] 257–67) for an argument that Deuteronomy makes the same distinction
between priests and Levites as that conventionally thought to be the case in P.
Nevertheless, the prevailing view remains the older one that there is no distinction
between priests and Levites in Deuteronomy; see, e.g., J. A. Emerton, "Priests and
Levites in Deuteronomy," *VT* 12 (1962) 129–38.

[11] A similar picture is found in Ezekiel 44–45, except that here the altar priests
are "Zadokites," descendents of Zadok. Many scholars think (rightly, in my opinion) that in these different conceptualizations of the priesthood, we see the remnants of struggles among different priestly groups for power and position during
the period of the "First Temple." In the Second Temple period, which may also
be the time of the compilation of P, the situation had resolved itself into altar priests
(Aaronites) and "Levites" (including Netinim, singers, gatekeepers, and the like). For
further information, see the discussion in L. Grabbe, *Judaic Religion in the Second
Temple Period: Belief and Practice from the Exile to Yavneh* (London: Routledge, 2000) 135–
37, and the literature cited there, especially R. Nurmela, *The Levites: Their Emergence
as a Second-Class Priesthood* (SFSHJ 193; Atlanta: Scholars Press, 1998). A recent study
on the question is J. Schaper, *Priester und Leviten im achämenidischen Juda: Studien zur
Kult- und Sozialgeschichte Israels in Persischer Zeit* (FAT 31; Tübingen: J. C. B. Mohr

The remnants were an inferior clergy whose responsibility was care of the physical tabernacle and serving the priests and the cultic service. Thus, the Levites became a sort of second-class clergy occupied with the tasks of physical serving but excluded from service at the altar. We cannot be certain that this interpretation is what Leviticus presupposes, but this appears to be the most likely scenario.

Anointing and Consecration of the Priests

An important section of Leviticus relates to the ceremony by which Aaron and his sons became priests: chapters 8–9. They were undergoing the passage from "common" to "sacred." Various purification and burnt offerings and washings were performed, a special ordination offering carried out (8:22–29), and the anointing done. Those involved were then required to remain a week segregated in the Tent of Meeting (transitional rite). The final act was a ritual of incorporation, in this case sacrifices and ceremonies on the eighth day (Leviticus 9).[12]

This story of Aaron and his sons' anointing is given for at least two reasons: it relates the once-upon-a-time, once-and-for-all, unrepeatable *Urtat* when the first priest was first anointed and the priestly line began (cf. also Exod 29:9; 40:15); secondly, it would set a pattern of the initiation which all subsequent new priests would have to undergo. Consequently, it might be expected that all new priests have to endure the same ceremonies as Aaron and his sons, yet there is no evidence that this happened. Rather, it seems that only the high priest was to be anointed on taking up his office (Lev 6:13–15 [ET 6:20–22]); if there was a ceremony for all new priests, it is nowhere described or even hinted at.

[Paul Siebeck], 2000) who argues for an extensive hypothesis about a struggle for position between the "Zadokite" priests and the Levites from the time of Josiah to the end of the Persian period. See my reviews forthcoming in *JQR* and *JSJ*.

[12] The lengthy ritual described in Leviticus 8–9 has many characteristics of what is often referred to as a "rite of passage" (see A. van Gennep, *The Rites of Passage* [London: Routledge & Kegan Paul, 1960]). This is an anthropological term for rites which take place as a person passes from one stage to another, such as from boyhood to manhood or girlhood to womanhood. There is first a rite of separation, next a transitional rite during which the person is in a "liminal" state. There may be dangers while in this liminal state, and various rituals have to be carefully performed to protect the one undergoing the transition.

Priestly Dues

The means by which the priesthood is supported are alluded to several times in Leviticus, though additional material is found elsewhere in P. One of the special concerns of Leviticus 6–7 is that of the sacrificial portions which go to the priests. Some offerings (the burnt offering in particular) were burned entirely, but for most sacrifices only certain parts of the animal went on the altar while the rest was divided between the offerer and the offering priest or went entirely to the priest. Two portions of most offerings from the herd or flock belonged to the priests. The breast was presented as the תנופה[13] before Yahweh and then given to all the priesthood ("Aaron and his sons"); the right thigh was presented as the תרומה[14] and allocated to the offering priest (7:29–32).

Leviticus 27 also discusses a means of support for the priesthood via vows and consecration of objects and property to God (vv. 1–29). It was possible to dedicate human beings, animals, houses, and land to God.[15] Firstfruits are mentioned in Leviticus (2:14–16) and elsewhere (especially Num 18:12–14; Deut 18:4; 26:1–11). The amount is nowhere precisely delineated, but the impression is that donations of this sort were to be made to the priesthood as well as the other priestly gifts.

Little is said about tithes in Leviticus, only a few brief verses at 27:30–33. Yet the main support of the priesthood would logically come from the tithes. Such things as the priestly portions of sacrifices or vows would not have been sufficient to sustain an active priesthood under normal circumstances. Two sources of tithes are indi-

---

[13] The term תנופה was applied especially to the thigh of the sacrifices of well-being which went to the priest, but it is also used in other passages. The precise meaning of the word is uncertain. Clues to the ceremony have been sought in the supposed etymology of the word, but there is no agreement on its origin. See further Grabbe, *Leviticus*, 67–68.

[14] With regard to תרומה, all occurrences of the word suggest a gift intended for God or the priest. Whatever the precise significance of the name, תרומה applies primarily to the breast of the sacrificial animals which was given to the priest; cf. further Grabbe, *Leviticus*, 67–68.

[15] If the dedicated object was a person, then he or she had to be redeemed by money. If an animal suitable for offering had been vowed, it had to be sacrificed; however, if it was an unclean animal, it had to be redeemed by its valuation plus 20 percent. A house could be redeemed by paying its value plus 20 percent. Land was valued in relation to the jubilee year.

cated: (1) the produce of the field: grain, fruits, and the like; (2) the livestock. The vegetable produce is only mentioned in passing here and not further discussed, though one might expect it to be the same as indicated in Num 18:25–32 which gives the most extensive resource for the support of the priesthood and cultic activities. See below for a further discussion of tithes.

Conclusion

Leviticus treats a number of topics important for the priesthood: the priestly duties, the structure of the priesthood, the initiation of new priests, and the financial support of the priests. Two things become immediately clear when this overview is considered: first, it is incomplete, because many aspects of the priesthood are omitted or treated cursorily; secondly, the picture in Leviticus does not always agree with that elsewhere. Sometimes these differences are relatively small, but some involve larger questions (e.g., whether the Levites were full priests or not).

Relationship to Actual Practice

If Leviticus is to be evaluated properly, the question must be answered as to whether, or to what extent, it describes actual practice at some point in Israelite society. This is a question too big to be answered in detail, but some examples will help us to get a handle on it.[16]

The description of the sacrificial cult is likely to be broadly correct. Most temples of the time had certain standard requirements, with a set of sacrifices being central to the cult. We cannot vouch for every detail, but the Jerusalem cult is likely to have been very conservative, retaining its essential outline over the centuries even as some of the details altered. There are some difficulties, particularly the distinction between the "guilt offering" (אשם) and the "sin offering (חטאת).[17] But the existence of a variety of ceremonies and modes of sacrifice for different sins and impurities would be unexceptional. They are attested for the Second Temple in a form that roughly corroborates the Leviticus account.[18]

---

[16] I had already given a discussion of the basic question in *Leviticus*, 22–23.
[17] Cf. Grabbe, *Leviticus*, 36–37.
[18] Cf. Grabbe, *Judaic Religion in the Second Temple Period*, 132–44.

What is obvious to most scholars is that the desert tabernacle is a fiction. Its outlines mimicked the Jerusalem temple, but it is unlikely that any portable tent shrine—even if there had been one at some point in Israel's history—would have survived at the time of Leviticus's writing.[19] The wood and metal altar could not have funcioned as the main place of burning portions of animals since the heat would have destroyed it in short order.[20] Some other items of its furniture are attested for the Second Temple, such as the lamp stand and the table for the show bread.[21]

Tithing serves as a useful example to illustrate the difficulties of understanding both the Old Testament law and its actual application in Israelite society. On few other subjects do we have more information in the Old Testament writings or in references in early Jewish literature. With regard to Leviticus explicitly, we have a description of the tithe of animals (Lev 27:32–33). Cattle were to be tithed apparently by running them past and cutting out every tenth animal. Nothing is said about how the tithe was to be used. By inference from other passages (2 Chron 31:6), it was to go to the priests as a a part of their income. A number of questions arise. Why is not the tithe of animals referred to elsewhere in the Old Testament (except 2 Chron 31:6)? If the entire herd or flock was run by each year, the breeding stock would gradually become decimated (literally). Would it just have been the new crop of calves, kids, and lambs each time? This makes sense, but no discussion is given. Giving the first-born of each breeding animal would equal roughly ten percent, so how did the tithe relate to the command about the first-born?

---

[19] On the possible background to the tabernacle, see F. M. Cross, "The Priestly Tabernacle," *BA* 10 (1947) 45–68 (also in G. E. Wright and D. N. Freedman [eds.], *Biblical Archaeologist Reader, Volume 1* [Anchor Books; Garden City, NY: Doubleday, 1961] 201–28); M. Haran, "Shilo and Jerusalem: The Origin of the Priestly Tradition in the Pentateuch," *JBL* 81 (1962) 14–24; *Temples and Temple-Service in Ancient Israel* (Oxford: Clarendon, 1978) 175–204; J. Milgrom, *Leviticus 1–16*, 29–34.

[20] Cf. P. Heger, *The Three Biblical Altar Laws: Developments in the Sacrificial Cult in Practice and Theology, Political and Economic Background* (BZAW 279; Berlin and New York: de Gruyter, 1999) 171–206.

[21] See Josephus, *War* 5 §§216–17; 7 §§148–51; and the discussion in T. A. Busink, *Der Tempel von Jerusalem von Salomo bis Herodes: Eine archäologisch-historische* (Studie unter Berücksichtigung des westsemitischen Tempelbaus 2. Von Ezechiel bis Middot; Leiden: Brill, 1980) 1156–74.

Outside Leviticus, other aspects of tithing in ancient Israel are equally surrounded by difficulties of understanding and relating the literary tradition to the actual situation. Numbers 18:21–32 states that all the tithes were to go to the Levites. The Levites in turn were to tithe this tithe and give it to the priests. Nehemiah 10:37–39 seems to give a similar picture. Deuteronomy 13:17–19 and 14:22–29, on the other hand, speak of eating the tithe in the "place that the Lord your God will choose." All the members of the household were to take part in the feast, and the Levite was to be included (Deut 13:18). In the third year, however, the tithe was to be brought into the settlements and given to the Levites, the stranger, the fatherless, and the widow.

How are these various instructions and statements to be related? It is not clear that they can be. What appears to be the most likely explanation is that various ideas about how to handle the matter have found their way into the text. Some passages may represent changes in practice over time and/or space: i.e., one practice was normal at a particular time or in a particular part of the land, but at a different time or place another practice (described in another passage) predominated. On the other hand, it may well be that some of the differences belong to an idealized cult which some groups wanted to impose but which were in fact never practiced. We do have some idea of what was done during the Second Temple period, but our knowledge still does not reconcile all the biblical data nor relieve all tensions.[22]

Two other observances can be considered. Leviticus 25 describes (a) a seventh or sabbatical year in which the land was to rest and (b) a jubilee year in which debts were to be canceled and property returned to its original owners. The sabbatical year (שמטה) was in fact observed during the Second Temple period, with enough evidence to show not only its observance but also the cycle followed by it.[23] However, although a 49-year jubilee chronological cycle is central to *Jubilees*, neither it nor any other writing of the Second Temple period—nor the biblical text—provides evidence that the

---

[22] For the data from the Second Temple period and a discussion of its significance, see Grabbe, *Leviticus*, 71; *Judaic Religion in the Second Temple Period*, 137–38.

[23] See Grabbe, "Maccabean Chronology: 167–164 or 168–165 BCE?" *JBL* 110 (1991) 59–74, esp. 60–63.

jubilee was ever observed. Indeed, its relationship to the sabbatical year is unclear in the text.[24]

A final example is found in Leviticus 17. The instructions in the first part of this chapter give as a command that all clean domestic animals (cattle, sheep, and goats) are not to be slain for food apart from the altar (17:2–7). Although an exception is made for wild animals who are ritually clean (17:13–14), this law seems totally impractical. Several attempts have been made to justify it. The standard explanation is that in the province of Yehud in the Persian period, no place was so far from Jerusalem that it would be a hardship to bring any animal to be slaughtered to the temple itself.[25] More recently Menahem Haran[26] and Jacob Milgrom[27] have associated the P document (including Leviticus) with a pre-monarchic tribal territory centered on Shiloh; however, the principle is the same: the territory was small enough that all animals for slaughter could be brought to the cultic center. Milgrom has also argued that Leviticus does not presuppose a single temple, and Douglas agrees with him.[28]

None of these explanations seems very likely. Although Leviticus may say nothing explicit about a single shrine, it is difficult to believe that P envisages anything else. There was only one tabernacle in the wilderness, not multiple ones. On the other hand, those who refer to a territory small enough to bring all of their animals for slaughter seem not to realize how inconvenient this would be. Even when most meat eaten may have been in conjunction with the annual festivals in Jerusalem, whenever it was necessary or desirable to kill of one's flock or herd for food, the Israelite was hardly likely to embark on a day or two's journey to sacrifice it. Also, how did he get the meat back home? There would be problems of transport and preservation of the meat. Thus, this passage appears to promulgate another utopian law.

---

[24] Despite *Jubilees* the jubilee year appears to be the fiftieth year, not the 49th. But then one must ask how there can be two fallow years in a row, when one alone often caused hardships? For a further discussion of the question, see Grabbe, *Leviticus*, 94–97.

[25] Cf. Gerstenberger, *Leviticus: A Commentary*, 236.

[26] Haran, "Shiloh and Jerusalem."

[27] Milgrom, *Leviticus 1–16*, 29–35.

[28] Milgrom, *Leviticus 1–16*, 29–34; "Does H Advocate the Centralization of Worship?" *JSOT* 88 (2000) 59–76; Douglas, *Leviticus as Literature*, 90–94.

In sum, Leviticus overall presupposes a functioning priesthood and cult, and the picture as a whole is likely to have conformed to reality. But there are also a number of laws that are unlikely to have been practiced; they probably represent a utopian vision that would not have worked. This suggests that Leviticus was never a practical manual but a theological work with a message whose primary concern went far beyond a description of how the cult and priesthood functioned, as the next section discusses.

What was the Purpose of Leviticus?

In asking about the purpose of Leviticus, I have in mind several things: What was its audience? (Priests? Lay Israelites?) Why was it written? (For example, to provide a manual for priests?) Was it a description of a working cult or only a theoretical or utopian one? The focus of the present section, like the rest of the essay, is on the priesthood, but some wider issues will inevitably come up.

What has become clear from our study is that Leviticus gives us neither a self-contained nor an independent account of the priesthood. It is obvious that it is not meant to stand alone but presupposes some significant aspects of the priesthood that are described only in other texts. The book begins with a temple in place, presupposing the chapters at the end of Exodus (or something similar to them) which describe the building of the portable temple known as the tabernacle. Whatever the message of Leviticus, it cannot have been intended as a complete statement about the cult and priesthood. Far too much of importance is omitted for it to be that.

Therefore, Leviticus cannot have been a manual for priests. But did the priests ever have a manual, anyway? We are used to the availability of guidebooks, job descriptions, and operating instructions for electrical appliances (even if they are often ignored), but for much of history knowledge and skills within various occupations and professions were handed down by a sort of apprenticeship. A novice priest is likely to have gained knowledge of how to carry out the priestly duties by learning under the supervision of older, more experienced priests. There must have been all sorts of details of the daily routine in the temple that were never written down but were learned by a process of oral teaching and example. Neither Leviticus nor any other known writing begins to convey this necessary information, and it is very unlikely that such a writing ever existed.

When the priestly information in Leviticus is looked at closely, however, most of it is actually relevant or useful for non-priests. A quick survey of this material will illustrate to what extent non-priests would need, or at least want, to know these data.

Leviticus 6–7 are primarily about what the priests do and can be said to be instructions for the priests; however, they hardly constitute esoteric information and would be the sort of thing that non-priests would be curious about. Furthermore, the lay Israelites would need to know what portions of each sacrifice went to the priests. Also, some of the material is really for the non-priests, such as information about what happens when something comes in contact with holy flesh (Lev 6:20–21) or about how the well-being offering (7:11–15) and votive offerings (7:16–18) are treated.

According to Leviticus 7–10 all Israelites, not just priests, would need to be aware of the story of how the priesthood supposedly began. The story of how God killed two of Aaron's sons would have been a warning not to treat the cult lightly or carelessly.

Leviticus 12–15 mentions the involvement of priests in the ceremonies of cleansing after various impurities relating to the reproductive organs or afflictions from "leprosy." In each case, this is information that would be of value to the lay Israelite. The priest had an important function in pronouncing on purity and in carrying out ceremonies of ritual cleansing, but all Israelites would need to know about these rites.

Leviticus 16 describes the ritual on the Day of Atonement. Although the high priest was central in the ceremony, all the community took part. There is nothing here that can be described as information needed solely by the priests.

Most of the references in 17–27 are ones in which the priest is mentioned because of natural involvement in the situations being described, but the perspective is from the lay point of view: slaughter of animals as sacrifice (17), bringing a guilt offering to the priest (19:20–22), the ceremonies of the Wave Sheaf and the Festival of Weeks and the various festival sacrifices (23), redemption of property (25:32–34; 27:8–23). One passage is different, however: 21:1–22:16 is addressed specifically to "the priests, the sons of Aaron" and discusses such matters as priestly marriage, mourning for the dead, and who may eat of the priestly portions (22:17–33 are instructions about sacrifice and would have applied to laymen as well as priests).

We can summarize by saying that in only two passages are the details so clearly aimed at a priestly audience that they might have been written solely for priests: 6:1–7:10 and 21:1–22:16. Everything else seems to apply to laity or at least could be useful for laity as well as priests. The picture we are left with is that Leviticus is not primarily a book for priests. Of course, since the book contains a variety of traditions, for a couple of passages to be perhaps originally solely for priests is not unexpected. Overall, though, the book has another purpose than to be a priest's manual or even a priestly book, as the "Conclusion" will now discuss.

Conclusions

The foregoing study has indicated several conclusions about Leviticus's teachings on the priesthood:

1. For historians today Leviticus is a valuable resource: by comparing its information with that of other sources, it is possible to learn a good deal about the ancient temple cult and priesthood. It is also possible to produce a synthesis of the book's teachings on the priesthood; indeed, some of the main teachings have been summarized above. But a number of considerations suggest that to produce a summary of its teachings about priesthood is to miss the book's message.

2. Despite its traditional title, the book of Leviticus is not primarily a book for priests. It is not a priestly manual, and it does not seem to have priests as its target audience, though priests were no doubt a *part* of the intended audience.

3. The relationship of its teachings to the reality of the cult and priesthood is a complex one. Broadly, as already noted, its description of the various sacrifices and the priestly duties and temple operations is likely to be similar to how these activities actually functioned. On the other hand, certain instructions are highly suspect and are probably idealistic teachings that were never carried out.

So, what can we say about the book and the priestly material in it? We must first ask about when it was written. Despite the arguments of Milgrom and others, I am not persuaded that Leviticus arose with the pre-monarchic shrine at Shiloh. Apart from the problems of using the biblical traditions about Shiloh as history,[29] the P

---

[29] Here is not the place to rehearse the current debate about whether and to what extent the biblical text can be used to reconstruct the history of Israel. Cf.

document in general and Leviticus in particular is still likely to belong to the Persian period as a composition/compilation.[30] The classic passage about the promulgation of the law is found in Nehemiah 8.[31] The picture presented here is of Ezra's bringing the "torah of Moses"/"torah of God" from Babylon and reading it to the people. What are the contents implied by this law? There is not a lot of information, but the observance of the Festival of Tabernacles is central to the chapter. The only passage of the present Pentateuch on which it could be based is Leviticus 23 which mentions the various kinds of vegetation that were to be used in celebrating the festival (Neh 8:14–17//Lev 23:40–42). Whatever the historicity of the events in Nehemiah 8, the author/compiler of the passage seems to have known the book of Leviticus. This and other indications give the strong presumption that the Pentateuch was complete by the end of the Persian period.[32]

We should, then, reckon with a book written/compiled sometime in the Persian period, most likely by a priest or priests. The book itself may have been written with a variety of purposes in mind, but it was not primarily an attempt to educate priests or provide a priestly manual, nor was it primarily aimed to give instructions to lay Israelites who would have grown up with the cultic routine and received instructions from priests and their own families from an early age. The primary message of Leviticus seems to have been theological.

---

my article, "Writing Israel's History at the End of the Twentieth Century," in A. Lemaire and M. Saebø (eds.), *Congress Volume: Oslo 1998* (VTSup 80; Leiden: Brill, 2000) 203–18.

[30] See J. Blenkinsopp ("An Assessment of the Alleged Pre-Exilic Date of the Priestly Material in the Pentateuch," *ZAW* 108 [1996] 495–578) and my discussion in *Judaic Religion on the Second Temple Period*, 26–28. This does not mean that some parts of the P tradition are not very old (see Grabbe, "The Book of Leviticus," *Currents in Research: Biblical Studies* 5 [1997] 91–110, for a discussion of some of those arguing this case). The arguments that there is clear evidence of pre-exilic language in P are well taken, but they do not settle the question of the final composition.

[31] See my discussions in *Ezra-Nehemiah* (Old Testament Readings; London: Routledge, 1998) 143–50; "The Law of Moses in the Ezra Tradition: More Virtual than Real?" in J. Watts (ed.), *Persia and Torah: The Theory of Imperial Authorization of the Pentateuch* (SBLSS 17; Atlanta: Society of Biblical Literature, 2001) 91–113.

[32] See my arguments in "Jewish Historiography and Scripture in the Hellenistic Period," in L. Grabbe (ed.), *Did Moses Speak Attic? Jewish Historiography and Scripture in the Hellenistic Period* (JSOTSup 317 = European Seminar in Historical Methodology 3; Sheffield Academic Press, 2001) 129–55, especially 142–48.

This has been demonstrated most recently—in masterly fashion—by Mary Douglas.[33]

Why did the writer of Leviticus use the format of cultic laws and discussion, then? Other means of presenting theology were also being developed and used at this time. These included narratives or stories about Israel's past, prophetic writings, tales about heroes and heroines, and various sorts of wisdom literature. It has sometimes been assumed that priestly writers would have confined themselves to particular sorts of writing, such as the medium of temple, purity, and cultic description; however, this is simplistic.[34] Many of the other types of writing were also likely to have been engaged in by priestly writers.[35] On the other hand, cultic description and laws about ritual purity were a priestly concern and were a natural choice for a priestly writer, especially in certain contexts. In this case, the writer of Leviticus wanted to express himself about conduct in the individual's daily life, and conduct with regard to ritual purity and cultic regulations was parallel to what we might call moral and ethical conduct.

The dry discussion of ritual details about animal sacrifice or cultic purity might seem the antithesis of deep theology. Far from it. In a number of recent writings Jacob Neusner has shown how the laws of the Mishnah express an entire world view.[36] Similarly, a

---

[33] Douglas, *Leviticus as Literature*.

[34] One might think about the more recent context of clergy in eighteenth and nineteenth century England who gained a reputation for pursuing all sorts of intellectual—and sometimes idiosyncratic—hobbies, including chemistry, anthropology, palaeontology, and the like, and writing about them. If the caricature of the priestly writer were true, these clergy would have confined their writings to sermons, biblical commentaries, and similar modes of expression. Many clergy did engage in such writings, but many other quite different treatises came from clerical pens.

[35] As argued elsewhere, the ones with the education and the leisure to compose literature were mainly the temple personnel; see my *Priests, Prophets, Diviners, Sages*: 160–61, 169–71; *Judaic Religion in the Second Temple Period*, 136. Despite frequent claims to the contrary, literacy in the sense of reading and writing extensively was unlikely to have been widespread (see most recently I. M. Young, "Israelite Literacy: Interpreting the Evidence," *VT* 48 [1998] 239–53, 408–22. However, the question is broader than just that of being able to read or write: it includes the important question of having the leisure to pursue such activities, which few would have enjoyed.

[36] J. Neusner, *Judaism: The Evidence of the Mishnah* (Chicago: University of Chicago Press, 1981); *A Religion of Pots and Pans? Modes of Philosophical and Theological Discourse in Ancient Judaism: Essays and a Program* (BJS 156; Atlanta: Scholars, 1988). Cf. also his *Judaism as Philosophy: The Method and Message of Mishnah* (Charleston: University of South Carolina Press, 1991); *The Transformation of Judaism: From Philosophy to Religion* (Champaign, IL: University of Illinois Press, 1992).

number of scholarly writings in the past decades have attempted to show how Leviticus also carried an important theological message.[37] Biblical theologians still too frequently forget that the second "great commandment" (Mark 12:28–31; Matt 22:35–40; Luke 10:25–28)—you shall love your neighbor as yourself—is found in Leviticus 19:18. Indeed, it can be argued that chapter 19 is the heart and focus of the entire book and its message.[38]

Mary Douglas titled her book, *Leviticus as Literature*; she could just as easily have called it, *Leviticus as Theology*. The book of Leviticus is starting to reclaim its place as a profoundly theological writing with a deep spiritual message.

---

[37] My own brief attempt to show this is given in *Leviticus*, 101–9.
[38] Cf. Douglas, *Leviticus as Literature*, 228–29, 239–40.

DEATH AND SEXUALITY AMONG PRIESTS
(LEVITICUS 21)

CALUM CARMICHAEL

A rule in Lev 21:1–6 restricts to close family members those persons a priest can mourn. A long recognized, very puzzling element presents itself. The rule excludes a wife from the circle of intimates. The following rule in Lev 21:7, 8, which is actually attached to the previous one, restricts in turn a priest from marrying certain types of women. The marital restrictions have given rise to views about a special link between sexuality and priests that has had considerable impact down through the centuries. I shall offer a solution to the puzzle in the opening rule of Leviticus 21 about the exclusion from mourning of a wife (and a married sister), and counter claims made about biblical attitudes to sexuality that have been based on a reading of the rule about priests' wives.

Priests and Mourning

With exceptions, priests are not to defile themselves for the dead. The rule in Lev 21:1–6 reads:

> And Yahweh said unto Moses, Speak unto the priests the sons of Aaron, and say unto them, There shall none be defiled for the dead among his people: But for his kin, that is near unto him, that is, for his mother, and for his father, and for his son, and for his daughter, and for his brother, And for his sister a virgin, that is nigh unto him, which hath had no husband; for he may he be defiled. He shall not defile himself as a husband among his people and so profane himself. They shall not make baldness upon their head, neither shall they shave off the corner of their beard, nor make any cuttings in their flesh. They shall be holy unto their God, and not profane the name of their God: for the offerings of Yahweh made by fire, and the bread of their God, they do offer: therefore they shall be holy.

The rule presents an obvious problem. Priests must not defile themselves on account of the dead, that is, make baldness upon their head, shave off the corner of their beard, and cut their flesh. Exceptions

apply, however. He—the rule switches from the plural to the singular—can defile himself for kin close to him, for his parents, for
his children, for his brother, and for his sister so long as she has
not been married. Remarkably, his wife finds no place in the list of
exceptions.[1] J. E. Hartley states bluntly: "The absence of any mention of a priest's wife is amazing."

Hartley's solution is to deny the existence of the problem by claiming that a wife is included in the term שאר in v. 2, "kin, relative."[2]
But v. 4 explicitly states that as a husband he shall not defile himself. To be sure, the meaning of this particular verse has caused
commentators great difficulties, so much so that the expression in it,
בעל בעמיו, literally "a husband among his peoples," is said to be the
most difficult one in the entire Book of Leviticus.[3] Baruch Levine
provides an example of a typical attempt to give a different meaning to the phrase.[4] It refers to, he says, kin by marriage, literally, a
husband among his kin (not some amorphous group עמיו, "peoples").
A priest in the role of a husband is not permitted to attend the bur-
ial of his wife because a man's wife is not his consanguineous relative, but his affinal one. She is not family, but kin. Aside from the
problem of translating עמיו as "kin," an obvious problem with this
explanation is that a priest cannot mourn his sister should she be
married. Yet she still remains a consanguineous relative. Two common but very free translations are "nor shall he make himself unclean
for any married woman among his father's kin" (NEB), and "related
to him by marriage" (NIV). Once we observe the inspiration for the
expression, the meaning turns out to be quite straightforward and
has nothing to do with kin in the narrow sense used by critics and
translators.

---

[1] The coupling of marital restrictions with rituals for the dead is found in sources
about the ancient Iranian priestly caste (the Magi), but unique considerations apply.
On the importance of the kinds of marriages the Magi could contact and their special role in regard to cadavers; also the importation of these matters into Zorastrianism,
see R. N. Frye, "Zoroastrian Incest," in G. Gnoli and L. Lanciotti (eds.), *Orientalia
I. Tucci memoriae dicata* (Rome: Istituto italiano per il Medio ed Estremo Oriente,
1985) 453.

[2] J. E. Hartley, *Leviticus* (WBC 4; Dallas, TX: Word Books, 1992) 347.

[3] R. Péter-Contesse and J. Ellington, *A Translator's Handbook on Leviticus* (New
York: United Bible Societies, 1990) 316. They summarize the various attempts to
explain it.

[4] B. Levine, *Leviticus* (JPS Torah Commentary; Philadelphia: Jewish Publication
Society, 1989) 142.

The Levite and His Concubine (Judges 19)

The rule, I submit, has been formulated with a specific tradition in focus, the incident in Judges 19 involving a single Levite whose concubine turns to prostitution. Why has the lawgiver gone to this tradition? In his previous rule (Lev 20:27) about those who make contact with the dead, familiar spirits and mediums, his concern was unacceptable actions on behalf of the dead.[5] What spurred his interest was Tamar's story in Genesis 38. On behalf of her dead husband she acts the harlot, and a sacred one at that, for the term used of her describes her as a temple priestess of the Canaanite cult. Her intent is to raise a child for him by his father, Judah. Her specific action on behalf of the dead in a context that suggests Canaanite ways prompts the lawgiver to prohibit the more familiar forms of Canaanite dealings with the dead. What transpires in the first Israelite family, among the twelve sons of Israel, is a harbinger of later untoward developments. The lawgiver consequently turns to Judges 19, to a tradition in a later generation that also concerns an unacceptable action on behalf of the dead; only in this instance it is a husband who acts on behalf of his dead wife.[6]

The grisly story is so bizarre that modern readers will find it incomprehensible. Its intent, however, is to illustrate the supposed chaos and anarchy that prevail when Israel lacked the institution of kingship. "In those days there was no king in Israel: every man did that which was right in his own eyes" is the comment by the

---

[5] See C. Carmichael, *Law, Legend, and Incest in the Bible. Leviticus 18–20* (Ithaca: Cornell University Press, 1997) 180–82.

[6] In his *Leviticus 17–22* (AB 3A; New York: Doubleday, 2000) 1591–93, in a section devoted to a critique of my thesis about the relationship between law and narrative, J. Milgrom chooses to ignore the role of a fundamental procedure that I attribute to the biblical scribe when setting out his laws, namely, he focuses primarily on matters that turn up for the first time in the nation's history but he also turns to similar matters that show up in succeeding generations. The procedure is similar to how the biblical narratives are themselves presented. There is a focus on beginnings and then on related developments in succeeding generations. Further noteworthy is that the collections of laws are placed at foundational moments in the legendary history (and pre-history) of the nation. The deity's rules about killing animals and humans are set down at the fresh start to the world after the flood. The rules of the Book of the Covenant and succeeding rules about the institution of the cult are set down at the start of the nation after the exodus from Egypt. We find the laws of Deuteronomy set down in anticipation of the Israelites starting up a new life in the land of Canaan.

biblical narrator at the conclusion to the episode about the Levite's wife and its consequences (Judg 21:25; cf. 19:1). The tale is about a woman who plays the harlot against her husband, a Levite, a priest of the Israelite cult. She leaves him and returns to her father's home. Some months go by and, despite his wife's egregious behavior, the Levite decides to take up with her again. Her father receives him well and for many nights detains him by plying him with food and drink. Eventually the priest leaves with his wife and a servant and the three of them settle for the night at the city of Gibeah. There someone who used to live in the Levite's own part of Israel provides hospitality to them. The men of Gibeah are Benjaminites who are described as "sons of Belial," a phrase signifying deviance and lawlessness. They demand sexual intercourse with the Levite. To protect his male guest, the host offers to the gang his virgin daughter and the Levite's wife. The hoodlums are not interested but, for whatever reason, when the Levite gives over his wife to them they accept her, and sexually abuse her all night long.

In the morning when the Levite starts out to continue his journey he finds his wife lying motionless at the threshold of the door. Addressing her, he tells her that they should go on their way, but there is no response from her for she is dead. He then lifts her onto his donkey and goes to his own home. There he cuts up her corpse into twelve pieces and sends them around the twelve tribes of Israel to tell them about the barbaric treatment of his wife by the men of the tribe of Benjamin. The other tribes are duly outraged and they convene an assembly at which they decide to exact vengeance and, further, to deny from their own numbers wives to the Benjaminites. A drawn out battle ensues with the outcome that all of the Benjaminites, save six hundred men, are slaughtered.

National sentiment, however, asserts itself and there is regret that one of the twelve tribes of Israel will disappear if these men do not obtain wives. A decision is then made that the surviving Benjaminites can acquire virgin daughters from the city of Jabesh-gilead because that city failed to send men to the original assembly deciding the fate of the Benjaminites. After its male inhabitants and their spouses (and children) are slaughtered four hundred young virgins are given to the Benjaminites. More virgins are needed and the men of Benjamin acquire them by going to an annual vintage festival at Shiloh and there, seizing the girls while they are dancing, carry them off as wives.

The story, then, involves a priest who, according to the Massoretic text, is on his way to serve in a sanctuary when the horrific event ensues (Judg 19:18). The law in Lev 21:1–6 links defilement that is caused by a priest's involvement with the dead to the priest's fitness for serving in the sanctuary: "They [the priests] shall be holy unto their God ... for the offerings of Yahweh made by fire, and the bread of their God, they do offer" (Lev 21:6). A succession of laws also takes up aspects of the priestly vocation (Leviticus 21).

The harlotry of the Levite's wife has aroused skepticism from ancient times. Most modern versions of the Bible accept the LXX reading that she left her husband because she was angry with him. Rejected is the MT reading that she played the harlot against him and left him. We should stay with the text of the MT.[7] The translation of the LXX may be an attempt to avoid the apparently shocking nature of her offense in the MT.[8] More persuasively, support for the MT reading comes from noting that the story, like the others in the Book of Judges, illustrates the lawlessness and anarchy of the times. When, moreover, she dies the victim of sexual abuse by many men the narrative, in typical biblical fashion, conveys *pars pro pari* the nature of her misdeed, sexual relations with many different male partners. Her end is heaven's way of punishing her for her sexual misconduct when married to the Levite, misconduct for which she had not been punished when it happened.[9]

The Levite's action of transporting her divided corpse throughout the land of Israel means that he presents himself among all his

---

[7] G. R. Driver unconvincingly argues that the verb זנה is not the usual "to whore" but another verb, attested nowhere else in the Old Testament, "to be angry." See "Mistranslations in the Old Testament," *Die Welt des Orients* 1 (1947) 29–30. One of R. G. Boling's arguments against accepting the MT is his claim that "As Israelite law did not allow for divorce by the wife, she became an adulteress by walking out on him." He is correct in stating that a woman could not divorce her husband, but she was indeed free to walk out on him, a quite different action. Boling cannot accept the view that she prostituted herself, but seems to introduce much the same idea by claiming that she is an adulteress. I presume he does so because he is trying to explain why the MT has the reading about harlotry. See *Judges. A New Translation with Introduction and Commentary* (AB 7; New York: Doubleday, 1975) 274.

[8] It may be another example of what I call "desexing," the inclination to remove (in selected instances) the sexual from language, actions, and institutions. The LXX is especially given to the process. See C. Carmichael, "Desexing," *Rechtshistorisches Journal* 17 (1998) 266–82.

[9] Compare how Lot's daughters sexually abuse him, in part, because it mirrors how he offered them for the sexual enjoyment of the men of Sodom (Genesis 19).

kindred Israelites (not just among his own kin) as a husband defiling
himself with his wife's dead body. The fact that he is the husband
of this woman is no ordinary fact in the story but a central feature,
as its sequel about the denial of wives to the perpetrators of the crime
brings out (Judg 21:1). The distinguishing feature of the Benjaminite
males who survive the onslaught against their tribe is the bar on
them becoming husbands in Israel because of their culpability for the
death of the wife of a Levite. The law in Lev 21:1–6 relates back
to the appalling incident involving the wife's corpse because no later
Israelite priest must be associated with the uncleanness of this early
member of the Israelite priesthood.

The law is an impressive example of how an odd reference in it
evokes, by a very precise use of language, an event in the history
of the nation. In ordinary circumstances involving the mortality of
certain females, no Israelite priest should defile himself by contact
with his wife's corpse because it would serve as a reminder of a
deeply defiling incident in the history of the nation. The fact that
the contact is of the kind that involves cutting his own body by way
of establishing a sympathetic link with the dead person makes all
the more noteworthy the connection between such customary mourning practices and the Levite's action with his wife.[10] Normally allowed
to mourn an intimate by cutting himself, a priest does not participate
in such permissible defilement when a wife dies because he must signal his freedom from uncleanness of the kind that dramatically attached
to his ancestor living in the time of the Judges. It is an act of omission that, having regard to the scar of national history, constitutes a
counter example to the one in that history. For the recipients of the
rule the odd requirement that a priest should not mourn his wife
invites the question "Why should he not?" The answer involves the
historical incident. The exclusion of the wife from the rule is based
not on ritual considerations or on grounds of blood-relatedness, but
on a historical development.

The exclusion of a married sister from the list of those whom the
priest can mourn is similarly explained. A Levitical priest will have
married her, a standard inter-tribal union among priestly families, and

---

[10] The practices in question were a feature of both Canaanite and Israelite culture
(Isa 15:2; 22:12; Jer 16:6; Amos 8:10, cf. 1 Kgs 18:28). On how food that is offered to
a deceased person establishes contact between the living and the dead, see S. R.
Driver, *Deuteronomy* (ICC; Edinburgh: T&T Clark, 1902) 291–92.

in the event of her death the ban, applying to her husband, carries over to her brother. He can mourn his sister so long as she is not married, but the unnecessary language that she is a virgin and that she has had no husband seems odd. The double description, however, is important in light of the Levite and his wife/harlot. When a priest's wife or married sister, also a priest's wife, dies, he must do nothing that associates him with this Levite. If a priest's sister has a husband she falls into the taboo category on the sole basis of the husband-wife incident in Judges 19. This part of the rule also incorporates the historical scar and the reference to the husband is important in pointing to it. Mention that she is a virgin is insufficient to achieve the association with the story.[11]

Although the expression בעל בעמיו seems an odd one, its literal meaning, "a husband among his peoples," is remarkably apt. It recalls the Levitical husband in Judges when throughout the territory of Israel he proclaims among his fellow Israelites the Benjaminites' outrage. The plural form עמיו designates the units that comprise the people of Israel. The term עם can refer to a smaller unit in the sense of those who make up the various inhabitants of a locality, or to a smaller unit in the sense of a single tribe with the plural often referring to the tribes of Israel.[12] A central feature of the story is the concern both with the totality of Israel and its constituent parts.

The rule switches from a reference to a priest to a prohibition that applies to all priests, from the third person singular to the third person plural (vv. 4 and 5). The change in number may reflect the move from the focus on the single Levite in Judges 19 to the general rule for all priests.

Marital Restrictions on Priests

The next, related rule reads:

> They [the priests] shall not take a wife that is a whore, or profane; neither shall they take a woman put away from her husband: for he is

---

[11] The text therefore affords no support to G. Wenham's claim that the additional designation of the sister having a husband is necessary because the term virgin by itself can simply mean a woman of marriageable age who may not be virginal. See "*Betulah* 'a girl of marriageable age,'" *VT* 22 (1972) 326–48.

[12] See F. Brown, S. R. Driver, and C. A. Briggs, *A Hebrew and English Lexicon of the Old Testament* (Oxford: Clarendon Press, 1906) 766.

holy unto his God. Thou shall sanctify him therefore; for he offereth
the bread of thy God: he shall be holy unto thee: for I Yahweh, which
sanctify you, am holy. (Lev 21:7, 8)

Why should the lawgiver, bewilderingly it would seem, switch from
the topic of a priest's becoming defiled from contact with a corpse to
the kind of woman he cannot marry, especially the three listed, a
prostitute, a profane woman, and a divorced woman? The Judges
tradition, I suggest, accounts for the odd juxtaposition of topics in the
two rules, mourning the dead and the status of a priest's wife. The
Levite's situation with his sharply raises the issue of a wife who is
a problem to her husband. This priest's spouse was promiscuous.
The rule's formulation, in turn, is negative; it is about the kind of
woman a priest cannot marry. Further, the rule is remarkable in that
it states that a priest has not to marry a harlot. In the ordinary
course of events it hardly seems a likely choice for a priest to make,
or anyone for that matter, and we might well wonder why a lawgiver pays the possibility any attention. Hartley recognizes the problem when he claims that a prohibition against marrying a harlot
would be obvious, hence there would be no need to state it. So he
weakens the sense of the rule when he states "the strong term [har-
lot] applies here to a woman who had lost her virginity without specifying the frequency."[13] Such a curious rationalization is not called for.

The Levite's wife played the harlot against him. The story does not
expand on why she did so, nor does it comment on what motivated
the Levite to choose to continue to live with her. No doubt the
entire matter comes under the judgment that everyone at that time
did what was right in his or her own eyes. The chaos communicated
in the story is in many respects the opposite of what would occur
under (it is thought) the orderly rule of a king. A priest's wife becomes
a harlot. He does not reject her but takes her back. To satisfy their
sexual needs the debased men of Gibeah demand the man not the
woman. The priest sends his wife to be raped and does not protect
her. After she dies he cuts up her body but does not cut his own,
as is the standard custom for a close relative.

Alert to the chaos in the story the lawgiver, I suggest, lays down
rules that will contribute toward some order in Israelite society, and
he fashions this order by reacting to the contents of the story. In his

---

[13] See J. E. Hartley, *Leviticus*, 348.

rule about priestly marriages, he thinks of the odd situation in which a priest might marry a harlot. While a law can lay down such a prohibition it cannot legislate for the possibility that a priest's wife might become a harlot, as happened with the Levite. (The law of adultery would apply in that event.)

The priest is not to marry a woman who is profane, or one whose husband has divorced her. The latter prohibition carried over into later Judaism, also into the Christian church for its clergy, and for Christian kings. Jacob Milgrom reckons that the term "profane" in the rule refers to a raped woman.[14] He may be correct because each description reflects the narrative. The Levite's wife ended up raped (and dead) from her experience, and earlier she had left her husband.[15] The rule would then have in focus less exceptional matters that can be legislated for, and which a priest can take into account before, not after, marrying. Thus the lawgiver might think of a woman who has been raped before marriage, or one whose previous marriage has been dissolved. I am inclined to think, however, that the rule's denial to a priest of a woman who is "profane" may represent a judgment on the Levite in Judges for taking his wife back after her promiscuous conduct. (He also was prepared to have her back after the Benjaminites had raped her.) The lawgiver might then have switched from the Levite's situation to the more manageable one where a priest is considering marriage. We might think of a woman who, before marriage had been a harlot but, like the woman in Judges 19, had quit the life of a prostitute. A priest is, nonetheless, not permitted to marry such a woman.

The sequel to the story about the Levite's spouse concerns restrictions on wives for the tribe of Benjamin. This aspect of the saga is further indication that the tradition in Judges influences the lawgiver in his choice of topics. As in the law, the issue in the story is about acquiring a wife, not about what takes place after a marriage. The other tribes refuse to marry their daughters to those Benjaminites who had survived the vengeance taken against the tribe for its treatment of the Levite's concubine. (We might note again the juxtaposition of the topics of marriage and the dead.) In the end, one way in

---

[14] See J. Milgrom, *Leviticus* 77–22, 1807. For other views, see Hartley, *Leviticus,* 343.

[15] Her returning to her father's home rather than the husband sending her out of his is a further example of the disorderly character of the times.

which the Benjaminites are allowed to obtain wives is by means of
an overly formalistic interpretation of the marital oath that the other
tribes had sworn. The oath reads, "There shall not any of us give his
daughter unto Benjamin to wife" (Judg 21:1). The Benjaminites are
encouraged to "seize" the women (at the vintage festival), an action
not quite the same as the women being given to the men. In any
event, the issue in the narrative is about restrictions on what kinds
of wives a certain group of Israelites, the tribe of Benjamin, can
acquire. The law, in turn, is about restrictions that apply to another
group of Israelites, namely, the priests, the tribe of Levi.

Once we relate the law to its influencing narrative, we can reject,
I think, commentators' claims about the special link that supposedly
prevails between a priest and his sexuality. There is no need to suggest, as Karl Elliger does, that special powers flow to a priest from
intercourse with an untouched woman; or to accept Erhard Gerstenberger's claim that "sexual intercourse between the woman and
another man conceals dangers affecting the priest's execution of his
office. It is as if the woman were infected with an alien power, one
possibly incompatible with the holiness of Yahweh's temple."[16] Such
theorizing arises because the rules are read on their own terms without awareness of the specific motivation inspiring them. Despite
appearances the contents of the rules do not support notions of the
sacred, mystical power of sexual relations, a power that, depending
on its source, can compete with or complement a priest's sacred
status.

The Harlotry of a Priest's Daughter and the Restrictions on a High Priest Concerning Mourning Customs and Concerning Wives

The next rule reads:

> And the daughter of any priest, if she profane herself by playing the
> harlot, she profaneth her father: she shall be burnt with fire. And he
> that is the high priest among his brethren, upon whose head the anoint-
> ing oil was poured, and that is consecrated to put on the garments,

---

[16] See K. Elliger, *Leviticus* (HAT; Tübingen: J. C. B. Mohr [Paul Siebeck], 1966) 290, and E. S. Gerstenberger, *Leviticus* (OTL; Louisville, KY: Westminster John Knox, 1996) 313. J. Milgrom similarly gets caught up in this thinking when he claims on the basis of this text in Lev 21:7 that the priests are "innately holy," *Leviticus 1–16* (AB 3; New York: Doubleday, 1991) 48.

shall not uncover his head, nor rend his clothes; Neither shall he go in to any dead body, nor defile himself for his father, or for his mother; Neither shall he go out of the sanctuary of his God; for the crown of the anointing oil of his God is upon him: I am Yahweh. And he shall take a wife in her virginity. A widow, or a divorced woman, or profane, or an harlot, these shall he not take: but he shall take a virgin of his own people to wife. Neither shall he profane his seed among his people: for I Yahweh do sanctify him. (Lev 21:9–15)

Eli's Sons

Insight into this rule is forthcoming if we assume that the lawgiver has under review two traditions about priestly offenses, those of the sons of Eli and those of the sons of Aaron (1 Samuel 2–4 and Leviticus 10). First is the tradition about damnable priestly sexual conduct in the generation of Eli's sons. It is the generation that comes after the Levite's of Judges 19. Issues similar to those that arose in the story in Judges 19 come up. The sexual offenses in question concern the sons of the high priest, Eli, and they die because of them. Second is a tradition about the deaths of the sons of the first high priest, Aaron.

An initial question is why the lawgiver might switch from the story of the Levite's wife whom "sons of Belial," the men of the Benjaminite city of Gibeah, sexually abused (Judg 19:22) to the tradition in 1 Samuel 2–4. One factor is the lawgiver's standard procedure of noting a similar problem in a succeeding generation, a procedure wholly in keeping with the overall presentation of the contents of Genesis-2 Kings. In Genesis, for example, the narrator presents problems encountered by Isaac similar to those encountered by Abraham in the preceding generation. The specific trigger for the lawgiver's move may then have been that the similarly described "sons of Belial," the high priest Eli's sons, Hophni and Phinehas, abused the women who assembled at the door of the tabernacle in Shiloh (1 Sam 2:12, 22) in a manner similar to the abuse of the Levite's wife.

A priest's wife should be morally upright but in Judges 19 non-priests profaned the Levite's wife both at her bidding and latterly at his. Likewise, the priests themselves should be morally proper in their conduct but Hophni and Phinehas profaned themselves by lying with the women at the sanctuary (1 Samuel 2). If the lawgiver has made this move from Judges 19 to 1 Samuel 2 why did he cite sexual misconduct by a priest's daughter and not a priest's son? The answer is two-fold. He does indeed go on to deal with the sexual life of priests but before doing so he covered the example that falls between the Levite's wife's harlotry and the sexual offenses of Eli's sons, namely, the harlotry of a priest's daughter. A priest's daughter who prostitutes herself is the equivalent to a priest's son who fornicates. Note how, as in the story where the sons profane their father, Eli, the rule focuses on the effect of the offspring's offense on the father, "by playing the harlot, she profaneth her father" (Lev 21:9). The rule is one example among a number of rules where what happens to a member of one sex prompts a rule in regard to the other.[17] This desire to include comparable matters beyond what comes up in the tradition is a feature characteristic of all lawgiving. The tendency to cover more ground is readily observable in the laws themselves. Deuteronomy 22:3, for example, requires assistance to be given to someone whose ox or sheep gets lost, and then extends to include an ass, a garment, or any lost thing. The Roman jurist Celsus, in regard to the third chapter of the *Lex Aquilia*, stated that it is common enough for a statute to enumerate specific matters and then add a general term to include all such (D.9.2.27.16).

The subject matter in the law switches from sexuality (a priest's daughter's) to banning a high priest from exhibiting any external sign of mourning. The story of Eli and his sons accounts for the sharp disparity in subject matter. Eli is high priest at the sanctuary in Shiloh, the sanctuary to which the Levite of Judges 19 was journeying.[18] Eli's sons commit fornication there and for their offense heaven visits death upon them. The rule prohibits a high priest from mourning any death, but instead of a blanket statement on the matter it formulates for "any dead body . . . for his father, or for his mother." Why did the lawgiver bother to specify family members, in particular, a father and a mother, and, if he has focussed on the deaths of Eli's sons, why did he cite parents and not sons?

Aaron's Sons

As he generally does, the lawgiver, I submit, turned to the first time the problem of the death of a priestly family member presented itself. That was the occasion involving the first family of priests ever. Aaron's

---

[17] Thus Tamar's sexual relations with men from different generations of the same family (Genesis 38) prompts a rule about a man's relations with women from different generations of the same family (Lev 18:17). See Carmichael, *Law, Legend and Incest in Leviticus 18–20*, 36–38.

[18] See Boling, *Judges*, 275.

two sons, Nadab and Abihu, die for their offense of offering strange fire at the sanctuary (Leviticus 10). Like the priest's daughter in the rule in Lev 21:9 who plays the harlot, these sons of a priest also die by fire (Lev 10:2). The tradition about the incident explicitly states that Moses commanded Aaron and his surviving sons not to uncover their heads or rend their clothes in dealing with the dead bodies of the offenders. The rule, in turn (Lev 21:10, 12), incorporated precisely these instructions for a high priest when he is confronted with the death of his offending daughter. It also incorporated the further instruction that he remain in the sanctuary on account of the fact that "the anointing oil of Yahweh" is upon him (Lev 10:7).

Eli's and Aaron's sons die but the rule singled out a father and a mother, not sons (or daughters). The explanation comes from noting the lawgiver's standard procedure of linking what he found in a tradition to a less unusual situation that may turn up in the future. He cited parents because ordinarily they pre-decease sons and daughters, unlike the sons of Aaron and those of Eli who die before their parents. In both stories, but especially in the one about Eli, the relationship between a parent and sons is prominent.

The rule switches back from the topic of a priest's involvement with the dead to the topic of marital restrictions for a priest, the chief priest in this instance. The reason is that the lawgiver has still to take up the wanton sexual conduct of Eli's sons. Neither of them is high priest at the time, but as the tradition brings out (1 Sam 2:30–36), one of them would have succeeded to the office if matters had not taken the turn they did. Equally important, Eli is held liable for his sons' conduct. His condoning it implies that he is just as guilty as if he had initiated it along the lines of Seneca's Agamemnon that he who forbids not sin when in control commands it (*Qui non vetat peccare cum possit iubet*).[19]

In the rule a high priest must take a virgin as a wife and cannot take a widow, a divorced woman, a profaned woman, or a harlot. In focus is how the sons of Eli, in having sexual relations with the women who did menial chores at the threshold to the tabernacle (cf. Exod 38:8), may well have encountered the women listed in the rule.[20]

---

[19] Seneca, *Troades*, 290.

[20] D. Jobling states, "These women are subject to the authority of the priests, so that they cannot be considered as entering voluntarily into these liaisons. The women are victims of exploitation. Their routinized rape continues the theme from the end

The rule concludes with the puzzling statement that the high priest must not "profane his seed among his people." The lawgiver may well have thought of Eli who did not stop his sons' sexual activity and paid a heavy penalty for failing to do so (1 Sam 2:22, 29; 3:13).

Physical Blemishes that Render Priests Unfit for Service in the Sanctuary

The next rule reads:

> And Yahweh spake unto Moses, saying, "Speak unto Aaron, saying,
> Whosoever he be of thy seed in their generations that hath any blemish,
> let him not approach to offer the bread of his God. For whatsoever man
> he be that hath a blemish, he shall not approach: a blind man, or lame,
> or he that hath a flat nose, or any thing superfluous, Or a man that is
> brokenfooted, or brokenhanded, Or crookbackt, or a dwarf, or that hath
> a blemish in his eye, or be scurvy, or scabbed, or hath his stones broken;
> No man that hath a blemish of the seed of Aaron the priest shall come
> nigh to offer the offerings of Yahweh made by fire: he hath a blemish; he
> shall not come nigh to offer the bread of his God. He shall eat the bread
> of his God, both of the most holy, and of the holy. Only he shall not
> go in unto the vail, nor come nigh unto the altar, because he hath a blem-
> ish; that he profane not my sanctuaries: for I Yahweh do sanctify them."
> And Moses told it unto Aaron, and to his sons, and unto all the children
> of Israel. (Lev 21:16–24)

The conduct of Eli's sons brings up the issue of fitness for the priest-hood. The deity declares that, even though he established Aaron's priesthood for all time, in the case of Eli's family, which belongs to the line of Aaron, he has to bring to an end its role as a priestly line (1 Sam 2:27–31). So there are instances, heinous in this example, when priests prove to be unfit for service. The faults at issue are the manifest moral deficiencies of this particular family of priests. The question is why did the lawgiver go on to judge that certain physical blemishes render a priest unfit for serving at the sanctuary, but do not disqualify him from eating the sacred dues that come from the worshippers at it?

Judgment has already been made by the lawgiver that a priest who has a self-inflicted bodily blemish on account of his mourning a dead

---

of Judges." He goes on to compare the treatment of the Levite's wife and the mass abduction of women in Judges 21. See *1 Samuel* (Berit Olam; Collegeville, MN: The Liturgical Press, 1998) 180.

relative becomes defiled. Presumably, he would be excluded from serving at the sanctuary until such time as the blemish disappeared. In the rule in Lev 21:16–24 other more naturally occurring and more permanent blemishes come into reckoning, none of them being specifically linked to mourning the dead. What, then, has triggered this particular topic?

The clue comes from the aftermath of Eli's learning that he and his family are no longer fit to be priests. The dramatic evidence that the priesthood has been taken from them comes in the form of the loss in battle to the Philistines of the Ark of the Covenant, and the accompanying deaths of Eli's two sons. Eli hears about the debacle while, sitting by the wayside, he awaits news of the Ark's forced removal from the sanctuary at Shiloh.

It is at this point in the narrative that much attention is paid to Eli's physical condition. He is old and blind (1 Sam 4:15). The narrator goes on to tell how a messenger conveys the terrible news about the fate of Eli's sons and the Ark. He then records, "And it came to pass, when he [the messenger] made mention of the ark of God, that he [Eli] fell from off the seat backward by the side of the gate, and his neck brake, and he died: for he was an old man and heavy" (1 Sam 4:18). It is tempting to see Eli's physical problems in light of his previous life, as external signs of his flawed internal state. Thus his blindness might relate to the fact that he saw the corruption of his sons but failed to do anything about it, and his heaviness, in turn, to the fact that he and his family made themselves "fat with the chiefest of all the offerings of Israel my people" (1 Sam 2:29).

The blemishes cited in the rule will not, however, reflect corresponding moral blemishes.[21] What has triggered the topic is the focus on Eli's physical state and the fact that it comes up in a context of fitness for the priestly vocation. Already in the lawgiver's time rules presumably did exist about physical blemishes that would disqualify someone from priestly service. The extreme situation in the tradition has brought up the less dramatic topic. Aside from the commonality of subject matter, unfitness for priestly service and a priest's

---

[21] I am reluctant to go as far as M. Douglas who indeed claims that "Leviticus makes physical blemish correspond to blemished judgement" (*Leviticus as Literature* [Oxford: Oxford University Press, 1999] 46). For one thing, there is no hint in the text for that view, for another, the physical blemish does not prevent the person from sharing in the sacred dues.

physical condition, two further pieces of evidence suggest a connection between law and narrative.

First is the fact that the list of blemishes in the rule begins with blindness and lameness. There is no obvious reason why the list should start with blindness, and then, having done so, proceed to lameness (cf. 2 Sam 5:8). As it happens, the narrator mentions first Eli's blindness and then presents a picture of him unable to stand because of his physical condition. The implication is that he can barely walk. The lameness cited in the rule may come from this aspect of the narrative. Suggestive too that Eli's physical state inspired some aspects of the handicaps listed in the rule is his broken neck. The list includes other broken limbs, foot and hand, disabilities that will not, unlike a broken neck, cause death. Again, but less persuasive, the fact that the rule cites crushed testes, with consequent infertility, may link up with the fate that befell Eli's immediate family. Its demise is a major feature of the narrative (1 Sam 2:31–34).

Secondly, in the rule, those who are physically disfigured in some way may nonetheless eat the sacred dues. In the narrative, in the same context in which Eli's physical problems and the issue of the fitness of his family for the priesthood are raised, there is comment about how future members of it will appeal to be admitted to a priest's office so that they can obtain food (1 Sam 2:36). There is, then, in the narrative as in the law a distinction made between unfit priests and priests nonetheless having a claim upon sacred dues.

Concluding Remarks

(1) Read against the idiosyncratic character of a particular incident, a rule takes on a different complexion from the one that might suggest itself if it is read on its own terms. Without awareness of the link to the idiosyncratic features of a story, critics often opt for what can be loosely labeled religious meaning. An example is the mystical character attributed to priestly sexuality by Elliger and Gerstenberger. Such an esoteric reading of the rule in question is not necessary once we identify the narrative that prompted it in the first instance. Where the specific motivation for a rule remains hidden, the temptation to resort to some general concept seems to be compelling.

(2) One key to comprehending biblical rules is that they function to counteract history (as it is presented in Genesis–2 Kings), to ensure

that wrongs of the past are not repeated. Rules are not founded on some set of fundamental theological suppositions. We have to resist the tyranny of large generalizations, for example, that some overriding notion of holiness pervades all of the rules.

(3) The attempt to relate biblical laws to social, political, and religious history cannot but be speculative. Much discussion goes back and forth between various historical reconstructions because the evidence for the realities of life in ancient Israel is largely nonexistent or inventively imagined. One opinion is as good as another. There is, in fact, no real method involved in the historical critical approach as applied to the biblical texts. The assumption is that the laws point directly to issues at the time they are compiled, but it is just that, an assumption. Now all one can ever ask of a hypothesis is: does evidence exist to support it? Even if evidence is forthcoming, the hypothesis may still be wrong. My own thesis faces the same inevitable limitation. However, whereas I can give detailed evidence for linking laws to narratives in support of my assumption that the one genre relates to the other, that is, the biblical scribes modified existing laws in response to narrative incidents, critics who rely on the historical method have no means of producing any evidence in support of their assumption. They lack written sources to back up their claims about how the laws address actual societal issues in the lawgiver's time and place. Consequently, they cannot compare like with like, the beginning of any kind of analysis.[22]

In biblical scholarship, the biases of religious apologists and ideological movements can prove burdensome as well as enlightening. What David Daube called the Zionist approach to the Bible has as its aim the attempt to suggest continuity between the history of modern Israel and the history of Israel in the Bible.[23] Christian apologists, in turn, put a high premium on the notion of historicity because of

---

[22] The classical historian E. Gruen is totally skeptical that the historical critical method as applied to Jewish-Hellenistic literature from the time of Alexander's conquests to the early Roman Empire provides us with conventional forms of historical knowledge; see *Heritage and Hellenism: The Reinvention of Jewish Tradition* (Hellenistic Culture and Society 30; Berkeley: University of California, 1998). See my review in *The American Historical Review* 105 (2000) 593–94.

[23] Milgrom is quite explicit: "When the first Zionists rebuilt the temple. . . ." See *Leviticus 1–16*, 1070.

the extraordinary historical claims they make about Jesus in the New Testament.[24]

One way to appreciate that biblical material is not a reliable source of historical information is to recognize that at all times and places literature is a fertile field for producing myths about a group's identity. A piece of writing has the power to create the impression that its delineation of the peculiarities of a people depicts the national character and constitutes the key to the nation's identity. The impression may have some basis in reality but is largely chimerical. Fielding's celebration of the eccentric amiability of his characters created the stereotype of the eccentricity of the English. Shakespeare's tragedies became popular in eighteenth century Europe and created the view that a gloomy spirit dwelt in the English nation.[25] Sir Walter Scott's novels greatly impacted notions about Scottish identity among Americans and Europeans. In each instance, and we can include the impact of the Bible on judgments about the people of Israel, we are not dealing with accurate historical depictions but with literary creations.

The biblical lawgivers, to be sure, may well have been interested in societal issues of their time, but—and I emphasize this point— addressing contemporary ills was not their main aim. Rather, they were set on creating a fiction about the origin of Israelite law, an aim found in so many legal systems.[26] It goes without saying that their judgments about what happened at the beginnings of the nation came from their own milieu.

---

[24] By contrast, scholarship about the classical world is less burdened by such biases and has largely freed itself from the illusions of the historical method that so dominated its inquiries in the nineteenth and much of the twentieth century. See D. Cohen, "Greek Law: Problems and Methods," *Zeitschrift der Savigny-Stiftung für Rechtsgeschichte* 106 (1989) 81–105.

[25] See P. Langford, *Englishness Identified: Manners and Character 1650–1850* (Oxford: Oxford University Press, 2000) 56–64, 289–311.

[26] For Greek law, see A. Szegedy-Maszak, "Legends of the Greek Lawgivers," *GRBS* 19 (1978) 199–209; for Roman Law, see H. F. Jolowitz, *Historical Introduction to Roman Law* (Cambridge: Cambridge University Press, 1952) 4, 10; and for Scotland, H. L. MacQueen, "Regiam Majestatem, Scots Law and National Identity," *Scottish Historical Review* 74 (1995) 1–20. The Vlax Rom (Gypsies) assert that their *kris* system of public assemblies to resolve disputes and formulate policies is an authentic, ancient form of Romani culture which may even go back to the Indian *panchajat* system. In fact, the origin of the *kris* system appears to be in the Romanian village assemblies of the sixteenth century at the time when the Vlax Rom became enslaved in Romanian neo-feudal society. See T. Acton, S. Caffrey, and G. Mundy, "Theorizing Gypsy Law," *American Journal of Comparative Law* 45 (1997) 237, 247–9.

(4) In conventional biblical scholarship there prevails a naïve view of the relationship between law and society, namely, that laws on the books are responses to problems in the society.[27] While the view is true in a banal sense—how can the laws not reflect what their creators experienced in their own time and place—it overlooks factors that render the link much more complex. Even a scrutiny of the contemporary situation in the United States casts doubt on a straight correlation. Most issues in law are settled, not adjudicated. In the United States over 90% of cases do not end up in court. The result is that we do not know the unwritten rules that apply when these cases are settled. Laws on the books are not the most accurate guides to what is going on in society. Even when cases come before the courts, although written rules will be cited by lawyers in their presentations to judge and jury and by judges in their judgments, closer inspection reveals that unwritten rules and social norms indirectly communicated, usually in anecdotal form and incorporating current myths, really determine the outcome.[28] The rules on the books furnish "directional signals or perhaps parameters for argument."[29] It follows that the link between a society's written rules and the issues in society that they appear to address is correspondingly complicated.

(5) It is crucial to decide what kind of material we are dealing with. I suggest that it has the following character. Those who set down the rules so immersed themselves in their folk traditions that, focussing on and rendering judgment about remarkable events recorded there, they produced a distinctive national body of laws. In keeping with the fiction that Moses delivers the laws during his lifetime, some rules explicitly refer to events that he experienced. Other rules, however, do not cite events before or after the time of Moses. Walter Benjamin's point applies as much to these rules as it does to storytelling: "It is half the art of storytelling to keep a story free from explanation as one reproduces it."[30] Jacob is paid back in kind for cheating his elder

---

[27] Montesquieu in the eighteenth century gave major impetus to this mirror theory of law; see *De l'esprit des lois*, book 1, ch. 3 (1748).

[28] See L. Lopucki and W. Weyrauch, "A Theory of Legal Strategy," *Duke Law Journal* 49 (2000) 1405.

[29] See W. Weyrauch, "Aspiration and Reality in American Law," in Alan Watson (ed.), *Law, Morality, and Religion: Global Perspectives* (Berkeley: Robbins Collection Publications, School of Law, University of California, 1996) 222. The parallel to how most critics assess the rules found in ancient Near Eastern law codes may be noted.

[30] See W. Benjamin, *Illuminations. Essays and Reflections* (New York: Harcourt, Brace & World, 1968) 89.

brother out of the birthright when he unwittingly receives the elder daughter Leah in marriage instead of her sister Rachel (Gen 25:27–34, 27, 29). The narrator leaves it to the reader to see the link—and the deity's judgment in the matter. The rules without narrative references function similarly. Time and again, they contain striking or odd or fantastic elements. The aim is to arouse curiosity and to trigger historical memory. The process lures the reader into an engagement with the narrative traditions recounted in Genesis-2 Kings. The Mosaic formulations of rules serve as inspiration either for actual life in the land of Israel or, more likely, for the exiled community. They function, not with a view to being enforced, but as a permanent stimulus for reflection.[31]

In systems of law where a good measure of institutionalization has occurred, law that is written down in the form of statutory legislation, for example, is seen to play an important role, even if unwritten rules might oftentimes prove more significant. The biblical era lacked such institutionalization and, consequently, there was more scope for lawgivers to give expression to legal and ethical concerns from a base that differs markedly from what we find in modern societies. There is not likely to be a sharp demarcation of literary activities between those who set down laws and those who set out stories. Law and storytelling can be much more closely related than has been hitherto realized. It is my contention that in the Hebrew Bible there does indeed exist an integral connection between the two. Every rule in the Book of Leviticus, not just those I have examined in Leviticus 21, serves to illustrate the nexus.[32]

---

[31] D. Allison writes, "While the pervasion of our [biblical] sources by the implicit is a stubborn fact which makes contemporary interpretation difficult, it is useless to complain about improbable literary complexity or subtly encoded messages. Why expect an ancient Jew to have floated everything with meaning to the surface of his text, so that its contents should be visible to us, bad readers with poor memories, as to those who shared his small literary canon and memorization skills?" See *The New Moses: A Matthean Typology* (Minneapolis: Fortress, 1993) 92.

[32] For other examples, see Carmichael, *Law, Legend, and Incest in Leviticus 18–20;* "The Sabbatical/Jubilee Cycle and the Seven-Year Famine in Egypt," *Bib* 80 (1999) 224–39; "The Origin of the Scapegoat Ritual," *VT* 50 (2000) 167–182.

PART FOUR

LEVITICUS IN TRANSLATION AND INTERPRETATION

THE OLD GREEK TRANSLATION OF LEVITICUS

SARIANNA METSO AND EUGENE ULRICH

The Old Greek (OG) translation of Leviticus is generally to be de-scribed as a faithful translation of the ancient Hebrew scroll from which it was translated. That ancient Hebrew text was not entirely identical with the one transmitted in the Masoretic *textus receptus* (MT) or with any other preserved Hebrew text, though it was closely related. One of the principal values of the OG, therefore, is as an additional witness to the Old Hebrew (OH) of Leviticus that lay behind it and the other primary witnesses: the Masoretic Text, the Samaritan Pentateuch (SP), and the scrolls from Qumran (Q) and Masada. Each of the witnesses makes contributions to our knowl-edge of the OG, but none is without its problems.

In his recent three-volume commentary on Leviticus Jacob Milgrom devotes only a brief paragraph to the state of the text:

> The text of Leviticus is in an excellent state of preservation. The vari-ations in the MT are few and nearly always insignificant. The rare meritorious variant in the LXX and Sam. is duly noted in this com-mentary. The LXX and Sam additions to 15:3 are supported by 11QLev.... The few interesting variations in 4QLev[b] and 4QLev[d] ... are also reported.[1]

With respect to the OG translation, John Wevers, in his commen-tary on the LXX of Leviticus, sees the consonantal MT as basically the textual standard by which to measure the work of the transla-tor, and attributes the vast majority of "changes" between the MT and the OG to the activity of the translator.[2]

Milgrom, however, does not mention several Qumran variants,[3] and Wevers' concentration on the OG translator as agent of most

---

[1] J. Milgrom, *Leviticus 1–16: A New Translation with Introduction and Commentary* (AB 3; New York: Doubleday, 1991) 2. The much longer text in 11QpaleoLev[a], SP, and LXX at 15:3 (as also at 17:4) may be an "addition," but perhaps weightier arguments can be made that they are the original text lost from the MT by parablepsis.

[2] J. W. Wevers, *Notes on the Greek Text of Leviticus* (Atlanta: Scholars Press, 1997) xxvii.

[3] The Qumran scrolls present variant readings not mentioned by Milgrom in the following cases: 14:42, 45, 51; 17:3, 4; 22:12, 31; 24:10; 25:46.

changes is open to question (see below). In an attempt to gain a good perspective on the OG of Leviticus, to determine whether there may not be a bit more merit to the OG than Milgrom allows, and to determine whether a yet-sharper focus can be attained on the work of the OG translator than Wevers has provided, this chapter will (1) present a general overview of the OG of Leviticus; (2) discuss the oldest Greek manuscripts of Leviticus; (3) analyse the light cast by the Qumran Hebrew MSS on the OG of this book; (4) and give a reappraisal of the value of the Qumran Greek MSS.

The Old Greek Translation

The most informative recent source for a comprehensive understanding of the OG translation of Leviticus is John Wevers' *Notes on the Greek Text of Leviticus*. During the last three decades of the twentieth century, Wevers published fifteen detailed volumes on the Greek Pentateuch: the Göttingen critical editions of the five books, the accompanying *Text History* for each, and single-volume commentaries on the each of the five translations.[4]

Also of high value is Paul Harlé and Didier Pralon's *Le Lévitique* in the series *La Bible d'Alexandrie*.[5] Since its emphasis is more on the Septuagint as subsequently received within Judaism and Christianity, more attention will be devoted in this chapter to Wevers' study, which focuses specifically on the OG as the original translation from the Hebrew into Greek.

Wevers concludes that the best witnesses in general to the OG for Leviticus are the uncials Alexandrinus (A) and Vaticanus (B) plus the minuscule 121 along with the *x* and *b* groups.[6] But the situation is complex, and "one cannot simplistically follow the A B text since their text is at times demonstrably secondary."[7] He produces in the

---

[4] The volumes for Leviticus are: J. W. Wevers (ed.), *Leviticus* (Septuaginta: Vetus Testamentum Graecum II.2; Göttingen: Vandenhoeck & Ruprecht, 1986); idem, *Text History of the Greek Leviticus* (MSU 19; Göttingen: Vandenhoeck & Ruprecht, 1986); and idem, *Notes*.

[5] P. Harlé and D. Pralon, *La Bible d'Alexandrie: Le Lévitique* (Paris: Cerf, 1988). For the general project of which this volume is a part, see M. Harl, G. Dorival, and O. Munnich, *La Bible grecque des Septante: Du judaïsme hellénistique au christianisme ancien* (Paris: Cerf/C.N.R.S., 1988).

[6] For details, see J. W. Wevers, *Text History*, 59–71, esp. 71.

[7] Ibid., 72.

Göttingen volume a critically established text which provides "as close an approximation to the original LXX as possible, limited only by the inadequacies of the editor."[8] It may be important to add his modest disclaimer that the approximation to the original LXX is also limited by the nature of the evidence, since all Greek MSS except the two fragmentary ones from Qumran are at least six hundred years removed from the original translation.

The lost original translation then is Wevers' ideal goal, and the task of the OG translator he delineates as follows:

> to render the intent of the Hebrew parent text into a Greek form which his synagogal audience and readers would understand. To do this well presupposes an artist who fully understood both the limitations and the possibilities of the two linguistic codes involved, viz. Hebrew and Hellenistic Greek. Stress [then, in Wevers' *Notes*] is intentionally placed on how well the translator carried out his work, thus on how he constructed his Greek text, on how and whether he avoided transferring the characteristics of the source language to the target language.[9]

Along that spectrum, Wevers concludes that the character of the OG translation of Leviticus is "more of an isolate type of translation than a contextual one" (*Notes*, p. ix), i.e., compared to the OG of Genesis and Exodus, it strives noticeably more to render the Hebrew closely than to achieve good Greek style. Wevers notes, however, that "the translator did not proceed mechanically, [for] though the syntax is more often translation Greek than compositional, the translator did try to make sense. The text must have communicated to its Alexandrian audience . . ." (p. x).

Nonetheless, Hebraisms permeate the translation, and a Greek reader who did not know Hebrew "would not readily understand such oddities as ἀνδρὶ ἀνδρί, ᾧ ἂν γένηται (15:2) as referring 'to any man to whom there should happen'" (p. ix). According to Wevers, "lexically the most extreme type of Hebraism is the calque, i.e. a word chosen from the target language to represent the lexemic content of the equivalent source word [e.g., διαθήκη for ברית] . . . In other words, to understand the Greek word one must consult the Hebrew, not the Greek, dictionary" (p. x). The translator "also created a number of neologisms . . . [and] hapax legomena" (pp. x–xi).

---

[8] Wevers, *Notes*, xxvi.
[9] Ibid., xxvii.

Wevers observes that "at times the translator betrays a lack of certainty in cultic matters" and that "particularly characteristic of the translator's work is his love of variation" (p. xi).

Wevers notes a number of cases in which "changes are . . . made in order to clarify the Hebrew text. Many of these are merely a matter of simplification" (p. xii), but there are "attempts at clarification which render the intent of a passage more precise" (p. xiii), and "often what is clearly implicit in MT is rendered explicit in LXX" (p. xiv). According to Wevers, "that the Alexandrian did not woodenly translate his text word-for-word without regard for the context is fully clear; he approached his text in a rational fashion quite aware of the context in which a passage stood" (p. xiv), so that "passages which might be considered inconsistent may often be rendered in a more consistent way by Lev" (p. xv). In order to avoid "any possible misunderstanding on the part of the reader," the translator ends up "in fact, at times actually 'correcting' the text" (p. xvi). Particularly interesting are cases in which the translator "put into Greek what he thought God actually meant to say" (p. xvii). Wevers concludes that "it is hardly surprising that in the translation of such a difficult book as the Hebrew Leviticus, the translator at times misunderstood the Hebrew text. Sometimes this resulted in a confused text, and MT is much clearer than LXX" (p. xvii).

For Wevers, "of greater interest are cases betraying an exegetical mindset on the part of the translator. Some of these involve reinterpreting or correcting MT over against what it actually says" (p. xix). The translator's "theological presuppositions can often be detected in his choice of lexeme for a particular concept, or in his prejudicial choice of certain renderings, even in slight changes of text which a close comparison of text and translation might reveal" (p. xxii).[10]

---

[10] It might be important to note here—especially in light of those who claim to find "theological variants" and "actualizing exegesis" at various points in the LXX—that Wevers (ibid., xviii) categorically states: "I have found little indication in Lev which might reflect the life and times of the Alexandrian translator." This judgment concurs with the more comprehensive conclusion of his colleague, Robert Hanhart, who for decades served as the director of the Septuaginta-Unternehmen. In "The Translation of the Septuagint in Light of Earlier Tradition and Subsequent Influences," in G. J. Brooke and B. Lindars (eds.), *Septuagint, Scrolls, and Cognate Writings: Papers Presented to the International Symposium on the Septuagint and Its Relations to the Dead Sea Scrolls and Other Writings (Manchester, 1990)* (SBLSCS 33; Atlanta: Scholars Press, 1992) 339–79 (esp. 342–43), Hanhart wrote: "The LXX—and this is true for all the books translated—is *interpretation* only insofar as a decision is made

While we stand grateful to Wevers for what he has taught us about the Greek Pentateuch, we must also ask whether the specific interpretation he gives to the evidence—especially with regard to the "exegetical mindset" of the translator—is always the most accurate interpretation.

One can readily agree with his assessment of the general style of translation. The Greek Leviticus is a rather literal translation of the Hebrew, as Pralon also concludes:

> Dans le spectre des variations de traduction, depuis le littéral jusqu'à la paraphrase, le *Lévitique* se situe plutôt du côté du littéral. Le texte grec diffère assez peu du texte massorétique si bien que les deux textes paraissent se fonder sur une tradition assez tôt unifiée."[11]

And Harlé agrees:

> le Lévitique grec était, dans le Pentateuque, le livre qui sans doute manifestait le plus haut degré de fidélité à ce qui avait été son modèle. Il faut pourtant annoncer aussitôt que des différences existent, et que ces différences sont nombreuses.[12]

On the other hand, it is appropriate to ask whether it is specifically the Masoretic form of the Hebrew that is the correct measuring stick for the OG translation. The MT, especially for the Pentateuch, has been quite faithfully transmitted from one form of the Hebrew texts as they existed in antiquity; but it represents only one of the available textual traditions that were in circulation in Judaism in the Second Temple period, and it has undergone repeated editorial scrutiny as the rabbinic period continued. For Leviticus the surviving MSS give evidence for only a single main edition of the Hebrew text circulating in the latter half of the Second Temple period, and the OG is rightly judged to derive from the same close textual tradition that the Qumran scrolls and the ancestors of the MT and the SP transmit. But none of the texts consistently agrees with another, and there are numerous variants, charting inconsistent patterns, between them. As Harlé says, "nous avons pu relever près de 600 différences avec le TM."[13] Again, most of these differences are minor,

---

between various possibilities of understanding which are already inherent in the formulation of the Hebrew *Vorlage* and thus given to the translator. . . . The LXX is essentially *conservation*."

[11] Harlé and Pralon, *Le Lévitique*, 49.
[12] Ibid., 24.
[13] Ibid.

but, as we will see below, the description of the character of the OG is fundamentally altered, depending upon whether the measuring stick is the MT or some other ancient Hebrew ms. Harlé is well aware of this: "En quelques cas, qui constituent des exceptions remarquables, le texte grec suppose un substrat hébreu différent du TM."[14]

Wevers is aware of the problem but takes a cautious position:

> Since Lev is by nature a translation text, a careful comparison at all levels between the presumed parent Hebrew and the resultant Greek texts is basic to the Notes. I have taken the parent text as the consonantal text of MT except where the evidence makes such a parent text unlikely. This consonantal text is an actual text, and throughout an attempt has been made to avoid speculative reconstructions as much as possible, even though at times these might be most attractive.[15]
>
> I am, however, as a general rule, chary of retroversions without any extant remains.[16]

At the theoretical level, one can only wish for a bolder approach, for several reasons. First, we have only a very small percentage of "extant remains" from the many thousands of texts from antiquity. Secondly, the greater the number of texts discovered, the greater the *number* of variants revealed and the richer the array of *types* of variants. Thirdly, though the MT is in one real sense "an actual text," it is, in the (consonantal) form that we have it, not an "actual text" that any Jewish reader in the Second Temple period ever read, since all must agree that there are not a few late secondary readings and scribal changes from the rabbinic period. Moreover, "speculative reconstruction" is not only not to be avoided; it is an essential task of the historian. That task is primarily one of reconstruction—hopefully educated and well-based reconstruction—of a past scene that has mostly vanished. The historian's task is to contemplate and assess the small percentage of evidence that remains and attempt to recreate the original full scene as best one can. Limiting the scene solely to the few bits of data that happen to survive seems a sure way of attaining an impoverished reconstruction.

At the practical level, one can, by perusing the variants in the biblical volumes of DJD, find examples at the Hebrew level of the

---

[14] Ibid., 25. Pralon (ibid., 49; italics in original) subtly concurs: "*l'original* (connu ou supposé). . . . "

[15] Wevers, *Notes*, xxvii.

[16] Ibid., 438 n. 3.

vast majority of "changes" that show up in the OG. There is no reason to posit these changes at the specifically Greek translation stage rather than at the Hebrew stage; most are routine variants—minor errors, explicitating clarifications of implicit meanings, formulaic levelings—that are richly documented at the Hebrew level, as we shall sample below. Perhaps it can be asked quite startlingly: If we are comfortable with the conclusion that the original Greek translation is no longer available and attainable except through critical judgment, why do we hesitate to accept that the original Hebrew is no longer available except through critical judgment? This all the more since prevailing scholarship presumes a single OG translation by a single translator only as far back as the third century BCE, while the origins of the Hebrew are significantly earlier and murkier.

In contrast, Wevers would argue:

> One should not automatically presuppose a different parent text when differences between the Greek and the Hebrew obtain; rather one should first seek for and pursue other explanations. It is only through such details that a picture of the attitudes, the theological prejudices, as well as of the cultural environment of these Jewish translators can emerge.[17]

Most would agree with Wevers that one should be cautious about retroversions without direct evidence; but we do have an immense amount of accumulated evidence from Qumran and elsewhere to make reconstruction generally not only possible but even to varying degrees more scientifically defensible than the reluctance to reconstruct. The Qumran and SP evidence demands that the first consideration, when the LXX reading is at variance with the MT, be whether it is likely that the LXX is faithfully rendering an alternate Hebrew reading.[18]

Let us consider but one example. Julius Wellhausen in 1871 proposed a "retroversion without any extant remains" at 2 Sam 13:39. He proposed that רוח המלך* had been in the Hebrew text where the MT has דוד המלך.[19] Subsequently, he discovered that the Lucianic

---

[17] Ibid., xxxii.

[18] See A. Aejmelaeus, "What Can We Know about the Hebrew *Vorlage* of the Septuagint?" *On the Trail of Septuagint Translators: Collected Essays* (Kampen: Kok Pharos, 1993) 77–115, esp. 92–93 [= *ZAW* 99 (1987) 58–89, esp. 71].

[19] J. Wellhausen, *Der Text der Bücher Samuelis* (Göttingen: Vandenhoeck & Ruprecht, 1871) 190–91.

tradition, and in fact the majority Greek tradition, had τὸ πνεῦμα
τοῦ βασιλέως (even though Vaticanus and Alexandrinus had Δαυεὶδ
/ ὁ βασιλεὺς meekly revised toward the errant MT!).[20] Thus he now
had some "extant remains," but no more than than others do when
they suggest the reconstruction of a common Hebrew reading when
the LXX has a variant from the MT. The *coup de grâce* was provided by 4QSam[a], a scroll which preserves that correct reading in
Hebrew: המלך ה[רו]ח—thus posthumously absolving Wellhausen from
the charge of "speculative reconstruction." The disciplined use of the
trained scholarly imagination is not only legitimate, it is an essential requirement in textual criticism. Countless examples have now
been accumulated of textual variants—correct readings, erroneous
readings, as well as synonymous variants—which supply the exact
Hebrew form upon which an LXX "variant" had had been based.

In addition to Wellhausen's, several additional voices should be
heard from the latter half of the twentieth century, i.e., with awareness of the significance of the Qumran scrolls for LXX studies in
general.

Frank Moore Cross was the insightful harbinger of the new era
in LXX studies with his article, "A New Qumran Biblical Fragment
Related to the Original Hebrew Underlying the Septuagint," docu-
menting for the first time in nearly two millennia a Hebrew MS of
Samuel much closer than the MT to the Hebrew original that provided the basis for the OG translation.[21]

Harry Orlinsky also stated the newly gained vision clearly:

> The LXX translation, no less than the MT itself, will have gained very
> considerable respect as a result of the Qumran discoveries in those cir-
> cles where it has long—overlong—been necessary. And the LXX trans-
> lators will no longer be blamed for dealing promiscuously with their
> Hebrew *Vorlage*; it is to the *Vorlagen* that we shall have to go, and it
> is their *Vorlagen* that will have to be compared with the preserved MT.[22]

The most comprehensive and fully developed study is Emanuel Tov's
The Text-Critical Use of the Septuagint in Biblical Research, which deals in

---

[20] Ibid., 223.
[21] F. M. Cross, "A New Qumran Biblical Fragment Related to the Original
Hebrew Underlying the Septuagint," *BASOR* 132 (1953) 15–26.
[22] H. M. Orlinsky, "The Textual Criticism of the Old Testament," in G. E.
Wright (ed.), *The Bible and the Ancient Near East: Essays in Honor of William Foxwell
Albright* (Garden City, N.J.: Doubleday, 1961) 113–32, esp. 121.

nuanced detail with the possibilities and limitations of understanding the original Hebrew upon which the Greek translations were based. After treating numerous examples in a careful distinction between "reliable" and "doubtful" retroversions, he says:

> If a retroverted reading is based on a reasonable Greek-Hebrew equivalence, and if it is contextually preferable to the reading of MT, the reconstruction should be considered reliable. The background of this argument is that it would have been unusual had the LXX translators preserved such [a] preferable reading coincidentally or changed their original text to that preferable reading. Rather, it is more natural to assume that the translators found such a reading in their *Vorlage*.[23]

Leonard Greenspoon judges similarly about the 4QLXXLev[a] variants:

> In our opinion, there is force to [the] arguments in favor of the originality of these Qumran readings as constituting the Old Greek text and as accurate reflections of a Hebrew *Vorlage* at variance with the MT. . . . Such arguments demand that we take seriously the fidelity of Old Greek translators to their Hebrew text, while not denying some elements of interpretation on their part. . . . At the very least, we must allow . . . for the "stratified" nature of almost all biblical manuscripts, in this instance especially those in Greek.[24]

Nonetheless, the agent for the bulk of the "changes" according to Wevers is the Greek translator: "the Notes deal principally with the work of the translator, i.e. they are concerned with how the translator, the original LXX, interpreted the text. . . ."[25] As we will note below, however, the important distinction must be kept in view between the Hebrew parent text taken up by the translator and the transforming work of the translator who understands (and occasionally misunderstands) that particular Hebrew text. As a first step, let us examine the oldest Greek evidence available.

---

[23] E. Tov, *The Text-Critical Use of the Septuagint in Biblical Research* (2d ed.; Jerusalem Biblical Studies 8; Simor: Jerusalem, 1997) 85. See also N. F. Marcos, *Introducción a las versiones griegas de la Biblia* (2d ed.; Madrid: Consejo Superior de Investigaciones Científicas, 1998) = *The Septuagint in Context: An Introduction to the Greek Versions of the Bible* (tr. W. G. E. Watson; Leiden: Brill, 2000); and K. H. Jobes and M. Silva, *Invitation to the Septuagint* (Grand Rapids: Baker, 2000) 168–71.

[24] L. J. Greenspoon, "The Dead Sea Scrolls and the Greek Bible," in P. W. Flint and J. C. VanderKam with A. E. Alvarez (eds.), *The Dead Sea Scrolls after Fifty Years: A Comprehensive Assessment* (vol. 1; Leiden: Brill, 1998) 101–27, esp. 109–10.

[25] Wevers, *Notes*, xxvii. This "tendance" is noted by G. Dorival in *La Bible grecque*, 199.

The Oldest Greek Manuscripts of Leviticus

Although the oldest MSS are not necessarily the best MSS, antiquity is nonetheless one potentially important feature that must be considered in the evaluation of MSS. In Cave 4 at Qumran two Greek MSS of Leviticus were discovered which are four centuries older than any other Greek MS of the book.[26]

4QLXXLev^a (4Q119 = Rahlfs 801)

Approximately a dozen fragments survive from this MS of the Greek Leviticus which was inscribed on a prepared skin. The MS dates "from about the late second or the first century BCE."[27] The handful of fragments can be pieced together to form a mostly vertical strip preserving the full height of a column containing Lev 26:2–16; only about one third of the width of the column is preserved. The appearance of the remains is consistent with someone's grasping the scroll at the top and bottom and twisting it to tear it in half, because the top and bottom, though damaged, are in much better physical condition than the more broken central section.[28]

The fragmentary scroll was first published by Patrick Skehan in 1957,[29] and the revised edition for DJD by Skehan and Ulrich in 1992. Both had shared with John Wevers the developing drafts of the edition, just as he graciously shared early drafts of his Göttingen Greek edition, which was published in 1986.

The text of 4QLXXLev^a is clearly a representative within the MS tradition of the OG of Leviticus. Fifteen variants from the critically established text of the Göttingen Greek edition (𝔊^{ed}) appear, apart from orthographic differences. None of these readings was selected for the critical text in 𝔊^{ed}. In contrast to that assessment which

---

[26] Fragments of the Greek Numbers and Deuteronomy were also found in Cave 4. Though no fragments of the Greek Genesis have been identified, some from Exodus as well as the Epistle of Jeremiah were found in Cave 7. For an overview of the Greek texts found in the Judean Desert, see E. Tov, "The Nature of the Greek Texts from the Judean Desert," NovT 43/1 (2001) 1–11.

[27] P. W. Skehan, E. Ulrich, and J. E. Sanderson, Qumran Cave 4.IV: Palaeo-Hebrew and Greek Biblical Manuscripts (DJD 9; Oxford: Clarendon, 1992) pl. XXXVIII and pp. 161–65 and 7–10, esp. 161.

[28] Ibid., pl. XXXVIII.

[29] P. W. Skehan, "The Qumran Manuscripts and Textual Criticism," Volume du congrès, Strasbourg 1956 (VTSup 4; Leiden: Brill, 1957) 148–60, esp. 157–60.

rejected all fifteen variants as witnesses to the OG, Ulrich proposed in the DJD edition that "it can be argued, on the basis not only of its antiquity but even more of its textual readings, that 4QLXXLev[a] penetrates further behind the other witnesses to provide a more authentic witness to the Old Greek translation."[30] We will return in part IV below to a closer analysis of the variants offered by this MS and to adjudicate the relative value of the Qumran Greek vs. the previously available Greek MS tradition.

4QpapLXXLev[b] (4Q120 = Rahlfs 802)

Nearly a hundred small fragments from a papyrus MS of Leviticus were also found in Cave 4.[31] The 31 fragments with identifiable text come from the first thirteen columns of the scroll and contain parts of Lev 1:11–6:5[5:24 LXX]. The scroll, which "could reasonably be assigned to the first century BCE,"[32] preserves one important variant plus a number of variants that appear to be minor but may still offer some clues about the early Greek text (see part IV below).

Prior to judging whether the Qumran Greek variants may offer superior or trustworthy readings, or whether they may witness more closely to the original Greek translation, it will be instructive to review the interrelationships of the Hebrew scrolls of Leviticus from Qumran with the OG and MT.

Light from the Hebrew Scrolls on the Old Greek

Fourteen Hebrew MSS (plus fragments of possibly two more) of Leviticus were found in the Judean caves, in addition to the two Greek MSS and one MS of a targum, for a total of seventeen (or possibly nineteen) MSS of the book.[33] The Hebrew MSS teach us a great

---

[30] DJD 9.163.

[31] Ibid., pls. XXXIX–XLI and pp. 167–86.

[32] Ibid., 11.

[33] The Qumran Leviticus MSS are: 1QpaleoLev-Num[a], 1QpaleoLev[b]?, 2QpaleoLev, 4QExod-Lev[f], 4QLev-Num[a], 4QLev[b-c, g], 4QLXXLev[a], 4QpapLXXLev[b], 4QtgLev, 4Qpap cryptA Lev[h]?, 6QpaleoLev, 11QpaleoLev[a], 11QLev[b]. Two additional Leviticus MSS were found at Masada: MasLev[a,b]. For the specific contents of the biblical scrolls, see E. Ulrich, "Index of Passages in the Biblical Scrolls," in P. W. Flint and J. C. VanderKam with A. E. Alvarez (eds.), *The Dead Sea Scrolls after Fifty Years: A Comprehensive Assessment*, (vol. 2; Leiden: Brill, 1999) 649–65.

deal about the OG. There are many variants, mostly minor, but they betray no clear patterns in the affiliations between the textual traditions. Thus, the ancient Hebrew text of Leviticus—as far as the evidence reveals—seems to have been relatively homogeneous in the latter part of the Second Temple period. Only one edition of the text is displayed by the various MSS, with minor variants randomly marring each of the individual witnesses. The single edition is understandable, insofar as there may well have been a single priestly tradition preserved and guarded by the temple priesthood in charge of administering the sacrificial rituals.[34]

The question guiding this chapter is the character of the OG translation of the ancient Hebrew text, and the formulation of the question with which many scholars would begin is twofold: (1) was the MT the *Vorlage* of the OG? and (2) is the OG a reliable witness to the ancient Hebrew? Both questions will be answered by the same set of readings. We could tersely anticipate the answer with a proleptic (1) no, and (2) yes, but those answers will be expounded methodically below.

A moderate number of the variants shows that the OG was based on ancient but still-extant Hebrew readings that differ from the MT. It is equally true that the OG very often agrees with the MT; but that is irrelevant for the present argument, since the hypothesis being analyzed is that the OG reflects an ancient Hebrew text which was partly in agreement with the MT (of course) but also partly in disagreement from it.

The set of readings in section A shows the OG not only in agreement with a Qumran MS against the MT, but also supported by the SP. A few clear examples are listed, followed by others which may not be decisive but which lend support:

---

[34] The uniformity of this edition, however, did not preclude fierce debates over its proper interpretation, as seen, e.g., in 4QMMT. The halakic disputes there include a number of points regarding the interpretation of Leviticus; see 4QMMT B 9–13 (4Q394 3–7 i 12–16 [Lev 7:15]), 4QMMT B 27–33 (4Q394 3–7 ii 14–19 [Lev 7:13]), etc. Nonetheless it was this single text of Leviticus that was being interpreted, and the interpretation was done outside the scriptural text. A diversity of interpretation, similar to that which persisted after the text had assumed its fixed status, should also be presumed to have been operative in earlier temple traditions. Religious practices of the early Second Temple may well have involved diversity, in which case our present text presumably records the resolution of that prior diversity.

A. $OG = Q\ SP \neq MT$

(1) Clear examples

15:3   [טמא הוא] בו כל ימי ז[ב בשרו או החתים בשרו מזובו]
         11QpaleoLev^a SP(> בו) = Q > 𝔐 (מזובו 1°∩2°; see B.2 below)[35]

17:4   [לעשות אתו עלה]אֹו שלמים ליהוה לרצֹנֹכֹם לריח ניחח
         4QLev^d SP 𝔊] וישחטהו בחוה ואל פתח אוהל מו[עֹד לוא יביאנו
         > 11QpaleoLev^a 𝔐

22:5   טמא 4QLev^e SP = 𝔊 > 1QpaleoLev(vid) 𝔐

22:31   אתם 4QLev^b SP = 𝔊 + אני יהוה 𝔐𝔊^mss

(2) Supporting examples

3:11   והק[ט]יר 4QLev^b SP = 𝔊 והקטירו 𝔐𝔊^ms

13:42   בקרחתו 11QpaleoLev^a SP 𝔊] בקרחת 𝔐

14:42   יקחו וטחו 4QLev-Num^a SP 𝔊] יקח וטח 𝔐[36]

14:45   ו[נֹתֹצֹו 4QLev-Num^a SP 𝔊 ℭ J S] ונתץ 𝔐

14:51   על 4QLev-Num^a SP 𝔊] אל 𝔐[37]

17:4   להקריבו 4QLev^d SP 𝔊^mss] להקריב 11QpaleoLev^a 𝔐 𝔊^ed ℭ^OJ

---

[35] K. A. Mathews correctly notes that the SP, though in the main agreeing with 11QpaleoLev^a and OG, nonetheless varies from them in lacking בו; see D. N. Freedman and K. A. Mathews, *The Paleo-Hebrew Leviticus Scroll (11QpaleoLev)* (Winona Lake, IN: ASOR/Eisenbrauns, 1985) 32; and K. A. Mathews, "The Leviticus Scroll (11QpaleoLev) and the Text of the Hebrew Bible," *CBQ* 48 (1986) 171–207, esp. 198. For the purposes of this limited chapter, however, focus will be kept on the main lines of affiliation, ignoring minor variants (such as לוא יביאנו 4QLev^d vs. לא הביאו SP in the next reading at 17:4) within readings which do demonstrate major affiliation.

[36] Though Milgrom (*Leviticus 1–16*, 873) does not mention the 4QLev-Num^a reading, he does note the other witnesses and correctly relegates the variant to negligible status: "The Sam., LXX, and Pesh. read the plural, but the changes of number are characteristic of this chapter's style." In contrast, Wevers (*Notes*, xxii) sees the OG translator's cultic exegesis at work: "it is the priests who are to do the slaughtering, not the worshiper. . . . The Alexandrian insists on the priestly slaughter of the sin offering." That the OG reading, however, is due to its Hebrew *Vorlage* and not the translator's exegetical insistence can readily be seen by the random attestation of singular-plural in the various witnesses at 14:13, 42 (note esp. ולקחו . . . יקח וטח in MT), 50. In all these cases the OG agrees with an extant Hebrew reading.

[37] Milgrom (*Leviticus 1–16*, 881) comments: "The proposition *'el* 'toward' may not be a synonym or a mistake for *'al* 'upon' because its intention may be to indicate that any part of the house will do. Indeed, the rabbis debate this very issue: one tradition opts for the whole house (*Sipra, Měṣōrāʿ Neg.* 5:14) and another just for the door lintel (*m. Neg.* 14:1), in other words, where it could be seen (*Tiferet Israel*)." Milgrom does not mention that the reading על is supported by 4QLev-Num^a, SP, and the LXX, or that the על/אל variant—due to the loss of pronunciation distinction between those laryngeals—is widespread and usually meaningless. It is perhaps more on target to argue that על is original and intended, and that the rabbis' debate was due to the fact that they had inherited a proto-MT text which had אל and therefore begged for explanation.

21:8   מקדשם 11QpaleoLevᵃ SP 𝕲] מקדשכם 𝔐
22:12   היא 4QLevᵇ SP 𝕲] הוא 𝔐

The set of readings in section B shows the OG in agreement with an extant Qumran MS against the MT, irrespective of the SP:[38]

B. *OG* = 𝕲 ≠ *MT*

(1) Clear examples

3:1   ליהוה 4QLevᵇ = La¹⁰⁰(*deo*)] > 𝔐 SP 𝕲ᵐˢ
17:3   אל בישראל ה[ג]ר [והגר] 4QLevᵈ (cf 𝕲ᴬᴮᶠᴹ ἢ τῶν προσηλύτων τῶν προσκειμένων ἐν ὑμῖν; and cf 16:29; 17:8, 10, 13)] > 11QpaleoLev 𝕲 SP 𝔐ᶜᵈ

(2) Supporting examples

2:8   והביא 4QLevᵇ 𝕲] והבאת 𝔐 SP
2:11   כל מנחה 4QLevᵇ 𝕲(vid)] כל המנחה 𝔐 SP
15:3   בו 11QpaleoLevᵃ 𝕲(ἐν αὐτῷ)] > SP; מזובו 1°ᵒ2° 𝔐 (see A.1 above)
17:11   כול בשר 4QLevᵈ 𝕲(πάσης σαρκός) 𝕾 (cf 17:14)] הבשר 𝔐 SP
17:11   בדמו 4QLevᵈ 𝕲(αἷμα αὐτοῦ, cf 17:14)] בדם 𝔐 SP
18:30   כי אני 11QpaleoLevᵃ 𝕲] אני 𝔐 SP
24:10   והאיש הׄ[ׄי]שראל[י] 4QLevᵇ 11QpaleoLevᵃ 𝕲] ואיש הישראלי 𝔐; ואיש ישראלי SP
25:46   ונחלתם 4QLevᵇ 𝕲(καὶ καταμεριεῖτε)] והתנחלתם 𝔐 SP

Section A shows variants in which at least two Hebrew MSS exhibit the reading attested by the OG, but against which the MT varies. Section B shows yet more OG ≠ MT variants for many of which it is plausible to judge that the OG accurately reflected a variant Hebrew text.[39] This evidence lay unavailable for two millennia until the discovery of the Scrolls, and thus the suggestion of these Hebrew readings, as opposed to the MT, as the basis for the OG translation would have appeared to be "speculative reconstruction." From these readings it should be clear that, though there is a large degree

---

[38] It does not matter that the SP disagrees with the OG, any more than it matters whether the MT disagrees with it, since the argument is not that the OG was translated from the SP, any more than it was translated from the MT. The agreement of the SP in section A was simply to support the existence of multiple Hebrew attestations of the basis for the OG translation.

[39] For additional readings outside Leviticus in which the OG agrees with a Qumran reading against the MT, see E. Ulrich, *The Dead Sea Scrolls and the Origins of the Bible* (Studies in the Dead Sea Scrolls and Related Literature 2; Grand Rapids: Eerdmans; Leiden: Brill, 1999) 165–83, esp. 177–79 [repr. of "The Septuagint Manuscripts from Qumran: A Reappraisal of Their Value," *Septuagint, Scrolls and Cognate Writings*, 49–80].

of agreement among all witnesses to Leviticus, the OG not infre-
quently shows faithful dependence upon an ancient Hebrew text
which was simply at variance with the form of the text transmitted
as the Masoretic *textus receptus*. Though some of the simple, routine
readings may have arisen separately and coincidentally, the majority of the more distinctive readings must be judged as direct Greek
dependence on the Hebrew parent text. Thus, it can be argued for
Leviticus, as it has also been demonstrated for many other books,
that generally the OG is a faithful translation of its ancient Hebrew
parent text, and that that parent text was similar to but not identical with the one handed down to become eventually the MT. The
similarities to the MT are due, not to the MT specifically, but to
the fact that most texts are generally faithful to the textual tradition
which they are attempting to copy, and thus texts not directly related
to each other will nevertheless show numerous agreements.

A Reappraisal of the Qumran Greek Scrolls

Having demonstrated that the OG at times differs from the MT but
nonetheless is based on a Hebrew text in circulation in the latter
half of the Second Temple period, we may now analyze the variants of 4QLXXLev^a against the Göttingen critical text and then consider 4QpapLXXLev^b:[40]

4QLXXLev^a

26:4	[τον υετον τ]ηι γηι υμων 𝕮 ^{J}(מיטריא דארעכון)] τον υετον υμιν 𝕲^{ed} = נשמיכם 𝔐𝔴 (cf. Ezek 34:26)
26:4	τον ξυλινον καρ[πον . . .]] τα ξυλα (ξυλινα G-426) των πεδιων αποδωσει τον καρπον αυτων 𝕲^{ed} = (ו)עץ השדה יתן פריו 𝔐𝔴
26:5	αμητος A B* 121 mss Philo Aeth] αλοητος 𝕲^{ed} = דיש 𝔐𝔴
26:6	[ο]εκφοβων / υμας F mss Arm Syh(υμας sub ÷) = 𝕮^P] tr 𝕲^{ed}(sub ÷ G); > υμας Bo = מחריד 𝔐𝔴𝕮^O
26:6^{fin}	[κ]αι πολεμος—[υμων 3°] ad fin 6 O mss La^{100} Co Syh = 𝔐𝔴] ad fin 5 𝕲^{ed}; ad fin 5 et 6 A B^{mg} F M' mss
26:8	πεντε υμων Syh(π. εξ υ.)] εξ υμων πεντε 𝕲^{ed}; מכם המשה 𝔐𝔴
26:9	[και εσται μο]υ η διαθηκη εν υμιν[ ]] και στησω την διαθηκην μου μεθ υμων 𝕲^{ed} = והקימתי את בריתי אתכם 𝔐𝔴

---

[40] Only textual variants are listed, ignoring purely orthographic differences which
do not affect meaning.

26:10 [εξοισετ]ε μετα των νεων] εκ προσωπου νεων εξοισετε 𝔊ᵉᵈ
= 𝔐 חדש תוציאו מפני

26:11 βδελυξομαι 126 (βδελλυξωμαι) Arab] βδελυξεται η ψυχη μου
𝔊ᵉᵈ
= 𝔐 נפשי תגעל

26:12 και εσομ[αι]] και εμπεριπατησω εν υμιν και εσομαι υμων
θεος 𝔊ᵉᵈ
= 𝔐 לאלהים לכם והייתי בתוככם והתהלכתי

26:12 μοι εθν[ος]] μου (μοι mss) λαος 𝔊ᵉᵈ La Arm Bo 2 Cor 6:16;
𝔐 לעם לי

26:13 τον ζυγον το[υ δεσμου] mss La¹⁰⁰] τον δεσμον του ζυγου 𝔊ᵉᵈ
= (עלי)כם מטת 𝔐(-עול מטות)

26:14 μου 2° mss La¹⁰⁰ Aeth Bo] +ταυτα 𝔊ᵉᵈ Arm = 𝔐 האלה

26:15 [προστα]/γμασι μου] κριμασιν μου 𝔊ᵉᵈ La = 𝔐 משפטי

26:15 α[λλα ωστε?]] ωστε (2°) 𝔊ᵉᵈ = (הפרכם)ל 𝔐; και ωστε 392
Aeth

Before analyzing these variants, it is useful to call several general
points to mind. First, there are crucial differences in the history of
the Greek text between (1) the Hebrew parent text from which the OG
of a book was translated, (2) the transformational work of the translator himself, (3) the multiple changes that occurred during the lengthy
and complex period of textual transmission, and (4) the intentional
revisions by the various Greek recensionists.

Secondly, because none of our texts are pure or free from strong
influence by at least three of these factors, we must accept that it
will frequently be the case that successive words will demonstrate
different influences; that is, one word may be the OG translation
[2] accurately reflecting its parent text [1], the following word may
be an error that crept in during the transmission stage [3], the next
word may be the OG translation [2] which misread or misunderstood the parent text [1], the following word may be a helpful but
secondary reading inserted for clarity in the transmission stage [3],
and the following word may be the result of proto-Theodotion's or
Origen's recensional activity [4]. Often the mix of these influences
is unpredictable.[41]

Thirdly, we should recall that

> Lagarde had discovered the general, but not universal, rule of thumb
> that if two variants occur in the manuscript tradition, both correct and

---

[41] This is the "stratified" nature of biblical mss, of which Greenspoon spoke in
part I above.

acceptable, one in literal agreement with the MT and the other more free, then the freer rendering is (other things being equal) to be selected as the OG and the literal rendering is to be seen as secondary revision toward the MT . . .[42]

Finally, however, since recensional activity, when it was applied, was usually noticeably pervasive within any given text, we should not normally expect spotty recensional activity in a pair of contrasting MSS. That is, with regard specifically to the Greek Leviticus variants, it is quite possible that either 4QLXXLev[a] or $\mathfrak{G}^B$ could have undergone revision toward the proto-MT as the recensional process ran its course; but it is not likely that both MSS would have been recensionally revised to similar extents. Implausible would be the hypothesis that 4QLXXLev[a] had been revised toward the proto-MT in half its readings while $\mathfrak{G}^B$ had been revised toward the proto-MT in another half of the readings.

Returning to the variants between 4QLXXLev[a] and $\mathfrak{G}^{ed}$, since there are detailed studies of these fifteen variants readily available,[43] we may focus here simply on whether the 4QLXXLev[a] evidence can contribute toward our quest of the original Greek translation,[44] or whether all its variant readings are to be relegated to the apparatus to the critical edition.[45] The question can be further elaborated:

> . . . whether an alternate Hebrew text [at variance with the MT] might lie behind the OG or might have influenced the Greek variants. Then the following pair of contrasting possibilities [needs to] be explored . . .: (a) If the reading in $\mathfrak{G}^{ed}$ represents the [OG], then how is the reading in 4QLXXLev[a] to be explained? (b) If the reading in 4QLXXLev[a] is the OG, then how is the reading in $\mathfrak{G}^{ed}$ to be explained?[46]

A systematic analysis according to that line of questioning yielded the following results.[47] None of the 4QLXXLev[a] variants turned out to be an error; all were readings that made sense in context. Seven were unique readings; three were attested by only one or two other MSS, while five had good support in the MS tradition. With respect to closeness to the MT, again none of the 4QLXXLev[a] variants was

---

[42] Ulrich, *Scrolls and Origins*, 180.
[43] See Ulrich, *Scrolls and Origins*, 168–74; and Wevers, *Notes*, 438–45.
[44] As claimed by Ulrich in DJD 9.163.
[45] As initially in Wevers, *Leviticus*.
[46] Ulrich, *Scrolls and Origins*, 168.
[47] Ibid., 168–74, 182–3.

an error, while all were reasonably accurate, acceptable translations of a Hebrew text close to the MT. For twelve of the fifteen variants the $\mathfrak{G}^{ed}$ reading appeared closer to the MT, while two were neutral ([ὁ]ἐκφοβῶν / ὑμας 26:6 and μοὶ ἔθν[ος] 26:12), and only one showed 4QLXXLev^a, as opposed to $\mathfrak{G}^{ed}$, in agreement with the MT (the placement of [κ]αὶ πόλεμος . . . 26:6^{fin}).[48] Certain readings could make a credible claim to being the OG, especially ἔθνος (v. 12, since λαός became the recensional standard), but also plausibly τὸν ξύλινον καρπόν (v. 4), ἄμητος (v. 5), the καὶ πόλεμος clause probably placed properly (at the end of v. 6), βδελύξομαι (v. 11), and προστάγμασι (v. 15, since κρίμα became the recensional standard).

Though 4QLXXLev^a antedates the other Greek MSS by four centuries and some of its readings appeared superior, none was selected for $\mathfrak{G}^{ed}$. Lagarde, however, would presumably have chosen some or—because of the general pattern—most of them as more representative of the OG translation, since, in accordance with his principle, the majority are correct and acceptable, with the $\mathfrak{G}^{ed}$ readings in literal agreement with the MT and the 4QLXXLev^a readings more free.

Wevers did subsequently accept μοὶ ἔθνοι and apparently ἄμητος as OG,[49] but he resisted the remainder. The larger picture, however, must also come into play. 4QLXXLev^a and $\mathfrak{G}^{ed}$ are clearly both representatives of the same general text tradition, and $\mathfrak{G}^{ed}$ appears to show revision toward closer approximation to the MT in twelve of the thirteen variants. In contrast, the 4QLXXLev^a readings are a free but reasonably literal translation of the MT or a yet more literal translation of a variant *Vorlage*. When faced with the question regarding the comprehensive pattern—

either seeing the Göttingen edition as an accurate translation (the OG) of the proto-MT and 4QLXXLev^a as secondary (simplification, smoothing, error, etc.), or seeing the Qumran text as an acceptably free trans-

---

[48] Insofar as the MT preserves the original text, this single agreement of 4QLXXLev^a with the MT against $\mathfrak{G}^{ed}$ is meaningless; both simply preserve the original text, independently, as do all other MSS which have not been corrupted. The variant is most likely due, not to "an attempt on the part of LXX at a more logical consecution of clauses" as Wevers suggests (*Notes*, 439), but to the loss of the clause through parablepsis באשרכבם followed by insertion of a marginal restoration at the wrong point. Note, e.g., that 4QLev-Num^a twice omits a full verse (Lev 14:24 and 45), with a later hand secondarily inserting the latter verse.

[49] Wevers, *Notes*, 442–43 and 439; see also L. J. Greenspoon, "The Dead Sea Scrolls," 101–27, esp. 109–110.

lation (the OG) of the proto-MT or a more literal translation of a slightly variant *Vorlage* and the text in the Göttingen edition as a revision toward the proto-MT—[50]

it is difficult to avoid the conclusion that 4QLXXLev[a] is a better witness to the OG, while the later LXX MS tradition shows a pattern of occasional revision of the OG toward a text like the MT.[51]

4QpapLXXLev[b]

This MS exhibits one highly important variant with a strong claim as a uniquely attested original reading. For the divine name it reads ΙΑΩ at Lev 4:27 (and also probably at 3:12) where the MT and SP have the Tetragrammaton and the (later) LXX MS tradition has κύριος; this last never occurs in 4QpapLXXLev[b] (or 4QLXXLev[a]).[52] Otherwise, the scroll has what appear to be only minor, routine variants; these nonetheless offer some useful clues about the development of the Greek text.

For example, 4QpapLXXLev[b] provides at least two original, correct readings in Lev 2:4 where A and B present an error and a minor addition. For the first 4QpapLXXLev[b] probably reads ἐν κλιβάνῳ correctly for "in the oven" (תנור in the MT and SP), whereas A and B read the *lectio facilior* ἐκ Λιβανου ("from Lebanon"). Immediately following, A and B add δῶρον κυρίῳ against the combined witness of the MT, the SP, and the OG.

At Lev 4:6b SP has the plus באצבעו whereas the MT does not; 4QpapLXXLev[b] joins 𝔊[ed] in reading τῷ δακτύλῳ in agreement with the SP, whereas A B agree with the MT in lacking it. In the next verse 4QpapLXXLev[b] 𝔊[ed] A and B all read the plus τοῦ μόσχου whereas the MT and SP lack it. Regarding the first, Wevers, considering whether the Greek readings are dependent upon the Hebrew readings, says:

> LXX . . . has τῷ δακτύλῳ in which it follows the Sam text באצבעו . . .
> This has no equivalent in MT, and A B *b* omit it entirely, thereby

---

[50] Ulrich, *Scrolls and Origins*, 183.

[51] Recall that Wevers (*Text History*, 72) had described "the A B text [as] at times demonstrably secondary."

[52] For a rich discussion of the occurrences of the divine name in ancient Hebrew and Greek texts see P. W. Skehan, "The Divine Name at Qumran, in the Masada Scroll, and in the Septuagint," *BIOSCS* 13 (1980) 14–44, esp. 28–29 and 34.

equalling MT. Whether or not this was omitted under Hebrew influence
is unknown, but that the omission is secondary is certain. Only an
original reading could have followed the Sam text.[53]

Regarding the next variant in 4:7, Wevers says:

> Over against MT, LXX designates the blood as τοῦ μόσχου, a quite
> unnecessary addition, since there is only one source of blood given in
> the context. Hex[apla] has placed the plus under the obelus to show
> that it is an addition.[54]

In response to the first, we can credit Wevers with attributing an
OG reading to a variant Hebrew *Vorlage*, and simply note that he
presumably meant that LXX follows not SP but some available
Hebrew text that had the same reading as SP. It is correct that
"Whether or not this was omitted under Hebrew influence is
unknown," but the pattern should be noted—on the hypothesis that
the 4QLXXLev[a] readings more closely represented the OG—that A
B repeatedly displayed secondary variants that would be classified as
"thereby equalling MT." In response to the second variant, one can
readily see that the same basic phenomenon is at work. In the second reading, just as in the first, the OG simply translated faithfully
from a Hebrew text that had a routine plus; in both cases the plus
is "a quite unnecessary addition," but in the first we can plainly see
that the "unnecessary addition" was added by a Hebrew scribe, not
the OG translator. The key insight is that the OG translator faithfully followed its Hebrew *Vorlage* in both readings. The key problem
is in thinking of the MT and the SP as standard texts by which to
judge Greek readings, whereas they are simply two of the texts that
survived from antiquity, out of the large number of Hebrew texts
that existed—one unknown member of which was used as the *Vorlage*
for the OG translation.

For other readings it is difficult to decide which reading is to be
preferred as the OG, but 4QpapLXXLev[b] exhibits some perfectly
good synonymous readings alongside the later Septuagint MS tradition, and using the same argumentation as that used for 4QLXXLev[a],
it can be argued that the scroll may more closely witness to the original translation, while the later LXX MS tradition has revised accord-

---

[53] Wevers, *Notes*, 37.
[54] Ibid.

ing to later vocabulary usage or for closer approximation to the emergent MT.[55]

Conclusion

The Hebrew text tradition of Leviticus had basically achieved a uniform state, to judge from the extant sources, by the second half of the Second Temple period. Especially since this contrasts with the pluriform state of Exodus and Numbers, which display two or more literary editions, it is plausible to assume that the Jerusalem priesthood had kept a watchful eye on the text of Leviticus. From that perspective, however, the rationale would not have been textual concern for a "standard text" of the scriptural book, but practical concern for clear uniform instructions for correct procedures in the traditional sacred rituals that were practiced in the temple and beyond.

The Old Greek translation of one of the ancient Hebrew scrolls of Leviticus should be seen generally as a faithful attempt to translate the contents of that scroll into a Greek form that had strong and primary fidelity to the details of the original rituals while still attempting to make sense to the Hellenistic Jewish community. The OG of Leviticus is the most literal of the Pentateuchal translations, perhaps due to its unique nature, and can be appreciated as an even more faithful and literal translation insofar as it is compared to its proper Hebrew parent text rather than to the MT. Vaticanus and Alexandrinus plus minuscule 121 are the best witnesses in general to the OG, but the fragmentary Greek scrolls from Qumran, four hundred years older, for some readings provide closer witness to the OG translation.

The LXX of most books traversed a history that shows influences from at least four different sources. Scholarly attention must focus on the different influences due to (1) the Hebrew parent text from which the OG of a book was translated, (2) the transformational work of the translator himself, (3) the multiple changes that occurred during the lengthy and complex period of textual transmission, and (4) the intentional revisions by the various Greek recensionists. A great deal of editorial and scribal activity had taken place in the

---

[55] A similar conclusion can be argued for 4QLXXNum; see Ulrich, *Scrolls and Origins*, 179–83.

Hebrew text which the OG translator received, but it was a single Hebrew text. The translator also should be viewed as basically performing a single operation, the transformation of the Hebrew original (as he found and understood it) into the Greek language. Some intentional change, including exegetical, undoubtedly occurred in stage 3, while stage 4 involved mostly mechanical revision with little exegetical activity.

John Wevers had asserted above that one "should not automatically presuppose a different parent text when differences between the Greek and the Hebrew obtain; rather one should first seek . . . the attitudes, the theological prejudices, as well as of the cultural environment of these Jewish translators."[56] The weight of the evidence, however, and the judgment of a range of scholars tip the scale in the opposite direction. One should not automatically presuppose, but one should automatically first test whether a variant parent text is the cause of the OG reading.

Wevers' *Notes*, it should nonetheless be explicitly affirmed, remain the most comprehensive commentary on and most valuable tool for understanding the OG of Leviticus. One simply now needs to study it with the additional perspective of judging in each case whether it is "the translator" or the translator's *Vorlage* that provided the alternate reading that is "changed from the MT." The secondary nature of some of those variants will be attributable to the MT text tradition, and some will be attributed to the Hebrew *Vorlage* of the OG. The MT should not be presumed to be "the standard text," but each case must be judged on its own merits.

---

[56] Ibid., xxxii.

RECEPTION OF THE HEBREW TEXT OF LEVITICUS IN THE TARGUMS

Martin McNamara, MSC

Introduction

The present volume will treat extensively and in depth of the composition of the book of Leviticus, of its chief themes and of the manner in which its text has been and still is understood and presented in various communities of believers, whether Jewish or Christian. This present essay is concerned with the manner in which the book was understood and presented in one section of Jewish literature, namely in the Targums or Aramaic translations.

The oldest Aramaic translation of part of this work known to us is the rendering of portions of Leviticus 16 (Lev 16:12–15, 18–21) in the fragments in 4Q156 (probably from the second century BCE).

The best known Targums of Leviticus are those transmitted by rabbinic Judaism, namely:

(a) *Targum Onqelos*

(b) The Palestinian Targums, for Leviticus represented by *Targum Neofiti I*; the *Fragment Targums*, extant for a number of verses in the manuscripts given the sigla P (fifteenth century) V (thirteenth century) N (thirteenth century), and for Lev 1:2 only in the Leipzig manuscript with the siglum L (thirteenth-fourteenth century). Fragments have also been preserved in the Cairo Genizah manuscript with the siglum F, of uncertain date, between the ninth and fourteenth centuries (with Lev 22:26–23:44) and three Toseftas in the Cairo Genizah manuscript FF (from the mid-eleventh-fourth century) (with toseftas for Lev 1:1; 10:19–20; 22:27).

(c) *Targum Pseudo-Jonathan*

There is also a *Samaritan Targum*, being a translation of the Hebrew text of the Samaritan Pentateuch into Palestinian Samaritan Aramaic. Abraham Tal has made a detailed study of the Samaritan renderings and given us a new critical edition of the Samaritan Targum,

based on all the extant material.[1] There is a great diversity among
the manuscripts, the cause of which lies in the evolution of the
Aramaic language down through the ages. Three types of recensions
are distinctly recognizable. The oldest type, represented by MS Or.
7562 of the British Library, reflects the Aramaic of the Samaritans
at the beginning of their independent literary activity. In Tal's opinion this is a stage of development from the pre-Talmudic period,
when the so-called Palestinian Targum was composed, and even
older, for it presents some affinities with the linguistic stratum to
which *Onqelos* and the Aramaic documents of the Dead Sea caves
belong. The second type, represented by MS 6 of the Shechem
Synagogue, reflecting a stage contemporary with Talmudic Aramaic,
evolved from the fourth century onwards. The third type, represented by MS 3 of the Shechem Synagogue, is the result of the
intervention of ignorant scribes. It was copied and its text thoroughly
revised when no Samaritan properly understood the contents of the
Targum. The *Samaritan Targum* texts reflect an evolving linguistic history of the Samaritan language, and likewise the changing manner
of presenting the biblical text in the vernacular rendering. This is
best illustrated by the difference in approach towards anthropomor-
phic descriptions of God in his deeds in the Hebrew text of the
Pentateuch. While targum manuscripts of the first type make no
attempt to remove personifications of God, in the younger manuscripts efforts are made to avoid such manuscripts.[2] The influence
of *Onqelos* is also noticeable in the later expressions.[3] No use of the
Samaritan Targum of Leviticus will be made in the present essay. Jacob
Milgrom does draw occasionally on it in his commentary on the
book of Leviticus.[4]

---

[1] A. Tal, *The Samaritan Targum of the Torah: A Critical Edition.* (3 vols.; Tel Aviv:
University of Tel Aviv, 1980–1983) (in Hebrew); idem, "Samaritan Literature," in
A. D. Crown (ed.), *The Samaritans* (Tübingen: J. C. B. Mohr [Paul Siebeck], 1989)
444–49.

[2] Tal, "Samaritan Literature," 447–49.

[3] Ibid., 445–47.

[4] See the corresponding entries in the Index to J. Milgrom, *Leviticus 1–16. A New
Translation with Introduction and Commentary* (AB 3; New York: Doubleday, 1991) 1150;
idem, *Leviticus 23–27. A New Translation with Introduction and Commentary* (AB 3B; New
York: Doubleday, 2001) 26, 93. Most of the references, however, are to the Hebrew
Samaritan Pentateuch.

The translation into the Syriac dialect of Aramaic (the Peshitta) might also be regarded as a Targum. Consideration of this translation, however, falls outside the remit of this present essay.

Origin and Nature of Extant Targums

In recent years there has been intense study of the Targums of the Pentateuch, especially of the Palestinian Targums. This holds true in a special manner with regard to the nature and date of the form or Aramaic in which they are composed, but has often passed beyond this to the nature and date of the contents of the translation, be these haggadic or halakhic. Any study bearing on the Targums as interpretation of the Hebrew text of Leviticus must take cognizance of these current discussions.

The traditional rabbinic view of the Pentateuch Targums was that they originated in the time and activity of Ezra the scribe, with special reference to the reading of the Law in Neh 8:1–3, 8 and the summary of this activity in Neh 8:8, "And they read from the book, from the law of God *mĕporaš* (NRSV: "with interpretation"), and gave the sense so that the people understood the reading," a text interpreted as follows in the Talmuds of Palestine and Babylon (*y. Meg.* 74d; *b. Meg.* 3a);[5] "*And they read in the book of the Law of the God*: this indicates the Hebrew text; מפרש *mĕporaš* this indicates Targum." While there are some scholars who believe that מפרש *mĕporaš* both here and in Ezra 4:18a denotes some kind of extempore translation, a Targum, such an understanding is generally rejected in favor of a meaning such as "paragraph by paragraph," "distinctly" (Neh 8:8), "verbatim, word for word" (Ezra 4:18).[6]

The origin of Targums in the time of Ezra is still defended by Menahem Kasher. In his view, all three Targums—*Onqelos, Pseudo-Jonathan,* and *Neofiti*—trace their origin to the time of Ezra, and the Tannaim and Amoraim used these three Targums in their rabbinic

---

[5] Not however in the LXX which renders Nehemiah 8:8 as: και ανεγνωσαν εν βιβλιω νομου του θεου και εδιδασκεν Εσδρας και διεστελλεν εν επιστημη κυριου και συνηκεν ο λαος εν τη αναγνωσει, "And they read in the book of the law of God, and Esdras taught, and instructed them distinctly in the knowledge of the Lord, and the people understood *the law* in the reading."

[6] See the discussion of the usage in H. G. M. Williamson, *Ezra, Nehemiah* (WBC 16; Waco, TX: Word, 1985) 56, 278.

texts, both halakhic and haggadic, found in the Talmud and Midrash.[7]

We shall return to the role of Ezra and the reading of the Law of Moses a little later. For the moment we may note that Kasher's view is shared by very few, if any, scholars today. A major difficulty with regard to the Targums of the Pentateuch (which include the Targum of Leviticus which concerns us here) is the time lag between the available manuscripts and any presumed early date of composition. Judged from the point of view of language rather than content, *Onqelos* may represent a state of the Aramaic language pre-132 CE, that is later than that of the Qumran texts. The language of the Palestinian Targums must be later than this, say third century CE at the earliest.[8] The age to be attributed to the contents of these Targums (their haggadah and halakha) is another matter. The contents may be much older than the language in which these are expressed. With regard to this opinions differ. A good amount of the content of the Palestinian Targums has been studied by reason of its supposed relationship with the New Testament. There has been a strong reaction to this use of the Targums by a number of scholars, some of whom would maintain that not just the targumic language but even the material used in these comparisons is demonstrably late.[9] R. Grossfeld has made a detailed analysis of the text of the *Targum Neofiti I* of Genesis in its relationship the Jewish midrash. He finds that it is most closely related to the midrash of *Genesis Rabbah*, representing

---

[7] M. Kasher, *Aramaic Versions of the Bible. A Comprehensive Study of Onkelos, Jonathan, Jerusalem Targums and the Full Jerusalem Targum of the Vatican Manuscript Neofiti I* (vol. 24 of *Torah Shelemah*; Jerusalem: Bet Torah Shelemah, 1974). The relevant texts of Kasher are given by B. Grossfeld, *Targum Neofiti I. An Exegetical Commentary to Genesis Including Full Rabbinic Parallels* (New York: Sepher-Hermon Press, 2000) xxiii–xxv, with his own translation of Kasher's original Hebrew. Grossfeld (p. xxviii) believes that Kasher has not proven his contention.

[8] See S. Kaufman, "Dating the Language of the Palestinian Targums and their Use in the Study of First Century CE Texts," in D. R. G. Beattie and M. J. McNamara (eds.), *The Aramaic Bible. Targums in their Historical Context* (JSOTSup 166; Sheffield: Sheffield Academic Press, 1994) 122.

[9] See J. A. Fitzmyer, review of M. McNamara, *The New Testament and the Palestinian Targum to the Pentateuch* (AnBib 27; Rome: Biblical Institute Press, 1966), in *TS* 29 (1968), 322–26; review of M. Black, *An Aramaic Approach to the Gospels and Acts* (Oxford: Blackwells, 1967), in *CBQ* 30 (1968) 417–28, esp. 420–22. For rejection of the view that in Rom 10:6–7 Paul knew or used the paraphrase of *Neof.* Deut 30:12–13 see J. Fitzmyer, *Romans. A New Translation with Introduction and Commentary* (AB 33; New York: Doubleday, 1993) 590–91. There is a different appreciation of the text of *Neofiti* in J. D. G. Dunn, *Romans 9–16* (WBC 38; Dallas: Word, 1988) 603–6, and in B. Byrne, *Romans* (SP 6; Collegeville, Minn.: The Liturgical Press, 1996) 321.

the views of fourth- and fifth-century Palestinian Rabbis. He is of the opinion that the Targumic rendering found in *Neofiti* is roughly contemporaneous with these, both Rabbis and *Targum Neofiti* probably depending on a common interpretative tradition.[10]

Dr. Grossfeld has also made a special study of the halakha of *Targum Onqelos*, and finds that it follows the halakha of R. Aqiba (early second century).[11]

Pseudo-Jonathan is a Targum with a difference. It is a curious combination of what appears to be passages with the text of *Targum Onqelos* with others carrying the Palestinian Targum. It has sections closely related to Jewish midrashim, the pseudepigrapha and also seems to have texts from hitherto unidentified sources. Some of its grammatical forms appear very old, while it has also some demonstrably late references, such as mention of Adisha and Fatima (Gen 21:21), the wife and daughter of Mohammed. A study of its contents seems to indicate that *Pseudo-Jonathan* was not a work intended for public worship. Rather is it a learned, literary, composition, intended for the compiler's own circles, and rather than a Targum proper may be a re-written Bible or a work on the way to this. The Aramaic language, or languages, of the text have been studied by S. A. Kaufman and E. M. Cook. Kaufman states that in these passages wherein *Pseudo-Jonathan* is not simply copying *Onqelos* and its language, or the Palestinian Targum and its language, or lifting a phrase straight out of one of its midrashic sources, *Pseudo-Jonathan* does have its own distinctive language. This language, he says, must be considered an authentic Aramaic dialect—undoubtedly exclusively a literary one—but a real dialect nonetheless. Thus considered, the work is variously dated between the seventh and tenth centuries.[12] It must be recalled, however, that other scholars consider *Pseudo-Jonathan* a much older work.[13]

---

[10] See R. Grossfeld, *Targum Neofiti I. An Exegetical Commentary*, xxix.

[11] R. Grossfeld, "Targum Onqelos, Halakha and the Halakhic Midrashim," in D. R. G. Beattie and M. J. McNamara (eds.), *The Aramaic Bible. Targums in their Historical Context* (JSOTSup 166; Sheffield: Sheffield Academic Press, 1994) 243–44.

[12] Kaufman, "Dating the Language," 124–25.

[13] See for instance, B. Mortensen, "Pseudo-Jonathan and Economics for Priests," *JSP* 20 (1999) 39–71; P. V. M. Flesher, "Is *Targum Onkelos* a Palestinian Targum? The Evidence of Genesis 28–50," *JSP* 19 (1999) 35–79; R. Hayward, "The Priestly Blessing in *Targum Pseudo-Jonathan*," *JSP* 19 (1999) 81–101.

A noteworthy feature of the Targums of the Pentateuch is that each group contains both indications of an internal unity and signs of a multiformity or composite history of composition. The unity appears in special terminology and phraseology proper to particular Targums as well as specific translational techniques. The diversity is detected especially in the manner in which additional paraphrase is attached to the fundamental translation. The translational techniques of individual targums will be pointed out in due course. In a special study of *Targum Neofiti I* B. Barry Levy makes much of this lack of unity between translation proper and the added or prefaced paraphrase of haggadah.[14] In Levy's view, while much of the text of *Neofiti I* remains literal, it seems obvious to him that many passages were added to it in the course of development and were not part of the original rendering, which, in his view, undoubtedly differs from the present document, that is *Neofiti I* as we now know it. His arguments for this claim come from the literary layering in the text (seams in many cases being still evident) and the linguistic differences evident in the text. The passages in question, he asserts, vary in size from a word or phrase to a column of text. G. Boccaccini advocates a systemic approach to Targum study. He notes that in rabbinic studies scholars have been tempted to study traditions instead of studying documents, and to compare parallels instead of comparing ideological systems. But rabbinic documents, he continues, are not chaotic collections of ancient material and parallels; they are consistent ideological documents.[15] Similarly with regard to the Targums. An examination of the system of *Neofiti* as a whole, he believes—not as a container of synoptic traditions and parallels—leads one to consider the second half of the second century CE as the period when its ideological system took shape around the idea of the eternal Torah. *Neofiti*, he believes, is a reliable source of formative rabbinic Judaism.[16] D. M. Golomb,[17] again with special ref-

---

[14] B. Barry Levy, *Targum Neophyti 1. A Textual Study* (2 vols.; Studies in Judaism; Lanham: University Press of America, 1986–1987).

[15] G. Boccaccini, "Targum Neofiti as a Proto-Rabbinic Document: A Systemic Analysis," in D. R. G. Beattie and M. J. McNamara (eds.), *The Aramaic Bible. Targums in their Historical Context* (JSOTSup 166; Sheffield: Sheffield Academic Press, 1994) 255.

[16] Ibid., 261.

[17] D. M. Golomb, "Methodological Considerations in Pentateuchal Targumic Research," *JSE* 18 (1988) 3–25.

erence to *Neofiti*, advocates greater respect for close connection between the longer and shorter added targumic haggadah (or halakha) and the immediate biblical text, and intertextual connections. A view that may accommodate both positions is one that sees evidence in our present Targums of growth and accumulation over the centuries. This view is advanced in particular with relation to the *Targum of the Prophets*. Targums have been compared to a tell, with various strata. Robert Gordon[18] makes the point that a sensitivity to the tell-like character of Targum is required in our investigation since the extant text probably includes stratified elements representing as much as several centuries of targumic development.

We shall bear this approach in mind in our study of the reception of Leviticus in the Targums.

The Law of Moses in the Books of Ezra-Nehemiah: Neh 8:15 and Lev 23:40

Ezra 7–8 and Nehemiah 8 tell of the activity of Ezra the scribe in making known to Israel the book of the Law of Moses which the Lord had commanded for Israel. Ezra saw to it that the book of the Law was read to the people and that they were helped to understand what was written in it. Nehemiah 7:22b–8:18 is all about the public reading and explanation of this Law.

Ezra is presented as having left Babylonia for Jerusalem on the first day of the first month of the seventh year of the Persian king Artaxerxes, and as having reached Jerusalem in the fifth month of that same year (Ezra 7:7–8). The solemn reading and explanation of the book of the Law of Moses took place on the seventh month of that same year (Neh 7:72). It is commonly accepted that the Persian king in question was Artaxerxes II, whose seventh year would have been 458 BCE. If Artaxerxes III was intended the date would be 389 BCE. For our purpose here it matters little whether the account of Ezra-Nehemiah is strictly historical, whether it is a lightly or heavily embellished narrative of a historical event, or whether it is merely a literary presentation of the role of the book of the Law of

---

[18] R. Gordon, *Studies in the Targum to the Twelve Prophets. From Nahum to Malachi* (VTSup 51: Leiden: Brill, 1994) 152–53.

Moses in the later post-exilic Jewish community. This last-mentioned
position it clearly is.

Most of the narrative in question throws little light on the interpretation of the Book of Moses in the age of Ezra or later. There
is at least one question where reference seems to be made to specific
texts in the Pentateuch. This is Neh 8:15, in the context of Ezra's
command to celebrate the feast of booths in accordance with command of the Law.

> On the second day [of the seven-day festal celebration] the heads of
> the ancestral houses of all the people, with the priests and the Levites,
> came together to the scribe Ezra in order to study the words of the
> law. And they found it written in the law, which the Lord had com-
> manded by Moses, that the people of Israel should live in booths dur-
> ing the festival of the seventh month, and that they should publish
> and proclaim in their towns and in Jerusalem as follows, "Go out to
> the hills and bring branches of olives, branches of wild olive, branches
> of myrtle, branches of palm, and branches of other leafy trees to make
> booths, as it is written" (Neh 8:13–15 [NRSV]; v. 15, צאו ההר והביאו
> עלי זית ועלי עץ שמן ועלי הדס ועלי תמרים ועלי עץ עבת לעשת סכת ככתוב).

Use of the phrase "as it is written" would seem to indicate reference to a specific text in the work known to the author as the Book
of the Law of Moses. Of the Pentateuchal passages dealing with the
feast of booths (Exod 23:16; Lev 23:39–43; Num 29:12–38; Deut
16:13–15) the only possible reference is to Lev 23:40, which says
that in the first of the seven-day festival the people shall take *the fruit
of majestic (?) trees, branches of palm trees, boughs of leafy trees,* and willows
of the brook (and rejoice before the Lord for seven days) (NRSV;
ולקחתם לכם ביום הראשון פרי עץ הדר כפת תמרים וענף עץ עבת וערבי נחל).

The trees indicated in the texts of Leviticus and Nehemiah are
not the same. Nor is the stated purpose for the trees identical in
both passages. In the text of Nehemiah they are intended for making the booths. No such purpose is indicated in the text of Leviticus.
No full explanation for the difference between the two texts has been
found.

It may be that the author of the text of Nehemiah is influenced
by what may already have become current practice with regard to
the tree branches and fruits carried during the feast of booths, and
that this has influenced his use of the Leviticus text. In later Judaism
this feast was coming into ever greater prominence. This feast is thus
described in 2 Macc 10:6–8:

They celebrated it for eight days with rejoicing, in the manner of the festival of booths, remembering how not long before, during the festival of booths, they had been wandering in the mountains and caves like wild animals. Therefore, *carrying ivy-wreathed wands and beautiful branches and also fronds of palm* (διὸ θύρσους καὶ κλάδους ὡραίους ἔτι δὲ καὶ φοίνικας ἔχοντες), they offered hymns of thanksgiving to him who had given success to the purifying of his own holy place. They decreed by public edict, ratified by vote, that the whole nation of the Jews should observe these days every year. (NRSV)

Josephus twice describes the procession during this festival, first in *Ant.* 3 §245 in his account of the Mosaic legislation on this feast. Moses, he says,

... bids each family tò fix up tents, apprehensive of the cold and as a protection against the years inclemency. Moreover, when they should have won their fatherland, they were to repair to that city which they would in honor of the temple regard as their metropolis, and there for eight days keep festival: they were to offer burnt-offerings and sacrifices and thanksgiving to God in those days, bearing in their hands a bouquet composed of myrtle an willow and a branch of palm, along with fruit of the perse (φεροντας εν ταις χερσιν ειρεσιωνην μυρσινης και ιτεας συν κραδη φοινικος πεποιημενην του μηλου του της περσεας προσοντος).

In this text Josephus is recalling the Mosaic legislation. In the second text (in *Ant.* 13 §372) Josephus mentions the same feast in connection with an incident involving Alexander (Jannaeus, 103–76 BCE), making explicit mention of the use of palm branches (the Jewish *lulabim*) and citrons (ethrogs). Josephus writes:

As for Alexander, his own people revolted against him—for the nation was aroused against him—at the celebration of the festival, and as he stood beside the altar and was about to sacrifice, they pelted him with citrons (κιτριοις), it being the custom among the Jews that at the festival of Tabernacles everyone holds wands made of palm branches and citrons (θυρσιους εκ φοινιων και κιτριων)—as we have described elsewhere.

The explicit mention of the citrons (ethrogs; *Neofiti trogin*) and the *lulabim* in the targumic renderings of Lev 23:40 must be due to this liturgical practice, not the underlying Hebrew text.

The Hebrew text, we may recall has: וּלְקַחְתֶּם לָכֶם בַּיּוֹם הָרִאשׁוֹן פְּרִי עֵץ הָדָר כַּפֹּת תְּמָרִים וַעֲנַף עֵץ עָבֹת וְעַרְבֵי נָחַל (Lev 23:40). *Onqelos* renders the relevant section as: פֵּירֵי אִילָנָא אֶתְרוֹגִין לוּלְבִין וְהַדַּסִּין (וְעַבְרִין דְּנַחַל),

"fruits of the tree, citrons (ethrogs), palm branches (*lulabim*) and myrtle branches."[19] The Palestinian Targum of Lev 23:40 may equally be dependent on liturgical practice. *Neofiti* renders as אילן משבח תרנין (והדס וערבה דנחלה) ולולבין, "a (fruit of) an excellent tree: *citrons* (ethrogs; in *Neofiti* written as *terogin*), and palm branches (*lulabim*) and myrtle branches."

Shared Interpretations in the Palestinian Targums of Leviticus and the Greek Versions

It is usual to look for the origins of the Targums of the Pentateuch within rabbinic Judaism, even when these origins are believed to have been relatively early, for instance *Targum Onqelos* within the traditions of the schools of Rabbis Aqiba and Ishmael from the second to the middle of the third century,[20] and the Palestinian Targum as represented by *Neofiti I* within rabbinic Judaism of the fourth and fifth centuries.[21] More recent scholarship invites us to look at another dimension of the Pentateuchal Targums, and to compare their rendering with that of the ancient Greek versions, especially the Septuagint and the others referred to in the Hexapla as *Allos*. Robert Hayward has done this for Leviticus in *Neofiti I* in his notes to the English translation of this Targum,[22] and Jacob Milgrom is doing likewise in his commentary on Leviticus.[23] Restricting ourselves to some examples from Leviticus we may note that the Hebrew אשה, "fire offerings (to the Lord)" in *Neofiti* regularly becomes קרבן "sacrifice(s) to the name of the Lord" (thus Lev 1:9, 13, 15, 17, etc.).[24] The LXX also frequently explains the expression as meaning κάρπωμα, "burnt offerings"

---

[19] See also the note on the rendering in Grossfeld, *The Targum Onqelos to Leviticus and the Targum Onqelos to Numbers. Translated, with Apparatus and Notes* (ArBib 8; Wilmington, Del.: Michael Glazier, 1988) 53, n. 11.

[20] See, for instance R. Grossfeld, *The Targum Onqelos to Genesis. Translated, with a Critical Introduction, Apparatus, and Notes* (ArBib 6; Wilmington, Del.: Michael Glazier, 1988) 16–17.

[21] See, for instance, R. Grossfeld, *Targum Neofiti I. An Exegetical Commentary*, xxix.

[22] M. McNamara and R. Hayward, *Targum Neofiti I: Leviticus. Translated, with Apparatus* (ArBib 3; Collegeville, Minn.: The Liturgical Press, 1994). For occurrences see the Index under "Allos" and "Septuagint," 230–32.

[23] See the entries for "Version. Septuagint" and "Targums" in the Index in J. Milgrom, *Leviticus 1–16*, 1148–50; see likewise, *Leviticus 23–27*, 2693.

[24] For a full list see McNamara and Hayward, *Targum Neofiti I: Leviticus*, 7.

or θυσια, "sacrifice." Similarly with regard to הקטיר, the *hiphil* of קטר, "to burn, offer (on the altar)." In *Targum Neofiti* this is regularly rendered as "set in order (סדר) on top of the altar." Thus in *Neof.* Lev 1:9, 13, 15, 17 etc. The LXX also very often uses the verb επιθημι, "set forth," to translate this same *hiphil*. The instances are noted by R. Hayward.[25] This new approach to the Pentateuchal Targum tradition is a very welcome one and is deserving of further research. It may be capable of shedding much light on the development of the exegetical tradition that became fixed in different ways in the Palestinian Targums and in *Onqelos*.

Leviticus 16 in 4Q156 (4QtgLev) and in The Other Targums (Onqelos, Palestinian Targums, Pseudo-Jonathan)

Chapter 16 of the book of Leviticus, with the Jewish ritual for the Day of Atonement, was one of the most important chapters for Jewish religion. It is given detailed introductions, textual comments and annotations in modern commentaries.[26] Given this, one may be somewhat surprised at the lack of paraphrase or expansive comment in the chief targums. This may be because, being halakha and ritual, there was agreement on the meaning of the text, and its sacred nature did not invite undue expansion in the Aramaic rendering.

The lack of expansion is clearest in *Targum Onqelos*. B. Grossfeld's annotated translation has little in italics (the usual way of indicating expansion in the *Aramaic Bible* series).[27] He has only ten notes for this entire chapter, only four of which are extensive. In a manner usual in *Onqelos* (and the Palestinian Targums), at 16:1 the Hebrew proposition אל ("to") is rendered as עם ("with"). This occurs only after the verb דבר (*dibber*), "to speak," "and the Lord spoke with," not after the verb אמר, "and the Lord said." A theological reason for this particular usage has been put forward.[28]

---

[25] For the Greek rendering of both Hebrew words see Milgrom, *Leviticus 1–16*, 582.

[26] See J. E. Hartley, *Leviticus* (WBC 4; Dallas, Tex.: Word, 1992) 216–46; J. Milgrom, *Leviticus 1–16*, 1009–1084.

[27] R. Grossfeld, *The Targum Onqelos*, 32–35 for Leviticus 16 text and notes.

[28] On this see Grossfeld, *The Targum Onqelos*, 3, referring to the view of Z. W. Chayoth (1864).

Leviticus 16:1 speaks of the death of the two sons of Aaron "when they drew near" (NRSV; בקרבתם; the root קרב can also mean "offer [in sacrifice]"). *Onqelos* paraphrases "when they offered an alien fire," this in keeping with the *Midrash Sifra* (*Aḥarê Mot* 1, p. 79b) which recounts a difference of opinion on the matter among the Rabbis:

> R. Jose, the Galilaean says: "They died on account of their approaching too close, but not on account of what they offered." R. Aqiba says: "One verse says: 'For approaching too close before the Lord they died' (Lev 16:1), while another verse states: 'And they offered an alien fire before the Lord' (Lev 10:1); (the verse) 'upon offering a strange fire before the Lord' (Num 3:4) is decisive. Thus they died on account of what they offered, not on account of approaching too close."

This text indicates the reflection that can stand behind a targumic rendering, and the attempts to understand Scripture by Scripture. In this verse the Targums follow the understanding of R. Aqiba: thus *Neofiti*, the *Fragment Targums*, *Neofiti* margins (which in good part reproduce *Fragment Targums* texts), *Pseudo-Jonathan*; likewise the LXX and Vulgate.

Neofiti is slightly more expansive than *Onqelos*; it reads: ". . . when they offered before the Lord a superfluous sacrifice, out of time, concerning which they had received no order."

At 16:2 the main text of *Onqelos* reads the plural "atonements," for "atonement," but without significance.

At 16:8–9 *Onqelos* inserts "(for) the Name of" before "the Lord" ("for the Name of the Lord" instead of "for the Lord"), a buffer word in *Targum Onqelos* fashion.

Leviticus 16:21 says that the live goat is to be sent into the wilderness by means of "a man," ביד איש עתי. The Hebrew word עתי occurs only here in the Hebrew Bible. While declared of uncertain meaning (as in the note to the NRSV rendering), it is generally taken to mean "timely, ready, waiting in readiness." The Targums render in like manner, מזמן, rendered differently in modern translations: "the designated man" (*Onqelos*), "who is in readiness" (*Neofiti*); "the man who has been designated previously" (*Pseudo-Jonathan*).

Little extra is said on the two goats (16:6–10). *Targum Onqelos* has a slight paraphrase on the place where the goat is to be sent. The Hebrew text speaks of it being sent to "a separated, cut off region," which in *Onqelos* is rendered as "an uninhabited area," in keeping with the understanding found in the *b. Yoma* 67b: "Our Rabbis taught: Azazel—it should be hard and rough. One might have assumed that it is to be an inhabited land, therefore the text reads: 'In the wilderness'" (Lev 16:22). *Neofiti* and *Pseudo-Jonathan* in the translation proper do not go beyond the Hebrew text.

In this chapter *Pseudo-Jonathan* goes its own way and adds brief and longer expansive paraphrases throughout. In *Neof.* Lev 16:1 Aaron is called the *high* Priest, in keeping with a translational technique of *Neofiti* to which we shall return later. In *Ps.-J.* Lev 16:1 the two sons of Aaron who have died are called *high* priests. They are said to have died in *glowing fire* as they offered *profane fire* before the Lord. In *Pseudo-Jonathan* (as indeed in *Neofiti*) at 16:2 mention is made of the *Shekinah* of the Lord being revealed in the clouds above the propitiatory. At 16:3 *Pseudo-Jonathan* is quite explicit that the bull to be offered is not to be a hybrid, a text to be compared with a text in *Sifra*,[29] although there is no mention in rabbinic writings of a hybrid bull. Leviticus 16:4 mentions the vestments that Aaron is to wear, noting that these are his sacred vestments. *Pseudo-Jonathan* adds: "But he shall not enter in garments of gold, lest the sin of the golden calf be remembered," a text which again can be compared with one in *Sifra*.[30] At Lev 16:5 *Pseudo-Jonathan* notes that the two male goats are not to be hybrids, and at 16:6 that Aaron shall buy the bull of the sin offering from his own money. *Equal* lots are to be placed on the two goats (16:8). The goat which has the lot for Azazel shall be set alive before the Lord to make atonement for *the sinfulness of the people of the house of Israel and shall be sent to die in a rough and stony place which is in the desert of Soq, that is Beth Haduri.* The Hebrew word סוק means "peak, precipice," but also designates the mountain from which the scapegoat was to be hurled according to the Jewish tradition registered here by *Pseudo-Jonathan*, also found in *b. Yoma* 67b (316), which is also mentioned in *m. Yoma* 6:8. This same tradition, with mention of Soq and Bet Haduri, is recalled again in *Ps.-J.* Lev 16:22: "The man shall let the goat go into the desert of Soq, and the goat shall go up on the mountain of Beth Haduri, and a blast of wind from before the Lord will thrust him down and he will die." All this is in keeping with *Pseudo-Jonathan*'s interest in miracles and wonders.[31]

---

[29] As noted by M. Maher, *Targum Pseudo-Jonathan: Leviticus. Translated, with Notes* (ArBib 3; Collegeville, Minn.: Liturgical Books, 1994) 168.

[30] See note by Maher, *Targum Pseudo-Jonathan: Leviticus*, 166.

[31] On this see M. Maher, *Targum Pseudo-Jonathan: Genesis* (ArBib 1B; Collegeville, Minn.: Liturgical Press, 1992) 6 (see pp. 5–8 for the "Haggadah of Ps.-J.").

Here he goes beyond his usual sources, since *m. Yoma* 6:6 says that it was the man (designated) who was to push the goat over.

After consideration of the rendering of the Hebrew text in these traditionally-known Targums, we can pass to the two fragments of Targum Leviticus 16 from Qumran. The text 4Q156 is fragmentary, with only some words of the Aramaic version of Lev 16:12–15, 18–21. The text is probably from the second century BCE, hence by far the oldest version extant of any Targum of the Pentateuch. We cannot say whether the fragments are from an original full Aramaic version of the Pentateuch, of the Book of Leviticus or just from a rendering of Leviticus chapter 16, translated separately possibly by reason of the role of the Hebrew text in the liturgy of the Day of Atonement. The text was published by J. T. Milik, together with a commentary.[32] The edition is accompanied by notes from the pen of M. H. Kasher on the edited Targum fragment and the commentary.

The Hebrew text in question has the divine name יהוה twice. The corresponding space for the Aramaic translation is lost, but is restored with the Hebrew letters. The occurrence or translation is not significant, since the other Targums (*Onqelos, Neofiti, Pseudo-Jonathan*) reproduce the divine Name (with series of yods) here, without use of any buffer word, such as *Memra*. At 16:12 the Hebrew קטרת is translated by a word beginning with כש, which Milik says may be completed either as כשת or כשרת, the name of a species of perfume, *costum*, mentioned in *Jub.* 16:24. He considers this term (כש?) too specific with regard to the meaning of the Hebrew word. The Hebrew term קטרת, Kasher notes, contains many ingredients. Kasher notes that this Hebrew word is simply transcribed in all its occurrences in the traditional Targums (*Onqelos, Neofiti, Pseudo-Jonathan*). The Samaritan has ולאועדות for ולקטרת (of the other Targums) and so throughout Scripture; the Syriac has ולעטרא and so throughout. In Kasher's view, this (Qumran) Targum had a third Aramaic word, beginning with the letters כש, which to his mind is כשרתא, found once in the Babylonian Talmud (*b. Ber.* 43a), apparently in the sense of "(twigs of) fragrance."

Fragment 1, line 6 renders the key word הכפרת of the Hebrew Text of Lev 16:14 as כסיא, "the covering." The traditional Targums

---

[32] In R. De Vaux, *Qumrân Grotte 4* (DJD 6; Oxford: Clarendon Press, 1977) 86–94. There is a translation in F. García Martínez, *The Dead Sea Scrolls Translated. The Qumran Texts in English* (trans. W. G. E. Watson; 2nd ed.; Leiden: Brill, 1994) 143.

(*Onqelos, Neofiti, Pseudo-Jonathan*) simply retain the Hebrew word (כפ[ו]רתה/א). The term used in the Qumran text has significance with regard to the nature and function of the *kapporet*, and whether it was a covering of the Ark or not. Despite the Qumran reading, the *kapporet* is not regarded as a covering by scholars.[33]

Kasher notes the rabbinic views denying that the *kapporet* was a mere cover to the ark, but also notes the opinion of Rashi on Exod 25:17 explaining the word as "a cover on the work" (i.e. the ark). At Lev 16:2b both *Onqelos* and *Pseudo-Jonathan* render כפרת of the Hebrew as בית כפורתא, "house (place) of the *kapporet*," *Neofiti*, however, simply as כפרתה (על). This leads Kasher to think that this may perhaps indicate some convergence with the view found in the Qumran fragment and the grammarians and Rashi, that *kapporet* does mean a cover, i.e. for the ark.

Kasher concludes with a note that in general, these two fragments lend some weight to the view that he has set forth in his work on the Targums that more than three extant Aramaic translations existed, and that in each of them elements of the Oral Law (which might not be written down but had to be transmitted orally) were blended or merged in the course of the translation.[34]

Reception of the Hebrew Book of Leviticus in the Traditional Targums

Whatever of a prehistory in such works as the Greek translation and a Qumran Targum, our present Targums of Leviticus are *Onqelos*, the Palestinian Targums and *Pseudo-Jonathan*. While these differ among themselves, they have traits in common which can be described as the typically targumic manner of translation and interpretation. Each of the three groups mentioned above have traits and translational techniques proper to themselves, and varying somewhat from book to book of the Pentateuch.

Leviticus, being mainly legal and ritual, with little narrative, is likely to have less of these than other books, while *Onqelos* in general is less rich in these traits than the other Pentateuch Targums. It follows that the targumic traits of *Targum Onqelos* of Leviticus is

---

[33] See Milgrom, *Leviticus 1–16*, 1014 (on the occurrence of the term in Lev 16:2); Hartley, *Leviticus*, 234–35.
[34] Kasher, "Appendix," 93; cf. idem, *Torah Shelemah*, vol. 24.

one of the least representative in targumic characteristics. They are present there, nonetheless. We shall return to a special consideration of *Onqelos* later.

A feature of the Targums is a reverential manner of speaking about God. God tends not to be made the direct subject or object of actions. Whether the reason is reverential approach or the avoidance of anthropomorphisms is not always clear, and for our purpose matters little.

Actions are said to be done *before God* (or *the Lord*). This usage is very frequent in *Onqelos*, as in the other Targums. Sacrificial offerings are made before the Lord (*Onq.* Lev 1:1, etc.), and received (or: received with favor) before the Lord (*Onq.* Lev 1:17).

One of the best known features of these Targum renderings is the use of the phrase "*Memra* of the Lord." Much has been written on this term *Memra* and its significance.[35] While less frequent in *Onqelos* than in the other Targums, it does occur there, and also in *Onqelos* Leviticus on a number of occasions (22 instances in all).[36] In *Onqelos* it occurs in verses where it is also present in other Targums on ten occasions, particularly in conjunction with observing the service of the *Memra* of the Lord (8:35; 10:30; 22:9; 26:23); of God's *Memra* rejecting sinners (20:23; 26:30; see also 26:11b). In *Neofiti* it is not of frequent occurrence, about fourteen times in all: five times in chapter 26 ("my *Memra*," "in my *Memra*"); three times in chapter 16 ("my *Memra*," twice, "in my *Memra*"), and six times elsewhere. It occurs rather frequently in chapter 26, where there is mention of the covenant.

Another term frequent in the Targums is the *Shekinah*, the Presence of God with his people. This is also true of *Targum Onqelos*. As Israel Drazin has noted, it occurs once in *Targum Onqelos* of Leviticus. Thus in *Onq.* Lev 26:11: "I will place my sanctuary in your midst, and

---

[35] Among the more recent works we may note, D. Muñoz Leon, *Dios-Palabra. Memra en los targumim del Pentateuco* (Granada: Institución San Jeronimo 4, 1974); R. Hayward, *Divine Name and Presence, The Memra* (Oxford Centre for Postgraduate Hebrew Studies; Totowa, N.J.: Allanheld, Osmun, 1981).

[36] For occurrences in *Onqelos*, see Muñoz Leon, *Dios-Palabra*, 712–17; for occurrences in *Onqelos* Leviticus in conjunction with other Targums, see idem, 687 (10 occurrences, mainly [7 times] in conjunction with *Pseudo-Jonathan*). For *Tg. Onq.* Leviticus see also the Index in Hayward, *Divine Name*, 181 (7 references). See also I. Drazin, *Targum Onkelos on Leviticus: An English Translation of the Text with Analysis and Commentary* (New York: Ktav, 1994) 13–14, and 22, n. 15.

my *Memra* will not reject you. (12) And I will rest my *Presence* (*Shekinah*) in your midst and be your God ... (14) But if you do not listen to my *Memra* and will not perform these commandments ... (15) ... but alter my covenant, (1) then I, too, will ... punish you." We may note here that in v. 15 the Hebrew text speaks of *breaking* (פרר) the covenant, the root meaning of which is preserved in all the other Targums except *Onqelos*. *Onqelos*, here as elsewhere, has שני, "to change." This is but one little indication of how *Targum Onqelos* Leviticus carries the peculiarities of the overall *Onqelos* rendering.

The *Shekinah* and the Glory of the Lord are central concepts in the Targums, in particular in the Targum of the Pentateuch. *Targum Neofiti* tends to bind the two together as "The Glory of the *Shekinah* of the Lord."[37] (The term יקר, "glory," as we shall note again, occurs only once in *Onqelos*, at Lev 9:6, 23.) In *Neofiti*, as for the other books of the Pentateuch, the two terms are used conjointly: "Glory of the *Shekinah*." However, in the text of *Neofiti* proper the occurrences are few: three in all (Lev 9:23; 15:31; 26:11). The expression is somewhat more frequent in the marginal annotations—five times in all: Lev 9:2; 9:6; 15:31; 26:1; 26:12. Usage is generally in the context of revelation ("the *Shekinah* of the Lord was revealed"), or of God's dwelling with Israel.

Another term employed in the Targums in relation to God's relationship with his people is *Dibbera* (a term also used in rabbinic theology). It is of much rarer use than the others, and is a technical term for God revealing his will to his people, or humankind.[38] The term does not occur in *Onqelos* but is found in a midrash on Lev 1:1 in all texts of the Palestinian Targums.

References to prayer are very frequent in the Targums,[39] including *Targum Onqelos*. As Drazin has noted[40] there is no instance in Leviticus in which *Targum Onqelos* has the opportunity to translate

---

[37] See D. Muñoz Leon, *Gloria de la Shekina en los Targumim del Pentateuco* (Madrid: Consejo Superior de Investigaciones Científicas, 1977); for Glory and *Shekinah* in *Onqelos*, see pp. 199–210; for the extent and significance of Glory and *Shekinah* in *Onqelos* as compared with the use in the Palestinian Targums, see pp. 465–85.

[38] On the *Dibbera* of the Lord, see M. McNamara, *Targum Neofiti 1: Genesis. Translated, with Apparatus and Notes* (ArBib 1A; Collegeville, MN: The Liturgical Press, 1992) 38.

[39] See M. Maher, "The Meturgemanim and Prayer," *JJS* 40 (1990) 226–46; 44 (1993) 220–34.

[40] Drazin, *Targum Onkelos*, 14,

words as שלי, "prayer." In Leviticus *Neofiti* does succeed in introducing mention of praying (שלי) on three occasions: at 19:30, 26:2,
and in the lengthy haggadah in 22:27. At 19:30 Neofiti renders "you
shall fear my sanctuary" of the Hebrew text as "You shall pray with
reverence in my sanctuary." Similarly at 26:2. We shall meet the
third text below, in which the substantive "prayer" (שלי) also occurs,
as it does in a marginal annotation at 9:24.

Leviticus has much to say on the priest, the priests, the sons of
Aaron the priest, and the sons of Aaron the priests. Together with
the noun כהן, the Hebrew text also has the verb כהן, "to officiate
as priest" twice (at 7:35; 16:32). *Onqelos* throughout the Pentateuch
generally retains the noun in its Aramaic rendering but paraphrases
the verb as שמש, "to serve (before the Lord)." This holds true also
for the occurrences in Leviticus. In both instances *Neofiti* renders the
verb as "to serve in the high priesthood (before the Lord)." In reference to the priests, Lev 21:4 says that none of them shall defile
himself as a husband among his people and so defile himself. The
ending is rendered in *Neofiti* as "lest he profane his priesthood." The
marginal text to *Neofiti* has, "The *high* priest shall not make himself
impure even for his own, to profane the *high* priesthood because of
them." Aaron is called the high priest in *Neof.* Lev 16:1 and in 21:1
Neofiti makes mention of a high priest, where in the Hebrew text
there is mention only of priests. Similarly in *Neofiti* margin, Lev 14:26
mention is made of a high priest where the Hebrew text and *Neofiti*
have only "priest." There is no mention of high priesthood, or high
priest in *Onqelos* Leviticus, and the question has been raised as to
whether such mention throughout *Neofiti*, and other texts of the
Palestinian Targum, represents later additions, or serves as indication of the late nature of the text of *Neofiti*. The view has been put
forward that the presence of the designation "high priesthood" indicates a later stage of evolution.[41] However, we may note that the
designation "high priesthood" occurs once in *Onqelos*, at Num 16:10.
Here in the Hebrew text God says to the sons of Korah: ". . . you
yet seek the priesthood as well (ובקשתם נם כהנה)." In all the Targums,

---

[41] On this question see M. McNamara, "Melchizedek: Gen 14,17–20 in the
Targums, in Rabbinic and Early Christian Literature," *Bib* 81 (2000) 22–26. The
Targumic texts with the designation "high priesthood" are given by M. Kasher,
Torah Shelemah (vol. 35 [= *Aramaic Versions of the Bible*, vol. 2]; Jerusalem: Beth Torah
Shelemah, 1983) 170–85.

in *Onqelos* and in the Palestinian Targums, "high" is here added to priesthood, and the text rendered as: "you wish to assume (*Targum Neofiti* and *Targum Onqelos*, "you seek") the high priesthood also." Nowhere else in *Onqelos* is "high" added to the terms "priest" or "priesthood," unless it is already in the Hebrew text (as it is in Num 35:25, 28, and possibly 35:32). The presence of the title "high priesthood" in *Onq.* Num 16:10 is to be borne in mind in any discussion as to whether the use of the same expression in the Palestinian Targums of the Pentateuch is due to later insertions, or even an indication of the late dates of the texts that carry them. It may be that the designation was once more frequently used in *Onqelos* and later erased from most texts.

In the Targums, particularly the Palestinian Targums of the Pentateuch, some Aramaic paraphrases are introduced by the words, "My people, children of Israel," עמי בני ישראל. The phrase is not found in *Onqelos*, but occurs seven times in Targum of Leviticus in *Pseudo-Jonathan* and *Neofiti*: Lev 19:11; 19:12 (*Pseudo-Jonathan* only); 19:26 (*Neofiti* only); 22:28; 25:15 (*Pseudo-Jonathan* only); 25:36 (*Pseudo-Jonathan* only); 25:37 (*Pseudo-Jonathan* only). In other books the phrase can introduce a long paraphrase; generally in Targum Leviticus the paraphrases so introduced are brief. The expression seems to be liturgical in character.[42] In *Neofiti* and *Pseudo-Jonathan* Exodus 20 the phrase is prefaced to the translation of each of the Ten Commandments. In Targum Leviticus also, the instances in question tend to be of the same kind. Thus *Neof.* and *Ps.-J.* Lev 19:11: "My people, children of Israel, you shall not steal"; *Neof.* Lev 22:28: "My people, children of Israel, you shall not sacrifice a cow or a ewe together with its young on the same day." *Pseudo-Jonathan* on this verse has a fuller development: "My people, children of Israel, just as I am (thus the London MS; the *editio princeps* has: "just as our Father is") merciful in heaven, you shall be merciful on earth. You shall not slaughter a cow or ewe and its young on the same day."[43]

---

[42] See I. Elbogen, *Der jüdische Gottesdienst in seiner geschichtlichen Entwicklung* (3rd ed.; Frankfurt, 1931) 188–92.

[43] See M. McNamara, *The New Testament and the Palestinian Targum to the Pentateuch* (AnBib 27 and 27A; Rome: Biblical Institute Press, 1966; repr. with additions 1978) 134–38.

Israel Drazin's Presentation of the Reception of the Hebrew Text
in Targum Onqelos of Leviticus

After this examination of aspects of the manner in which the biblical book of Leviticus has been presented in the Targums in general
it is well to pay attention to *Onqelos* in particular. This has been
done in a special manner by Israel Drazin.[44] In his introduction
Drazin notes that his study of the translation of *Onqelos* reveals that,
in addition to replacing anrthropomorphisms and anthropopathisms
and deviating from the original Hebrew text for the honor of God
and Israelite ancestors, *Targum Onqelos* renders the Masoretic Text's
peshat, its plain meaning, even when this meaning is contrary to rabbinic tradition and halakha.[45] Drazin's study shows, he believes, that
since *Targum Onqelos* focuses on the plain, simple meaning, it does
not follow the view of any particular school. In an introductory section on statistics, Drazin notes that while *Targum Onqelos* is the most
exact of all the Aramaic Bible translations, its rendering of Leviticus
deviates 2,432 times from the literal biblical text, which is about
three changes in each of Leviticus' 859 verses. However, about 92
percent of the differences, 2,247 instances, simply clarify the text,
including 465 times when the Targumist only inserts ד and 552 occasions when the Aramaic letter for "the" (א) is added. These two
insertions total 41.9 percent of all alterations. *Targum Onqelos*'s differences
clarify some, but not all, ambiguities; they render figurative language
concretely; avoid questions, negative statements, and exaggerations
which could be misunderstood; and replace ambiguous, indirect, and
passive language with clear, forceful, and vivid words. Because of its
attempt to clarify the text's simple meaning, and because of the general context of the verse, the Targum may be the opposite of the
Masoretic Text.[46] About seven percent of *Targum Onqelos*'s deviations,
167 in all, were made to enhance respect for God. The Targumist
replaces many, but not all, anthropomorphisms and anthropopathisms,
and otherwise deviates for God's honor in Leviticus only twenty
times. In twenty-two instances *Memra* is used. The term יְקָרא ("glory")
is inserted once (at Lev 9:4); *Shekinah* is included once (Lev 26:12).

---

[44] Drazin, *Targun Onkelos*.
[45] Ibid., 1.
[46] Drazin, *Targum Onkelos*, 13, and n. 9 (p. 20). There are only two instances of
this at Lev 13:2.

In addition קדם is added 115 times, and דחל is included once as a disparaging substitute for an idol (Lev 19:4). There are many instances where *Targum Onqelos* does not avoid anthropomorphisms and anthropopathisms (it renders "face, פני (of God)" as God's "anger" in 20:3, 5, 6 and 26:7), nor add *Memra, Shekinah,* קדם, דחל, or render Elohim by the Tetragrammaton, even though the other, more prolix Targums (Palestinian, *Pseudo-Jonathan*) do so.[47] Eighteen deviations from the Hebrew text were intended to preserve the honor of Israel's ancestors. Many derogatory statements are deleted, changed or softened. Israel's ancestors' attitudes and reactions are depicted with delicacy, and sometimes even the remotest suggestion of any wrongdoing on their part is avoided.[48]

Drazin has given us an important summary of the manner in which the Hebrew text has been received in *Targum Onqelos*. The author also notes the remarkable relationship between *Targum Onqelos* and *Sifra*'s *peshat* exegeses in the rendering of Leviticus as in the other four books of the Pentateuch. There are 129 instances where *Onqelos* parallels *Sifra*, including 82 where the former uses the latter's words. *Targum Onqelos* never explains Leviticus contrary to *Sifra*'s *peshat. Onqelos* incorporates all, or virtually all, of *Sifra*'s interpretations that are *peshat* and neglects its *derash*. From this Drazin concludes that *Onqelos* reflects the midrashic traditions of Palestine rather than those of Babylonia, and that it depends on *Sifra* and is to be dated after *Sifra* and the other tannaitic midrashim, that is, after the fourth century CE, and not about 135 CE as is commonly supposed.[49] These positions on the dependence on *Sifra* and the late dating are highly questionable, but need not detain us here.

Some Thoughts on Halakha of the Targums of Leviticus and its Affiliations

Leviticus is chiefly concerned with the practical issues of cult and ritual. It is only to be expected that in its reception within the Jewish communities there would be concern to link the understanding of its text with Jewish law as understood and expounded by the Jewish sages, and possibly private individuals, of different ages. An

---

[47] Ibid., 14, with references.
[48] Ibid., with the evidence in n. 28.
[49] Ibid., 10–11, 14.

examination of the halakhic interpretation of these Targums will need to pay attention to the tradition represented by each of the individual texts: *Onqelos*, *Neofiti*, the margins of *Neofiti*, the *Fragment Targums*, and *Pseudo-Jonathan*.

This is not the place to enter in any detail into these questions, as there is a variety of views among scholars on the issues involved, in particular the presence and significance of anti-halakhic interpretations in the Targums, in particular the Palestinian Targums of the Pentateuch, and whether such presence there is due to the private views of the Targumist rather than to the synagogue.

We have seen that I. Drazin maintains that *Targum Onqelos* of Leviticus renders the *peshat*, the plain sense of the Hebrew text, even when this meaning is contrary to rabbinic tradition and halakha, and since it focuses on the text's simple meaning, it does not follow the view of any particular school.[50] The tradition represented by *Targum Onqelos* has also been examined by B. Grossfeld. In his view, the exegetical tradition of *Onqelos* is related to the halakhic midrashim which are attributed to the school of Aqiba.[51] With regard to *Targum Onqelos* of Leviticus (as for the other books) he sees abundant parallels with both the haggadic as well as halakhic midrashim, as well as with the Talmuds, although to a much greater extent with the Babylonian than with the Jerusalem one: for Leviticus in the ratio of Babylonian Talmud 17; Jerusalem Talmud 1; midrashim 42 (*Sifra* 36; *Leviticus Rabbah* 2, others 2 + 1). This evidence is consonant with a Palestinian origin for *Onqelos*, together with a later redaction in Babylonia.[52]

The halakha of the Palestinian Targum, particularly of *Neofiti*, and of the book of Leviticus in particular, still awaits a full treatment. B. J. Bamberger has given a preliminary statement on halakhic elements in *Neofiti*, for Leviticus, Numbers, Deuteronomy, although most of his examples are from the Targums of Leviticus.[53] While his chief concern is *Targum Neofiti*, he also notes the renderings in the other

---

[50] Drazin, *Targum Onkelos*, 1.
[51] Grossfeld, *The Targum Onqelos to Genesis*, 15–18.
[52] Ibid., 15.
[53] See B. J. Bamberger, "Halakic Elements in the Neofiti Targum: A Preliminary Statement," *JQR* 66 (1975) 27–38. His examples from Leviticus have been noted by R. Hayward, throughout M. McNamara and R. Hayward, *Targum Neofiti 1: Leviticus*.

Targums (*Onqelos*, *Pseudo-Jonathan*, and the *Fragment Targums*, in the form then known in the Rabbinic Bible and in M. Ginsburger's edition). He is of the opinion that in *Neofiti* distinctive halakhic views are expressed chiefly through exceptional renderings of the biblical text, rarely through additional comments. He examines the material under three headings: ancient halakot, tannaitic halakot, anomalous readings. Under the heading "Ancient Halakot" Bamberger examines Targum Lev 23:11, 15 ("the day after the sabbath" of the biblical text rendered as "the day after the first festal day of Passover") and Lev 23:20 (with the rendering *etrog* and *lulabin* examined above). Under the heading "Tannaitic Halakot" he examines six texts from Targum Leviticus. In Lev 19:9 and 23:22 he believes that *Neofiti* has the view of R. Simeon. In Lev 19:26 *Neofiti* could reflect the view either of R. Dosa or Aqiba. In its rendering of Lev 20:14 *Neofiti* is said to adopt R. Aqiba's view explicitly. The final text he considers under this subheading is Lev 21:20, where the text of *Neofiti* is particularly difficult.[54] Under the heading "Anomalous Renderings" Bamberger examines five texts from Leviticus (Lev 1:8; 5:21; 10:6 [translation of the Hebrew פרע, unbind the hair, or let it grow loose, as "cover"; also in *Neof.* Lev 10:13, 45 and 21:10], 20:9 and 21:13). These instances show peculiarities of *Neofiti*'s rendering and differences within it from the closely related tradition of the *Fragment Targums*. This "preliminary" examination indicates the value of a fuller study.

M. J. Bernstein has written on the halakha in the marginal annotations of *Codex Neofiti I*,[55] a study I did not have the opportunity to see.

Whereas the additional halakha in *Targum Onqelos* and in the Palestinian Targums of Leviticus seems to be minimal, *Pseudo-Jonathan* has a few notable additions, two of which I note here.

The first is on the first commandment and the use of synagogue decorations. The first commandment is restated thus in Lev 26:1: "You shall make for yourselves no idols and erect no carved images or pillars, and you shall not place figured stones in your land, to worship at them; for I am the Lord your God" (NRSV). The text

---

[54] See R. Hayward's the note on the text in M. McNamara and R. Hayward, *Targum Neofiti 1: Leviticus*, 83.

[55] See M. Bernstein, "The Halakhah in the Marginalia of Targum Neofiti," *Proceedings of the Eleventh World Congress of Jewish Studies* (vol. A; Jerusalem: Magnes, 1995) 223–30.

is retained practically unchanged, without addition, in *Neofiti* ("to bow down before it"). The same might be said of *Onqelos*: "you shall not place any stone for worship in your land to worship upon it." The biblical text and Aramaic paraphrases, however, had to take account of the growing Jewish practice of decorating synagogue floors with mosaics. The matter was discussed (and resolved) by the rabbis, and *Pseudo-Jonathan* going on rabbinic texts paraphrases: "You shall not make idols for yourselves; you shall not erect for yourselves images or pillars to bow down (to them), and you shall not set up a figured stone in your land to bow down to it. However, you may put a pavement with figures and images in the floors of your sanctuaries, but not bow down to it. For I am the Lord your God."[56]

The next example concerns a development of a prohibition in Lev 19:17. The Hebrew text of Lev 19:17 says: "You shall not hate in your heart anyone of your kin; you shall reprove your neighbor, or you will incur guilt yourself" (NRSV). *Onqelos* renders it literally. So, too, does *Neofiti*. Not so *Pseudo-Jonathan* which paraphrases as follows: "You shall not speak flattering words with your mouth while hating your brother in your heart. You shall reprove your neighbor; but if he is put to shame you shall not incur guilt because of him." *Pseudo-Jonathan* is here in the rabbinic tradition of some of his favorite sources (*Sifra, Kedoshim, Perek* 4.8; *b. 'Arak.* 16b; *b. Mez.* 31a), which are but part of the history of the exegesis of this verse, the earlier stages of which have been researched by J. L. Kugel.[57]

Haggadic Additions in the Palestinian Targums of Leviticus

While there is little extended paraphrase and no additional haggadah in the *Targum Onqelos* of Leviticus, the Palestinian Targums and *Pseudo-Jonathan* do include three rather extended midrashim which merit consideration here.

---

[56] For the rabbinic texts in question see the note to *Pseudo-Jonathan* by M. Maher, *Pseudo-Jonathan: Leviticus. Translated with Notes* (ArBib 3; Collegeville, Minn.: The Liturgical Press, 1994) 204. See also M. Klein, "Palestinian Targum and Synagogue Mosaics," *Immanuel* 11 (1980) 33–45; also G. Vermes, "Bible and Midrash," in P. R. Ackroyd and C. F. Evans (eds.), *The Cambridge History of the Bible* (vol. 1; Cambridge: Cambridge University Press, 1970) 217–18.

[57] See J. L. Kugel, "On Hidden Hatred and Open Reproach: Early Exegesis of Leviticus 19:17," *HTR* 80 (1987) 43–61 (with treatment of the texts of *Sifra* and *Pseudo-Jonathan*, pp. 55–57).

Targums Lev 1:1. Moses' Reflection at the Setting of the Tent of Meeting

The book of Leviticus opens abruptly with the words: "The Lord (YHWH) called Moses and spoke (וידבר) to him from the Tent of Meeting, saying (לאמר). . . ." Modern commentators note this, and link this opening with earlier narratives on the newly erected ten at Sinai (Exod 24:15–18; 25:1; Exod 40:34–38; Lev 1:1)[58] or some other passage. In *Exodus Rabbah* 19:3 and 46:3 Lev 1:1 is linked with Exod 19:3 in a midrash on the three things that Moses did (on his own initiative) and which the Almighty retrospectively approved.[59] The second of these instances was in the case of the tent of Meeting, when Moses argued thus: "If I might not ascend Sinai, hallowed only during Revelation, without first obtaining divine permission, as it says: 'And the Lord called to him out of the mountain saying' (Exod 19:3), how can I enter, without divine permission, the Tent of Meeting, which is consecrated for all generations? God agreed, for it says: 'And the Lord called to Moses, and spoke to him out of the Tent of Meeting' (Lev 1:1)." This midrash is found to Lev 1:1 in *Neofiti*, the *Fragment Targums*, MSS PVN, and in *Pseudo-Jonathan*. Its insertion at the beginning of the otherwise rather non-haggadic Targum of Leviticus may have been facilitated by the fact that Lev 1:1 was the opening of a synagogue liturgical reading (*seder*), and some of the longer Palestinian Targum paraphrases correspond to the beginning of such *sedarim*, including Lev 22:27 to be considered below. *Neofiti* opens its paraphrase with a text which is identical almost verbatim with its rendering of Num 7:1. The text of *Neofiti* reads:

> And when Moses had finished erecting the tent and had anointed and consecrated it, and all its accessories, and the altar and all its accessories, Moses thought in his heart and said: "Mount Sinai, whose consecration is but the consecration of a moment (i.e. *temporary*), and whose anointing is but the anointing of a moment, I did not ascend it until the time it was spoken with me from before the Lord; the tent of meeting, whose consecration is an eternal consecration and whose anointing is an eternal anointing, it is but just that I should not enter

---

[58] Thus Milgrom, *Leviticus 1–16*, 134–39, on Lev 1:1, with reference to R. Rendtorff, *Leviticus* (vol. 3.1; Neukirchen-Vluyn: Neukirchener Verlag, 1985) 22.

[59] See R. Le Déaut, with J. Robert, *Targum du Pentateuque. Traduction des deux recensions Palestiniennes complètes* (SC 245; vol. 1 of *Genèse*; Paris: Cerf, 1978) 167; McNamara, *Targum Neofiti I: Genesis*, 93, n. 1 to Gen 15:1.

within it until the time it is spoken with me from before the Lord."
Then the *Dibbera* called to Moses, and the Lord spoke with him from
the tent of meeting, saying: "Speak to the children of Israel and you
shall say to them: 'If anyone of you brings an offering before the
Lord—from the herd, from the oxen or from the sheep you shall bring
your offerings'."

*Targums Lev 22:27. The Merits of the Patriarchs and the Abolition of
Sacrifice*

The Hebrew Text (as in NRSV) stipulates that: "When an ox or a
sheep or a goat is born, it shall remain seven days with its mother,
and from the eighth day on it shall be acceptable as the Lord's
offering by fire" (לקרבן אשה ליהוה). Onqelos consistently renders אשה
as "offerings" (קרבן), and so also here, with a certain tautology: "to
be offered as an offering before the Lord," as does also *Pseudo-
Jonathan*. *Neofiti* in its translation proper simply ignores the Hebrew
קרבן, rendering "it is ritually permitted to offer it before the Lord."
For Jews after the cessation of sacrifice on the destruction of the
Temple in 70 CE the verse recalled that the law applied no longer.
None of the animals mentioned could now be sacrificed. The midrash
recalls how these three animals were connected with the Patriarchs,
and asks that the prayers of the Fathers be now accepted in their
stead.

The well-constructed midrash has been preserved in *Neofiti*, PVN
of the *Fragment Targums*, and in a lengthy gloss to *Neofiti*, which coincides with the text CtG F from the Cairo Genizah. It also has been
preserved in *Pseudo-Jonathan*. I reproduce here the translation of
Neofiti.[60] The biblical references in the midrash are to incidents recalled
in Genesis 18, 22 and 27.

Neof. Lev 22:26–27

And the Lord spoke to Moses saying: "(This is) a time that you recall
in our favor our offerings which we used to offer, and atonement was
made for our sins. But now that we have nothing to offer of our flocks

---

[60] For studies of the midrash see R. Le Déaut, "Lévitique XXII 26–XXIII 44
dans le Targum palestinien: De l'importance des gloses du codex Neofiti I," *VT* 18
(1968) 458–71; idem, *La nuit pascale. Essai sur la signification de la Pâque juive à partir
du Targum d'Exode XII 41* (Rome: Biblical Institute Press, 1965) 170–74; G. Vermes,
"Redemption and Genesis 22," in *Scripture and Tradition in Judaism* (2nd ed.; Leiden:

of sheep, atonement can be made for our sins; the ox has been chosen first, to recall before me the merit of the man of the East who in
his old age was blessed in everything; he ran to his cattle-yard and
brought a calf, fat and good, and gave it to the boy-servant who hur-
ried to prepare it. And he baked unleavened bread and gave to eat
to the angels; and immediately it was announced to Sarah that Sarah
would give birth to Isaac. And after that the lamb was chosen to recall
the merit of a man, the unique one, who was bound on one of the
mountains like a lamb for a burnt offering upon the altar. But (God)
delivered him in his good mercies; and when his sons pray they will
say in their hours of tribulation: 'Answer us in this hour and listen to
the voice of our prayer and remember in our favor the Binding of
Isaac our father.' And after this kid-goat was chosen in order to recall
the merit of the perfect man who clothed his hands with goat-skins
and prepared dishes and gave them to eat to his righteous father, to
receive the order of blessings." These are the three sacrifices, the
sacrifices of the three fathers of the World, that is Abraham, Isaac and
Jacob; therefore it is written in the book of the law of the Lord: "A
bull, a lamb or a goat, when it is born shall be brought up for seven
days behind its mother and from the eighth day onwards it is ritually
permitted to offer it before the Lord."

Palestinian Targums Lev 24:12. Midrash on Moses as a Model for Judges

This is a long haggadah around four texts in the Pentateuch in
which Moses said "I have not heard (a similar case to be judged)."
The texts are Lev 24:12; Num 9:8; 15:34 and 25:7 and the midrash
is inserted in the Palestinian Targums in almost identical form at
each of those four places. In it Moses is presented as a model for
rabbinic judges. The haggadah has been preserved in *Neofiti*, in PVN
of the *Fragment Targums*, and in a gloss to *Neofiti*, which reproduces
the text of P. It is also in *Pseudo-Jonathan*.[61] I give the translation of
the text of *Neofiti* here. There is no real parallel in rabbinic literature to this midrash.[62]

Brill, 1973) 211; J. Heinemann, "Ancient Exegetical Traditions in the Aggadah and
the Targumim," *Tarbiz* 35 (1965–1966) 84–89 (Hebrew); C. T. R. Hayward, "The
Date of Targum Pseudo-Jonathan: Some Comments," *JJS* 40 (1989) 20–21.

[61] On this midrash see B. Barry Levy, *Leviticus, Numbers, Deuteronomy* (vol. 2 of
Targum Neophyti I: A Textual Study; Lanham, New York, London: University Press of
America, 1987) 44–47. See also the annotations by R. Le Déaut, *Targum du Pentateuque*
II. *Exode et Lévitique* (Paris: Cerf, 1979) 488–91, and of R. Hayward, in M. McNamara
and R. Hayward, *Targum Neofiti 1: Leviticus*, 96–97

[62] See A. Shinan, "The Aggadah of the Palestinian Targums of the Pentateuch

Neofiti Lev 24:11–12

> And the son of the Israelite woman expressed "the Holy Name" with blasphemies and he reviled (it). And they brought him to Moses. And the name of the woman was Shelomith, the daughter of Dibri, from the tribe of the sons of Dan. This was one of the four legal cases that rose up before Moses, and he decided them in the understanding from above. In two of them Moses was quick, and in two of them Moses was slow. In the former and in the latter he said: "I did not hear." In (the judgment of) impure persons who were not able to do the Passover, and in the judgment of the daughters of Zelophehad Moses was quick, because their cases were civil cases. (In the judgment) of him who gathering wood desecrated the sabbath willfully, and (in the judgment) of the blasphemer who expressed his Holy Name with blasphemies, Moses was slow, because their cases were capital cases, and in order to teach the judges who would rise up after Moses to be quick in civil cases and slow in capital cases, so that those would not kill quickly (even) one deserving according to the law to be killed, lest acquittal be found for him from another angle in the trial; lest they be ashamed to say "We have not heard." And they guarded him in prison until it is declared to them from before the Lord by which judgment they should put him to death.

Translation Techniques in Neofiti and Pseudo-Jonathan

Translation of the Aramaic text of *Targum Neofiti* into English soon led the present writer to a realization that the original translator or redactor was following certain translational techniques, evident in the translation of the words or phrases of the original Hebrew almost always in the same manner in the Aramaic version. In this the translational principles of the Aramaic text looked somewhat similar to those found in the Revised Standard Version. The introduction to the English translation of *Neofiti* Leviticus lists eighteen of these, for instance Hebrew text "peace offerings" becomes "sacrifices of holy things"; "torah" (law) becomes "decree/instruction of the Torah"; the adjective "precious/good" is added to "crimson"; "to pardon/for-

and Rabbinic Aggadah: Some Methodological Considerations," in D. R. G. Beattie and M. J. McNamara (eds.), *The Aramaic Bible: Targums in Their Historical Context* (JSOTSup 166; Sheffield: Sheffield Academic Press, 1994) 213–14. L. Ginsberg, *Notes on Vols. 3 and 6: From Moses in the Wilderness to Esther* (vol. 6 of *Legends of the Jews*; Philadelphia: Jewish Publication Society, 1968) 85, n. 455.

give" is rendered "remit and forgive." What is seen in *Neofiti* Leviticus holds good for the other books of the Pentateuch in *Neofiti*'s rendering. A similar examination has found that by and large the same holds for *Pseudo-Jonathan*. Most probably similar principles are valid for *Onqelos*.

What this evidence indicates is that there is a certain unity running throughout the Palestinian Targum as found in *Neofiti* (and probably in the other texts of the Palestinian Targum as well). We are in the presence not of haphazard ad hoc translations of individual passages but of well-thought through renderings of the Pentateuch, presumably the work of scholars, active within an exegetical tradition.

Purpose of Targumic Renderings: To Give the Sense of the Hebrew and Help the People Understand the Reading

At the end of its description on the work of Ezra and his helpers with regard to the reading of the Law of Moses, Neh 8:8 tells us that "they read from the book, from the law of God, with interpretation (NRSV; or "section by section"?). They gave the sense (of the Book of the Law), so that the people understood the reading."

ויקראו בספר בתורת האלהים מפרש ושום שכל ויבינו במקרא

Onqelos and the Palestinian Targums, true to their name, are primarily translations, intended to give the sense of the Hebrew text. In the attempt to do so the presence of translational techniques indicate that they are witnesses to an intensive exegetical activity. In the effort to have generations down through the ages understand the message of the Hebrew text there is also evidence from their texts of interpretation with this in view, varying from Targum to Targum.

If one were to answer the question as to how the Hebrew text of Leviticus was received, transmitted, in the Targums I think it would be fair to say that by and large *Onqelos* and the Palestinian Targums faithfully render the Hebrew text, in accord with certain translational techniques, but also show the influence of an exegetical activity in many of their paraphrases. Most translations can be presumed to originate within an exegetical activity, and we can presume that the same holds good for the Targums. How old this exegetical tradition was is more difficult to say. Much of it is also clearly witnessed to by related rabbinic writings on the books in question. But the exegetical tradition to which part at least of the Targum exegetical tradition bears witness seems older than the age of the Tannaim, bearing witness to a tradition also attested to by the LXX and other old Greek translations. This older exegetical tradition would have been further developed by the rabbis, in the ages of the Tannaim and the Amoraim, in the halakhic midrashim, and in the two Talmuds, and the later midrashim.

Some scholars today are trying to reconstruct the history of a Palestinian Targum which in due time gave raise to a Proto-*Onqelos*, and the various extant forms of the Palestinian Targum. An awareness of the likelihood of an old and lengthy exegetical history for the interpretation and translation of the Book of Leviticus may help in this.

THE RECEPTION OF LEVITICUS: PESHITTA VERSION

D. J. LANE

Introduction

Orient

The Peshitta version is not the only rendering of Hebrew Leviticus into Syriac, but it is the version that has maintained itself as the authoritative one for Oriental Christianity: here it had its origin and medium of transmission. The term Oriental Christianity indicates the Syriac-using churches which lie to the east of the Mediterranean, and whose chief centers were the more westerly Antioch on the Orontes and the more easterly Seleucia-Ctesiphon (Mahoze) between the Euphrates and the Tigris. Their adherents were, and still are, to be found in present eastern Turkey, southern Russian states, Iraq, Iran, the Gulf States, and South India. Formerly they were to be found also in Central Asia and China; they now have a diaspora of their own, chiefly in North America, Sweden, the Netherlands and Germany.

This Christianity of the Peshitta was (and is) a Christianity with varying degrees of closeness and distance from the Greek church of the east. It has, too, a history and culture which is marked by invasions from Roman, Byzantine or Frankish forces from the West; Persian, Hun or Mongol invasions from the East; Islamic invasion from the South; or a twentieth century Middle Eastern holocaust. It never had more than toleration from either its own or invading rulers, and its story is one of martyrs, displacement and monasticism rather than protection by a royally favored episcopate. Its earlier years were colored by the eclectic philosophies of oriental Hellenism, and both these and later ones were marked by association or conflict with its companion seeker for their Zoroastrian (and later Islamic) rulers' tolerance and approval: Judaism.

The ninth and tenth Christian centuries, however, saw a period of stability and favor under the rule of the Abbasids and the leadership of such Patriarchs as Timothy the Great, Isho bar Nun, and Abdisho. In this period, notably at the Upper Monastery of Abraham

and Gabriel in Mosul, the text of the Peshitta, Old and New Testament
alike, and of the Syriac liturgies, were given an integrity and authority. In biblical terms, the Syriac Vulgate became the Syriac Authorized
Version. The reception of Hebrew Leviticus in the Syriac churches
is an integral part of the history of those churches. The character
of its translation into Syriac, the history of its transmission, its authority against other renderings whether official or unofficial, and its use
are corollaries and consequences of this Oriental Christianity.[1]

Orientalists

But the reception of Hebrew Leviticus as Syriac Peshitta has a second context: that of the Western scholarly world. After the Fifth
Lateran Council (1512–17) Syriac bible manuscripts were known in
the West, and in the seventeenth century appeared as components
of two successive polyglot bibles. Syriac studies flourished after the
sixteenth century founding of the Maronite College in Rome, which
facilitated the work of such Maronite scholars as Sergius Risius,
Abraham Ecchellensis and Gabriel Sionita, and the manuscript collecting and cataloguing of the Assemani family. Syriac Old Testament
provisions became part of the basic versional material used for critical assessment of the Hebrew (Masoretic) text. Leviticus came to
play a crucial part: its ceremonial components became a touchstone
as to whether Peshitta Pentateuch could be regarded as a Jewish or
Christian textual witness.[2] What follows shows that the reception of
Leviticus as Peshitta is one episode within the larger picture of the
symbiosis of a book from the Hebrew Pentateuch and the worlds of
Oriental Christianity and Western biblical scholarship.

Definition of the Peshitta

The Term

The term Peshitta must be regarded cautiously: it is an adjective,
not a noun. The feminine adjective ܦܫܝܛܬܐ means "simple," either

---

[1] D. J. Lane, *The Peshitta of Leviticus* (Monographs of the Peshitta Institute Leiden
6; Leiden: Brill, 1994) 156–76.
[2] J. A. Emerton, "Unclean Birds and the Origin of the Peshitta," *JSS* 7 (1962)
204–11.

in the sense of ordinary or everyday, or of uncomplicated. In conjunction with the noun ܦܫܝܛܬܐ "version" it has been taken to signify the Syriac bible text in common use, or a text without such marginal notes or sigla as the Syrohexapla, or a translation which is straightforward. The term has been used with reference to the Syriac bible since Moses bar Kepha in the ninth century, who contrasts it with the Syrohexapla, and Bar Hebraeus in the thirteenth, who identifies its simplicity with rejection of ornate language.[3] It may best be understood in the third of the senses just given: a version which stands close to that from which it was made. It is not so halting as to be virtually a transliteration of its model, nor so embroidered as to be a free composition. Two instances of idiom in translation illustrate this. At 22:7 the plain Hebrew ובא השמש is rendered by the idiomatic ܘܡܪܒܥܬ ܫܡܫܐ; at 26:36 the idiomatic מנסת חרב by pedestrian ܐܝܟ ܕܥܪܩܝܢ ܡܢ ܩܪܒ ܣܝܦܐ. From the ninth century there is, then, a descriptive term for a Syriac translation. There is, too, from that and the next century, virtually a standard text to which the term applies.

Its Dangers

But two warnings are needed. The first one is that Peshitta, as a descriptive term, is a blanket one for all the books of the Old and New Testament in the Syriac canon. The origin and the translation history and method of the New and Old Testaments differ greatly; within each Testament the books do not all show the same detailed characteristics. In the Old Testament the combination of general resemblances in translation method and detailed differences of vocabulary and syntax suggest that anything up to half a century lies between the rendering of Pentateuch and that of Ezekiel or Chronicles. For example, Leviticus, Numbers and Deuteronomy are half way between the conservatism of Genesis and the tendency to innovate of Ezekiel. Leviticus prefers ܩܪܝܬܐ to ܡܕܝܢܬܐ to render עיר, and ܩܝܡܐ to ܕܝܬܩܐ for ברית.[4] Ezek 22:26 prefers ܚܘܠ to ܚܠܘܬܐ for חול and ܡܚܘܐ to ܡܘܕܥ for אמם.[5] A curious

---

[3] M. P. Weitzman, *The Syriac Version of the Old Testament: An Introduction* (University of Cambridge Oriental Publications 56; Cambridge: Cambridge University Press, 1999) 3.

[4] Weitzman, *Syriac Version*, 179. See, however, Weitzman's whole argument, 164–205.

[5] Ibid., 165.

instance of dependence or interbreeding is seen at, e.g. 1:17. The
earlier manuscripts prefer ܠܝܚ ܪܝܚ as the equivalent of ריח ניחח,
the later ones ܠܝܚ ܣܘܐܬ. This might be the influence of a
Septuagintal ὀσμὴ εὐδωδίας on later manuscripts: but at Gen 8:21
(except for 5b1) manuscripts give both readings.

The second warning is that a hasty use of the term Peshitta brings
the response "In which text? In which manuscript?" Text and manuscript are no more than witness to a type of text: in the Leiden
edition 19 manuscripts are used as evidence of Peshitta Leviticus,
and a further 37 consulted; three printed ecclesiastical editions and
one academic edition of the Peshitta version are currently available.
A search for "the real Peshitta" is a quest for fools' gold, because
each edition is a compromise with the manuscript evidence on which
it rests, and each manuscript hangs upon its exemplar and its scribe.[6]
The search is a progress of infinite regression to the point where
manuscripts now cease, in the fifth century. Behind that point lies
guesswork, with (as appears below) only the doubtful reed of patristic sources as support.

The Printed Texts

The Beginnings

For the Westerner, the final stage of the reception of a text is the
production of a definitive printed edition. There are currently three
ecclesiastical texts: that is, they do not have scholarly apparatus, and
were produced primarily for the use of the Syriac speaking churches
in the Near East or South India. They were basically made in the
nineteenth century in circles where theories of biblical inspiration
disallowed the inclusion of variants on the grounds that a biblical
text was an inspired text. They are: (a) United Bible Societies, 1979,
1987 (reprint of Lee, 1823); (b) Beirut, 1951 (reprint of Dominicans'
Mosul edition of 1887–92) (c) Trinitarian Bible Society, 1911/13,
1954 (reprint of Urmia edition of Dr. Justin Perkins, 1852).[7] They

---

[6] D. J. Lane, "Text, Scholar and Church: the Place of the Leiden Peshitta Within
the Context of Scholastically and Ecclesiastically Definitive Versions," *JSS* 38 (1993)
33–47.

[7] Lane, *Leviticus*, 127–44.

are mongrel texts, offspring by interbreeding of printed and manuscript sources; nevertheless they served as a control in text criticism
of the MT.

Their origin is the Syriac bible *editio princeps*. This is the contribution made by the Maronite Gabriel Sionita to the seventeenth
century polyglot bible of Guido le Jay. Leviticus, in common with
the other OT books, was based, with some modifications from a
thirteenth century manuscript (13a1), on a seventeenth century copy
(17a5) of a fifteenth century manuscript which had been written in
Jerusalem (15a1), slightly modified by 10m3. 15a1 derived from a
twelfth century manuscript (12a1) which had its home in the Tur
Abdin monasteries, heartland of Western Syriac monasticism in present Eastern Turkey.[8] It was written in Edessa, key city of Syriac
life and culture. The Paris polyglot has, therefore, a text with an
accumulation of scribal errors within a consistent pattern. They are
chiefly lacunae *per homoeteleuton*, or omission or addition of the conjunction *waw* or the particle *dalath*. However, by virtue of being
printed, this text had an assertive authoritativeness, even if subsequent editors of printed texts modified or tampered with it in attempts
to provide a "better" text through use of manuscripts. Inevitably a
criterion of a manuscript's excellence was how good a mirror it was
of the MT.[9]

The Middle Period

The text was mediated to later printed editions by the London
Polyglot, 1657, of Brian Walton. Walton reproduced the Paris text,
and his collaborator Thorndike added lists of variants from one
twelfth (12b1) and two seventeenth century manuscripts (17a3,4)
which last, in fact, are closely related to 17a5. This Walton text was
taken over by Samuel Lee who had been charged by the British and
Foreign Bible Society to produce a Syriac bible for Syriac Christians
in India. In Leviticus, Lee made about 90 changes to Walton's text.
He could do no other than exercise his judgement, but what actually happened was that in about 30 of these changes he modified a

---

[8] The sigla used for manuscripts are those of the Leiden Peshitta. See also Peshitta
Institute Leiden University (ed.), *List of Old Testament Peshitta Manuscripts (Preliminary
Issue)* (Leiden: Brill, 1961).
[9] Lane, *Leviticus*, 145–56.

text deriving from West Syriac sources (coming from 17a5) with elements from mixed West and East Syriac sources. He had access to the key Western 12a1, giving preference to that and to another twelfth century manuscript (12b2). This second twelfth century manuscript muddied the waters, since it derives from the East Syriac or Mosul, pattern of text: for Leviticus, showing some 96 resemblances. The result was to exclude some old errors and import some new ones, albeit of the same kind. Larger omissions are by now corrected, but as between the editions there is variation of suffixed/non-suffixed nouns, and the presence or absence of particle, preposition or copula.

Next in order comes the Urmia edition, prepared by the American missionary Justin Perkins for Syriac Christians around Lake Van. This seems to be little more than a reworking of Lee's edition. It was stated that sources not in print were used (twelfth century and sometimes older manuscripts), but these are not specified, and departures from Lee suggest that the tendency to modify in line with the Mosul or Eastern tradition seems continued, as for example presenting ܪܟܠܬ for ܪܟܠܪ at 25:8. The Mosul edition follows much the same pattern: there are claims that it uses manuscript evidence, and the suspicion remains that any used were nineteenth century copies in the East Syriac text tradition. In effect it is based on Lee, and borrows from Urmia.

The use of Peshitta in *Biblia Hebraica* 3[10] must be understood in the light of these remarks. The main siglum refers to Walton's edition, but to Barnes for the Pentateuch. Otherwise 7a1 is the only manuscript referred to (presumably in Ceriani's photolithographic edition),[11] Aphrahat (presumably in *Patrologia Syriaca*)[12] the only other early source, and Lee and Urmia are the other printed texts. An attempt by these means to recover an early Peshitta as a control for the MT is not likely to succeed. In fact all that emerges is that the MT and Peshitta have been subject to the same scribal vagaries, notably of the omission or addition of conjunctions and particles.

[10] A. Alt and O. Eissfeldt (eds.), *Biblia Hebraica* (3d ed.; Stuttgart: Privilgierte Württembergische Bibelanstalt, 1937).

[11] A. M. Ceriani (ed.), *Translatio Syra Pescitto: Veteris Testamenti ex codice Ambrosiano sec. Fere VI photolithographice edite* (Milan, 1876–1883).

[12] D. I. Parisot (ed., trans.), *Aphraatis Sapientis Persae Demonstrationes* in R. Graffin (ed.), *Patrologia Syriaca* (I.1–2; Paris: Firmin-Didot, 1894–1907).

The most accessible Peshitta printed text is that of the United Bible Societies 1979/1987: a reprint of Lee, with the addition of the apocryphal books. However notice must be taken of the Pentateuch originally prepared for the British and Foreign Bible Society by William Emery Barnes,[13] and for this more information is available. With two collaborators, Barnes provided a revision of Lee's edition. He referred to the Urmia edition, making some 24 changes on that basis, but for the most part he used manuscripts which had became available after Lee's work. One hundred thirty departures from Lee pulled his addition away from Lee's tendency towards the East Syriac and into the direction of older manuscripts from West Syriac sources which Koster designated Basic Textus Receptus: they might also be called proto-Peshitta.[14] For Leviticus the key manuscripts are 6b1, 8b1, 9a1, and 7a1: preference was given to the first two. The result was to provide an eclectic text which had characteristics of a fluid manuscript tradition which ante-dated ninth/tenth century standardization. Where Barnes repudiates or reproduces Lee, 6b1 and 8b1 provide the clue. On this basis he has reached something approaching a text without the cumulative scribal inaccuracies of the five hundred years between 12a1 and 17a5. But this cluster of four early manuscripts highlights the difficulty of Peshitta studies: there are very few early manuscripts, either of the whole Old Testament or separate books. It is significant that there are very few readings in Leviticus where the Leiden text differs from Barnes.

The Leiden Text

The current Leiden edition of the Peshitta is a scholarly one, and tries to come to terms with two opposing principles: one, that excellence of readings is guaranteed by the age of a manuscript; second, that authenticity of text is guaranteed by multiplicity of shared readings. As a result the edition lays out as a basic text the most intact and best preserved ancient manuscripts, a seventh century complete bible (7a1), but alters its readings where the majority of tenth century and earlier manuscripts concur. This method in fact avoids

---

[13] W. E. Barnes, C. W. Mitchell and J. Pinkerton (eds.), *Pentateuchus Syriace* (London: Apud Societatem Bibliophilorum Britannicam et externam, 1914) 7.

[14] M. D. Koster, *The Peshitta of Exodus. The Development of its Text in the Course of Fifteen Centuries* (Assen/Amsterdam: Van Gorcum, 1977). Although dealing with Exodus, this work gives the definitive overall discussion of manuscript text history.

taking issue with the problem it suggests. The question is a simple one, of whether Peshitta, as a normative text, derived from a single hypothetical exemplar copied more or less accurately, or is the result of increasing conformity to a norm. The base is presumed to be a Hebrew text or text type: the Masoretic, from which or to which reference was made.

The present writer has described this manuscript, 7a1 in the Leiden notation, as a median text.[15] That is, a text which has characteristics both of its predecessors and successors. It can therefore, on the basis of both earlier and later manuscripts, provide a Syriac text that might have been. While it is fair to regard the dominant text tradition of the ninth/tenth centuries and later as a standard or received text (that is, more of them have survived and have a coherence), the earlier ones are clearly before *Textus Receptus* and were influential in forming it. In this sense they are proto-Peshitta.

The strengths of the edition are that it provides evidence of all the readings of manuscripts of the twelfth century and earlier, and has a fair claim to take note of all the Syriac biblical manuscripts currently known and available.

The work of all these successive editors has made possible an understanding of the way in which Peshitta was received and transmitted in its Western and Eastern Syriac homelands. *Biblia Stuttgartensis*[16] has made a move to avoid the errors of its predecessor, concerning itself with agreements between 7a1 (Ceriani) and Walton. Lee, Urmia, Mosul, and unspecified manuscripts are also listed; Aphrahat has been abandoned, but readings from Bar Hebraeus' *Scholia* brought into play. Here again, there is little of significance: readings of a plural verb for a singular or the addition of an explanatory noun, indicate scribal acts. The reading of passive ܐܬܦܩܕܬ for active צוית at 8:31 (concurring with LXX, Targum) suggests that the Hebrew was originally an unpointed צות which the Masoretes (or a scribe) mistook as active. Cumulatively, on such arguments rests the case that the Peshitta ante-dated the MT.

---

[15] Lane, *Leviticus*, 2–12.

[16] K. Elliger and W. Rudolph (eds.), *Biblia Hebraica Stuttgartensia* (Stuttgart: Deutsche Bibelstiftung, 1967/77).

Manuscripts and Their Relations

Scribes and Translators

The editors of the printed texts had only those manuscripts which chance allowed them to consult. Of the regrettably few available for Leviticus, two stand out: the similar 6b1 and 9a1. The latter, however, lacks the first fifteen chapters and the former the first three. Two related issues are raised. The first is that of differences between other manuscripts and these two. They may indicate a difference of *Vorlage*, or scribal changes which are accidental or a matter of preference. Hence the second issue raised is that of basic translation method: namely, choice of vocabulary and syntax.

If variants do not come from difference of *Vorlage*, then the character of Peshitta is set entirely by the basic translator, and is not subject to attempts to adapt the version towards or away from Masoretic or Septuagintal patterns.

The first issue is fairly simply dealt with: the variations are scribal, and are either mechanical accidents or subconscious adaptations. There are omissions, repetitions, conflations, and syntheses: yet with a good standard of accuracy. The second requires more discussion, and is the subject of a later section of this chapter. In anticipation it can be said that there is no evidence of revision or adaptation: the basic translation rests upon something like the MT. But it needs to be remembered that the earliest surviving Leviticus manuscripts are coeval with or even antedate the presumed period of the fixing of the Masoretic vocalized text and its firming of hermeneutic givens.[17]

Patterns of Text

The Leiden edition's concentration on manuscripts of the twelfth century and earlier makes it possible to identify patterns in the transmission of Syriac Leviticus text before the ninth/tenth century standardization, and to suggest reasons for the pattern. In its simplest form there are manuscripts, usually of complete bibles, which can be associated with West Syriac:[18] 7a1, 8a1, 9a1, 12a1. On the other

---

[17] E. Tov, *Textual Criticism of the Hebrew Bible* (Minneapolis: Fortress; Assen and Maastricht: Van Gorcum, 1992) 19; in addition see 22–79.

[18] On the difference between West and East Syriac, see below on the Karkaphensian manuscripts.

hand there are manuscripts, usually of the Pentateuch alone, which
can be associated with East Syriac: 8b1, 9b1, 10b1.2, 12b1,2. The
association is primarily with place: the former with monasteries of
Tur Abdin or the related churches of Takrit, the latter with churches
or monasteries in or near Mosul. 7a1 certainly, and probably 9a1
also came to Europe from the Coptic/Syriac monastery in the Nitrian
desert[19] to which they had been given in the ninth century by the
West Syriac church in Takrit, the chief center of the Maphrianate,
or chief bishopric. A general consistency between manuscripts of the
same area is not surprising: local texts cannot help but have a mutual
coherence. But manuscripts and persons may move. 8a1 has been
altered by at least two later hands, the effect being to replace readings associated with the West by those associated with the East. But
the clustering of manuscripts in or around centers raises the questions about the nature of characteristic differences between these
types of text.

Local Characteristics

The characteristics or differences may be of three kinds. The first is
that of simple mechanical scribal error: for example homoearcton,
homoeteleuton, dittography, haplography, or mistaken letters. These
errors arise, but not in such numbers as to question the general level
of accuracy in copying: those of homoearcton and homoeteleuton
are frequently corrected by the first hand.[20] Most of the errors are
of single letters omitted: the conjunction *waw* or the particle *dalath*.
The second is of inner-Syriac development: either changes of vocabulary or style, or attempts to clarify words or phrases. Here there is
a general tendency for the later manuscripts to have a longer text:
at 4:31 an explanatory ܩܘܼܒܪܐ (neither in 6b1 nor the MT) is
added. At 7:6 ܕܗܘܐ (possibly with *sey*) becomes ܕܗܒܘ ܐܡܪܘ; at
11:45 ܐܠܗܟܘܢ) (neither in 6b1 nor the MT) is added. Two further examples may be clarifications, or attempts at more exact renderings of the MT. At 15:26 ܠܡܐܟܘܠܬܐ becomes (8a1ᶜ and 9a1,
the latter here in later manuscript company,) ܢܩܝܘܬܐ: correctly
understanding that the point of comparison of not the uncleanness,

---

[19] I. H. C. Fraser, *The Heir of Parham: Robert Curzon, 14th Baron Zouche* (Harleston: Paradigm Press, 1986) 118–34.
[20] Leiden Peshitta *Leviticus*, xii–xxv.

but its cultic consequences. At 16:32 6b1 and 9a1 (the earlier tradition) present ܪܩܒܠܐ: the later manuscripts present ܪܐܢܐ. Both readings have an otiose *waw*, but each understands a different type of clothing or reflects a change of usage.

The third is that the traditions represent different attempts, in whole or part, at rendering a similar *Vorlage*. Within the manuscript tradition, as stated above, the differences are not so great that there is a likelihood of differences of *Vorlage*. At 20:15 6b1, 8b1, 9a1, with the MT, present ܬܩܛܠܘܢ: the later manuscripts ܬܩܪܒܘܢ. There has been a conscious or unconscious enhancement of the sentence's logic. At 21:20, concerning disqualifications for priesthood, the MT מרוח אשך (with a crushed testicle) 9a1 has the equivalent ܫܠܝܚ (blear eyed) and the rest ܕܚܕܐ ܐܫܟܗ (mono-testicular), neither of which in fact is correct. In conclusion, geographical distancing has led to copyists' habits cumulatively setting or confirming different developmental paths.

Proto-peshitta

Character

The questions now are those of the intention behind the translation, and the basis on which it was made. There is no question but that the Peshitta is based upon the Hebrew scriptures: the only questions being those of source, method and means. The source for Leviticus is clearly the pre-Masoretic Hebrew bible text tradition: no manuscript variants suggest otherwise. The method is also clear enough. Broadly translation can search for the formal or the dynamic equivalent in the target language of what is found in the base language.[21] As mentioned above, Peshitta is a mean between the two. However, there is always to be noted that however closely languages are related, there are differences of vocabulary and syntax which necessitate adaptation. As against Biblical Hebrew, Syriac has a wider vocabulary, a more nuanced verbal system, a more flexible approach to subordinate clauses. Hence the Syriac translator(s) had to come to a mind as to what the Hebrew meant as well as said. This is especially

---

[21] E. A. Nida and C. R. Taber, *The Theory and Practice of Translation* (Leiden: Brill, 1969).

notable in cases where Hebrew can use an infinitive, or especially an infinitive construct and suffix which may be either a final or a consecutive clause. For example, at 8:11 לקשדם ... וימשח is rendered מה.ר־.גוּ מסמ.ר־ב; and at 16:17 בבאו ... עד שׁאתו as תה ג.ר־בוּ ר־גוּ.בּ ותה.

However, the means of translation raises questions of the version's dependence, in whole or part, on existing translations of the Hebrew scriptures. Jewish and Greek influences played a part in the culture in which Peshitta was made, transmitted, and circulated. Hence there is the possibility that where the Leviticus translator found a phrase or passage which was opaque or incomprehensible there was consultation or even reliance placed on other versions: Targum or LXX at some stage of their development.[22] The best interpretation of the evidence are as follows. The Hebrew text upon which Peshitta Leviticus is based is an unpointed consonantal one, although Leviticus provides little hard evidence. But at 9:4 תהבוּ.שׁר־ takes נראה as passive, and in 9:21 ותהבּ־־סוּ.בּ similarly takes צוה as a passive. There is not a clear direct dependence on other versions, targumic or septuagintal, but there is clear evidence of a shared reservoir of interpretation as is found in the later written versions or in such other texts as *Sifra*, the second century CE commentary on Leviticus. At 17:10 and 20:5 ונתתי פני and ושׂמתי אני את פני suggest divine favor: but the opposite is intended. Peshitta, however, presents תהוּ.לגוּ.ר־גוּ and תהוּ.לגוּ.ר־גוּ ר־יכ־ר־ ר־בכ־ר־ in the tradition of *Onqelos* and LXX. At 15:3 טמאתו הוא is ambiguous: either the person or the issue is contagious. Targums *Onqelos* and *Pseudo-Jonathan* coincide with Peshitta ר־שׁוּהוּ.גּ מתסהּ.בּ.גּ: it is the issue. LXX takes the contrary part. A more complex situation arises with equivalents for גר. 16:29 האזרח והגר הגר בתוככם has the equivalent אוּהתה, וּסמ.ר־ם לוּ.ר־ם.ר־ה.גּ ותהב.סלוּ תה.בכ־ר־ לוּ.ר־גּ.ר־התהוּ.בּ. This raises the whole question of the proselyte, and the different significations of the word גר.[23] *Onqelos* and *Pseudo-Jonathan* are close to this, LXX is not. An instance where social custom and philology seem to suggest Peshitta is at 19:27. לא תקפו פאת ראשכם appears as לר־ אוּבוּ.ם סה רוּ.ר־ם, ם.גּ.ר־.בּ.גהּ.בּ. This gives the opposite sense: not to "let grow long" instead of not to "cut off." This might simply be an acknowledgement of cultural practice or disfavor, or

---

[22] Lane, *Leviticus*, 99–126; Weitzman, *Syriac Version*, 68–107.
[23] E. Schürer, *The History of the Jewish People in the Time of Jesus Christ* (rev. ed. Geza Vermes et al.; Edinburgh: T&T Clark 1986) III.1.169–76.

Syriac has thought of the root רפא (Job 10:10) "thicken, heap up," or its own ܩܘܐ "heap up" as an approximation to נקף.

The need for clarity and elegance in the target language led to an improvement in the logic of the first eight chapters. The use of language about sacrifices proceeds with greater logic: the generic term) ܩܘܪܒܢܐ is replaced by specific terms only when the precise requirement and terminology is determined.[24] The present writer allows more place to translational interpretative skill than does Weitzman, who allows more to inner Syriac corruption.

Origin

The question of Christian or Jewish origin for Peshitta is one that does not seem capable of final answer. Chronicles shows signs of Christian translation, the earlier books give conflicting messages. They are clearly Jewish in origin, in that they derive from a Hebrew text and stand in a Jewish exegetical context. Arguments that a lax approach to cultic matters indicates Christian origin are not sustainable, as Torah and Temple requirements were properly fulfillable only in Palestine and its center Jerusalem: things were done in differently in Osrhoene and Adiabene. Hence Weitzman proposes a sectarian Jewish group for the version's origin.[25] However, it is not possible to draw firm lines between Jewish sectarians and Christians: such terms as Jewish and Christian are late rather than early, and have definition only when self-realized one against the other. Differentiation between Jews and Christians, even the adoption of those terms, was process rather than event. In any case Christianity to the east of Antioch was a less formally structured matter than in the world of the Mediterranean. It is not possible to give a final response on the evidence in Leviticus as to whether the version was one which "Christians" found and made their own, or one which they had created for them in their own language. That they spoke Syriac, and that the version is in Syriac may not be causally connected. Yet it is worth pointing out that use of Leviticus, as other books of the Pentateuch, was as much in controversy with Jews as in exegesis and liturgy: had the version been of Christian origin it

---

[24] D. J. Lane, "'The best words in the best order': Some Comments on the 'Syriacing' of Leviticus," *VT* 39 (Peshitta Institute Communication 21) (1989) 468–79.
[25] Weitzman, *Syriac Version*, 252–62.

could not have been an agreed basis for debate. It is also to be
noted that in later years when there was a high value placed on
Greek versions, these were unofficial and for scholarship rather than
debate: as the official version the Peshitta held ground. On balance,
the Pentateuch Peshitta is of Jewish origin.

Use of Peshitta

Lectionary

The main use of Peshitta was as bible text for worship: its origin
was most likely in the running translations provided for worship where
the participants were unfamiliar with the basic language, Hebrew.
Some manuscripts are marked with section divisions which sometimes but not always agree with the section divisions of Hebrew Masoretic texts: suggesting traditions of *lectio continua*. Some manuscripts
have annotations in text or margin to mark out appropriate passages
for specific liturgical occasions. In the fragmentary manuscript 6k2
a marginal note indicates that chapter 16 (the day of atonement ceremony) is used for a day in Easter week. Elsewhere in that manuscript there is a set of notes, indicating quire and page numbers,
which designate sections for nine occasions[26] including a time of
intercession. An eighth century Eastern Pentateuch manuscript, 8b1,
notes five lections: including chapter 8 (the anointing of Aaron and
his sons) for Ordination and the consecration of the holy oil, Muron;
chapter 12 (ceremony of purification and offering of a woman after
male child-birth) for our Lord's entry to the Temple at childhood;
chapter 26 (If you walk in my statutes . . . Then if you walk contrary to my statutes) for a time of prayer. However it is likely that
these lectionary notations are later than the time of the original
scribe. An interesting case is 8a1, where there are a number of lectionary notations, probably from a later hand, and which have been
subsequently deleted: they did not match other lectionary systems.

From the ninth century there are lectionary manuscripts, that is
manuscripts containing only the extracts necessary for the liturgical
day. The extracts are an unreliable evidence for text: they are extracts
which stand alone, and so have introductory phrases (e.g. ܘܐܡܪ

---

[26] Leiden Peshitta *Leviticus*, xxiv–vi, xxviii–ix.

ܝܘܡܝܢ ܟܗܢܐ before the third extract of 914) and explicatory
additions, notably replacement of pronouns by proper names. That
compiled for the church of Bar Sauma in Antioch in 1000 (1111)
provides nine lections from Leviticus. Among them are 26:42–46 (I
will remember my covenant with Jacob . . . Isaac . . . and Abraham . . .
I will remember the land") for the annunciation to Zechariah; 8:1–13
(the anointing of Aaron and his sons at the entry to the tabernacle)
for Epiphany; 23:23–32 ("Afflict yourselves . . . and present an offering
to the Lord") for the first Sunday in Lent; 24:11–23 ("Bring out of
the camp one who is accursed . . .") for Good Friday. The East
Syriac lectionary from the Mosul area, BL Manuscript Rich 7168
(not used by the Leiden Peshitta) is more sparing, using only three
passages for Sundays after the Ascension: 23:9–22 (presentation of
harvest offerings) for the fifth; 19:1, 2 + ? ("You shall be holy . . .")
for the sixth; and 19:15–19; 20:9–14 ("You shall do no injustice . . .")
for the seventh. This last lectionary extracts moral instruction, the
others draw resemblances between Old Testament and figures of the
New, and allusively provide inter-textual illumination. This distinction reflects the difference between a Greek-influenced willingness to
go beyond metaphor, and a concurrence with Theodore of Mopsuestia,
who was not.

Exegesis and Exposition

In the Syriac world scholarship is closely related to the ecclesiastical, in that it is related to exposition and exegesis. By exposition is
meant the setting out of ideas derived from biblical terms, and by
exegesis the explanation of passages with reference to vocabulary,
syntax, context and general knowledge. Again, Leviticus is less heavily used than other biblical books, so a few examples can easily be
given. It must be noted that this use of biblical quotation is an uncertain tool for text history or criticism: copyists of the authors' texts
may have assimilated quotations to that which was familiar to them;
writers use passages to substantiate an argument, not to demonstrate
a text. For Leviticus, the pattern is shown in Owens' discussion of
Aphrahat's use of the book. The title "Aphrahat as a Witness to the
Early Syriac Text of Leviticus" reflects the older scholarship, though
his discussion reflects a sounder method. While it may seem that
patristic quotations are testimony to Peshitta text at its various stages,

conclusions are difficult to draw. It is not, therefore, a simple matter of an author quoting directly from a manuscript under his eyes,
or of quoting by memory with varying degrees of exactness; it is
more a question of rhetoric molding its components.

Owens discusses in detail all the 14 quotations from Leviticus that
he finds, and concludes that they fall within the text pattern of
Peshitta manuscripts, and that deviations are the result of argument
rather than use of manuscript(s) with readings different from those
we know.

> ... the typical Bible passage is quoted loosely, partially, with an intro-
> duction that often obscures the beginning of the text quoted, and is
> thoroughly integrated into the stream of Aphrahat's discussion.[27]

Two examples may be given.

> It is written in the law, that when there is a leper in Israel he is to
> have a covering over his lips, and his clothes are to be torn, and his
> hair is to hang down, and his dwelling is to be outside the camp and
> he is to proclaim himself unclean all the days of his leprosy. xix.3(4),
> Lev 13:45–46.[28]

The beginning is adapted to the character of a quotation, and
emphases shifted to make it suitable as illustration of a discussion of
Mic 3:7 on the covered lips of seers and diviners.[29] The second
example has a greater inwardness. There are nine quotations of Lev
26:12, "I will dwell with them and walk with them." Each has an
introduction indicating a prophetic source for the citation—but in
fact the quotations are quotations of a quotation: its immediate source
is Paul in 2 Cor 6:16.[30] Aphrahat has made Peshitta his own, and
has used it as a friend, relying on good-natured flexibility.

Examples from two other writers support these conclusions. This
last quotation used by Aphrahat is found elsewhere. Philoxenus uses
it to clinch a tortuous argument to the effect that the nature of the
Word was not changed to flesh: were that so, and the Word had
taken another man and dwelt in him the text would have been

---

[27] R. J. Owens, "Aphrahat as a Witness to the Early Text History of Leviticus,"
in P. B. Dirksen and M. J. Mulder (eds.), *The Peshitta: Its Early Text and History*
(Monographs of the Peshitta Institute Leiden 4; Leiden: Brill, 1988) 1–48.47.
[28] Ibid., 47.
[29] Ibid., 16.
[30] Ibid., 42–43.

"dwelt in him . . ."[31] It appears in the eighth century Dialogue between Sergius and a Jew to settle an argument that the living are not defied by contact with a dead man's finger. It also appears in a scholion in Manuscript V of Ishodad of Merv's commentary on Ps 90:1–2.[32] More oblique quotations are found in Bar Hebraeus: he uses the command that an animal participant in bestiality is to be stoned is an instance of a physical punishment being an analogy for one which is spiritual and non-physical.[33] There are frequent general references to the text to demonstrate that the ceremonies of Leviticus are portrayals of events in the life of Jesus, e.g. the wilderness fast or the passion.[34] In these and so many other instances the text is subordinate to the argument. As Hayman says with reference to the Jew's quotation of 11:3, 4, 7 (classification of herbivores) in reply to Sergius:

> Both Sergius's quotations from Lev. 11 and those of the Jew show a certain amount of confusion. Both ignore the item "parts the hoof," both never quite the text exactly, and in some cases they both quote only their own inferences from it.[35]

The longest quotation of all from the distinction of herbivores (11:13–31) is in Jacob of Edessa's *Hexaemeron*: but that is neither straight Peshitta nor straight Syrohexapla—as might be expected.[36]

The more exegetical commentaries might be expected to help with more extensive exact quotations of biblical text. However that is not the case in such a work as Ishodad of Merv's commentary on Leviticus. His aim is to comment on words or phrases of difficulty,

---

[31] M. Brière, *Sancti Philoxeni Episcopi Mabbugensis. Disssertationes Decem: de Uno e Sancta Trinitate Incorporato et Passo* (PO 39; Paris: Firmin-Didot, 1979) 8:130 (Dissertations 6a, 7a, 8a).

[32] C. van den Eynde, *Commentaire d'Is'o'dad de Merv sur l'Ancien Testament VI Psaumes* (CSCO 433/4 Syr 185/6; Louvain: Peeters, 1981).

[33] N. Sed, *Le Candélarbre du Sanctuaire de Grégoire Abou'lfaradj dit Bar Hebraeus, Douzieme Base: du Paradis Suivé du Livre des Rayons: Traité X* (PO 40; Turnhout: Brepols 1981) 50:11–6.

[34] F. Rilliet, *Jacques de Saroug, Six homélies festales en prose* (PO 43; Turnhout: Brepols, 1986) *Lent III:20*; M. Albert, *Homélies contre les Juifs par Jacques de Saroug* (PO 38; Turnhout: Brepols, 1976) IV:193–4.

[35] A. P. Hayman, *The Disputation of Sergius the Stylite against a Jew* (CSCO 339 Syri 152; Louvain: Peeters, 1973) 61. See also D. J. Lane "'There is no need of turtle doves or young pigeons' (Jacob of Sarug): Quotations and Non-Quotations of Leviticus in Selected Syriac Writers," in *III Peshitta Symposium* (Forthcoming).

[36] I.-B. Chabot, *Jacobi Edesseni Hexaemeron Seu in Opus Creationis Libri Septem* (CSCO Scr Syri II vol. 56; Paris, Louvain: CSCO 1928, 1932) 182–227.

or where information from other writers on history or philosophy assists understanding of the text. But he quotes only the word necessary, otherwise summarizes the passage which is the basis of comment. For example, in chapter 11, on the distinction of animals, fish and birds, he gives only the term, e.g. ܪܚܫܐ or ܢܘܢܐ ܐܪܥ. Or he gives a paraphrase, and picks up points from that, notably at the beginning of the commentary. Although citing Greek versions and other writers, his basic text is Peshitta.[37]

Karkaphensian (Masoretic) Manuscripts

Underlying this use of biblical text there needs to be a comprehension of it. A very different approach to Peshitta text is evidence of scholarly, or at any rate educational use. There are some manuscripts, known as Masoretic or Karkaphensian, which are selective. They give only those words which are problematic: they may be patent of more than one vocalization and may have differences of meaning; there may be concerns of grammar; they may be illuminated by other versions or manuscripts. For example at Lev 26:22 7a1 presents ܘܬܫܠ ܒܟܘܢ but other manuscripts ܘܬܫܠ ܒܟܘܢ: which is noted in BL Add Ms 12,138 as being a distinction without a difference. The same root has two forms, as middle or third letter weak. A little further on there is the word ܐܫܬܝ. It is noted that this may be vocalized in three ways, ESHTAY (ptāhā) as a masculine singular imperative; ESHTAY (zqāphā) as a feminine singular imperative; or ESHTY (hbāsā)) as a simple past tense. In other places there are different possibilities of interpretation, and glosses of other readings from Syriac or even Greek text types are given. These manuscripts come from between the ninth and twelfth centuries, and represent two different text traditions. One, for example, BL Add Ms 12,138 is the work of an East Syriac scribe in the monastery of Mar Gabriel at Harran, and others, for example, BL Add Ms 12,178 are from the Monastery of the Skull near Reshaina, and are the work of West Syriac scribes. These latter give readings from Syriac manuscripts, and from Greek texts, as well as church fathers and teachers. It is from them that the mystery of differences between West and East Syriac manuscript traditions is cleared up. The

---

[37] C. van den Eynde, *Commentaire d'Is'o'dad de Merv sur l'Ancien Testament II Exode-Deuteronome* (CSCO 176,179; Syr 80, 81; Louvain: CSCO, 1958).

difference is of dialect, because Syriac was spread over such a wide area: the difference therefore is comparative rather than abslute. The western Bar Hebraeus commented acidly on the introduction of (an inferior) dialect from the East in the sixth century school of Nisibis, reckoning the Syria of the area around Edessa, Melitene and Mardin to be the best and purest. The number of ninth and tenth century "Masoretic" manuscripts seems to go with a revival of the Western Syriac literary tradition in the area around Kartamin and Mardin under the influence of the successive Patriarchs Denis, Abraham, John and Athansius, to the great fury of the Greeks. The activity is also associated with the earlier activity of Jacob of Edessa and his ability in drawing on Greek as well as Syriac material for elucidation of the text.[38] Two important conclusions are to be drawn. The first is that the difference between Western and Eastern manuscripts lies in their origin in areas of Syriac Christianity which had dialectic differences which were accentuated by their separation by new the frontier between Sassanian and Roman Empires drawn in 393. This difference was accentuated by the Arab conquest of the old Sasanian empire in the sixth century. The second is that the curious resemblance between 9a1 and 6b1 can be explained by the resurgence of West Syriac intellectual activity of which the Karkaphensian manuscripts are evidence. It is now hardly to be wondered at that 9a1 follows so closely the sixth century Western type of manuscript 6b1.[39]

Rivals to Peshitta

The foregoing remarks bring to mind the multicultural and multilingual nature of Oriental Christianity, and especially the part played by Greek learning and language. The making of the Syrohexapla, and its use in some of the lectionary readings in Athanasius of Antioch's collection, draw attention to the predilection for things

---

[38] P. Martin, "Tradition Karkaphienne ou la massore chez les Syriens," *Revue Asiatique* 5:14 (1869) 249–53.

[39] The argument is plausibility rather than certainty. 9a1, in Florence, seems to have had an provenance in the Deir es Suryan collection, being removed in the Assemani collecting expedition. The Deir es Suryan collection came to a great extent from the gifts of Takrit people. It is certainly a likelihood that a newly made complete bible made at the time of a literary resurgence and re-introduction of Serta script would be presented to a significant monastery. On this subject, see especially P. Martin, *La Massore*, 250–52.

Greek in the western part of Oriental Christianity. The ninth century Eastern writer Ishodad of Merv also made use of the version.
This comes partly from culture, and partly from the engagement
with Greek writers in controversy over the natures of Christ between
the supporters of Cyril of Alexandria and Theodore of Mopsuestia
which made agreement on biblical text an important element.

The Syrohexapla itself was made in the early seventh century by
Paul of Tella for Philoxenus of Mabbug, as a translation based on
Origen's revision of the LXX, and indeed Philoxenus may have been
the instigator of another Syriac version of a Greek text, though only
fragments of Isaiah remain. Finally, some relics of a Christian Syriac
version survive, in lectionary sections: from Lev 8:18–30; 11:42–12:18.[40]
It is not strictly Syriac, but in Palestinian Aramaic, though re-written in a script similar to Estrangela. This too has a Greek base: not
surprisingly, since it was the work of Aramaic Christians in Palestine
who adhered to the Chalcedonian decrees and earned the nickname
"Melkites."

Two figures highlight the interculturation prevalent in Oriental
Christianity proper. One is Jacob of Edessa. Not long before his
death in 708 he produced a version of the Old Testament, surviving in a single manuscript each for the Pentateuch (Bibliothèque
Nationale, Paris, Syriac manuscript 27), Ezekiel, Isaiah, Daniel,
Susanna and a section of Wisdom. It did not maintain itself as a
rival to Peshitta: possibly because the East Syriac Christians were
suspicious of it, possibly because it differed too greatly from Peshitta,
possibly because it was a scholarly tool rather than a general purpose version. The basic text, at least in Samuel, is Peshitta, with
much additional material from the Lucianic recension and Syrohexapla
and his own rendering of Septuagint, together with explanatory
expansions and additions. It is to be noted that Jacob had studied
in Alexandria, where he would have become aware of the range of
Greek possibilities. Salvesen's conclusion is

> Jacob's aim in his Old Testament version is likely to have been . . .
> primarily the clarification of the biblical text as it existed in Syriac
> and Greek, rather than the creation of a new standard text.[41]

---

[40] M. H. Goshen-Gottstein and H. Shirun, *The Bible in the Syropalestinian Version.
Part I, Pentateuch and Prophets* (Hebrew University Bible Project, Monograph Series
4; Jerusalem: Magnes, 1973).
[41] A. Salvesen, *The Books of Samuel in the Syriac Version of Jacob of Edessa* (Monographs
of the Peshitta Institute Leiden 10; Leiden: Brill, 1999) 15.

Jacob is credited with initiating the textual, grammatical and critical activity of the Karkaphensians mentioned above. Another, earlier, figure of interest is Eusebius of Emesa. He was born in 300 in Edessa, where he had his early education. But he spent other parts of his life in Caesarea, Antioch and Alexandria. While he wrote in Greek, he made use of Hebrew and Syriac biblical texts and exegetical traditions to explicate his version of Scripture.[42] It must not be forgotten, that even though there were periods of turmoil and difficulty, there was much interchange of trade and culture between the different parts of the Orient: a not inconsiderable factor in the circulation and reception of texts.

Reception as Process

The Current Acceptance

Reception of a text is a continuous rather than momentary affair. There are definitive periods, rather than moments, for the reception of Hebrew Leviticus as Peshitta. For the Syriac churches such moments are clearly the period of translation and transmission of Proto-Peshitta in the first Christian century; the stabilizing of the text in the ninth century; the conservation of key manuscripts in the Coptic/Syriac monastery of Dair es Suryan in Egypt. For the Western world the key periods were firstly that of the work of the Maronites in Rome, who brought Peshitta to the attention of Western scholars; secondly the work of editors who engaged in text criticism of the Hebrew bible and also made possible the provision of printed material for church use in India and the Middle east. The final period is that of study of the whole context and culture of Syriac Christianity and the symbiosis between its society and its literature. The end point of reception is when, within successive vernacular liturgies translated from Syriac, the Peshitta finds its own lodging in vernacular tongue. There the nuances and interpretative edge influence a version within a new target language. Within these settings Leviticus has its own role, because of the clarity and simplicity of its structure and genre which make the book's salient points easier to observe.

---

[42] R. B. ter Haar Romeny, *A Syrian in Greek Dress: The Use of Greek, Hebrew, and Syriac Biblical Texts in Eusebius of Emesa's Commentary on Genesis* (Traditio Exegetica Graeca 6; Louvain: Peeters, 1997) 71–82.

Select Bibliography

Detailed bibliographies are to be found in the relevant books noted because they indicate the conclusions reached in the summary given above.

1. The Peshitta version of Leviticus is to be found in:
a. Ecclesiastical versions

Barnes, W. E., C. W. Mitchell and J. Pinkerton (eds.). *Pentateuchus Syriace* (London: Apud Societatem Bibliophilorum Britannicam et externam, 1914).
David, C. J. and G. Ebed-Jesus-Khakyat (eds.). *Biblia Sacra Juxta Versionem Simplicem quae dicitur Peschitta* (Mosul, 1887–1891).
Le Jay, G. M. et al. (eds.). *Biblia Hebraica. Samaritana, Chaldaica, Graeca, Syriaca, Latina, Arabica* (9 vols., Paris, 1629–1645) vol. 6, *Polyglot Syriac text of Pentateuch*, ed. Gabriel Sionita.
Lee, S. (ed.). *Vetus Testamentum Syriace* (London: Apud Societatem Bibliophilorum Britannicam et externam, 1823.)
Perkins, J. (ed.), *K^etaba Qaddi_a ha(naw):d^e-diyatiqi ʿattiqti suryaʿit* (Urmia, 1852).
Walton, B. (ed.). *Biblia Sacra Polyglotta* (6 vol., London, 1657).

b. Scholarly Version
Peshitta Institute, Leiden (ed.). *The Old Testament in Syriac According to the Peshitta Version*, I, 2 + II, 1b. *Leviticus* (D. J. Lane), *Numbers* (A. P. Hayman), *Deuteronomy* (W. M. van Vliet, based on material collected by J. H. Hospers and H. J. W. Drijvers), *Joshua* (J. E. Erbes), (Leiden: Brill 1991)—Note that the method of desig-nating Syriac OT manuscripts used in this chapter is that of the Leiden edition.

2. The definitive bibliography for Old Testament Peshitta studies and some general overviews are:

Dirksen, P. B. *An Annotated Bibliography of the Peshitta of the Old Testament* (Monographs of the Peshitta Institute Leiden V; Leiden: Brill, 1989). The definitive bibliography for Old Testament Peshitta studies.
———. "The Old Testament Peshitta" in M. J. Mulder ed. *Mikra: Text, Translation, Reading and Interpretation of the Hebrew Bible in Ancient Judaism and Christianity* (Assen and Maastricht: Van Gorcum; Philadelphia: Fortress, 1988). Gives an overview of the text history of the version.
Koster, M. D. *The Peshitta of Exodus. The development of its text in the course of fifteen centuries* (Assen and Amsterdam: Van Gorcum, 1977). A key volume for Peshitta Pentateuch studies.
Lane, D. J. *The Peshitta of Leviticus* (Monographs of the Peshitta Institute Leiden 6; Leiden: Brill 1994). A study of the Leviticus text, manuscripts, translation method, printed editions and church context.
———. "Text, Scholar and Church: the place of the Leiden Peshitta within the context of scholastically and ecclesiastically definitive versions," *JSS* 38 (1993) 33–47. Discusses the vagaries of editors and manuscripts.
Weitzman, M. P. *The Syriac Version of the Old Testament: An Introduction* (University of Cambridge Oriental Publications 56; Cambridge: Cambridge University Press, 1999). A magisterial overview of the Peshitta as translation and discussion of its origin.

3. The Oriental churches are discussed in:

Fiey, J. M. *Assyrie Chrétienne* (3 vols.; Beirut: Imprimerie Catholique, 1986).
———. *Jalons pour une Histoire de l'Église en Iraq* (CSCO 310 Subsidia 36; Louvain: CSCO, 1970).
———. *Mossoul Chrétienne* (Beirut: Imprimerie Catholique, 1959).

4. Individual manuscripts are discussed in:

Hunt, L.-A. "The Syriac Buchanan Bible in Cambridge: Book Illumination in Syria, Cilicia and Jerusalem of the later Twelfth Century," *OCP* 57 (1991) 331–69.
Jenner, K. D. "Some Introductory Remarks Concerning the Study of 8a1," in P. B. Dirksen and M. J. Mulder (eds.), *The Peshitta: Its Early Text and History* (Monographs of the Peshitta Institute Leiden 4; Brill, 1988) 235–40.

5. Patristic use of Leviticus is discussed in:

Lane, D. J. "'There is no need of turtle doves or young pigeons' (Jacob of Sarug): Quotations and non-quotations of Leviticus in selected Syriac writers," in *III Peshitta Symposium* (forthcoming).
Owens, R. J. "Aphrahat as a Witness to the Early Text History of Leviticus," in P. B. Dirksen and M. J. Mulder (eds.), *The Peshitta: Its Early Text and History* (Monographs of the Peshitta Institute Leiden 4; Leiden: Brill, 1988) 1–48.

6. Lectionary Manuscripts are discussed in:

Heiming, O. "Ein Jakobitisches Doppellektionar des Jahres 824 aus Harran in den HSS Add 14,485 bis 14,487," in P. Granfield and J. A. Jungmann (eds.), *Kyriakon: Festschrift Johannes Quasten*, (2 vols.; Munster: Aschendorff, 1970–1972) II.768–99.
Jenner, K. D. "De Perikopentitels van de Geïllustreerde Syrische Kanselbijbel van Paris" (Ph.D. diss., Leiden, 1993).

7. The Masoretic Manuscripts and Eastern and Western Syriac are discussed in:

P. Martin "Tradition Karkaphienne ou la massore chez les Syriens," *Revue Asiatique* 5 (1869) 245– 379.
——. "Essai sur les deux principaux dialectes Araméens," *Revue Asiatique* 6 (1872) 305–483.
——. "Histoire de la Ponctuation ou de la massore chez les Syriens," *Revue Asiatique* 7 (1875) 81–208.

8. On the multicultural and lingual context of Syriac churches:

Baars, W. "Ein neugefundenes Bruchstück aus der Syrischen Bibelrevision des Jakob von Edessa," *VT* 18 (1968) 548–54.
ter Haar Romeny, R. B. *A Syrian in Greek Dress: the Use of Greek, Hebrew, and Syriac Biblical Texts in Eusebius of Emesa's Commentary on Genesis* (Traditio Exegetica Graeca 6; Louvain: Peeters, 1997).
Saley, R. J. *The Samuel Manuscript of Jacob of Edessa. A Study in its Underlying Textual Traditions* (Monographs of the Peshitta Institute Leiden 9; Leiden: Brill, 1998).
Salvesen, A. *The Books of Samuel in the Syriac Version of Jacob of Edessa* (Monographs of the Peshitta Institute Leiden 10; Leiden: Brill, 1999).
Vööbus, A. *The Pentateuch in the Version of the Syro-Hexapla* (CSCO 369, Subsidia 45; Louvain: Peeters, 1975).

9. Christian Palestinian Syriac:

Goshen-Gottstein, M. H. and H. Shirun. *The Bible in the Syropalestinian Version. Part I, Pentateuch and Prophets* (Hebrew University Bible Project, Monograph Series 4; Jerusalem: Magnes Press, 1973).

10. The shifting emphases in Peshitta studies is shown in the proceedings of the three conferences organized by the Peshitta Institute, Leiden:

Dirksen, P. B. and M. J. Mulder (eds.). *The Peshitta: Its Early Text and History: Papers read at the Peshitta Symposium held at Leiden 30–31 August 1985* (Monographs of the Peshitta Institute Leiden 4; Leiden: Brill, 1988).

Dirksen, P. B. and A. van der Kooij (eds.). *The Peshitta as Translation: Papers Read at the II Peshitta Symposium Held at Leiden 19–21 August 1993*, (Monographs of the Peshitta Institute Leiden 8; Leiden: Brill, 1995).

The Peshitta: its use in Literature and Liturgy: III Peshitta Symposium, Leiden August 12–15 2001 (forthcoming).

THE BOOK OF LEVITICUS IN THE
DEAD SEA SCROLLS

Peter W. Flint

1. *Introduction*

This essay surveys and discusses the Leviticus scrolls found at Qumran and other sites in the Judean Desert.[1] In terms of manuscripts discovered, Leviticus was the sixth most popular, both overall and at Qumran. The significance of this book for the Qumran community is also indicated by the many times it is referenced in their writings, a topic which is explored elsewhere in the present volume.[2]

Following a survey of the seventeen Leviticus manuscripts, we shall offer several observations arising from this ancient material, assess the text of Leviticus in the Dead Sea Scrolls, present a selection of significant readings, and close with a bibliography and three Appendices: (1) a table with data on the Leviticus Scrolls; (2) an index of contents by manuscript; and (3) an index of contents by chapter and verse.

2. *The Leviticus Scrolls from Qumran and Other Sites*

2.1 *Comment*

A grand total of seventeen copies of the Book of Leviticus were discovered in the Judaean Desert (including the *Targum* of Leviticus and two Greek copies found in Cave 4). Fifteen manuscripts were unearthed in the vicinity of Wadi Qumran: one each from Caves 1, 2, and 6,[3] ten from Cave 4,[4] and two from Cave 11.[5] Two more scrolls were

---

[1] For an earlier treatment of the Leviticus scrolls, see E. Eshel, "Leviticus, Book of," in *EDSS* 488–93.
[2] R. Kugler, "Rethinking the Notion of 'Scripture' in the Dead Sea Scrolls: Leviticus as a Test Case" in this volume.
[3] 1QpaleoLev, 2QpaleoLev, and 6QpaleoLev.
[4] 4QExod-Lev^f, 4QLev-Num^a, 4QLev^b, 4QLev^c, 4QLev^d, 4QLev^e, 4QLev^g, 4QLXXLev^a, pap4QLXXLev^b, and pap4QtgLev.
[5] 11QpaleoLev^a and 11QLev^b.

discovered in the ruins atop Masada further down the western coast of the Dead Sea.[6]

Between them, these manuscripts have several rich and interesting features; for example, two Hebrew scripts (palaeo and square), three languages (Hebrew, Aramaic, Greek), and the rare phenomenon of two books on the same manuscript (see section 2.2. below).

The profile of each Leviticus scroll includes, where possible, a textual classification in one of the following categories: (1) *proto-Masoretic* (i.e. with affinities to the Masoretic Text); (2) *pre-Samaritan*; (3) *pre-Septuagint* (i.e. with affinities to the *Vorlage* or Hebrew source of the Septuagint); (4) *mixed* (i.e. with affinities to two or more of the Masoretic Text, the Samaritan Pentateuch, and the Septuagint); and (5) *non-aligned* (i.e. with affinities to two or more of the other witnesses, but also with independent readings not known from these later texts texts).

2.2   *The Seventeen Leviticus Scrolls*

(a) *The Five Scrolls from Caves 1, 2, 6, and 11 at Qumran*
*1QpaleoLev (1Q3) preserves material from chapters 11–23 of Leviticus, as well as portions of Numbers (see Appendix 2). Written in the palaeo-Hebrew script, this scroll preserves a text identical to that of the Masoretic Text (𝔐), except for some variations in orthography or spelling, which is sparing (or defective). 1QpaleoLev could be classed as a *proto-Masoretic* (or *proto-Rabbinic*) text.[7] In fact, however, the textual form in this scroll is equally close to the Masoretic Text (𝔐) and to the Samaritan Pentateuch (𝔐),[8] and so it is better listed as *mixed*.

*2QpaleoLev (2Q5) was also copied in palaeo-Hebrew, somewhere in the first century BCE. Although very little text remains (only part of Lev 11:22–29), differences against the Masoretic Text (𝔐) are evident. In two cases 2QpaleoLev is in agreement with the Samaritan

---

[6] MasLev[a] and MasLev[b].

[7] Thus E. Tov, "The Biblical Texts from the Judean Desert—An Overview and Analysis of all the Published Texts," in E. D. Herbert and E. Tov (eds.), *The Bible as Book: The Hebrew Bible and the Judaean Desert Discoveries. Proceedings of the Conference Held at Hampton Court, Herefordshire, 18–21 June 2000* (London: The British Library, 2002) forthcoming.

[8] Tov, "The Biblical Texts from the Judean Desert," 155.

Pentateuch (𝔚) and the Septuagint (𝔊) against 𝔐. This text, therefore, may be classified as *mixed*.

*6QpaleoLev (6Q2) is likewise written in palaeo-Hebrew script,
and the spelling is full (or *plene*). The single fragment only preserves
text from Lev 13:12–13; with such little evidence to assess, no date
is offered in the *editio princeps*.

*11Qpaleo-Levᵃ (11Q1), also in palaeo-Hebrew, was copied about
100 BCE. Preserving text from chapters 4, 10–11, and 13–21, and
chapters 22–27 in full, this is the longest of all the palaeo-Hebrew
scrolls. The complete manuscript most likely contained twenty-three
columns.[9] Since 11Qpaleo-Levᵃ ends with a ruled but uninscribed
area that covers a complete column, and also with a separate handle sheet, Leviticus was not followed by Numbers in this scroll. The
text of 11Qpaleo-Levᵃ is not especially close to the Masoretic Text,
the Samaritan Pentateuch, or the Septuagint, and contains several
independent readings; it is thus classified as *non-aligned*.[10]

*11QLevᵇ (11Q2) is the only manuscript from the Minor Caves
at Qumran not written in palaeo-Hebrew. Copied about 50 CE, it
preserves text from chapters 7–10, 13–15, and 25. Featuring full
orthography, 11QLevᵇ agrees three times with the Masoretic Text
against the Septuagint, three times with the Septuagint against the
Masoretic Text, and has five unique readings. Like 11Qpaleo-Levᵃ,
this scroll preserves a text that is best classified as *non-aligned*, in view
of its unique readings and inconsistent pattern of agreements and
disagreements with the ancient witnesses.

(b) *The Ten Leviticus Scrolls from Cave 4 at Qumran*
*4QExod-Levᶠ (4Q17) preserves text from chapters 38–40 of Exodus
and chapters 1–2 of Leviticus. Copied in the mid-third century BCE,
this is one of the two oldest Dead Sea Scrolls. The surviving material is closest to the Samaritan tradition, and thus is classified as
Palestinian (Frank More Cross's preferred term) or *pre-Samaritan* (Emanuel
Tov's nomenclature).[11] Its tendency towards expansion and fuller
spelling should also be noted.

---

[9] See E. Eshel, "Leviticus, Book of," 488–93, esp. 490–91.
[10] Tov, "The Biblical Texts from the Judean Desert," 156.
[11] See F. M. Cross, "4QExod-Levᶠ" in E. Ulrich, F. M. Cross et al. (eds.), *Qumran
Cave 4, Genesis to Numbers* (DJD 12; Oxford: Clarendon, 1994) 136.

*4QLev-Num[a] (4Q23) is a substantial manuscript, preserving text from nine chapters of Leviticus (13–16, 18–19, 24, 26–27), as well as sixteen chapters of Numbers (1–4, 8–13, 22, 26, 30, 32–33, 35). The manuscript is carefully inscribed in an early Hasmonaean script, dating to the middle or later half of the second century BCE. The orthography is similar to that of the Masoretic Text and the Samaritan Pentateuch. To judge from the variant readings listed in the *editio princeps*,[12] the text of this scroll is equally close to 𝔐 and 𝔴 (which differ little from each other in the case of Leviticus). In Leviticus 14, however, the copyist omitted two entire verses: 24, most likely through parablepsis, and 45. In the second instance, the missing text was then added above the line, probably by a second scribe. Emanuel Tov lists 4QLev-Num[a] as *proto-Masoretic*,[13] but it is better classified as *mixed*, in view of its affiliations to both 𝔐 and 𝔴 (but not 𝔊).

*4QLev[b] (4Q24), which was copied in the mid-first century BCE, preserves text from chapters 1–3 and 21–25 of Leviticus. The orthography is similar to that of the Masoretic Text and the Samaritan Pentateuch, although none of the three are fully consistent. Since the text of 4QLev[b] is generally close to that of both 𝔐 and 𝔴, it may be classified as *mixed* (see 4QLev-Num[a] above). However, the scroll seems not to have contained the text of Lev 3:1–11, and preserves a small longer reading against 𝔐, 𝔴, and 𝔊 at Lev 22:22.

*4QLev[c] (4Q25) comprises only nine fragments, with only five chapters of Leviticus (1, 3–5, 8) represented. A survey of the variant readings in the *editio princeps* suggests that 4QLev[c] is textually close to the Masoretic Text and the Samaritan Pentateuch, but less so to the Septuagint; it is thus classified as *mixed*. This manuscript also agrees with 𝔐 and 𝔴 with respect to orthography, but with small differences. No date is suggested for this scroll in the critical edition.

*4QLev[d] (4Q26) was written in an early Herodian script, and is dated between 30 BCE and 20 CE. The letters are very difficult to read, since the ink has corroded and eaten through the leather. The four identifiable fragments preserve text from chapters 14, 15, and 17 of Leviticus. The preserved variant readings suggest a text that

---

[12] E. Ulrich, "4QLev-Num[a]," in E. Ulrich, F. M. Cross et al. (eds.), *Qumran Cave 4, Genesis to Numbers* (DJD 12; Oxford: Clarendon, 1994) 154–62.
[13] For Tov's methodology, see section 4.1 below.

is *mixed*, since it is close to the Samaritan Pentateuch and the Septuagint, but less so to the Masoretic Text. The orthography is fuller than that of 𝔐 and 𝔪.

*4QLevᶜ (4Q26a), for which no date is offered in the *editio princeps*, preserves portions of five chapters of Leviticus (3, 19–22). The preserved variants suggest a text closer to that of the Masoretic Text and the Samaritan Pentateuch than to the Septuagint, yielding a classification of *mixed*. One interesting reading is in Lev 19:36, where 4QLevᶜ simply reads אבני צ[ד]ק (*just weights*), as opposed to 𝔐𝔪𝔊, which read מאזני צדק אבני (*just balances, just weights*); the omission is most likely explained by homoioteleuton.

*4QLevᵍ (4Q26b) differs from the other Leviticus scrolls by featuring fuller orthography and the tetragrammaton in the paleo-Hebrew script (𐤉𐤄𐤅𐤄). Because so little text survives (only portions of 7:19–26), no date is suggested for this scroll in the *editio princeps*.

*4QLXXLevᵃ (4Q119) is one of the relatively few Greek scrolls found at Qumran. Copied in the late second or first century BCE, 4QLXXLevᵃ survives in only two pieces, the first preserving text from Lev 26:2–6 and the second fragment thus far unidentified. The orthography is generally close to that in the Septuagint codices, but *iota* adscript is used. Together with pap4QLXXLevᵇ (see below), this scroll antedates other Greek witnesses to Leviticus by some four centuries. It contains fifteen variant readings from the critical (Göttingen) edition of the Septuagint, seven of which are unique and three are attested in other manuscripts. While none of these readings has been adopted in the Göttingen edition, the antiquity of this scroll and the readings it preserves suggest that 4QLXXLevᵃ "penetrates further behind the other witnesses to provide a more authentic witness to the Old Greek translation."[14]

*pap4QLXXLevᵇ (4Q120), which was copied in the first century BCE, is one of two Leviticus scrolls written on papyrus. Of the ninety-seven fragments allocated to this scroll, the contents of only thirty-one have been identified; the other, however, are all small, often preserving only a letter to two. As was the case with 4QLXXLevᵃ, the orthography is similar to that of the Septuagint codices and *iota*

---

[14] E. Ulrich, "4QLXXLevᵃ," in P. Skehan, E. Ulrich, and J. Sanderson (eds.), *Qumran Cave 4, IV Palaeo-Hebrew and Greek Biblical Manuscripts* (DJD 9; Oxford: Clarendon, 1992) 161–65, esp. 163.

adscript is used. One interesting feature in this scroll is the use of Ιαω to translate the divine name (transliterating יהוה), rather than the more usual κυρίος.

*pap4QtgLev (4Q156) is one of only three *targums* (translations into Aramaic) among the Scrolls (the other two are of Job). Copied in about 150 BCE, this papyrus scroll only preserves Lev 16:12–15 and 16:18–21; however, it may have originally contained all of Leviticus, or a ritual text for the Day of Atonement. Comparison with the Masoretic Text and later Aramaic translations of Leviticus show pap4QtgLev to be a literal translation, similar to *Targum Onqelos* and *Targum Neofiti I.*[15]

(c) *The Two Leviticus Scrolls Found at Masada*

*MasLev^a (Mas1a) and MasLev^b (see below) were discovered during Yigael Yadin's excavations of the Jewish mountain fortress. The scroll was copied in the second half of the first century BCE by a highly-skilled scribe. The single surviving fragments preserves text from Lev 4:3–9 that is identical with the Masoretic Text, except for one longer spelling in verse 7. The textual form preserved is thus classified as *proto-Masoretic*.

*MasLev^b (Mas1b) is far more substantial than MasLev^a, with forty-five fragments surviving, and was copied almost a century later (mid-first century CE). Much of Lev 8:3–11:40 is preserved in this manuscript, which is classified as *proto-Masoretic*. Its textual form is virtually identical with the Masoretic Text, including its spelling, although the scribe made several corrections in the scroll.

3. *Observations Arising from the Leviticus Scrolls*

Between them, the seventeen Leviticus scrolls offer several insights as to the importance of this book at Qumran, the evidence for the Pentateuch as a collection, the use of Hebrew scripts, the earliest translations of Leviticus, and writing materials.

3.1   *The Relative Number of Manuscripts*

The large number of Leviticus scrolls found at Qumran (15) is indicative of the importance of this book for the community that lived

---

[15] Eshel, "Leviticus, Book of," 492.

there. The only other books represented by more manuscripts at Qumran are: Psalms (36), Deuteronomy (30), Isaiah (21), Genesis (20), and Exodus (17).

The significance of Leviticus for the Qumran community is also indicated by the extent to which it is referenced in their writings; each of the book's twenty-seven chapters is quoted or alluded to somewhere in the non-biblical scrolls (many of which were specific to the Qumranites). For example, the *Temple Scroll* alone quotes or paraphrases portions of twenty-three chapters, and more than half of the two dozen rulings in the work called *Some of the Works of the Law* (4QMMT) are based on legal issues concerning ritual purity from the text of Leviticus. The key to understanding the Qumran community's emphasis on purity is summed up in Lev 15:31: "Thus you shall keep the people of Israel separate from their uncleanness, so that they do not die in their uncleanness by defiling my tabernacle that is in their midst."[16]

3.2   *Evidence for the Pentateuch as a Collection*

Three Leviticus manuscripts (4QExod-Lev[f], 1QpaleoLev, and 4QLev-Num[a]) each preserve portions of more than one book, thereby confirming the traditional order of Exodus–Leviticus–Numbers. When we add the evidence of additional scrolls that preserve material from more than one book (4QGen-Exod[a], 4QpaleoGen-Exod[l], 4QExod[b]), we may reasonably conclude that the Pentateuch was viewed as a collection at Qumran. The preserved data also suggest that all five books from Genesis to Deuteronomy were sometimes written on a single scroll.[17] Some Leviticus, manuscripts, however, contained only a single book; see the comments above on 11Qpaleo-Lev[a], which ends with a ruled, blank column and has a separate handle sheet.

3.3   *The Palaeo-Hebrew Leviticus Scrolls*

Four of the Leviticus scrolls (24% of the total) are written in palaeo-Hebrew, rather than the square script in which the vast majority of the Dead Sea Scrolls were copied: 1QpaleoLev, 2QpaleoLev,

[16] See M. G. Abegg, P. W. Flint, and E. Ulrich, *The Dead Sea Scrolls Bible* (San Francisco: Harper San Francisco; Edinburgh: T&T Clark, 1999) 78.

[17] For further comments, see J. VanderKam and P. Flint, *The Meaning of the Dead Sea Scrolls* (San Francisco: Harper San Francisco, 2002) 108, 105–51.

6QpaleoLev, and 11QpaleoLev^a. Among the Qumran scrolls classified as *biblical*, only eight more are written in this script: 4QpaleoGen^m, 6QpaleoGen, 4QpaleoGen-Exod^l, 4QpaleoExod^m, 4QpaleoDeut^r, 4QpaleoDeut^s, and 4QpaleoJob^c. It seems that the ancient palaeo-Hebrew script—which was common before the Exile (587–539 BCE)—was used for books that were considered especially important, of great antiquity, and attributed to Moses. (The inclusion of Job may well reflect the Rabbinic tradition that Moses wrote this book [see *b. B. Bat.* 14b, 15a]). Four more Qumran texts copied in palaeo-Hebrew are 4Q124, 4Q125 and 11Q22 (each listed as *Unidentified Text*), and 4Q123 (*paleoParaJoshua*), which contains portions of Joshua 21. In addition to the Qumran copies, two more texts in this script—both nonbiblical and written on papyrus—were found at Masada (*paleoText of Sam. Origin* [recto], and *paleoUnidentified Text* [verso]).

3.4   *Leviticus Scrolls in Greek and Aramaic*

Relatively few Dead Sea Scrolls were written in Greek, most of them biblical manuscripts and from the Pentateuch. Besides the two Leviticus copies (4QLXXLev^b and pap4QLXXLev^b), there is one Greek scroll of Exodus (pap7QLXXExod), one of Numbers (4QLXXNum), and one of Deuteronomy (4QLXXDeut). Another important item is the Minor Prophets Scroll (8ḤevXII gr) that was found in Cave 8 at Naḥal Ḥever. Also noteworthy are a Greek *Paraphrase of Exodus* (4Q127), the apocryphal Letter of Jeremiah (pap7QepJer gr), the recently-identified *1 Enoch* (pap7QEn gr), and the fascinating *Unidentified Greek Scroll* (4Q126).

One of the three *Targums* among the Scrolls is of Leviticus (4QtgLev); the other two are of Job (4QtgJob and 11QtgJob). In light of the tradition that Moses wrote Job (*b. B. Bat.* 14b, 15a), it appears that only books of Moses were considered eligible for translation into Aramaic.

3.5   *Biblical Scrolls Written on Papyrus*

The Dead Sea Scrolls, especially the biblical ones, were almost always written on leather parchment, while letters and bills were written on papyrus. Some 100 papyri were discovered at Qumran, of which only eight contain biblical books. Four papyri are of the Pentateuch (pap4QLXXLev^b, as well as pap4QGen, pap7QLXXExod, and pap6QDeut?), one is of the Historical Books (pap6QKings), one of the Poetic Books (pap6QPs), two of the Prophets (pap4QIsaᵖ and pap6QDan). To these may be added a scroll of *1 Enoch* (pap7QEn gr) and a possible biblical text from Cave 7 that was written in Greek: *pap7QBiblical Text gr* (7Q3).

The scarcity of biblical texts written on papyrus is partly due to the expense and scarcity of this material, which had to be imported from Egypt. More significant, perhaps, is that parchment was prepared from ritually pure animals. This would have been more acceptable to the Qumran community, and Jewish scribes in general, for copying biblical texts than papyrus, which was made by non-Jews in Egypt and thus was considered by many to be impure.[18] Compare the later Jewish tradition that biblical scrolls were to be written on parchment (the *m. Meg.* 2:2 and *y. Meg.* 1.71d).

4. *The Text of Leviticus in the Scrolls*

4.1 *Textual assessment*

As observed in section 2 above, most Leviticus scrolls contain at least some variant readings against the Masoretic text, the Samaritan Pentateuch, and the Septuagint, but several are textually close to 𝔐 or 𝔰 or both. According to our assessments in section 2, the following summary is given for the fourteen manuscripts written in Hebrew—i.e. excluding the Greek copies and the *targum* of Leviticus. Only one scroll (4QExod-Levᶠ) is properly classified as *pre-Samaritan*, two (MasLevᵃ and MasLevᵇ) as *proto-Masoretic*, two (11Qpaleo-Levᵃ and 11QLevᵇ) as *non-aligned*, and seven as *mixed* (1QpaleoLev, 2QpaleoLev, 4QLev-Numᵃ, 4QLevᵇ, 4QLevᶜ, 4QLevᵈ, 4QLevᵉ). For the remaining two scrolls (6QpaleoLev and 4QLevᵍ), no assessment was offered, since too little text survives for a proper judgment to be made.

---

[18] For further details, see M. Bar-Ilan, "Writing Materials," *EDSS* 2.996–97; VanderKam and Flint, *The Meaning of the Dead Sea Scrolls*, 52–53.

Textual Affinities of the Fourteen Leviticus Scrolls
(Differing Assessments in Italics)

Scroll	P. Flint	E. Tov
1QpaleoLev	*mixed*	*proto-Masoretic*
2QpaleoLev	*mixed*	*no assessment*
4QExod-Lev^f	pre-Samaritan	pre-Samaritan
4QLev-Num^a	*mixed*	*proto-Masoretic*
4QLev^b	*mixed*	*proto-Masoretic*
4QLev^c	*mixed*	*proto-Masoretic*
4QLev^d	mixed	pre-Samaritan/LXX
4QLev^e	*mixed*	*proto-Masoretic*
4QLev^g	no assessment	no assessment
6QpaleoLev	no assessment	no assessment
11QpaleoLev^a	non-aligned	non-aligned
11QLev^b	non-aligned	non-aligned
MasLev^a	proto-Masoretic	proto-Masoretic
MasLev^b	proto-Masoretic	proto-Masoretic

Several of these classifications differ from those of Emanuel Tov. His assessment concurs with ours for five of the twelve scrolls: the single *pre-Samaritan* manuscript, the two *proto-Masoretic* ones, and the two *non-aligned* ones. The following scrolls, however, are listed by Tov as *proto-Masoretic*, whereas we class them as *mixed*: 1QpaleoLev, 4QLev-Num^a, 4QLev^b, 4QLev^c, and 4QLev^e. Moreover, Tov offers no assessment of 2QpaleoLev, but there seems to be sufficient evidence to view it as *mixed*. The final scroll, 4QLev^e (which we list as *mixed*), is classed by Tov as *pre-Samaritan*, but also features in his list of texts close to the *Vorlage* of the Septuagint.

These discrepancies arise mainly from Tov's stated principle: "in accord with statistical probability, texts which are equally close to MT and SP in the Torah and to MT and the LXX in the other books are counted as MT."[19] Laying aside the question of "MT and LXX in the other books" (which is a separate but related issue), in our opinion such methodology is lacking with respect to the Pentateuch. Indeed, in the Appendix at the end of his article Tov lists the following manuscripts under both the MT and SP columns: 1QpaleoLev, 4QLev-Num^a, 4QLev^b, 4QLev^c, and 4QLev^e. Classing these texts as *proto-Masoretic*, however, gives undue weight to the early precursor of

---

[19] Tov, "The Biblical Texts from the Judean Desert," 153.

the Masoretic Text and is misleading to the reader. Our research indicates that only the two Masada scrolls (MasLev^a and MasLev^b) may be viewed as especially close to the precursor of the Masoretic text.

Tov's treatment of 4QLev^d is closer to the approach advocated in the present article: by giving this scroll equal mention among the "Pre-Samaritan Texts" and the "Texts Close to the Presumed Hebrew Source of the LXX," he makes it clear that 4QLev^d is close to these two witnesses but not to the Masoretic Text.

The solution proposed here is relatively straightforward. First, we recognize with Tov the existence of many texts among the Scrolls that are equally close to two of the main ancient witnesses (𝔐, 𝔴, or 𝔊). These texts, however, cannot be classified as *non-aligned*, since that category also features several independent readings, which are present in scrolls such as 11QpaleoLev^a but not in many others.

Rather than listing these texts as *proto-Masoretic*, as Tov does, we suggest a *mixed* category. This accounts for the evidence more clearly, without placing the texts concerned in a group where they do not belong. It is possible that with further research this category can be further refined; for example, how many independent readings are required for a text to be classed as *non-aligned* rather than *mixed*? (A case in point is 4QLev^b, which apparently lacked Lev 3:1–11 and preserves a small longer reading at Lev 22:22.)

Despite the variety that is evident in many Leviticus scrolls, there are no large-scale variations in content. The form of this book seems to have stabilized early, perhaps because it was a work containing specific cultic regulations. It appears that a single textual tradition is preserved in the seventeen Leviticus manuscripts, although they are variously classified as *proto-Masoretic, pre-Samaritan, mixed* or *non-aligned*.

It appears that none of the variant readings found in the Leviticus manuscripts have so far been accepted by modern Bible translators, although this may change as the readings are carefully analyzed and weighed.

4.2   Some Significant Readings

Several interesting or significant variant readings preserved in the seventeen Leviticus scrolls appear below. Many more may be found in the critical editions of these manuscripts (see the Bibliography).

Lev 14:24 om totum comma(?) 𝕲ᵐˢ 4QLev-Numᵃ] hab 𝔐𝔰𝔤𝕲

> Here the copyist of 4QLev-Numᵃ has omitted all of verse 24 (וְלָקַח
> אֶת־כֶּבֶשׂ הָאָשָׁם וְאֶת־לֹג הַשֶּׁמֶן וְהֵנִיף אֹתָם הַכֹּהֵן תְּנוּפָה לִפְנֵי יְהוָה הַכֹּהֵן,
> *and the priest shall take the lamb of the guilt offering and the log of oil, and the
> priest shall raise them as an elevation offering before the L*ORD). Rather than
> using a different Hebrew Text, the scribe most likely erred by para-
> blepsis, his eye skipping from יהוה at the end of verse 23 to יהוה at the
> end of verse 24.

Lev 17:3 וְהַגֵּר הַ[גָּ֯ר בִּישׂ֯רָאֵל (cf. 𝕲ᴬᴮꟳᴹ ἢ τῶν προσηλύτων τῶν προσκειμένων
ἐν ὑμῖν; and cf. 16:29; 17:8, 10, 13) 4QLevᵈ] > 11QpaleoLev 𝔐𝔰𝔪

> This variant reading concerns the inclusion or resident aliens in the
> prohibition given in verse 3; compare verses 8, 10, 12, 15, which refer
> to resident aliens.[20] Whereas 11QpaleoLev, the Masoretic Text, and
> the Samaritan Pentateuch begin the verse with *If anyone of the house of
> Israel*, 4QLevᵈ broadens the referents to include "[*and the stranger who*]
> *resides in Israel* (וְהַגֵּר הַ[גָּר בִּישׂרָאֵל). The Septuagint is similarly more
> embracing: *Each one of the children of Israel or of the proselytes who reside
> among you.*

Lev 19:36 אבני צֶ֯[דֶ֯ק 4QLevᵉ] מאזני צדק אבני צדק 𝔐𝔰𝔪𝕲. Calculations
of space make it unlikely that 4QLevᵉ included the first two words
were included, by way of inversion, in 4QLevᵉ.

> 4QLevᵉ simply has אבני צֶ֯[דֶ֯ק (*just weights*), as opposed to 𝔐𝔰𝔪𝕲, which
> read *just balances, just weights* (מאזני צדק אבני צדק 𝔐). This omission is
> most likely explained by homoioteleuton, the scribe's eye skipping from
> the first צדק to the second.

Lev 22:5 טמא 4QLevᵉ 𝔰𝕲] > 1QpaleoLev(vid)~

> The reading in 4QLevᵉ agrees with the Samaritan Pentateuch and the
> Septuagint: או איש אשר יגע בכל שׁ[רֶ֯ץ טמא (*and whoever touches any*] *unclean
> [swa]rming thing*). The effect of טמא, which is not found in the Masoretic
> Text, or, apparently, in 1QpaleoLev, is to intensify the notion of
> uncleanness.

Lev 22:22 יַ[לֶּפֶת או מזֹ֯רֹ֯וֹחַ [אשׁ֯ךָ֯ 4QLevᵇ] ילפת 𝔐𝔰𝔪𝕲 (cf. 21:20)

> Lev 22:21–22 specifies that a sacrifice of made to the Lord in fulfillment
> of a vow or as a freewill offering must be a perfect and unblemished
> animal. The Masoretic Text and other witnesses refer in verse 22 to
> *anything blind, or injured, or maimed, or having a discharge or an itch or*

---

[20] For comments, see Eshel, "Leviticus, Book of," 489.

scabs. . . . 4QLev[b], however, has a longer text at this point, by adding *or crushed [testic]les*, thus further extending the scope of blemish and imperfection.

Select Bibliography

Editions of the Leviticus Scrolls

Caves 1, 2, and 6:

Barthélemy, D. and J. T. Milik (eds.). *Qumran Cave I* (DJD 1; Oxford: Clarendon Press, 1955) 51–53 + pls. 8–9.
Baillet, M., J. T. Milik, and R. de Vaux. *Les 'Petites Grottes' de Qumran: Exploration de la falaise Les grottes 2Q, 3Q, 5Q, 6Q, 7Q, à 10Q, Le rouleau de cuivre. 1. Texte 2. Planches* (DJD 3; Oxford: Clarendon Press, 1962) 56–57, 106 + pls. 12, 20.

Cave 4:

Vaux, R. de and J. T. Milik (eds.). *Qumrân Grotte 4:II 1. Archéologie; 2. Tefillin, Mezuzot et Targums (4Q128–4Q157)* (DJD 6; Oxford: Clarendon Press, 1977) 86–89, 92–93 + pl. 28.
Skehan, P. W., E. Ulrich, and J. E. Sanderson (eds.). *Qumran Cave 4.IV: Palaeo-Hebrew and Greek Biblical Manuscripts* (DJD 9; Oxford: Clarendon Press, 1992) 161–86 + pls. 38–41.
Ulrich, E., F. M. Cross et al. (eds.). *Qumran Cave 4.VII: Genesis to Numbers* (DJD 12; Oxford: Clarendon Press, 1994) 133–44, 153–204 + pls. 22–37.

Cave 11:

Freedman, D. N. and K. A. Mathews. *The Paleo-Hebrew Leviticus Scroll (11QpaleoLev[b])* (Winona lake, Ind.: ASOR, 1985). [abbreviated PHLS]
García Martínez, F., A. S. van der Woude, and E. J. C. Tigchelaar. *Qumran Cave 11.II: 11Q2–18, 11Q20–31* (DJD 23; Oxford: Clarendon Press, 1992) 1–9 + pl. 1.
Puech, É. "Notes en marge de 11QpaléoLévitique: Le fragment L, des fragments inédits et une jarred de la grotte 11," *RB* 96 (1989) 161–83.

Masada:

Talmon, S. "Hebrew Fragments from Masada," in *Masada VI: Yigael Yadin Excavations 1963–1965, Final Reports* (Jerusalem: Israel Exploration Society and the Hebrew University of Jerusalem, 1999) 36–50.

Other books and articles

Abegg, M. G., P. W. Flint, and E. Ulrich. *The Dead Sea Scrolls Bible* (San Francisco: Harper San Francisco: Edinburgh: T&T Clark 1999) 77–107.
Eshel, E. "A Possible Source for the Temple Scroll and *Miqsat Ma'ase Ha-torah*," *DSD* 2 (1995) 1–13.
Fitzmyer, J. A. "The Targum of Leviticus from Qumran Cave 4." *Maarev* 1 (1978) 5–21
Freedman, D. N. "Variant Readings in the Leviticus Scroll from Qumran Cave 11," *CBQ* 36 (1974) 525–34.
Mathews, K. A. "The Paleo-Hebrew Leviticus Scroll from Qumran," *BA* 50 (1987) 45–54.
—— "The Leviticus Scroll (11QpaleoLev) and the Text of the Hebrew Bible," *CBQ* 48 (1986) 171–207.

Skehan, P. W. "The Qumran Manuscripts and Textual Criticism," *VTSup* 4 (1957), 153–54.

Tov, E. "מקומראן 11 אופייה הטקסטואלי של מגילת ויקרא ממערה" ("Textual Character of the Leviticus Scroll from Qumran Cave 11"), *Shnaton* 3 (1978) 238–44.

—— "4QLevᵈ (4Q26)," in F. García Martínez, A. Hilhorst and C. J. Labuschagne (eds.), *The Scriptures and the Scrolls: Studies in Honour of A. S. van der Woude on the Occasion of His 65th Birthday* (Leiden: Brill, 1992) 1–5.

—— "The Biblical Texts from the Judean Desert—An Overview and Analysis of all the Published Texts," in *The Bible as Book: The Hebrew Bible and the Judaean Desert Discoveries. Proceedings of the Conference Held at Hampton Court, Herefordshire, 18–21 June 2000*, edited by E. D. Herbert and E. Tov (London: The British Library, 2002) 139–66.

Ulrich, E. "The Greek Manuscripts of the Pentateuch from Qumrân, Including Newly Identified Fragments of Deuteronomy (4QLXXDeut)," in A. Pietersma and C. Cox (eds.), *De Septuaginta: Studies in Honor of John William Wevers on His Sixty-Fifth Birthday* (Mississuaga, ON: Benben, 1984) 71–82.

—— "The Septuagint Manuscripts from Qumran: A Reappraisal of Their Value," in G. J. Brooke and B. Lindars (eds.), *Septuagint, Scrolls and Cognate Writings: Papers Presented to the International Symposium on the Septuagint and Its Relations to the Dead Sea Scrolls and Other Writings* (Atlanta, GA: Scholars Press, 1992) 49–80.

—— "The Palaeo-Hebrew Biblical Manuscripts from Qumran Cave 4," in D. Dimant and L. H. Schiffman (eds.), *Time to Prepare the Way in the Wilderness: Papers on the Qumran Scrolls by Fellows of the Institute for Advanced Studies of the Hebrew University, Jerusalem (1989–1990)* (Leiden: Brill, 1995) 103–29.

VanderKam, J. C. and P. W. Flint. *The Meaning of the Dead Sea Scrolls* (San Francisco: Harper San Francisco, 2002).

APPENDIX 1

LEVITICUS SCROLLS FROM THE JUDAEAN DESERT

Details of the seventeen Leviticus scrolls are summarized in the Table below. Note that Column III (*Range of Contents*) lists a manuscript's earliest and latest verses in terms of their Masoretic order, without implying that the intervening text is also preserved in these fragmentary scrolls. Column IV (*Date when Copied*) indicates the approximate date of each manuscript on the basis of palaeographic analysis. In some cases the *editio princeps* does not offer a date since too little text survives for a judgment to be made.

I *Siglum*	II *Number*	III *Range of Contents*	IV *Date When Copied*	V *Publication Details*
1QpaleoLev	1Q3	11:10 to Num 36:8?	?	DJD 1.51–53 + pls. 8–9
2QpaleoLev	2Q5	11:22–29	1st c. BCE	DJD 3. 56–57 + pl. 12
4QExod-Lev[f]	4Q17	Ex 38:18 to Lev 2:1	Mid 3rd c. BCE	DJD 12.133–44 + pl. 22
4QLev-Num[a]	4Q23	13:32 to Num 35:5	Mid or later 2nd c. BCE	DJD 12.153–76 + pls. 23–30
4QLev[b]	4Q24	1:11 to 25:52	Mid 1st c. BCE	DJD 12.177–87 + pls. 31–34
4QLev[c]	4Q25	1:1 to 8:28	?	DJD 12.189–92 + pl. 35
4QLev[d]	4Q26	14:27 to 17:11	30 BCE to 20 CE	DJD 12.193–95 + pl. 36
4QLev[e]	4Q26a	3:2 to 22:17	?	DJD 12.197–201 + pl. 37
4QLev[g]	4Q26b	7:19–26	?	DJD 12.203–204 + pl. 37
4QLXXLev[a]	4Q119	2:2–16	Late 2nd to 1st c. BCE	DJD 9.161–65 + pl. 38
pap4QLXX Lev[b]	4Q120	1:11 to 6:5[𝔐5:24]	1st c. BCE	DJD 9.168–86 + pls. 39–41
pap4QtgLev	4Q156	16:12 to 16:21	ca. 150 BCE	DJD 6.86–89, 92–93 + pl. 28
6QpaleoLev	6Q2	8:12–13	?	DJD 3.106 + pl. 20
11Qpaleo Lev[a]	11Q1	4:24 to 27:19	100 BCE	*PHLS*, Puech, Tigchelaar
11QLev[b]	11Q2	7:34 to 25:33	ca. 50 CE	DJD 23.1–9 + pl. 1
MasLev[a]	Mas1a	4:3–9	2nd half of 1st c. BCE	Masada 6.36–38 + illustration 3
MasLev[b]	Mas1b	8:31 to 11:40	Mid 1st c. CE	Masada 6.38–50 + illustration 4

APPENDIX 2

CONTENTS OF THE LEVITICUS SCROLLS
BY MANUSCRIPT

The contents of each of the seventeen Leviticus scrolls are presented below, based in the various volumes given in the Bibliography and detailed in Appendix 1. The Masada material is from S. Talmon's 1999 edition in *Masada VI: Yigael Yadin Excavations 1963–1965*; and the Qumran material is from six volumes in the series "Discoveries in the Judaean Desert (of Jordan)," the 1985 book by D. N. Freedman and K. A. Mathews (*PHLS*), and the 1989 article by É. Puech.

1QpaleoLev (1Q3)
  11:10–11
  19:30–34
  20:20–24
  21:24
  22:1–6
  23:4–8
  Num 1:48–50
  Num 36:7–8(?)
  Lev 27:30–31(?)
  plus fragments

2QpaleoLev (2Q5)
  11:22–29

4QExod-Lev^f (4Q17)
  Exod 38:18–22
  39:3–24
  40:8–27
  Lev 1:13–15, 17
  2:1

4QLev-Num^a (4Q23)
  Lev 13:32–33
  14:22–34, 40–54
  15:10–11, 19–24
  16:15–29
  18:16–21
  19:3–8
  24:11–12
  26:26–33
  27:5–22
  Num 1:1–5, 21–22,
    36–40

2:18–20, 31–32
3:3–19, 51
4:1–12, 40–49
5:1–9
8:7–12, 21–22
9:3–10, 19–20
10:13–23
11:4–5, 16–22
12:3–11
13:21
22:5–6, 22–24
26:5–7
30:3?, 7? (9?, 13?)
32:8–15, 23–42
33:5–9, 22–34, 52–54
35:4–5

4QLev^b (4Q24)
  1:11–17
  2:1–16
  3:1, 8–14
  21:17–20, 24
  22:2–33
  23:1–8, 10–25, 40
  24:2–23
  25:28–29, 45–49,
    51–52

4QLev^c (4Q25)
  1:1–7
  3:16–17
  4:1–6, 12–14, 23–28
  5:12–13
  8:26–28

4QLevᵈ (4Q26)
  14:27–29, 33–36
  15:20–24
  17:2–11

4QLevᵉ (4Q26a)
  3:2–8
  19:34–37
  20:1–3, 27
  21:1–4, 9–12, 21–24
  22:4–6, 11–17

4QLevᵍ (4Q26b)
  7:19–26

4QLXXLevᵃ (4Q119)
  26:2–16
  plus a fragment

pap4QLXXLevᵇ (4Q120)
  1:11
  2:3–5, 7–8?
  3:4, 7, 9–14
  4:3–4, 6–8, 10–11, 18–19, 26–28, 30
  5:6, 8–10, 16–19
  6:1–5[˜ 5:20–24]
  plus fragments

pap4QtgLev
  16:1–15, 18–21

6QpaleoLev (6Q2)
  8:12–13

11Qpaleo-Levᵃ (11Q1)
  4:24–26
  10:4–7

  11:27–32
  13:3–9, 39–43
  14:16–21, 52–57
  15:1–5
  16:1–6, 34
  17:1–5
  18:27–30
  19:1–4
  20:1–6
  21:6–12
  22:21–27
  23:22–29
  24:9–14
  25:28–36
  26:17–26
  27:11–19

11QLevᵇ (11Q2)
  7:34–35
  8:8 or 9
  9:23–24
  10:1–2
  13:58–59
  14:16–17
  15:18–19
  25:31–33
  plus fragments

MasLevᵃ (Mas1a)
  4:3–9

MasLevᵃ (Mas1b)
  8:31, 33–34
  9:1–10, 12–13, 15, 22–24
  10:1, 9–20
  11:1–21, 24–40

APPENDIX 3

CONTENTS OF THE LEVITICUS SCROLLS
BY CHAPTER AND VERSE

For earlier listings of contents by chapter and verse, see E. Ulrich, "Appendix I: Index Of Passages in the Biblical Scrolls," in P. W. Flint and J. C. VanderKam (eds.), *The Dead Sea Scrolls After Fifty Years: A Comprehensive Assessment* (2 vols., Leiden: Brill, 1998–99) 2.649–65, esp. 656–58; P. W. Flint, "Appendix: Index of Passages in the Biblical, Apocryphal, and 'Pseudepigraphal' Scrolls," in A. J. Avery-Peck, J. Neusner and B. D. Chiton (eds.), *Judaism in Late Antiquity, Part Five. The Judaism of Qumran: A Systematic Reading of the Dead Sea Scrolls. Volume One: Way of Life* (HO series; Leiden: Brill, 2000) 87–103, esp. 89–90.

Passage	Scroll	Passage	Scroll
1:1–7	4QLev^c	11:22–29	2QpaleoLev
1:11–17	4QLev^b	11:27–32	11QpaleoLev^a
1:11	pap4QLXXLev^b	13:3–9, 39–43	11QpaleoLev^a
1:13–15, 17	4QExod-Lev^f	13:32–33	4QLev-Num^a
2:1	4QExod-Lev^f	13:58–59	11QLev^b
2:1–16	4QLev^b	14:16–17	11QLev^b
2:3–5, 7–8?	pap4QLXXLev^b	14:16–21, 52–57	11QpaleoLev^a
3:1, 8–14	4QLev^b	14:22–34, 40–54	4QLev-Num^a
3:2–8	4QLev^c	14:27–29, 33–36	4QLev^d
3:4, 7, 9–14	pap4QLXXLev^b	15:1–5	11QpaleoLev^a
3:16–17	4QLev^c	15:10–11, 19–24	4QLev-Num^a
4:1–6, 12–14, 23–28	4QLev^c	14:16–17	11QLev^b
4:3–4, 6–8, 10–11, 18–19,		15:18–19	11QLev^b
26–28, 30	pap4QLXXLev^b	15:20–24	4QLev^d
4:3–9	MasLev^a	16:1–6, 34	11QpaleoLev^a
4:24–26	11QpaleoLev^a	16:1–15, 18–21	pap4QtgLev
5:6, 8–10, 16–19	pap4QLXXLev^b	16:15–29	4QLev-Num^a
5:12–13	4QLev^c	17:1–5	11QpaleoLev^a
6:1–5[⁓ 5:20–24]	pap4QLXXLev^b	17:2–11	4QLev^d
7:19–26	4QLev^g	18:16–21	4QLev-Num^a
7:34–35	11QLev^b	18:27–30	11QpaleoLev^a
8:8 or 9	11QLev^b	19:1–4	11QpaleoLev^a
8:12–13	6QpaleoLev	19:3–8	4QLev-Num^a
8:26–28	4QLev^c	19:30–34	1QpaleoLev
8:31, 33–34	MasLev^b	19:34–37	4QLev^e
9:1–10, 12–13, 15, 22–24	MasLev^b	20:1–6	11QpaleoLev^a
9:23–24	11QLev^b	20:1–3, 27	4QLev^e
10:1–2	11QLev^b	20:20–24	1QpaleoLev
10:1, 9–20	MasLev^b	21:1–4, 9–12, 21–24	4QLev^e
10:4–7	11QpaleoLev^a	21:6–12	11QpaleoLev^a
11:1–21, 24–40	MasLev^b	21:17–20, 24	4QLev^b
11:10–11	1QpaleoLev	21:24	1QpaleoLev

22:1–6	1QpaleoLev	24:11–12	4QLev-Num[a]
22:2–33	4QLev[b]	25:28–36	11QpaleoLev[a]
22:4–6, 11–17	4QLev[c]	25:28–29, 45–49, 51–52	4QLev[b]
22:21–27	11QpaleoLev[a]	25:31–33	11QLev[b]
23:1–8, 10–25, 40	4QLev[b]	26:2–16	4QLXXLev[a]
23:1–3? (or Num 18:8–9?)	2QNum[d?]	26:17–26	11QpaleoLev[a]
23:4–8	1QpaleoLev	26:26–33	4QLev-Num[a]
23:22–29	11QpaleoLev[a]	27:5–22	4QLev-Num[a]
24:2–23	4QLev[b]	27:11–19	11QpaleoLev[a]
24:9–14	11QpaleoLev[a]	27:30–31(?)	1QpaleoLev

RETHINKING THE NOTION OF "SCRIPTURE" IN THE DEAD SEA SCROLLS: LEVITICUS AS A TEST CASE

Robert A. Kugler

The study of scripture in the Dead Sea Scrolls is shaped by the rock-solid conviction that "the Bible" for the Essenes was a revered textual object which they interpreted at will in the course of expressing their theological convictions. Hence scholars are preoccupied with establishing the scope of the Essene's Bible, the precise character of the biblical text, and the nature and consequences of their exegetical methods. Yet the results of the search for the Qumran canon, text, and interpretive method urge us to adopt a very different notion of scripture among the Essenes. We have discovered that there was no canon at Qumran, only an open-ended appreciation of a vast number of texts and traditions, many of which are not in our Hebrew Bible. We have learned that the biblical scrolls exhibit unrestrained textual diversity, a fact that seemed not to worry the Essenes. And we have determined that their exegetical practices, although in some respects like those of the Jews of their day, were just as often their own unique methods of making sense of the texts and traditions they inherited. In short, we discover—with the help of the following survey of research and glimpse into the presence of Leviticus at Qumran—that scripture for the Essenes was no static entity, a revered textual object that could be manipulated at will. Instead, in the words of William Graham, "'scripture' is not a literary genre but a religio-historical one"; as such it should be studied not as a static textual reality, but as a relational phenomenon, a dynamic human process.[1]

The Study of Scripture in the Dead Sea Scrolls: a Critical Review

Interest in the Qumran "canon" has been driven in part by an even greater interest in ascertaining the moment when the Hebrew

---

[1] W. Graham, *Beyond the Written Word: Oral Aspects of Scripture in the History of Religion* (Cambridge: Cambridge University Press, 1987) 6.

Bible/Old Testament canon first took its present shape.[2] In any case, besides pointing to possible "canonical" language in the scrolls,[3] scholars have sought to determine the Essenes' authoritative texts by a variety of criteria:[4] the number of times a book appears in the community library,[5] the quotation of a book with a citation formula,[6] or

---

[2] Some of the essays on the topic include D. Carr, "Canonization in the Context of Community: An Outline of the Formation of the Tanakh and the Christian Bible," in R. D. Weiss and D. M. Carr (eds.), *A Gift of God in Due Season: Essays on Scripture and Community in Honor of James A. Sanders* (JSOTSup 225; Sheffield: Shieffield Academic Press, 1997) 22–64; I. H. Eybers, "Some Light on the Canon of the Qumran Sect," in S. Z. Leiman (ed.), *The Canon and Masorah of the Hebrew Bible: An Introductory Reader* (New York: Ktav, 1974) 23–36; J. A. Sanders, "The Scrolls and the Canonical Process," in P. W. Flint and J. C. VanderKam (eds.), *The Dead Sea Scrolls After Fifty Years: A Comprehensive Assessment* (2 vols.; Leiden: Brill, 1998, 1999) 2.1–23; J. C. VanderKam, "Authoritative Literature in the Dead Sea Scrolls," *DSD* 5 (1998) 382–402; E. Ulrich, "The Canonical Process, Textual Criticism, and Latter Stages in the Composition of the Bible," in M. Fishbane and E. Tov with W. Field (eds.), *"Sha'arei Talmon": Studies in the Bible, Qumran, and the Ancient Near East Presented to Shemaryahu Talmon* (Winona Lake, IN: Eisenbraun, 1992) 267–91 (repr. in *The Dead Sea Scrolls and the Origins of the Bible* [Grand Rapids: Eerdmans, 1999] 51–78); idem, "Canon," in L. Schiffman and J. VanderKam (eds.), *Encyclopedia of the Dead Sea Scrolls* [henceforth *EDSS*] (Oxford: Oxford University, 2000) 117–20.

[3] See 1QS 1:1–3, which urges the *maskil* to instruct the community to "seek God with all their heart and with their soul, to do that which is good and upright before him, just as he commanded through Moses and all his servants the prophets", and 4QMMT C 9–10, "that you may have understanding in the book of Moses [and] in the book[s of the p]rophets and in Dav[id]."

[4] In addition to those listed here, others cite the presence of God's direct speech in a work (11QTemple) or the presence of unusual graphic characteristics (e.g., the separation of lemmata from interpretive comments in the *pesharim*).

[5] By this measure the Psalms (36), Deuteronomy (29), Isaiah (21), Exodus (17), Genesis (15), and Leviticus (13) would be the most important books for the community, and books like Joshua (2), Proverbs (2), Ezra (1) would be the least significant. Completely unimportant would be Nehemiah and Esther, no copies of which survive!

[6] Phrases like אשר כתוב, כאשר כתוב, כי כן כתוב, כי כתוב על, כי כתוב, as well as כאשר אמר, אשר אמר are generally understood to denote the authority of the quotation that follows. For a collection of direct quotes in the scrolls, see J. Fitzmyer, "The Use of Explicit Old Testament Quotations in Qumran Literature and in the New Testament," *NTS* 7 (1960–61) 297–333 (repr. in J. A. Fitzmyer, *The Semitic Background of the New Testament* [Biblical Resource Series; Grand Rapids: Eerdmans/ Livonia, MI: Dove, 1997] 3–58). Although Fitzmyer is reluctant to draw conclusions from his research about the authority of some books at Qumran, J. VanderKam willingly takes that next step in his essay, "Authoritative Literature." Note as well M. Bernstein, "Introductory Formulas for Citation and Re-citation of Biblical Verses in the Qumran Pesharim," *DSD* 1 (1994) 30–70; idem, "Scripture: Quotation and Use," *EDSS* 2.839–42; F. M. Horton, "Formulas of Introduction in the Qumran Literature," *RevQ* 28 (1971) 505–14; J. Lust, "Quotation Formulae and Canon in Qumran," in A. van der Kooij and K. van der Toorn (eds.), *Canonization and Decanonization* (SHR 82; Leiden: Brill, 1998) 67–77.

the existence of a commentary on a book.[7] But the effort has done
little to reveal a Qumran canon. Instead it has proven that preservational whimsy and accidents make book counting a vain effort,[8] the
Essenes were inconsistent in introducing quotes with formulae,[9] and
their commentaries were not reserved so much for authoritative books

---

[7] See Eybers, "Some Light," 24; Ulrich, "Canon," 119; cf. VanderKam,
"Authoritative Literature," 386–87. Commentaries, or *pesharim*, are usually distin-
guished from more diffuse interpretive works that "rewrite" existing compositions.
See especially the similar distinction made between expositional (= commentary)
and compositional (= rewritten Bible) works in D. Dimant, "Use and Interpretation
of Mikra in the Apocrypha and Pseudepigrapha," in M. J. Mulder (ed.), *Mikra: Text,
Translation, Reading and Interpretation of the Hebrew Bible in Ancient Judaism and Early
Christianity* (CRINT 2.1; Assen and Maastricht Van Gorcum; Philadelphia: Fortress,
1988) 381–84; and J. C. Reeves, "Scriptural Authority in Early Judaism," in J. E.
Bowley (ed.), *Living Traditions in the Bible: Scripture in Jewish, Christian, and Muslim Practice*
(St. Louis, MO: Chalice, 1999) 63–84, esp. 74–77. Reeves also cites J. M. Harris,
"From Inner-Biblical Interpretation to Early Rabbinic Exegesis," in M. Sæbø (ed.),
Hebrew Bible/Old Testament: The History of Its Interpretation (Göttingen: Vandenhoeck &
Ruprecht, 1996) 256–69, esp. 258.
[8] For example, it may be purely a matter of preservational accident that no
copies of Esther or Nehemiah survive.
[9] While Exodus, Leviticus, Numbers, Deuteronomy, 2 Samuel, the three major
prophets, five of the minor prophets, and Psalms, Proverbs, and Daniel make the
list, other compositions that were surely authoritative for the group are left off, most
notably Genesis and Joshua, both of which spawned as many or more exegetical
works among the scrolls than the number of their own manuscripts (on Genesis,
see M. Bernstein, "Contours of Genesis Interpretation at Qumran: Contents, Context,
and Nomenclature," in J. Kugel [ed.], *Studies in Ancient Midrash* [Cambridge, MA:
Harvard University Press, 2000] 57–85; and E. Eshel, "Hermeneutical Approaches
to Genesis in the Dead Sea Scrolls," in J. Fishman and L. von Rompay [eds.], *The
Book of Genesis in Jewish and Oriental Christian Interpretation* [Louvain: Peeters, 1997]
1–12; on Joshua, see E. Tov, "The Rewritten Book of Joshua as Found at Qumran
and Masada," in M. Stone and E. Chazon [eds.], *Biblical Perspectives: Early Use and
Interpretation of the Bible in Light of the Dead Sea Scrolls* [STDJ 28; Leiden: Brill, 1998]
232–56). And the supposition that when a speaker or writer denotes something as
written he is also acknowledging its special authority may stretch the evidence too
far. While using the quoted source to support his views *does* indicate its value for
the interpreter, it is equally possible that the author means only to say that he
knows this source to exist in written form. In fact, it may not be any more authoritative for him than other sources known to him only in oral form which are introduced with formulae using the verb אמר, or are not introduced at all. Also with
regard to this criterion it is important to note that citation formulae introduce a
quote from *Jubilees* (4Q228 1 i 9, using כי כן כתוב) and words of Levi which are
not traceable to any known work (CD 4:15), suggesting that the range of works
understood by the Essenes to be of value extended well beyond what later became
the Hebrew Bible canon. Finally, one should note that there are also many occasions when works that were undoubtedly authoritative for the community were
quoted without any citation formulae at all (see, for example, the many citations
of Deuteronomy in 4Q174; see also the impressive list of citation-less allusions to
and quotations of scripture in the *Community Rule* listed by P. Wernberg-Møller,

as they were for works that lent themselves to their peculiar commentary genre.[10] Most of all the effort has demonstrated that at Qumran there was no closed collection of authoritative books. Instead there was an open-ended collection of texts and traditions about God and God's people which the Essenes deemed to be useful resources in the struggle to make sense of life in God's sight.

Similarly, the facts turned up by the study of the text of the Bible at Qumran have disappointed readers hoping to settle longstanding questions about the development of the biblical text. That those who view the Masoretic tradition as the closest thing to an *Urtext* of the Hebrew Bible find comfort from the scrolls[11] as readily as those who say it emerged from ancient, nearly limitless diversity,[12] or from a

---

"Some Reflections on the Biblical Material in the Manual of Disciples," *ST* 9 [1955] 40–66, esp. 41–42, n. 1).

[10] Works in this category comment on Isaiah (3Q4; 4Q161–165), Hosea 4Q166–167), Micah (1Q14), Nahum (4Q169), Habakkuk (1QpHab), Zephaniah (1Q15; 4Q170) and Psalms (1Q16; 4Q171; 4Q173), hardly a complete list of the books one would have expected the Qumran community to hold dear. In addition, the category is not as easily separated from Rewritten Bible, on one side, and "Bible" on the other, as one would think: 4Q252, the so-called *Commentary on Genesis* mixes the *pesher* technique with that of reproducing and/or rewriting material from Genesis, while the *Reworked Pentateuch* at Qumran (4Q158; 4Q364–367) seamlessly merges large portions of the biblical books as we know them with quasi-interpretive comments and passages from other parts of the Pentateuch.

[11] This is roughly the view of E. Tov, although his position has evolved over the years; see especially, "The Orthography and Language of the Hebrew Scrolls Found at Qumran and the Origins of These Scrolls," *Textus* 19 (1986) 31–57; idem, "A Modern Textual Outlook Based on the Qumran Scrolls," *HUCA* 53 (1982) 11–27; idem, "Hebrew Biblical Manuscripts From the Judaean Desert: Their Contribution to Textual Criticism," *JJS* 39 (1988) 5–37; idem, "Some Notes on a Generation of Qumran Studies (by Frank M. Cross): A Reply by Emanuel Tov," in J. Trebolle Barrera and L. Vegas Montaner (eds.), *The Madrid Qumran Congress: Proceedings of the International Congress on the Dead Sea Scrolls, Madrid, 18–21 March 1991* (STDJ 11; 2 vols.; Leiden: Brill, 1991) 15–21; idem, *Textual Criticism of the Hebrew Bible* (Minneapolis/Assen and Maastricht: Fortress/Van Gorcum, 1992) 114–17, 313–49. Tov's commitment to the Masoretic text as at least the *best* text form is evident in his claim that the Proto-Masoretic text is the point toward which textual criticism should direct its focus; it should seek to recover that "original text that signals the end of a long compositional history and the start of the history of textual transmission" (*Textual Criticism*, 171).

[12] S. Talmon, "The Old Testament Text," in *The Cambridge History of the Bible. 1. From the Beginnings to Jerome* (Cambridge: Cambridge University Press, 1970) 159–99 (repr. in F. M. Cross and S. Talmon [eds.], *Qumran and the History of the Biblical Text* [Cambridge, Mass.: Harvard University Press, 1975] 1–40); "The Textual Study of the Bible—A New Outlook," in *Qumran and the History of the Biblical Text*, 321–400. Talmon perceives less evidence for text-types in the scrolls, and much more for textual diversity. From this he concludes that the three major types emerged from an

process of textual development that moved from singularity to diversity and back to singularity again[13] speaks volumes about the inconclusive character of the evidence. Indeed, to the barely-concealed chagrin of many text critics the scrolls have provided us with a treasure trove of variant texts existing side by side in a single library. Instead of solving text-critical problems, as was once hoped,[14] the scrolls present a startling new vision of textuality, one in which a community evidently reveled not only in a vast and open collection of texts and traditions, but also in multiple textual editions of those works.[15]

The attempt to define Essene exegetical methods and their results has likewise disappointed some and surprised many.[16] Rather than

---

even wider variety of texts, and that they survived only because the groups that used them were those that endured (the Christian, Samaritan, and Rabbinic groups). Other texts also depended on a community's "sponsorship" and expired with their communities, although traces of their existence survive in the scrolls.

[13] See W. F. Albright, "New Light on Early Recensions of the Bible," *BASOR* 140 (1955) 27–33 (repr. in *Qumran and the History of the Biblical Text*, 140–46); and F. M. Cross, "The Contribution of the Qumran Discoveries to the Study of the Biblical Text," *IEJ* 16 (1966) 81–95 (repr. in *Qumran and the History of the Biblical Text*, 278–92); "The Evolution of a Theory of Local Texts," in R. A. Kraft (ed.), *1972 Proceedings: IOSCS and Pseudepigrapha* (Missoula, Mont.: Scholars, 1972) 108–26 (repr. in *Qumran and the History of the Biblical Text*, 306–20); and "The History of the Biblical Text in Light of Discoveries in the Judean Desert," *HTR* (1964) 281–99. Cross' most recent defense of his thesis is "Some Notes on a Generation of Qumran Studies," in *The Madrid Qumran Congress*, 1–14, esp. 6–11. Using the evidence of the scrolls and the major versions Albright and Cross posited three text families. Some scrolls reflect the Samaritan text tradition (e.g., 4QpaleoExod[m]; 4QNum[b]), others relate best to the Septuagint (e.g., 4QSam[b]; 4QJer[b]), and still others match most closely the Masoretic text tradition (1QIsa[a]).

[14] See, for example, the words of W. H. Brownlee, "The most obvious value of the Qumrân Scrolls is for determining the authentic text of the Old Testament, since indeed every book of the Hebrew Bible (unless it be Esther) is represented among the manuscript fragments of the fourth Qumrân cave alone" (*The Meaning of the Qumrân Scrolls for the Bible* [New York: Oxford University Press, 1964] 3).

[15] Eugene Ulrich was one of the first to recognize this situation, and is one of the few to appreciate its significance; see his collection of essays, *The Dead Sea Scrolls and the Origins of the Bible* (SDSRL; Grand Rapids, Mich.: Eerdmans, 1999).

[16] The literature on this topic is enormous. Some general treatments incude M. Bernstein, "Interpretation of Scriptures," in *EDSS*, 376–83; idem, "Scriptures: Quotation and Use," in *EDSS*, 839–42; G. Brooke, *Exegesis at Qumran* (JSOTSup 29; Sheffield: JSOT, 1985); W. H. Brownlee, "Biblical Interpretation Among the Sectaries of the Dead Sea Scrolls," *BA* 14 (1951) 54–76; idem, *The Meaning of the Qumrân Scrolls for the Bible* (New York: Oxford University Press, 1964); F. F. Bruce, *Biblical Texts in the Qumran Texts* (Grand Rapids: Eerdmans, 1959); D. Dimant, "Qumran Sectarian Literature," in *Jewish Writings of the Second Temple Period* (ed. M. E. Stone; CRINT 2.2; Philadelphia: Fortress, 1984) 503–514; M. Fishbane, "Use,

discover consistent practices among the Essene interpreters comparable to those used by other Jews of the era, scholars have uncovered
almost unrestrained freedom in the Qumran approach to scripture.
The uses of scripture at Qumran range from barely paraphrasing
it[17] to echoing it without citation formulae[18] to quoting it after various citation formulae[19] to rewriting it altogether[20] to systematically
commenting on it.[21] And any hope that the Essenes would at least
have been consistent in the use of their varied exegetical techniques,
reserving certain approaches for certain kinds of texts, has long since
evaporated.[22] Here too unrestrained diversity rules, a diversity that
is governed only by a passion for engaging existing texts and traditions through any means possible.

Authority, and Interpretation of Mikra at Qumran," in *Mikra: Text, Translation,
Reading, and Interpretation of the Hebrew Bible in Ancient Judaism and Early Christianity*,
339–77; H. Gabrion, "L'interprétation de l'Ecriture dans la littérature de Qumrân,"
ANRW 19.1 (1979) 779–848; M. Horgan, *Pesharim: Qumran Interpretations of Biblical
Books* (Washington, DC; Catholic Biblical Association, 1979); S. Lowy, "Some Aspects
of Normative and Sectarian Interpretation of the Scriptures," *ALUOS* 6 (1969)
98–163; J. Maier, "Early Biblical Interpretation in the Qumran Literature," in
Hebrew Bible/Old Testament, 108–121; J. Milgrom, "The Qumran Cult: Its Exegetical
Principles," in G. Brooke (ed.), *Temple Scroll Studies* (Sheffield: Sheffield Academic
Press, 1989) 165–80; D. Patte, *Early Jewish Hermeneutic in Palestine* (SBLDS 22; Missoula,
Mont.: Scholars Press, 1975); E. Slomovic, "Toward an Understanding of the Exegesis
in the Dead Sea Scrolls," *RevQ* 7 (1969–71) 3–15; G. Vermes, "Biblical Interpretation
at Qumran," *ErIs* 20 (1989) 184–91; idem, "Biblical Proof-Texts in Qumran
Literature," *JSS* 34 (1989) 493–508; idem, *Post-Biblical Jewish Studies* (SJLA 8; Leiden:
Brill 1975); idem, *Scripture and Tradition in Judaism* (StPB 4; Leiden: Brill, 1961);
P. Wernberg-Møller, "Some Reflections."
   [17] See, for example, 4Q364–67 4Q158.
   [18] See, for instance, the long list of allusions identified in 1QS by Wernberg-
Møller, "Some Reflections," 41–42, n. 2; likewise, see J. Carmignac, "Les citations
de l'ancien testament, et spécialiement des poèmes du serviteur, dans les hymnes
de Qumran," *RevQ* 2 (1959–60) 357–94.
   [19] Among others, see A. Chester, "Citing the Old Testament," in D. A. Carson
and H. G. M. Williamson (eds.), *It Is Written: Scripture Citing Scripture. Essays in Honour
of Barnabas Lindars, SSF* (Cambridge: Cambridge University Press, 1988) 141–69; and
Fitzmyer, "The Use of Explicit Old Testament Quotations," passim; on the question of variants in quotations and the possibility of misquotations, see most recently
the article and bibliography in E. L. Greenstein, "Misquotations of Scripture in the
Dead Sea Scrolls," in B. Walfish (ed.), *The Frank Talmage Memorial Volume I* (Haifa:
Haifa University Press, 1993) 71–83.
   [20] The term "Rewritten Bible" was developed by Vermes, *Scripture and Tradition
in Judaism*; exemplars at Qumran include 4Q225; the *Jubilees* manuscripts; and perhaps the *Temple Scroll*. Debate as to what constitutes this genre continues.
   [21] See, among other texts, 1Q14–16; 1QpHab; 3Q4; 4Q161–167; 4Q169–71;
4Q173. The most important treatment remains Horgan, *Pesharim*; but see also
Brooke, *Qumran Exegesis*; and Dimant, "Use and Interpretation of Mikra."
   [22] One need only cite the case of 4Q252, the so-called *Commentary on Genesis*. It

The evidence of previous research, then, indicates that scripture at Qumran was not merely a textual artifact for the Essenes to circumscribe, copy faithfully, and interpret in a disciplined and regular fashion. Instead it was a wide variety of texts that inspired reflection on what it means to be human in relationship to God, reflection that produced in turn more such texts which in turn prompted more such reflection. In other words, scripture for the Essenes seems to have been a matter of relationships among people, texts, and traditions, and a process of interpretation and reinterpretation. If this is true, we need to find new ways to study "scripture in the Dead Sea Scrolls" which take into account these characteristics. But first we must offer evidence from the scrolls themselves to raise this suspicion to a reasonable hypothesis. For that I turn to a brief look at Leviticus in the scrolls.

Leviticus at Qumran: Evidence for an Alternative View of Scripture at Qumran

The Book of Leviticus was both richly preserved and widely interpreted at Qumran. No fewer than fifteen Hebrew, Greek, and Aramaic manuscripts from Caves 1, 2, 4, 6, and 11 provide evidence of the book,[23] and the seemingly boundless number of quotations and echoes of Leviticus in the nonbiblical scrolls still remain to be tallied and analyzed. In what follows I offer only a summary of the evidence for the biblical text[24] and analysis of a handful of interpretive passages. That will be quite enough, though, to make an initial case for a revised notion of scripture in the Dead Sea Scrolls, and to set the stage for a larger treatment of Leviticus at Qumran in particular.[25]

---

mixes the *pesher* technique with that of reproducing and/or rewriting material from Genesis. See also the *Reworked Pentateuch* (4Q158; 4Q364–367) which seamlessly merges large portions of the biblical books as we know them with quasi-interpretive comments and passages from other parts of the Pentateuch (especially noteworthy in this regard is the recent study of M. Segal, "Biblical Exegesis in 4Q158: Techniques and Strategy," *Textus* 19 [1998] 45–62).

[23] 1Q3; 2Q5; 4Q17; 4Q23–26, 26a, 26b; 4Q119–120; 4Q156; 6Q2; 11Q1–2.

[24] See in this volume the complete treatment of the text of Leviticus at Qumran by Peter Flint.

[25] See my forthcoming volume treating Leviticus in the Brill series on "The Bible at Qumran: Text and Interpreted."

The first thing that strikes an observer of the Leviticus manuscripts is the variety of forms in which they appear.[26] While most of them seem to have been preserved alone as single manuscripts, one is joined on a scroll with Exodus (4QExod-Lev^f) and another is copied with Numbers (4QLev-Num^a). Square-script Hebrew manuscripts account for the greatest number (4QExod-Lev^f; 4QLev-Num^a; 4Q-Lev$^{b-e, g}$; 11QLev^b), but there are four other manuscripts written in paleo-Hebrew (1QpaleoLev; 2QpaleoLev; 6QpaleoLev; 11QpaleoLev), a mode of text production usually thought to signify the community's reverence for a text. Yet at the same time Leviticus appears in two Greek manuscripts (4QLXXLev; 4QpapLXXLev), a language not thought to have been deeply appreciated by the Essenes. In addition, there is a fairly faithful Aramaic translation of Leviticus (4Q156).

Further indication of textual variety is the fact that while none of the Leviticus manuscripts coheres entirely with the Masoretic, Septuagint, or Samaritan texts alone, they do on occasion agree with one of those traditions against other Leviticus scrolls. For instance, 4QExod-Lev^f adds היא מנחה at Lev 2:1 in agreement with the LXX and the Samaritan texts against the Masoretic text and 4QLev^b, both of which omit the phrase. Similarly, at Lev 17:3 4QLev^d adds the sojourner (והגר ה[גר בישראל) to the list of those prohibited from slaughtering outside the camp in agreement with the LXX and Samaritan texts against the Masoretic text and 11QpaleoLev.

From even these few examples it should be evident that the Leviticus manuscripts at Qumran are mixed. But their diversity and individuality goes even further in that they nearly all preserve unique readings as well. For example, 4QLev-Num^a is missing Lev 14:24, and 14:43 may be shorter than in any other known text. 4QLev^b lacks redundant material in Lev 3:1–11 and at Lev 22:22 the same manuscript adds bruised testicles to the list of characteristics that disqualify an animal for sacrifice (probably by analogy with Lev 21:20). 4QLev^d adds a directive ה- to the phrase מחוץ, "from outside" in Lev 17:3, a change considered by at least one commentator to have halakhic significance.[27] Both Greek manuscripts of Leviticus, though generally like the Old Greek, also go their own way; for instance

---

[26] For a summary of the evidence for Leviticus at Qumran, see E. Eshel, "Leviticus, Book of," *EDSS* 488–93.

[27] E. Eshel, "4QLev^d: A Possible Source for the Temple Scroll and Miqsat Ma'ase ha-Torah," *DSD* 2 (1995) 1–13.

4QLXXLev[a] preserves in a single column of text (Lev 26:2–16) fifteen variants from the Old Greek, seven of which are unique. And among the many one-time readings offered by 11QpaleoLev is the use of additional language from Lev 20:23–24 in 18:27 to harmonize two passages that deal with the presence of the nations in the land. This last example proves that the users of texts at Qumran were aware of the differences among their manuscripts of Leviticus: the supplementary language in Lev 18:27 has been bracketed by the scribe to set it off from the surrounding text.

What we learn from this brief overview is that the text of Leviticus at Qumran remained fluid throughout the life of the community. Moreover, its fluidity often preserved conflicting testimony, a sure sign of the community's sense that "scripture" was not a settled textual phenomenon, the parameters of which were determined for all time. Indeed, the evidence suggests that scripture was still growing and developing, perhaps in response to the needs of the community that revered it. Our look at just a trio of examples of exegesis of Leviticus in the scrolls adds weight to this suspicion.

That the laws of the Pentateuch were interpreted by the people of Qumran is a certainty. There is much evidence to support this claim, not the least of which is the assertion in 1QS 6:7–8 that community members were obliged to spend a part of each night interpreting the law. One of the best-known texts to take up especially the laws in Leviticus is 4QMMT, "Some Works of the Law."[28] Most regard MMT as an early group document that nevertheless retained currency in the community throughout the duration of the group's residence at Qumran. Strugnell and Qimron divide the work into three parts: part A is a calendar; part B is a collection of first person plural speeches addressed to a second person party on disputed halakhic issues; and part C is a first person plural hortatory address to a second person urging the addressee to side with the authors in

---

[28] For the official edition, see E. Qimron and J. Strugnell, *Qumran Cave 4, V. Miqsat Ma'aseh Ha-Torah* (DJD 10; Oxford: Clarendon, 1994). The secondary literature on MMT is abundant and grows ever more enormous. For a good selection of essays, see J. Kampen and M. J. Bernstein (eds.), *Reading 4QMMT: New Perspectives on Qumran Law and History* (SBLSS 2; Atlanta: Scholars, 1996); and the more recent contributions by G. Brooke, L. L. Grabbe, and H. K. Harrington in M. Bernstein, F. García Martínez and J. Kampen (eds.), *Legal Texts and Legal Issues: Proceedings of the Second Meeting of the International Organization for Qumran Studies, Published in Honour of Joseph M. Baumgarten* (STDJ 23; Leiden: Brill, 1997).

the halakhic disputes surveyed in part B. While the supposedly epis-
tolary genre of MMT as a whole is legitimately disputed, parts B
and C together do include the elements of a letter, and part A is
now thought to have been a later addition to the letter.[29] Thus it
seems likely that MMT was, at least at an early stage of its development, a memorandum from the community to an external authority encouraging him to accept the community's views and to reject
those of another, unnamed group. In the course of making his argument, the sectarian author repeatedly takes up laws known from
Leviticus and interprets them for the sake of his particular situation.
I summarize here only two uses of Leviticus in this composition.[30]
Even this little bit of evidence supports the notion articulated
earlier in this paper that "scripture" at Qumran was indeed a fluid
concept.

In what Lawrence Schiffman calls "an almost certain restoration"
MMT B 21–22 seems to prohibit the use of hide or bone from the
carcass of an unclean animal to fashion a carrying handle.[31]

21 [   ] ה] ואף על עור]ות ועצמות הבהמה הטמאה אין לעשות[

22 [מן עצמותמה] ומן ע]ו[ר]ות[מה ידות כ]לים

And concerning the hides and bones of unclean animals: it is forbidden to make handles of vessels from their bones and hides.

The editors, though perhaps less confident of their own restoration
than Schiffman,[32] make the conjecture by comparison with 11QTᵃ

---

[29] See especially J. Strugnell, "Appendix 3; Additional Observations on 4QMMT,"
in DJD 10.203–6; idem, "MMT: Second Thoughts on a Forthcoming Edition," in
E. Ulrich and J. VanderKam (eds.), *The Community of the Renewed Covenant: The Notre
Dame Symposium on the Dead Sea Scrolls* (CJA 10; Notre Dame: University of Notre
Dame Press, 1994) 57–73. For the definitive argument in favor of separating the
calendar from the rest of the work, see J. VanderKam, "The Calendar, 4Q327,
and 4Q395," in *Legal Texts and Legal Issues*, 179–94.

[30] For a fuller treatment of Leviticus in MMT, see my "Rewriting Rubrics:
Sacrifice and Religion in the Dead Sea Scrolls," in J. J. Collins and R. A. Kugler
(eds.), *Religion in the Dead Sea Scrolls* (Grand Rapids, Mich.: Eerdmans, 2000) 90–112.

[31] L. Schiffman, "The Place of 4QMMT in the Corpus of Qumran Manuscripts,"
in J. Kampen and M. J. Bernstein (eds.), *Reading 4QMMT: New Perspectives on Qumran
Law and History* (SBLSS 2; Atlanta: Scholars Press, 1996) 81–98, esp. 88; see also
idem, "*Miqsat Ma'aseh Ha-Torah* and the *Temple Scroll*," *RevQ* 14 (1990) 448–51; idem,
"The Prohibition of Skins of Animals in the *Temple Scroll* and *Miqsat Ma'aseh Ha-
Torah*," *Proceedings of the Tenth World Congress of Jewish Studies: Division A* (Jerusalem:
World Union of Jewish Studies, 1993) 191–98.

[32] L. Schiffman, DJD 10.49, n. 22, 155. See Qimron's slightly more sanguine

51:4–5 (a text that prohibits carrying the flesh, hide, bones or nails of an unclean animal; see also 47:7–15), and with reference to the decree of Antiochus III against bringing the hides of unclean animals into Jerusalem (*Ant.* 12 §146), the mishnaic ruling that defilement comes from the flesh of unclean animals, but not their hide or bones (*m. Hul.* 9:1–2), and the apparently contrasting, strict Sadducean view of related matters alluded to it *m. Yad.* 4:6. Indeed, commentators agree that this ruling, like others in MMT, reflects a stricter "Sadducean" view over against that of the more lenient Pharisees.[33]

This discussion of the MMT ruling may be unnecessarily biased by reliance on the later polemical discussions found in the rabbinic corpus. The debate referred to by Schiffman and others has to do with the bringing of hides and other body parts of unclean animals into Jerusalem, or with carrying the parts of slaughtered animals of any kind. By contrast, the remains of the MMT B 21–22 at least permit conviction on the fact that the ruling deals with hides of animals made into carrying handles (ידות), a much narrower concern than that of any of the related texts cited by the editors of MMT, Schiffman, and Sussmann. Where might the authors of MMT have come upon such a slender interest?

Leviticus 11:25 may have been the hook on which this ruling was developed. With respect to unclean animals the Masoretic text of the verse reads וכל הנשא מנבלתם יכבס בנדיו וטמא עד הערב, "And all who carry *from* their [unclean animals] carcass shall wash his garments and remain unclean until evening." By contrast, where Leviticus 11 again takes up the issue of one rendered unclean by carrying the carcass of an animal or something of it, the text reads וכל הנשא את נבלתה/והנשא את נבלתם (Lev 11:28, 40). A glance at the versional evidence for vv. 25, 28, and 40 proves that the different reading in v. 25 was a puzzle to ancient readers. In v. 25 the Targums and some Syriac manuscripts correct the text to give the equivalent of את נבלתם; in v. 28 the Samaritan Pentateuch and the Greek text read מנבלתם and its equivalent (τῶν θνησιμαίων); and in v. 40 the Greek

---

view expressed in "The Nature of the Reconstructed Composite Text of 4QMMT," in J. Kampen and M. J. Bernstein (eds.), *Reading 4QMMT: New Perspectives on Qumran Law and History* (SBLSS 2; Atlanta: Scholars, 1996) 11–12.

[33] Schiffman, "*Miqsat Ma'aseh*," 442–48; Sussmann, DJD 10.189. For a contrasting view, see Grabbe, "4QMMT and Second Temple Jewish Society," in Bernstein, García Martínez and Kampen (eds.), *Legal Texts and Legal Issues*, 95–97.

reads ἀπὸ θνησιμαίων αὐτῶν. It appears that MMT B 21–22 simply solves the problem in a different way, taking the מן preposition of הנשא מנבלתם as a causative: someone carries *by means of* [a part of] the carcass.[34]

Thus what we encounter here is a text that works to clarify an ambiguous biblical witness on a matter of cultic purity. In doing so the text's authors exhibit the sort of flexibility regarding "scripture" we posited above.[35]

Another ruling in MMT, against sacrificing a parent animal and its offspring on the same day, echoes Lev 22:28 (4QMMT B 36–38). While it is largely reconstructed, the editors and most commentators are confident of the general contours of the halakha.[36]

36 [על העברות אנחנו חושבים שאין לזבוח א]ת האם ואת הולד ביום אחד
37 [ ]ועל האוכל אנח]נו חושבים שיאכל את הולד
38 [שבמעי אמו לאחר שחיטתו ואתם יודעים שהו]א כן והדבר כתוב עברה

> And concerning pregnant animals: we think that one should not sacrifice the mother and its fetus on the same day. Concerning consumption [of the fetus]: we think that the fetus may be eaten, the one that was in the womb of its mother, after it has been slaughtered. And you know that this is so, for the ruling refers to a pregnant animal.

Assuming that the reconstruction in line 36 is correct,[37] the first part of the ruling prohibits *sacrificing* a mother and its fetus on the same day and the second part permits the priests or the one making sacrifice to eat the fetus after properly *slaughtering* it rather than let it go to waste.

Commentators puzzle over this ruling, finding it difficult to relate it to Lev 22:28, and especially hard to explain the use of the כתוב

---

[34] See GKC §119x.

[35] 4QMMT B 22–23 is a logical follow-up to this ruling based on Lev 11:25. It attends to Lev 11:39–40, addressing the case of carrying the hide of a clean animal, saying that such a person is also unclean.

[36] However, Brooke, "Explicit Presentation," in Bernstein, García Martínez and Kampen (eds.), *Legal Texts and Legal Issues*, 72–73, does not share in the confidence others express regarding the reconstruction. As a consequence he resists associating the passage with Lev 22:28.

[37] It is certainly the most likely reconstruction; Qimron and Strugnell, DJD 10. 157–58, explain that they posit העברות because of the same word in the singular at the end of the ruling (line 38). Moreover, they supply לזבוח because in a similar ruling in 11QT 52:5–7 the text uses זבה instead of the שחט of Lev 22:28; the previous ruling dealt with matters relating to animal sacrifice and the sanctuary (see במקדש in line 35); and the second part of this ruling—using the word אכל—has clearly shifted to the question of non-sacral slaughter.

formula prior to a single, non-biblical word.[38] However, it may not be all that much of a puzzle. Leviticus 22:28 only rules against *slaughtering* (שחט) a parent animal (*gender unspecified*) and its offspring on the same day. By contrast this halakha takes up a narrower form of that problem, asking whether one can *sacrifice* (זבח) a *mother* (אם) and the fetus of its womb on the same day. In light of Lev 22:28 and Deut 22:6, no one thinks that it was accepted practice, even among the corrupt Jerusalem priests, to *knowingly* slaughter for sacrifice a pregnant beast. Thus the MMT ruling must address the case of a pregnancy discovered only after the beast had been killed for sacrifice. What should be done under those circumstances, asks the author of MMT? The answer, predicated on the biblical prohibition of *slaughtering* both parent and child beast on the same day, is that both certainly may not be *sacrificed* on the same day. But having gone that far, what is to be done with the fetus that remains? (Apparently the mother would become the sacrificial animal in such circumstances.) MMT says that it should be slaughtered since it cannot survive outside its mother's womb, and it should be eaten (perhaps so that its food value not go to waste). Thus when the ruling closes with the words והדבר כתוב עברה, "And the ruling refers to a pregnant animal," the author is likely claiming that Lev 22:28 can be understood to refer to precisely this sort of case, namely a pregnant animal.[39]

We see a consistent thread in these two reflections on Leviticus in MMT. If a situation presented a question unanswered by the law, there was no hesitancy to construct from the existing legal stipulations found in "scripture" new laws to govern the novel predicament. Thus this interpretation of scripture at Qumran fuels our suspicion that for the Essenes scripture was not just a textual artifact, but an

---

[38] Qimron and Strugnell, DJD 10.157–58, think that the halakha only aims to rule against the intentional slaughter and sacrifice of a pregnant mother and its fetus on the same day. They relate their claim to the widespread debate in early Judaism as to whether a mother and its fetus are separate entities (for citations and secondary literature, see DJD 10.157, n. 115). Schiffman, "*Miqsat Ma'aseh*," 448–51, mentions this passage, but deals mostly with 11QT 52:5–7. His view of the MMT passage is apparently similar to that of Qimron and Strugnell. Qimron and Strugnell, Bernstein ("The Employment and Interpretation of Scripture," in Kampen and Bernstein [eds.], *Reading 4QMMT*, 41) and Brooke ("Explicit Presentation," 73) all express varying degrees of discomfort with the use of the כתוב formula in this instance.

[39] Bernstein, "The Employment and Interpretation of Scripture," 40–41, holds much the same view of the ruling.

ongoing process, one that involved the interaction among existing texts or traditions, the group's context and needs, and questions about what it meant to be human in relationship to God in that particular context.

We turn now to a single instance of Leviticus interpretation outside of MMT to underscore and add to the preceding observations. 4Q265, an enigmatic text related to the *Community Rule*, includes a section that relates the laws in Leviticus 12 regarding impurity after childbirth to the timing for Adam's and Eve's entry into to the Garden of Eden (7 ii 11–17).[40]

11 בשבוע הראיש]ון נברא האדם וכל קודש לא היה לו עד]
12 אשר לא הובא אל נן עדן ועצם [מעצמיו לקחה לאשה ושם לא]
13 [ה]יה לה עד אשר לא הובאה אצ]לו בשבוע השני [
14 [כי] קדוש נן עדן וכול האב אשר בתוכי קדוש [על כן כתוב אשה אשר ילדה זכר]
15 וטמאה שבעת ימים כימי נדת דוותה תטמא וש]לשים ושלשת ימים תשב בדמי]
16 טהרה ואם נקבה תלד וטמאה [שבעים כנדתה וששים יום וששת ימים]
17 [תש]ב בדם טהרה בכול קודש [לא תגע ואל המקדש לא תבוא עד מלאת]

11 In the first week [Adam was created, but he did not have anything holy before 12 he was brought into the Garden of Eden. And a bone [from his bones was taken for the woman . . . but she had no name <?>] 13 before she was brought to him [in the second week . . . 14 for] the Garden of Eden is sacred and all its young shoots are sacred. [Therefore it is written, a woman who bears a male] 15 shall be impure for seven days, as in the days of her menstruation shall she be impure, and th[irty-three days shall she remain in the blood] 16 of her impurity. But if she bears a female, she shall be impure [two weeks as in her mestruation, and sixty-six days] 17 [shall she rem]ain in the blood of her purity. No hallowed thing [shall she touch, nor come into the sanctuary until the days of her purification are fulfilled.]

In spite of the reservations of this text's editor, it seems clear enough that the passage offers an etiology for the rules in Leviticus 12: a woman is impure after childbirth because parturition itself renders all those associated with it unclean.[41] In the case of Adam and Eve at their "birth" there was no woman to become unclean, but they

---

[40] The text and translation are taken from J. Baumgarten, "Purification After Childbirth and the Sacred Garden in 4Q265 and Jubilees," in G. J. Brooke (ed.), *New Qumran Texts and Studies: Proceedings of the First Meeting of the International Organization for Qumran Studies, Paris 1992* (Leiden: Brill, 1994) 3–10, esp. pp. 3–4.

[41] Baumgarten, "Purification," 5–6.

were themselves made so by the process; thus arose the extrabibli-
cal tradition of the delay before they entered the temple-like sanctuary of the Garden of Eden. Notably, though, this view is expressed
somewhat elliptically and it uses an already-interpreted version of
Genesis 2. The elliptical character of the passage can be attributed
to its likely reliance on an otherwise-known exegetical motif, one
that also relies on the expanded account of Genesis 2.[42] A fuller version of the motif appears in *Jub.* 3:8–14. Obviously the author(s) of
4Q265 could trust the audience to be familiar with a more complete account like that of *Jubilees* and with the idea that there was
a delay between the creation of Adam and Eve and their entry into
the garden. So not only does this passage treat the existing "scripture" synoptically, but it does so by including within the scope of
scripture substantially more than what modern readers would call
"Bible." Thus here we have further evidence for a broader and still-
developing notion of scripture at Qumran. The audience there could
be expected to "track" such a sophisticated interpretation as this
because it was their habit to know—apparently by memory—exegetical motifs and to hear them in conjunction with one another, with
the result being new insights gained from the artful merger of motifs.
Once again we see that for the Essenes, it would seem, scripture
was a process of reflection on and interpretation of existing traditions in light of their peculiar circumstances.

Conclusion

From our survey of the texts of Leviticus at Qumran we learned
that there was no established text of the Bible shared among the
Essenes; rather, there were many texts, some of which were in conflict
with one another, but all of which seem to have been taken up and
used with equal freedom, in spite of the group's clear awareness of
the conflicts among them. Our look at the use of Leviticus in MMT
proves that the group, though evidently revering the power of Leviticus to address them in their wonderings about what God would
have them do, felt free to develop from Leviticus new rules by reading it more narrowly here, more expansively there, and synoptically

---

[42] For the notion of exegetical motifs, see J. Kugel, *The Traditions of the Bible*
(Cambridge: Harvard University Press, 1998) 1–41, esp. pp. 24–29.

elsewhere. And we discovered from our brief encounter with 4Q265 that these people swam in a much larger ocean of "scripture" and exegetical motifs than we do, one that they apparently knew well and considered to have some power over their imaginations.

All of this points again in the direction of William Graham's judgment regarding the nature of scripture: at least at Qumran it was not a literary genre, but a religiohistorical one; it was not a static entity, but a dynamic human process of engaging texts and traditions and being engaged by them in the effort to understand life in God's sight. If this judgment is deemed accurate we now must move beyond the fascination with canon, text, and method and develop instead more suitable ways to study scripture in the Dead Sea Scrolls.

JESUS, LEVITICAL PURITY, AND THE DEVELOPMENT OF PRIMITIVE CHRISTIANITY

BRUCE CHILTON

Jesus' practice of commensality is still commonly treated as equivalent to "cleansing all foods" (Mark 7:19)—as if that uniquely Markan construct held for Jesus' whole program, and as if food were the beginning and end of the issue of purity.

Neither proposal has much to offer any more, but a liberal consensus, usually speaking in a Pauline idiom, makes Jesus into a cipher for grace and purity into a cipher for law. In that way, the Gospels support the argument that the Torah and anything like it have been relativized by the revelation of Christ. In its present form, the consensus appears to stretch back to Adolf von Harnack.[1] Many "conservative" scholars attribute such a transcendence of purity to "the historical Jesus" they believe the Gospels attest. In a different idiom, some scholars who proudly insist there is not much at all to be said about the figure of Jesus nonetheless find a way to have him make all foods clean: they make the Hellenistic matrix of the Gospels into an alternative to Judaic conceptions of purity.[2]

Why contest such a powerful consensus? The liberal paradigm encounters and creates more and more anomalies, the greater our

---

[1] See W. Pauck, *Harnack and Troeltsch. Two Historical Theologians* (New York: Oxford University Press, 1968). He aptly and approvingly cites (pp. 31–2) Harnack's formulation in his *Wesen des Christentums*, "The Christian religion is something lofty and simple and is concerned only about one point: Eternal life in the midst of time through God's power and in his presence. It is not an ethical or social arcanum for the purpose of preserving all sorts of things or of improving them." It is the burden of Pauck's study that Harnack's liberal historical approach was consciously framed to challenge ecclesiasticism, a program which is easily instanced in the literature today.

[2] For a searching criticism of this Pauline reading of Jesus, courtesy of the concept of purity, see E. P. Sanders, *Jesus and Judaism* (Philadelphia: Fortress, 1985) 172–87. More recently, see the cautions of R. Horsley, "Jesus, Itinerant Cynic or Israelite Prophet?" in J. H. Charlesworth and W. P. Weaver (eds.), *Images of Jesus Today* (Faith and Scholarship Colloquies 3; Valley Forge, PA: Trinity Press International, 1994) 68–97, as well as his *Archaeology, History and Society in Galilee. The Social Context of Jesus and the Rabbis* (Valley Forge, PA: Trinity Press International, 1996).

knowledge of the New Testament's development and the better our familiarity with the anthropology of purity.

"Cleansing all foods" has the sheen of a general principle, until you see it demolished as such in Acts 15:13–21. Not even the liberal Jesus is up to denying the laws of *kashrut*, only to have his own brother invoke them afresh. That we are dealing with a gloss in Mark is commonly agreed (although who did the glossing is a perennial debate).[3] Had anything like the Markan policy been widely accepted as the dominical position, the early Christian centuries would have seen much less controversy regarding what might be eaten, and with whom.

A closer look at Mark 7 reveals a variety of policies about purity, all of which are attributed to Jesus. An aphorism (7:14–15) speaks of the direction in which impurity flows. The assertion is easily construed in Aramaic attested from Jesus' period and place,[4] and is attractive when it is so rendered:

> *la' demin bar bar-'enasha' / da'teh bey demtamey*
> *bera' min da'tan min / bar-'enasha' 'elen demtamyey.*

Representation in English can preserve its structure:

> nothing that is outside a person / entering one defiles one,
> except that things coming from / a person, these defile one.

To this teaching there are attached distinct instructions about different kinds of purity: not to make the vow of *qorban* to protect one's wealth from one's parents (7:6–13), not to engage in impure thoughts (7:17–23), not to insist upon hand-washing (7:1–5), and—as we have seen—a bold gloss about the significance of the teaching as a whole in regard to foods (7:19c).

The dispute described in Mark 7:6–13 insists that what is owed to one's parents cannot be sheltered by declaring it dedicated to the Temple. The crucial point of such a gambit of sheltering is that one might continue to use the property after its dedication, while what

---

[3] See H. B. Swete, *The Gospel according to St Mark. The Greek Text with Introduction, Notes and Indices* (London: Macmillan, 1913) 152.

[4] For a discussion of the Aramaic *mashal* and its wider setting, see B. Chilton, "A Generative Exegesis of Mark 7:1–23," *The Journal of Higher Criticism* 3 (1996) 18–37; also in B. Chilton with C. A. Evans (eds.), *Jesus in Context. Temple, Purity and Restoration* (AGJU 39; Leiden: Brill, 1997) 297–317.

was given to a person would be transferred forthwith.[5] Complaint about the practice, especially as stated in the simple epigram of Mark 7:11–12, is consistent with taking offense at commercial arrangements associated with the cult (see Matt 17:24–27; Mark 12:41–44 = Luke 21:1–4). The epigram about *qorban* is also hyperbolic, involving the claim that Jesus' opponents do not permit one to do *anything* for one's parents (Mark 7:12). It is reminiscent of the imagery of pearls and swine (Matt 7:6), needles and camels (Matt 19:24 = Mark 10:25 = Luke 18:25), outwardly clean cups which are grossly impure (Matt 23:25 = Luke 11:39).

The hyperbolic epigram has here been enveloped in a much more elaborate argument, which makes the policy about *qorban* seem different from the aphorism about defilement in rhetoric as well as substance. Mark 7:6–13 is a syllogism, developed by means of scriptural terms of reference. Isaiah's complaint[6] frames the entire argument: the people claim to honor God, but their heart is as far from him as their vain worship, rooted in human commandments (Mark 7:6b-7). That statement is related in Mark 7:10–12 to the tradition of *qorban*, taken as an invalidation of the Mosaic prescription to honor parents, in both its positive[7] and its negative[8] forms. The simple and unavoidable conclusion is that the tradition violates the command of God (Mark 7:8–9, 13).

There is nothing complicated about the logic of the argument, and it can easily be structured in a different way. Matthew, in fact, takes us from the conclusion, through the Mosaic prescription in its contradiction by *qorban*, and on to the citation of Isaiah (see Matt 15:3–9). The association of similar passages is reminiscent of the rabbinic rule of interpretation, that a principle expressed in a text may be related to another passage of Scripture, without identity of wording between the two passages.[9] But the scriptural syllogism by no

---

[5] Cf. *m. Ned.* 1:2; 3:2; 5:6; 8:7; 9:1; Z. W. Falk, "Notes and Observations on Talmudic Vows," *HTR* 59 (1966) 309–12; E. Bammel, "Gottes DIATHHKH (Gal. III.7–17) und das jüdische Rechtsdenken," *NTS* 6 (1959–60) 313–19; K. H. Rengstorf, "*korban, korbanas*," *TDNT* 3.860–66.

[6] In Isa 29:13; the form of the quotation is closest to that of the Septuagint, but is identical to no known ancient version.

[7] See Exod 20:12; Deut 5:16.

[8] See Exod 21:17; Lev 20:9.

[9] See B. Chilton and C. A. Evans, "Jesus and Israel's Scriptures," in Chilton and Evans (eds.), *Studying the Historical Jesus. Evaluations of the State of Current Research* (NTTS 19; Leiden: Brill, 1994) 281–335, esp. 294–95.

means requires the invocation of any such formal principle. The fundamental argument is that the Law and the Prophets (the latter in a Septuagintal form, referring to the "commandments of men" in Isa 29:13) are antithetical to the practice of authorities in the Temple.

The next change in rhetoric and setting, however, is of far greater importance in shaping the received meaning of the passage. The rhetorical moves involved are, to begin with, private comment and catalogue (Mark 7:17–23).[10] In a house, apart from the crowd, the disciples ask Jesus what he means in his parabolic aphorism concerning what defiles (7:17). He replies in a way that makes "what goes into a person" the exact equivalent of food, passing through the stomach and into the latrine, where its risible lack of importance at last becomes obvious even to the uninitiated (7:18–19). What proceeds from a person, however, is equated with a list of "bad thoughts": fornications, thefts, murders, adulteries, covetings, evil, deceit, debauchery, envy, blasphemy, arrogance, and foolishness, these are the evils which are said to defile a person (7:20–23).

The two forms of rhetoric, the comment and the catalogue, are symmetrical. The comment, in response to a question (vv. 17–19), specifies that Jesus' original saying had refuted the impurity of foods. The explicit gloss at the end of v. 19, "cleansing all foods," draws out the logic of the comment.[11] The catalogue insists, on the other hand, that defilement is to be taken seriously, once it is understood to be moral instead of alimentary (see the references to defilement, by means of the verb koinow, in v. 20 and in v. 23). The list of intellectual vices defines them as the most dangerous impurities. The two rhetorical forms correspond to two complementary redefinitions of purity. It can no longer be a matter of what is eaten, but must be seen as a matter of what is thought.

Both of those concerns are characteristic of Hellenistic Christianity. Paul reports favorably on the practice in Antioch before emissaries from James came, when meals could be conducted with common fellowship among Jewish and non-Jewish followers of Jesus (see Gal 2:12). According to Paul, the arrival of those emissaries caused Peter

---

[10] It is common to see the section as offering an interpretation of Jesus' aphorism; cf. W. L. Lane, *The Gospel According to Mark* (NIC; Grand Rapids: Eerdmans, 1974) 255–56.

[11] It might be attributed to the present sphere of usage, or—as seems more probable—to the next, Markan phase (see below).

to separate from non-Jews, and even his partner Barnabas acceded
to the separation (Gal 2:12–13). The tendency of Hellenistic communities of Christians to mix their Jewish and non-Jewish con-
stituencies, and therefore to relax or ignore issues of purity in foods,
is here documented by Paul (c. 53 CE).[12]

Vincent Taylor long ago pointed out that the vocabulary of the
list of vices in Mark 7 is more typical of the Pauline corpus (in the
broadest sense) than of any other body of literature in the New
Testament.[13] What is even more interesting is the express connection between such vices and the term "impurity" (akatharsia) in Rom
1:24; Gal 5:19; Eph 4:19; 5:3; Col 3:5. It appears that early Christianity
(which Paul and the deutero-Pauline corpus reflect together with
Mark) saw a shift in the understanding of the medium of impurity:
no longer foods, but moral intentions, conveyed the danger of
defilement.

In order to recast the whole of the tradition as an assertion of a
new medium of impurity, defined on Jesus' authority, a rhetorical
method needed to be found which would point all of the arguments
in the same direction which the latest developments indicated. The
solution was a synthetic device of enormous power: narrative context. The arguments generally—with their varying rhetorics and
different topics—are presented in the context of a dispute. Pharisees
and scribes observe that Jesus' disciples do not wash their hands
before meals; they object, and Jesus goes on to reply by means of
the material already described (Matt 15:1–2; Mark 7:1–2, 5).[14]

The new context, of course, has nothing precisely to do with the
arguments that are then attributed to Jesus. Qorban, the direction of
defilement, the comparative danger of foods and vices are all interesting matters, more or less related by a common interest in what
true purity is, but none of those arguments actually answers the
Pharisaic/scribal objection to not washing prior to a meal. The narrative context proceeds on the supreme and laconic assurance that

---

[12] Cf. Lane, Mark, 256; and B. Chilton, A Feast of Meanings: Eucharistic Theologies
from Jesus through Johannine Circles (NovTSup 72; Leiden: Brill, 1994) 109–30.

[13] V. Taylor, The Gospel According to St. Mark (New York: St. Martin's, 1966) 347.
A comparative table of usages appears on p. 346.

[14] In Luke 11:37–38 the narrative context is developed further. A single Pharisee
invites Jesus to dine, and is astonished when his guest does not wash. Luke permits us to see an alternative development of this cycle of tradition at the time of
that Gospel's redaction.

the readership *already understands* that all Pharisaic/scribal practices
are to be grouped together, and accorded the same sort of weight
one would attribute to washing one's hands. How the community
eats, and with whom, is the central concern, which then determines
one's stance in respect of all that pertains to purity. The context
assumed is very much like that of Galatians 2, although the position taken is different from Paul's, insofar as a positive place is found
for purity.

The power of the new rhetorical device is demonstrated by the
fact that Jesus never answers the question that is posed to him by
the Pharisees concerning the washing of hands. The response needs
to be filled in by the hearer or reader, who has been catechized to
the point that it seems evident that there is a new, inner purity of
moral intention that supersedes the usual practices of Judaism.[15]

What is striking about all these policies is that in their different
ways they map the territory of the clean and unclean, and explain
how to negotiate the boundary. It is quite true that the territory
looks increasingly "moral," and less "cultic," the closer one approaches
the preferred idiom of Mark, but that in no way diminishes the sense
of the contagion which an impure thought can provoke. Indeed, *The
Shepherd of Hermas* opens with a disturbing thought-experiment which
a serious reading of Mark 7 might encourage:[16] what happens when
one of the proscribed designs actually does proceed from one's heart?

That is to say: moving from the "cultic" to the "moral" realm
does not by itself entail a denial of purity. Such moves rather map
a fresh territory of the clean and unclean. Mark 7 in any case not
only deals with the map of the moral "heart," but also with the map
of the household, the map of the Temple, and the map of the human
body.

These changes in the maps and territories of purity suggest that
they might provide us with some purchase for understanding the
cultural development of the Gospels' traditions. With that possibility in mind, I undertook a review more than a decade ago of anthro-

---

[15] In a recent thesis, J. Klawans correctly observes that both sorts of purity are
at issue in Judaism, but he does not take account of variegations and shifts within
Christian practice; see *Impurity and Sin in Ancient Judaism* (Oxford: Oxford University
Press, 2000) 136–57.

[16] See Chilton, "Christianity," in J. Neusner (ed.), *Women and Families* (The Pilgrim
Library of World Religions; Cleveland: Pilgrim, 1999) 26–49.

pological literature concerning purity and sacrifice (purity's first cousin).
What emerged was a model of religions as framing the pragmatic,
affective, and ideological lives of communities with distinct but comparable systems; the whole analysis was related to Jesus' raid on the
Temple.[17]

The link between social eating and sacrifice has been widely attested
in the literature. When I placed Jesus' resistance to Caiaphas' administration of the Temple in that anthropological context, the result
surprised me. When Jesus said "This is my blood" and "This is my
flesh," he referred—not to his personal body and blood in the first
instance—but to the wine and bread of his meals as substitutes for
offering in the Temple from which his action had effectively banned
him.

During the period of that project, Bernhard Lang was pursuing
his interest in anthropology and the Hebrew Bible. He developed
the idea of Jesus' categorical concern for the Temple and the evolution of his meal practice, and went on to write a comprehensive
history of the Eucharist.[18] Meanwhile, I was working at his suggestion on an exegetical study, discerning how different meanings and
practices of the meal developed during the period of the New
Testament's formation.[19]

Lang's historical study and my exegetical study both concerned
how the remembrance of Jesus' words corresponded to distinct practices and beliefs. I left to the side how and why Jesus himself framed
the initial practices that generated those developments. Those inferences are developed in my recent narrative of Jesus' life.[20]

Now if Jesus and his movement are to be understood within practices of purity rather than against them, our liberal myth is evidently
in trouble. An alternative is at a fledgling stage, where much remains to be worked out. Fortunately, that task has been undertaken
vigorously.

---

[17] B. Chilton, *The Temple of Jesus. His Sacrificial Program Within a Cultural History of
Sacrifice* (University Park, Pa.: The Pennsylvania State University Press, 1992).
[18] B. Lang, *Sacred Games. A History of Christian Worship* (New Haven and London:
Yale University Press, 1997).
[19] B. Chilton, *A Feast of Meanings. Eucharistic Theologies from Jesus through Johannine
Circles* (SNT 72; Leiden: Brill, 1994).
[20] B. Chilton, *Rabbi Jesus: An Intimate Biography* (New York: Doubleday, 2000).

One of the inhibitions against seeing Jesus in the context of purity was that, in North American scholarship during the '80's, Galilee was virtually annexed in Athens. If pig bones were found in Sephhoris, the surmise has sometimes run, why would Jesus not have eaten a ham sandwich? Eric Meyers has commented:

> Why so many scholars have associated the rural landscape of Galilee with all its towns and villages as being devoid of Jewish learning as well as lacking in the everyday accoutrements of a Greco-Roman lifestyle is hard to understand, and I leave it for others in the discipline of New Testament to reflect on.[21]

More reflective archaeology has indeed stressed the regionalism of Galilee, evinced by artifacts and architectures that relate to the practice of purity. Marianne Sawicki's "cognitive archaeology"[22] and continuing study of synagogues and *miqvaot*[23] are especially eloquent in this regard, although the earlier contributions of Sean Freyne, James Strange, Eric Meyers and Richard Horsley are also very much a part of the same reevaluation.[24]

The immersion of John the Baptist has obvious implications for the study of Jesus, and my own address of that topic has been ancillary to other concerns. So it was a delight for me to be involved with the rich treatment of Joan E. Taylor, which establishes that John is chiefly to be understood as a purifier. At long last the apologetic picture of John as a prophet of Jesus has been replaced with an appropriate emphasis upon his practice of repeated immersion with repentance.[25]

Of course, shifts in practices of purity as reflected within Christian sources are never likely to be understood apart from an appreciation of cognate shifts within Judaic sources. For this reason, the

---

[21] E. Meyers, "Jesus and His Galilean Context," in D. R. Edwards, C. T. McCollough (eds.), *Archaeology and the Galilee. Texts and Contents in the Graeco-Roman and Byzantine Periods* (SFSHJ 143; Atlanta: Scholars Press, 1997) 57–66, 65–65.

[22] M. Sawicki, *Crossing Galilee. Architectures of Contact in the Occupied Land of Jesus* (Harrisburg: Trinity Press international, 2000).

[23] See D. Urman and P. V. M. Flesher (eds.), *Ancient Synagogues. Historical Analysis and Archaeological Discovery* (StPB 47; Leiden: Brill, 1995, 1998).

[24] See especially in D. Edwards and C. T. McCollough (eds.), *Archaeology and the Galilee: Texts and Contexts in the Byzantine Period* (Atlanta: Scholars Press, 1997), and R. Horsley, *Archaeology, History and Society in Galilee: The Social Context of Jesus and the Rabbis* (Valley Forge, PA: Trinity Press International, 1996).

[25] J. E. Taylor, *The Immerser: John the Baptist within Second Temple Judaism* (Studying the Historical Jesus 2; Grand Rapids: Eerdmans, 1997).

social-historical work of Craig Evans and the systemic analyses of
Jacob Neusner have been fountains of light, and collaborating with
them on several volumes has taught me more than I can say.[26]
Recently, the books of Paula Fredricksen,[27] Elizabeth Schüssler
Fiorenza,[28] Jostein Ådna,[29] and Christian Grappe[30] represent positive
engagement with the issue of purity, and in that they are taking up
the clear if less emphatic leads in the earlier works of James D. G.
Dunn,[31] Ben F. Meyer,[32] Marcus Borg,[33] E. P. Sanders (cf. n. 2),
and N. T. Wright.[34] Indeed, I would suggest that an adjustment to
the cultural issue of purity, together with a willingness to correct the
positivism often associated with "the historical Jesus," represent gen-
uine advances during the past quarter century.

So having learned so much from scholars who have contributed
within the field of purity, what do I believe we can say, and what
questions remains to be answered? By referring to some texts that
have featured centrally in discussion, I will attempt both questions.[35]

The analogy of a map may prove useful again at this point. Rural
Galilee defines Jesus' characteristic activity in the Gospels, and
Jerusalem is the only major city that concerns him. His venture east
of the sea of Galilee is a disaster for a local herd of swine, and for
any probability that he would find accommodation in Decapolis

---

[26] See, for example, B. Chilton and C. A. Evans, *Jesus in Context. Temple, Purity
and Restoration* (AGAJU 39; Leiden: Brill, 1997); B. Chilton and J. Neusner, *Judaism
in the New Testament. Practices and Beliefs* (London and New York: Routledge, 1995).

[27] P. Fredrickson, *Jesus of Nazareth, King of the Jews: A Jewish Life and the Emergence
of Christianity* (New York: Knopf, 1999).

[28] E. Schüssler Fiorenza, *Jesus and the Politics of Interpretation* (New York: Continuum,
2000).

[29] J. Ådna, *Jesu Stellung zum Tempel. Die Tempelaktion und das Tempelwort als Ausdruck
seiner messianischen* (WUNT 119; Tübingen: J. C. B. Mohr [Paul Siebeck], 2000).

[30] C. Grappe, *Le Royaume de Dieu. Avant, avec et après Jésus* (Le Monde de la Bible
42; Geneva: Labor et Fides, 2001).

[31] J. D. G. Dunn, *Jesus and the Spirit: A Study of the Religious and Charismatic Experience
of Jesus and the First Christians as Reflected in the New Testament* (London: SCM, 1975).

[32] B. F. Meyer, *The Aims of Jesus* (London: SCM, 1979).

[33] M. Borg, *Conflict, Holiness and Politics in the Teachings of Jesus* (Studies in the Bible
& Early Christianity 5; New York: Edwin Mellen, 1984). Klawans (pp. 144–45)
attacks Borg for globally distancing Jesus from any system of purity, but it is a
credit to his scholarship that he develops evidence that disconfirms the liberal paradigm he defends.

[34] N. T. Wright, *Jesus and the Victory of God: Christian Origins and the Question of God*
(Minneapolis: Augsburg, 1993, 1996).

[35] For a fuller discussion, and citation of the associated passages, see my *The
Temple of Jesus* and *Rabbi Jesus*.

(Mark 5:1–20); his venture west of Nazareth, into Syro-Phoenecian territory, finds him comparing a Gentile and her sick daughter to dogs (Mark 7:24–30). His exorcisms target unclean spirits (Mark 1:21–28), while his theory of healing is the forgiveness of sin (Mark 2:1–12). Although he keeps his distance form the Temple except for pilgrimage, his cleansing a "leper" allows for a sacrifice demanded by the book of Leviticus (Mark 1:40–44).

The last case deserves a second look, however, because Jesus famously truncates the Levitical procedure. He tells the scabby man to go directly to the Temple, not to the local priest for the preliminary sacrifice of cleansing mandated in the book of Leviticus (Lev 14:1–20). Within the Levitical map, then, Jesus keeps his bearings, but also takes a short cut.

And this is not the only one. He also travels through Samaria (John 4:1–42), sends followers to eat in towns and villages in Galilee on the assumption that what is set before them to eat is pure (Luke 10:1–12), and commends a local centurion near Capernaum for his faith (Matt 8:5–13). When he makes his final visit to Jerusalem, he attacks the merchants of the Temple to insist upon the short cut that ends them all (Mark 11:15–18): Israelite offerings in the sanctuary, without commercial mediation.

As Cecil Roth suggested long ago,[36] Zechariah 14 is central to the events in Jerusalem (at least from the perspective of Jesus' movement). But the prophetic text accounts for more than that. It almost goes without saying—although T. W. Manson did say it, and very convincingly[37]—that the entry into Jerusalem is accounted for, because so many of the elements of Zechariah and its connection with the festal procession of Sukkoth are taken up in the narratives. But beyond that, we also have in Zechariah the forgiveness of sins before the Throne of God (Zech 3:1–5, 9–10; 13:1), the promise of Spirit (4:6;[38] cf. 7:12), criticism of fasting (7:2–7; 8:18–19), the prophecy of bad shepherding in the Temple (11:1–12:9), as well as the removal

[36] C. Roth, "The Cleansing of the Temple and Zechariah xiv 21," *NovT* 4 (1960) 174–81.

[37] T. W. Manson, "The Cleansing of the Temple," *BJRL* 33 (1951) 271–82.

[38] As I have argued elsewhere, this usage is resonant with the principle of contagious purity in Hag 1:14; 2:4–5, 10–19; see B. Chilton, *Jesus' Baptism and Jesus' Healing. His Personal Practice of Spirituality* (Harrisburg: Trinity Press International, 1998) 5, 71–78.

of an unclean spirit (13:2) and the climactic vision of a Sukkoth of universal range and terrible violence in a Temple cleared of merchants (14:1–21).

To deny the relevance of this prophetic and apocalyptic scenario to an understanding of the likely motivation of Jesus is only possible by setting aside many levels of tradition in the New Testament. I understand that the liberal myth would like us to do that, reducing resonances with "the Old Testament" to prooftexts, and discounting cultural resonance with Judaism—even as attested in the Dead Sea Scrolls—on the alleged grounds of the chronology of Rabbinic sources. But were concerns for purity a figment of later authors, that would not account for their rich representations within different layers of the Gospels, nor for the policies later attributed to teachers such as James and Paul.

These policies and their variants support the inference of Jesus' Zecharian program of purity, a practice suited to the conviction that God's Spirit was transforming the world so as to establish the divine kingdom. The great question remains, however, that of the relationship between practice and vision in Jesus' activity and in his movement. When a prophecy is deployed practically, how much must be done on the ground to justify the image in one's mind?

The circles of James, Peter, Barnabas and Paul evidently wrestled with the issue of purity. All four, against their Pharisaic colleagues, could imagine uncircumcised believers, and put their imaginations into baptismal practice (Acts 15:1–30). But their visions, policies, and preferences were far from uniform in regard to the value of circumcision, and the issues of *kashrut* and sexuality saw them busily redrawing maps of purity for the new worlds they were living in. In a sense, it seems easier to trace the application of Jesus' orientation than to specify it. Be that as it may, we can characterize the impact of Jesus' purity on disciplines and passions in his movement after his death.

James and the Question of Purity

The remarkable and early agreement that Jews and non-Jews could be included in the same movement by baptism established a radical principle of inclusion. But it also brought about controversies within the early Church. Although Peter, James, Barnabas, and Paul agreed that circumcision could not be demanded of non-Jews who received baptism, there were strong factions which did not concur (see Acts 11:1–18; 15:1–5). After all, they had the covenant of circumcision (Gen 17:9–14) as a counter argument: although Acts refers only tangentially to those loyal to that covenant as a requirement implied within baptism, they were obviously a considerable contingent within primitive Christianity.

Even among those teachers who extended baptism to non-Jews without requiring circumcision, disagreements arose. The best attested argument occurred at Antioch, where non-Jews had begun to eat together with Jews in the context of Christian practice of Eucharist and other common meals (see Gal 2:11–21). The conflict involved Paul, Peter, James, and Barnabas as its principals. Barnabas, a Levite from Cyprus, was a prominent, loyal recruit in Jerusalem, who enjoyed the trust of the apostles and mediated relations between them and Paul.[39]

The radical quality of Paul's position needs to be appreciated. He was isolated from every other Christian Jew (by his own account in Gal 2:11–13, James, Peter, Barnabas, and "the rest of the Jews"). His isolation required that he develop an alternative view of authority in order to justify his own practice. Within Galatians, Paul quickly articulates the distinctive approach to Scripture as authoritative which characterizes his writings as a whole. His invention of the dialectic between grace and law, between Israel as defined by faith and Israel after the flesh, became a founding principle in the intellectual evolution of Christianity in its formative period.[40] But the Pauline character of that evolution was by no means predictable at the time Paul himself wrote, and Paulinism can become an obstacle to historical study, insofar as it prevents us from imagining other forms of theological commitment to Jesus.

The confrontation at Antioch which Paul recounts to his audience in Galatia did not turn out happily for him at the time. His explanation of his own point of view is triumphant and ringing only in retrospect. Indeed, by the time he recollects his argument for the benefit of the Galatians (to whom he writes some four years after

---

[39] See Acts 4:36–7; 9:26–30; 11:19–26.
[40] See J. Neusner and B. Chilton, *The Intellectual Foundations of Christian and Jewish Discourse: The Philosophy of Religious Argument* (New York: Routledge, 1997) 26–46.

this confrontation), he seems so confident that one might overlook
the fact that he was the loser in the battle with the representatives
of James. It was he, not they, who left the area of Antioch (so Acts
15:22–41).

The position of James is not represented, as is Paul's, by a writing of James himself.[41] But the book of Acts does clearly reflect his
perspective in regard to both circumcision and the issue of purity
(Acts 15), the two principal matters of concern in Galatians. The
account in Acts 15 is romanticized; one sees much less of the tension and controversy which Paul attests. But once allowance has
been made for the tendency in Acts to portray the ancient Church
as a body at harmonious unity, the nature and force of James' position become clear.

The two issues in dispute, circumcision and purity, are dealt with
in Acts 15 as if they were the agenda of a single meeting of leaders in Jerusalem. (Paul in Galatians 2 more accurately describes the
meeting he had with the leaders as distinct from a later decision to
return to the question of purity.) The first item on the agenda is
settled by having Peter declare that, since God gave his Holy Spirit
to Gentiles who believed, no attempt should be made to add requirements such as circumcision to them (Acts 15:6–11). Paul could scarcely
have said it better himself; and that is consistent with the version of
Paulinism represented in Acts.

The second item on the agenda is settled on James' authority, not
Peter's, and the outcome is not in line with Paul's thought. James
first confirms the position of Peter, but he states the position in a
very different way: "Symeon has related how God first visited the
Gentiles, to take a people in his name" (Acts 15:14). James' perspective here is not that all who believe are Israel (the Pauline
definition), but that in addition to Israel God has established a people in his name. How the new people are to be regarded in relation to Israel is a question which is implicit in the statement, and
James goes on to answer it.

---

[41] The Letter of James is at best a derivative reflection of his position; see M.
Dibelius, *Der Brief des Jakobus* (Göttingen: Vandenhoeck & Ruprecht, 1984). Some
recent work would suggest that the letter does reflect a Jacobean position, but actual
attribution to James is difficult to sustain; cf. P. H. Davids, *James* (NIBCNT; Peabody:
Hendrickson, 1989).

James develops the relationship between those taken from the Gentiles and Israel in two ways. The first method is the use of Scripture, while the second is a requirement of purity. The logic of them both inevitably involves a rejection of Paul's position (along the lines laid out in Galatians 2).

The use of Scripture, like the argument itself, is quite unlike Paul's. James claims that "with this (that is, his statement of Peter's position) the words of the prophets agree, just as it is written" (Acts 15:15), and he goes on to cite from the book of Amos. The passage cited will concern us in a moment; the form of James interpretation is an immediate indication of a substantial difference from Paul. As James has it, there is actual agreement between Symeon and the words of the prophets, as two people might agree: the use of the verb συμφονεω is nowhere else in the New Testament used in respect of Scripture. The continuity of Christian experience with Scripture is marked as a greater concern than within Paul's interpretation, and James expects that continuity to be verbal, a matter of agreement with the prophets' words, not merely with possible ways of looking at what they mean.[42]

The citation from Amos (9:11–12, from the version of the Septuagint, which was the Bible of Luke-Acts) comports well with James' concern that the position of the Church agree with the principal vocabulary of the prophets (Acts 15:16–17):

> After this I will come back and restore the tent of David which has fallen, and rebuild its ruins and set it up anew, that the rest of men may seek the Lord, and all the Gentiles upon whom my name is called . . .

In the argument of James as represented here, what the belief of Gentiles achieves is, not the redefinition of Israel (as in Paul's thought), but the restoration of the house of David. The argument is possible because a Davidic genealogy of Jesus—and, therefore, of his brother James—is assumed.

The account of James' preaching in the Temple given by Hegesippus (see Eusebius, *Hist. eccl.* 2.23.1–18) represents Jesus as the son of man who is to come from heaven to judge the world. Those who agree

---

[42] See B. Chilton and J. Neusner, *Judaism in the New Testament. Practice and Beliefs* (London: Routledge, 1996) 104–108.

cry out, "Hosanna to the Son of David!" Hegesippus shows that James' view of his brother came to be that he was related to David (as was the family generally) and was also a heavenly figure who was coming to judge the world. When Acts and Hegesippus are taken together, they indicate that James contended Jesus was restoring the house of David because he was the agent of final judgment, and was being accepted as such by Gentiles with his Davidic pedigree.

But on James' view, Gentiles remain Gentiles; they are not to be identified with Israel. His position was not anti-Pauline, at least not at first. His focus was on Jesus' role as the ultimate arbiter within the Davidic line, and there was never any question in his mind but that the Temple was the natural place to worship God and acknowledge Jesus. Embracing the Temple as central meant for James, as it meant for everyone associated with worship there, maintaining the purity which it was understood that God required in his house. Purity involved excluding Gentiles from the interior courts of the Temple, where Israel was involved in sacrifice. The line of demarcation between Israel and non-Israel was no invention within the circle of James, but a natural result of seeing Jesus as the triumphant branch of the house of David.

Gentile belief in Jesus was therefore in James' understanding a vindication of his Davidic triumph, but it did not involve a fundamental change in the status of Gentiles vis-à-vis Israel. That characterization of the Gentiles, developed by means of the reference to Amos, enables James to proceed to his requirement of their recognition of purity. He first states that "I determine not to trouble those of the Gentiles who turn to God" (15:19) as if he were simply repeating the policy of Peter in regard to circumcision. (The implicit authority of that "I" contrasts sharply with the usual portrayal in Acts of apostolic decision as communal.) But he then continues that his determination is also "to write to them to abstain from the pollutions of the idols, and from fornication, and from what is strangled, and from blood" (15:20).

The rules set out by James tended naturally to separate believing Gentiles from their ambient environment (rather in the manner of *Sib. Or.* 4:24–34). They are to refrain from feasts in honor of the gods and from foods sacrificed to idols in the course of being butchered and sold. (The notional devotion of animals in the market to one god or another was a common practice in the Hellenistic world.)[43] They are to observe stricter limits than usual on the type of sexual activity they might engage with, and with whom. (Gross promiscuity need not be at issue here; marriage with cousins is also included within the likely area of concern. That was fashionable in the Hellenistic world, and proscribed in the book of Leviticus [see chapter 18 and 20:17–21]). They are to avoid the flesh of animals that had been strangled instead of bled, and they are not to consume blood itself. The proscription of blood, of course, was basic within Judaism. And strangling an animal (as distinct from cutting its throat) increased the availability of blood in the meat. Such strictures are consistent with James' initial observation, that God had taken a people from the Gentiles (15:14); they were to be similar to Israel and supportive of Israel in their distinction from the Hellenistic world at large.

The motive behind the rules is not separation in itself, however. James links them to the fact that the Mosaic legislation regarding purity is well and widely known (15:21):

> For Moses from early generations has had those preaching him city by city, being read in the synagogues every Sabbath.

Because the law is well known, James insists that believers, even Gentile believers, are not to live in flagrant violation of what Moses enjoined. In the words of Amos, they are to behave as "all the Gentiles upon whom my name is called." As a result of James' insistence, the meeting in Jerusalem decides to send envoys and a letter to Antioch, in order to require Gentiles to honor the prohibitions set out by James (Acts 15:22–35).

The same chapter of Leviticus that commands, "love your neighbor as yourself" (19:18) also forbids blood to be eaten (19:26) and fornication (19:29 see also 18:6–30). The canonical (but secondhand) letter of James calls the commandment of love "the royal law" (Jas 2:8), acknowledging that Jesus had accorded it privilege by citing it alongside the commandment to love God as the two greatest commandments (see Mark 12:28–32). In Acts James himself, while accepting

---

[43] See V. J. Rosivach, *The System of Public Sacrifice in Fourth-Century Athens* (ACS 34; Atlanta: Scholars Press, 1994). The constraints are sometimes compared to the so-called Noachic commandments of *b. Sanh.* 56a–b, which are held to be binding on non-Jews.

that Gentiles cannot be required to keep the whole law, insists that they should acknowledge it, by observing basic requirements concerning fornication and blood and idolatry.

It is of interest that Leviticus forbids the eating of blood by sojourners as well as Israelites, and associates that prohibition with how animals are to be killed for the purpose of eating (17:10–16). Moreover, a principle of exclusivity in sacrifice is trenchantly maintained: anyone, whether of Israel or a sojourner dwelling among them, who offers a sacrifice which is not brought to the LORD's honor in the Temple is to be cut off from the people (17:8–9). In other words, the prohibitions of James, involving sacrifice, fornication, strangled meat produce, and blood, all derive easily from the very context in Leviticus from which the commandment to love is derived. They are elementary, and involve interest in what Gentiles as well as Israelites do.

James' prohibitions as presented in Acts are designed to show that believing Gentiles honor the law which is commonly read, without in any way changing their status as Gentiles. Thereby, the tent of David is erected again, in the midst of Gentiles who show their awareness of the restoration by means of their respect for the Torah. The interpretation attributed to James involves an application of Davidic vocabulary to Jesus, as is consistent with the claim of Jesus' family to Davidic ancestry. The transfer of Davidic promises to Jesus is accomplished within an acceptance of the terms of reference of the Scripture generally: to embrace David is to embrace Moses. There is no trace in James' interpretation of the Pauline gambit, setting one biblical principle (justification in the manner of Abraham) against another (obedience in the manner of Moses). Where Paul divided the Scripture against itself in order to maintain the integrity of a single fellowship of Jews and Gentiles, James insisted upon the integrity of Scripture, even at the cost of separating Christians from one another. In both cases, the interpretation of Scripture was also— at the same moment as the sacred text was apprehended—a matter of social policy.

In a recent conference at Trinity Western University, John J. Collins referred to the two citations of Amos 9:11 which are attested at Qumran.[44] He relied on his findings in an earlier work that the

---

[44] See C. A. Evans and P. W. Flint (eds), *Eschatology, Messianism, and the Dead Sea*

two exegeses are quite different from one another, and from James'
exegesis.[45] For reasons that will emerge shortly, I would be inclined
to describe the relationship among the interpretations as complementary. The more recently identified usage (in 4Q174 3:10–13, a
florilegium) is the more straightforward, in that the image of the
restoration of the hut of David is associated with the promise to
David in 2 Sam 7:13–14 and with the Davidic "branch" (cf. Isa
11:1–10), all taken in a messianic sense.[46] Given the expectation of
a son of David as messianic king (see *Pss. Sol.* 17:21–43), such an
application of the passage in Amos, whether at Qumran or by James,
is hardly strange. On the other hand, it is striking at first sight that
the passage in Amos—particularly, "the fallen hut of David"—is
applied in the *Damascus Document* (CD 7:15–17), not to a messianic
figure, but to the law which is restored. Now the book of Amos itself
makes Judah's contempt for the Torah a pivotal issue (Amos 2:4),
and calls for a program of seeking the Lord and his ways (Amos
5:6–15), so it is perhaps not surprising that "the seeker of the law"
is predicted to restore it in the *Damascus Document*. Still, CD 7:15–20
directly refers to the "books of the Torah" as "the huts of the king,"
interpreted by means of the "fallen hut of David." Evidently, there
is a precise correspondence between the strength of the messiah and
the establishment of the Torah, as is further suggested by the association with the seeker of the law *not only here*, in the *Damascus Document*,
but also in the *Florilegium*. A contextual reading of the two passages
demonstrates a dual focus, on messiah and Torah in each case, such
that they stand in a complementary relationship. The possibility of
influence on James' interpretation of Amos as presented in Acts 15
may not be discounted.

Eusebius on several occasions refers to James as having been the
first bishop of Jerusalem, and once cites a source of the second century to do so (*Hist. eccl.* 2.1.1–6, 23.1; 7.19; referring in the first passage to Clement's *Hyostyposeis*). James died in the year 62 CE, so that

---

Scrolls (Grand Rapids: Eerdmans, 1997) 151. For an accessible and interesting presentation of the texts in English, see M. Wise, M. Abegg, E. Cook (eds.), *The Dead
Sea Scrolls. A New Translation* (San Franscisco: Harper, 1996).

[45] See J. J. Collins, *The Scepter and the Star: The Messiahs of the Dead Sea Scrolls and
other Ancient Literature* (ABRL; New York: Doubleday, 1995). He develops his reading of the difference between this interpretation and that contained in the *Damascus
Document* on pp. 64–65, following the lead of J. A. Fitzmyer.

[46] Collins, *Scepter and the Star*, 61.

his example had been there to influence the emerging model of hierarchy within the church for more than three decades before the
Pastoral Epistles were written (*ca.* 100 CE). James was clearly a local
leader, who made decisions on the basis of Scripture, and the exercise of his authority—owing to his familial relationship—brought with
it a personal link to Jesus himself on the basis of his own "good
confession" (as the language of 1 Tim 6:13 would have us put it)
before both friendly and hostile witnesses. The personal model of
James as bishop was evidently sufficient to elevate that office above
other possible contenders for what was to be the predominant authority within the church by the end of the first century.

There is, no doubt, a degree of anachronism in Eusebius' portrait
of James' episcopal authority. He conceived of it as being a "throne,"[47]
in the manner of the image of dominant power which only the fourth
century saw fully achieved, and he imagines a formal election as
being involved. In fact, if one sees the espicopate as an entirely
Hellenistic invention with the life of the church, it is easy enough
to dismiss the entire reference to James as bishop. But that would
be a hasty judgment. Eusebius' reference is persistent, and grounded
in an identification of James' office from the second century. Moreover,
if Eusebius helps us correctly to identify that office (for all his own
anachronism), then we can explain the key shift in the hierarchy of
the Church during the first century, from apostolate to episcopate.

Still, the objection remains that *episkopos* is an odd title for James—
or for any Aramaic speaker—to bear. In just this regard, a suggestion made many years ago by Joachim Jeremias turns out to be
crucially important. Jeremias fastened his attention on the office of
the *mebaqqer* at Qumran.[48] That term means "overseer," just as *episkopos* does, and the *mebaqqer* was charged to do many of the same
things that an *episkopos* was do to: he was to teach the Torah (even
to priests) as well as the particular traditions of the Essenes, to admin-
ister discipline, and to see to the distribution of wealth (see CD
13.7–8; 14.8–9, 13–14) As Jeremias points out, comparisons are
made between the *mebaqqer* and a father and a shepherd (CD 13.9);
he does not mention, but the point is worth making, that Christ

---

[47] See *Hist. eccl.* 2.1, 23; 7.19.
[48] His views are accessibly presented in *Jerusalem in the Time of Jesus: An Investigation
into Economic and Social Conditions during the New Testament Period* (London: SCM, 1969)
260–62.

himself is said to be an *episkopos*, to care as a shepherd does in bringing us to God (so 1 Pet 2:25; a letter, like the Pastorals, written around 90 CE). Divine care and the institution of the overseer appear to have been linked in both Essene theology and primitive Christianity.

The connection as Jeremias attempted to make it was vitiated by his surmise that the community at Qumran somehow represented the Pharisaic ethos.[49] In fact, the Essenes pursued their own system of purity, ethics, and initiation, followed their own calendar, and withdrew into their own communities, either within cities or in isolated sites such as Qumran. There they awaited a coming, apocalyptic war, when they, as "the sons of light," would triumph over "the sons of darkness": not only the Gentiles, but also anyone not of their vision (see the *War Scroll* and the *Community Rule*). The culmination of those efforts was to be complete control of Jerusalem and the Temple, where worship would be offered according to their revelation, the correct understanding of the law of Moses (cf. CD 5:17–6:11).

Now James is quite unlike the Essenes in his acceptance of uncircumcised followers of his brother, as well as in his fellowship in Jerusalem with a group centered on the Temple, unassociated with Qumran.[50] But his devotion to the Temple involved tension with the administration there (tension severe enough ultimately to bring about his death), and he appears to have recourse to an interpretation of Scripture which may be compared to that of the Essenes.

The Conflicting Strategies of Peter, James and Paul

Peter seems to have shared with Jesus the hope of a climactic disclosure of divine power, signaled in the willingness of nations to worship on Mount Zion. His offer at the time of the Transfiguration, to build "huts" or *sukkoth*, is not the inept suggestion it is often made

---

[49] For this criticism, see H. W. Beyer, "*episkeptomai*," *TDNT* 1.599–622, 618–619. He develops some of the basic philological evidence in favor of the solution, but then opts for the hypothesis of "something new and distinctive." The problem with that hypothesis is the commonality of the term within Hellenistic culture. A successful solution must explain why it was taken up, not why it was invented. The application of *mebaqqar* to James seems to meet the case.

[50] Another central point of tension is that *mamzerim* were excluded from the *yachad* of Qumran, and Jesus himself was a *mamzer*; see M. Bar-Ilan, "The attitude toward *mamzerim* in Jewish society in late antiquity," *Jewish History* 14 (2000) 125–70.

out to be, but signals his awareness of the sources of Jesus' vision.[51]

Peter perpetuated that vision by means of his fidelity both to breaking bread at home with the disciples and in worship within the
Temple (Acts 2:43–47). At the same time, Acts portrays Peter's activity much further afield. The key to connection between Peter's residence in Jerusalem and his activity in Syria and beyond is provided
by the vision which he relates as the warrant for his visit to the
house of Cornelius, the Roman centurion (Acts 10:1–48).

Peter defends his baptisms in the house of Cornelius on the basis
of his vision in the course of a dispute with those who argued that
circumcision was a requirement of adherence to the movement (Acts
11:1–18). He cites his activity among non-Jews at a later point, in
the context of the so-called the Apostolic Council (Acts 15:7–11).
Throughout, the position of Peter appears to have been consistent:
God may make, and has made, eschatological exceptions to the usual
practice of purity. Those exceptions include the acceptance of uncircumcised men in baptism, and fellowship with them.

The policy of accepting non-Jews, who were baptized but not circumcised, was perhaps the most important decision, which the primitive Church made. As we have seen, it is presented as formalized
in the book of Acts in a single session (Acts 15:1–35), but the reference to the dispute earlier (in Acts 11:1–3) shows that the policy
was framed over a number of years.

In his letter to Galatians, Paul reflects not only the discussion at
the "Council," but the attempt to grapple with the consequences of
baptizing non-Jews in Jesus' name at an earlier stage (Gal 2:1–10).
Paul records the agreement of the "pillars" of the Church in Jerusalem
that there should be an apostolate to the circumcised (represented
by Paul) as well as to the circumcised (represented by Peter). (Of
course, other apostolates—such as James'—also concentrated on the
circumcised; Paul's point is that Peter was especially concerned with
the circumcised outside of Jerusalem and even territorial Israel.) Those
pillars include James, Jesus' brother, Peter himself, and John. Paul
goes on to describe the contention which emerged in Antioch, a dispute which split the Church for decades, but the remarkable agreement on a central point should not be overlooked: James, Peter, and

---

[51] See B. Chilton, "The Transfiguration: Dominical Assurance and Apostolic
Vision," *NTS* 27 (1980) 115–124.

Paul agreed that there was a place for non-Jews within the movement. Those who disagreed with them, the adherents to the Abrahamic requirement of circumcision (see Gen 17:10–14), were not silenced, and maintained their position (see Acts 11:2–3; 15:1; Gal 5:2–12). Ebionite Christianity appears to have been the principal wing of the Church in the second century in which their stance prevailed (see Irenaeus, *Haer.* 1.26.2). However much the position of the circumcisers could claim the warrant of Scripture, the vision of Peter represents the dominant tendency towards an acceptance of non-Jews.

Yet while Paul held that all believers were a new "Israel of God" (Gal 6:16), defined by having faith in Jesus just as Abraham had faith in God (Gal 3:6–9), Peter conceived of the acceptance non-Jews in baptism more as a gracious inclusion than the "new creation" of which Paul spoke (Gal 6:15). Once non-Jews had been accepted in baptism, Peter might sometimes have fellowship with them, and sometimes not. As an apostle, such contact might be necessary; as a faithful Jew, it was not natural. Within Paul's perspective, that was hypocrisy; within Peter's perspective, it was a consistent consequence of proceeding by the revelation of whom and what God accepts (and when), rather than a predetermined policy. James, while accepting the baptism of non-Jews, nonetheless maintained that a policy of their separation from Jews should be followed, unless they observed enough of the commonly acknowledged rules of purity to honor in practice the status of the Torah as the revelation to Moses, warranted in Scripture.

The Resolution of Purity and Virtue in Hellenistic Christianity

The logical extension of Paul's conception was that all things are pure to the pure, precisely the formulation attributed to him in Titus 1:15. But Paul's actual practice turned out to be otherwise. He indeed departs from the policy of James in 1 Corinthians 8, by accepting that food offered to idols might be eaten, on the grounds that idols represent entirely fictional gods (1 Cor 8:4–6). But he also warns against eating such food if those who believe in such gods are confirmed in their idolatry, "and their conscience, being weak, is defiled" (1 Cor 8:7–13, especially v. 7). The defilement here is internal and moral, rather than alimentary, but it is nonetheless dangerous; Paul declares that he would prefer not to eat meat at all, rather than cause a brother to sin (1 Cor 8:13; see the restatement of the principle in Rom 14:13–23). By means of his own, characteristic argument, Paul approximates to what the Rabbis would come to teach concerning the danger of idolatrous feasts (see '*Abod. Zar.* 8a, instruction in the name of R. Ishmael). Even more signally, from the point of view of the development of Christianity, Paul attests the tendency to collapse the categories of sin and purity into a single conception of mortal error.

Paul in this aspect reflects a more general tendency in Hellenistic Christianity. In his letters and in letters attributed to him there is an express connection between named vices (which are catalogued) and "impurity" (Rom 1:24; Gal 5:19; Eph 4:19; 5:3; Col 3:5). Early Christianity saw a shift in the understanding of the medium of impurity: no longer foods, but moral intentions, conveyed the danger of defilement. And those intentions are as specifically identified in the New Testament as impure foods are discussed in Rabbinic literature, because the danger in both cases was understood to be an impurity which made a real and dangerous separation from God.

The cataloguing of sins, and their classification with impurity, is scarcely a Christian invention. It is represented, for example, in Wis 14:22–31. But the genre is mastered to brilliant effect in Rom 1:24–32; Gal 5:19–21; Eph 5:3–5; Col 3:5–6, and is taken up in the period after the New Testament (see *Didache* 5; Shepherd of Hermas, *Mandate* 8). What is striking in each case is not only the equation of impurity and sin, but a clear indication that impurity as such remains a fundamental category: sexual contact, a concern from at least the time of Leviticus 18, survives the declining significance of alimentary purity, even within Paul's thought. There is no question, therefore, of purity simply being abstracted into the realm of intention. Rather, intentionality of practice, as well as observation of the integrity of one's body, are together held to define an ambit of purity. On such an understanding, one's body was indeed a temple of the holy spirit (see 1 Cor 6:18–20; see 3:16–17), and a rigorous attitude towards marriage is completely coherent with the emphasis that a new purity is required by God for the inheritance of his kingdom (see Matt 5:27–28, 31–32; 19:3–12; Mark 10:2–12; Luke 16:18; 1 Cor 7:10–16).

The success of the gospel of Jesus within the Hellenistic environment of primitive Christianity was in no small measure a function of its ability to frame a rational, practical, but stringent system of purity. The marketplace is declared pure in itself, provided it does not encourage the defilement of idolatry, and the requirements of James are largely forgotten. But moral, and especially sexual, requirements make it clear that purity has not been abandoned as a regulatory system, despite the efforts of Paul in regard to alimentary purity.

The success of the resolution of virtue and purity within primitive Christianity was sealed by the attribution to Jesus of the identification between the two. The attribution appears in Mark (and the Matthean parallel) just after Jesus' own teaching about what truly defiles (Mark 7:15). First by means of comment in response to a question (Mark 7:17–19), and then by means of comment and catalogue (Mark 7:20–23), the rhetoric attributes the shift in the medium of impurity to Jesus himself. The rhetoric is the product of an interpretative community, a circle sufficiently influential to cast what it had been taught concerning Jesus' principle into the terms of reference of the Hellenistic mission.

The circle is concerned with issues of fellowship at meals, but is unwilling to dismiss purity as a divine category, as Pauline rhetoric could do (see Rom 14:14). The circle responsible for Mark 7:20–23, on the other hand, insists upon the danger of impurity but sees the contagion in moral terms. Such an attitude is closer to that of the lists of vices which Paul repeats than it is to the innovative aspects of his argument and rhetoric. The identification of the authority behind the circle is obviously a matter of inference, but—among the possibilities given by Paul in Galatians 2—the most plausible suggestion is that it represents the apostolate of Barnabas. Barnabas is described by Paul as being less engaged with purity than either James or Peter, but also as having been taken up in their "hypocrisy" (Gal 2:11–13). In effect, once Jesus enters the house in Mark 7:17, a new social setting is addressed, and the point of his teaching, as commented upon and expanded by means of a catalogue, is that vices rather than foods are sources of impurity. The categories of the pure and the impure are maintained, but they are worked out on the basis of moral rather than alimentary materials.

The dramatic shift in rhetoric and meaning within the Barnaban circle could not have succeeded by means of the comment (Mark 7:17–19) and the catalogue (Mark 7:20–23) alone. After all, they were by way of appendix to the principal matter of the emerging text, which still concerned *qorban* (Mark 7:6–13) and the direction of impurity (Mark 7:14–15). Beginning from the aphorism of Jesus in regard to the direction of defilement, his movement developed a palimpsest of policies in regard to purity. James' circle—focused on the Temple and a literal interpretation of Scripture by an authoritative *mebaqqer*—likely developed the syllogism about *qorban*, just as Barnabas' circle defined a purity of moral intent.

In order to recast the whole of the tradition as an assertion of a new medium of impurity, defined on Jesus' authority, the narrative context of Mark, with its metonym of washing hands (Mark 7:1–5), succeeded brilliantly. So brilliantly that its theological argument has been swallowed by a liberal Christianity which claims its interests are historical. The Gospels, as well as the more obviously Hellenistic documents of the New Testament, attest the resolution of virtue and purity that was a vital part of the genius of Christianity. That fusion, far from transcending purity, provided the category with an inextricably moral dimension.

THE RABBINIC RECEPTION OF LEVITICUS

Hannah Harrington

This article is an exploration of the way in which Leviticus was interpreted among the early Rabbis. I would like to challenge recent
claims about the relationship of Leviticus to three rabbinic documents: the Mishnah, the *Sifra* and *Leviticus Rabbah*. My conclusions,
in advance, are 1) the Mishnah depends on Leviticus; 2) the agenda
of the *Sifra* is not to critique the logic of the Mishnah; and 3) *Leviticus
Rabbah* did not invent the equation of holiness and ethics. Finally, I
would like to bring into relief elements of the agenda behind these
rabbinic texts.

Jacob Neusner (the most prolific writer on the rabbinic understanding of cult and purity) has stated that rabbinic documents reveal a
radical diachronic development in their approach to Leviticus, and
indeed all of Scripture. According to Neusner, at the end of the second century CE the Mishnah's writers selected certain ideas from
Scripture and developed them along the lines of philosophical logic,
sometimes even contradicting Scripture. This "philosophy" was
acclaimed by Jews to the highest degree, and Neusner argues that
"rabbinic literature responds to the crisis precipitated by Mishnah's
style, content, and success." In the third century, the author of the
Sifra, disturbed by Mishnah's lack of appeal to Scripture, provided
exegetical links to keep the Mishnah tethered by Scripture claiming
that the Mishnah really did get its ideas from Scripture. However,
Neusner argues repeatedly that the Mishnah does not depend on
Scripture but is an autonomous document "which appeals to the
intrinsic traits of things to accomplish classification and hierarchization."[1] The third link in the chain is *Leviticus Rabbah* (fourth-fifth century), which, according to Neusner, interprets Leviticus in terms of
the salvation of Israel through ethics rather than through the cult.

---

[1] For example, J. Neusner, *Tosefta, Tractate Abot, and Earlier Midrash Compilations:
Sifra, Sifré to Numbers, and Sifré to Deuteronomy* (vol. 2 of *The Judaism Behind the Texts:
The Generative Premises of Rabbinic Literature*; Atlanta: Scholars Press, 1994) 56.

In Neusner's view, rabbinic texts represent different worldviews, and sometimes he states that they represent separate Judaisms.[2]

In my view, all of the above rabbinic texts presuppose a thorough knowledge of Scripture which forms a base for discussion. This is not to say, by any means, that these texts form a harmonious whole. To be sure, disagreement is not scarce among the Rabbis. Nevertheless, the ideological puzzle pieces of the individual texts fit together surprisingly well when Scripture is allowed into the equation.[3] I claim that Neusner has compartmentalized the rabbinic texts excessively. He has not taken into sufficient account the biblical pillars supporting the entire enterprise.

Let us now examine each of these three documents and their relationship to Leviticus. First, the Mishnah. Neusner approaches the Mishnah with the assumption that since the Mishnah does not formally appeal to Scripture, it is not a religious text.[4] Does Neusner mean that the Rabbis first began reading Leviticus seriously only when the Sifra compiled its exegesis in the third century? He states, "Between 200 and 400, Judasim changed from a philosophy to a religion. . . . When, finally a religious sytem appeals as an important part of its authoritative literature or canon to the Hebrew Scriptures of ancient Israel or 'Old Testament' we have a Judaism."[5] Do we then conclude that Judaism as a religion did not begin until the *Sifra* appealed to Scripture? Rather, Scripture is at the very heart of the

---

[2] For example, sometimes Neusner calls the Mishnah a separate Judaism from the *Sifra* and other times he insists that it is not a Judaism at all but a philosophical law code; J. Neusner, *The Canonical History of Ideas, The Place of the So-called Tannaitic Midrashim: Mekhilta Attributed to R. Ishmael, Sifra, Sifre to Numbers, and Sifre to Deuteronomy* (Atlanta: Scholars Press, 1990) 8, 33–34.

[3] Neusner is certainly right that the final redactors do shape the texts in light of their own "ideological positions." The documents are not harmonious, internally consistent texts. "Nevertheless," as Daniel Boyarin says, "the texts cannot be made to reveal the autonomous worldviews of autonomous socio-cultural groups, either by any modern theory of texts or culture, or by their specific nature"; see D. Boyarin, "On the Status of the Tannaitic Midrashim" *JAOS* 112 (1992) 457–58.

[4] Boyarin, "On the Status," 461, check also J. Neusner, *Sifra in Perspective: The Documentary Comparison of the Midrashim of Ancient Judaism* (Atlanta: Scholars Press, 1988) 205.

[5] Neusner, *The Canonical History of Ideas*, 33–35. Cf. Boyarin's point that there must have been a Judaism during the time of the Mishnah even if one says it is not reflected in the Mishnah, and this Judaism would have appealed to Scripture; such an appeal is exactly what we find in the Midrash; see Boyarin, "On the Status," 461.

Mishnah, and a careful reading of both will uncover the logic of the Mishnah since the latter does not explain its exegetical processes.

Now the Mishnah does not spend its time with the obvious, explicit parts of Leviticus. For example, a list of acceptable sacrifices or forbidden foods is nowhere to be found. This information is presupposed as common knowledge (cf. *m. Hul.* 3:6). The Mishnah is interested rather in deciding the ambiguous cases, filling in the vague fabric between the explicit seams of Scripture, as it were. The Rabbis fill in the gaps of Leviticus by utilizing information and principles from Scripture itself. Even though the Mishnah does not make formal appeal to Scripture, the reader will recognize its support in the background. To illustrate this, I will examine three Mishnaic concepts Neusner uses to uncover the Mishnah's philosophy: מקוה, טבול, יום and כונה. My claim is that all of these concepts are based squarely on Leviticus and simply would not have existed without it.

Let us start with the טבול יום, a person who has completed immersion after impurity but has not completed the appropriate waiting period before he can be pronounced "pure." For example, a person who has had sexual intercourse on a given night bathes in the morning and then, according to the Rabbis, may go about normal business affairs as long as the person waits until evening to handle sacred items or enter sacred areas. Scripture refers to this individual as "impure until the evening" (Lev 15:16–18). Thus, even though bathing may have occurred a few hours after sexual intercourse, the couple is not truly pure until the following sunset. Now the Rabbis refer to the טבול יום as "pure" even though the person is forbidden to the sacred until the sun sets. Neusner makes much of this apparent contradiction of the Mishnah and Scripture. Scripture labels this intermediary status, impure; the Rabbis label it pure. He also infers from this data that while the Rabbis regard immersion in water as purifying, Scripture implies that water ablutions have no purifying effect since the purifying person is "impure" until evening even though he may have bathed in water before evening. Neusner concludes that for Scripture, "It is perfectly clear, therefore, that ordinary water is ... not understood as a substance capable of purifying anything from uncleanness."[6]

---

[6] J. Neusner, *A History of the Mishnaic Law of Purities* (vol. 19; Leiden: Brill, 1977) 4.

In my view, there is no blatant contradiction between the view of the Mishnah and that of Leviticus with regard to purification. The Torah itself ascribes value to water ablutions even if the purification time period is not up. First, the leper who has not completed all of his purification but has bathed is admitted to the camp and is even described as טהור, "pure" (Lev 14:8). He is clearly not totally pure because he is not allowed to go home until the end of the seventh day at which time he completes the rest of the purification rites. Another example of water purging impurity without any other requirement is the rinsing of hands by a זב. The זב, probably a gonorrheic, is highly contagious to others with whom he comes into contact. However, if he washes his hands before contact, he will not transmit impurity (Lev 15:11). Another example of water sufficing to shed a certain amount of impurity is the man who lets the scapegoat go on Yom Kippur (Lev 16:26). This person becomes impure by virtue of this task and must launder his clothes and bathe. As soon as he does this, however, he is allowed to return to the camp. He does not have to wait for sunset or perform any other ritual to be granted this permission. Therefore, Scripture supplies clear precedents for the effective purifying value of water on its own without which the Rabbis would never have been able to institute the category of טבול יום. The fact is, Scripture is ambiguous on the issue of intermediary status. Its statement that the purifying person is impure until evening has to be qualified by several examples of individuals who, while not completely pure, are not completely impure either.

As additional proof that the טבול יום is a valid reading of Scripture, some of the Qumran authors concur with the principle, if not the term, of טבול יום. 4Q514 states that the corpse-contaminated person is allowed back into the city once he bathes even though he remains impure to a lesser degree for an entire week (4Q514 lines 3–9; cf. 1QM 14:2–3).[7]

---

[7] J. Milgrom, "Studies in the Temple Scroll," *JBL* 97 (1978) 513–14; *Leviticus 1–16* (AB 3; New York: Doubleday, 1991) 970–71. The writer of the Temple Scroll is adamant that the impurity bearer remains impure until the end of the prescribed period, but then he is primarily concerned about the sacred realm; cf. 11QT 49:16–17. The Temple Scroll requires two immersions for impure persons who wish to enter the Holy City: the first probably allows contact within the lay sphere and the second with sancta (11QT 45:7–10). Why have two immersions if neither has any purificatory effect without sunset?

The מִקְוֶה, or immersion pool, is another rabbinic concept at issue. Neusner claims that the מִקְוֶה is a rabbinic innovation which reflects the Mishnah's stance that stasis is the proper response to persecution.[8] Still water is associated with this stasis.

> The Mishnaic system to begin with thus provides a mode of purification different from that specified in the Written Torah for the Temple, but analogous to that suitable for the Temple. ... They bathe not in running water, in anticipation of the end of days and for the sake of eschatological purity, but in still water, to attain the cleanness appropriate to the eternal Temple, the cycle of cleanness and the perpetual sacrifice. ... As sun sets, bringing purification for the Temple, so rain falls, bringing purification for the Table.[9]

Here Neusner makes a claim about the Mishnah's eschatology based on a comparison of its purification laws with those found in Scripture. However, I argue that the Mishnah does not require a different mode of purification than Scripture, but is, in fact, interpreting Scripture in a manner consistent with the text. Leviticus 15:11 insists that persons who engage in sexual intercourse, for example, must immerse in water enough to cover the entire body. Leviticus 11:36 states that both a spring and a cistern connected to a source of water are impenetrable to impurity. The Rabbis logically infer here that the immunity of the spring and cistern makes both prime sources of purification. The Rabbis, nevertheless, probe the question of why a cistern shares the immunity of a spring when water in other vessels is subject to impurity (Lev 11:32–33). They conclude that the cistern, like the spring, must be connected to a natural source of water. Thus, the concept of the reservoir, אוֹצָר, is born to ensure that still pools not only remain sufficient but that they are connected to a natural source of water (Sifra Shem. Sher. par. 9:1). Only rain or spring water which comes from God will affect purification. The Damascus Document too apparently regards these notions as Scriptural, stating that im-mersion in a rock pool purifies if its water is sufficient to

---

[8] Neusner claims that the Rabbis' selection of ritual purity as the most central component of the Mishnah reflects their position that only by extending the purity of the biblical sanctuary into common homes can Jews cope with and even ignore the catastrophes of Temple loss (70 CE) and national disintegration (135 CE). The Mishnah's focus on ritual purity, according to Neusner, creates a new worldview, one which has little need of Scripture; J. Neusner, Purities, vol. 22, 301–3.

[9] Ibid., 87.

cover a person (CD 10:11–13). Thus, the notion of the מקוה is not
a rabbinic invention but rather a valid interpretation of Scripture.

A third levitical concept which is associated with the Rabbis is
that of כונה, intention. Throughout the Mishnah the intention of a
person often shapes the law in a given situation. For example, as
soon as the owner intentionally separates an animal from his flock
(by word or deed) and designates it holy, it is treated as such. As
the Mishnah says, "One's word of mouth [dedication of an object]
to the Most High is equivalent to one's act of delivery to an ordinary person" (m. Qidd. 1:6; cf. Jub. 17:3; cf. Lev 6:18; cf. Exod 29:27).
Improper intention can render a sacrifice unfit.[10] Similarly, intention
alone can render an item susceptible to impurity. For example, intentional irrigation of one's crops will render them susceptible to impurity; accidental watering or rain will not (cf. m. Mak. 2:3–4).

Now Neusner concludes from these and other examples that, in
contrast to Scripture, the Rabbis' "fundamental question" is "What
can a man do?" He explains, "The evidence of the Mishnah points
to a Judaism which answers that question simply: Man, like God,
makes the world work. . . . The Mishnah's Judaism is a system built
to celebrate that power of man to form intention, willfully to make
the world with full deliberation, in entire awareness, through decision and articulated intent."[11]

Now the question is, are the Rabbis introducing a new worldview
by emphasizing human intention? Does the Torah take intention
into account? One need not look beyond Leviticus to find that the
answer is yes. First, Lev 5:5 makes it clear, that the sinner's offering
is not accepted unless there is sincere confession of wrongdoing.[12]

---

[10] J. Neusner, A History of the Mishnaic Law of Holy Things (vol. 6; Leiden: Brill,
1980) 26–27.

[11] J. Neusner, Judaism: The Evidence of the Mishnah (Chicago: University of Chicago
Press, 1981) 282–83: "And . . . so does the Mishnah assess the condition of Israel,
defeated and helpless, yet in its Land: without power, yet holy; lacking all focus,
in no particular place, certainly without Jerusalem, yet set apart from the nations. . . .
The evidence of the Mishnah points to a Judaism defiant of the human condition
of Israel, triumphant over the circumstance of subjugation and humiliation, thus
surpassing all reality."

[12] R. Simeon b. Lakish explains: "Great is repentance, which converts intentional
sins into unintentional ones" (b. Yoma 86b). Likewise, "How is the high priest's deliberate sins atoned by the bull? Because he has confessed his brazen and rebellious
deeds it is as if they become unintentional ones before him" (Sifra Ahare par. 2:4,
6; cf. t. Yoma 2:1; Lev 5:20–26 [Heb]).

Jacob Milgrom has demonstrated that already in Leviticus human intention is the key element in determining the sanctity of all offerings.[13] The offerings of Leviticus are holy before they are brought to the sanctuary while they are still with the owner (cf. Lev 6:18).[14] Leviticus 27 catalogs a number of offerings, animals, houses, other property, which are dedicated simply by an individual's intentional designation. In fact, the term תרומה, offering, derives from the verb הרם *hif'il*, whose basic meaning is "remove, set aside." Thus, offerings are dedicated by the offerer's expressed intention, either in word or deed. With regard to irrigation, Lev 11:33 states that if water is put on crops (יותן), it renders them susceptible to impurity. The Rabbis notice this from this verbal form that a subject has acted purposefully on the water, i.e., someone has intentionally irrigated the crop. Thus, a farmer's irrigation of his crops renders them susceptible to impurity but rain, an uncontrollable factor, does not. Hence, it should come as no surprise that intention, already a key factor in Scripture, is utilized by the Rabbis in determining the law.

Our next document is the *Sifra*. The *Sifra* is a compilation of tannaitic exegesis on Leviticus that was compiled shortly after the Mishnah in the third century CE.[15] Its Rabbis are by-and-large the same as those credited in the Mishnah. The *Sifra* is a commentary on Leviticus which reveals the process by which the Mishnah's conclusions were exegeted from Scripture. Neusner, however, understands the *Sifra* to be a *de novo* composition of the third century, the primary motivation of which is to critique the Mishnah's logic and lack of appeal to Scripture.[16] Neusner assumes that the process of exegesis detailed in the *Sifra* is not the process which brought the Mishnah to its conclusions. Rather, "*Sifra*'s great theme is the critique of classification without Scripture."[17] According to Neusner, the *Sifra* is against classification and codification without explicit reference to Scripture.

---

[13] Milgrom, *Leviticus 1–16*, 486; cf. also H. Eilberg-Schwartz, *The Human Will in Judaism: The Mishnah's Philosphy of Intention* (Atlanta: Scholars Press, 1986) 148, who recognizes biblical antecedents in the Mishnah's laws of intention.

[14] In fact, it is the label of "most holy" or "lesser holy" that determines where the animal is to be slaughtered, Milgrom, *Leviticus 1–16*, 486.

[15] Boyarin, "On the Status," 460.

[16] Neusner, *Sifra in Perspective: The Documentary Comparison of the Midrashim of Ancient Judaism* (Atlanta: Scholars Press, 1988) 204, writes, "Scripture occupies an odd position in *Sifra*, dominant for everything, definitive, as to the message of the document, of nothing."

[17] Neusner, *Sifra in Perspective*, 205.

Neusner discusses the difference between the logic of the Mishnah and *Sifra* on Leviticus. The Mishnah "appeals to the intrinsic traits of things to accomplish classification and hierarchization." By this, Neusner means that the Mishnah's authors studied various topics of interest and imposed rules on analogous cases. In contrast to Mishnah's analytical reasoning, Neusner says the *Sifra* links the law of the Mishnah to Scripture by "exegetical construction"; the *Sifra* is a "lavish exposition of the exegetical process, its extravagant articulation of the steps and stages of reasoning, from proposition to text, from text to proposition."[18] That is, the *Sifra* starts with Scripture's terms and then uses exegetical reasoning to derive its lists and categories forming the whole of the law from its parts.

Neusner is correct that the Mishnah and *Sifra* reveal two different kinds of reasoning processes, however, this does not place the two documents at odds with each other. As E. P. Sanders and others have pointed out, Neusner does not take into sufficient account the notion of genre.[19] The *Sifra* is a commentary whereas the Mishnah resembles a law code In his efforts to understand each work on its own terms, Neusner has come up with a separate worldview and circle of Rabbis for each document even though the documents attribute their data by and large to the same sages. He assumes that since the *Sifra* is a Bible commentary, its compilers are opposed to

---

[18] J. Neusner and W. S. Green (eds.), *Approaches to Ancient Judaism: Theory and Practice* (vol. XI/1; Missoula, MT: Scholars Press, 1978) 89.

[19] E. P. Sanders, *Jewish Law from Jesus to the Mishnah* (London: SCM, 1990) 312–22. The Rabbis omit theology (sin/atonement issues; suffering/penitence; divine power/grace) and history so they must think it is unimportant. According to Neusner, the Mishnah is opposed to what it omits. Sanders rightly complains that Neusner claims he only knows what he can show, but then says the Mishnah is a philosophy about "creation and revelation and redemption," and then goes on to say "but it does not speak of these things." Mishnah's real meaning can be found only in "the deep structure of [a] tractate." Mishnah "rarely bothers to spell out what we know." Thus, as Sanders concludes, "Neusner's proposed world view is actually based not on the contents of the Mishnah and inferences backwards from them, but on what, according to him, is not there: prophecy, history and eschatology," thus, an argument from silence. Also, cf. Boyarin, "On the Status," 460, who writes, "The Mishnah simply does not treat eschatology, any more than the Constitution of the US does, but you may be sure that many of the framers of that document heard sermons about the Day of Judgment, and some of them may even have delivered such sermons." The Tannaitic Midrashim are what they claim to be: "collections of biblical interpretations that were produced, by and large, by tannaim and then edited (and indeed shaped and often modified) by redactors of probably the late third and fourth centuries.

codifications. Since the Mishnah resembles an independent law code, it must be at odds with biblical exegesis.[20] However, as demonstrated above, the Mishnah writers turn out to be reading Scripture very carefully and thus Neusner's agenda for the *Sifra* collapses.

In addition, one-third of the *Sifra* does not intersect with the Mishnah. What is the purpose of this material? Why include it at all if the sole agenda of the document is to criticize Mishnah's lack of appeal to Scripture? It does not substantiate or criticize the Mishnah; it is simply unrelated. Neusner has not supplied adequate proof that the *Sifra* is anything more than it claims to be: a compilation of early rabbinic exegesis on Leviticus.

Finally, *Leviticus Rabbah*. Neusner's suggestion that *Leviticus Rabbah* has transformed Leviticus from a text about the cult into one about ethics, is also questionable. He says,

> The laws of the book of Leviticus, focused as they are on the sanctification of the nation through its cult, in *Leviticus Rabbah* indicate the rules of salvation as well . . . The biblical book that deals with the tabernacle . . . now is shown to address the holy people. Leviticus really discusses not the consecration of the cult but the sanctification of the nation . . . it turns out that the sanctification of the cult stands for the salvation of the nation. So the nation now is like the cult then. The ordinary Israelite now like the priest then. The holy way of life lived now, through acts to which merit accrues, corresponds to the holy rites then. The process of metamorphosis is full, rich, complete. When everything stands for something else, the something else repeatedly turns out to be the nation.[21]

First of all, the biblical text of Leviticus itself already addresses the "holy people" and is very interested in their sanctification. Many passages are directed to the entire nation of Israel, not just the priests or Levites, exhorting it to be a holy people (e.g. Lev 11:1, 44; 19:2). Secondly, Neusner describes *Leviticus Rabbah* as a sort of mirror image of Leviticus, in which everything stands for something else, in this quote, a "metamorphosis," in other places, a "paradoxical syllogism" or an "as-if reading, the opposite of how things seem." This claim is hardly supported by the texts discussed below.

---

[20] H. Maccoby, "Uniting the Dual Torah. A Review of *Sifra and the Problem of the Mishnah*, by Jacob Neusner (1991)," *JTS* 44 (1993) 317–38.

[21] J. Neusner, *Leviticus Rabbah* (vol. 10/1 of *The Components of the Rabbinic Documents: From the Whole to the Parts*; Atlanta: Scholars Press, 1997) 1.

Neusner finds an example of "metamorphosis" in *Leviticus Rabbah*'s use of the forbidden foods from Leviticus 11 to symbolize foreign nations. Indeed the threat and future of the foreign nations opposing Israel takes up almost the entirety of *par.* 13.[22] However, what led the Rabbis to connect forbidden foods and Gentiles? The basis of the connection of forbidden foods and foreign nations is already in Lev 20:24b–26 [JPS]:

> I the LORD am your God who has set you apart from other peoples. So you shall set apart the clean beast from the unclean, the unclean bird from the clean. You shall not draw abominations upon yourselves through beast or bird or anything with which the ground is alive, which I have set apart for you to treat as unclean. You shall be holy to Me, for I the LORD am holy, and I have set you apart from other peoples to be Mine.

This passage is the closest Scripture comes to providing a rationale for forbidden foods: they are a marker separating Israel from non-Israel. Every time Israel eats a meal she reinforces that distinction between herself and other nations. Thus, pure animals become representative of the pure nation, and impure animals of impure nations and this notion is developed by other biblical authors as well (e.g. Gen 15:9–14; Isa 40:11; Ezek 34:7–31; cf. Acts 10:12–28).

As another example of this "as-if" reading, Neusner claims that the authors of *Leviticus Rabbah* read about the skin diseases of Leviticus as if they were reading about something else entirely, e.g. gossip.[23] In support of this view, Leviticus 13–14 provides details about leprosy, a cultic matter, but *Leviticus Rabbah* seems to change the discussion to abstract, moral issues, in which leprosy stands for various sins (e.g., *par.* 17). However, while the emphasis of *Leviticus Rabbah* is definitely ethical and homiletical, Neusner has not given sufficient credit to the influence of Leviticus upon *Leviticus Rabbah*. What made the Rabbis associate leprosy with various sins? The authors of *Leviticus Rabbah* formed their association of sin and leprosy not by mere speculation but by reading Leviticus carefully. According to Leviticus 14, the leper does not just perform water ablutions but must bring four atoning sacrifices in order to be cleansed. In addition, Lev 14:34

---

[22] Ibid., xlviii.

[23] J. Neusner, *The Later Midrash Compilations: Genesis Rabbah, Leviticus Rabbah and Pesiqta deRab Kahana* (vol. 3 of *The Judaism behind the Texts: The Generative Premises of Rabbinic Literature*; Atlanta: Scholars Press, 1994) 91.

warns that God will afflict Israel with leprosy as punishment for sin (cf. also Num 12:9–11; Job 11:6; 22:5; 2 Chron 26:23).

My claim, then, is that *Leviticus Rabbah*, while it focuses primarily, but not exclusively, on moral interpretations of Leviticus, recognizes the seeds of moral teaching already in the biblical text.[24] Ethics is not a foreign notion to Leviticus, and so *Leviticus Rabbah* is not an inversion or a mirror image opposite of the biblical text.[25] Leviticus 19 begins with the exhortation to be holy and then spells out how this is done with a long exhortation on ethics, including injunctions against withholding wages, bearing grudges, and dishonesty. The notion that ethics is essential to holiness was recognized by Jews long before the writing of *Leviticus Rabbah* and is discussed by other Jews in antiquity (cf. 1 Pet 1:15). A prime example is the *Sifra* which devotes an entire *parashah, Qedoshim*, to explicating Leviticus 19 on the subject of maintaining holiness by imitating God's ethics.

Neusner understands the thinking behind *Leviticus Rabbah* to be that of "philosophers and scientists." Their *modus operandi* is "identifying and classifying the facts of Israel's social life. . . . Once discovered, the social rules of Israel's national life yield explicit statements, such as that God hates the arrogant and loves the humble." Neusner describes the process of *Leviticus Rabbah* like that of the Mishnah— the work of philosophers classifying data, "sound, scientific philosophy."[26] However, nowhere do the Rabbis of *Leviticus Rabbah* (or the Mishnah) discuss the questions of philosophers, e.g., what is the meaning of life? What is prime reality? The Rabbis of *Leviticus Rabbah*, in particular, demonstrate their complete trust in Scripture's all-sufficiency, by quoting it at every turn to support their claims. Furthermore, Neusner's claim is difficult to support in light of his own findings on *Leviticus Rabbah*. In his analytical work on the pre-suppositions of rabbinic documents he imposes a three category grid

---

[24] In a recent lecture Neusner argued that ethics was an important part of holiness in the rabbinic canon in which he includes "Scripture as mediated in the Mishnah, Taluds and Midrash of 200 through 600 CE." However, he still sees this in contradistinction to Judaism's earlier "classical" definitions of holiness by which he must mean Scripture itself, "The Ethical Imperatives of Holiness: How in Formative Judaism Theology and Law Come to Realization in Workaday Conduct," paper presented for The Mathers Lecture, Queens University, Kingston, Ont., Nov. 26, 2001.

[25] Cf. J. Milgrom, *Leviticus 17–22* (AB 3; New York: Doubleday, 2000) 1594–1726, on chapter 19.

[26] Neusner, *Components of the Rabbinic Documents*, xlii.

to uncover unarticulated premises behind the texts: 1) Unarticulated
Premises: The Givens of Religious Conduct; II) Unarticulated Premises:
The Givens of Religious Conviction; and III) Matters of Philosophy,
Natural Science and Metaphysics. After subjecting every chapter of
Leviticus Rabbah to this grid, Neusner repeatedly states that this third
category is empty. In the entire text there is not one datum of phi-
losophy, natural sciences or metaphysics.[27]

Now Neusner is quite right that *Leviticus Rabbah* selects isolated
verses from Leviticus as a sparse framework for discussions which
often center on subjects related to current problems, not necessarily
the ones in the mind of the priests of Leviticus. This should not be
surprising. The average preacher comes to his/her congregation with
a selected text and a clear agenda to promote, but in the course of
the sermon Scripture is usually used both explicitly and implicitly.
As the above examples demonstrate, the pillars of Leviticus are in
both the foreground and the background of *Leviticus Rabbah*.

Neusner makes too much of the differences in form between rabbinic documents. True, the Mishnah is not organized by the sequence
of topics in Scripture nor does it make formal appeal to Scripture.
The *Sifra*, using a completely different form, follows the order of
Leviticus and links its comments to particular verses. Finally, *Leviticus
Rabbah* quotes only a framework of verses from Leviticus and often
steers the discussion into other topics. Nevertheless, the differences
in the formal presentations of these three texts should not lead us
to the conclusion that the Mishnah and *Leviticus Rabbah* are framed
by philosophers with an agenda far removed from the Torah and
only the *Sifra* is really reading Leviticus. Instead of making so much
of form, we need to take more account of substance. Then, assuming the most logical scenario, i.e., that the Rabbis really were informed
by the Scripture they were reading, we should ask, "Is it possible to
read Scripture as a coherent system and come up with the conclusions of the Mishnah? Is there support for *Sifra*'s claim that the
Rabbis have formed their halakha on the basis of Leviticus? Is there
support in Leviticus for *Leviticus Rabbah*'s emphasis on morals?" Given
the evidence, I continue to answer all of these questions in the
affirmative.

---

[27] Neusner, *The Later Midrash Compilations: Genesis Rabbah, Leviticus Rabbah and Pesiqta
deRab Kahana*, 85–189.

In conclusion, Neusner has concluded more than the evidence allows. Claiming to treat each rabbinic text on its own terms, Neusner has constructed opposing philosophies for each one. He claims that, in contrast to Leviticus, the Mishnah's worldview has to do with stasis, represented by still pools of purification water used by determined Jews who intended to maintain their sanctification in the midst of the chaos created by the loss of land and temple. However, the mishnaic concepts discussed above (טבול יום, מקוה, and כונה) do not support a philosophy in competition with Scripture. They can be understood as completely consonant with Leviticus as demonstrated above. According to Neusner, the *Sifra*'s raison d'etre is to criticize the Mishnah for not appealing to Scripture, but, as demonstrated above, the Mishnah is guided by Scripture. Furthermore, one-third of the *Sifra* is irrelevant to the Mishnah and the rest supports the Mishnah's conclusions. Finally, to say that *Leviticus Rabbah* reads Leviticus in an "as if" manner converting the cult into a tool for moral teaching is an overstatement. Leviticus itself is clear that without the observance of ethics, the ritual of the cult fails to keep Israel holy.

Using Scripture to inform Scripture, the Rabbis have filled in many gaps of the text of Leviticus. Their focus has been, not on restating the obvious message of the text nor on constructing a competing ideology, but on settling ambiguity. Their way is not the only way to read the text, nor do they lack biases and diversity of opinions. Nevertheless, as the above examples give evidence, there are certain principles at work within these rabbinic texts which were not created out of philosophical speculation but were rooted in the soil of Leviticus.

Recognizing that Leviticus is foundational to the rabbinic texts discussed above, let us examine them once again in order to uncover particular biases in interpretation. While the perspective of *Sifra*'s compilers is not exactly the same as that of the Mishnah's nor the interest of the contributors to *Sifra* the same as those of *Leviticus Rabbah*, still, some shared ideological undercurrents can be detected. These biases can be brought into sharper relief by comparing rabbinic interpretations of Scripture with those of other ancient Jewish communities.

One motive of the Rabbis of the Mishnah is to alleviate the laws of Leviticus as much as possible.[28] While this leniency may not be

---

[28] Some may argue that in the Gospels, Jesus attacks the Pharisees for laying

apparent in all areas of the law, as apparent already from the above discussion.[29] The טבול יום, discussed above, is free to do business immediately after bathing and is considered טהור for all intents and purposes except the sacred. While this is in root based on Scripture, it does represent a lenient interpretation, especially when compared with that of other early exegetes, e.g. the Qumran community.[30] For the latter, purifying persons are repeatedly identified as טמא, impure, until all purification rites are completed (cf. 11Q19 49:20; 50:9–12; 4Q277 1 ii 2–13).

In contrast to the rabbinic interpretation of impurity, the Scrolls seem to extend its power beyond the plain meaning of Scripture. Impure foods include even gnats and larvae, items explicitly excluded from the forbidden list by the Rabbis (CD 12:11–13; *m. Ter.* 7:11). Items which are susceptible to impurity are limited by the Rabbis to only those mentioned in Scripture. Thus, when Num 19:18 states that "everything" in the house of the dead becomes impure, "everything" is understood within the context of the impurity laws, i.e., it only refers to those items explicitly said to be susceptible to impurity by Scripture (e.g., Lev 11:32–33; Num 31:20–23). At Qumran, susceptible items to impurity include all of the rabbinic list as well as stone; the corpse-contaminated house is impure in all of its parts, including locks, lintels and soil (11Q19 49:12–16).

Similarly, מדרס, the transfer of sexual impurity by pressure, was limited by the *Sifra* only to objects which could be used for sitting or lying without losing their normal function (*Sifra Mes. Zab.* 2:1–4; cf. *b. Šabb.* 59a). This is a limitation of Lev 15:10 which states clearly

---

excessive burdens upon Jews by their rigid traditions. This accusation must be tempered by at least the following two considerations: 1) Jesus may be accusing the Pharisees from within the tradition, as an insider, just as similar accusations against them exist in the Talmud; and 2) at the time of the rabbinic documents (after 200 CE) alleviation is the norm rather than stringency due to the impossibiltiy of observing so much of the law without political power and without the Temple.

[29] T. Frymer-Kensky (private communication) has pointed out that the rabbis are not lenient with regard to women, tithing, and the עם הארץ.

[30] The Qumran sectarians tend to emphasize the level of impurity in an item rather than its purity (J. Baumgarten, personal note, 2000). Baumgarten notes, for example, that the one who gathers the ash of the red cow, prescribed by Scripture as an איש טהור, Num 19:9, may be a טבול יום, according to the Rabbis (*Sif. Num.* 157, [Horovitz]), but not according to the sectarians (4Q277 1 ii 2); see J. Baumgarten, *Qumram Cave 4.XXV. Halakhic Texts* (DJD 35; Oxford: Clarendon Press, 1999) 117.

that everything under the זב becomes unclean. According to the Rabbis, one has to infer here that Scripture's "everything" is everything in the context of chapter 15, that is, everything which can be used for lying, sitting, and riding, the special modes of impurity transfer introduced in chapter 15.

The Rabbis use the concept of intention, כונה, also, to limit the effect of impurity. As noted above, if a person did not mean to put water on his crops, they are not rendered susceptible to impurity. Thus, rain will not defile a crop since it was not intentionally put there by the farmer. This stands in stark contrast to the view found at Qumran that even rain and dew render crops susceptible to impurity, creating an enormous hardship for the farmer (4Q274 3 ii 8).

Neusner is right that the Rabbis have an agenda, they have certain emphases and interests; but they are not the ones he is suggesting, they are not interested in beginning a new Judaism, a new philosophy or worldview. They wish rather to alleviate the sacred text they have inherited while still remaining true to it.

Another item on the rabbinic agenda is an emphasis on the laity. Sometimes Leviticus is unclear who actually receives a holy offering. Sometimes an offering is simply "holy to the Lord" and the beneficiary is not stated. For example, the fourth year fruit offering is designated holy (Lev 19:24), but who is eligible to eat it? The Rabbis assign it to the farmer, who worships God in Jerusalem with the fruit or its value (Sif. Num. 6 [9]). As a striking contrast, the Dead Sea Scrolls assign the fruit entirely to the priests (4QMMT B 62–63; 11Q19 60:3–4; 4Q251 10:6–8). The bias of the Rabbis toward the laity here is evident.

The rabbinic bias toward the laity is especially evident when discussing the matter of profane or sacred slaughter. Leviticus 17:1–3 states that all sacrificial animals must be sacrificed at the sanctuary first before they may be eaten by the owner. Deuteronomy 12:12 allows those living "too far" from the sanctuary to slaughter their animals at home as long as the blood is properly disposed of. The question is, how far is "too far"? The Scroll authors define "too far" as over a 3–day journey from Jerusalem (11QT 52:13–15). The Rabbis define "too far" as applicable to anyone living outside of Jerusalem (Sifre Deut 71 [134]). The two interpretations are readily explained once one realizes who would benefit most from each. The priests receive choice parts of every well-being offering, thus if every

lamb, goat or cow eaten had to be first presented as a sacrifice, the
priestly coffers would definitely swell.[31] By contrast, the Rabbis allow
profane slaughtering, from which no priestly portions are taken, for
those living outside of Jerusalem. The Qumran authors favor the
priests; the Rabbis prefer the laity.

Again reflecting their bias toward the laity, the Rabbis, on sacred
festivals, had the sacred vessels brought out of the sanctuary into full
view of the people in the courts (m. Suk. 4:5). Even the עמי הארץ,
who were not trusted throughout the year in matters of tithes and
purity, were invited to participate in the festival on these occasions.
All Israel, priests and laity, were allowed to process around the brazen
altar which was located in the court of the priests.[32]

In addition, the Rabbis limit the power of the priest to determine
leprosy, restricting its examination and pronouncement. Scripture
states that a priest must pronounce the leper pure or impure (Lev
14:7, 48). The Rabbis insist that the priest be informed by a sage
(m. Neg. 3:1). According to their interpretation the leper has to be
examined under optimum conditions in order for the examination
to be valid: the priest must be able to see all of the affected area
at one glance (t. Neg. 2:12); the suspected leper must be in the correct position for the examination (m. Neg. 2:4); the affected area must
be of a certain size and color (m. Neg. 7;4; Sifra Taz. Neg. 2:17, par.
2:4), and must be examined under sufficient light at certain times
of the day (Sifra Taz. Neg. 2:3; m. Neg. 2:2). This method would no
doubt give the suspected leper a decided advantage. The Rabbis
define leprosy and gonorrhea so narrowly that these afflictions almost
ceased, at least theoretically, to exist.[33] In a time when no temple

---

[31] In addition to the amount of sacrifices to be offered, the sect also increased
the portions of these animals to be given to the priests. Leviticus designates the
right thigh and the breast of all Israelite well-being offerings for the priests (Lev
7:33). Deuteronomy requires the shoulder, jowls, and inner parts of all firstborn
animals to be given to the priests (Deut 18:3). Thus, according to the sectarians,
Jews should add the two requirements and give all of these portions to the priests
from every offering they bring; Y. Yadin, The Temple Scroll (3 vols.; Jerusalem: The
Israel Exploration Society, 1983) 1.154; J. Milgrom, "The Shoulder for the Levites"
in Yadin, Temple Scroll, 1.169– 76.

[32] I. Knohl, "Post-Biblical Sectarianism and the Priestly Schools of the Pentateuch:
the Issue of Popular Participation in the Temple Cult on Festivals" in J. Trebolle
Barrera and L. V. Montaner (eds.), The Madrid Qumran Congress: Proceedings of the
International Congress on the Dead Sea Scrolls, Madrid, 18–21 March, 1991 (2 vols.; Leiden:
Brill, 1992) 2.602–603, esp. n. 4.

[33] By contrast, in the Dead Sea Scrolls, leprosy and gonorrhea are defined more

existed, the Rabbis tried to alleviate the law which required the cult for the purification of those afflicted with these diseases.

Finally, the Rabbis have inherited a very distinctive concept of holiness from Leviticus which stands in sharp contrast to notions of the sacred in the Graeco-Roman world. In addition to detailing numerous priestly laws for the implementation of the cult, Leviticus requires all Israel to be "holy as the Lord your God is holy" (Lev 11:45; 19:2). The Rabbis understand this command to teach separation from evil as well as commitment to ethical goodness. The *Sifra* interprets holiness as separation: "'As I am [holy] separated, so be ye separated [holy]': this means separation from things impure and defiling, foremost among which are idolatry (see chapter 1), adultery and other illicit sexual relations, and murder" (*Sifra* on Lev 16:16, 57b, Weiss, 81c; cf. *Sifra* 81a). "By separating oneself from sin, a person can become holy" (*Sif. Qedosh.* 93b; cf. *Lev. R.* 23 end). Even the fear of sin leads a person to holiness (*b. 'Abod. Zar.* 20b; cf. also *y. Sheq.* 3:3).

But dissociation from these basic evils is not the whole of the matter. The exhortation of Lev 19:2 to be holy is followed by a list of commands which legislate ethical goodness among Israel, including such good deeds as leaving gleanings for the poor (19:10), paying wages on time (19:13), and loving one's neighbor as oneself (19:18). The Rabbis refer to Leviticus 19 as "the passage on holiness" and debate exactly how many duties are required by it (*Lev. Rab.* 24:5). The point is that for the Rabbis holiness depends upon fulfilling ethical obligations (Lev 19:13).[34]

Reading the rabbinic material in its Greco-Roman context brings into relief the strong ethical component in the Jewish definition of holiness and the lack of it among Greco-Roman cults. Among the Greeks and Romans the terms *ethos* and *mores* indicated social norms and had little, if anything, to do with the holy sphere.[35] Holiness

---

broadly, the former is the product of an evil spirit and the latter may even be incurred by sexual fantasies. Lepers were to be isolated even from each other according to the scrolls (11Q19 46:16–18; 48:14–15; 4Q276 2); the Rabbis allow them to exist unconfined as long as they remained outside of city walls (*m. Kel.* 1:7; *b. Zeb.* 117a; *b. Pesah* 66b–67a; *Sif. Num.* 5:2).

[34] B. Leiser, "The Sanctity of the Profane: A Pharisaic Critique of Rudolf Otto," *Judaism* 20 (1971) 92.

[35] B. Cohen, *Jewish and Roman Law: A Comparative Study* (2 vols.; New York: Jewish Theological Seminary of America, 1966) 1.66.

did not indicate a moral lifestyle prescribed by the Greco-Roman
gods. Greeks and Romans were not asked to submit to an organized
system of beliefs or identify with a special "holy people" as among
the Jews.[36] While morality is discussed by philosophers and law-
makers, it was not dictated or controlled by the gods. Morality was
simply not the purview of the priests, who were, rather, experts in
implementing correct rituals.[37] As Liebeschuetz says, although the
Romans

> were even obsessively convinced of the need to placate the gods, belief
> in the gods seems to have had little effect on their conduct. The reader
> of Latin literature feels that fear of divine displeasure was very rarely
> a motive when a Roman decided on a course of action . . . nor is there
> much evidence that a divine command was used as an excuse to jus-
> tify any individual's behaviour retrospectively.[38]

A potentially immoral or aggressive individual would probably not
be deterred by reflection on the gods. As Cicero said: Jupiter is the
best and greatest "not because he makes us just or sober or wise
but healthy and rich and prosperous."[39]

The Jewish cult itself cannot be properly implemented without
attention to ethics. Confession and repentance are preconditions for
an effective sacrifice for sin (*Sif. Zut.* on Num 4:4; *t. Menah.* 10:12;
m. Yoma 8:8; *t. Yoma* 4:9; cf. Lev 5:5; *b. Sebu.* 13a). Violation of
another person's rights is considered on a par with sacrilege. The
Rabbis regard restitution of wrongs done to one's fellow Jew as a
matter of holiness and it had to be made along with payment of a
fine to the injured party (*m. Yoma* 8:9; *t. Ta'an.* 1:8; Lev 6:2–5; cf.
m. Yoma 3:8; Philo, *Leg.* 1.235). In addition, the Holy One himself
was violated by this breach of ethics and had to be appeased. Ritual
alone was not enough to create holiness in Israel. Only the Jew with
the "pure heart" could "ascend the holy hill" (Pss 15:1–5; 24:3–4).

---

[36] J. North, "The Development of Religious Pluralism" in J. Lieu et al. (eds.),
The Jews among Pagans and Christians (London: Routledge, 1992) 187.

[37] North, "The Development of Religious Pluralism," 188; E. Gruen, personal
communication, 1997. As K. Dowden says, Romans "reckoned their moral behav-
iour was up to them and what others thought of them" in *Religion and the Romans*
(London: Bristol Classical Press, 1992) 8.

[38] J. H. W. G. Liebeschuetz, *Continuity and Change in Roman Religion* (Oxford:
Clarendon, 1979) 3.

[39] Cited by Liebeschuetz, *Continuity*, 39; cf. also 307; North, "The Development
of Religious Pluralism," 188.

By contrast, Greco-Roman cults are characterized by the precision of their rituals. The Latin for religion is not *religio*, but *cultus deorum*, the cult of the gods.[40] Rituals had to be exact, prayers word-perfect, gestures without variance. Of these rituals the single most important act is animal sacrifice, the main focus of which is the moment of divination.[41] Extispicy, i.e. the examination of entrails for signs, was probably part of every sacrifice. In fact, the Greek word kalleireisqai "to look for good sacrificial signs," simply means "to sacrifice."[42] Offerers prayed to the deity and the deity was expected to reply by signs in the animal's body.

In summary, let us review the process of the rabbinic reception of Leviticus. What we find is 1) Scripture is read and studied, comments are made, ambiguous texts are discussed at length and conclusions are drawn; a system is codified for belief and practice; 2) In the third century CE two major texts emerge, of two different genres, one a law code which presents the law as a system for belief and practice by classification, analogy, and other logical means and the second, a commentary on Leviticus which presents a collection of sayings and decisions of earlier Rabbis in order to remind the reader of the Scriptural underpinnings of the system which they espouse. The Mishnah, as a code of law, records classifications and codifications of prior exegesis. The *Sifra* comes to largely the same conclusions as the Mishnah but reveals the process by which they were formed. Finally, 3) *Leviticus Rabbah* emphasizes the ethical side of sanctification in a series of homilies based on principles inherent in Leviticus and other parts of Scripture.

Once we take seriously the role of Scripture as foundational for all of these texts, we begin to see the affinity between them. Concepts such as טבול יום, מקוה, and כונה are understood as the products of careful readings of Scripture rather than as *de novo* philosophical ideas. Using Scripture to inform Scripture, the Rabbis focused on settling ambiguity, not on restating the obvious message of the text.

---

[40] J. Ferguson, "Roman Cults" in M. Grant and R. Kitzmyer (eds.), *Civilization of the Ancient Mediterranean* (3 vols.; New York: Charles Scribner & Sons, 1988) 2.909.

[41] E. E. Evans-Pritchard, *Nuer Religion* (Oxford: Clarendon, 1956); C. Levi-Strauss, *The Savage Mind* (Chicago: University of Chicago Press, 1966) 223–38; for a study of biblical sacrifices from a structural perspective, cf. D. Davies, "An Interpretation of Sacrifice in Leviticus," *ZAW* 89 (1977) 387–98.

[42] M. H. Jameson, "Sacrifice and Ritual: Greece" in *Civilization of the Ancient Mediterranean*, 2.962.

When one takes into account the undisputed statements of Leviticus, the rabbinic discussions are more easily understood. Without recognizing the Rabbis' scriptural orientation, any presentation of the rabbinic reception of Leviticus is in danger of distortion.

Nevertheless, in settling Scripture's ambiguity, biases of the Rabbis do come into relief. Their choices reveal a certain agenda which includes, but is not limited to, the following components: 1) The Rabbis are interested in alleviating difficulties of observing the law. It is because the Rabbis took Scripture so seriously that they capitalized on ambiguous passages where they could alleviate the law; 2) The Rabbis are found to be a pro-laity party. Rabbinic interpretation invariably prefers the laity over the priests granting the former perquisites and privileges not conceded by other Jewish groups in antiquity. 3) The Rabbis, in contrast to their pagan neighbors, are interested in the realization of holiness among all Israel as expressed in both ritual and ethical practice. Religion without ethics was considered no religion at all.

אֲנִי יהוה: GOD'S SELF-INTRODUCTORY FORMULA IN LEVITICUS IN MIDRASH *SIFRA*

Gerhard Bodendorfer

God's self-introductory formula has been examined extensively in research. Walther Zimmerli[1] and Karl Elliger[2] devoted long essays to it, and Hans-Peter Mathys[3] went into it in some detail in his research on Lev 19:18. While one distinguishes between short and long forms of the formula,[4] there is no difference as regards their content. Neither are they indications of editorial layers. Besides that, we also find אֲנִי יהוה מקדשכם (20:8; 21:8:15:23; 22:9:16:32). Both forms occur very frequently in the Holiness Code. They have a primarily structuring function as concluding formulas. The short forms subdivide the various series of commands, whereas the long forms set the main sections apart from the subdivisions.[5] Though this rather formal aspect of the formula is foregrounded, their functional importance should not be overlooked. The self-introductory formula is a means for demanding God's recognition as a form of obedience, thus emphasizing the relationship between God and man. God's authority, i.e. that of his name: the significance of YHWH being the God of the Israelites, is an element not to be neglected in priestly theology. Thus it is worth examining the formula as regards its function in the rabbinic interpretation of the text in Midrash *Sifra*, with a brief look also at *Leviticus Rabbah*. For convenience's sake I shall quote

---

[1] "Ich bin Jahwe," in W. Zimmerli, *Gottes Offenbarung. Gesammelte Aufsätze zum Alten Testament* (TB 19; München: Kaiser, 1963) 11–40.

[2] K. Elliger, "Ich bin der Herr—euer Gott," in H. Gese und O. Kaiser (eds.), *Kleine Schriften zum Alten Testament* (TB 32; München: Kaiser, 1966) 211–31.

[3] H.-P. Mathys, *Liebe deinen Nächsten wie dich selbst. Untersuchungen zum alttestamentlichen Gebot der Nächstenliebe (Lev 19, 18)* (OBO 71; Göttingen: Vandenhoeck & Ruprecht, 1986) 109–12.

[4] The short form, always asyndetically linked: 11:45; 18:5, 6, 21; 19:12, 14, 16, 18, 28, 30, 32, 37; 20:26; 21:12; 22:2, 3, 8, 30, 31, 33; 26:2. The long form: 11:44; 18:2, 4, 30; 19:2, 3, 4, 10, 25, 31, 34, 36; 20:7, 8, 24; 21:8, 15, 23; 22:9, 16, 32; 23:22, 43; 24:22; 25:17, 38, 55; 26:1, 13, 44.

[5] Cf. A. Ruwe, *"Heiligkeitsgesetz" und "Priesterschrift." Literatur-geschichtliche und rechtssystematische Untersuchungen zu Leviticus 17,1–26,2* (FAT 26; Tübingen: J. C. B. Mohr [Paul Siebeck], 1999) 72.

from the text using the translation and text division by Jacob Neusner,[6] which is based on the edition by Koleditzky.[7] I will also add references to the edition by Weiss, whose pagination and textual division often differ from Neusner and Koleditzky.

1. *Midrash Sifra*

Traditionally, *Sifra*, "the book," is considered to be one of the oldest Midrashim, written some time between 200 and 400 CE. Because of its material *Sifra* is classified as halakhic midrash, as it is interested almost exclusively in legal issues.[8] Due to its exegetic terminology *Sifra* is usually ascribed to the so-called "School of Aqiba," although Aqiba's significance for this school stands on a historically weak foundation. The fact that no other halakhic midrash is documented in so many different manuscripts is a clear sign of the significance of the Leviticus halakha.[9] Despite the work's importance usable editions are rare. After the 1862 edition by I. H. Weiss from Vienna, it was only between 1983–90 that a usable textual basis for research was provided by L. Finkelstein, whose volumes, published in New York, contain the material from *Nedaba* and *Hoba* of the MS Vatican 66.[10] It is due to Jacob Neusner that research on *Sifra* has been greatly advanced in the past ten years. A number of his publications explicitly deal with the phenomenon of *Sifra*.[11] Genetic history, authorship, literary structure and above all the difficult relation

---

[6] J. Neusner, *Sifra. An Analytical Translation* (3 vols.; BJS 138–140; Atlanta: Scholars Press, 1988).

[7] S. Koleditzky, *Sifra de-ve Rab. Hu Sefer Torat Kohanim* (Jerusalem, 1961).

[8] The only narrative text, Lev 8:1–10:7 is commented on by *Mekhilta de-Milluim*, which was added to *Sifra* only at a late stage.

[9] Two of the most important ones are MS Vatican 66 from the ninth to tenth centuries and MS Vatican 31 of 1073.

[10] L. Finkelstein, *Sifra on Leviticus According to Vatican Manuscript Assemani 66 with Variants from the Other Manuscripts, Genizah Fragments, Early Editions and Quotations by Medieval Authorities and with References to Parallel Passages and Commentaries* (4 vols.; New York: Jewish Theological Seminary, 1983–1990). The fourth volume contains the commentary.

[11] E.g. J. Neusner, *Sifra in Perspective: The Documentary Comparison of the Midrashim of Ancient Judaism* (BJS 146; Atlanta: Scholars Press, 1988); idem, *Uniting the Dual Torah: Sifra and the Problem of the Mishnah* (BJS 147; Cambridge: Cambridge University Press, 1990); idem, *The Canonical History of Ideas. The Place of the So-Called Tannaite Midrashim: Mekhilta Attributed to R. Ishmael, Sifra, Sifré to Numbers, and Sifré to Deuteronomy* (SFSHJ 4; Atlanta: Scholars Press, 1990).

to Mishnah have been dealt with extensively by Neusner. Two areas may be of considerable interest also in this context. First, there is the question of a text's editorial history, which is of some importance also to exegetes, and second, there is the significance attached to the biblical text in the relation between Mishnah and *Sifra*. As concerns the first question, Günter Stemberger has recently published a groundbreaking article, "Zur Redaktionsgeschichte von Sifra," in a series edited by Neusner.[12] In this essay, Stemberger (partly) concurs with Neusner[13] that the text of *Sifra* evolved in at least three stages. At the beginning there was a so-called *Grundschrift*, which is to be characterized as a simple exegetic commentary on Leviticus. This first text was followed by a so-called

> dialektische Auslegung als Erweiterung des Grundtextes die ein begrenztes Repertoire logischer Kontrollverfahren mit feststehenden Wendungen auf die in der einfachen Auslegung gebotenen Aussagen anwendet und diese letztlich als richtig erweist, wie der stereotype Abschluß mit *talmud lomar* plus Wiederholung der einfachen Auslegung zum Ausdruck bringt.[14]

This development is completed by the interpolation of Mishnah and Tosefta passages, which was meant to express the coherence with the basic rabbinic text, thus providing the students with a complex learning aid which saved them the time of perpetually consulting the Mishnah itself. Stemberger's detailed analysis goes far beyond Neusner, and contradicts him primarily concerning the complex relationship between Mishnah and *Sifra*. In his publications, Neusner had always maintained that the polemic against Mishnah was a specific concern of *Sifra*.

> In his interpretation, the general thrust of *Sifra* is an overall polemic against Mishnah and its purely logical classification of reality; *Sifra*, by contrast, always tries to show—usually by quoting from Mishnah and

---

[12] G. Stemberger, "Zur Redaktionsgeschichte von Sifra" in J. Neusner (ed.), *Approaches to Ancient Judaism XI* (SFSHJ 4; Atlanta: Scholars Press, 1997) 39–82. Cf. on the editing and early reception of *Sifra* also "Sifra—Tosefta—Yerushalmi: Zur Redaktion und frühen Rezeption von Sifra," *JSJ* 30 (1999) 277–311.

[13] Not entirely, however, since Neusner distinguishes between the three levels only from a literary point of view, whereas he ignores the question whether all three are from the same "authorship" or whether they were created over a longer period of time. To Neusner, moreover, the syllogistic part and the Mishnah parallels belong to the same concept.

[14] Stemberger, "Redaktionsgeschichte," 55.

Tosefta—that mere logic is misleading and that without Scriptural evidence true insight is impossible.[15]

Stemberger contests this view. He clearly distinguishes the interpolation of Mishnah texts from phase two, i.e. from the dialectic commentary, and thinks it can be dated some time between the fifth and eighth century. Such a late date, of course, makes the controversy between Mishnah, which was completed around 200, and *Sifra* more than unlikely. Stemberger rather believes that the purpose of this *Sifra* version was to defend Mishnah as conforming to Scripture. The question of the Bible's significance in Mishnah and *Sifra* would have to be answered to the effect that *Sifra* in its final version was reacting to the increasing critique of tradition and to the call for a return to the Scripture. In contrast to Neusner's Mishnah polemic, *Sifra* would thus be the very proof that Mishnah presupposes the Bible as its basis, though without referring to it in every instance. Stemberger admits, however, that at this stage his view still contains many hypothetical elements which need to be corroborated by further investigations.

Concerning the age of the various genetic stages of Midrash, Stemberger voices his opinion cautiously, but without avoiding the major problems. The question whether a text like *Sifra* might contain material from before the destruction of the Temple is naturally of particular interest to biblical scholars. The *Temple Scroll* in particular has shown how Leviticus could be interpreted during the Second Temple period. Did something like a textbook for priestly education exist, which may have left its traces in *Sifra*? After all, the important *Sifra* scholar Finkelstein did postulate the existence of such a book predating the times of Jochanan ben Zakkai and R. Eliezer, i.e. clearly before 70 CE. An early version of *Sifra* even dates back to Hasmonean times.[16] Stemberger, however, can prove that Finkelstein's arguments do not bear close examination. The preferred exegetical rules of *Ribbui* (amplification) und *Miut* (restriction) rather show that the text in its oldest version can hardly have been written before 70 and in any case has to be dated to rabbinic times, to the decades after the Bar Kochba revolt at the earliest. For the

---

[15] Ibid., 40.
[16] L. Finkelstein, "The Core of the Sifra: A Temple Textbook for Priests," *JQR* 80 (1989–90) 15–34.

anonymous dialectic commentary of the second phase Stemberger assumes the third century as the earliest possible date of composition. Since the third text version was written between the fifth and eighth centuries, a development of up to 600 years has to be estimated for *Sifra*.

But let us come back to our question: How is the formula being used?

2. *The Formula's Hermeneutic Function*

God's self-introductory formula plays an important role in Midrash *Sifra*. Its first occurrence[17] is in *Ṣaw* 13.7 (Weiss 13.4 37a) on Lev 7:11–18, where 22:2 is quoted:

> As to bird-offerings and meal-offerings, which do not fall into the category of sacrifices at all? And while encompassing a variety of cases, what about the log of oil that is presented by the person afflicted with the skin disease? Scripture says, "[Instruct Aaron and his sons] to be scrupulous about the sacred donations that the Israelite people consecrate to me, lest they profane my holy name. I am the Lord." This serves to encompass all of them.

The reference to God's self-introduction emphasizes the force of the regulation, which pertains to all sacred donations. Here already it is undoubtedly clear that "I am the Lord" reinforces and enjoins the significance of a rule. In this passage, however, it serves above all as a means of rabbinic hermeneutics, here specifically as a strategy for extending the purview of a certain rule (*Ribbui*).

In *Sifra Emor*, too, like in *Ṣaw*, "I am the Lord" functions as reinforcement in the context of defining the purview of certain rules, and likewise in *Aḥarê Mot* 13.II.2f (Weiss 13.3 85b), in relation to laws against incest.

Emor 2.9 (Weiss 2.9 95a) on 21:15 reads:

> "... among his people": this serves to encompass under the law the daughter of a male priest who has been profaned, indicating that she is invalid for marriage into the priesthood. R. Judah says: The daughter of a male proselyte is in the status of the daughter of a male priest

---

[17] *Mekhilta de-Milluim* on *Ṣaw* quotes the formula after Num 3:41 (Weiss 40b) and Isa 61:8 (Weiss 41b).

who has been profaned. . . ."for I am the Lord who sanctifies him."
This once more serves to indicate the reason for the rule.

In *Emor par.* 2.10 (Weiss *par.* 2.6 94b) "I am the Lord" in Lev 21:12
(consecrated oil) functions as an explanation for extending the law
also to "a high priest who was consecrated by being vested with
many priestly garments."

In *Emor par.* 4.I.3 (Weiss *par.* 4.1 97a), relating to Lev 22:2, the
formula serves to include also the priests' holy implements, which
are not explicitly named. At the conclusion of 4.I.4 (Weiss *par.* 4.2
97a) there is a comparison between Lev 19:10 and 22:2. The identical (linguistic) usage in the two passages is taken to mean by analogy that in both instances the formula "involves extirpation as a
penalty." The context "extirpation" also determines *Emor* 4.III.3 (*par.*
4.10 97b) on Lev 22:3, where it rules that extirpation of a priest
who consumes consecrated meat during bodily impurity extends to
every place where God may dwell.

At the end of *Emor* 6 (Weiss 6.10 98a) the term "the purpose"
emphasizes the force of the regulation in Lev 22:16.

In each of these passages, then, the formula expresses the significance
of the biblical command and serves as a marker for an exegetic
operation, amplification or analogy for example.

Emor par. 11.2 (Weiss 11.1–3 101b) on Lev 23:23–25 (28) contains
a text which is largely based on *t. Roš Haš.* 2.10 and later on 2.11.
In between it reads:

> R. Yose b. R. Judah says: That proof[18] is not required. It is written,
> "[the trumpets] shall serve you for remembrance before your God: I
> am the Lord your God" (Num 10:10). Now, when Scripture says, "I
> am the Lord your God," it serves as a generative analogy (*binyan ab*),
> to indicate that at every passage at which you make mention of verses
> which have to do with remembrance, you join that passage with verses
> having to do with divine dominion.

Thus, here too, the formula's main function is hermeneutic. Numbers
10:10 is closely connected to Lev 23:23. Moreover, the formula is
to be found also in Lev 23:22, though not referring to the holidays
of the seventh month.

---

[18] That is, the proof that the formula refers to *Roš Haššanah*, thus indicating that
the recitation of the verses has to do with divine dominion.

In *Qedoshim* 6 end (Weiss 6.10 90b) on Lev 19:28, a quotation from *m. Mak.* 3.6 E-G is used, according to which one is found guilty only if a tattoo contains a divine name. The formula serves here to specify and restrict the rule.

3. *The Formula as Motivation and Sign of Intention*

In relation to a command to honor a sage/elder the formula is invoked as a motivation meant to touch the heart. Near the end of *Qedoshim* 7 (Weiss 7.14 91a) it says:

Lo, the matter is handed over to the heart, for it is said, "you shall fear your God, I am the Lord"—in connection with anything that is handed over to the heart, the fear of God is invoked.

Qedoshim par. 2 end (Weiss *par.* 2.14 88b) on Lev 19:14 enjoins not to give inappropriate council to anyone by referring to the intention inherent in "but you shall fear your God: I am the Lord." In both passages it is the formula's connection with fear which expresses its specific parenetic function.

4. *The Formula as Conclusion, ". . . Faithful to Pay a Reward":*
Its Function with Regard to Structure and Meaning

In five instances the formula appears as the conclusion of a paragraph (in the following way): "'I am the Lord (your God)': Faithful to pay a reward." See *Aharê Mot par.* 8.11 (Weiss *par.* 9.10 85b) on 18:5; 13.II.16 (Weiss 13.15 86a) on 18:5 and 22:31–32; *Qedoshim* 8.II.8 (Weiss 8.11 91a) on 19:37; *Emor* 9.8 (Weiss 9.6 99b) on 22:33; *Behar* 9.II.7 (Weiss 9.6 110b) on 25:55; likewise in *Aharê Mot* 13.III.3 (Weiss 13.16 86a) on 18:21 as well as in *Emor* 9.3 (Weiss 9.3 99b) (on 22:31), in the middle of a longer paragraph; with some variation also in *Aharê Mot par.* 8.1 (Weiss *par.* 9.1 85b) on 18:2; 13.II.6 (Weiss 13.5 86a) on 18:2 and *Qedoshim* 10.3 (Weiss 9.2 91b) on 20:7. Two of them have a clearly eschatological perspective: *Aharê Mot par.* 8.11 on 18:5 relates to the next life which follows from the observance of the commandments. *Aharê Mot par.* 13.II.16 affirms the resurrection of the dead and the punishment of all peoples who hate Israel.

In *Qedoshim* 8.II.8 and *Emor* 9.3 we read: "'And you shall observe all my statutes and all my ordinances and do them': This serves to

assign both keeping and doing to the ordinances and keeping and
doing to the statutes. 'I am the Lord': I am faithful to pay a reward."
The basis for this is the identical regulation in Lev 19:37 and 22:31.
Again, there seems to be no difference between the short and the
long form. One could, however, argue that the *topos* of the punishing God is ultimately to be inferred from the term "your God"
(אלהיכם). The wording in *Aḥarê Mot par.* 8 (Weiss *par.* 9.1 85b) on
Lev 18:2 seems to support this interpretation:

> The Lord spoke to Moses saying, "Speak to the Israelite people and
> say to them, I am the Lord your God": "I am the Lord," for I spoke
> and the world came into being. "I am full of mercy." I am Judge to
> exact punishment and faithful to pay recompense. I am the one who
> exacted punishment from the generation of the Flood and the men of
> Sodom and Egypt, and I shall exact punishment from you if you act
> like them.

The association of YHWH with mercy is very common in rabbinic
tradition.[19] In contrast to this, Elohim is usually identified with justice. This division is however not fully consistent in rabbinic literature. The judicial activity as expressed through the use of the formula
might thus have its origin in this understanding of אלהיכם and it
might have been taken over at the end of a paragraph where the
short form occurs. It is equally possible—and in my opinion more
plausible—to assume that the formula, be it in its short or long form,
has a connotation referring to God judging in the divine court.

The text takes up themes which are found elsewhere too, particularly separation and distance from other peoples, from Egypt among
others. Leviticus 18:2 is unique in that within the entire Holiness
Code it is the only passage where the formula precedes a series of
apodictic laws. It is therefore not surprising that the rabbis used this
passage as a basis for general statements about God's function as
judge and ruler of history. It is equally clear that *Sifra* establishes a
close connection between Lev 18:2–5 and 22:31–33, which arises
also from a linguistic similarity. Both texts impress the keeping of
the laws (חקות and משפטים or מצות, respectively). Leviticus 19:37, too,

---

[19] Cf. G. Bodendorfer, "Die Spannung von Gerechtigkeit und Barmherzigkeit
in der rabbinischen Auslegung mit Schwerpunkt auf der Psalmeninterpretation," in
R. Scoralick (ed.), *Das Drama der Barmherzigkeit Gottes. Studien zur biblischen Gottesrede
und ihrer Wirkungsgeschichte in Judentum und Christentum* (SBS 183; Stuttgart: Katholisches
Bibelwerk, 2000) 157–92.

contains the element of preserving and keeping the laws (מִשְׁפָּטִים and חֻקּוֹת). Leviticus 20:7 is continued in v. 8, which again demands the keeping of the statutes (חֻקּוֹת). It is thus, in my view, above all this regulation to keep and abide by the statutes which stands behind the topos of the faithful God.

At first glance, Lev 18:21 does not fit into this picture, since it lacks any reference to laws. This is however to be found in the wider context, in 18:26 (חֻקּוֹת and מִשְׁפָּטִים).

Moreover, these are important parenetic parts, which are linguistically interconnected. This explains the insertion in Lev 25:55, which is quite far away from the reference to laws in v. 8. But v. 55 is a prominent concluding paragraph. *Sifra* quite clearly takes it to be a summary of all laws, and hence the formula of the faithful God is here absolutely appropriate.

The formula occurs at another place, too, if only in the wider context of a reference to the laws, though here the rabbis do not comment on it in the same way. It is in Lev 18:30 (especially in relation to v. 26), which also marks a major break. It becomes clear that there is no simple all-around key and that one has to consider *Sifra*'s long genetic process, during which elements were changed and further developed. With regard to chapter 18 in particular I think that *Aḥarê Mot* 13.II presents a very fundamental and comprehensive interpretation, which has to be assessed in its relation to the entire chapter.

5. *The Exodus from Egypt*

In an important essay, Frank Crüsemann[20] has pointed out the function of the exodus from Egypt in the Holiness Code as "sanctification." The exodus is sanctification and means separation from the other peoples. As such it is a legal status for the Israelites, which demands Israel to behave accordingly. At the same time, however, a text like Leviticus 26 particularly shows that irrespective of Israel's behavior God's deed will remain.

---

[20] F. Crüsemann, "Der Exodus als Heiligung. Zur rechtsgeschichtlichen Bedeutung des Heiligkeitsgesetzes," in E. Blum, C. Macholz, E. W. Stegemann (ed.), *Die Hebräische Bibel und ihre zweifache Nachgeschichte. Festschrift für Rolf Rendtorff zum 65. Geburtstag* (Neukirchen-Vluyn: Neukirchener Verlag, 1990) 117–29.

In *Sifra*, the rabbis confirm Crüsemann's main thesis in a particular way.

The exodus from Egypt is mentioned in *Shemini* 12.II.5 (Weiss 12.3f 57a); *Aharê Mot* 13.II.1 (Weiss 13.3 85b); *Qedoshim* 8.II.6 (Weiss 8.10 91a); *Emor* 9.6–8 (Weiss 9.6 99b); *Behar par.* 5.I.10 (Weiss par. 5.3 109b); 9.I.3f (Weiss 9.4 110a). In *Shemini* and *Emor* it is connected with the topic of holiness. The exodus is connected with the acceptance of Torah and is also applied to various single commands. Concerning Lev 11:45, *Shemini* puts it in general terms: "It was on this stipulation that I brought you up out of the land of Egypt, on the condition that you accept on yourselves the yoke of the religious duties."

Aharê Mot 13.II.1 similarly emphasizes that already in Egypt Israel had committed itself to God. The people's self-commitment is then expressed through the formula. In this context it is interpreted as a question leading to a binding answer.

> The Lord spoke to Moses saying, "Speak to the Israelite people and say to them, 'I am the Lord your God'" (Lev 18:6): R. Simeon b. Yohai says: That is in line with what is said elsewhere: "I am the Lord your God [who brought you out of the land of Egypt, out of the house of bondage]" (Exod 20:2). Am I the Lord, whose sovereignty you took upon yourself in Egypt? They said to him, "Indeed." Indeed you have accepted my dominion. They accepted my decrees: "You will have no other gods before me" (Exod 20:3). That is what is said here: "I am the Lord your God," meaning, Am I the one whose dominion you accepted at Sinai? They said to him, "Indeed." Indeed you accepted my dominion. They accepted my decrees: "You shall not copy the practices of the land of Egypt where you dwelt, or of the land of Canaan to which I am taking you; nor shall you follow their laws."

To my knowledge this is the only passage in *Sifra* (apart from Mekhilta de-Milluim), which deliberately refers to an instance of the formula outside Leviticus. Exodus 20:2 is certainly a most significant passage. It is, so to speak, the decisive evidence of the connection between the exodus and Sinai and also to the main commandment. Through the exodus Israel was separated from the other peoples. The commitment to the one God was identical with the acceptance of this God as the single and exclusive authority. The question which God asks mirrors the linguistic openness of the formula, which can also be translated as: "Am I YHWH your God?" In his essay Zimmerli had already referred to Hos 13:4, where in the context of his self-introduction God refers to his uniqueness and connects it with the exodus from Egypt.[21] Ezekiel 20:5–7 makes it yet more clear that even at the very beginning of the exodus story legislation plays a part. The first and second commandment occur here already. *Aḥarê Mot* 13 does not mention the Ezekiel reference, but the implicit statement that Israel had committed itself to God already in Egypt is clear. The exodus itself is to be understood only in the context of adopting the commandments, i.e. of the acceptance of the only God who rules over Israel.

In *Aḥarê Mot* 13.III, according to Leviticus 18, the Egyptians and Canaanites serve as a deterrent example of incest, which is prohibited with particular force. In Lev 18:21 the formula is used as in 18:30, in order to indicate that these are serious prohibitions, the transgression of which will be punished by extirpation.

Qedoshim comments on 19:36:

> "I am the Lord your God who brought you out of the land of Egypt": It was on this stipulation that I brought you out of the land of Egypt, that you accept responsibility for yourselves the duties concerning just weights. For whoever accepts the religious duties involving just weights affirms the exodus from Egypt, and whoever denies the religious duties involving just weights denies the exodus from Egypt.

Emor on Lev 22:33 speaks of radical self-devotion to God:

> "Who brought you out of the land of Egypt" (Lev 22:33): I brought you out of the land of Egypt on a stipulation that you be prepared to give yourselves to sanctify my name. "I will be your God": like it or not. "I am the Lord": I am faithful to pay a reward.

Behar par. 5 on 25:38 in turn brings up the taking of interest as an example of a special prohibition connected to the exodus from Egypt:

> "I am the Lord your God who brought you forth" (Lev 25:38). It was on this stipulation that I brought you out of the land of Egypt, that you accept upon yourself the religious duty of not taking interest. For whoever accepts the prohibition of usury accepts the exodus from Egypt and whoever denies the religious duty of not accepting usury denies the exodus from Egypt.

The formula takes a somewhat different turn in the last instance, *Behar* 9.I.3–4 on 25:55:

---

[21] See Zimmerli, "Ich bin Jahwe," 11–40.

"For to me the people of Israel are servants, they are my servants, whom I brought forth out of the land of Egypt" (Lev 25:55): It was on the stipulation that they not be subjugated to them. "I am the Lord your God": What is the point of this verse? It teaches that whoever enslaves himself to them here below is regarded as though he had enslaved himself above as well.

Israel is only God's slave, not the slave of other peoples. The purpose of the exodus from Egypt was to subject Israel to God alone.[22]

6. *The Exodus from Egypt is Closely Connected to the Concept of Holiness*

Several texts speak of holiness and separation. These are Lev 11:44–45; 19:2; 20:7,26; 22:31–32:

Shemini 12.II.3–7 (Weiss 12.3f 57a) on Lev 11:41–45, which was already mentioned, is connected three times with holiness (for the sake of clarity and in order to point out certain connections I shall subdivide the text):

> 3 "For I am the Lord your God; consecrate yourselves therefore and be holy, for I am holy": Just a I am holy, so are you holy. Just as I am separate, so you be separate.
> 4 "You shall not defile yourselves with any swarming things that crawl upon the earth": even though it does not reproduce through sexual activity.
> 5 "For I am the Lord who brought you up out of the Land of Egypt"; it was on this stipulation that I brought you up out of the land of Egypt, on the condition that you accept on yourselves the yoke of the religious duties. For whoever accepts the yoke of the religious duties also affirms the exodus from Egypt, but whoever rejects the yoke of the commandments rejects the exodus from Egypt.
> 6 ". . . to be your God": whether you like it or not.[23]
> 7 ". . . you shall therefore be holy, for I am holy": Just as I am holy, so are you holy. Just as I am separate, so you be separate.

Holiness thus means separation. Here it defines the reason for the dietary laws, which are exclusively based on the sole veneration and sanctification of God. The exodus from Egypt is viewed as dependent on the acceptance of the commandments. In fact, the two are

---

[22] In *Emor* 17.II.7 there is no exegesis of אני יהוה in Lev 23:43. In this passage the "booths" are seen "as a memorial to the exodus."
[23] Literally: "against your will."

considered to be two aspects the same. Rejection of the exodus is to be understood in the light of the thesis as put by Crüsemann, that exodus means the same as sanctification and that the consequence of both is separation.

Aḥarê Mot 13 on 18:5 takes up Lev 22:31–32 in 16. On this see below under heading 8. *Aḥarê Mot* 13.II.

Qedoshim par. 1.I. (Weiss 86b) on Lev 19:2:

> 1 "And the Lord said to Moses. Say to all the congregation of the people of Israel. You shall be holy etc.": This teaches that this chapter was stated in the assembly of all Israel. And why was it stated in the assembly of all Israel? It is because most of the principles of the Torah depend upon its contents.
> 2 "You shall be holy": You shall be separate.
> 3 "You shall be holy, for I the Lord your God am holy": That is to say, if you sanctify yourselves, I shall credit it to you as though you had sanctified me, and if you do not sanctify yourselves, I shall hold that it is as if you have not sanctified me. Or perhaps the sense is this: If you sanctify me, then lo, I shall be sanctified, and if not, I shall not be sanctified? Scripture says, "For I . . . am holy," meaning, I remain in my state of sanctification, whether or not you sanctify me. Abba Saul says: The king has a retinue, and what is the task thereof? It is to imitate the king.

In *Qedoshim* 10.2 (Weiss 9.2 91b) Lev 19:1 is understood as a "reference to the sanctification involved in carrying out all of the religious duties" and distinguished from Lev 20:7. Though their contents are closely related, 20:7 is interpreted as "separation from idolatry." This has primarily hermeneutic reasons and is not meant as a conclusive understanding of 19:2. The assignation of meaning to the so-called *gufê torah* in particular is somewhat indeterminate in rabbinic literature.[24] It is however clear that something important and decisive is at stake here. Sanctification is conditionally connected to the

---

[24] The principles of the Torah, the *gufê torah*, are variously specified in rabbinic tradition. According to *m. Ḥag.* 1.8 the laws concerning civil cases and temple services, levitical cleanness and uncleanness, and the forbidden relations are *gufê torah*. *B. Ḥag.* 11b expands this list. In *b. Ber.* 63a it says, "Bar Kappara expounded: What short text is there upon which all the essential principles of the Torah depend? 'In all thy ways acknowledge Him and He will direct thy paths' (Prov 3:6). Raba remarked: Even for a matter of transgression. Bar Kappara [further] expounded: A man should always teach his son a clean and not laborious trade. What, for example? R. Hisda said: 'Needle-stitching.'" According to *b. Šabb.* 32a "the laws of *hekdesh*, *terumoth* and tithes are indeed essential parts of the law." According to *b. Ker.* 5a, with reference to Lev 19:8, *piggul* (an offering disqualified by improper

commandments. All in all, the *gufê torah* are not meant to be reduced to Lev 19:18, which nevertheless is of special importance in *Sifra*.[25] After all, Aqiba calls it there the "encompassing principle of the Torah" (*kelal gadol*), whereas Ben Azzai following Gen 5:1 singles out the equality of all human beings as the "encompassing principle" (*Qedoshim* 4.III.7; Weiss 4.12 89a).

Whereas in the second unit holiness is again explained as separation, a more differentiated interpretation follows in the third unit. First, the sanctification of Israel is tantamount to the sanctification of God, whereby the former gains special importance. From this, it may however be concluded that God is made dependent on the sanctification of the people. Consequently, the statement is qualified; God does not need the sanctification of Israel, he remains holy in any case. Abba Saul, finally, reads the verse as a reference to man being made in God's image.

Qedoshim 10.2–5 (Weiss 9.2–4 91b) on 20:7 has already been mentioned. It reads:

> 2 "Consecrate yourselves, therefore, and be holy": This refers to the sanctification achieved through separation from idolatry.
> Or perhaps it refers to the sanctification involved in carrying out all religious duties? When Scripture says, "You shall be holy" (Lev 19:1), lo, we find reference to the sanctification involved in carrying out all the religious duties.
> When then is the sense of the statement, "consecrate yourselves, therefore, and be holy, for I am the Lord your God?" This refers to the sanctification achieved through separation from idolatry.
> 3 "for I am the Lord your God":
> I am the Judge for exacting penalty and faithful to pay a reward.
> 4 "Keep my statutes and do them": I know only the matters that Scripture has spelled out in detail. How do I derive the rest of the details of the passage? Scripture says, "Keep my statutes and do them."
> 5. I am the Lord who sanctifies you: Just as I am holy, so you be holy.

Qedoshim 9.II[26] on Lev 20:22–26, in accordance with the biblical text, connects the specific questions of cleanness concerning creeping animals to the question of separation for the sake of God:

---

intention) is a *gufê torah*. According to the late *Num. Rab.* 13.15–16 they are the orders of Mishnah.

[25] Cf. R. Neudecker, "'And You Shall Love Your Neighbour as Yourself—I Am the Lord' (Lev 19,18) in Jewish Interpretation," *Bib* 73 (1992) 496–517.

[26] In this part of *Sifra* everything in the MSS and prints is mixed up (primarily

10 "... and between the unclean bird and the clean; you shall not make yourselves abominable by beast or by bird or by anything with which the ground teems, which I have set apart for you to hold unclean": that is, to subject to such a prohibition.

11 "You must be holy to me, for I the Lord am holy": Just as I am holy, so you be holy. Just as I am separate, so you be separate.

12 "... and have separated you from the peoples, that you should be mine": If you are separated from the nations, lo, you are for my Name, and if not, lo, you belong to Nebuchadnezzar, king of Babylonia, and his associates.

13 R. Eleazar b. Azariah says: How do we know that someone should not say, I do not want to wear mixed fibers, I don't want to eat pork, I don't want to have incestuous sexual relations. Rather: I do want. But what can I do? For my father in heaven has made a decree for me! So Scripture says, "and have separated you from the peoples, that you should be mine." So one will turn out to keep far from transgression and accept upon himself the rule of Heaven.

This explanation of the commandment is very significant as it makes the biblical text topical in a most drastic way. It is put down to the unconditional divine will and on the next level is connected to sanctification. A comparable explanation is to be found in the passage from *Aharê Mot* (13.II.7–13) explained below under heading eight.

Leviticus 21:6 does not use the formula, but there is nevertheless a connection to the holiness of the people, which the authors of *Sifra* also take as an indication of an unquestionable, absolute relation:

Thus *Emor* 1.III (Weiss 1.6 94a) on 21:6:

1 "They shall be holy to their God": whether they like it or not.
"... and not profane the name of their God; for they offer the offerings by fire to the Lord, the bread of their God; therefore they shall be holy": this explains the reason for these rules.
"... they offer": and not the Levites.
"... therefore they shall be holy": encompassing blemished priests.

In *Emor* 1.IV.1–5 (Weiss 1.12f 94b) on 21:8, the hermeneutic procedure of the Midrash again becomes particularly clear as it tries to

---

due to the insertion of *Mekhilta de-Arayot*). Neusner's counting corresponds to that on the *Davka* CD-ROM as well as to the edition *Torat Kohanim* (Jerusalem, 1959) (*Hotsa'at Sifra*). Weiss chapter 9—Neusner chapter 10; Neusner chapter 9—Vatican 66, 411–13; Vatican 31, 170–71. This shows the need for a collation of MSS and editions of *Sifra*. I suppose that Shlomo Naeh did this; see S. Naeh, "The Structure and Division of *Torat Kohanim* (A): Scrolls," *Tarbiz* 66 (1996–97) 483–515 (Hebrew); idem, "(B) Parashot, Peraqim, Halakhot," *Tarbiz* 69 (1999–2000) 59–104 (Hebrew); but in any case there is no publication of the collation.

interpret the various textual building bricks as explications of the biblical verse.

> 1 "They shall not marry a harlot, neither shall they marry a woman divorced from her husband": The use of "marry" twice teaches that a woman bears an admonition on account of her husband's status.
> 2 And how do we know that if the man does not concur, he is flogged? Scripture says, "You shall consecrate him," even against his will.
> 3 "... for he offers the bread of your God": this tells the reason for it all.
> 4 "... he shall be holy to you": this encompasses blemished priests.
> 5 "... for I the Lord, who sanctify you, am holy": this constitutes an admonition to the court in this matter.

A commandment needs to be clearly specified. In those cases where transgressions will be legally prosecuted, the commandment consists in rabbinic view not only of a clear definition but is also preceded by a warning. Here, God's self-introductory formula serves this purpose. This is to say, the redundant manner of representation is analyzed as a hint to hidden dimensions of the text yet to be worked out. The text thus contains both the commandment's explanation and a closer definition of its purview, as well as a warning.

Emor 9 (Weiss 99b) has already been mentioned several times. Its exegesis of Lev 22:29–33 very forcefully shows the different facets of *Sifra*. First, it examines the halakha on 22:29–30 and defines the purview of the commandment. This is followed by an exact definition of v. 31 the essence of which reads: "'So you shall keep my commandments and do them: I am the Lord': this serves to assign to the commandments the duties of both keeping and doing them."

This part is concluded by the well-known formula: "'I am the Lord': faithful to pay a reward." It occurs a second time in the same paragraph as the conclusion of *Pereq* 9. In between it frames comments on the sanctification of the divine name on v. 32. The topic there is martyrdom. According to the sages, no one who sacrifices his life in order to sanctify the divine name can hope for a miracle. On the contrary: those who are ready to do so only on that condition will not experience one. The famous story of Dan 3:16–18 serves as explanation. It is supplemented by another well-known parable, which is to be found also in *b. Ta'an.* 18b.[27] Trajan[28] intends to

---

[27] Cf. *Y. Ta'an.* II.13.66a; *y. Meg.* I.6.70c. On this see G. Stemberger, "Rom in der rabbinischen Literatur," *ANRW* 19.2:358–59.

[28] In *Sifra Emor*, Vatican 66 (p. 442) reads Trogiyanus (likewise Vatican 31

have Pappos and Julianos executed, but he himself is killed by a delegation from Rome. This use of the text aims at the positive example given by the two condemned to death. Upon the dictator's mocking request to ask God for a miracle, they reply that they too are sinners and that moreover Trajan is not worth having a miracle arranged for his sake. Nevertheless would God in the end give him the just punishment for an unjust execution, which eventually does happen. In this context, the ensuing passage becomes enormously explosive as an invitation to self-devotion:

> "who brought you out of the land of Egypt" (Lev 22:33): I brought you out of the land of Egypt on a stipulation that you be prepared to give yourselves to sanctify my name. "I will be your God": like it or not. "I am the Lord": I am faithful to pay a reward.

Leviticus 19:30 and 26:1–2 mention the formula in connection with the keeping of the Sabbaths and with the sanctuary. On this the authors comment in *Qedoshim* 7 (Weiss 7.7 90b):

> [And you shall keep my Sabbaths and revere my sanctuary: I am the Lord:] might one suppose that the building of the house of the sanctuary will override the restrictions of the Sabbath?
> Scripture says, "You shall keep my Sabbaths and revere my sanctuary: I am the Lord."
> Scripture has said that the Sabbath is on account of keeping the rule and the sanctuary is on account of reverence. Might one suppose that one should have fear of the sanctuary in particular?
> Scripture says, "You shall keep my Sabbaths and revere my sanctuary: I am the Lord."
> Now just as in the case of the Sabbath, it is not the Sabbath that you fear but the one who gave the commandment concerning the Sabbath, so in the case of the sanctuary it is not the sanctuary that you are to fear, but the one who gave a commandment concerning the sanctuary.

The term used for fear, יָרֵא, occurs only here in connection with the "sanctuary." The rabbis confirmed at this point what Ruwe suspected:

> Since a parallel phrasing is lacking in the Old Testament the demand to fear the sanctuary must be closely connected with the demand to

---

p. 184, though with only one *yod*). In the Bavli MSS, the name is spelled with only slight variation. In Stemberger's view, this is probably a "revision of the tradition concerning the execution of Lusius Quietus, who under Trajan had suppressed the Jewish revolt in the diaspora" ("Rom," 358).

fear YHWH, which particularly in Deuteronomy functions as a guiding principle for justifying laws. It is possible that, influenced by the prohibition of image worship, the demand to fear YHWH was modified into a demand to fear the sanctuary, which no longer orients the deduction of legal regulations to God himself, but more indirectly to the sanctuary as the special locus of divine presence.[29]

Behar 9.II (Weiss 9.5f 110ab):

4 ". . . and you shall set up a figured stone in your land, to bow down to them": In your land you shall now bow down on stones, but you may bow down on stones that are in the sanctuary.
5 ". . . for I am the Lord your God. You shall keep my Sabbaths and reverence my sanctuary": It is concerning a Jew who sells himself to a gentile that Scripture speaks. He should not say, Since my master serves an idol, so shall I serve an idol; since my master fornicates, so shall I fornicate; since my master profanes the Sabbath day, so shall I profane the Sabbath day. Scripture says, "You shall make for yourselves no idols . . . You shall keep my Sabbaths."
6 ". . . and reverence my sanctuary": In this passage Scripture has given an admonition concerning all the commandments.
7 ". . . for I am the Lord your God": faithful to pay a reward.

With regard to 26:1–2. Ruwe comments:

These verses stand isolated in their immediate context . . . Since the passage 26:1–2 comes at the end of all material legal paragraphs of the holiness code, immediately before the concluding paraenesis referring to the whole code, it is only reasonable to assume that 26:1–2 too is referring to the holiness code in its entirety and hence functions as a kind of signature to 17:1–25:55.[30]

Behar 9.II.6 takes that fact into account by seeing in it a warning relating to all commandments.

7. *The Last Occurrences of the Formula are Interpreted with a Strong Eschatological Emphasis, and its Meaning here is to Console*

Beḥuqqotai 3 (Weiss 3.4 111a) on Lev 26:13:

6 Might one suppose that my fear will not be upon you? Scripture says, "and I will be your God and you shall be my people." If you do not believe in me through all these things, nonetheless I am the

---

[29] Ruwe, *"Heiligkeitsgesetz"*, 102.
[30] Ibid., 99.

Lord your God, who brought you forth out of the land of Egypt. I am the one who did wonders for you in Egypt. I am the one who is going to do for you all these wonders.

Beḥuqqotai 8.II.12 (Weiss 8.10 112b) offers a synopsis of the story.

Here, the separation of the Israelites according to the Torah is important. God is with his people in times of danger and of exile. The Torah is being preserved for Israel.
"'... for I am the Lord their God'—in the time of Gog" finally is the last comforting affirmation.

8. Aḥarê Mot 13.II

One text has turned out to be particularly rewarding upon closer examination and it seems to summarize the various aspects of meaning in an exemplary way. While I cannot go into its genesis or composition in detail I put it at the end of my reflections on Sifra. The text in question is Aḥarê Mot 13.II. (Weiss 85b/86a).

The first part focuses on the obedience which began in Egypt and was fulfilled at Sinai. Egypt and Canaan are the two metaphors which symbolize separation. This was an important topic already in Par. 8 and it is taken up here:

1 The Lord spoke to Moses saying, "Speak to the Israelite people and say to them, 'I am the Lord your God'" (Lev 18:6):
R. Simeon b. Yohai says: That is in line with what is said elsewhere: "I am the Lord your God [who brought you out of the land of Egypt, out of the house of bondage]" (Exod 20:2). Am I the Lord, whose sovereignty you took upon yourself in Egypt? They said to him, "Indeed." Indeed you have accepted my dominion. They accepted my decrees: "You will have no other gods before me." That is what is said here: "I am the Lord your God," meaning, Am I the one whose dominion you accepted at Sinai? They said to him, "Indeed." Indeed you accepted my dominion. They accepted my decrees:
"You shall not copy the practices of the land of Egypt where you dwelt, or of the land of Canaan to which I am taking you; nor shall you follow their laws."

Paragraph 2 insists on the force of the commandments, which is said to be expressed by the formula:

2 R. Ishmael says: The weighty character of the laws against incest is shown by the fact that Scripture begins and ends its presentation of them by invoking the name of the Lord. At the beginning: "None of you shall come near anyone of his own flesh to uncover nakedness; I

am the Lord". And at the end: "You shall keep my charge not to
engage in any of the abhorrent practices that were carried on before
you, and you shall not defile yourselves through them; I am the Lord
your God." Lo, the weighty character of the laws against incest is
shown by the fact that Scripture begins and ends its presentation of
them by invoking the name of the Lord.

Paragraph 3 (which I do not quote in full) takes up paragraph 1, while
it emphasizes the involuntary acceptance of the commandments:

> 3 Rabbi says: It is self evident to the One who spoke and brought
> the world into being that in the end they would bear unwillingly the
> restrictive laws concerning sexual relations. That is why he set the mat-
> ter forth for them through a decree. "I am the Lord, your God."
> Know who it is who makes this decree over you. And so we find that
> they actually did unwillingly bear the restrictive laws concerning sex-
> ual relations.

God's self-communication is a decree, it brings the commandments
into force irrespective of whether Israel wants them or not. And
more than this, God needs the radical self-communication in order
to counteract Israel's unwillingness to obey certain commandments.
    Paragraph 4 enters into a dialogue with Moses:

> 4 Rabbi says: Speak to the Israelite people and say to them, I am the
> Lord your God": Say to them, I too am admonished just as I have
> spoken to you, and you have accepted. So speak so that they will
> accept it.

Paragraphs 5 and 6 belong together. They show the formula's hermeneutical function in the juridical context. The biblical text is interpreted so as to harmonize with the terms "admonition" and "judgment
to the court," which are necessary preconditions for punishment.

> 5–6 "'. . . and say to them': lo, this is an admonition to the court. 'I
> am the Lord your God': I am Judge to exact punishment and reli-
> able to pay a reward."

Parasha 8 already explained in detail what the grounds are for the
topos of the faithful God. Therefore it does not need another explanation here and occurs only as formula. *Behar* 9.II. on 25:55 has a
very similar reference, so that between 18:2 and 25:55 we come full
circle once again, which creates a strong textual unity.
    This is followed by warnings against idolatry starting from the
keywords "Egypt" and "Canaan." Paragraph 11 again enjoins the

significance of God's self-revelation as a justification of the commandments.

Whereas the commandments concerning thievery, fornication, idolatry, blasphemy and murder are presented as logically understandable, paragraphs 11–12 significantly read:

> for instance, the prohibition against eating pork, wearing mixed species, the rite of removing the shoe in the case of the deceased childless brother's widow, the purification-rite for the person afflicted with the skin ailment, the goat that is sent forth—cases in which the impulse to do evil raises doubt, the nations of the world, idolaters, raise doubt. In this regard Scripture says, "I the Lord have made these ordinances, and you have no right to raise doubts concerning them."

> 12 "[My rules alone shall you observe] and faithfully follow [my laws]": Treat them as principal and do not treat them as peripheral.

In paragraph 13, "and faithfully follow" is again interpreted as separation from foreign nations. Here, however, it is followed by a remarkable extension to the world to come, which again recalls *Par.* 8:

> "When you walk it will lead you": in this world.
> "when you lie down it will watch over you": in the hour of death.
> "and when you are awake it will talk with you": in the age to come.
> And so Scripture says, "Awake and shout for joy, you who dwell in the dust, for your dew is like the dew on fresh growth, you make the land of the shades to come to life" (Isa 26:18).
> And might you say: "My hope is lost, my prospects are lost?"
> Scripture says, "I am the Lord." I am your hope, I am your prospects, in my is your trust . . . (quotes from Isaiah follow: Isa 46:4; 44:6; 41:4).

This paragraph confirms the lasting relation to God also in difficult times.

Paragraphs 14 and 15 discuss 18:5, declaring that from there it may be inferred that even a gentile who obeys the commandments is to be regarded like a high priest.

Paragraph 16 once more makes reference to the formula, creating a link to 22:31–32. In this passage, the topic is no other than the threatening of Israel by the other peoples. They force it to idolatry and threaten the people which remains faithful to the one God with death. May one practice idolatry in order to survive? Is it allowed in privacy, without witnesses, since Torah itself is meant to lead to life and not to death? And what about doing so in public? Concerning this we read:

"If you sanctify my name, then I shall sanctify my name through you. For that is just as Hananiah, Mishael, and Azariah did." Here, then, the sanctification of the name is taken as readiness to die. The conclusion, on the other hand, in turn promises a glorious end for Israel: because the day on which the idolaters bend down in front of the idols, while Israel stands upright like a palm tree (Song 7:8 and Ps 7:9), this day will be the day of revenge, on which God will resurrect the dead. "'I am the Lord': I am Judge to exact punishment and faithful to pay a reward."

This passage is closely related in meaning to *Emor* 9.

All in all, one has to agree with Neusner, who writes concerning *Aḥarê Mot* 13.II, "that we have ... a kind of scrapbook of diverse materials, all of them pertinent to a fundamental proposition, if not particular to the details of the formulation of that proposition in the passage at hand."[31] To me, diverse materials seem to converge here from other parts and they seem to be inserted into the striking exegesis of 18:2 on purpose. The great theme is the recognition of the one God against all ills and the separation from peoples practicing idolatry. It is following the Torah which decides everything. The Torah is open to everyone, not only Israel.

9. *A Summary in Keywords*

Let me summarize briefly: The use of the formula in *Sifra* accomplishes the following:

- It emphasizes God's right and privilege vis-à-vis Israel.
- It has a structuring function. This is particularly true of the parenetic passages, which stress the keeping of the commandments.
- In connection with the exodus from Egypt the formula also serves as an indication regarding the commitment to the commandments, which began with the exodus as sanctification.
- Sanctification means separation and is connected to the radical acceptance of the commandments, which God decreed solely by virtue of his authority. Here the rabbis reject a rational explanation of the commandments.

---

[31] Neusner, *The Canonical History of Ideas*, 81.

Rabbis and modern exegetes alike have elucidated both the formal usage and the meaning of the formula. The rabbis moreover pointed out that it is particularly in these parenetic passages that God appears emphatically as judge. This is meant as warning and insistent exhortation; at the same time however it contains an aspect of hope and consolation, especially in view of the apocalyptic redemption. This is all the more necessary in the face of the consequences which radical acceptance of the commandments as sanctification may have, i.e. persecution and death.

Beyond this, the formula as it appears in *Sifra* served the rabbis as an argument in rabbinic hermeneutics in defining the purview of the commandments. This is closely connected to the meaning of God's role as ruler, which is expressed through the formula.

10. A Brief Look at Leviticus Rabbah

In contrast to the halakhic Midrash *Sifra*, *Leviticus Rabbah* belongs to the genre of the so-called homiletic Midrashim. In its present form it consists of thirty-seven thematically unified paragraphs. Five of them are identical with *Pesiqta de Rab Kahana*. Parallels are to be found primarily in *Pesiqta de Rab Kahana*, in *Genesis Rabbah* and in the *Yerushalmi*. The time of composition is usually dated to the fifth century. The edition by M. Margulies,[32] which is most frequently quoted today, is mainly based on the text form of ms British Museum Add. 27169 No. 340.

The Midrash *Leviticus Rabbah* has only six passages in which the formula occurs. These are 23.2, 9; 24.1, 5; 29.7 and 35.3.

Leviticus Rabbah 23.2 and 23.9 take up Exod 18:3 as their theme. 23.2 creates a link to Deut 4:34. Here it reads:

> R. Samuel b. Nahmani remarked: Had it not been for the fact that the Holy One, blessed be He, had bound himself by an oath, Israel would indeed never have been redeemed. Hence it is written, "Wherefore (לכן) say unto the children of Israel: I am the Lord, and I will bring you out from under the burdens of the Egyptians, etc." (Exod 6:6), and the expression לכן denotes nothing but an oath; as you read, לכן

---

[32] M. Margulies, *Midrash Wayyikra Rabbah. A Critical Edition Based on Manuscripts and Genizah Fragments with Variants and Notes* (5 vols., Jerusalem: Keren Epstein, 1953–60).

have I sworn unto the house of Eli" (1 Sam 3:14). R. Berekiah quoted, "you have with your arm redeemed your people" (Ps 77:16), where "with your arm" signifies, "with despotic power." R. Judan said: From the words, "To go and take Him a nation from the midst of another nation" to the words, "great terrors" (Deut 4:34) there are seventy-two letters. Should any one tell you that there are seventy-five, bid him deduct from this the second "nation" which is not to be included in the number. R. Abin commented: He redeemed them by His name; for the name of the Holy One, blessed be He, consists of seventy-two letters.

The connection with Exod 6:6 is significant, which is an important instance of the priestly covenant theology. The emphasis here is on God's active role independent of his people's assistance. The reference to God's name serves a similar purpose: it is God's free decision to liberate Israel.

In 23.9 the self-introductory formula of 18:2 and 4 appears as a formula of punishment. The text speaks for itself. Its theme is God's impatience with the crime of whoring. It says for instance:

> R. Hiyya taught: Why is "I am the Lord" written twice? It implies: I am He who inflicted punishment upon the Generation of the Flood, upon Sodom, and upon Egypt, and I am the same who will inflict punishment upon any one who will act in accordance with their practices. The Generations of the Flood were blotted out from the world because they were steeped in whoredom.... "I am the Lord" implies: I am He who inflicted punishment upon Samson, Amnon, and Zimri, and who will inflict punishment upon any one who will act in accordance with their practices. I am He who requited Joseph, Jael, and Palti the son of Laish, and I will in the future pay reward to any one who acts in accordance with their deeds.

In *Sifra*, in *Aḥarê Mot Par.* 8.1, the first part of Hiyya's statement had occurred in similar words, though anonymously. The assumption that behind this understanding of the formula lies the rabbinic equation of אלהים and judge is not corroborated here. One might interpret the double occurrence in relation to vv. 2 and 4, where in both instances the long form with אלהיכם appears, but the text makes no reference to אלהים. Here the issue is rather God's judicial aspect which demands separation and distance from the other peoples. This is also confirmed by the next instance.

Leviticus Rabbah 24.1 is the beginning of *Qedoshim*. God's holiness is understood as an expression of his punishing justice. It is the real reason for his glorification. The primary reference for it is Isa 5:16, which is further explained by Ezek 38:23; Ps 9:16; Jer 16:21 and Mic 6:5.

Leviticus Rabbah 24.5 recalls *Sifra Qedoshim Par.* 1, while it points out the connection to the decalogue more clearly:

> R. Hiyya taught: This section was spoken in the presence of a gathering of the whole assembly, because most of the essential principles of the Torah are attached to it. R. Levi said: Because the Ten Commandments are included therein."[33]

This is subsequently explicated in more detail.[34] God's self-introductory formula in Exod 20:2 stands for the First Commandment, which has its correspondence in Lev 19:3. God's sovereignty is connected to the First Commandment, or rather it *is* the First

---

[33] For the assessment of Leviticus 19 as a central Pentateuchal text it may be interesting to note that in *b. Ber.* 63a the Talmud quotes Prov 3:6 as the text to which all central principles of the Torah are attached, i.e. a text from the *Ketubim* (see footnote 24). From this it may be inferred that the statements about isolated passages which implicitly contain the essence of the Torah do not make an assessment of the texts' overall value within the Tanakh as a whole. We may rather assume that it is an attempt to paraphrase essential tenets of faith. R. Levi does so by recognizing the decalogue as the core of the Torah and relating Leviticus 19 to it. At this point, then, the text goes beyond *Sifra*. According to *Leviticus Rabbah* 24 the holiness of the people arises from its acceptance of the Torah at Sinai, where the Israelites were endowed with two crowns of holiness, God however with only one. Israel receives the second crown for fighting its evil inclination. Altogether, then, God and Israel have three crowns of holiness, which also explains Isa 6:3. According to R. Yudan, holiness is moreover given as an eternal present to Israel in Leviticus 19, which he compares with David's eternal royal dignity and Aaron's eternal priestly dignity. At this point, we can clearly see the important role of the holiness topos in Leviticus 19 and the high value put on the text. In addition to this, in *Leviticus Rabbah* 24, the text was subsequently seen as equivalent to the tractates *Pesaḥim* (*Pisha*) and *Neziqin*. *Pesaḥim* deals with Exod 12:1–13:8 (and 13:16 respectively), *Neziqin* with Exod 21:1–23:9 (and 23:33 respectively), and *Qedoshim* with Lev 19:1–20:8 (and 20:27 respectively). Depending on how the endings of the *parashot* are determined, there are 60 or 70 single instructions in each *parasha*. In this context, a reference to *b.Qid.* 30a is interesting, according to which the "*waw*" in נחון in Lev 11:42 stands in the middle of the letters of the Torah, Lev 10:16 דרוש דרש is in the middle of the words and Lev 13:33 והתגלח in the middle of the verses. This shows that the rabbis cared about the "middle," or the center, of the Torah also in a material sense.

[34] According to the Jewish counting of the Ten Commandments the following verses are put in parallel: Exod 20:2 and Lev 19:3 (First Commandment); Exod 20:3 and Lev 19:4 (Second Commandment); Exod 20:7 and Lev 19:12 (Third Commandment); Exod 20:8 and Lev 19:3 (Fourth Commandment); Exod 20:12 and Lev 19:3 (Fifth Commandment); Exod 20:13 and Lev 19:16 (Sixth Commandment); Exod 20:13 and Lev 20:10 (Seventh Commandment); Exod 20:13 and Lev 19:11 (Eighth Commandment); Exod 20:16 and Lev 19:16 (Ninth Commandment); Exod 20:17 and Lev 19:18 (Tenth Commandment).

Commandment. This view had implicitly occurred already in *Sifra*, in *Aḥarê Mot* 13:II.1, there in connection with Lev 18:2. In *Sifra*, however, there was no conscious reflection on the Ten Commandments.

Leviticus Rabbah 29.7 interprets 23:24 by using Isa 48:17, the emphasis being on an understanding of מלמד as trainer. God trained Israel. Another aspect, brought up in a parable, lies in the reference to the patriarchs as advocates in court, so that there is again an element of judgement.

A contrasting parable explains Lev 19:32 in 35.3. The issue here is God's model character:

> R. Eleazar observed: It is the way of the world that when a mortal king issues an order, then if he wishes to execute it he does so, but if not then he ultimately has it performed through others. The Holy One, blessed be He, however, is not so, but He issues a decree and Himself performs it first. Thus for example, it is written, "You shall rise up before the hoary head, and honour the face of the old man, and you shall fear your God: I am the Lord" (Lev. 19:32). "I am the Lord" means: I am He who was first to carry out the precept of rising before an old man. Hence it says, "if you walk in my statutes."

As concerns the interpretation of the self-introductory formula, *Leviticus Rabbah* is altogether in accordance with *Sifra*. The judgement of God, the connection of Leviticus 19 to the so-called *gufê torah*, fear as motivation: all these aspects were already present in *Sifra*. And 23.2 does create textual associations with Deut 4:34 and Exod 6:6 which are absent in *Sifra*, but are nevertheless obvious.

DOUBLE TIME... DOUBLE TROUBLE?
GENDER, SIN, AND LEVITICUS 12

Linda S. Schearing

> Our Daughters Ask: Does Jewish tradition consider
> giving birth a religious experience? You'd never know
> it from this parasha!
>
> · · ·
>
> Our Daughters Ask: Why is the woman who's given
> birth required to bring... sacrifices.... Why a sin
> offering? What's she done wrong?
> —*The Five Books of Miriam: A Woman's Commentary
> on the Torah*[1]

Leviticus 12:1–8, with its regulations concerning childbirth, evokes a
myriad of responses from contemporary readers. For some it is a
"rabbi killer,"[2] while others ask plaintively, "What's a feminist to do
with the opening verses of this portion?"[3] Its ideas—labeled "anti-
sexual" by more acerbic readers[4]—are understood by others as divine
mandates for twenty-first century women.[5] From distaste to despair,
from ridicule to pious adherence, this passage retains its power to
stir the emotions of its readers.

This article explores the history of Leviticus 12's reception. Through
two millennia and across the confines of at least two faith traditions, readers produced readings of (or responses to) Leviticus 12
that shaped the social construction of gender and women's worship
practices. Was childbirth a cause for celebration? Should a mother's

---

[1] E. Frankel, *The Five Books of Miriam: A Woman's Commentary on the Torah* (San
Francisco: HarperSanFrancisco, 1996) 163, 165.

[2] J. Magonet, "'But if it is a Girl, She is Unclean for Twice Seven Days...'
The Riddle of Leviticus 12.5," in J. F. A. Sawyer (ed.), *Reading Leviticus: A Conversation
With Mary Douglas* (JSOTSup 227; Sheffield: Sheffield Academic Press, 1996) 144–52,
esp. 144.

[3] M. Drucker, "Parshat Tazria: The Unbearable Lightness of Childbirth," n.p.
[cited 25 May 2001]. Online: http://www.malkadrucker.com/birth.html.

[4] B. E. Akerley, *The X-Rated Bible: An Irreverent Survey of Sex in the Scriptures* (Austin,
Tex.: American Atheist Press, 1985) 51.

[5] Both Orthodox Jews and Eastern Orthodox Christians follow a more literalist
appropriation of Lev 12:1–5.

faith community welcome her back into their midst after giving birth? Or should childbirth isolate her from worship? Although a study of this length cannot, by its very nature, deal with all interpretive trajectories concerning gender and Leviticus 12, it will examine three interpretive periods: 1) early and medieval Judaism, 2) patristic and medieval Christianity, and 3) contemporary liturgical responses in Judaism and Christianity.

Before we address Leviticus 12 in antiquity, a quick examination of the text itself is necessary. Leviticus 12:1–8 is found in the so-called "Manual of Purity" that extends from Leviticus 11:1–15:33 and is sandwiched between regulations concerning clean and unclean creatures (chapter 11) and the diagnosis of skin disease (chapter 13). Moreover, it shares some elements in common with chapter 15, the chapter dealing with bodily discharges like menstruation.

Leviticus 12:1–5 describes the duration of the mother's purification after childbirth. If she gives birth to a son she is unclean for 7 days (as at the time of her menstruation). On the eighth day the baby is circumcised. This time of uncleanness is followed by a period of 33 days of blood purification (for a total of 40 days). If she gives birth to a daughter, these times are doubled (14 days of uncleanness followed by 66 days of blood purification for a total of 80 days). No explanation is given for the difference in these times. During her period of purification, the mother can neither come into the sanctuary nor touch holy objects (v. 4).

Verses 6–8 concentrate on the offerings required at the end of the 40 or 80–day period of purification. The new mother is to make a burnt offering (a lamb) and a sin offering (either a pigeon or a turtle dove). A "sliding scale" of sacrifices is provided in v. 8 should she be unable to afford a lamb. In that case, two turtle doves (one for the burnt offering and one for the sin offering) suffice. Unlike the legislation in vv. 1–5, no distinction is made between the birth of a son or daughter. Male and female babies alike call for the same offerings before their mothers become "clean" again.

The general rationale for the purity guidelines like those found in Leviticus 12 is the object of extensive debate. Scholars offer explanations ranging from health awareness to anthropological/socio-religious concerns as they attempt to understand the mentality behind such legislation. But while others deal with this debate, the concern of this essay is not (per se) how the original author and audience understood Leviticus 12, but how subsequent readers understood (and applied) it.

Early and Medieval Judaism

At least three approaches to the issue of women, childbirth, and Leviticus 12's purity legislation characterize Jewish readings from the second century BCE to the fifteenth century CE: 1) reading Genesis 1–3 as an etiology of Leviticus 12, 2) using midrash to address questions about Leviticus 12, and 3) understanding Leviticus 12's restrictions concerning the Temple as having validity for synagogue worship practices.

Leviticus 12 and Genesis 1–3

One of the earliest attempts to explain the origins of the Leviticus 12's purity laws is found in the pseudepigrahical book of *Jubilees* (second century BCE):

> [3:8]In the first week Adam and his wife—the rib—were created, and in the second week he showed her to him. Therefore, a commandment was given to keep (women) in their defilement seven days for a male (child) and for a female two (units) of seven days. [3:9]After 40 days had come to an end for Adam in the land where he had been created, we brought him into the Garden of Eden to work and keep it. His wife was brought (there) on the eightieth day. After this she entered the Garden of Eden. [3:10]For this reason a commandment was written in the heavenly tablets for the one who gives birth to a child: if she gives birth to a male, she is to remain in her impurity for seven days like the first seven days; then for 33 days she is to remain in the blood of purification. She is not to touch any sacred thing nor to enter the sanctuary until she completes these days for a male. [3:11]As for a female she is to remain in her impurity for two weeks of days like the two first weeks and 66 days in the blood of purification. Their total is 80 days. [3:12]After she had completed these 80 days, we brought her into the Garden of Eden because it is holiest in the entire earth, and every tree which is planted in it is holy. [3:13]For this reason the law of these days has been ordained for the one who gives birth to a male or a female. She is not to touch any sacred thing nor to enter the sanctuary until the time when those days for a male or female are completed. [3:14]These are the law and testimony that were written for Israel to keep for all times.[6]

While Leviticus 12 stipulates different lengths for a mother's impurity following the birth of a son (7 days) or a daughter (14 days), it

---

[6] *The Book of Jubilees* (trans. J. C. Vanderkam; CSCO 88; Leuven: Peeters, 1989) 17–18.

does not disclose the rationale for this difference. The writer of *Jubilees* rectifies this omission by connecting the mother's impurity to the creation of the first male and female. According to *Jub.* 3:8, Adam was created in the first 7 days (thus sons render their mothers unclean for 7 days), while Eve was shown to Adam in the second week (thus daughters make their mothers unclean for 14 days [v. 11]). It is interesting to note that in linking the "doubling effect" of the mother's impurity to Eve, the writer gives no explicitly pejorative reason in explanation.

In addition to explaining the differences in purification periods, *Jubilees* links the length of the mother's purification to Adam and Eve. According to *Jubilees*, the period following the birth of a male (7 + 33 = 40 days) corresponds to the fortieth day after Adam's creation (when God brought Adam into the Garden), while the time following the birth of a girl (14 + 66 = 80 days) corresponds to Eve's introduction to the Garden on the eightieth day after her creation (vv. 9–11). Again, like the legislation governing the mother's days of impurity, there is no pejorative dimension given to this "doubling" effect.

Jubilees also explains the prohibition against the postpartum woman's touching of holy objects and her entrance into the sanctuary (Lev 12:4). In *Jubilees*, the Garden and all of its trees are "holy" (as is the land itself). This fact (no doubt reenforced by Eve's report that God told them not to "touch" the tree in Gen 3:2) is understood by the writer as the foundation for Lev 12:4's prohibitions. Moreover, the Garden's sanctity demands that the writer of *Jubilees* locate both the creation of Adam and Eve, as well as the birth of their children, outside the Garden's boundaries. By having Eve enter the Garden on the eightieth day—and having this form the basis of Leviticus 12's prohibition of the postpartum woman's entrance into the sanctuary—the writer presents the Garden as a prototype of the Temple.[7] Moreover, this explanation grounds Leviticus 12's purity legislation in the time shortly after creation (long before the Temple's actual construction).

---

[7] J. M. Baumgarten, "Purification After Childbirth and the Sacred Garden in 4Q265 and Jubilees," in G. J. Brook (ed.), *New Qumran Texts and Studies: Proceedings of the first Meeting of the International Organization for Qumran Studies, Paris, 1992* (Leiden: Brill, 1994) 3–10; esp. pp. 6–10.

Echoes of the reading found in *Jubilees* can be found in 4Q265[8] and 4Q266. Although both restate *Jubilees'* etiological treatment of Leviticus 12, 4Q266 6 ii 5–11 adds the note, ‏[התן את הי[לד למנקת‎ ‏[בטוה]רה‎, indicating that a wet-nurse suckles a child "in purity."[9] This might imply that while the mother was considered impure following birth, the child itself was not (the purity status of the child is not addressed in Leviticus 12). If this is true then the child—although pure at birth—might afterwards be in danger of contamination by contact with its mother's breast during her period of impurity (hence the necessity of a wet-nurse until the mother is purified).[10]

Leviticus 12 and the Rabbis

Rabbinical approaches to Leviticus 12 are as varied as they are creative and offer a wealth of comment on details not covered in Leviticus 12.[11] For the sake of brevity, our treatment will be limited to five questions: 1) What defines a "birth?" 2) When does a woman bear a child but is not considered *niddah*? 3) What if the sex of the child cannot be determined? 4) Why does Leviticus 12 stipulate 40/80 days for the mother's purification? and, 5) Why does the woman bring a sacrifice at the end of her purification?

What defines a "birth?" Since Leviticus 12 details the stipulations surrounding a child's birth, one question that emerged was how to discern *when* a birth had actually taken place. Some rabbis suggested that the child's *form* (either in its totality or in part—hand, arm, etc.) was necessary. *B. Hullin* 71a, for example, quotes the sages as saying that: "Whatsoever has not the human form is not considered a child." *B. Niddah* 24b underscores this idea by noting that when a woman delivers either blood or water the sages ruled it was not a valid birth. Both rulings were subject to debate. In regards to the argument based on *form*, R. Meir insisted that even if a woman birthed an animal-like object, it was a "birth" and it rendered her unclean (*b. Hul.* 71a). As for delivering blood and water, who is to

---

[8] "265. 4QMiscellaneous Rules: Plates V–VIII" in J. Baumgarten et al. (eds.), *Qumran Cave 4.XXV: Halakhic Texts* (DJD 35; Oxford: Clarendon Press, 1999) 60; see also Baumgarten, "Purification After Childbirth," 6.

[9] "265. 4QMiscellaneous Rules," 60.

[10] Ibid.

[11] The scope of the following treatment is highly selective—focusing on questions of particular concern to this article and limited primarily to the Babylonian Talmud.

say, some rabbis argued, that a child might have been squashed in
the process of birth and thus blood and water was all that was left
of its original form (*m. Nid.* 24b)?

A different type of argument revolved around the stage of the
pregnancy at which the "birth" in question happened. In relation to
miscarriages, for example, a woman who miscarried up to the fortieth day had not birthed a "child," but the same could not be said
of the woman whose miscarriage happened on the 41st day (*m. Nid.*
3.7). Sometimes a birth was considered to have taken place even
though a child had yet to be delivered! R. Huna addressed the status of the woman whose child has put its hand out and then taken
it back. He ruled that such a woman is considered unclean as if the
birth was complete (*b. Nid.* 28a).

When does a woman bear a child but is not considered niddah? According
to some rabbis, to be considered *niddah* a mother has to give birth
through her "normal passage" (*b. Mak.* 14b, *b. Šabb.* 135a). Focusing
on the *method* of birth, this position argues that to be considered *niddah* a woman must deliver vaginally. Delivery though any other means
(like a caesarean section) does not render the mother unclean and
exempts her from Leviticus 12's purity stipulations. These rulings
were challenged, however, by rabbis such as R. Simeon, who argued
that Leviticus 12's focus was not the *method* of birth but its *result*—
a child. Since a child could be delivered in more than one way
(vaginally and "from the side") all such births rendered women *niddah* (*b. Nid.* 40a).

What if the sex of the child cannot be determined? Although Leviticus 12
clearly states times of uncleanness and purification for the mothers
of male and female babies, it does not address the birth of the
androgyne or hermaphrodite. Rabbinic resolutions to this quandary
varied. Some argued that one should add the times for male and
females babies together (and perhaps the time for menstruants too)
and produced an extended period for uncleanness and purification
(*b. B. Bat.* 127a). Others argued that hermaphrodites called for both
a selection and combination of male and female legislation. For
example, *b. Bik.* IV suggests that:

> Hermaphrodites are LIKE men—thus their mothers have 33 days of
>   purification
> Hermaphrodites are LIKE women—thus their mothers have 14 days
>   of uncleanness
> Hermaphrodites are LIKE men and women—thus mothers must bring
>   offerings.

At least one rabbi—Sherabya—argued that the birth of a hermaphrodite rendered the mother outside of Leviticus 12's purview entirely, thus allowing for her to be exempt from *niddah* status (*b. B. Bat.* 127a).

Why does Leviticus 12 stipulate 40/80 days? As to why the periods of 40 days and 80 days are mandated, some rabbis suggested that these times mirrored the formation of the embryo. For males, the embryo was developed on the fortieth day, while females took twice as long to develop (the eightieth day). To substantiate this, the rabbis report an alleged experiment by Cleopatra that scientifically verified these findings (*b. Nid.* 30b).

Why does the woman bring a sacrifice at the end of her purification? Identifying the offering in Lev 12:6 as a "sin" offering, some rabbis simply said that the mother brings it because she is a sinner. Others specified her sin by suggesting that the pain of birth was so extreme that she swore, in her pain, that she would never have intercourse with her husband again. In so swearing she violated God's procreative command and thus expiation was necessary (*b. Nid.* 31b). Such rendering laid open the possibility of linking Eve's actions with Leviticus 12's legislation. Implicit in Gen 3:16's mandate for increased pain in childbirth is Eve's culpability for the postpartum woman's later rejection of her conjugal duties.

Aside from these questions, Leviticus 12 evoked interest in other ways as well. For example, rabbinical thought connected the sexual act with Leviticus 12. In *b. Ḥul.* 109b the rabbis admonish their readers that for everything God forbids there is an equivalent that God grants. Although it is forbidden for Jews to have sex during menstruation, sex is permitted in blood of purification. In this way the rabbis limited sexual abstinence after birth to 7–14 days. Another situation arose concerning time limits for men's vows of abstinence. While the rabbinical schools of Shammai and Hillel differed in their conclusions, they both appealed to Leviticus 12 for their rationale. According to Beth Hillel, wives had to contend with 7 days of their spouse's abstinence (derived from the days of uncleanness for a male child) while Beth Shammai counseled wives to consent to 14 days (in keeping with the period of uncleanness for a girl child) (*b. Ketub.* 61b; *b. 'Ed.* IV).

The Synagogue as Surrogate Temple

An intriguing development concerning Leviticus 12's interpretation in medieval Judaism is the equation of the Temple with the Jewish synagogue.[12] Leviticus 12:4 warns against postpartum women touching holy objects and entering into the sanctuary while vv. 6–8 describes the appropriate offering they should give following their days of purification. All of which, one would think, would become rather moot (in practice) following the Temple's destruction in 70 CE. Instead, some readers superimposed selected regulations concerning the Temple over the liturgical practices of the synagogue. The result was a series of injunctions against postpartum women's participation in various synagogue activities.

In the wake of the Temple's destruction in 70 CE, Jewish worship shifted both ritually (from sacrifice to prayer/study of Torah) and spatially (from the Jerusalem Temple to the local synagogue). Whereas much of Levitical law became obsolete at this point, some legislation survived the transition. It is in the "highly controversial and problematic"[13] extra-Talmudic text *Baraita de Niddah* (ca. sixth to seventh century CE) that one finds menstruants and postpartum women imaged as "dangerously" impure. The *Baraita de Niddah* thus "updates" Lev 12:4 for post 70 CE Jews. In a passage from the *Ma'aseh HaGe'onim* (thought to be "lifted entirely" out of the *Sefer Baraita de Niddah*) the writer warns menstruating women and postpartum women not to touch sacred books, pray, say God's name, or enter the synagogue.[14]

While we do not know who wrote the *Baraita de Niddah* or to whom it was written, we do know that its prescriptions did not go unchallenged. The *Sefer HaPardes* (a twelfth century collection of rulings from Rashi (1040–1105) contains the following observation:

> Some women refrain from entering a synagogue and from touching a Hebrew book during their menstrual periods. This is only superogation ... and they are not obliged to act in this manner. For what is the reason for them to act this way? If it is because they think that the synagogue is like the Temple, then even after their immersion why do they enter it? ... Thus, you see that (the synagogue) is not like the Temple, and they may enter it [even during their periods].[15]

---

[12] For an extended discussion of this association of Temple with synagogue see J. R. Woolf, "Medieval Models of Purity and Sanctity: Ashkenazic Women in the Synagogue," in M. Poorthuis and J. Schwartz (eds.), *Purity and Holiness: The Heritage of Leviticus* (Jewish and Christian Perspectives Series 2; Leiden: Brill, 2000) 263–80; 273–78.

[13] Ibid., 269.

[14] Ibid.

[15] *Sefer ha-Pardes* (ed. Ehrenreich) 3, as cited in S. J. D. Cohen, "Purity and Piety:

This controversy over whether the menstruant and the postpartum woman should be separated or integrated into synagogue worship is further documented in R. Karo's *Shulḥan Arukh* (a rabbinic law code) and R. Isserles's subsequent gloss. In the *Shulḥan Arukh*, the Sephardic authority R. Karo (1488–1575) comments on *halakah* and on *minhag* (received custom):

> All those who are impure may read the Torah, recite the *Shema*, and pray, except for the ejaculant, because Ezra removed him from the general category of the impure and prohibited him [to engage] either in the words of Torah or in the recitation of the *Shema*, or in prayer, until he immerses [in a *mikveh*] so that the Sages should not frequent their wives like roosters. Afterward, however, this enactment was abolished and the original law was re-established, that even an ejaculant is permitted [to engage] in the words of Torah, the recitation of the *Shema*, and prayer, without immersion and without washing in nine *kabim* of water. And this is the common practice.[16]

But in a gloss to this statement, the Ashkenazic authority R. Isserles (1525–1572) writes:

> Some have written that a menstruant, during the days of her discharge, may not enter a synagogue or pray or mention God's name or touch a Hebrew book, but some say she is permitted [to do] all these, and this view is correct. However, the practice in these countries accords with the first opinion. However, in the white days the custom is to permit [her to do all these]. And even in a place that follows the stringent practice, on the Days of Awe and other such occasions when many gather to enter the synagogue, they are permitted to enter the synagogue like other women because it will be great sadness for them if everyone gather [in synagogue] but they stand outside.[17]

Shaye J. D. Cohen[18] and Jeffrey Robert Woolf, after examining the historical context of Isserles' gloss, conclude that Isserles' reference to "these countries" refers to an appropriation of Leviticis 12 found in Franco-German (Ashkenazic) medieval Judaism. Woolf argues that up until the end of the eleventh century the *halakhic* tradition followed by such groups was more diverse than that of other Jewish communities. While most Jews by the mid to late medieval period

The Separation of Menstruants from the Sancta," *Daughters of the King* (Philadelphia: Jewish Publication Society, 1992) 103–15; 109–10.

[16] *Shulḥan Arukh*, Oraḥ Ḥayyim 88, as cited in Cohen, "Purity and Piety," 104.

[17] Ibid.

[18] Cohen, "Purity and Piety," 109–11.

viewed the Babylonian Talmud as the primary arbitrator of *halakhic* truth, Woolf argues that Franco-German Jews' *corpus receptus legalis* was more open. It recognized "received custom" such as the *Baraita de Niddah* as authoritative.[19]

Leviticus 12 in Patristic and Medieval Christianity

Somewhat surprisingly, Leviticus 12's purity legislation has enjoyed a tenacious history in Christian interpretation. In spite of what might be called a "slow" interpretive start,[20] it played an important role in post-third century CE thought concerning liturgical practices and the development of Marian ideology.

The Church as Surrogate Temple

Throughout the first millennium, obedience to practices inspired by Leviticus 12 became the object of Christian debate. This debate can be best examined in the exchanges between Augustine of Canterbury (597–604), Pope Gregory the Great (590–604), and in the writings of Theodore of Canterbury (668–690).[21] All three addressed the issue of the Christian postpartum woman in relation to religious objects/ actions and entrance into the sanctuary. Moreover, a great deal of the medieval debate that followed these writers used their writings as a foundation for their own arguments.[22]

In 598, one year after his arrival in Canterbury, Augustine wrote a letter to Pope Gregory in Rome. Aside from asking for more help in his task of instructing converts, Augustine sought pastoral (and administrative) advice on a number of different issues. Among other questions, Augustine asked Gregory whether or not a pregnant woman

---

[19] Woolf, "Medieval Models of Purity and Sanctity," 270–71.

[20] For a detailed discussion of Leviticus' use in early Christian literature see G. Rouwhorst, "Leviticus 12–15 in Early Christianity," in *Purity and Holiness*, 181–93.

[21] Although this debate is striking, it is certainly not the first time this question emerged in Christian writings. One of the earliest witnesses to the "purification" of Christian postpartum women is found in the *Canons of Hippolytus* (fourth century).

[22] R. Meens, "Questioning Ritual Purity: The Influence of Gregory the Great's Answers to Augustine's Queries about Childbirth, Menstruation and Sexuality," in R. Gameson (ed.), *St. Augustine and the Conversion of England* (Stroud: Sutton Publishing, 1999) 174–86; and "'A Relic of Superstition Bodily Impurity and the Church form Gregory the Great to the Twelfth Century Decretists," in *Purity and Holiness*, 281–93.

should be baptized, how long a postpartum woman has to wait before entering a church after her baby is born, how long she and her husband have to wait before having intercourse, and whether or not she should be allowed the sacrament of holy communion during the time of her period.[23] Augustine's questions imply that by this time (at least in the British-Irish church), some Christians were applying the purity injunctions in Lev 12:3–4 to Christian worship practices. As the Jewish postpartum woman was to refrain from coming into contact with sacred objects/rituals, so the Christian one was to abstain from baptism and communion. As the Jewish postpartum woman was to wait 40/80 days after childbirth before offering a sacrifice, so the Christian one was to stay away from Church for a time and then enter into a reconciliation ceremony before re-entrance into public Christian worship. It was about the above practices that Augustine sought aid from his pope. Gregory responded by affirming that pregnant/postpartum women could be baptized, take communion, and enter the church.

Whether Theodore of Canterbury knew about Gregory's instruction and ignored it, or whether he simply was unaware of Gregory's previous correspondence with Augustine on these matters is unclear.[24] What is clear, however, is that Theodore took a position quite contrary to Gregory's in his writings. In *The Penitential of Theodore*, a collection of decisions made on various issues, Theodore addresses the plight of the postpartum woman. In paragraph 17 he notes that "During the time of menstruation women should not enter into church or receive communion, neither lay woman nor religious. If they presume to do so all the same, they should fast for three weeks."[25] Paragraph 18 extends this regulation to the postpartum woman: "In the same way those women should do penance, who enter a church before their blood is purified after birth, that is for forty days."[26]

The positions of Gregory the Great and Theodore of Canterbury established the poles of the argument for centuries afterwards. In the ninth century, for example, Pope Nicholas I (d. 867) had to rule on a question concerning the length of time a new mother should be absent from church services. He did so by citing Gregory's ruling.

---

[23] Meens, "A Relic," 282.
[24] Ibid., 286–87; idem, "Questioning Ritual Purity," 178.
[25] *Theodori Poenitentiale* I, 14, para. 17.
[26] *Theodori Poenitentiale* I, 14, para. 18.

However, when a similar situation confronted the Regino of Prüm (abbot, d. 915) and Burchard of Worms (archbishop, d. 1125), neither cited Gregory. Instead they cited sources that forbid postpartum women from entering church following their deliveries.[27]

Somewhat ironically, this concept of keeping postpartum women away from the site of worship would later be known in Christianity as "churching."

Leviticus 12, Luke 2, and Mariology

Luke 2:21 contains the account of Jesus' circumcision while vv. 22–24 record Mary's visit to Jerusalem forty days after his birth. Apparently, she and Joseph were rather poor because Luke records that they offered two turtledoves (instead of the lamb and turtledove stipulated in Leviticus 12). It wasn't the Holy Family's finances, however, that drew the most attention from readers, but the fact that Mary offered what was understood as a "sin" offering. Such an action raised a host of questions about Mary's nature. Was the mother of the Christ a "normal" woman? Did she menstruate? Did she bleed when giving birth to Jesus? In either of these cases, Leviticus 12 and 15 would have labeled Mary ceremonially "unclean." In the early centuries following Jesus' death, however, Christian communities claimed that Mary was "more than" other women. As this happened, such "normal" aspects of female physicality such as menstruation and parturition became the objects of controversy. For example, while some thought that Mary's piety exempted her from the "normal" pain of childbirth, others insisted that even Mary's hymen was left intact during Jesus's birth!

A more serious issue arose concerning the sin offering Mary offered in Lk 2:24. The dogma of Mary's Immaculate Conception insisted that Mary was without sin. If this was the case then why would she need to be purified? How could the birth of the Savior render his mother unclean? As Mary's visit to Jerusalem for her purification became immortalized in the church's festival of Candlemas, focus on her purification was kept cultically alive each calendar year.[28]

---

[27] Meens, "A Relic," 288–89; idem, "Questioning Ritual Purity," 179–80.

[28] For an interesting treatment connecting the themes of purification and Mary's presentation see C. Caspers, "Leviticus 12, Mary and Wax: Purification and Churching in Late Medieval Christianity," *Purity and Holiness*, 295–309.

Perhaps one of the most well-conceived medieval treatments of Mary's presentation and its relationship to Leviticus 12 is found in the writings of Thomas Aquinas. In his *Summa Theologica*, he addressed Lk 2:21–24, Leviticus 12, and Mary's sinlessness and perpetual virginity:

> *Obj*[ection] 1. It would seem that Christ was unbe-comingly presented in the Temple. For it is written (Ex 13:2): *Sanctify unto Me every first-born that openeth the womb among the children of Israel.* But Christ came forth from the closed womb of the Virgin; and thus He did not open His Mother's womb. Therefore Christ was not bound by this law to be presented in the Temple.

> . . .

> Reply Obj[ection] 1. As Gregory of Nyssa says (*De Occursu Dom.*): *It seems that this precept of the Law was fulfilled in God incarnate alone in a special manner exclusively proper to Him. For He alone, whose conception was ineffable, and whose birth was incomprehensible, opened the virginal womb which had been closed to sexual union, in such a way that after birth the seal of chastity remained inviolate.* Consequently the words *opening the womb* imply that nothing hitherto had entered or gone forth therefrom. Again, for a special reason is it written *"a male,"* because *He contracted nothing of the woman's sin*: and in a singular way *is He called 'holy,' because He felt no contagion of earthly corruption, whose birth was wondrously immaculate* (Ambrose, on Luke 2:23).[29]

In another section of his treatment, Aquinas addressed the question of whether or not Mary ought to have gone to the Temple for purification in the first place:

> *Obj*[ection] 1: It would seem that it was unfitting for the Mother of God to go to the Temple to be purified. For purification presupposes uncleanness. But there was no uncleanness in the Blessed Virgin, as stated above (QQ. 27, 28). Therefore she should not have gone to the Temple to be purified.

> Obj[ection] 2: Further, it is written (Lev 12:2–4): *If a woman, having received seed, shall bear a man-child, she shall be unclean seven days*; and consequently she is forbidden *to enter into the sanctuary until the* days *of her purification be fulfilled.* But the blessed[sic] Virgin brought forth a male child without receiving the seed of man. Therefore she had no need to come to the Temple to be purified.

---

[29] Thomas Aquinas, "Question 37, Third Article: Whether Christ Was Becomingly Presented in the Temple?" in *Summa Theologica* (vol. 2; New York: Benziger, 1947) 2221.

Obj[ection] 3: Further, purification from uncleanness is accomplished by grace alone. But the sacraments of the Old Law did not confer grace; rather, indeed, did she have the very Author of grace with her. Therefore it was not fitting that the Blessed Virgin should come to the Temple to be purified.

On the contrary is the authority of Scripture, where it is stated (Luke 2:22) that *the days of* Mary's *purification were accomplished according to the law of Moses.*

I answer that, As the fulness of grace flowed from Christ on to His Mother, so it was becoming that the mother should be like her Son in humility: for *God giveth grace to the humble,* as is written James 4:6. And therefore, just as Christ, though not subject to the Law, wished, nevertheless, to submit to circumcision and the other burdens of the Law, in order to give an example of humility and obedience; and in order to show His approval of the Law; and, again, in order to take away from the Jews an excuse for calumniating Him: for the same reasons He wished His Mother also to fulfil the prescriptions of the Law, to which, nevertheless, she was not subject.

Reply Obj[ection] 1: Although the Blessed Virgin had no uncleanness, yet she wished to fulfil the observance of purification, not because she needed it, but on account of the precept of the Law. Thus the Evangelist says pointedly that the days of her purification *according to the Law* were accomplished; for she needed no purification in herself.

Reply Obj[ection] 2: Moses seems to have chosen his words in order to exclude uncleanness from the Mother of God, who was with child "without receiving seed." It is therefore clear that she was not bound to fulfil that precept, but fulfilled the observance of purification of her own accord, as stated above.

Reply Obj[ection] 3: The sacraments of the Law did not cleanse from the uncleanness of sin which is accomplished by grace, but they fore-shadowed this purification: for they cleansed by a kind of carnal purification, from the uncleanness of a certain irregularity, as stated in the Second Part (I–II, Q. 102, A. 5; Q 103, A. 2). But the Blessed Virgin contracted neither uncleanness, and consequently did not need to be purified.[30]

In both cases—her perpetual virginity and her sinlessness—Aquinas felt it necessary to defend Mary's actions in Lk 2:21–24 in light Leviticus 12's association with impurity. Nor was such concern solely

---

[30] Thomas Aquinas, "Question 37, Fourth Article: Whether It Was Fitting That the Mother of God Should Go To the Temple to Be Purified?" in *Summa Theologica*, Vol. 2, 2222.

the purview of theologians like Aquinas. A similar point of view can be found in the liturgy of a mid-eleventh century Bavarian Candlemas ceremony:

1 [Veneration of Mary, daughter of Abraham]

2 (a, b) Be glad, noble mother and virgin, who, believing in the archangelic prophecy, bore a son in obscurity,

In whose most precious blood all of the lost human race was cleansed, as God had promised Abraham.

3 (a, b) [Virginity of Mary—blossoming rod, ever-closed gate]

4 (a, b) But nonetheless, since you wished to show us an example of the virtues of a mother, you subjected yourself to a legal remedy for (ritually) impure mothers; Spotless mother, you brought with you to the temple to one to be cleansed, God made flesh, who gave to you the adornment of virginity

5 (a, b) [Mary rejoice and exult in the child]

6 (a, b) Therefore we who honor feasts of the infant Christ born for us, and of his sweet mother Mary,

If we, the latecomers, cannot follow the great humility of God, may his mother be a model for us.

7 (a,b)–8 [trinitarian doxology . . .][31]

For historians like Joanne Pierce, this rite, with its imperative to let Mary "be a model for us" exemplifies how the Feast of Candlemas connected the themes of Mary and purification while at the same time exhorting women to follow Mary's example."[32]

Leviticus 12 and Contemporary Jewish and Christian Women

While there are contemporary groups—both fringe[33] and not-so-fringe[34]—who recognize Lev 12:1–5 as authoritative for contemporary women, the majority of Jewish and Christian readers either mitigate what they see as Leviticus 12's negative implications or

---

[31] J. M. Pierce, "'Green woman' and Blood Pollution: Some Medieval Rituals for the Churching of Women after Childbirth," *Studia Liturgica* 29 (1999) 191–215, see esp. pp. 208–9.
[32] Ibid., 209, 213–14.
[33] African Hebrew Israelites of Jerusalem.
[34] Ethiopian Jews, Orthodox Jews, and Eastern Orthodox Christians.

simply reject its authority outright. Thus, contemporary liturgical responses to Leviticus 12:1–5 (aside from those groups who preserve a literalist reading/application of Lev 12:1–5) fall into at least two main categories: 1) attempts to "recover" Lev 12:1–5 liturgically for contemporary women, or 2) attempts to invent new rituals to replace it.

Recovering Leviticus 12:1–5

One liturgical response to Lev 12:1–5's purity legislation is to recover the text by modifying its negative associations. This "modification process" took place in quite different ways for Jews and Christians. While certain sectors in Judaism, for example, sought a gender balanced reading of Lev 12:3 (bringing girl babies as well as boy babies into the covenant), many Christians shifted the ritual's locus from purification to celebration. Thus "Churching" became a rite of thanksgiving and blessing for Christians—a rite intentionally separated from the idea of purification.

In the latter half of the twentieth century, Conservative, Reform, and Reconstructionist Jews developed birth rituals for their newborn daughters. Known by a variety of labels—*Shalom Bat* ("Welcome to the daughter"), *Simḥat Ha-bat* ("Joy of the daughter"), *Brit Bat* ("Covenant for a daughter"), *Shalom Nekeva* ("Welcome to the female"), and *Brit Ha-hayim* ("Covenant of life")[35]—one of the ritual's purposes was to counter the gender asymmetry of Lev 12:3. Although the ritual has no real moorings historically in Jewish tradition, it appears to be gaining popularity. Jewish feminist Blu Greenberg, for example, predicts that:

> Within the next century, this ritual will surely become uniform and fixed; Jews living a hundred years from now will probably celebrate the birth ceremony for a baby girl as if it had been part of Judaism since revelation at Sinai.[36]

What allows Greenberg to be so optimistic concerning the future of this ritual? It is her firm belief that such recasting (expansion?) of

---

[35] N.a., "What about Baby Girls? The *Brit Bat*" in *Ritual Reality: The Ultimate Jewish Baby Resource*. Online. [Accessed 18 May 2001.] Http://www.ritualr.com/britbat.htm.

[36] B. Greenberg, "Female Sexuality and Bodily Functions in the Jewish Tradition," in J. Becher (ed.), *Women, Religion and Sexuality: Studies on the Impact of Religious Teachings on Women* (Philadelphia: Trinity Press International, 1990) 1–44, esp. 14.

Lev 12:3 is in keeping with the spirit of Judaism. As Greenberg reflects:

> Where does the solution lie? Certainly we cannot rewrite the sources; nor would we want to for that is part of our history and our tradition. Nor does the solution lie in a hostile confrontation with the sources.
>
> How, then, do we overcome thousands of years of ambivalence regarding female sexuality and bodily functions—fear, power, respect, temptation, infatuation, disgust, admiration, defilement, glorification, subordination, appreciation?
>
> There are ... methods ... drawing on fundamental characteristics of Judaism. One is the continuous explication and interpretation of inherited tradition. The strength of Judaism is that it has often incorporated, gradually and in varying degrees, the values of contemporaneous culture. ... Thus the process of hermeneutic made it possible for *halakha* to remain continuous with revelation, yet adapt itself to the needs of a living community
>
> ... New interpretations of hallowed texts will use feminism as an hermeneutic. The new understanding of women that we have arrived at in this very moment of human history will become an integral part of Jewish values, not at odds with them.[37]

A quite different approach to Leviticus 12's negative connotations is found in the changing understanding of the Christian ritual of "Churching." From at least the eleventh century, Christians had a rite that "re-introduced" the postpartum woman into the church.[38] In analyzing medieval churching rites, historian Joanne Pierce identifies five characteristic themes:

1) purification (blood pollution or sexual pleasure);
2) repentance (forgiveness/reconciliation; connected with purification);
3) blessing (connected with reconciliation and celebration);
4) thanksgiving (for a safe delivery/survival of childbirth);
5) celebration (private/social/official).[39]

While even a simplistic survey of the history of churching is not possible in a short treatment such as this, it is nevertheless important to note several key points as a backdrop to what happens with this ritual in the twentieth century. Although for the sake of brevity we

---

[37] Ibid., 38–39.
[38] W. Coster, "Purity, Profanity, and Puritanism: The Churching of Women (1300–1700)," *SCH* 27 (1990) 377–87; esp. 377.
[39] Pierce, "'Green Woman,'" 205.

will look at Anglican and Roman Catholic examples, it is important
to realize that it wasn't only Anglican and Catholic women who
wrestled with this ritual. While some reformers "denounced the ritual as Judaising," others struggled with its place in newly formed
liturgical systems.[40] In the words of one historian:

> ... churching was one of the most hotly debated practical manifes-
> tations of English religion in the sixteenth and seventeenth centuries.
> Defended by bishops and conformists, given new prominence by Laud-
> ians, it was strongly condemned, satirized, and dismissed by more rad-
> ical and reforming Protestants.[41]

Both Anglicans and Catholics shifted the focus of churching away
from women's *purification* following childbirth to *thanksgiving* com-
memorating the birth. For Anglicans, this can be readily seen in
rite's title in the Book of Common Prayer. While the 1549 Book of
Common Prayer contains "The Order of the Purification of Women,"[42]
three years later (in the 1552 edition) this same rite is called "The
Thanksgiving of Women After Childbirth, Commonly Called the
Churching of Women."[43]

For Catholics, the shift from purification to celebration is evident
in the liturgical directions taken by the Council of Trent emphasizing the *blessing* of the mother rather than her *purification*. The Council
also noted that churching was voluntary and not an obligation for
Roman Catholic mothers.[44] In spite of the Council's intent, however, Catholic women continued to connect churching with purification.
As one historian notes:

> By preserving the main gestures and prayers ... it [the Council of
> Trent] maintained the elements referring to purification. In so far as
> the perception of church can be traced, oral accounts from north-west-
> ern European women suggest that they themselves perceived the ritual
> as a form of (obligatory) purification.[45]

Indeed, this distance between official rhetoric and actual prac-
tice/perception marks the history of churching in the Catholic church.

---

[40] Caspers, "Leviticus 12," 303.
[41] Coster, "Purity, Profanity, and Puritanism," 377–78.
[42] F. F. Brightman, *The English Rite* (vol. 2; London: Rivingtons, 1915) 883ff.
[43] Ibid., 880ff.
[44] A.-M. Korte, "Reclaiming Ritual: A Gendered Approach to (Im)purity," *Purity and Holiness*, 313–27; 315–16.
[45] Ibid., 315.

For example, the *Catholic Encyclopaedic Dictionary* defined the "churching of women" as:

> . . . an act of thanksgiving after childbirth; the mother coming to church to receive the blessing contained in the 'Rituale Romanum.' No idea of purification whatsoever is contained in the rite, for in childbearing is incurred no sort of taint. A mother is not bound but recommended to receive it; the common idea that she should not got to church for any purpose before being churched is a pernicious superstition.[46]

But pernicious superstition or not, the practice continued. For example, Irish women who were interviewed about pre-Vatican II churching practices described their own observations and feelings:

> 1—Another belief firmly held by the older generations of women was that the mother didn't get strong until she was churched, nor that any food she cooked, or even served, would be fully nutritional until the churching was done, usually three weeks after the birth. It was a ceremony in the Catholic Church, a cleansing ceremony . . . I don't know if it was obligatory but every woman was churched. If she weren't, the neighbours would not be pleased, as she might 'bring a plague of rats about the place. A neighbour woman now deceased told me it was a privilege bestowed by the church on married mothers only, that it was not for 'sluts that had children outside of marriage'. An old school teacher told my mother many years ago that a woman who gave birth to a son first was privileged, because our blessed lady had a son first, and so she did not need to be churched after any subsequent birth, only after the first one.

> 2—On the first Sunday the mother went to mass after having a baby. She went up to the altar boy when everyone was left the church and told him she wanted to be churched. The priest would come out with his stole, the altar boy with a lighted candle and holy water. The priest would give the woman the end of the stole and pray over her while she held the lighted candle and sprinkle holy water over her. She was then 'clean' and back in the church.

> 3—If the mother was well enough to attend christening she went to the church and took no part in Christening, but as soon as she entered the church she went to the side altar of the Blessed Virgin and knelt down at the altar rails until the Christening of her baby was finished . . . When the priest was ready, he went inside the rails and went to where the mother was and he prayed over her for almost five minutes, blessed

---

[46] A. O'Connor, "Listening to Tradition," in L. Steiner-Scott (ed.), *Personally Speaking: Women's Thoughts on Women's Issues* (Dublin: Attic Press, 1985), as cited. N.p. [cited 12 April 2001] Online: http://iol.ie/~pcassudt/ARC/churching.html.

her with holy water and made the sign of the cross with his thumb
on her forehead. There was a blessed candle alight during the time
the woman was being churched. The people who had attended the
Christening waited for the mother at the bottom of the church ...
Now if the mother could not go to be churched the day of the
Christening, she was churched the first Sunday she went to mass after
the birth of the baby ... There was a custom around here at that
time that a woman that was not churched did not enter any other
house, only her own. No neighbour wanted her to visit them until she
was churched as she was considered a very bad omen to see her enter
anybody's house. She was supposed to bring bad luck to the house
until she was blessed by the priest, some misfortune would befall one
of the people in the house she went to, or something belonging to
them would have some mishap.

4—The baby was usually christened before the midwife finished with
the mother, usually within one week, the mother was also churched
at the same time. It wasn't considered right for the mother to leave
the house for any reason until she had been churched. I never knew
for a long time what this ceremony meant. I thought that the mother
was living in sin until this was done ... Any mother who didn't have
it done was considered to be almost pagan. The usual procedure was
for the mother to kneel at the altar and hold a lighted candle while
the priest prayed over her and blessed her with holy water. To me it
was very similar to the Christening of the baby when the devil was
driven out.[47]

Although anecdotal, these women's memories and observations are
not anomalies. A sociological study (1950) of mothers in East London
reveals that over 90% still participated in churching.[48] Thus, it is
not surprising in the documents that emerged from Vatican II
(1962–1965), the revised liturgy omitted the blessing on the mother
and instead included a blessing for both parents at the end of the
baptismal rite.

Replacing Leviticus 12:1–5

A second type of contemporary liturgical response to Lev 12:1–5 is
the invention of new rituals marking childbirth—rituals that re-

---

[47] Ibid.
[48] M. Young and P. Wilmott, *Family and Kinship in East London* (Institute of Community Studies, Reports, 1; London: Routledge and Kegan Paul, 1957) 57 as cited in
Coster, 387.

place those historically connected with Leviticus 12. A good example of this reasoning can be found in the writings of various Jewish feminists.

Not all Jewish women are satisfied with balancing Lev 12:3 with a corresponding ceremony for their newborn daughters. For example, in her article "Jewish Feminism and 'New' Jewish Rituals: Imitative or Inventive?" Rabbi Elyse Goldstein notes that:

> In the progressive movements we have encouraged what I term *imitative* ritual. In imitative ritual we redesign the traditional model, but we do not reimagine it. We imitate it, with a "female" twist on the end. . . . A baby naming looks like a *brit*, but without the cutting.[49]

Goldstein argues that contemporary Jews should not try to "balance the scale" with traditional rituals celebrated by men, but instead invent new rituals that reflect women's unique experiences. She calls these ceremonies "inventive rituals" and asks her Jewish readers:

> . . . do we want to *invent* our own? If we choose to be inventive, what will our rituals look like? How will they be uniquely our own? . . . Will they focus on our biological womanhood—menstruation, childbirth, lactation—or a more inner sense of womanhood, not defined by physicality?[50]

This is a bold move, she realizes, and not without its own problems. She admits that:

> Inventive rituals are risky. They are not linked to thousands of years of practice. They do not look like what your *bubbe* did. A menstruation ceremony, a menopause *mikveh* celebration, a silk and applique tallis-cape with hood does not look or feel familiar . . . How do we as non-Orthodox Jews balance the tightrope between accepted traditional rituals that gives us collective context and memory . . . and new rituals that continue our goal of inclusivity and personal meaning? . . . We add, we subtract, we change, we adapt, and at what point do we say: enough, this ritual is now exactly the way we want it?[51]

[49] E. Goldstein, "Jewish Feminism and 'New' Jewish Rituals: Imitative or Inventive?" *The Reconstructionist: A Journal of Contemporary Jewish Thought & Practice.* n.p. [cited 18 May 2001]. Online version http://www.rrc.edu/journal/recon63_1/goldstein.htm.
[50] Ibid.
[51] Ibid.

Concluding Remarks

Leviticus 12, with its ancient legislation linking impurity with child-birth and childbirth with the mother's isolation from her faith com-munity, has shown a remarkable ability to influence readers over two millennia and across two faith traditions. Nor has its influence been abolished today. As Rabbi Melissa Crespy notes: "perhaps these verses and commentaries would not be so painful if the reality they reflect existed only in the distant past. But this is not true."[52]

The question that fairly begs to be asked is simply: "Why?" Why—when other legislation was set aside after 70 CE did this passage get recycled and applied to synagogue worship practices? Why—when Christians rejected so much of the legal traditions inherited from Judaism—did the church see fit to retain liturgical practices inspired by Leviticus 12? When scholars reconstruct the rationale behind ancient Israel's purity legislation, should we assume that these dynam-ics remained the same throughout the centuries of Leviticus 12's reception? Or could it be that whatever fuels Leviticus 12's recy-cling is founded on sociological bedrock far deeper than the topsoil of Israel's purity system?

---

[52] Rabbi M. Crespy, "Tazria-Metsora 5761: Leviticus 12:1–15:33," in *Parashat HaShavuah*, n.p. [cited 25 May 2001]. Online: http://jtsa.edu/topics/parashah/5761/tazriametsora.shtml.

"COMING BEFORE THE LORD": THE EXCLUSION OF WOMEN FROM THE PUBLIC DOMAIN OF THE ISRAELITE PRIESTLY CULT[1]

JUDITH ROMNEY WEGNER

Prologue

Feminist analysis of sacred texts involves a broad interdisciplinary approach that takes account of the insights of the social sciences. Though often couched in theological terms, the portrayal of women in religious scriptures is more usefully understood as rooted primarily in anthropology, and thus needs to be analyzed from that perspective among others.

Anthropologists, sociologists and historians of religion like Mary Douglas, Peter Berger and Mircea Eliade have persuasively argued that religious doctrines and practices reflect human efforts to make sense of the cosmos.[2] The innate human craving for harmony and order prompts the hope that the world is fundamentally ordered rather than chaotic. In the Israelite priestly cult of Leviticus, the preservation of cosmic harmony in nature and society depended in part on a sacrificial cult based on the premises of *quid pro quo* and *do ut des*, and in part on the "holiness" and "purity" of the hereditary priesthood that conducted the cult—and by extension, on the purity of Israelites at large, characterized in Exod 19:6 as "a kingdom of priests and a holy nation."

This paramount concern with purity and fear of pollution led the framers of the priestly code to regulate the movements of persons exhibiting grave physical abnormalities such as scaly skin diseases or genital discharges; sufferers might be placed in isolation until the priest pronounced them cured. The androcentric mindset of those

---

[1] A shorter version of this article appears in J. Magness and S. Gitin (eds.), *HESED VE-EMET: Studies in Honor of Ernest S. Frerichs* (BJS 320; Atlanta, GA: Scholars Press, 1998.

[2] M. Douglas, *Purity and Danger* (London: Routledge and Kegan Paul, 1966); P. Berger, *The Sacred Canopy* (Garden City, NY: Doubleday, 1967); M. Eliade, *The Sacred and the Profane* (New York: Harcourt Brace Jovanovich, 1959).

who made the rules viewed one important group as so anomalous that it came to epitomize *otherness*: namely, the entire class of women. So it is no surprise that priestly regulation of cultic pollution included taboos involving women, designed to control the pollution generated by such "abnormal" phenomena as childbirth, menstruation, vaginal discharges and illicit sexual relations.

Israelite priests, like those of many other religions of the biblical period (including Zoroastrianism and Hinduism to the east and early Greek paganism to the west[3]) believed that the miasma of cultic pollution was generated by anomalous phenomena, especially abnormal flows of blood or other uncontrollable discharges connected with poorly understood processes of life and death. Humans tend to fear things they do not understand and hedge them about with taboos.[4] Uncontrollable discharges frequently and obviously occurred in women (who routinely lose blood during menstruation and at parturition) as well as to persons of either sex who suffer from chronic genital discharges. So priestly laws regulated the *post-partem* purification of new mothers (Leviticus 12) and the cleansing of cultic impurity generated by various bodily emissions (Leviticus 15). In addition, the Holiness Code proscribed various types of sexual activity thought to produce cultic contamination (Leviticus 18 and 20).

זב *and* זבה

The present paper focuses on the rules of Leviticus 15, dealing with male and female genital discharges. These regulations had far wider repercussions on women than most biblical scholars have realized; in fact, they were doubly effective, as they sociologically reflected and theologically reinforced the "establishment view" of the place of women in biblical Israelite society. Priestly concern with sexuality and its attendant pollution inevitably affected the image and status

---

[3] G. C. Haughton, *The Institutes of Manu: Compromising the Indian System of Duties, Religious and Civil* (ed., P. Percival; 4th ed.; New Delhi: Asian Educational Services, 1982); M. Boyce, *Zoroastrianism* (Totowa, NJ: Barnes & Noble Books, 1984); R. Parker, *MIASMA: Pollution and Purification in early Greek Religion* (Oxford: Clarendon Press, 1983).

[4] H. Eilberg-Schwartz, *The Savage in Judaism: An Anthropology of Israelite Religion and Ancient Judaism* (Bloomington, IN: Indiana University Press, 1990).

of women as a group, even though the primary goal of the priestly
rules was surely not to complicate women's lives but simply to maintain harmony in the sacred cosmos. To preserve the holiness and
purity of individual Israelites and thus of the community as a whole,
it was necessary that women keep to their assigned "place" in Israelite
culture; and in the priestly system that meant strict confinement to
the private domain of the culture where they would pose no threat
to men's cultural enterprises in the public domain. This accounts for
the explicit disqualification of women from the conduct of the priestly
cult, repeatedly declared (along with the eating of specified portions
of the sacrifices) to be the preserve of the "*sons* of Aaron" (Lev 1:6,
2:2, 3:2) but not his *daughters*. Thus, only the *male* descendants of
priests may partake of the meal-offering (מנחה, Lev 6:7–11) the sin-
offering (חטאת, Lev 6:17–22), the guilt-offering (אשם, Lev 7:1–6) and
so forth. The sole exceptions were the elevation-offering (תנופה) and
sacred gift-offering (תרומה), placed by Scripture in a special category
that may be eaten outside the sanctuary. This fact alone made it
accessible to a priest's daughters living at home (as specified in Lev
10:14 and 22:12–13)—important evidence of the deliberate exclusion of females from the sacred precinct.

Conformity with priestly regulations was designed to maintain or
restore *holiness* and its inseparable companion, *cultic purity*. The concept of cultic purity takes for granted that certain bodily states or
processes generate an invisible, intangible, yet nonetheless palpable
miasma of pollution, whose most important effect was to impede
access of the human to the divine. This was expressed in the priestly
world view, which insisted that a man in a state of cultic impurity
could not "come before YHWH" (that is, "into the presence of YHWH")
until he had taken appropriate steps to remove the impurity.

The Term לפני יהוה

The biblical expression לפני יהוה, far more prevalent in the Priestly
source than elsewhere, is usually rendered "before the LORD." But
this translation obscures its technical significance in the rites of the
priestly cult, where it more strictly denotes "in/into the presence of
YHWH." Scholars have made strenuous efforts to pinpoint the precise physical location connoted by לפני יהוה as used in P; yet scant
attention has been paid to the far more important figurative significance

of the phrase, which defines a crucial aspect of human relationship to the divine, namely the capacity to approach close enough to communicate with the Deity or at least to perceive oneself as being in the Presence of God.

Scholars addressing the question of coming "into the presence of YHWH" have focused mainly on the distinction between priesthood and laity in this regard. But until now, no one seems to have noticed an equally important dichotomy, based not on caste but on gender: the priestly use of the phrase לפני יהוה for the Divine Presence contemplates the public domain of Israelite worship into which males alone may enter and from which females are routinely barred. Such exclusion is not unique to Israelite religion or Judaism, but is a normal incident of the status of women in religious systems that reflect and endorse patriarchal culture—in particular, it is a commonplace in the classical rules of the three religions based directly or indirectly on the Hebrew Bible.

We shall now explore how P's use of language subtly reinforces social mores that bar women's access to the public domain of Israelite culture and provide a model for the subsequent exclusion of women from public religious enterprises of rabbinic Judaism, patristic Christianity, and Islam—thereby effectively depriving women of principal means of access to the life of mind and spirit and the world of ideas that elevates humankind above all other forms of life.

While the expression לפני יהוה occurs mainly in the context of the priestly sacrificial cult, it occurs also in connection with offerings brought by lay Israelites in specified circumstances. As earlier research by N. Raban has established, the location connoted by לפני יהוה may vary, depending on who is doing what, when and where.[5] Thus when a member of the hereditary caste of כהנים performs cultic rites like sprinkling sacrificial blood, the location is inside the Tent of Meeting (אהל מועד).[6] But when a lay Israelite brings a sacrifice of wellbeing (זבח שלמים), which he himself will slaughter as prescribed in Leviticus 3, the offeror does not physically enter the Tent but presents and slaughters his sacrifice at its entrance. Nonetheless, this lay Israelite is described as acting לפני יהוה (Lev 3:1–2, 3:7, 3:12).

---

[5] N. Raban: "Lipne YHWH," *Tarbiz* 1 (1930) 1–8 (Hebrew). See also, most recently, A. M. Cooper and B. H. Goldstein, "At the Entrance to the Tent: More Cultic Resonances in Biblical Narrative," *JBL* 116 (1997) 201–15.

This fact indicates that the phrase can have a purely abstract significance; the present discussion will concern itself with this figurative or symbolic meaning.

Readers may have noticed that I referred to the offerer as "he himself." That is because P's references to the sacrifice of זבח שלמים slaughtered by the offerer contemplate solely Israelite males. The ineligibility of women to participate actively in this sacrificial rite, if not absolutely explicit, seems to be taken for granted. The two cases where P does explicitly command a woman to bring an offering (Lev 12:6 and 15:29), do not have her slaughtering the victim, nor do they describe her as "coming before YHWH." The exclusion of women is likewise implied in a commandment repeated in J, E, and D (Exod 34:23, Exod 23:14 and Deut 16:16 respectively), which explicitly requires Israelite *males* to bring offerings before the LORD on the three pilgrimage feasts known as חגים.[7] But whereas it is theoretically possible that the non-priestly rule mandating the pilgrimage for men left it optional for women,[8] the priestly corpus leaves us in no doubt that its use of the expression לפני יהוה contemplates men only and specifically excludes women, as we shall see from the following example.

Leviticus, chapter 15 discusses cultic pollution incurred through male and female genital discharges and prescribes a process of purification to "cure" that pollution. In the case of a male sufferer, Lev 15:13–15 decrees as follows: [9]

---

[6] Also termed משכן (Tabernacle) and מקדש (Sanctuary), depending on the source.

[7] The pilgrimage festivals of Pesaḥ/Passover, Shavu'ot/Weeks and Sukkot/Booths. While the Deuteronomic formula את פני יהוה שלוש פעמים בשנה יראה כל זכורך, "three times a year shall all your males appear before YHWH" (Deut 16:16) may constitute a non-priestly precursor of P's exclusion of women, it is more likely that the Deuteronomist chose to exempt women because of the practical difficulty of requiring mothers and young children to make thrice-yearly pilgrimages to distant Jerusalem. By contrast, in the priestly rules concerning festivals, the redactor's interpolation at Lev 23:39–43 casts the commandment of the palm branch ושמחתם לפני יהוה אלהיכם, Lev 23:40) in a cultic context that contemplates males alone. It is clear that he deliberately excludes women (along with slaves and children) by omitting the inclusive formula אתה ובתיך (or אתם וביתכם) "you and your household(s)" as found in the Deuteronomic versions of festival regulations (Deut 12:7; 14:26).

[8] The Mishnah would later explicitly exempt women from this מצוה along with most others of a cultic nature. Similarly in classical Islam to this day, the *hajj* is the only one of the "five pillars of Islam" that the Qur'an makes optional for women (by excluding any reference to it in Sura 33:35, which makes the first four pillars mandatory for *muslimīn* and *muslimāt* alike).

[9] Lengthy biblical citations are taken from *TANAKH: The Holy Scriptures* (Philadelphia: JPS, 1985).

13 When one with a discharge becomes clean of his discharge, he shall count off seven days *for his cleansing, wash his clothes, and bathe his body in fresh water* [emphasis added]; then he shall be clean.

14 On the eighth day he shall take two turtledoves or two pigeons and *come before YHWH* at the entrance of the Tent of Meeting and *give* them to the priest (ובא לפני יהוה אל פתח אהל מועד ונתנם אל הכהן).

15 The priest shall offer them, the one as a sin offering and the other as a burnt offering. Thus the priest shall make expiation on his behalf, before YHWH for his discharge (מזובו).

In the case of a woman, 15:28–30 decrees as follows:

28 When she becomes clean of her discharge, she shall count off seven days, and after that she shall be clean.

29 On the eighth day, she shall take two turtledoves or two pigeons and *bring* them to the priest at the entrance of the Tent of Meeting (והביאה אותם אל הכהן אל פתח אהל מועד).

30 The priest shall offer the one as a sin offering and the other as a burnt offering. Thus the priest shall make expiation on her behalf, *before YHWH* [emphasis added] for her unclean discharge (טמאתה מזוב).

A cursory reading may suggest equivalence between the problems of the זב and the זבה, and likewise between the solutions; the prescribed offerings and purification rituals seem at first glance virtually identical. But closer scrutiny reveals a spurious parallelism masking a significant discrepancy—a fact that went unnoticed (or at least undiscussed), until I pointed it out some years ago in my book *Chattel or Person?*[10] More recently, Jacob Milgrom, commenting on Lev 15:29 in his Leviticus volume in the Anchor Bible, dismissed this crucial discrepancy as follows:

29 and [she shall] *bring* them [to the priest] (*wehebi'a 'otam*). A shortened form for *uba' lipne YHWH . . . unetanam ['el hakkohen]*, "he shall come before the LORD . . . and give them [to the priest]" (v. 14), and the indication that the pericope on the *zaba* is structured on that of the *zab but in a condensed form* [emphasis added]. (Square-bracketed words added by the present writer for purposes of clarification.) [11]

Given the meticulous attention to detail for which Professor Milgrom is justly renowned, this arbitrary dismissal of so glaring a discrep-

---

[10] J. R. Wegner, *Chattel or Person? The Status of Women in the Mishnah* (Oxford: Oxford University Press, 1988) 147.

[11] J. Milgrom, *Leviticus 1–16* (AB 3; New York: Doubleday, 1991) 944.

ancy is astounding—and not merely because Milgrom (uncharacteristically for him) ignores the well-known rabbinic maxim אין אות מיתרת בתורה, "there is no superfluous letter in the Torah." It is equally surprising that a scholar of Milgrom's caliber, in today's climate of raised consciousness to gender issues, seems to have overlooked the fact that the omission of a phrase as significant as לפני יהוה in the woman's case can hardly be due to "condensation" or even mere inadvertence, but undoubtedly *reflects* the priestly view of women's ineligibility to enter, still more participate in, the public domain of the cult.

Specifically, the inclusion of לפני יהוה in the man's case distinguishes him from the woman in an otherwise identical situation *by according him a symbolic location that brings him much closer to God.* This becomes obvious from a careful comparison of 15:14 with 15:29. Whereas verse 14 enjoins the זב to *come before the* LORD (לפני יהוה) to the entrance of the Tent of Meeting and *give* [his offering] to the priest (ובא לפני יהוה אל פתח אהל מועד ונתנם אל הכהן), verse 29 describes the woman as merely *bringing* her offering to the priest *at the entrance of the Tent of Meeting* (והביאה אותם אל הכהן אל פתח אהל מועד). Symbolically, she is not seen to perform an act of the same cultic quality; by omitting the crucial words לפני יהוה, the text purposefully avoids placing the woman in the Divine Presence. This cannot arbitrarily be dismissed as a distinction without a difference! On the contrary, it deliberately highlights the contrast between the *legal capacity* of a male and the *legal incapacity* of a female to play an active cultic role.

Furthermore, verse 14 instructs the זב to *give* his offering to the priest (ונתנם אל הכהן)—that is, to hand the birds over directly, thereby making a meaningful physical contact with the priest as his intermediary to God. But verse 29's instruction to the זבה carefully avoids direct priestly contact with her, by instructing her not to *give* her offering to the priest, but only to *bring* it to him "to the door of the Tent of Meeting" (והביאה אותם אל הכהן אל פתח אהל מועד). She approaches the entrance, but presumably sets her offering down somewhere outside; unlike her male counterpart, she does not place the birds directly into the hands of the priest.[12] Whatever the topographical niceties here, it is clear that the text contemplates the man

---

[12] In this context we note that (as Milgrom himself points out in connection with

as symbolically bringing his offering *"into the presence of YHWH"* in a manner consciously denied to the woman.

My analysis is further supported by a second discrepancy between the cases of זב and זבה. Whereas Scripture mandates ritual bathing and clothes-laundering for the man in 15:13, that requirement is not specified in the parallel case of the woman in 15:28. Milgrom circumvents the lacuna by explaining as follows the statement that "after that she shall be pure" (15:28):

> that is, after the seven days and *implicitly after she has laundered her clothes and bathed her body in spring water* (v. 13).[13]

In other words, Milgrom simply assumes that the woman's putative bathing requirement (not mentioned in verse 28) was taken for granted by analogy to the man's bathing requirement in verse 13.

With great respect, I believe Milgrom to be mistaken. A more logical explanation of the failure to mention a bathing requirement for the woman in verse 28 is this: the priestly system mandates ritual purity only for the performance of cultic acts, i.e., it is required of one who will be either literally or figuratively entering the presence of YHWH. But, unlike the זב, the זבה does *not* come symbolically לפני יהוה, because as a woman she is ineligible to do so; consequently, *in this context*, her state of cultic purity is irrelevant.[14]

In general, priestly interest in a woman's state of cultic purity or impurity stems from fear that a menstruant (נדה) or זבה may transmit cultic pollution to any man who touches her, which will in turn disqualify that man from engaging in cultic activities—clearly a matter of crucial import to men of the priestly caste. Yet we note that P (unlike later rabbinic law) never states *explicitly* that a menstruant

---

one who hands a carcass directly to a non-Israelite resident alien in Deut 14:21), the verb נתן necessarily implies handing an object over directly, thus making physical contact with the recipient—which, in Milgrom's own words (p. 703), would violate "P's obsession" with defilement by contact.

[13] Milgrom, *Leviticus 1–16*, 944 [emphasis added].

[14] The same is true of the parturient in chapter 12, which does not specify that she must immerse herself before bringing her offering to the priest. The language of 12:6 parallels that of 15:29 also in omitting the words לפני יהוה, which in 12:7 refer only to the priest who offers the gift on her behalf. She herself does not proceed further than the entrance of the Tent of Meeting, i.e., does not enter the Sanctuary proper; most translations misleadingly translate אל המקדש in 12:4 as "into" the Sanctuary, when in fact the woman is required to bring her offerings only "to" the Sanctuary and to deposit them at some designated spot outside the entrance.

or זבה must ritually immerse herself before resuming intercourse with her husband—but only that the *man* who has had intercourse with her must *himself* undergo ritual immersion to remove the invisible, intangible contamination.

This is clearly spelled out in the asymmetry of chapter 15's bottom line, which recapitulates the subject matter (in relevant part) as follows:

> 32 Such is the ritual . . .
>
> 33 concerning *anyone, male or female, who has a discharge,* and concerning a *man who lies with an unclean woman* (והזב את זובו לזכר ולנקבה ולאיש אשר ישכב עם טמאה). [15]

The asymmetry here is blatant: after speaking of the uncleanness of both males and females who suffer from discharges, v. 33 concludes the list with the case of "a man who lies with an unclean woman" (earlier mentioned in 15:24), but ignores its contextual mirror-image, "a woman who lies with an unclean man." Why is this woman missing? The simple answer is that contamination of a clean woman by an unclean man is irrelevant to a system in which women do not perform cultic rituals requiring them to be in a state of cultic purity.

The Exception Proves the Rule

P describes one scenario that may superficially appear to contradict my assertion that the priestly system does not permit a woman to come into the presence of YHWH. This is the rite of the סטה, the suspected adulteress whose jealous husband lacks the two witnesses he needs to convict her (Deut 17:6 and 19:15). P's solution for this problem is the ordeal spelled out in Numbers 5. The rite of the סטה (or, as P itself more significantly calls it, the "jealousy ritual" (הקנאות תורת)—as it clearly has more to do with a husband's jealousy than a wife's straying) commands the priest to "*bring her* forward and *stand her* before YHWH": והקריב אתה הכהן והעמדה לפני יהוה

---

[15] This comports with the fact that the prohibition of intercourse with a menstruant (Lev 18:19, 20:18) is unmatched by any corresponding prohibition of intercourse by a "clean" woman with a man in a state of cultic pollution due for instance to an emission of semen (Lev 15:16). Note also that rabbinic law grounded in the rules of Leviticus does not require a young unmarried menstruant (assumed to be uninvolved in sexual encounters) to visit the מקוה until just before marriage.

(Num 5:16). But closer scrutiny exposes this as the proverbial exception that proves the rule; or rather, that it is not strictly an exception at all. Careful analysis of text and context shows that the rule itself does not apply here, because the סטה does not *enter* the divine Presence in the normal active sense of that verb.

The ordeal procedure does not constitute active participation by the woman in a cultic rite, because it is *not a voluntary act on her part.* The terminology הקריב אתה ("bring her near") and העמדה ("stand her up") contemplates her as a *passive object*—indeed, this vocabulary precisely matches that used by P of sacrificial victims.[16] The woman does not actively *come* into the presence of YHWH; she *is brought* there (we may imagine her paralyzed with fear, being dragged by the priest into the Sanctuary) in a procedure that graphically presents her not as a person but as an object.

Aside from the סטה, the only other biblical woman described as being "in the presence of YHWH" appears neither in P nor elsewhere in the Torah, but in the Deuteronomic history—namely, the story of Hannah (1 Samuel 1–2). But Hannah's story does not refute my present thesis, since the use of the phrase לפני יהוה in that JE text is unconnected with the Aaronide cult in Jerusalem contemplated by P's use of the phrase.[17]

Thus far, we have seen that the mindset of Israelite religious culture, as represented in the rules of the priestly cult of the Jerusalem Temple, viewed women (even those of the priestly caste) as ineligible to enter the Divine Presence. This gender disqualification is a separate issue from the requirement of membership in the hereditary priestly class that actually administers the cult, as was clearly demonstrated in the paradigm of the the זב and the זבה, whereby only the former, and not the latter, is said to bring his offering לפני יהוה.[18]

---

[16] Most strikingly in the ritual described in Lev 16:5–10, where the High Priest Aaron takes two goats and "stands them" (והעמד אתם) before YHWH; one he "brings near" (והקריב) to be offered as a sacrifice, while the other is "left standing alive" (יעמד חי) before YHWH, prior to its dispatch to Azazel as a scapegoat bearing the people's sins.

[17] The primary source of 1 Samuel 1–2 is E, an author who does not share P's understanding of the term לפני יהוה, but focuses on the levitical priests at Shiloh—a shrine which in any case is called not בית יהוה but היכל יהוה, and hence is not a true analogue to the Jerusalem Temple

[18] The separate significance of gender is adumbrated also by the rules in Lev

Religious Activities Outside the Divine Presence

The Aaronide cult of the Temple at Jerusalem did not permit women
to "enter the presence of YHWH." Does this mean that the system
precluded women from engaging in any religious activity whatsoever? Not so; for we do find women performing some quasi-cultic
activities that did not technically require entering the Divine Presence.
The Hebrew Bible portrays at least three instances of the involvement of women in cult-related activities; but close scrutiny reveals
that none of these cases describes the women as coming לפני יהוה.
The most significant example appears in the P corpus itself: namely,
a woman's eligibility for naziritehood as specified in Numbers 6.
  Numbers 6:1–21 (excerpts)

> 2 . . . If anyone, *man or woman*, explicitly utters a nazirite's vow to set
> himself *apart for the LORD* (ליהוה), . . .
>
> 5 Throughout the term of his vow as nazirite, no razor shall touch
> his head; it shall remain consecrated until the completion of his term
> as nazirite *of the LORD* (אשר יזיר ליהוה) . . .
>
> 6 Throughout the term that he has set apart *for the LORD* (ליהוה), he
> shall not go in where there is a dead person.
>
> 7 . . . he must not defile himself for them, since hair set apart for his
> God is upon his head;
>
> 8 Throughout his terms as nazirite he is consecrated to the LORD
> (ליהוה).
>
> 9 If a person dies suddenly near him, defiling his consecrated hair, he
> shall shave his head on the day he becomes clean; he shall shave it
> on the seventh day.
>
> 10 On the eighth day, he shall bring two turtle doves or two pigeons
> to the priest, at the entrance of the Tent of Meeting.
>
> 11 The priest shall . . . make expiation on his behalf . . . That same
> day he shall reconsecrate his head
>
> 12 and rededicate *to the LORD* (ליהוה) his term as nazirite; and he shall
> bring a lamb in its first year as a penalty offering . . .

22:10–13 concerning the disqualification of a priest's daughter, who has ceased
(through marriage to a lay Israelite) to be a member of a priestly household, from
eating special priestly rations from the תרומה offering. This was not an issue for
a priestly male who married a lay Israelite woman.

13 This is the ritual for the nazirite. On the day that his term as
nazirite is completed, he shall be brought to the entrance of the Tent
of Meeting.

14 As his offering *to the Lord* (ליהוה), he shall present: [details of a substantial offering are here spelled out].

Even a cursory glance at these rules establishes that both males and
females (6:2) may take a nazirite vow ליהוה ("to YHWH"). But nothing suggests that this occurs in the Divine Presence; from start to
finish, no part of the process requires the nazirite to come לפני יהוה.[19]
True, this fact applies to male and female alike; but it is also precisely what makes naziritehood possible for a woman; she can acquire
the status and perform the duties of a נזיר without ever entering the
Divine Presence.

In light of P's general aversion to admitting women to cultic activities, what motivation could be strong enough to generate rules per-
mitting a female to become a nazirite—clearly a cult-related status?
The answer here is the same for a woman as for a man, at least as
indicated by what is both literally and metaphorically the bottom
line:

20 ... and this shall be a sacred donation for the priest, ...

21 Such is the obligation of a nazirite, *except that* he who vows an
offering to the LORD of what he can afford, *beyond his nazirite requirements*, must do exactly according to the vow that he has made, *beyond
his obligation as a nazirite*.

Here we learn that the nazirite gift goes to the priests; moreover, if
the nazirite's enthusiasm has led him to pledge more than the min-
imum gift specified in 6:14–15, he is held to his vow to donate the
actual amount of his pledge. Obviously, it would be poor fiscal policy indeed to deprive half the Israelite population of this opportunity to express their devotion to YHWH by contributing a nazirite
gift to the priestly coffers.[20] So we may reasonably surmise that the

---

[19] Significantly, the only participant in the Nazirite ritual who is said to come
לפני יהוה is the priest who actually presents the nazirite's offering "before the LORD"
in Num 6:16 and 6:20.

[20] The same rationale may partially explain the case of the זבה, whose offering
(without access to the Divine Presence) likewise generated pickings for the priest. It
seems that whenever God could offer women a chance to contribute without actually violating the cultic norm that barred them from entering the Divine Presence,
He was quite willing to do so!

obviation of any need for nazirites to enter the divine Presence is no mere accident!

The Bible mentions two further examples of women's cult-related activity. One is the unspecified (but presumably P-sanctioned) enterprise of the "women who thronged" (הצבאת אשר צבאו) "at the entrance of the Tent of Meeting" (Exod 38:8).[21] The other case involved women who "wove coverings for the Asherah" (2 Kgs 23:7), which likewise, seems to be a Temple-connected (though scarcely P-sanctioned) activity. But since the phrase לפני יהוה is lacking in both cases, neither this nor the unspecified activity of the thronging women[22] seems to have involved actually entering the divine Presence.

The activity in Exod 38:8 (like that of the parturient in Lev 12:6 and the זבה in Lev 15:29) occurs "at [i.e., outside] the entrance to the Tent of Meeting" and not in the *Divine Presence itself*. The female weavers in 2 Kgs 23:7 operated in the vicinity of cubicles housing certain temple functionaries called קדשים,[23] who offered unspecified services "in the House of YHWH" (2 Kgs 23:7). But even here, the text does not place the weavers inside the Sanctuary itself; it speaks of "the cubicles of the קדשים in the House of YHWH, where the women wove coverings for the Asherah" (בתי הקדשים אשר בבית יהוה אשר הנשים ארגות שם בתים לאשרה). The first אשר, somewhat ambiguous, may refer either to the קדשים themselves or to their cubicles "in the house of YHWH" and the second אשר refers to the cubicles. But we know that the term בית יהוה is not limited to the

---

[21] The unspecified character of the purpose of these הצבאת (female "crowds" or "throngers") is compounded by their presentation in a cognate accusative construction that matches the verb to the noun, thus affording no clue to their intended activity (see n. 23 below). S. Mandelkern (*Concordance of the Bible* [New York: Schulsinger, 1955] *s.v.*) implies that the women were doing something cultic, in his final comment, following a list of strictly military definitions of צבא, where he concludes with the following definition, apparently referring to the women in Exod 38:8: "per vices militares convenire ad ministeria sacra obeunda." Some scholars have suggested that they may have engaged in sacred prostitution; but nothing in the text itself supports this conclusion.

[22] The *New JPS Tanakh*, noting the difficulty, translates הצבאת אשר צבאו as "the women who performed tasks." The NRSV gives, "the women who served" and the NEB, "the women who were on duty."

[23] Recent scholarship on the topic of קדשים/קדשות claims that even these temple functionaries may not necessarily have been engaged in sexual activity of any kind. Mandelkern (*s.v.* צבא) implies merely that they were doing something cultic; following several strictly military definitions of צבאים, he offers a final definition, perhaps for the צבאת in Exod 38:8: per vices militares convenire ad ministeria sacra obeunda.

interior of the Sanctuary itself; any part of the Temple precincts can be subsumed under the general terms בית יהוה or בית המקדש (whose imprecision, indeed, has led to a widespread misunderstanding of a much-quoted New Testament account).[24]

Epilogue

The cultic regulations of the priestly corpus had far wider repercussions on women than have been noted (or perhaps even noticed) by most biblical scholars, even in modern times. The laws sociologically reflected and theologically reinforced a particular view of the place of women in biblical Israelite society—a view that would later ground rabbinic and patristic rulings to bar women from active participation in the public cultural domain of the communal religious enterprise. This exclusion of women embodied a fundamental aspect of the priestly worldview concerning the respective places of men and women in the divine cosmic plan.

Thus the discrimination between זב and זבה gave overt expression to a taboo based largely on male fears of potential cultic contamination by females, a taboo that became enshrined in a (perhaps subliminal) assumption that a woman may not enter the divine Presence.[25] In the view of the Israelite priesthood (as in many other religions from that day to this), women were simply unfit and hence ineligible to participate in cultic rites. In the priestly system, short of the drastic step of coming under suspicion of adultery, the ancient Israelite woman could never hope to find herself standing לפני יהוה, in the presence of God.[26]

---

[24] The Gospel accounts of Christ overturning the moneychangers' tables at the entrance to the Temple Mount (Mark 11:15–19; Matt 21:10–17; Luke 19:45–48) describe him as coming "into the Temple" (εις τον ιερον) to do this—thereby confusing generations of readers, who (not surprisingly) have drawn the incorrect conclusion that the money-changing took place inside the Sanctuary itself!

[25] Exactly how and why the exclusion of women from the public religious enterprise is related to the problem of cultic contamination generated by menstruation and by illicit sexual relationships has been spelled out by myself and others elsewhere, and will be further discussed in a longer version of the present paper, now in preparation.

[26] As noted above, the סטה was brought (or even dragged) into the Presence. Even Hannah (in a tradition of non-Aaronide provenance, in which the expression לפני יהוה was probably less technically employed) was assumed by the priest Eli to be drunk (1 Sam 1:13)—and thus to have entered the shrine more through inadvertence than by design.

This disqualification of women (even those of the priestly caste) from ritual or cultic activities would ultimately come to symbolize something far more oppressive. It expressed the worldview and mind-set of an intensely patriarchal culture, in which a woman's place was always and only in the private domain of the home, never in the public domain of the Temple, which would become a paradigm for her later exclusion from active participation in the public forums of rabbinic Judaism: synagogue, study house and courthouse. Jewish women, like women elsewhere, were thus denied access to the most satisfying and rewarding of human enterprises: the life of mind and spirit and the world of ideas.

INDEX OF SELECTED SCRIPTURAL CITATIONS
AND ANCIENT SOURCES

ANCIENT NEAR EASTERN SOURCES

NEW TESTAMENT

APOCRYPHA

PSEUDEPIGRAPHA

1 Enoch		20:12–13	138
1:5–7	126, 127	30	138
		34:18–19	138
Jubilees			
3:8–14	356, 431–33		

DEAD SEA SCROLLS

4Q265	355–56, 433	4QLev^g	327, 331, 349
4Q266 6 ii 5–11	433	4QLXXLev^a	256–57,
1QpaleoLev	259, 324,		259–60,
	329, 331		261–63, 327,
2QpaleoLev	324–25, 331		349
2QpaleoLev		4QpapLXXLev^b	257, 259–61,
4QExod-Lev^f	325, 329,		265–67, 327,
	331, 349		349
4QLev-Num^a	259, 326,	4QpaptgLev	282–83, 328
	329, 331, 349	4QMMT B 21–22	351–53
4QLev^b	259–60, 326,	4QMMT B 21–22	353–54
	331, 349	6QpaleoLev	325, 331
4QLev^c	326, 331, 349	11QLev^b	325, 331
4QLev^d	259–60, 326,	11QpaleoLev^a	259–60, 325,
	331, 349		331
4QLev^e	259, 327,	MasLev^a	328, 331
	331, 349	MasLev^b	328, 331

RABBINIC LITERATURE

Mishnah	384–88	*Leviticus Rabbah*	391–94,
			425–28
Sifra	389–91,		
	404–25		

TARGUMIM

Fragment Targums,	
Samaritan Targum,	
Neofiti I, Onqelos,	
Targum of the Prophets,	
Pseudo-Jonathan	269–98

OTHER EARLY JEWISH AND CHRISTIAN TEXTS

Josephus		*Thomas Aquinas, Summa Theologica*	
Ant. 3 §245	277	Question 37	441–43
Ant. 13 §372	277		
Penitential of Theodore	439–40		

INDEX OF MODERN AUTHORS